Soviet Leaders

Soviet Leaders

Edited by George W. Simmonds

THOMAS Y. CROWELL COMPANY

New York, Established 1834

Preface

The tremendous growth of American involvement abroad and of international communication has indeed brought the world into every man's home: the names of important figures, such as Touré, Sukarno, Brezhnev, Ho Chi-minh, Mao Tse-tung, Gandhi, Shelepin, Ky, Nasser, Tito, Moro, Gomulka, from countries large and small, are heard and seen every day on television, radio, and in the press. Yet even the well-informed citizen, in following events around the world, must perforce struggle to grasp the nature of the men behind the names and the qualities of life in societies so different from his own—a task made infinitely more difficult by the absence, frequently, of readily accessible and illuminating biographical material in English about many parts of the non-English-speaking world.

We hope that the present volume, entitled *Soviet Leaders,* will help to fill part of this gap. The book contains forty-two biographical sketches of important figures selected from all walks of Soviet life, including the political, governmental, military, economic, scientific, and cultural. The contributors have not rested content merely with a bare narrative of events, but have tried—so far as possible—to leave the reader with a definite impression of the personalities of the subjects of the sketches, not merely stating but appraising their achievements and their influence both at home and abroad. They have avoided a partisan approach and striven to present the technical material in a clear, simple, graceful manner, even while maintaining a high level of scholarship. Since many aspects of Soviet life not generally well known to the English-speaking public are inevitably touched upon in the accounts, an extensive glossary has been provided at the end of the book.

In the expectation that this volume will be used not simply for reference but also for study of current developments, through the medium of biography, we have provided a comprehensive index as well as an introduction containing an overview of the major developments in the Soviet Union since the downfall of Khrushchev. Finally, at the end of each sketch an up-to-date bibliographical survey of the most authoritative sources in the Russian, English, and other languages may be found.

The preparation of a comprehensive volume such as this raised special problems, of which the three most thorny ones were those of calendar, transliteration, and above all the selection of figures to be included. In this book all dates are given in accordance with the Gregorian calendar, which is now in use in Russia and in the West. The reader wishing to determine the actual dates in effect in Russia before the Soviet government abandoned the Julian calendar and shifted to the Gregorian should subtract twelve days from any date in the nineteenth century and thirteen from any in the twentieth century prior to February 14, 1918.

The second difficulty faced was that of transliterating from the Russian. As a rule the system of the Library of Congress was used, though we permitted numerous departures from uniformity for the sake of readability and in order to minimize the element of the unfamiliar and the bizarre. Our contributors were asked to employ, often in violation of the Library of Congress system, the conventional or most sensible English forms of Russian proper names (e.g., Malinovsky for Malinovskii, Polyansky for Polianskii) and to avoid whenever possible those unsightly transliterated forms of lugubrious titles and designations of which the Russians are so fond by using instead the simplest and most accurate English equivalent. However, all direct citation of Russian printed matter, especially in the bibliographies, is strictly in accord with the system of the Library of Congress, except for diacritical marks.

The greatest difficulty in planning this book involved the selection of forty-two prominent Soviet men as subjects for the biographical sketches. A preliminary list was sent to dozens of specialists and scholars, and their suggestions formed the basis for the final selection by the editor. It proved impossible, of course, to include all the figures that should have been included and, in some cases, to reconcile the conflicting estimates even of the specialists in the same field. The final selection represents an attempt on our part to include figures that are not only among the most influential and well known in their own fields, but whose lives and work typify the problems and achievements in these areas of Soviet life. It was on such grounds that we decided to retain the sketch on the former Premier Nikita Khrushchev, for example, even though his political career ended while this book was still in preparation; we felt that his failures and accomplishments are, after all, the starting point for understanding the efforts of the current leadership.

I am most sincerely grateful to all our contributors for their unusual, unflagging patience in meeting the many demands of a complicated project such as this one, even in the face of their own intense professional preoccupations. Dozens of scholars contributed criticisms and suggestions, and their help is gratefully acknowledged. Finally, whatever success our venture may have is in no small part due to Mr. Edward Tripp, chief editor of the reference division of Thomas Y. Crowell Company, who initiated the project and provided encouragement and guidance at every step of the way; to Dr. Severyn Bialer, of Columbia University, who not only wrote a number of the sketches but generously shared his previous experience with me at a crucial point in the early stages of planning; to Mr. Abraham Brumberg, editor of *Problems of Communism,* who read the introduction; and to Miss Joan Cenedella, house editor at Crowell, about whose cheerful, persistent, and perspicacious attention to every detail I have not words enough to say.

GEORGE W. SIMMONDS

Contents

ECONOMIC THEORY AND PRACTICE

SCIENCE AND PHILOSOPHY

THE ARTS

Introduction

by George W. Simmonds

The contributors have tried to discover not only the basic facts but also the import of the lives of forty-two of the most influential figures in contemporary Soviet society, including the personal sources of their power and creativity, the nature of their work, and their influence at home and abroad. Consequently, the reader who digs deeply and broadly enough will find here not only basic information about those Soviet citizens whose names make the headlines most frequently, but also a fascinating composite portrait of the current Soviet elite.

There is a remarkable similarity in the background, careers, and outlook of the chief leaders of the Soviet party and government. They emerge in these sketches as political executives par excellence, a fact that should occasion no surprise when it is remembered that Soviet society, greatly altered since its revolutionary origin almost fifty years ago, is today run from top to bottom by professional bureaucrats, with the party occupying the dominant position in Soviet life, and that this system has not only helped to shape the characters and views of the present leaders, but is in turn affected by their actions. The similarity among them can be seen in many particulars: a humble origin; birth in the first decade of the century; menial positions in industry or agriculture prior to their receiving—rather late in life—some education and technical training; a brief stint thereafter in a technical vocation, usually coupled with entrance into the party; rapid promotion in the party in the 1930's, when the headlong pace of collectivization and industrialization and the brutal sweep of party purges created many opportunities for advancement; a long mid-career existence in the provinces (though some, like Kosygin, Suslov, or Shelepin, moved immediately into the central economic or party bureaucracy); finally, thanks to Khrushchev, promotion to key posts in Moscow after 1957. The men who run Soviet Russia's armed forces also followed a remarkably homogeneous career pattern: a peasant origin; early enlistment; participation in the Civil War; party membership since the 1920's; education in the military institutions of higher learning, such as the Frunze military academy; rapid advancement in the 1930's and during the Second World War; the assumption of the highest positions under Khrushchev; an average age of sixty-one years at present; and a lifetime spent in an army in which a high degree of social discipline, political concerns, and ideology are part of the profession itself. Here, too, are portraits of great Soviet scientists and professionals—revealing their intense, lifelong battle for new frontiers in technology and science; their devotion to teaching and research; their antibureaucratism; their cosmopolitanism—and of leading cultural figures, whose lives and views are remarkably diverse.

But all of them—politicians, officials, generals, scientists, artists—live alike within the confines of one of the most integrated and managed of modern societies, in which the present and the past constantly impinge on the individual. Let us turn, therefore, to an examination of the events of the recent past, the better to assess the significance of the parts played by the chief actors on the Soviet scene.

Early on the morning of Tuesday, October 13, 1964, the telephone rang in Sochi, where Nikita Khrushchev was taking his Black Sea holiday. Leonid Brezhnev, who was on the line, asked him to return immediately to the capital for a meeting with the top party leaders. Premier Khrushchev, having cut short his meeting with the French science minister Gaston Palewski, hastened to the neighboring airport of Adler and flew back to Moscow. Arriving shortly after noon, he was driven straight to the Kremlin, only to find the nine active Presidium members and a hand-picked, carefully prepared quorum of the Central Committee on hand ready to ask for his dismissal. He defended himself, but to no avail, and after midnight drove away from the Kremlin to his house on the Lenin Hills where, faithful to the tradition of Russian political recantation, he wrote a letter to the Central Committee admitting his errors and submitting his resignation.

The charges against Khrushchev were many: major blunders in agricultural and industrial policy, excessive pragmatism and ideological weakness, adventurism in foreign policy, and irrational leadership in party affairs. But whatever the truth of the charges brought against this extraordinary and colorful man, he contributed a great deal to the abolition of Stalinist totalitarianism and to the restoration of normality during his ten years in the highest councils of the Soviet government.

To be sure, in the four years prior to Nikita Khrushchev's formal assumption of leadership (in June 1957), forces were already at work altering the nature of Stalin's Russia. During the period of Malenkov's premiership, from 1953 to 1955, the totalitarian apparatus utilized by Stalin began to be dismantled, the first steps in the "debunking" of Stalin were taken, Beria (the head of security and terror) and his assistants were executed, the virtual autonomy of the security police was abolished, and most forced labor camps were broken up after hundreds of thousands had been amnestied. Then too, Stalin's successors went to great lengths to show the world that the tyranny of individual dictatorship was over, that "collective leadership" would work: they went everywhere together, and mixed, and laughed, and chattered; their names appeared not in order of rank, but alphabetically; and party organs again began to meet regularly and report publicly. Important concessions were made to the peasants, and for the first time even the possibility of switching from emphasis on heavy industry to the manufacture of consumer goods was envisaged on the pages of Soviet newspapers. The Russian intelligentsia, and particularly the writers, experienced the first thaw—and the first freeze. More normal contacts with the West were resumed, and the Soviet leaders relaxed their hold over the other Communist parties—and they began to travel abroad, occasionally at first, and then more and more frequently.

Perhaps the circumstances prevailing after Stalin's death dictated the major direction of the changes undertaken by the leadership. It is unquestionably true that Malenkov actually initiated many of the original reforms, particularly in industry and agriculture. Still, in retrospect, it seems certain that much credit must go to Nikita Khrushchev personally. A man of great native shrewdness, of boldness verging on recklessness, a pragmatist, and a born boss with a strong turn of independence which he managed to preserve even in the Stalin era, he wanted to breathe new life into the numbed body of Soviet society, to push its development forward, and to win a greater place for it in the community of nations, all the while retaining the traditional authoritarian political and administrative edifice at home.

Toward that end he continued the reforms begun by Malenkov, and fostered experimentation on his own in agriculture and industry. In 1954 Khrushchev persuaded his colleagues to undertake the most radical agricultural innovation during the first decade after Stalin, the "virgin lands" program, in which hitherto fallow or marginal lands in the Volga valley and Siberia were to be cultivated posthaste. In the next half decade, the government also increased sharply capital investment in agriculture and introduced a number of important institutional changes. The poorest collective farms were converted into state farms; the Machine Tractor Stations (MTS) were abolished and their equipment sold to the farms; the quality of agricultural planning was improved. The peasants were also given greater incentives, as the government began to pay higher prices for compulsory farm deliveries, abolished the required compulsory deliveries from the peasants' garden plots, and reformed the complicated Soviet price and purchase system for agricultural products. The government also pushed the development of corn as the major feed-crop for Soviet livestock.

Important efforts were also made to improve industrial production. Studies of industry operation were undertaken, and Soviet technicians in ever greater numbers traveled to the West to gather data and acquaint themselves with Western techniques. Particularly anxious to achieve the most economical and rational use of capital, Khrushchev called for the revamping of the traditional Soviet planning system. Troubled by the notoriously low productivity of labor, the Soviet government revoked the laws freezing workers to their jobs; raised minimum wages and pensions; reduced the workday from eight hours to seven or six; undertook a massive reform of the whole Soviet wage system; reorganized the trade unions; and, in view of the impending labor shortage arising from the increased flow of young people into professional and white-collar occupations, undertook a radical reform of the educational system, which forced young people in general to begin work after the eighth grade, continuing their education from then on only after hours. Finally, in what was perhaps the most radical re-organization of Soviet economic administration in over two decades—and the most bitterly contested because of its political implications, as we shall see below—Khrushchev in May 1957 began dismantling the vast and often highly inefficient central economic administration in Moscow and re-establishing it closer to the grass roots in each major area of the country in the form of 105 regional economic administrative bodies (*sovnarkhozy*), the better to facilitate planning, interindustry cooperation, and the growth of the consumer industries.

As fresh winds blowing from the West were permitted to reach Soviet Russia, the sciences began to flourish too. Computer research grew, though not nearly so quickly as in the West, and so did cybernetics. Nuclear research and the space sciences moved into high gear, and considerable attention began to be devoted also to quantum radio-physics and radio-electronics. Lysenkoism, though not obliterated, was permitted to wane, and the study of biology began again to revive. Only chemistry appeared to lag. In general there was growing emphasis on basic research or pure science as opposed to applied science, in which the Russians had been strong traditionally. In the social sciences, too, there was considerable innovation. The field of communications and the information services were modernized, as the Soviets began to experiment with programmed learning and new audio-visual techniques. Much attention was focused on educational psychology. Public-opinion polling made its first appearance, though to be sure, it has never been used since more than very marginally and only on certain subjects. Nothing perhaps illustrates so well the general renaissance as the spectacular advances made in the field of statistical economics, which, as we shall see below, threatens to revolutionize both Soviet economic theory and practice.

The death of Stalin saw a revival in the arts as well. In novels such as Ilya Ehrenburg's *The Thaw* and Vladimir Dudintsev's *Not by Bread Alone,* in plays such as Leonid Zorin's *The Guests,* and in a growing number of poems, Soviet writers, poets, and dramatists attempted not only to break away from the typical stylistic devices of Soviet postwar potboilers written in accordance with the principles of Socialist Realism—loose and episodic structure; heavy and frequently verbose exposition; dramatic devices such as the eventual solution of the personal problems of the heroes and heroines simply as a by-product of the successful fulfillment of labor norms or farm quotas; the introduction of a *deus ex machina* for the unraveling of knotted plots, usually in the person of the district party secretary—but also to turn to meaningful nonpolitical themes such as personal love or even profound social problems like the "organization man" or the problem created by the permeation of the upper layers of Soviet society with "middle-class" values—conformism, conspicuous consumption, social climbing, material comforts, and the like—which threaten to undermine the Communist way of life. During these years, too, genuine literary criticism revived. The first great controversy raged in the winter of 1953–54 in regard to the nature of Socialist Realism, with criticism tending to be both indirect and direct, as in Ilya Ehrenburg's famous lectures on Stendhal (later published in *Literaturnaia gazeta*), in which he praised the famous French writer and poet for the very qualities lacking, by implication, in Soviet writing in general: sincerity, total devotion to the craft, originality ("the longer I study the history of literature, the less I understand the classification of schools, trends, and authors"), and distance from politics ("for Stendhal politics was one of the human passions—large, but not all-encompassing").

In the midst of this ferment many older writers, critics, artists, and poets (for example, Alexei Surkov, Vsevolod Kochetov, Alexander Korneichuk, Alexander Prokofiev, Leonid Sobolev, Vladimir Serov, Alexander Gerasimov) rose to defend traditional Socialist Realism in literature and the arts while many others—such as Ilya Ehrenburg, Victor Nekrasov, Konstantin Paustovsky, Alexander Tvardovsky, and Mikhail Romm, to mention but a few—fought for the new and broader artistic horizons. Perhaps most important of all, a new generation of liberal artists and writers appeared, notably, the poets Andrei Voznesensky, Yevgeny Yevtushenko, Bella Akhmadulina, Robert Rozhdestvensky; the fiction writers Vasily Aksyonov, Yuri Kazakov, Vladimir Tendryakov, Vladimir Dudintsev, Alexander Solzhenitsyn; the artists Ely Belyutin and Ernst Neizvestny, both of whom were attacked by Khrushchev as "abstractionists"; Bulat Okudzhava (poet, short-story writer, and popular guitarist); and Andrei Sinyavsky (pseudonym—Abram Tertz), Yuri Daniel (pseudonym—Nikolai Arzhak), and Valery Tarsis, whose nonconformist political satires and essays were clandestinely published abroad.

In Soviet foreign policy, too, there were basic changes during the Khrushchev era. Stalin had worked hard to preserve Soviet hegemony in interparty relations, making sure that the Communist parties around the world were obedient instruments of the Soviet party; not even the expansion of Soviet power into Eastern Europe and China and the installation of "people's democratic" regimes after 1945 had altered the traditional monolithic pattern of interparty relations. Yet after Stalin's death Soviet control faded and pluralism grew in international Communism. These developments led to the Polish and Hungarian revolutions, in 1956, which almost destroyed the Communist alliance. Khrushchev had contributed to these developments by pushing de-Stalinization both at home and abroad. At the

Twentieth Congress of the Communist Party of the Soviet Union (CPSU), in February 1956, the Stalinist assumption that world war between capitalism and Communism was inevitable was found wanting: Khrushchev declared that war was no longer "fatalistically inevitable" in a world possessing nuclear weapons; that "peaceful coexistence" between capitalism and Communism was possible; and that ultimately Communism would prove superior, not "through armed interference by the socialist countries in the internal affairs of capitalist nations" but, rather, by the economic defeat of capitalism. To meet these new conditions, the Soviet Union began to develop an effective foreign policy, as distinct from mere propaganda, in many parts of the world by utilizing for the first time every bona-fide diplomatic device from cultural exchange and trade to arms shipments (to Egypt and the Congo, for example). Khrushchev even resorted to vigorous personal diplomacy. Just as he traveled incessantly the length and breadth of his own country—lecturing, admonishing, praising local peasants and party chiefs—so he traveled indefatigably abroad, appearing in the capital of every country of Eastern Europe (except Albania), in Peking, in Jakarta, in Delhi and Burma, and in the United States.

But in all of these whirlwind measures designed to modernize Russia and expand her role in the world, Khrushchev never lost sight of two central aims: to gain and hold power for himself, and to revitalize the party and reassert its dominant position in Soviet life. The policies of the Soviet government, during the first four years after Stalin's death, were the result of collective decision-making, though Khrushchev, as first secretary, often played a key role. To gain the firmest possible grip over the party, he promoted his own most loyal and trusted supporters—many of them from the Ukraine—to key positions in the central apparatus and throughout the country, finally obtaining the expulsion from the party of the majority of the party leadership (including Malenkov, Molotov, Kaganovich, Shepilov, Bulganin, Saburov, and Pervukhin) after they had outvoted him in the Presidium in June 1957. Still, his victory was incomplete and he remained, at best, chairman of the board until his fall in October 1964.

However—and this was far more important for the course of history— Khrushchev wished to revive the party in order that it might once again occupy a position of leadership in the Soviet state, for Stalin, in exerting personal rule, had increasingly bypassed the party (demoralized and cowed as its members had become after the purges) and relied more and more on the technical and economic bureaucracy. Wishing to restore the former to its position as keeper of ideology and as the dominant political force in the USSR, Khrushchev worked for the reassertion of party sway over every institution in Soviet society, most notably perhaps the economic. To break the industrial bureaucracy (insofar as it represented a cohesive force), he abolished in 1957 the centralized industrial ministries, establishing in their stead the *sovnarkhozy* and scattering Moscow bureaucrats far and wide to serve under the regional party secretaries. By weeding out old-timers and introducing into high party office men who had proved themselves in technical and scientific fields, Khrushchev hoped to make the party more fitted for assuming real leadership in a complex modern society.

During his remaining years in office, from 1960 to 1964, Khrushchev was beset by many problems. Though he had hoped to continue stressing the development of consumer goods and light industry, sharp domestic opposition as well as the continuing international tension forced a reversion to more traditional planning goals emphasizing heavy industry and the military and space capabilities. The economic gains were also threatened by the continuing debacle in agriculture during the years 1959 to 1963. Khrushchev's hopes that the cultivation of marginal land could provide a long-term solution to Soviet grain problems proved illusory, as both natural causes and incorrect methods of cultivation brought low yields and soil erosion, dust blowing as far as the Balkan shores of the Black Sea. In June 1962 the government was forced to increase meat and butter prices sharply, a move that provoked widespread discontent, and to suspend indefinitely its program for abolishing the income tax. Most important of all, it was becoming obvious that a more deep-seated problem faced the Soviet leadership, namely, the actual obsolescence of parts of the economic system. For thirty years the Soviet economic system had worked, clumsily, wastefully, and cruelly to be sure, yet—starting from very low levels—it had made possible the enormous increases in production; now the old methods no longer fitted an economy parts of which were highly developed. That the planning and distribution systems no longer worked adequately was becoming clear from the frightening slowing down of the rate of economic growth, accompanied by capital shortages; by nonfulfillment of production plans, a quarter of all firms falling short in carrying out their production norms; and by a vast accumulation of unwanted and unsalable goods that created waste in a society so hard up that it could afford no waste at all.

In the arts, too, the *Ausgleich* apparently established in 1959 between the liberal and conservative factions, and between both of them and the party, appeared in danger. By the autumn of 1962 a revolt of the intellectuals against the *ancien régime* in the arts, of proportion greater than anything since the death of Stalin, was in the making. Yevtushenko and Axyonov were elected editors of the journal *Yunost;* the Moscow writers' organization passed into the hands of the liberals through the election of liberal board members; modern art was defended in an article even in *Izvestiia;* prerevolutionary Russian experimental paintings were hung in Moscow's Tretyakov gallery; Yevtushenko's poem "Stalin's Heirs" (an attack on Soviet reactionary bureaucrats in general) and Solzhenitsyn's powerful story about forced labor, *One Day in the Life of Ivan Denisovich,* appeared in *Pravda* and in the literary monthly *Novyi mir,* respectively; and the conservative leaders of nearly all of the creative unions in Moscow were under fire from the liberals.

When, at the same time, Khrushchev's efforts to break through Western containment in both Berlin and Cuba failed, the growing Sino-Soviet split proving equally deleterious, as hardly an international gathering passed without a show of open conflict and dissension between Moscow and Peking and other Communist parties, and as the criticism from China of Khrushchev's policies at home and abroad grew, he began to encounter the most serious opposition from the conservatives in the inner circles of the party. This opposition reached its height during the winter and spring of 1962–63 and culminated, apparently, in a bitter row between Khrushchev and Frol Kozlov (alleged to have been designated as his heir) in the Presidium, in which Kozlov attacked Khrushchev for the failure of various policies and raised openly the charge of one-man rule, thus bringing down on his head a brutal verbal counterattack by Khrushchev. The strain of these events evidently contributed to Kozlov's stroke in April 1963, and his retirement from politics.

Faced with these difficulties, Khrushchev appears to have followed increasingly chaotic and contradictory policies during his last year and a half in office. In the economic realm he pushed both the traditional (and outmoded) methods as well as modernization. On the one hand, although during the late summer and early fall of 1962 the intensive discussion in the Soviet press seemed to presage the institution of sound modern economic reforms, Khrushchev nevertheless reverted instead to one of his favorite devices: sweeping reorganization. Asserting that the existing territorial organization of the party was unsuitable for proper supervision over both agriculture and industry, the multitude of responsibilities borne by party and state officials causing them to scatter their energies, Khrushchev instituted—despite bitter opposition—the most radical reorganization of the party and government in decades: namely, the division of local party organizations into two parallel hierarchies, one exclusively and constantly concerned with supervision over agriculture, the other with industry, the whole paralleled by similarly bifurcated local-state organs. Far from providing a solution for Russia's economic ills, the reorganization soon led to vast confusion and chaos, bureaucratic rivalry, empire-building in the localities, and greater interference of the party in economic management. Khrushchev also began a crash program, amid much ballyhoo, for expanding the chemical industry.

Yet at the same time he permitted continuing discussion of radical methods for economic reform, in which some argued that Soviet centralized planning (which was clearly no longer suitable in its traditional form for current Soviet needs) could be saved by the application of far-reaching modern mathematical techniques and computers; others, pessimistic about the task of macroeconomic planning, urged that economic decision-making be genuinely decentralized, with individual firms and enterprises drafting their own plans based on supply and demand and making their own production decisions—all of this implying that economic reform could no longer be a matter of superficial reorganization, increased party guidance, or a mere relabeling of government offices, which Khrushchev was in effect doing. To compound the confusion, the Soviet government decided to try some radical experiments. In July 1964 two clothing firms were experimentally freed from all detailed supervision and were left free to seek out customers, draft their own output and production plans, and even alter some of the official prices by agreement with state retailers who bought their clothing. Then, late in September 1964, Khrushchev, reverting to his old favorite theme, publicly called for abandoning the recently proclaimed priorities to heavy industry and armaments in favor of giving the greatest attention to raising the Soviet standard of living.

In foreign policy, too, Khrushchev made striking innovations during his last year and a half in office. The confrontation between the United States and the Soviet Union during the Cuban crisis of October 1962, when (in Averell Harriman's words) President Kennedy and Premier Khrushchev looked down the nuclear barrel, had persuaded Khrushchev that he could not hurdle the Western-imposed containment; yet Sino-Soviet relations were constantly worsening, thus undermining not only the traditional primacy of the Soviet Union in interparty relations, but hastening the fragmentation of the Communist world as well. During the fall and winter of 1962–63 his policies were seriously opposed in the higher echelons of the party; by the end of spring 1963, when Khrushchev had succeeded in overcoming his opponents, he initiated a novel foreign policy: to cooperate directly with the United States, as the most powerful capitalist country; to secure for this the backing of important Western nations as well as the Communist-bloc countries; and to put Peking on the spot, thus leaving her increasingly isolated. Toward this end he negotiated the limited test-ban agreement with the United States in July 1963, while continuing the denunciation of the Chinese and threatening a showdown.

The portentous policy and political disputes in the higher echelons of the party appear also to have led, during the winter and spring of 1962–63, to an enormous public attack on the writers, artists, and intellectuals. It began with Khrushchev's completely unexpected denunciation of a handful of abstract paintings during his visit to an exhibition held in the huge Manezh Hall on December 1, 1962, and it developed into a campaign more vast and threatening than anything of its kind since the death of Stalin. Before it was over, writers, artists, and intellectuals had been dragooned into major meetings with party officials; Neizvestny, Rozhdestvensky, Shostakovich, Yevtushenko, Axyonov, and Vosnesensky had issued "recantations"; the liberals had been ejected from the Moscow writers' organization, far and away the largest and most important writers' group in the USSR; a new State Committee for the Press had been set up to supervise book publishing around the country, thus clamping down on the possibility of publication in the provinces of the works of writers refused publication in the capital cities; and the conservatives in literature and art, fearful of the success of the liberals, appeared to have regained much lost ground. Yet the campaign began to peter out at the end of April 1963, Khrushchev having become aware that when the cultural offensive gathered fury and turned into an attack on de-Stalinization, it was being used by his political opponents as a weapon to defend their personal positions (which had been imperiled by de-Stalinization) and to weaken his own, since he was publicly known as the architect of de-Stalinization. Moreover, the subjection of the cultural community in his own country appeared to be clearly inconsistent with the new direction in foreign policy, since the East European and Western nations, which he was trying to rally, as well as the United States (with which he was seeking a *rapprochement*) were openly critical of the cultural offensive.

The campaign showed that while few artists or writers challenged Communism as an ideal or the right of the party to direct their work, they did struggle to expand the opportunities for genuine creativity. At the same time, it became equally clear that Khrushchev had used first the liberals and then the conservatives, never giving up control or committing himself to either, since he viewed the artist, writer, and intellectual as essentially a political instrument to be turned on and off at the party's pleasure. The campaign also showed some serious flaws in Khrushchev's manner of governing. The cultural drive itself was handled in an extremely clumsy and erratic fashion. Khrushchev's own part was flamboyant and often quixotic. On the one hand, he had intervened personally to help Solzhenitsyn publish his controversial novel in the fall of 1962; on the other, he suddenly and viciously turned on the liberals during his visit to the Manezh, thus setting off the cultural offensive. In the course of the campaign, he denounced Valentin Katayev who, as editor of the journal *Yunost,* had helped many young writers in getting a start; Victor Nekrasov, former Stalin Prize winner and novelist, for his favorable travel notes on France; and Voznesensky and Paustovsky. Yet Khrushchev praised Yevtushenko, whose own five-part autobiography had begun to appear illegally in the French weekly *L'Express;* and, though at first denouncing Ilya Ehrenburg, he later urged Ehrenburg to finish publishing his controversial memoirs. Then, too, with Khrushchev frequently preoccupied with more pressing matters, lower-ranking officials were left to their own devices and often used the campaign for their own ends.

Surely an important factor in bringing Khrushchev's colleagues together to force his resignation was their increasing awareness that Khrushchev's personal style of leadership often resulted actually in negating his—as well as their—goal of dynamic but orderly process of government under party leadership. During his years in office Khrushchev had never been able to achieve general popularity and respect, despite his real accomplishments and his unceasing efforts to move among the people, to talk to them, and to make himself known to them. He talked too much, and in the early days he drank too much and clowned in public, appearing to lack dignity in his behavior both at home and abroad. He was never able to build a political image of the kind that perhaps Russians still expect, namely, the stern and remote father figure. During his last years in office there was no day that he or his lieutenants were not mentioned in the newspapers. He managed to hang on to his office despite major blunders, sometimes cowing his rivals by means of extreme recrimination (as was allegedly the case with Kozlov) or else relying on rotation to make them insecure and to prevent them from establishing solid, personal bases of power. The establishment of the dual system in the party and government that he pushed through in the spring of 1963, against violent opposition, was at least in part designed as a means of shaking up both the economic as well as the party administration. Moreover, under his individualistic rule, personal likes and dislikes apparently often outweighed objective factors: officials who for one reason or another incurred his displeasure were removed from responsible positions and relegated to jobs of lesser significance. He frequently washed the party's dirty linen in public. In the end, he appears to have increasingly bypassed his colleagues, relying more and more on his extremely able son-in-law Alexei Adzhubei (editor of *Izvestiia*) as a sounding board and channel for public communication, and even appealing over the heads of his colleagues to the Soviet people, as with the proposals for agricultural reform in the summer of 1964. These actions no doubt appeared to his colleagues to vitiate the ideal of a Soviet political system based on order, regularity, the division of labor, and professionalism.

Khrushchev's ouster on October 13, 1964, carefully planned and quietly and efficiently executed, startled the world but caused hardly a ripple among the Soviet public. His former colleagues (including Leonid Brezhnev, Nikolai Shvernik, Pyotr Shelest, Nikolai Podgorny, Alexei Kosygin, Dimitri Polyansky, Anastas Mikoyan, Mikhail Suslov, Gennady Voronov, Alexander Shelepin, Alexander Kirilenko), who now constituted the new "collective leadership," appeared relaxed and self-assured. Intending to restore confidence in the party as well as calm, efficient government, they stepped out of the limelight. Whereas Khrushchev, a temperamental, colorful figure, had been constantly in the public eye, under his successors days and weeks went by without any mention in the news of the activities of any of the leaders specifically. They called off the traditional New Year's gala reception and dance for foreign diplomats and correspondents at the great Kremlin Palace and sent only a modest message to the nation. They refrained from talking privately with foreigners, and their own personal statements seldom went beyond repetition of public statements of the government.

After more than two years, "collective leadership" still seems to function effectively—no mean feat—buttressed by continuity in leadership (essentially the same men who took over from Khrushchev are still in office) and by an apparently efficient division of labor. Although Brezhnev, as general secretary of the party, Podgorny, as chief of state, and Kosygin, as premier, appear to have the major responsibility for political, foreign, and economic problems, respectively, the members of the group nevertheless seem to operate as a genuine team, each looking out for his own area of concern, arriving at decisions through consensus, and cooperating frequently in similar endeavors. Thus, for example, the leadership divided up the speeches at the sessions of the Supreme Soviet and the plenary meeting of the Central Committee of the party in 1965 and at the Twenty-third Congress of the CPSU in March 1966, and no better example of cooperative endeavor can be found than the great Soviet "peace offensive" in Asia in January 1966, when simultaneously Kosygin helped to negotiate the India-Pakistan cease-fire in Tashkent, Shelepin headed a Soviet mission to Hanoi, and Brezhnev negotiated renewal of the Soviet-Mongolian treaty in Ulan Bator.

The team has accomplished a great deal since its inception. In the economic field, the new leaders eschewed Khrushchev's utopian visions as well as his penchant for solving problems through organizational restructuring; they have been more willing to introduce genuine economic reforms. It took only a month before the new leaders issued a decree abolishing the party and governmental reform of 1962 (which instituted two separate party and governmental hierarchies for industry and agriculture) and restoring unity in party committees at the local level. Within a year, too, the regional councils for industrial planning (*sovnarkhozy*), established by Khrushchev in the spring of 1957, were abolished and the ministries resurrected. The new leaders have also undertaken major reforms in agriculture, the area in the Soviet economy in which there are the greatest shortcomings. In March 1965 Brezhnev announced a major program of capital investment in agriculture, stressing that the Khrushchevian farm panaceas—such as his corn program and the virgin lands scheme—were to be either abandoned or de-emphasized. In June 1966 the Central Committee approved a vast land reclamation project, which provides for extension of irrigation over arid but usable lands in the southern Ukraine, Central Asia, and the northern Caucasus as well as (and this appears even more promising) the drainage and refurbishment of marshy land in northwestern Russia, Byelorussia, and the Baltic states, where weather conditions are reliable. Apparently devoid of gimmickry or crash psychology (a characteristic of so many previous Soviet efforts at land improvement), these projects seem to represent a slow, sound, traditional, long-range program for installing good practices of cultivation on both new (and suitable) land or on land already in use—an effort which, if successful, could ultimately go a long way toward solving one of Soviet Russia's basic economic problems. The new leadership also sanctioned the effort to destroy the last vestiges of Lysenkoism, which for so many years kept Soviet agriculture from benefiting from the results of modern research. The fraudulent nature of agricultural investigations carried out under Lysenko's direction were published in a report filling the entire November 1965 issue of *Vestnik,* the journal of the Soviet Academy of Sciences, which contained the reports of the investigating commission, Lysenko's replies, and the deliberations on the report by a joint meeting of representatives from the Soviet Academy of Agricultural Sciences, the Soviet Academy of Sciences, and the Ministry of Agriculture.

All talk about quick panaceas in industrial production and in consumption appears also to have faded, since the new leaders would seem to be aware that although Khrushchev contributed personally to the disarray in Soviet economic life by imposing erratic schemes on, and unpredictably interfering with, the planning and running of both agriculture and industry, the problems he faced were not of his own making: the Soviet economy is in need of radical reform. Thus, after an initial series of temporary corrective actions—including a crash program to get rid of a mountain of formerly accumulated unsalable goods, the repeal of Khrushchev's overly ambitious chemical expansion program, a round of sizable wage increases, and the scrapping of the entire structure of regional economic councils (*sovnarkhozy*)—the new leaders have begun to institute a very expensive long-range program, clearly on the basis of careful study, that will take years to implement, but that may well become one of the important steps in the economic development of the country.

The over-all goal of a ground-breaking series of measures taken by the new leaders since September 1965 is the abolition of the antiquated parts of the centralized system of economic planning and production inherited from Stalin and continued under Khrushchev. Under the old system, the whole range of basic decisions on economic planning, production, and even consumption were all made in Moscow so that, in the end, every enterprise or firm was told what to produce, at what cost to produce, to whom to sell and at what price, and how much to spend on what amounts of wages, fuel, materials, and components. Yet it has become obvious in recent years that the economy has grown much too big and too complicated for the old methods to work, and that even Khrushchev's efforts to devolve some powers to the regions—carried out without real economic modernization—led merely to further bottlenecks, confusion, and slowing down in economic growth. But in their efforts to introduce a new rationality into the Soviet economy, the Soviet leaders were faced with choosing among rival methods for reform, of which the two most important are those advocated by Professor Yevsei Liberman—whose ideals call for letting economic institutions at the local level make their own decisions based on a quasi supply-and-demand situation—and by the mathematical economists, such as Professor Leonid Kantorovich who, while urging the retention of central planning and direction, would adopt modern complex mathematical techniques for resource allocation applied with the help of computers. Either method contains problems. On the one hand, the abolition of centralized planning and direction in heavy industry would bring about a decline of production in that field, since this sector of the economy has always lent itself particularly well to centralized planning in both socialist and capitalist economies. On the other hand, the attempt to apply central computerized planning techniques to the whole area of consumer goods appears to be a manifest impossibility, when it is remembered that in the growing field of consumer-goods production in the Soviet Union there are at present millions of definably different types of products; no computer system or organization of information flows could possibly cope with a system of products of this magnitude. Keeping all of this in mind, the new Soviet leaders are instituting a mixed system in which the elements of central planning for the realization of national goals are to be preserved, and at the same time, independent managerial initiative, wider commercial freedom, more flexible prices, and more reliance on profits are to be encouraged through decentralization at the local level.

After a year of testing—in which experiments begun under Khrushchev were extended to many more firms and enterprises in various parts of the Soviet Union—the new system of "market socialism" was introduced on a nationwide basis in September 1965. It calls for the reduction of detailed planning of factory operations on the part of central government agencies; the evaluation of plant performance on the basis of sales rather than gross output; the greater handling of profits; the financing of large investment for plant expansion and the construction of new enterprises through interest-bearing loans rather than outright governmental budgetary grants; the payment of a fixed return to the government from profits; and the introduction of new wholesale prices based on actual production costs. In order to help Soviet managers understand their new functions, the government published a *Statute on the Socialist State Productive Enterprise,* set up a national market-research organization (the All-Union Scientific Research Institute for the Study of the Demand and Trade Fluctuations), worked out regulations for granting long-term bank loans, and in general shifted some of the budgetary priorities from producer to consumer goods and to the long-neglected service industries. In order to help rationalize both central planning as well as flexible market practices, the government also set up a new State Committee on Prices, which is expected to work out a general price policy under the new conditions and determine the category of goods for which the government must continue to fix prices as well as a list of commodities for which the laws of the market may be permitted to operate to some extent. Finally, in order to place full credit for the "new wave" in economics where it belongs, the new leaders awarded Lenin Prizes to three of the top mathematical economists.

Yet, despite these striking reforms, or perhaps because of them, many problems have still to be faced. In the first place, there are a number of technical problems. Although managers cannot begin to operate genuinely on the basis of profit until the prices at which their goods are sold are determined, the reform in price structure is expected to take years. Market research is only in its infancy in the USSR, and yet it is crucial to the new flexible operation of firms and enterprises and the wholesale and retail organizations. Nor has it been established whether the latter or the former should assume the burdens, responsibilities, and risks for establishing what consumers want. Indeed, servicing and merchandising are the most notoriously underdeveloped sectors of Soviet economic life, thus providing a major obstacle that will have to be overcome. There are personnel problems as well. A vast retraining program for managerial personnel seems inevitable, as the shift from a production orientation to focus on sales and profits becomes increasingly widespread. Moreover, the establishment of a major employment program seems unavoidable, as industrial plants increasingly rationalize their production; indeed, there is already growing unemployment, the result of automation, technical progress, and flight from the countryside. Finally, the massive economic reforms appear to be producing also a rich harvest of bureaucratic squabbles, as the old economic organizations seek to inhibit progress or to reclaim lost power and functions under the new system.

On the cultural scene, however, the new team has moved much more cautiously than in the economic realm. Indeed, it may be said that they have followed essentially the guide lines developed by Khrushchev—keeping the cultural liberals and conservatives in balance, permitting neither to dominate the other; containing carefully the radicals on the right and on the left; always permitting some progress; following a policy of "divide and conquer" in the event of broadly based opposition; always insisting on the party's place in the arts and literature and on the general primacy of Socialist Realism—without, however, resorting to Khrushchev's penchant for personal interference, or his flummery, or permitting subordinates to follow policies of extreme repression or liberality.

In the winter and spring of 1965 Khrushchev's successors made it clear that while they eschewed Khrushchev's highly personalized and erratic approach in the cultural field, they expected to follow a sober middle course—and that they expected "searching young artists and writers" to do the same. *Pravda*'s new editor, Alexei Rumyantsev, issued an apology—for the sharp cultural freeze of 1962–63—and a promise, namely, prohibiting the use of the command technique in artistic matters. Thus the arts again revived: new and unorthodox writers and artists were once again elected to office in the unions; Ilychev, the chief party cultural official under Khrushchev, was dropped from office in March 1965; jazz was for the first time officially accepted, and a Moscow Jazz Festival was held in the Composers' Club of Moscow in June 1965; Pasternak's poems were again reprinted in July 1965; and in March 1965 official recognition was finally accorded to Alexander Tyshler, the sixty-seven-year-old modern painter considered one of the leading pupils of the turn-of-the-century experimental artists, by means of a one-man show of his paintings and graphics held at the Pushkin Museum in Moscow—although, only a couple of months later, the press denounced Oscar Rabin, a young expressionist painter, for permitting an exhibition in London of his "neurotic" paintings.

By the end of the summer of 1965, however, a quiet movement again appeared to have been under way, directed not against the conservatives or liberals in the cultural community, but against nonconformist writers and their readers among the younger generation. Coupled with efforts to restore traditional Communist ideals in Soviet life and particularly in the education of youth, it reflected the serious high-level concern over what was felt to be the "negativism" and "maladjustment to life" on the part of the younger generation. The new cultural offensive got under way at the beginning of August with a series of reviews in *Pravda* and *Izvestiia* that contained criticism of a recent play, *My Poor Marat,* by Alexei Arbuzov, in which he described the declining idealism of Soviet youth, and of the experimental and allegedly "obscure" poetry of Andrei Voznesensky. Although Rumyantsev himself appears to have attempted to curtail the campaign (obviously with some high-level backing) by criticizing in an editorial both *Izvestiia* and *Selskaia zhizn* (the party's farm affairs paper) for condemning authors who exposed the seamier side of Soviet life, the criticisms continued, and in October Andrei Sinyavsky and Yuri Daniel, two nonconformist Moscow writers, were quietly arrested and held for interrogation. Both had lived ordinary lives as employees of the Gorky Literary Institute in Moscow, the former as teacher and critic who wrote perfectly acceptable reviews for *Novy mir* and the latter as translator, but both had also clandestinely published in the West widely read political fantasies and essays, under the pen names of Abram Tertz and Nikolai Arzhak, respectively, including the former's *The Trial Begins, Fantastic Tales, Liubimov,* and a brilliant essay, *On Socialist Realism,* and the latter's *Moscow Calling* and other stories. In February 1966 Valery Tarsis, an outspokenly anti-Soviet, nonconformist writer who had once been declared "insane" by the Soviet authorities and as a consequence gained international fame for his stinging memoir of the Soviet mental home in which he had been confined, *Ward 7* (he managed to have it published in Britain), was given permission to deliver a series of lectures at a British university, no doubt in the hope that he would defect—which he did.

These efforts, conducted thus with rapier rather than bludgeon, appear to have culminated in two important events: the now famous court trial of Sinyavsky and Daniel that was held on February 10–14 before a select audience in a small courtroom in Moscow to which only Soviet newsmen were admitted, at which the defendants, having pleaded not guilty, were sentenced, respectively, to seven and five years' hard labor on charges of having published abroad works of an allegedly anti-Soviet character; and the cultural pronouncements in Brezhnev's keynote speech at the Twenty-third Congress of the CPSU, on March 29, 1966, in which, though paying tribute to experimentation in the arts, he reaffirmed the orthodox position of the party on literature ("we are invariably guided by the principles of the partisanship of art, a class approach to the appraisal of everything that is being done in the sphere of culture") and justified the recent trial ("the Soviet people cannot ignore the disgraceful activity of such people"). The general tone of official orthodoxy in the arts was strengthened by the presence at the congress of conservative writers such as Viacheslav Kochetov and Alexei Surkov and the absence of the well-known liberals Alexander Tvardovsky and Boris Polevoi (who had been passed over in the party elections to the congress), and by having an address given by the venerable Mikhail Sholokhov, whose lifelong hatred of the urban intellectual prompted him this time too to denounce the two writers as "traitors" and their writings as "mud from a puddle." The government also arrested and sentenced Ivan Svetlichny and Ivan Dzyuba, two well-known liberal Ukrainian literary critics who had evidently been involved in smuggling "unacceptable" works abroad. But apart from these actions, and apart from reiterating the traditional position of the party in the realm of the arts, the new Soviet leadership made no attempt to alter the established balance between the artists and the state, being sensitive certainly to the vigorous protests by the Soviet cultural community and to the critical publicity emanating in the West, particularly from the Western Communists.

Important changes have also been made in foreign policy. The new leaders have cast aside the flamboyant Khrushchevian style and reverted to quiet, firm diplomacy, and they have also changed considerably the direction and goals of their foreign endeavors. Whereas during his last year and a half in office Khrushchev coupled direct opposition to China with direct approaches to the United States, seeking a major *détente* with the latter, the new men have embarked on a new path, being fearful that Sino-Soviet tension might erupt into border skirmishes or lead into a final breach that would shatter irrevocably what was left of the Communist world movement. Immediately after Khrushchev's ouster, the new leaders suspended the public polemics with the Chinese, and soon Chou En-lai, China's premier, was on his way to Moscow for exploratory talks. Cooperation proving impossible, however, the regime shifted its policy away from direct opposition to China (for example, public denunciations of the Chinese, a regular feature of the Moscow press from 1961 to 1964, ceased) to indirect competition for influence on China's allies and on the anti-Western nationalist governments in Asia, Africa, and Latin America.[1] At the same time, without returning to the all-embracing offensive against the Western alliance that Khrushchev had pursued, with disastrous results, until the Cuban missile crisis, the new leaders have resorted again to a traditional diplomatic policy: while permitting their zeal for major bilateral negotiations with the United States to cool down, they have transferred their main efforts to indirect maneuvers for exploiting differences within the Western alliance.

Their efforts have borne considerable fruit. Their patient diplomacy, their distaste for foreign adventures, their ability to provide genuine economic and technical assistance, and their willingness to state that the development of socialism in the new nationalist regimes may be possible, under certain conditions, without the leadership, or even separate existence, of the local Communist parties—all this has won for them again considerable influence both among the Communist-bloc countries, including Cuba, North Vietnam, and North Korea as well as among the underdeveloped nations, whereas the Communist Chinese (still a symbol of dogmatic, revolutionary intransigence), have been steadily discredited in the eyes of the Afro-Asians, the Latins, and lately even the Romanians. The patience of the new Soviet leaders in the Vietnam crisis has also been rewarded. While it has led to a cooling of Soviet-American relations, and while the regime was obviously not displeased over the American failures in Vietnam in the fall and winter of 1965–66, the new leadership obviously feared that the development of a Korea-type war might force Moscow to honor her commitments to the North Vietnamese—a war which, from the Kremlin's point of view, would have been the wrong war at the wrong time and place. But the stage appears to have long passed when Soviet Russia would have to react sharply. Finally, in probing the weak spots of the Western position both in Europe and among the new nations, the new leaders have hit upon a most powerful instrument for disrupting the Western alliance: President de Gaulle's ambition to build up an independent world power based on a French-led Western Europe. First begun in March 1964, when Nikolai Podgorny visited Paris; nourished by the Soviet sympathy for de Gaulle's views on the United Nations, his proposal for a return to the gold standard, his opposition to the American-sponsored plan for a multilateral nuclear force in NATO, his interest in expanding trade with Eastern Europe, and

---

[1] In the face of the steadily deteriorating relations between the Soviet Union and China, the Soviet leaders—in the fall of 1966—began once again an effort to marshal support from the "fraternal" parties around the world for calling a conference expelling the Chinese from the international Communist movement.

his outlook on—though not his specific proposals for—the restoration of peace in Vietnam; and brought to a high pitch by de Gaulle's extended visit to the Soviet Union in June 1966—the Franco-Soviet *rapprochement* must be considered an important factor in world diplomacy in the immediate future.

All of these policies—economic, cultural, diplomatic—were confirmed by the party's Twenty-third Congress, held in Moscow from March 29 to April 8, 1966. The congress also laid to rest any doubts that may have remained about the reality of "collective leadership." The sessions were quiet and businesslike, the speeches pedestrian in style and notable for their avoidance of the thorniest issues. The sobriety of Brezhnev's keynote speech contrasted sharply with the flamboyance and boldness of Khrushchev's speeches at the party congresses of 1956, 1959, and 1961.

These features may be ascribed not to excessive bureaucratism perhaps but, rather, to the efforts made by the new team to win friends and influence people abroad and, at home, to maintain the party's historical primacy as well as an ideologically integrated society, even in the face of the increasing sophistication and modernization of the Soviet nation. The moderation and forbearance of the new Soviet leaders was undoubtedly responsible for drawing the leaders of almost all of the world's Communist parties to Moscow, a major feat of Communist intramural maneuvering, despite the Chinese Communists' boycott; thus only the parties of Albania, Japan, and New Zealand joined the Chinese in spurning the Soviet invitation, whereas the North Koreans and North Vietnamese attended.

In order to strengthen party discipline, increase the authority of the leadership over the party and of the party over Soviet society, the congress approved measures that would henceforth restrict admission to the party, make expulsion of undesirables from the party easier, annul automatic rotation of party officials and, at the central level of the organization, abolish the Central Committee's Bureau for the Russian republic, enlarge the Central Committee from 340 to 360 members, and readopt the old designations "Politburo" for the Presidium and "general secretary" for the office of first secretary. Moreover, the membership of the party's executive committees remained virtually unchanged. Of the Presidium's twelve members (Brezhnev, Voronov, Kirilenko, Kosygin, Mazurov, Mikoyan, Podgorny, Polyansky, Suslov, Shvernik, Shelepin, Shelest), all were re-elected to the Politburo except Mikoyan and Shvernik. Arvid Pelshe, the first secretary of the Latvian party, was also promoted to the Politburo. Six of the seven previous candidate members of the Presidium—Demichev, Grishin, Mzhavanadze, Rashidov, Ustinov, Shcherbitsky—were reappointed as candidate members of the Politburo (Leonid Yefremov having been dropped), along with two new candidate members, Kunayev and Masherov, and all but one (Podgorny) of the previous eleven members of the party Secretariat were re-elected, including Brezhnev (as general secretary),

Suslov, Shelepin, Demichev, Ustinov, Andropov, Ponomarev, Kapitonov, Kulakov, and Rudakov,[2] with Kirilenko taking over Podgorny's vacated place. Thus once again continuity prevailed.

The last two years have seen the nearest thing to government by consensus that Russia in all its history has ever achieved, except for the period of provisional government (1917) and part of the 1920's—a remarkable phenomenon in a country governed for decades, indeed for centuries, by a single ruler. How has it been possible? A number of reasons come to mind. Perhaps Khrushchev's fall was the outcome not of any determination on the part of his closest comrades to reverse all of his policies, but to drop some and clarify, coordinate, and develop others, to cut out the nonsense and flamboyance. In other words, to a remarkable extent the present leadership see eye to eye on many of the key issues in foreign and domestic policy, and where there are disagreements—these are inevitable—conflicts often appear to be worked out first on the lower levels. Moreover, the present leaders undoubtedly keep in mind the deleterious consequences of one-man rule in a complex modern society. But whether the governing team can continue to live with some of the long-standing problems that are as yet unresolved—such as polycentrism in the international Communist movement, the continuing tensions with China, the nagging coolness in Soviet-American relations—and make far-reaching changes that must ultimately threaten the jobs of many thousands of tough officials and bring about much movement in Soviet society without a strong hand at the helm, remains to be seen.

[2] Alexander Rudakov died on July 10, 1966.

Leonid Ilyich Brezhnev

by Grey Hodnett

In the Hall of Catherine the Great in the Kremlin on April 17, 1964, Leonid Brezhnev, acting as chairman of the Presidium of the Supreme Soviet, presented Nikita Khrushchev on his seventieth birthday with the highest award of the Soviet Union—the Order of Lenin and the Gold Star of Hero of the Soviet Union. Having lauded Khrushchev's virtues, Brezhnev delivered the hug and three kisses required by "ancient Russian custom," amid the applause of the assembled leaders of party and state. Barely six months later, however, *Pravda* announced to a startled world that a plenum of the Central Committee of the Communist Party of the Soviet Union (CPSU) held on October 14, 1964, had "satisfied the request of N. S. Khrushchev to be released from the duties of first secretary of the Central Committee of the CPSU, and of chairman of the Council of Ministers of the USSR in connection with advanced age and a deterioration of his health." The man chosen to fill the highest, most coveted position in the Soviet Union—first secretary of the CPSU—was Khrushchev's former protégé, loyal supporter, and heir apparent, Leonid Brezhnev.

Leonid Ilyich Brezhnev was born on December 19, 1906, in the eastern Ukrainian village of Kamensk (now the city of Dneprodzerzhinsk) in what is today Dnepropetrovsk Oblast. The village was situated on the right bank of the Dnieper, in a dry yet fertile region, near Krivoi Rog, whose vast iron ore deposits continue to feed the metallurgical industry of Dnepropetrovsk, Zaporozhe, and the coal-mining Donbass region just to the east. Little is known about Brezhnev's early family life except that his father was a Russian by nationality and a metallurgical worker by profession. Leonid was eight years old when the First World War erupted, and eleven when the Bolshevik Revolution in far-off Petrograd (now Leningrad) precipitated the brief Austro-German occupation of the eastern Ukraine and the long months of civil war in which the White Volunteer Army, Red Army detachments, Cossack forces, Makhnovite guerrillas, Petlurists, and Socialist Revolutionaries met each other in fighting of unparalleled ferocity. What role, if any, his father played in this revolutionary upheaval is not known; but the future first secretary was old enough to have been deeply impressed by these dramatic events of the early phase of Soviet history.

In 1921, at fifteen, the young Brezhnev held his first job—probably some form of manual labor. Two years later he took the first step in his political career by joining the Komsomol (Young Communist League). Simultaneously, and while continuing to work, he pursued his secondary education, graduating in 1927 from a land-surveying vocational high school in Kursk, a city in the southwestern corner of the Russian republic. He then worked briefly as a surveyor in the Kursk provincial agricultural administration. Later in 1927 he made the long move to the Ural (now Sverdlovsk) Oblast where until 1930, during the initial years of the drive toward collectivization and industrialization, he worked briefly as a surveyor in a local agricultural administration and then held in rapid succession the posts of chief of a district agricultural department, deputy chairman of the Bissertsk district executive committee, and deputy chief of the Ural Oblast Agricultural Administration in the city of Sverdlovsk—all branches of the state machinery which were immediately concerned with governing the Russian peasantry. Thus, at twenty-four, Brezhnev had already managed to rise to a responsible administrative position involving active participation in the most traumatic undertaking of Stalin's "third revolution"—the collectivization of Soviet agriculture.

Suddenly, for reasons unknown, Brezhnev returned to the western part of the Soviet Union, apparently attending an agricultural institute in Moscow during 1930 and 1931. In the latter year he joined the Communist party, and also went back to his native Dneprodzerzhinsk, where he entered the Dneprodzerzhinsk Metallurgical Institute. After graduating from the Institute in 1935, it seems that he worked briefly at the F. E. Dzerzhinsky Metallurgical Factory before being called into the Red Army that same year. It is likely that he served as a political worker while in the army. Upon leaving military service in 1937, he is said by a recent official Soviet source to have spent a few months as director of a vocational high school in Dneprodzerzhinsk. Higher education apart, the popular stereotype of Brezhnev as an "engineer" is therefore misleading.

Brezhnev's unexceptional life was soon interrupted by the sinister course of Ukrainian political affairs in 1937. On March 17 it was announced that Pavel Postyshev, Stalin's emissary in the Ukraine and the man who since 1933 had relentlessly implemented a policy of exterminating the slightest sign of real or fancied opposition to Stalin's will, had been removed from his position as second secretary of the Communist Party of the Ukraine, shortly to vanish without a trace. Soon after, Postyshev's followers and appointees began to suffer the same fate. In late August, it is thought by some observers, a special commission consisting of Viacheslav Molotov, Nikolai I. Yezhov, and Khrushchev arrived in Kiev to purge the top Ukrainian party and government leadership and to install Khrushchev as the successor to Postyshev in the secretariat of the Ukrainian party. In any event Khrushchev soon became first secretary of the Ukrainian party. His appointment in January 1938 coincided with a lethal purge of thousands of party and state officials. Into the posts of the dead and departed stepped a younger and more docile generation of functionaries, among them Brezhnev.

In May 1937 Brezhnev had been appointed deputy chairman of the Dneprodzerzhinsk Executive Committee (city government). Evidently he met whatever expectations were held concerning his performance, for in May 1938 he was promoted to chief of a department of the Dnepropetrovsk Oblast Party Committee, and a year later he became secretary of this committee for propaganda affairs. Although it is conceivable that he was not involved in the frenzied political denunciations of these years, it is most implausible to suppose that he suffered no contamination whatever. As a result of the purges, Brezhnev, like many of his peers, achieved a position beyond all reasonable expectation for a person of his age and limited experience.

Brezhnev's brief career as a local party official was soon interrupted by the German invasion of the Soviet Union. From 1941 to 1945 he was a political worker in the Soviet Army, serving as deputy chief of the Political Administration of the Southern Front, chief of the political department of an army, and chief of the Political Administration of the Fourth Ukrainian Front, receiving in 1943 the rank of general-major. In 1946 he served as chief of the political administration of a military district. For a time he served directly under Khrushchev, thereby strengthening ties that later were to prove of great value. As a political worker Brezhnev supervised propaganda, Komsomol work, and party affairs; unlike Khrushchev he did not enjoy the status of membership in a military council, which carried with it some voice in the actual conduct of military operations.

Among the first postwar fruits of his affiliation with Khrushchev may probably be counted Brezhnev's appointment in 1946 as first secretary of the Zaporozhe Oblast Party Committee in the southeastern Ukraine. During this period wartime destruction of farm machinery and livestock and the drought of 1946 combined to produce near-famine conditions in the Ukraine. Large quantities of UNRRA (United Nations Relief and Rehabilitation Administration) aid helped to alleviate the crisis—a crisis that loomed sufficiently large in Stalin's eyes, it seems, to have led to Khrushchev's replacement in March 1947 as first secretary of the Ukraine by Lazar Kaganovich. Brezhnev's performance during this tense year may help to explain the promotion he received in November 1947 to first secretary of the Dnepropetrovsk Oblast Party Committee, preceding by one month Khrushchev's recall to his post of Ukrainian first secretary. Dnepropetrovsk is known both for its metallurgical industry and for its agriculture, although its population is predominantly urban.

Brezhnev continued to serve as first secretary in Dnepropetrovsk until 1950, when he followed Khrushchev to Moscow. The few months he worked in the Central Committee apparatus during 1950 exposed him for the first time to the conduct of party affairs at the highest level. But his job in Moscow—in retrospect—was merely routine preparation for a more important task. In July 1950, at forty-four, Brezhnev "arrived" as a top Soviet leader; with Khrushchev's apparent support and with Stalin's blessing, he was appointed first secretary of the Communist Party of Moldavia.

In the summer of 1940, following the Nazi-Soviet Pact, the Soviet Union invaded and annexed Bessarabia, which had been lost to Romania after the First World War. Shortly thereafter a "Moldavian Soviet Socialist Republic" was established—incorporating the newly acquired territory and a part of the territory in the southwestern Ukraine known until then as the Moldavian Autonomous Socialist Republic. During the Second World War the Romanians reoccupied the region, but Soviet control was restored in 1944. Soviet interest in the area was, and remains, largely geopolitical. There are few mineral resources in the region and little heavy industry; wine, tobacco, and other agricultural commodities are Moldavia's predominant contribution to the Soviet economy. The "Moldavian" inhabitants of the republic are ethnically close to, if not identical with, Romanians, though before the Soviet occupation there was also a significant indigenous Ukrainian peasant population. Some Russians and a large concentration of Jews lived in the towns, especially in the capital of Moldavia, Kishinev. The vast majority of the population lived in the countryside, where—even by 1950—few Communist party members could be found. Brezhnev's task as first secretary of the Moldavian party was to extend party membership and control in the countryside, solidify the newly established collective farm system, extract the largest possible agricultural surpluses from a recalcitrant peasantry, and enforce the Russifying nationality policy of the Soviet party.

Brezhnev's efforts were rewarded at the Nineteenth Congress of the CPSU in October 1952. Not only was he elected to the Central Committee, which was automatic in view of his status as head of a republic party; he was elevated by Stalin to candidate membership in what had become the highest formal policy-making body of the CPSU—the Presidium. Given Stalin's personal manner of determining major policy, this promotion was largely symbolic, reflecting the great rise in Brezhnev's status brought about by Stalin's decision—perhaps at Khrushchev's urging—to summon Brezhnev back to Moscow as a secretary of the party's Central Committee. It may be assumed that Stalin would hardly have entrusted such a sensitive position to anyone concerning whose personal loyalty he harbored even the faintest doubts.

As Brezhnev entered the Secretariat, the storm signals of a new purge were visible even to the most superficial observer. Clearly Brezhnev was among the group being jockeyed into position to replace those leaders whom Stalin intended (as Khrushchev put it) to "shorten by a head." Stalin's death on March 5, 1953, prevented the drama from progressing to its conclusion. It is unlikely that the full story of the months preceding Stalin's death will soon be revealed; and what role Brezhnev played during this period is simply unknown. Nevertheless, it is known that Brezhnev was removed from both the Presidium and the Secretariat immediately after Stalin's death and downgraded to the post of first deputy chief of the Main Political Administration of the Ministry of Defense, with responsibility for political supervision of the navy. This demotion may have reflected not only an attempt by the "collective leadership" to restrict Khrushchev's political power, but personal animus toward Brezhnev as well. Yet two factors—the depressed condition of Soviet argiculture and Khrushchev's political ambitions—were soon to propel Brezhnev once again toward high office.

In February 1954, at a plenary meeting of the Central Committee, Khrushchev unveiled a bold scheme to achieve rapid increases in agricultural output by plowing up 90 million acres of so-called virgin lands located east of the Volga, in western Siberia, and especially in the northern part of Kazakhstan. This agricultural campaign, entailing a massive mobilization of people and physical resources, was an enormous gamble, its success depending to no small degree on the vigor of the leadership of the Communist Party of Kazakhstan.

Several weeks before the February plenum convened, Zhumabai Shaiakhmetov, a Kazakh and the first secretary of the Kazakh party, had been driven from office, being charged with favoritism toward Kazakhs in employment and therefore, by implication, with discrimination against Slavs. Later hints indicated, however, that the personnel issue may have been related to an even more fundamental clash over policy. The Kazakh leaders, it has been speculated, resisted the virgin lands program because they correctly foresaw that plowing up the grazing lands of northern Kazakhstan—an area larger than France—would inevitably mean that the native Kazakhs would be swamped by an influx of Russians and Ukrainians.

Leading the immigration that did occur was Pantaleimon Ponomarenko, a candidate member of the Presidium of the CPSU, who replaced Shaiakhmetov as first secretary of the Communist Party of Kazakhstan. The new second secretary of the Kazakh party, whose duties included supervising the purge of Shaiakhmetov's adherents, was Leonid Brezhnev. Following Ponomarenko's departure in August 1954, Brezhnev moved up to first secretary of Kazakhstan, a post of great power and prestige, but a dangerous one; Brezhnev is so far the only man who has held it in the post-Stalin period without being purged.

Fortunately for Khrushchev and Brezhnev, the first few years of the virgin lands program did not produce the resounding failure that many Soviet leaders seem to have anticipated. The record 33-million-ton wheat harvest in 1956 may well have been a crucial contribution to Khrushchev's victory over the "anti-party group." Brezhnev, whose work in Kazakhstan had helped to lay the groundwork for the large harvests of the early years, was rewarded at the Twentieth Congress of the CPSU in February 1956 by re-election to the positions he had held three years earlier: candidate member of the Presidium and secretary of the Central Committee of the CPSU. Safely back in Moscow, he was now in a position to support Khrushchev in the latter's struggle for power.

On July 4, 1957, following a bitter battle in the party Presidium, far-reaching changes in the Presidium membership were announced. Because of apparent assistance from the party apparatus, the army, and (perhaps) the secret police, Khrushchev had managed to turn the tables on his opponents—constituting a majority of the eleven-man Presidium—and to expel Georgi Malenkov, Molotov, Kaganovich, and Maxim Saburov, while demoting Mikhail Pervukhin to candidate membership. These five full members of the supreme policy-making body of the USSR were replaced by nine newcomers, most of whom had risen to high office under Khrushchev's sponsorship. Six of the nine were recruited from the party apparatus —reflecting Khrushchev's indebtedness to the apparatus or his estimate of where loyal followers were to be found, or both. Brezhnev was one of these six.

There is little reason to doubt that before June 1957, Brezhnev was a protégé of Khrushchev, largely obliged to the latter for his rapid rise to the heights of power. Brezhnev's relationship to Khrushchev after this date cannot be described with such assurance, because it was in large measure determined by the extent of Khrushchev's influence over the other members of the Soviet elite—still a much disputed question. What can be stated is that Brezhnev remained a secretary of the Central Committee for three years—the three years in which Khrushchev's foreign and domestic policies achieved their greatest general success—leaving in July 1960 to become chairman of the Presidium of the Supreme Soviet, a position previously held by the aging Kliment Voroshilov and one often considered in the West to be inferior to membership in the Secretariat. Brezhnev's departure from the Secretariat followed soon after a sharpening of economic difficulties, the embarrassment of the U-2 affair and the aborted summit conference, the dismissal from the party Presidium of a number of persons believed to be Khrushchev's close followers (including the then heir apparent and de facto second secretary, Alexei Kirichenko), and the promotion to the Secretariat of Frol Kozlov. Some observers interpret these personnel changes as signs of Khrushchev's weakening power; Brezhnev, in their view, was one of "Khrushchev's men," sacrificed to protect Khrushchev's flanks. Others argue that Khrushchev shifted the leadership in 1960 simply because he was dissatisfied with the work of certain individuals.

If his departure from the Secretariat in 1960 deprived Brezhnev of actual administrative power, his tenure as chairman of the Presidium of the Supreme Soviet may have partly compensated for this loss by giving him more publicity than is usually accorded a secretary of the Central Committee and by broadening his experience in areas heretofore outside his field of responsibility—especially foreign affairs.

Brezhnev's life before 1960 was to some extent that of a typical, successful, territorial party official: humble family background; some technical training; brief professional employment; a rather long mid-career residence in the provinces, with economic (especially agricultural) affairs the focus of interest and efficient execution of commands from above the main criterion of success; and some staff and line experience in the central party apparatus. In Brezhnev's case this pattern was augmented to some degree by membership in the Presidium of the Central Committee. On the other hand, if in one sense it may be said that Brezhnev's past had been narrowly confined to organizational manipulation, in another sense it may likewise be said that he had already been exposed to an unusually broad range of the substantive problems of Soviet political life—in local government, party-military relations, industrial and agricultural management, political indoctrination, and control over non-Russian nationality groups.

Being chairman of the Presidium of the Supreme Soviet involved frequent contact—however ceremonial—with foreigners, many of whom were not Communists. This is an experience that most party officials have not had. Thus, for example, in 1961 Brezhnev went to Morocco, Guinea, Ghana, Sudan, and India, and led a party delegation to Czechoslovakia. The chairmanship also involved frequent contact and communication with a different cross-section of top Soviet officials from that normally encountered by an ordinary secretary of the Central Committee. In a political system as highly bureaucratized, compartmentalized, and secretive as that of the Soviet Union, access to people and information that cuts across institutional and hierarchical barriers is an advantage not to be underestimated. It should also be noted that in 1961 Brezhnev was awarded the title Hero of Socialist Labor for his "outstanding services in the development of rocket technology and in promoting the successful flight of a Soviet man into cosmic space in the 'Vostok' sputnik." This award indicated not only that Brezhnev had not been spending all his time performing ceremonial functions, but that he had been in close contact with the Soviet military establishment, precision engineering-armaments industry, and scientific elite.

Although it is necessary to distinguish between the Supreme Soviet as a powerless institution on the one hand, and on the other, the chairman of its Presidium, who enjoys high prestige, broad visibility, personal influence, and potential political power in crisis situations, it is true nevertheless that the chairmanship has seemed in the past to hold out little hope for advancement to the top. Brezhnev must surely have been relieved, then, when he was permitted to exchange the shadow of power for its substance.

On May 4, 1963, after Frol Kozlov's disappearance from public view for several weeks, it was belatedly announced that poor health was preventing him from performing his duties as secretary of the Central Committee. Kozlov's withdrawal from political life, which proved to be final, came toward the end of a winter that had offered numerous signs of indecision and conflict in the Kremlin; after his demise—he was at the time the heir apparent and second in command of the party—many observers thought they detected an upswing in Khrushchev's fortunes. Capping this observed trend was Brezhnev's reappointment to the Secretariat at the June 1963 plenum of the Central Committee. Brezhnev had been picked, it soon became evident, to occupy Kozlov's position as the man charged with general supervision of the party apparatus, with probable partial control over personnel matters and, no less important, as the man being groomed to succeed Khrushchev. Since, however, the Soviet political system lacks a regularized procedure for transferring power at the top, the danger exists at any moment that the heir may decide not to wait for nature to deliver the prize of the first secretaryship. In apparent recognition of this fact, Khrushchev at the same time secured the appointment to the Secretariat of another follower from the Ukrainian apparatus, Nikolai Podgorny, an ethnic Ukrainian, then first secretary of the Ukrainian Central Committee. Podgorny, it seems, was meant to counterbalance Brezhnev and keep the latter's ambitions in check.

When the showdown came in October 1964, Podgorny proved unable to prevent Khrushchev's overthrow—if indeed his sympathies did lie with Khrushchev. A conspiracy within the Presidium, abetted by passive acquiescence in the army and secret police, stripped Khrushchev of his three key positions: first secretary of the Central Committee, chairman of the Central Committee Bureau for the Russian republic, and chairman of the Council of Ministers, not to mention his membership in the party Presidium. With the sanction of the Central Committee one—but only one— of these titles was conferred upon Brezhnev: first secretary of the Central Committee of the CPSU.

In the post-Khrushchev period the procedures of the Soviet government as well as the distribution of top positions indicate that Brezhnev's authority as head of the party remains far lower than Khrushchev's. Brezhnev is hardly in a position to overwhelm his colleagues with his own talent or with the uniqueness of his past experience. He has no widespread domestic popularity, and he lacks the prestige abroad that Khrushchev was able to use to exert pressure against his associates. Nor could the lesson of Khrushchev's rise to power have been lost on the remaining Presidium members, including those, like Kosygin, whose own security depends on maintaining a certain autonomy of the state administration. Thus while Brezhnev remains the top man in the party, and was even vested with Stalin's title of "general secretary" at the party's Twenty-third Congress in April 1966, his freedom of action and his chances of achieving total power should not be overestimated.

It would be premature to speak of a clearly defined "Brezhnev policy." However, his actions after taking office appear to follow a "centrist" line in both foreign and domestic policy. Whether the social and economic forces at work in the Soviet Union will permit him to continue his attempt to satisfy, at least partially, the interests of all major groups remains to be seen. The answer should become clearer as attempts are made to implement the innovations announced at the September 1965 plenary session of the Central Committee and the October meeting of the Supreme Soviet of the USSR—an unstable compromise between traditionalist notions of a centrally directed economy and the views of those reformers who in recent years have argued in favor of a variety of measures aimed at rationalizing the Soviet economy.

Brezhnev and his wife, Victoria, have at least two children: a daughter, Galina, who has accompanied him on foreign trips and works for the Novosti press agency, and a son, Yuri, who is an engineer. More gregarious and colorful than his colleague Kosygin, Brezhnev is fond of Western European clothing and enjoys the various diversions of social life. He is also known to be the owner of one of the finest collections of live birds in Moscow. When abroad he has a reputation for being correct and businesslike; at home he could not have risen to his present eminence without being a skilled and ruthless master of intra-party combat—as Khrushchev, to his own misfortune, discovered in October 1964.

SELECTED BIBLIOGRAPHY

In Russian, the main sources of biographical information about Brezhnev are the following: *Deputaty verkhovnogo soveta SSSR*, Moskva, 1959, p. 63; *Deputaty verkhovnogo soveta SSSR*, Moskva, 1963, p. 66; *Bol'shaia sovetskaia entsiklopediia*, vypusk 2, LI, Moskva, 1958, p. 42; *Malaia sovetskaia entsiklopediia*, vypusk 3, I, Moskva, 1958, p. 1203; *Politicheskii slovar'*, Moskva, 1958, pp. 56–57; *Ezhegodnik bol'shoi sovetskoi entsiklopedii 1958*, Moskva, 1958, p. 627; *Ezhegodnik bol'shoi sovetskoi entsiklopedii 1962*, Moskva, 1962, pp. 588–89; *Ukrains'ka radians'ka entsiklopediia*, II, Kiev, 1960, p. 84. A Western source is J. Marin, "Breshnew, Leonid Iljitsch," *Porträts Der UdSSR-Prominenz*, München: Institut Zur Erforschung Der UdSSR, 1960.

In English, information about Brezhnev can be found in *Biographic Directory of the USSR*, New York: Scarecrow Press, 1958, pp. 97–98, and *Who's Who in the USSR, 1965–1966*, New York and London: Scarecrow Press, 1966, pp. 142–43. Brezhnev's career is discussed by Myron Rush in *Political Succession in the USSR*, New York: Columbia University Press, 1965, pp. 166–68 and by Robert Conquest in *Russia after Khrushchev*, New York: Praeger, 1965, pp. 135–39.

Nikita Sergeevich Khrushchev

by Myron Rush

Nikita Khrushchev was born April 17, 1894, in the village of Kalinovka, in a corner of Russia close to the Ukraine. Here he spent his early years. Little is known of his mother, Ksenia Khrushcheva, who died in 1945. His father, Sergei, was a peasant-become-miner. For a time the young Khrushchev attended a parochial elementary school, where he acquired the tools of learning. He began to tend cattle and continued to do so until he was fifteen; despite his engrossment in later life with agricultural problems, his early experience was largely limited to his work with livestock. Not until he became the responsible political leader in the Ukraine at the age of forty-three did he learn the arts of crop cultivation.

When Khrushchev was fifteen his father brought him to Yuzovka, a growing industrial center in the Ukraine. Here he made the transition from peasant to proletarian. He worked in the coal pits repairing mining machinery until the age of twenty-four. Although he lived and worked in an industrial center where there were numerous strikes and considerable underground revolutionary activity from 1912 until 1918, he took no important part in them. Not until 1918, when he was twenty-four, did he join the Communist party. He was in the Red Army for the next three years, but it is doubtful that he fought with distinction or occupied a responsible post. He was demobilized in 1921.

Khrushchev was to find his late entrance into politics no great hindrance to his career; it may even have helped it. Since he had not been inspired by idealism to enter the struggle against Tsarism, he had no need to rid himself of superfluous ideals during the hardships of civil war and the great compromises of the next period (the New Economic Policy). The Civil War was won by the Bolsheviks because of their decisive advantages in discipline and cohesiveness, and this was a lesson that Khrushchev learned well.

Khrushchev married in 1915, and had two children, a daughter in 1916 and a son in 1918. His wife died during the years of famine and epidemic after the Civil War. In 1924 he was again married, to Nina Khrushcheva. Though a Communist since 1918, she was a motherly figure who won the affection of a wide American audience when she visited the United States with her husband in 1959. She bore him a son and two daughters.

The Bolshevik victory in the Civil War was the making of Khrushchev's career. Upon leaving the Red Army, he returned to the Yuzovka coal pits as the assistant manager of a mine. He was also a part-time party functionary and remained one during his five years in technical schools in the next decade. At the age of thirty-one he became a full-time party official as the responsible leader of a district, and shortly afterward he attended the Fourteenth Congress of the Communist Party of the Soviet Union (CPSU) in Moscow.

Two years later Khrushchev was transferred to Stalino province as chief of the party's key organizational department. In this capacity he attended his second party Congress, the Fifteenth, in Moscow, this time as a voting delegate. Shortly after his transfer to Stalino, an extensive purge was initiated there. Khrushchev's exact role in this purge is not clear, but he was not a victim. After a few months he was transferred to a responsible post in Kiev, where he worked for a year, his last in the Ukraine for almost a decade. Thus this first phase of Khrushchev's party work in the Ukraine (1918–28) was spent in provincial posts, both line and staff, and none of it in Kharkov where the headquarters of the Communist Party of the Ukraine were then located.

In 1929 Khrushchev was transferred to Moscow, to the elite party Industrial Academy which trained economic administrators. As secretary of its party organization—the responsible political figure in the Academy—he played a key role in purging it of Stalin's opponents. After completing only half the training course, Khrushchev left the Academy to head the Bauman party district of Moscow where the Academy was located. After six months as secretary of the Bauman district, he was chosen to conduct a purge similar to the one at the Academy in the proletarian district of Krasnopresnenskaya. In January 1932, at the age of thirty-seven, he became second secretary of the Moscow City Party Committee. In this capacity he had an important part in maintaining a furious and hazardous pace in building the Moscow subway.

At the Seventeenth Congress of the CPSU, in 1934, men who had joined the party after the Revolution were for the first time elected to the Central Committee, and Khrushchev was among the few so honored. Although he was to attack the cult of Stalin after Stalin's death, Khrushchev bears a responsibility for its coming into existence. He put himself in the party's vanguard in praising Stalin. His career advanced rapidly after its late start.

The assassination of Khrushchev's opposite number in Leningrad, Sergei Kirov, in 1934, led to a blood purge which lasted from 1936 until 1938. Khrushchev's activity was divided in these years between Moscow and the Ukraine, whose party organizations he headed after January 1938. Like so much relating to those difficult times, Khrushchev's role in these events is not altogether clear. As head of the Moscow party organization, at the very least he was instrumental in removing numerous leaders from their posts in that city.

Khrushchev evidently was a hard-core supporter of Stalin at this time, and he was soon elevated to candidate membership in the Politburo. In 1938 he was sent to the Ukraine to impose Stalin's harsh policy toward Ukrainian nationals more ruthlessly than previous leaders had, and to purge the Ukrainian party of those leaders' following. Only three of the almost 100 members of the Ukrainian Central Committee were still members six months after Khrushchev arrived in the Ukraine. Even while destroying party organizations in the Ukraine, Khrushchev had the task of rebuilding them. The numerous young party functionaries he elevated became his protégés and supporters, and many were to play crucial roles in his bid for personal rule after Stalin's death.

Khrushchev's task in the Ukraine was not only to purge remaining followers of the previous leadership, but also to further suppress national feelings in the Ukrainian people. Under his direction, Ukrainian history was rewritten, and literature in the Ukrainian language was sharply criticized as an expression of the "national deviation" from the party line. During the war a considerable relaxation of ideological standards was permitted, but afterward, at Moscow's prompting, Khrushchev renewed his attacks on deviations in the Ukraine.

As boss of the Ukraine, Khrushchev was the political leader in occupying Poland's eastern territory, which was annexed in accordance with a secret protocol of the Nazi-Soviet Pact of August 1939. His activities during the campaign against Polish military forces were well publicized. Subsequently he cooperated with the Soviet political police (NKVD) in repressing the middle classes and non-Communist political leaders in the occupied area. The official in charge of these measures, Ivan Serov, later became head of the political police under Khrushchev (1954–58).

When the Ukraine was invaded by Nazi Germany in June 1941, Khrushchev represented the Ukrainian party organization in the local Military Council, and throughout the war he worked in this capacity on various fronts, along with the military commander and the chief of staff. His performance would seem to have been at least adequate, since Stalin, who did not hesitate to demote even his closest lieutenants when they failed him, did not demote Khrushchev. Even so, the scope of his activities was restricted by dint of the German occupation. Khrushchev suffered a personal loss during the war, the death of his oldest son.

As the Red Army drove the Germans back, Khrushchev returned to the Ukraine as head of the party and government. Because of severe drought in 1946 the grain harvest was poor, and food supplies for the entire country were jeopardized. Ukrainian leadership was held responsible. Khrushchev was replaced as head of the Ukrainian party by his former patron, Lazar Kaganovich. While Khrushchev remained head of the Ukrainian government, he played no public role in affairs from May till September. By the end of the year, however, Kaganovich's assignment as trouble-shooter was completed and Khrushchev regained his former post as first secretary of the Ukrainian party. Though he had suffered a setback, he had not been discredited.

In December 1949 Khrushchev left the Ukraine to become a secretary of the party's Central Committee in Moscow, his first post in the nerve center of the party. Had this promotion not occurred, he would have had slight chance of succeeding Stalin. As it happened, his coming to Moscow was an important part of Stalin's plan for maintaining a balance of power among his lieutenants.

Beginning in 1948 Stalin had been conferring important additional powers on Georgi Malenkov, who became in effect the heir presumptive. Now Khrushchev was brought to Moscow to balance Malenkov and to become the third Politburo member, with Stalin and Malenkov, in the party Secretariat. To judge by the assignments he gave him, however, Stalin apparently valued Khrushchev for his administrative abilities and his skill in maneuvering for power, not for his capacity to elaborate a grand policy or to realize it.

On his arrival in Moscow, Khrushchev became the spokesman on agricultural matters, and he promulgated, and subsequently directed, a major policy: the merger of collective farms, which reduced their number by four-fifths. Against his success here was the sharp setback he suffered when his proposal, published in 1951, for resettling collective farmers in "agrocities," was rejected. Though he continued to have responsibility for agriculture, he clearly did not have a free hand.

He was at the same time head of the key party organization in the Moscow area, and supervised aspects of the party's work throughout the country. He gave the report on the new party statute when the Nineteenth Congress of the CPSU met in 1952; that report was second in importance to Malenkov's. Stalin remained in the background until the end of the congress, when he spoke briefly on the world Communist movement.

In January 1953, a few weeks before Stalin's sudden death, Soviet newspapers announced the discovery of a conspiracy of doctors who had allegedly sabotaged the medical treatment of top Soviet leaders in the postwar period in order to shorten their lives, and who were then engaged in plotting the medical murder of a number of top military leaders. A month after Stalin's death it was officially announced that the alleged conspiracy was a fabrication. The reason for the fabrication remains obscure, but it was clearly directed by Stalin and certain of his lieutenants against others among his lieutenants, including Beria. There is little reason to believe that Khrushchev was a target. On the other hand, he may have been one of Stalin's tools: five key figures in the Ministry of State Security at the time the "doctors' plot" was being fabricated had either been closely associated with Khrushchev previously or were subsequently defended by him.

Whatever Stalin's objectives in the doctors' plot his death on March 5, 1953, prevented their realization. In the comprehensive reorganization of the leadership announced the day after his death, an unstable oligarchy, or "collective leadership," took charge. It appeared that Malenkov was trying to arrogate much of Stalin's former powers. Khrushchev, on the other hand, did not fare very well. During the next ten days, however, Malenkov's opponents succeeded in radically modifying the first arrangements. Malenkov was forced out of the party Secretariat, leaving Khrushchev the only top leader in that body.

Khrushchev's position at this time corresponded to Stalin's at the time of Lenin's death, and his strategy for winning succession was to be patterned on Stalin's. He would use his commanding position in the party Secretariat to gain control of the party administrative apparatus throughout the country, thus enabling him to control the party's "elective" machinery (which is actually appointive). By controlling appointments, Khrushchev could alter the composition of the Central Committee and thus dominate its executive body, the party Presidium.

In "the hundred days" following Stalin's death, there was acute struggle within the top leadership. Khrushchev's role in these developments is not clear. With the elimination of Beria, who was arrested in June 1953, the struggle for succession emerged as a rivalry between Malenkov, basing himself in the government bureaucracy, and Khrushchev, basing himself in the party apparatus.

In a speech to the government legislature in August 1953, Malenkov outlined a comprehensive domestic and foreign policy. In order to limit Malenkov's power, the other leaders supported Khrushchev, whom they apparently thought they could control. In September 1953 Khrushchev regained responsibility for agriculture. Even more important, his special position in the party was recognized by his designation as *first* secretary of the Central Committee. In the next years he worked strenuously to build up the power and authority of that office.

Khrushchev used his responsibility for agriculture as a basis for extending his influence over Soviet policy as a whole. In February 1954 he proposed and got adopted a crash program (the so-called virgin lands program) to cultivate millions of acres of untilled land in Siberia. Its successful execution required the application of vast economic means—money, transportation, technicians, workers, machinery—which would have been required for the competing programs of other leaders, particularly Malenkov's program for a sharp increase in consumer goods production. As a result the struggle between Khrushchev and Malenkov intensified, and with it the struggle between the state bureaucracy and the party, culminating in

Malenkov's defeat and replacement as head of the government in February 1955 by Nikolai Bulganin, an ally of Khrushchev.

With Bulganin's succession, Khrushchev's personal authority extended from agriculture to include economic organization, industrial and defense policy, and policy toward the world Communist movement. In the spring of 1955 he undertook a series of initiatives in the sphere of foreign policy. He went to Belgrade to end the USSR's quarrel with Tito, for which Stalin had been largely responsible. He ended the occupation of Austria, thereby satisfying United States conditions for a four-power summit meeting. Held in July 1955 in Geneva, the meeting helped to establish Khrushchev as the Soviet spokesman for foreign affairs and led to reduced tension between the two sides in the cold war, thus increasing Soviet room for maneuvering on the world scene. To further his policy of cultivating neutralist states, Khrushchev visited Southeast Asia, accompanied by Bulganin, the formal head of government.

Khrushchev's power and authority were confirmed and considerably extended by the work of the party's Twentieth Congress in 1956, and continued to grow during the summer of that year. In October 1956, however, the rebellion in Poland and armed revolt in Hungary, both caused in part by Khrushchev's attack on Stalin at the Twentieth Congress, jeopardized his position. After an interval, Khrushchev counterattacked. He proposed dissolution of the economic ministries, which were the basis of his opponents' political influence in the leadership. In desperation they conspired in the Presidium to limit his power, but Khrushchev used the occasion to summon the Central Committee, which by then he largely controlled. His chief opponents were expelled from the Central Committee and, in the Soviet political tradition, were dubbed "the antiparty group." Soon afterward Khrushchev purged Marshal Georgi Zhukov as a would-be "Bonaparte," thereby gaining personal control over the military, and in March 1958 he assumed the post of chairman of the Council of Ministers, clearly establishing himself as head of the government as well as the party. Within five years of Stalin's death, Khrushchev had made himself the personal ruler in the Soviet Union.

De-Stalinization is Khrushchev's greatest achievement, yet in the controversy over Stalin from 1953 to 1956 he originally tended to take Stalin's part. During the last hours of the Twentieth Congress of the party in February 1956, however, the delegates assembled in closed session heard his "secret speech" against Stalin, in which he contrived to exculpate himself from Stalin's crimes, while inculpating his chief rivals. He reassured his followers and prospective domestic allies, like the military, that he would not victimize them as Stalin had. The secret speech was not published in the USSR, but its contents were revealed to select audiences and spread to the populace. This led to minor disturbances in the USSR, and to more serious ones in the Soviet-dominated regimes of Eastern Europe. In the years following, Khrushchev did not pursue de-Stalinization single-mindedly, but only as circumstances required. Not until the Twenty-second Congress of the party in October 1961 did he repeat in public what he had said in closed session in 1956.

Among his domestic reforms, Khrushchev's most far-reaching was to make close party supervision and an intrusive public opinion the chief means of social control. Although the political police remained a key agency, it was no longer permitted to terrorize the people.

Khrushchev increased agricultural production considerably by 1958, largely by giving it the attention and capital Stalin had withheld; but it remained grossly inefficient and provided the Soviet people with only relatively small quantities of meat and dairy products. Khrushchev promised to remedy this. In 1958 he boldly abolished the state-owned Machine Tractor Stations (MTS) and sold their machinery to the collective farms. Successful here, he attempted further reforms and innovations. While the collective farms were encouraged to choose what crops to grow, they had at the same time to heed Khrushchev's demand for large quantities of corn. Though the virgin lands program was a doubtful success, Khrushchev continued to extend the area of cultivation. He inaugurated a program of increased production of chemical fertilizers and insecticides, but provided inadequate capital, and as a result Soviet agriculture after 1958 was largely stagnant, hardly keeping up with the growth of the population. Khrushchev's pet proposals and repeated reorganizations of the administrative system only caused disruption and lost motion. His agricultural policy after 1958, on which he staked so much of his personal prestige, must be judged an abysmal failure. Indeed, one of the first measures taken by his successors—encouraging peasants to cultivate their privately worked plots of land—had been neglected by Khrushchev.

Khrushchev's decentralization of industrial administration in 1957 reportedly led to an initial spurt of growth, but subsequently the rate steadily fell. Khrushchev attempted to reverse this trend by piecemeal recentralization, undermining his original reform, but with only slight success. While industry continued to grow at an impressive rate, the USSR manifestly failed to realize Khrushchev's repeated boast that its economy would overtake that of the United States. If anything, Soviet agriculture, industry, and defense capabilities fell even further behind those of the United States during Khrushchev's rule from 1957 to 1964.

Khrushchev's policy toward minority nationalities for the most part continued along the relatively moderate lines established after Stalin's death, though there was occasional wavering, and the Great Russian people were still strongly favored. Because of Khrushchev's long residence in the Ukraine, ethnic Ukrainians and Russians residing in the Ukraine were brought into the chief organs of leadership in large numbers, reversing Stalin's policy, which had tended to exclude all minority nationalities save his own—the Georgian. Khrushchev's chief lieutenants were ethnic Ukrainians—among them Nikolai Podgorny, Dimitri Polyansky, and Pyotr Shelest—and Russians who had lived most of their lives in the Ukraine, among them Leonid Brezhnev, who became Khrushchev's chief deputy and heir presumptive, Alexander Kirilenko and Leonid Yefremov. While these men did not participate equally in the conspiracy that removed Khrushchev, most of them increased their personal power as a result of it.

In 1958 Khrushchev proposed a radical reform in the educational system. Students were required to work in productive enterprises while in secondary school and for a period after graduation, before they could proceed to higher education. Khrushchev's intention was to break down emergent class barriers and to prevent the well-to-do from conferring career advantages on their offspring. But it was apparent that the reform would impair the training of scientists and scholars, and resistance developed. The measure was watered down, and its most radical provisions were gradually abandoned in the following years.

Khrushchev's policy toward the arts was variable. He was no lover of the arts but, unlike Stalin, he had little fear of its power to subvert the regime. As a result he preferred to have the organizations of artists and writers police themselves, with a minimum of party control. He did not hesitate, however, to intervene arbitrarily in their affairs, either to suppress their works or to use them for his own political purposes as, for example, in the de-Stalinization campaign. He showed contempt for most writers and artists on various occasions, especially in his vitriolic attack on abstract painters in December 1962.

The advent of thermonuclear weapons has been the central fact for Soviet foreign policy in the decade following Stalin's death. Khrushchev originated and chiefly executed this policy, although he did not create it as a unitary concept. After defeating Malenkov, he began his venture into personal diplomacy, for which there was no precedent in Soviet history, apart from the war years. The Summit Conference at Geneva in July 1955 initiated a new phase in Soviet foreign policy by convincing Khrushchev that the United States, despite its great preponderance in strategic forces, would attack the USSR only under the most extreme provocation. Thus assured, Khrushchev undertook to make the USSR a truly global power, extending Soviet influence into the far corners of the world where it had been absent or slight. In the summer of 1957, after the successful testing of an ICBM (Intercontinental Ballistics Missile) and launching of Sputnik, Khrushchev was emboldened to use the emergent Soviet strategic power as a means of pressure against the West. In November 1958 he personally initiated a crisis by demanding that Allied occupation of West Berlin be ended within six months, though he was unwilling—despite the West's vulnerability—to heighten the risk of war by carrying out his threats. Because the United States refused to yield, Khrushchev, after three years of alternating calm and bluster, was unable to achieve his objective.

Despite his threats, Khrushchev had in fact failed to acquire a large ICBM force before the United States did. By 1962 it was apparent that American leaders would not make large concessions on Berlin unless they believed the United States to be vulnerable to Soviet nuclear missiles. Therefore, in the spring of 1962 Khrushchev began installing short-range nuclear missiles clandestinely in Castro's Cuba. But before the deployment was completed, the installations were discovered. Rather than risk imminent war, Khrushchev removed them. After his ignominious defeat, Khrushchev lacked means of threatening the West, and thus began the final phase of his nuclear policy: relaxation of international tension. To this end he accepted the West's terms for a three-power agreement to prohibit atmospheric tests. He continued to support the "anti-imperialist" movement as a means of exacerbating relations between the West and the formerly colonial peoples, but even here he found it necessary to act cautiously.

Initially, Khrushchev's personal relations with the rulers of Communist China (the People's Republic of China, CPR) were excellent. He headed a delegation to Peking in October 1954 that offered large-scale aid to the CPR's industrialization program. In return, Mao and his lieutenants assisted Khrushchev against his domestic opponents. Signs of friction appeared, however, during Mao's return visit to Moscow in November 1957. Apparently rebuffed in his efforts to gain Khrushchev's support for measures against Taiwan (which the CPR claimed as an integral part of China), Mao decided on an independent course of action: in the summer of 1958 he initiated a test of will with the United States over Quemoy. Khrushchev made a sudden visit to Peking, apparently to discover how far Mao meant to go, and perhaps to advise restraint. For whatever reason, the Quemoy confrontation ended in victory for the United States. Khrushchev's relations with Mao continued to deteriorate in 1959 because he visited the United States in an atmosphere of *détente,* although his object was to win concessions. Following this visit Khrushchev made his third trip to Peking, this time to reassure Mao that he would not sacrifice the CPR's interests in his effort to reach an accommodation with President Eisenhower. Nevertheless, in 1960 at a conference of Communist leaders in Bucharest, Romania, Khrushchev found himself under personal attack by the CPR's representative. The dispute was concealed during the months following, only to break into the open in October 1961 when Khrushchev launched a verbal attack upon Communist Albania, whose side had been taken by Peking. After intermittent efforts over the next three years to avoid a break with the CPR, Khrushchev began to move toward a showdown in the summer of 1964. He had difficulty in mustering support from other Communist parties, however, and was overthrown by his own lieutenants before the intended showdown could take place.

The Sino-Soviet conflict involved a fundamental dispute over questions of national interest as well as the objectives of the world Communist movement. At the same time there was a strong element of personal rivalry. Khrushchev evidently let himself be provoked by the CPR, and his passionate feelings in the matter adversely affected his judgment and conduct. Khrushchev's ouster in October 1964 was highly gratifying to the CPR leadership, yet it did not greatly abate the hostility between the two countries.

Khrushchev's basic policies in the early 1960's—domestic and foreign, as well as those for the world Communist movement—had met basic failure by 1964. In the early fall it appeared that he might be planning to cease his efforts at simultaneous advance on all fronts in order to concentrate on raising Soviet living standards. But before he could carry out his new plans, or even elaborate on them publicly, he was suddenly overthrown in mid-October.

Khrushchev's rule accomplished one of the most difficult feats of the political art: to reform and moderate an absolutist regime without losing control of events. As a result, the Soviet regime is less evil than it was under Stalin; the people of the USSR are far less miserable; the world, even with the spread and accumulation of nuclear weapons, is a safer place to live in. What Khrushchev aimed at and achieved is the more surprising as he emerged from the closed and narrow circle of Stalin's heirs—those who survived Stalin's purges because they lacked the courage or decency to stand against him.

A man of powerful intellect and simple, direct speech, Khrushchev nevertheless remained a true descendant of his forebears—the cunning and devious Russian peasant. He had powerful passions, but Stalin's tyranny taught him to control them on the whole or to give them a relatively harmless expression. By his photographs he was an ugly man, short and fat; yet in his presence one felt his attractiveness and warmth, his strength and power of command. He had a penchant for large schemes and crash programs, pushing them through wherever possible without adequate preparation or anticipation of consequences.

As might be expected of one who achieved a remarkable series of personal victories in the decade after Stalin's death, Khrushchev was a man of great optimism and self-confidence. These qualities were of use to him in his effort to reform Stalinist Russia; yet in the end they were his undoing. As his programs and policies met increasingly with setbacks and failure, his lieutenants conspired and at an opportune moment overthrew him.

SELECTED BIBLIOGRAPHY

Biographical data on Khrushchev in Russian may be found in the *Bol'shaia sovetskaia entsiklopediia*, XLVI, Moskva, 1958, pp. 390–91; *Entsiklopedicheskii slovar'*, III, Moskva, 1955, p. 567; and *Politicheskii slovar'*, Moskva, 1958.

Biographical sources in English include the following: Bertram D. Wolfe, *Khrushchev and Stalin's Ghost*, New York: Praeger, 1957; Myron Rush, *The Rise of Khrushchev*, Washington D. C.: Public Affairs Press, 1958 and *Political Succession in the USSR*, New York: Columbia University Press, 1965; John Armstrong, *The Politics of Totalitarianism*, New York: Random House, 1961; Robert Conquest, *Power and Policy in the USSR*, New York: St. Martin's Press, 1961; Wolfgang Leonhard, *The Kremlin Since Stalin*, New York: Praeger, 1961; Edward Crankshaw, *Khrushchev's Russia*, Baltimore, Md.: Penguin Books, 1962; and Howard Swearer, ed., *The Politics of Succession in the USSR. Materials on Khrushchev's Rise to Leadership*, Boston: Little, Brown, 1964; Edward Crankshaw, *Khrushchev*, New York: Viking, 1966; Carl Linden, *Khrushchev and the Soviet Leadership*, Baltimore: John Hopkins Press, 1966.

Khrushchev's chief published works are: *K pobede mirnom sorevnovanii c kapitalizmom*, Moskva, 1959; *Zhit' v mire i druzhbe*, Moskva, 1959; *Mir bez oruzhiia—mir bez voin*, Moskva, 1960; *O vneshnei politike sovetskogo soiuza, 1960*, Moskva, 1961; *K pobede pazuma nad silami voini*, Moskva, 1964; *Stroitel'stvo kommunizma v SSSR i razvitie sel'skogo khoziaistva*, Moskva, 1962–64; *Vyskoe prizvanie literaturi i iskusstva*, Moskva, 1963.

Alexei Nikolaevich Kosygin

by Grey Hodnett

At the height of his power, Nikita Khrushchev held the positions of first secretary of the Central Committee of the Communist Party of the Soviet Union (CPSU), unofficial "head" of the Presidium of the Central Committee, chairman of the Bureau of the Central Committee for the Russian republic, and chairman of the Council of Ministers. It was some measure of the distance separating Khrushchev's power—however fragile it ultimately proved to be—and that of his heirs, that after his "retirement" on October 14, 1964, there was no longer any "head" of the Presidium and no individual held more than one of the three coveted official positions. As in the months following Stalin's death, "collective leadership" was the order of the day. This dispersal of power brought about a relative strengthening of the influence of lower bureaucratic authorities, including—most significantly—the Presidium of the Council of Ministers. Although this body's power has fluctuated in the past, it has been at times (e.g., before Stalin's death) one of the three most influential institutions in the Soviet

Union. Alexei Kosygin, formerly first deputy chairman of the Council of Ministers of the USSR, moved up, on October 15, 1964, to the post of chairman—that is, top man in the Presidium of the Council of Ministers.

Kosygin was born on February 21, 1904, in St. Petersburg (now Leningrad) the capital of the Russian empire, founded by Peter the Great early in the eighteenth century. The fact alone of being born in a metropolis sets Kosygin apart from most other contemporary Soviet leaders, who were reared in more rural or at least provincial settings. At the turn of the century St. Petersburg was a hotbed of clandestine revolutionary activity, due in no small measure to the city's rapid industrialization and large working-class population. Less than a year after Kosygin's birth, the grievances of the people and blundering of the autocracy led to the massacre of "Bloody Sunday" and the turmoil of the Revolution of 1905. The events of 1905 in turn helped to release the forces that brought Lenin to power in 1917. St. Petersburg, far more than Moscow, was identified in the mind of the public as the home of the Russian working class, the birthplace of Bolshevism, and the scene of the most stirring episodes of the Russian Revolution. The intangible advantages of being born in a city of such favorable associations were greatly enhanced for Kosygin by his working-class background; his father was a full-fledged proletarian, a lathe operator named Nikolai Kosygin.

Although nothing is known of his childhood, there is no reason to suppose that Kosygin was any more sheltered from the revolutionary agitation that swept through the working-class districts of the capital than were other youths his age. At thirteen he was old enough to appreciate the drama and revolutionary pageantry of 1917, if not to reflect deeply about its meaning. He must have seen at least some of the great heroes of the Revolution, including those who were later declared to have been schemers and traitors.

In 1919, when he was only fifteen, Kosygin is said to have volunteered for and become a private soldier in the Red Army. The fact that he committed himself to the defense of the Soviet regime at its hour of greatest trial must have stood him in good stead later in his career. Very few contemporary Soviet political leaders can say that they fought in the Civil War.

At the end of the war Kosygin returned to his home city for a secondary education. Like many Soviet officials of humble social origin, he received much of his schooling at a relatively advanced age, having already experienced life outside the schoolroom; but unlike many of his peers he was educated in a metropolitan environment. From 1921 to 1924 he attended the Leningrad Cooperative Vocational High School. Why he entered this school is unclear. Perhaps Lenin's New Economic Policy seemed to promise a future for cooperative light industry and trade; perhaps he was simply directed to this school by the Komsomol (Young Communist League) or party authorities. In any case, the move had a substantial effect on the course of his later career. In 1924 Kosygin finished his secondary education and set out on the long trip to his first job—in the Siberian consumer cooperatives.

The cooperative movement had laid down strong organizational roots in Russia early in the twentieth century, developing great popular support and—equally important—fulfilling a necessary economic function. In his last writings, Lenin urged that the party use the consumer cooperatives, for an indeterminate but lengthy period, as a bridge linking the petty proprietorship of the past with the fully collectivized economy of the future. The major task of the Bolsheviks during the 1920's was not merely—in Lenin's words—to "learn to trade," but to gain control of trade through two major levers: the state wholesale network and the consumer cooperatives. The latter played a key role in this process because, dealing with food, they were the main channel of trade between city and countryside. The Soviet regime therefore began to train its own trade cadres to replace the old cooperative officials whose political sympathies on the whole did not lie with the Bolsheviks. Kosygin was one of these new and loyal recruits.

After the Civil War the cooperatives were largely an appendage of the state bureaucracy; thus Kosygin was really a state trade official. He began his work in the junior position of instructor in an oblast consumer cooperative union, and was then promoted to the administrative board of the Lena Consumer Cooperative Union of Irkutsk Oblast. From this job he moved on to the more responsible position of chief of the planning department of the Siberian Territorial (Cooperative) Union; this appointment coincided closely with his admission in 1927 to membership in the Communist party. By 1929, when he ceased to work in the cooperatives, cooperative trade was fast losing the prominence it had enjoyed in the 1920's. Official attention shifted to industrialization, and with this redefinition of the party's main objective there developed an acute need for large numbers of trained industrial engineers and administrators. Kosygin was swept along with thousands of others who streamed into establishments providing a higher technical education.

Kosygin matriculated around 1930 in the Leningrad Textile Institute, a leading institution of its kind in the Soviet Union. He graduated in 1935, several months after the murder of Sergei Kirov, the party boss of Leningrad, on December 1, 1934. The man whom Stalin appointed in Kirov's place was Andrei Zhdanov, a rising party official with whom Kosygin was later to be associated.

For the first two years after his graduation, Kosygin's career was no different from that of any other young specialist trained by the Soviet regime. He was given a job as foreman in the Zheliabov Textile Factory in Leningrad and then promoted to shop chief in the same plant. In 1937, however, his career was given an unanticipated push forward. As the terror of the late 1930's gathered momentum, devastating the ranks of managerial personnel, Kosygin was appointed director of the October Cloth Weaving Plant in Leningrad, a post that carried with it ex-officio membership in the bureau of the Vyborg District Party Committee. Thus, at thirty-three, Kosygin held an important district-level economic-administrative position that gave him concurrent status as technical expert in deliberations of the party apparatus—a combination of responsibilities that would be repeated throughout his career.

Probably Zhdanov first noticed Kosygin in 1937, mentally enrolling him in the "reserves" for future promotion. In July 1938 Kosygin was granted the honor of serving directly under Zhdanov as chief of the Industrial-Transport Department of the Leningrad Oblast Party Committee. This was indeed an extraordinary leap in status, and proved to be the only exclusively party post Kosygin was ever to hold. With this short exposure to life in the inner sanctum of the party behind him, but without having held the customary preliminary position of secretary of an oblast party committee, he was promoted in October 1938 to the relatively high office of chairman of the Executive Committee of the Leningrad City Soviet—in effect, mayor of the second most important city of the Soviet Union. Now Kosygin was a junior associate of Zhdanov, rather than a mere employee, and responsible for all the municipal services of Leningrad, which were administered by the various departments under his control. Some industry of local importance also fell within his jurisdiction. Among his subordinates, especially those in economic planning, were men who had worked closely with Nikolai Voznesensky, an economist and a protégé of Zhdanov who had left the position of chief of the Leningrad City Planning Commission at the end of 1937 to become chairman of the State Planning Commission of the USSR (Gosplan).

In his rapid rise from obscurity, Kosygin had hardly gained his bearings as chairman of the Leningrad City Executive Committee when he was chosen (January 2, 1939) to fill the newly created post of people's commissar for the Textile Industry of the USSR. Presumably he owed this promotion to national office to Zhdanov's intervention with Stalin. Even so, without the conditions created by the "great purge" it would have been unthinkable to rise from plant director to minister in less than two years. Shortly afterward, at the Eighteenth Congress of the Communist Party of the Soviet Union (CPSU) in March 1939, Zhdanov clearly made his appearance as one of Stalin's closest collaborators. Zhdanov's increasing influence may to some extent have helped Kosygin gain election to the Central Committee at the same party congress, if his new post alone did not make his election virtually automatic. Only thirty-five years old, and head of a commissariat that, lacking political prestige, was nonetheless *the* light industry ministry, Kosygin could count himself among the select seventy-one members of a body that represented the uppermost stratum of the Soviet elite.

Though Kosygin's rise was made possible by the right political connections, it would be wrong to underestimate his own ability in explaining his success. The posts he held required high administrative and technical capabilities, without which he could not have ascended as he did in the state administration. These considerations apply particularly to his next promotion (April 17, 1940) to the position of deputy chairman of the Council of People's Commissars, a post he occupied until 1953.[1] He was now a member of what might be termed the "cabinet" of the Soviet government. His main responsibility at first consisted in fulfilling his duties as a member of the Economic Council (*Ekonomsovet*) under the Council of People's Commissars. The Economic Council was chaired by Vyacheslav Molotov, the chairman of the Council of Ministers; its membership included Anastas Mikoyan, Nikolai Bulganin, Alexei Voznesensky, V. A. Malyshev, and Mikhail Pervukhin. It performed a coordinating function for the entire economy, having the power to issue decrees binding for all state institutions. In essence it was the inner cabinet for economic affairs of the Soviet government. Kosygin had thus become an observer of and participant in economic management at the highest level of government.

Soon after the Nazi invasion of Soviet territory in June 1941, a new wartime supreme political organ was established—the State Defense Committee with a subordinate Council for Evacuation, whose chairman was Nikolai Shvernik and whose two other leading members were Mikoyan and Kosygin. A critical task facing the council was the evacuation of 500,000 people from Leningrad, which had been almost encircled by the Germans (and remained blockaded until January 1944), to prevent death by starvation of a large number of Leningraders. Kosygin was made responsible for this operation. As a Leningrader, he must have experienced particular satisfaction in having been able to make what turned out to be a successful contribution to the war effort. He was also deeply involved during the first years of the war in the gigantic effort to expand the military production capacity of Soviet industry—work that brought him into frequent contact with Alexei Voznesensky and his current political associate, Dimitri Ustinov.

In 1943 Stalin indicated his high regard for Kosygin's efforts and abilities by appointing him chairman of the Council of People's Commissars for the Russian republic—in effect, premier of the vast region stretching from Byelorussia in the West to the Bering Straits in the East. Kosygin held this post until 1946, at the same time retaining his deputy chairmanship of the USSR Council of People's Commissars. Three years of responsibility for the multitude of activities associated with the premiership of the Russian republic entitled Kosygin from this time on to be regarded

---

[1] In 1946 the title was changed to deputy chairman of the Council of Ministers.

as much more than a narrow economic specialist, though he continued to devote much of his time to light industry. In due course his labors received public recognition and Kosygin was elected in March 1946 to candidate membership in the party's Politburo, and to full membership in February 1948.

On February 17, 1948, Kosygin assumed still another role—that of minister of finance, a post he relinquished that same December after having reorganized the Ministry of Finance, introducing some order into chaotic postwar finances of the USSR. Stalin then immediately appointed him to head the new Ministry of Light Industry concerned with the production of consumer goods. In this office, which he held under various titles until February 1954, Kosygin was in the frustrating position of being responsible for that range of economic activities to which Communist doctrine has traditionally assigned low priority. Deficiencies in light industry cannot be attributed by Soviet leaders to the favored status of heavy industry, because this would imply that the regime was neglecting the welfare of the Soviet people. Rather, such deficiencies are explained as the result of poor administration, individual carelessness, lack of patriotism, and the like. For anybody supervising Soviet light industry, save an ideological fanatic (which Kosygin is not), there must be constant tension among conflicting interests: emotional and intellectual commitment to the accelerated growth of heavy industry, with an awareness that in any event advancement demands acceptance of this ideologically sanctioned pattern of economic growth; and, at the same time, a nagging professional dissatisfaction at not meeting the needs of the people, with an appreciation that the cause for existing shortcomings is not nearly so much human weakness as the underinvestment, shortage of raw materials, and inadequate incentives that characterize this stepchild sector of the Soviet economy.

Just as Kosygin was coming to grips with the intractable problems of consumer goods production, he found himself confronted with what may have been the most serious crisis in his life. On August 31, 1948, his political protector, Andrei Zhdanov, died of a heart attack—or so it was said. Georgi Malenkov, an opponent of Zhdanov, was one of the prime movers in a scheme, soon under way, to gain Stalin's authorization for a purge of Zhdanov's base of power—the Leningrad party organization. Whatever his reasons may have been, Stalin agreed to the purge. The result of this Byzantine intrigue was that several thousand party and state leaders who had been associated with Zhdanov in Leningrad lost their lives. Among them was Nikolai Voznesensky, chairman of the State Planning Commission, with whom Kosygin had worked closely during and after the war. In the political atmosphere of Stalin's time, contacts of this nature—however much in the line of duty—provided more than enough cause for incrimination; but for reasons still obscure, Kosygin survived. Presumably he was saved by some combination of friendly assistance by one or more of Stalin's entourage and recognition of his demonstrated capacities as a "nonpolitical" administrator and trouble shooter.

Whether Kosygin's luck would have continued had Stalin lived longer is doubtful. At the Nineteenth Congress of the CPSU, held in October 1952, Stalin demoted Kosygin to candidate membership in the Presidium —the new highest organ of the party, supplanting the former Politburo and Orgburo, and having a much larger membership than the Politburo. Simultaneously Mikoyan, Kosygin's former senior associate and colleague in the field of light industry and consumer goods, came under verbal attack by Stalin. It seems that Kosygin was probably marked for the purge that Stalin was preparing to unleash against leaders whom he now mistrusted. Fortunately for Kosygin and indeed many others, Stalin died on March 5, 1953.

In the redistribution of offices following Stalin's death, Kosygin did not fare particularly well. Probably none of the main contenders for power had ties with Kosygin. He was excluded from membership in the party Presidium and dropped from his position as deputy chairman of the Council of Ministers, although he was allowed to continue as chief of the renamed Ministry of Light and Food Industry. The ministry existed only until August 1953, when it was split into two new bodies: one for food, and the other for consumer goods. Kosygin became the new minister of the Consumer Goods Industry.

Kosygin had the good fortune to be a specialist in light industry and consumer goods production during a period when the policy of the Soviet government—as expressed by Malenkov, chairman of the Council of Ministers—had shifted to stress the objective of paying greater attention to consumer needs. This conjunction of government policy and his own personal ability brought Kosygin back into the "cabinet" in December 1953 as a deputy chairman of the Council of Ministers—although he was by no means a supporter of Malenkov. His departure from the Ministry of Consumer Goods Industry in February 1954 apparently signified merely that he was to devote his full energies to the general supervision of light industries in his capacity of deputy chairman of the Council of Ministers.

Despite this success of late 1953 Kosygin did not return to the limelight for another three years. At the December 1956 plenary meeting of the Central Committee, a decision was taken to convert the State Economic Commission for Current Planning of the National Economy (*Gosekonomkomissiia*) into a powerful, quasi independent economic high command. Created in May 1955 to handle short-term planning (long-range planning was left to Gosplan), *Gosekonomkomissiia* had been headed by Maxim Saburov, an economist of moderate tendencies. He was now replaced by Mikhail Pervukhin, a technocrat known for both his personal ambition and his strong predilection for centralized state control of the economy. At the same time Kosygin, released as a deputy chairman of the Council of Ministers, was appointed first deputy chairman of *Gosekonomkomissiia,* directly beneath Pervukhin.

The plenum of December 1956, and in particular the enhanced status of *Gosekonomkomissiia,* undoubtedly represented a setback to Khrushchev, who had been left by the Hungarian Revolution in a politically vulnerable position. One of the fundamental issues in dispute at this time was the role of the party apparatus—and hence of "political" considerations—in the routine management of the Soviet economy. The existence of the new *Gosekonomkomissiia* tended to minimize party influence over economic affairs at lower administrative levels and to reduce the weight of Khrushchev's party Secretariat in economic decision-making at the top. Khrushchev mounted a rapid counterattack at the plenary session of the Central Committee in February 1957, proposing dissolution of *Gosekonomkomissiia* and root-and-branch decentralization of economic administrative authority to local *sovnarkhozy* (councils of national economy). After strenuous resistance and several compromises, Khrushchev managed to put through his reorganization proposals in the late spring of 1957. *Gosekonomkomissiia* was dismantled along with a number of ministries; the *sovnarkhozy* were created; and a little-known party official with some economic experience, Joseph Kuzmin, was made chairman of the State Planning Commission (Gosplan) and first deputy chairman of the Council of Ministers. Kosygin was appointed to serve under Kuzmin as first deputy chairman of Gosplan, and in this capacity, he was elected on May 24, 1957, to the Council of Ministers (together with six lesser Gosplan officials) as a rank-and-file minister.

This reorganization of the Soviet economy contributed to the crystallization in the party Presidium of an anti-Khrushchev coalition, which, however, failed in an attempt to overthrow Khrushchev in June 1957 and was thenceforth stigmatized as the "antiparty group." Kosygin had neither the position nor the power to exert a significant influence on the outcome of this climactic struggle, though he could easily have ended his career by siding with the losers. He did not, after all, owe any political favors to Khrushchev—they had never been on noticeably close terms—and he may well have sympathized to a greater extent with the policy views of one or more of the conspirators. Native caution, however, and perhaps an antipathy toward Malenkov, restrained him from supporting the Presidium majority. As one of the few top-level economic officials who did not line up against Khrushchev, and as one of Malenkov's near-victims in 1949 (therefore indirectly to be trusted), Kosygin was rewarded, after Khrushchev's victory at the June 1957 plenum of the Central Committee, with election to candidate membership in the party Presidium and reappointment as deputy chairman of the Council of Ministers. Nevertheless, considering his past experience, these advancements indicated that he enjoyed something less than Khrushchev's complete confidence; and the reverse was probably also true.

In spite of his advancements, Kosygin ranked for two years lower than his less experienced former chief in Gosplan, Kuzmin, who, as first deputy chairman of the Council of Ministers, was responsible for over-all supervision as well as daily execution of economic planning. Kosygin's status began to change in March 1959, when he relieved Kuzmin as chairman of Gosplan. A year later it took a decisive upturn with his dual appointment (May 4, 1960) as a full member of the party Presidium and first deputy chairman of the Council of Ministers. He gave up the post of chairman of Gosplan at this time to Vladimir Novikov.

Kosygin's rise coincided with the dismissal from the party Presidium and Secretariat in June and July 1960 of a number of persons closely associated with Khrushchev (including his presumed successor, Alexei Kirichenko), and the promotion to the Secretariat of Frol Kozlov, until then first deputy chairman of the Council of Ministers and widely believed to have been more "conservative" than Khrushchev on such questions as political de-Stalinization and allocation of resources. Economic failures, apparent dissatisfaction on the part of the military with Khrushchev's intention to reduce the size of the armed forces, and the embarrassment of the U-2 incident provided the broader context for these personnel and organizational changes. Thus Kosygin assumed the extremely powerful position he was to occupy for the remainder of Khrushchev's reign at a time when it was not at all obvious that Khrushchev was appointing only political friends to high office; although it can be assumed that even if Kosygin did not owe his promotion to Khrushchev, the latter could have blocked Kosygin's way had he wished to do so.

As first deputy chairman of the Council of Ministers, Kosygin was directly subordinate to Khrushchev—who had become chairman in March 1958—and equal in rank with Mikoyan, the other first deputy chairman. Kosygin was primarily responsible for coordinating the domestic affairs of the Soviet state administration, with particular emphasis on nonagricultural economic activities. At the same time, however, he was frequently assigned the task of delivering speeches on the Soviet Union's relations with various foreign countries. He had become one of the half-dozen most important men in the Soviet Union, with a post that traditionally entailed a dangerously high degree of visibility and accountability. Yet, among the top figures, he remained the least publicized, the most "unpolitical," and seemingly, the least likely to assume leadership of the Soviet state.

The duumvirate of Brezhnev and Kosygin came to power in October 1964 amid signs of administrative chaos and deep-rooted malfunctioning in the Soviet economy. Khrushchev, with his "hare-brained scheming" and constant reorganizations, was naturally saddled with the blame for this state of affairs. But there remained the same problems that had vexed Khrushchev—a lagging agriculture and vast industrial inefficiency.

It soon became clear that at least some elements in the new leadership were sensitive to the need for economic reforms. For example, partial market relationships were experimentally introduced in some branches of light industry, an innovation attributable to Kosygin. How much further Kosygin, for one, would like to go remains to be seen. In general, the new leadership revealed an intention not to take precipitate action, not to disrupt what already seemed to work in the economy. However, caution may not turn out to be a substitute for decisive action. The elimination in September and October 1965 of the *sovnarkhozy* (local economic councils) and re-establishment of centralized ministries, and the half-hearted introduction of profit-maximization as a guide to managerial decision-making may have momentarily satisfied (or at least not antagonized) important elements of the Soviet elite, including the party apparatus, the high state economic bureaucracy, and the military. It does not appear, however, that these steps provide a consistent and effective answer to the dilemmas of the Soviet economy.

Kosygin conveys an impression to many observers of sobriety, administrative professionalism, and hardheaded realism. These are certainly qualities that are indispensable if the Soviet economy is to be made more rational; and they are backed by long years of experience. Whether he will be able to retain his position in the present unstable equilibrium, much less implement basic economic reforms, is not yet clear. Unlike Brezhnev, Kosygin possesses no base of support in the party apparatus, whose vital interests are likely to be threatened in the long run by genuine reform.

Kosygin has a wife, Klavdia, and two daughters. His son-in-law, Dzhermen Gvishiani, is a deputy chairman of the important State Committee for Coordination of Scientific Research. In the past Kosygin has been one of the Soviet leaders most frequently seen at Western diplomatic receptions in Moscow, and on his trips abroad he has impressed some observers—especially industrialists—as a "good businessman" who strikes a hard bargain but keeps his word. He has seemingly tried to convey the image of being a "technician" rather than a "politician"; although naturally, a man does not survive for a quarter of a century near the top of the Soviet system without being an accomplished politician. Kosygin is known to be an extraordinarily hard worker. The little free time he leaves himself is reportedly devoted to intellectual pursuits, including keeping abreast of Soviet and foreign belles-lettres, and attending the theater. He also skis, ice skates, and plays volleyball, it is said, in order to keep physically fit.

SELECTED BIBLIOGRAPHY

In Russian, the main sources of biographical information about Kosygin are the following: *Bol'shaia sovetskaia entsiklopediia,* vypusk 2, XXIII, Moskva, 1953, pp. 141–42; *Leningrad: Entsiklopedicheskii spravochnik,* Moskva and

Leningrad, 1957, p. 557; *Politicheskii slovar'*, Moskva, 1958, pp. 290–91; *Ezhe-godnik bol'shoi sovetskoi entsiklopedii 1958*, Moskva, 1958, p. 634; *Ezhegodnik bol'shoi sovetskoi entsiklopedii 1962*, Moskva, 1962, p. 601; *Malaia sovetskaia entsiklopediia*, vypusk 3, IV, Moskva, 1959, p. 1305; *Deputaty verkhovnogo soveta SSSR*, Moskva, 1959, p. 206; *Deputaty verkhovnogo soveta SSSR*, Moskva, 1963, p. 227. A Western source is J. Marin, "Kosygin, Alexej Nikola-jewitsch," *Porträts der UdSSR-Prominenz*, München: Institut Zur Erforschung Der UdSSR, 1960.

In English, information about Kosygin may be found in *Biographic Direc-tory of the USSR*, New York: Scarecrow Press, 1958, pp. 306–7, and *Who's Who in the USSR, 1965–1966*, New York and London: Scarecrow Press, 1966, p. 429. Kosygin's career is discussed by Myron Rush, *Political Succession in the USSR*, New York: Columbia University Press, 1965, pp. 176–77, and by Robert Conquest in *Russia after Khrushchev*, New York: Praeger, 1965, pp. 139–40.

Anastas Ivanovich Mikoyan*

by Kermit E. McKenzie

Anastas Ivanovich Mikoyan, close to the apex of the Soviet power structure for many years, terminated in April 1966 four decades of service as a member of the Politburo of the Central Committee. No other individual has equaled or exceeded his forty-year record in the Politburo, as candidate member since 1926 and full member since 1935. In the government hierarchy, also since 1926, Mikoyan has continuously held high office—until 1964 in the USSR Council of Ministers (formerly the Council of People's Commissars) and more recently in the Presidium of the USSR Supreme Soviet.

An Armenian by birth, Mikoyan comes from one of the ethnically most complex areas of the world, the Caucasus, lying to the southeast of Russia proper and including the North Caucasus plain, the intermediate mountain range, and the Transcaucasus. Here Christian Armenians and Georgians and Muslim Azerbaijanians, to mention only the most numerous peoples, lived for ages before the imperial conquests and annexations of the nineteenth century brought an influx of Russian soldiers, bureaucrats,

* The author wishes to express his thanks to the Research Committee of Emory University for a grant in support of this study of Mikoyan's career. Thanks are also due to the librarians at Radio Liberty Committee headquarters in New York City for their kind cooperation in making available the committee's extensive files on Mikoyan.

workers, and others into the area. In this multi-national arena there was at work during Mikoyan's childhood an ever-quickening competition among not only diverse nationalities and religions but also such change-espousing doctrines as liberalism, Bolshevism, Menshevism, and the radical populism of the Socialist Revolutionaries.

Mikoyan was born in the Transcaucasus on November 25, 1895, in the small village of Sanain, which at that time was included in Tiflis province of the Russian empire and now lies within the Alaverdi district of the Armenian Soviet Socialist Republic. Situated in a copper-mining region, Sanain is chiefly noted today for its monastery and other architectural monuments dating back to the tenth century.

Not much is known of Mikoyan's family and youth. Official biographies simply state that his father was a worker or, when he is identified more precisely, a carpenter. One source (Avtorkhanov, see bibliography) asserts that Mikoyan's father was a small merchant and thus denies Mikoyan the proletarian class origin desired for Soviet leaders. Likewise, in the official accounts there is little respecting Mikoyan's education, except that he graduated from the Armenian theological seminary in Tiflis. But tourists in Sanain are shown the parochial elementary school that he attended. Upon completing his seminary training, Mikoyan did not, however, become a priest. Rather, he is credited with having once remarked that he graduated from the seminary as an atheist and a materialist. Avtorkhanov reports that while in the seminary Mikoyan began his political activity as a member of the liberal Constitutional Democratic party and later switched to Marxism, but official biographies state only that in 1915 he joined the Bolshevik wing of the Russian Social Democratic Labor party. With this step Mikoyan committed his life to the Marxist cause as interpreted and led by Lenin.

Mikoyan's career as a Communist may with reason be seen as falling into four stages: first, the years 1915–20, when his activity was confined to his native Caucasus; second, the years 1920–26, during which he worked as a local party secretary outside the Caucasus and attained membership in the Central Committee of the Communist Party of the Soviet Union (CPSU); third, his long period of service under Stalin in the topmost organs of party and government; and last, the post-Stalin years.

The first or Caucasian phase of Mikoyan's career was enacted mainly in the large cities of Tiflis and Baku. About fifty miles to the north of Sanain lies Tiflis, where Mikoyan studied, chiefly Georgian in population and then the second largest city in the Caucasus. Roughly 250 miles to the east is the Caspian port and oil center of Baku, at that time the most populous city of the region and the center of Azerbaijanian nationalism. Mikoyan's political activity in these two cities, as well as his theological training, offer an interesting parallel to the career of his fellow Transcaucasian, the Georgian Stalin. But Mikoyan's provincial Caucasian period coincided with the tumultuous era of the First World War, Russian Revolution, and Civil War, by which time Stalin had already graduated to national leadership in the Bolshevik movement. Yet Mikoyan, by virtue of his participation in the revolutionary movement during the twilight of the Old Regime, also belongs in the category of Old Bolsheviks.

After entering Bolshevik ranks in 1915, Mikoyan carried on youth work in Tiflis, then went to the village of Echmiadzin as party organizer and propagandist, and also collaborated with the Tiflis Marxist newspaper *Paikar*.

With the beginning of the Russian Revolution in Petrograd during March 1917, Nicholas II was compelled to abdicate, and formal authority devolved upon a Provisional Government that was recognized by the emperor, the generals, and the Allies. However, its power was seriously limited by the simultaneous appearance of workers' soviets or councils. Later, peasant soviets also arose in the countryside, and soldiers' committees were formed in the military units. In this new and chaotic era of freedom the underground Bolshevik organizations began open political struggle, at first aiming to obtain influence and control in the soviets and soldiers' committees and later aiming at the wresting of power from the Provisional Government. In November 1917, under the leadership of Lenin and Trotsky, the Bolsheviks seized power in Petrograd and throughout much of the former empire, but three years of civil war were necessary before the Bolshevik dominion was consolidated. In the peripheral region of the Transcaucasus, the forces of nationalism and Menshevism proved at first generally stronger than Bolshevism, and, until Red Army units entered the picture in 1920 and 1921, the Bolsheviks made slight impression except in Baku.

During 1917, after organizing a soviet of soldiers' deputies in Echmiadzin, Mikoyan was in Baku from the end of March until August, then in Tiflis until October, and thereafter back in Baku. Here he must certainly have worked under the direction of such veterans as Stepan G. Shaumyan and Prokofii A. Djaparidze, both of whom had been Bolsheviks since 1903. Yet in many Soviet accounts of this period Mikoyan is represented as a peer of these and other more experienced Bolsheviks. Shaumyan was perhaps the leading Bolshevik working in the Caucasus at that time. His considerable status is illustrated by his election in August 1917 to the Central Committee of the party at its Sixth Congress and by his appointment in December as extraordinary commissar over the entire Transcaucasus Bolshevik movement. Djaparidze's status was somewhat lower; he was elected a candidate member of the Central Committee by the Sixth Congress. Under their guidance Mikoyan's activity included organizational work, journalistic endeavors, and speechmaking on such themes as the war, the nature of the Russian Revolution, and the nationality question. With these matters Mikoyan busied himself before departing for Tiflis, a Menshevik stronghold, in August.

During his short stay in Tiflis, Mikoyan participated in the First Caucasian Regional Congress of Bolsheviks, which met October 15–20, 1917. This assembly embraced Bolsheviks of all nationalities (it was only in 1920 that, for example, separate Georgian, Armenian, and Azerbaijanian Communist parties were created). Along with Shaumyan, Djaparidze, and several others, Mikoyan was elected to the regional committee that was intended to function as the executive organ of all party groups in the Caucasus, under the chairmanship of Philip I. Makharadze, a Georgian. The committee planned to seize power in early December and thereby link the Caucasus with the Russian Soviet Republic. But energetic action by Mensheviks and other anti-Bolsheviks forestalled this effort, and the regional committee had no success. With the establishment of firmly anti-Bolshevik governments in Armenia and Georgia, Bolshevik influence, at the end of 1917, was largely confined to Azerbaijan and the city of Baku. Shaumyan now was made extraordinary commissar for the Transcaucasus, and he and his followers in Baku, including Mikoyan, enjoyed the attention and personified the hopes of the party leaders viewing Caucasian developments from Petrograd and Moscow.

In Baku the Bolsheviks successfully maneuvered to exploit the hostility existing between the Armenians and the Azerbaijanians. In late April 1918, under the threat of a Turkish invasion of the Caucasus, the Armenian nationalists supported the establishment of a Bolshevik-dominated government in Baku, which became advertised as the Baku Commune. Up to this time Mikoyan had been active as a journalist, editing the Armenian-language newspaper *Social Democrat* and contributing to the *Baku Worker* and other newspapers. In March, during fighting between Bolshevik units and Azerbaijanian nationalists, he had put aside his pen for the sword and was wounded in action as a squad leader. Following his recovery, he became editor of *Izvestiia,* organ of the Baku soviet.

The so-called Baku Commune represented the high tide of Bolshevik influence in 1918. Based on the Baku soviet, it was headed by a Council of People's Commissars, including Shaumyan as chairman and eleven other persons but not Mikoyan. That Mikoyan was not included suggests his still relatively minor position in party ranks. Acknowledging the authority of Lenin's All-Russian Council of People's Commissars, the Baku Commune undertook several radical measures, in which Mikoyan is credited with a leading role: nationalization of the oil industry and the banks, levying of compulsory contributions on the bourgeoisie, and arrests of oil industrialists.

By July 1918, threatened by the advance of Turkish forces into the Transcaucasus and weakened by opposition to its policies, the Baku Commune was hard put to maintain itself. Mikoyan again participated in the persistent military activity arising in the area and rose to the rank of commissar of a brigade. In this hour of mounting threats against the Baku Commune, Mikoyan, according to official biographies, adopted an especially intransigent line, even disagreeing with the majority of the Baku Communist leadership. He opposed, unsuccessfully, the decision of the Bolshevik members of the Baku soviet to surrender power to those elements—Mensheviks, Socialist Revolutionaries, and Armenian nationalists—who had decided to invite British forces then stationed in Mesopotamia to come to aid in the defense of that city against the Turks. At the very end of July the Bolshevik-dominated commune reluctantly abdicated its powers. At this point Mikoyan opposed, again unsuccessfully, the Bolshevik decision to evacuate Baku and sail for Astrakhan, the port at the mouth of the Volga which was a Bolshevik stronghold throughout 1918–20. Mikoyan urged the Bolsheviks to remain in Baku and conduct a continuing struggle for a return to power. But the overwhelming majority of the party members boarded ship on July 31, leaving Mikoyan behind to create and lead an underground movement. The vessel transporting the Bolsheviks was stopped at sea by ships of the new Baku government, the Centro-Caspian Dictatorship, which incarcerated the captured Bolsheviks in the Bailov prison in Baku.

The Centro-Caspian Dictatorship, composed chiefly of Russian Socialist Revolutionaries and supported by Armenian nationalists and British forces under General Dunsterville, survived only one and one-half months against the pressure of the Turks and their Azerbaijanian allies. The British evacuated on September 14, and Baku was overrun the following day. In this confused moment Mikoyan succeeded in liberating the Bailov prisoners and together with them boarded the ship *Turkmen* in another effort to reach friendly Astrakhan; but the group was taken by the Socialist Revolutionaries and Mensheviks commanding the vessel to Krasnovodsk, directly across the Caspian Sea from Baku. There, on September 17, Mikoyan and his fellow Bolsheviks, thirty-five in all, were arrested by the local Socialist Revolutionary government and imprisoned in Krasnovodsk.

Now occurred the famous incident of the shooting of the Baku commissars, including such leaders as Shaumyan and Djaparidze. Having scrutinized various documents taken from the prisoners and lists of names of those who had been arrested earlier in Baku, the Socialist Revolutionary government singled out for execution those whom it considered the ringleaders of the Baku Commune, twenty-six in all, and shot them on September 20, 1918. Mikoyan's name, according to Soviet accounts, was fortuitously not on any of these documents and, therefore, he as well as others who had been prominent in the Baku Commune escaped execution, while certain lesser figures, including non-Bolsheviks, suffered this fate. Various anti-Communist writers have not been satisfied with this explanation of Mikoyan's survival; allegations of sinister conduct on Mikoyan's part have been made, and it has been suggested that Stalin later used similar allegations to keep Mikoyan in line. But satisfactory evidence supporting this interpretation is lacking. On the other hand, the Soviet charge that British military forces in the Transcaspian area were responsible for the executions does not seem substantiated.

Mikoyan remained in prison until the end of February 1919, first at Krasnovodsk, then further inland at Kyzyl-Arbat and Ashkhabad. Afflicted with scurvy, he spent about a month in the Ashkhabad hospital, where he busied himself organizing a secret Bolshevik circle. He also was able to establish contact with Baku, where the local Bolshevik organization revived following the withdrawal of the Turks upon the signing of the armistice of Mudros. Preparations for Mikoyan's escape from the hospital were forestalled by a general strike of the Baku workers, who successfully demanded that the British military forces in the Caspian area transfer him and the other Bolshevik prisoners to Baku.

For somewhat more than a year following his return to Baku in March 1919, Mikoyan's efforts were directed toward the re-establishment of Communist power there and throughout Azerbaijan. During this period an Azerbaijanian nationalist government sought, with the support until July 1920 of British troops, to maintain an independent statehood for Azerbaijan. Mikoyan now seems to have risen to the very top position among the Baku Communists; the execution of the twenty-six Baku commissars had removed the more experienced leaders. Mikoyan took part in an illegal Baku party conference in May 1919 that called for the creation of a workers' and peasants' soviet republic in Azerbaijan. He established contact with Sergei M. Kirov, then the Communist chief in Astrakhan, and organized the secret supply of oil from Baku to that city. Extending his activities beyond Baku, Mikoyan helped to create a short-lived soviet in the town of Lenkoran to the south and also coordinated the activities of Communists in the Daghestan region to the north, behind the lines of the anti-Bolshevik forces of General Denikin.

For his role in a general strike in May 1919, Mikoyan was arrested and put in Tagiev prison, but escaped with the help of comrades. Sometime later he was again arrested and held in Bailov and Tagiev prisons, then expelled to Georgia, which was under Menshevik control. From Georgia he was able to return illegally to Baku. There, in the summer of 1919 which saw considerable fighting between Red and White forces in the North Caucasus, Mikoyan arranged the safe passage to Astrakhan of Grigorii K. Ordjonikidze, the North Caucasus Bolshevik chieftain who had fled to Baku from Denikin's forces. In September, while attending an illegal meeting in Tiflis of the Caucasus regional committee of Bolsheviks, Mikoyan was arrested by the Georgian Mensheviks but again escaped, this time with the help of bribes.

At the end of September 1919 Mikoyan traveled to Moscow. Apparently this was his first trip outside the Caucasus-Caspian area and resulted in his first meetings with Lenin and Stalin. In Moscow the broad strategy of the future Communist seizure of power in Azerbaijan was outlined. Plans were to be made for the coordination of Communist uprisings in the towns with an invasion by Soviet troops from the North Caucasus. Following these talks, Mikoyan made his way to Tashkent in Central Asia, accompanied by the Bolshevik military leader, Mikhail V. Frunze. From there he traveled to Daghestan, where he met with Ordjonikidze and Kirov, who were to be the political leaders of the Soviet forces invading Azerbaijan the following spring.

It is not clear whether Mikoyan was present at the founding congress of the Communist Party of Azerbaijan when it convened illegally in Baku in February 1920. But he is credited in Soviet accounts, together with Ordjonikidze, Kirov, and Lavrentii L. Beria, with the practical work of creating the party. Mikoyan was back in Baku during March, for an exchange of messages with Kirov is on record: on March 9 Kirov directs Mikoyan to maintain regular contact with the Eleventh Red Army, then waiting in the North Caucasus. And Mikoyan confidently states that Kirov should inform Moscow of the growing strength of the Communists in Azerbaijan. All was ready for the coordinated actions of revolutionaries and Red Army forces.

The planned uprising in Baku occurred during the night of April 28, 1920. Mikoyan must have secretly left Baku shortly before, probably to make his expert knowledge of the area available to the invading Red forces. The first edition of the *Great Soviet Encyclopedia* states that Mikoyan returned to Baku on April 28 on the first armored train of the invaders. The second edition, however, has Mikoyan arriving with Ordjonikidze and Kirov on May 1, at the head of the Eleventh Red Army. In his memoirs, Mikoyan has confirmed the former version.

Until the end of 1920 Mikoyan remained in Baku to consolidate Communist authority. On May 5–6, he was present with Ordjonikidze and Kirov at the First All-Baku Party Conference. During July 16–19 Mikoyan and Ordjonikidze led the work of the First Congress of the Komsomol (Young Communist League) of Azerbaijan. In August Mikoyan was elected chairman of the council created by the First Congress of Trade Unions. It may be noted that Mikoyan did not attain the post of secretary of the Azerbaijanian party, which went to Kirov. And even higher stood Ordjonikidze, the secretary of the Transcaucasus Regional Committee of the party. Thus Mikoyan, while at the head of the Baku party organization, still remained at a relatively modest station in party ranks.

Near the close of 1920 Mikoyan's Caucasian period came to an end with his transfer to Nizhni-Novgorod (now Gorki), a large industrial and commercial center on the upper Volga east of Moscow. Here he was to assume new party tasks.

The chief aspects of the second phase (1920–26) of Mikoyan's career are his support of Stalin in the struggle for party leadership following the incapacitation of Lenin and his steady rise to positions of greater influence and responsibility. At the Eleventh Congress of the CPSU in March–April 1922, Mikoyan was elected a candidate member of the new Central Committee, becoming a full member one year later at the Twelfth Congress. In 1926 he attained membership in the top organs of party and government with election as candidate member of the Politburo and appointment as commissar of Foreign and Domestic Trade.

These years thus constitute for Mikoyan a transitional phase from provincial to national status. During this period Mikoyan participated as a delegate in every congress of the Communist party beginning with the Tenth in March 1921. And, in the governmental structure, beginning even in 1919, he was regularly a deputy to the All-Russian and, later, to the All-Union Congress of Soviets, which consistently elected him to its Central Executive Committee.

Even before he decided to support Stalin, Mikoyan displayed in his local party work a zeal for struggle against opponents both outside and within the party. There is no hint that he resisted the steady constriction of party democracy engineered by Lenin in his struggle against such early oppositional groups as the Democratic Centralists and the Workers' Opposition. The available evidence indicates the contrary.

From October 1920 until July 1922 Mikoyan worked in the Nizhni-Novgorod party organization, eventually becoming secretary of the provincial committee. There he is credited favorably in official Soviet accounts for his struggle against anarcho-syndicalists and the followers of Trotsky. In 1922 he was transferred to Rostov-on-Don, where he served for two years as secretary of the Southeastern Bureau of the Central Committee. His chief associate was Kliment E. Voroshilov, an intimate coworker with Stalin from Civil War days, then commander of the armed forces of the North Caucasus military district. With Voroshilov he purged local party organizations of Menshevik and "kulak-anarchist" elements. From August 1924 to August 1926 Mikoyan was secretary of the North Caucasus Regional Committee of the party. Official biographies attribute to him considerable success in rallying ordinary Cossacks and peasants to support the party's position against the opposition of surviving anti-Communist influences. He was also a member of the Revolutionary Military Council of the North Caucasus military district.

In politics at a higher level, it is not clear why and when Mikoyan elected to become an ally of Stalin. In his biography of Stalin, Trotsky states that Mikoyan, as a delegate from Nizhni-Novgorod to the party's Tenth Congress in March 1921, was already one of Stalin's close political allies. Yet at the congress Mikoyan criticized at length Stalin's report on the nationality question on grounds of its lack of practical recommendations and implied that Stalin had done little beyond restating general Leninist principles. Subsequently, at the congress, Mikoyan was elected, along with others including Stalin, to a commission to draw up concrete proposals for the implementation of Soviet nationality policy.

At the Eleventh Congress of the CPSU in March–April 1922, Mikoyan was elected one of the three secretaries of the congress (with Kirov and Abel S. Yenukidze). More important was his election to membership on a commission—on which Stalin and the Cheka-chief Felix E. Dzerzhinsky also served—which was to investigate the case of the so-called Declaration of the Twenty-Two. This declaration was a complaint that had been directed to the Communist International by twenty-two leaders of the Workers' Opposition, charging that democracy in Russia was being destroyed by the party bureaucracy. The commission condemned the Workers' Opposition as an antiparty faction and, in its demand for the expulsion of five of its leaders, simply continued the existing policy of constricting party debate. Mikoyan was also elected to membership on the commission on party structure, after he had criticized at some length Grigorii E. Zinoviev's report on this subject.

It was also at the Eleventh Congress that Mikoyan was promoted to the high position of candidate member of the Central Committee of the CPSU. Now he entered that small number of Communist leaders who exercised authority over the entire party and state and from whose ranks was chosen the all-powerful Politburo. The Central Committee was at that time composed of only twenty-seven full members and nineteen candidates, and thus was a much more select group than it is now with its total membership of 360. It was this Central Committee that elected Stalin as general secretary of the party on April 3, 1922. One month later Lenin suffered his first stroke of arteriosclerotic paralysis which virtually removed him from further political activity.

Having obtained high office, Mikoyan thereafter consistently linked his political fortune with Stalin's. At the party's Twelfth Congress in April 1923 Mikoyan became a full member of the Central Committee, now enlarged to include forty full members and seventeen candidates. The stenographic record of the proceedings does not indicate that he was a speaker at this congress. At the Thirteenth Conference, which met in January 1924 a few days before Lenin's death, Mikoyan did speak out against the followers of Trotsky and in support of the ruling triumvirate, Stalin, Zinoviev, and Lev B. Kamenev. At the Thirteenth Congress in May 1924, Mikoyan was re-elected a full member of the Central Committee (now composed of fifty-three full members and thirty-four candidates). The subsequent breakup of the triumvirate and the creation of the Left Opposition, headed by Zinoviev and Kamenev, produced a fierce struggle within the party. In December 1925, at the Fourteenth Congress, Mikoyan called for the Opposition to "submit to the iron will of the majority of the Central Committee," and added pointedly: "When Zinoviev has a majority, he is for iron discipline, for submission. When he doesn't have this majority, even if only for a minute, he is against it." But Mikoyan was conciliatory, flattering the Leningrad proletariat (the Opposition stronghold), and even holding Trotsky up as an example of one who, having been defeated, scrupulously observed party discipline. While the congress was still meeting, Mikoyan, Molotov, Kirov, and others journeyed to Leningrad to attempt to win over the party organization there. The congress, which ended in a decisive victory for Stalin, again saw Mikoyan elected to the new Central Committee (made up of sixty-three full members and forty-three candidates).

Stalin's victory over the Left Opposition soon brought promotion for Mikoyan. In July 1926 the plenary meeting of the Central Committee added five new candidate members to the Politburo, among them Mikoyan and two comrades from Civil War days, Kirov and Ordjonikidze. In August of that year Mikoyan succeeded Kamenev as commissar of Foreign and Domestic Trade. Now he was at the apex of the Soviet power structure.

In the third phase (1926-53) of Mikoyan's career, which spanned more than a quarter-century of service under Stalin, two fundamental facts may be immediately noted: first, there is no real evidence whatever that Mikoyan opposed Stalin's policies and measures in any field, except in statements made by Mikoyan and Khrushchev after Stalin's death; second, Mikoyan survived these years as a holder of high positions both in the party and in the government.

Among the major domestic and foreign developments during these years are the following: Stalin's victories over the United Opposition (Trotsky, Zinoviev, and Kamenev) and the Right Opposition (Bukharin, Rykov, and Tomsky); collectivization in agriculture; high-tempo industrialization with emphasis on heavy industry during the first Five-Year Plans; the "great purges" of the middle and late 1930's; the establishment of Stalin's personal and terrorizing supremacy over the leadership of the Communist party; Soviet participation in the Second World War; the creation of the Communist satellites; Soviet postwar economic recovery and growth; and the high tide of the cold war.

Mikoyan's positions in the party structure may be indicated first. He attended each of the five congresses of the period, from the Fifteenth Congress in December 1927 through the Nineteenth Congress in October 1952. He was a full member of each Central Committee elected by the successive congresses. He remained a candidate member of the Politburo until February 1, 1935, when a plenary meeting of the Central Committee promoted him to full membership. At that time there were ten full members and five candidates. Mikoyan remained in the Politburo (called the Presidium from 1952 to 1966) until April 1966. It may be noted that Mikoyan has never held office in either the Orgburo or the Secretariat.

Next may be listed Mikoyan's positions in the governmental structure during the Stalin era. He was consistently elected a deputy to each All-Union Congress of Soviets and was a member of its Central Executive

Committee until 1936, when the new constitution of that year replaced these two organs with the Supreme Soviet. Mikoyan was elected to all three Supreme Soviets of this period (in 1937, 1946, and 1950). He was a member of the Council of People's Commissars from 1926 to 1946 and, under its new name of Council of Ministers, from 1946 until 1953. His specific posts as a commissar (after 1946, minister) were as follows: from 1926 to 1930, commissar of Foreign and Domestic Trade; 1930–34, commissar of Supply; 1934–38, commissar of Food Industry; 1938–March 1946, commissar of Foreign Trade; March 1946–49, minister of Foreign Trade. From 1949 until Stalin's death Mikoyan, while remaining in the Council of Ministers, did not head up any specific ministry. From August 1937 to March 1946 Mikoyan also held the high rank of deputy chairman of the Council of People's Commissars; and, from March 1946 until Stalin's death in March 1953, the rank of deputy chairman of the Council of Ministers.

It may be convenient to subdivide this third phase in Mikoyan's career, when he served Stalin for twenty-seven years in high party and governmental posts, into three parts: the period from 1926 to 1941, the years of war from 1941 to 1945, and the postwar years until Stalin's death in 1953.

During the first period, from 1926 to 1941, the salient features of Mikoyan's activity included his apparently consistent support of Stalin in the latter's rise to complete personal supremacy over the party, his domestic labors in the areas of trade and supply of food and consumer goods, and his participation as a trade expert in Soviet foreign relations.

In support of Stalin at the Fifteenth Congress in December 1927, Mikoyan's major speech attacked the leaders of the United Opposition (Trotsky, Zinoviev, and Kamenev) and cited Lenin's "Testament" of December 25, 1922, against the latter two. Showing greater sternness than at the preceding congress in 1925, Mikoyan declared that reconciliation was impossible with such enemies of the party. Following the final defeat and expulsion of the United Opposition, Mikoyan again supported Stalin in 1928–30. This time the struggle was waged against those right-wing leaders in the Politburo who resisted Stalin's decision to terminate NEP (New Economic Policy) and launch the country upon a program of forced collectivization in agriculture and high-tempo heavy industrialization. At the Sixteenth Congress in June–July 1930, Mikoyan devoted about half of his major speech to an attack on the Right Opposition, insisting that its spokesmen had not yet sincerely acknowledged their mistakes.

During the tense years of the early 1930's, amid the strains and tensions produced by the strenuous pace of economic change and development, there is no evidence that Mikoyan was other than a stalwart Stalinist. All reasonable speculation concerning the existence of a supposedly moderate faction within the Politburo at this time does not identify Mikoyan as even to a modest degree anti-Stalinist. Of the five candidate members of the Politburo elected after the Seventeenth Congress in February 1934, Mikoyan was probably the only completely reliable supporter of Stalin. (The other candidates were then Pavel P. Postyshev, Grigorii I. Petrovsky, Yan E. Rudzutak, and Vlas Y. Chubar.) Mikoyan's speeches at the Seventeenth Congress, largely concerned with the growth of production in the light and food industries, were frequently laced with glowing acknowledgments of Stalin's qualities as a leader.

During the era of the great purges it appears that Mikoyan took an unusual interest in the NKVD (secret police). At a joint meeting (July 20, 1936) of the Moscow party *aktiv* and Moscow workers in the NKVD, he gave a report dedicated to the tenth anniversary of the death of Felix E. Dzerzhinsky, the first head of the security police. The report was published in 75,000 copies as a pamphlet of thirty-one pages, and republished in 1937 in 110,000 copies. Throughout, Dzerzhinsky and Stalin were depicted by Mikoyan as noble, self-sacrificing leaders. Also in 1937 there appeared, under the editorship of Mikoyan and others, including the future NKVD head, Beria, an edition of articles and speeches by Ordjonikidze, whose death (by suicide, according to Khrushchev in his "secret speech") had occurred in February of that year. Mikoyan himself was one of the few members of the 1934 Central Committee who survived the purges unscathed. Of the 139 full and candidate members elected in 1934 by the Seventeenth Congress, only twenty-three, including Mikoyan, were carried over to membership in the new Central Committee of 1939. In March 1939, at the Eighteenth Congress, which was the last to be held for thirteen years, Mikoyan extolled once again the practical and theoretical contributions of Stalin. Emphasizing Stalin's primary or exclusive authorship in each case, Mikoyan identified as the four major Soviet documents emanating since the Seventeenth Congress the following: the 1935 model charter of the collective farm, the 1936 Constitution of the USSR, the 1938 *History of the All-Union Communist Party* (*Bolsheviks*), and Stalin's report to the Eighteenth Congress.

In his capacity as commissar of Food during the middle 1930's, Mikoyan delivered a major report in January 1936 to the Central Executive Committee of the All-Union Congress of Soviets. The report was subsequently widely published as a pamphlet of some seventy-five pages. Using as his basic theme Stalin's assertion that life had become "more joyous" in the Soviet Union, Mikoyan sketched out a program promising new or expanded production of cigarettes, canned goods, mayonnaise, ice cream, etc. Emphasizing the need to follow American examples and acknowledging his debt to American production techniques, Mikoyan rather quaintly urged upon his audience the merits of ice cream for adults as well as children. "I have obtained," he noted, "information regarding the production of ice cream in America." Later that year, during August, Mikoyan traveled to the United States to observe American techniques first hand. He thereby became the first member of the Politburo to visit America and the second member (after Litvinov) of the Council of People's Commissars to do so. Accompanied by his wife and nine engineers he traveled to several cities to study especially the techniques of meat packing, canning, bottling, and the manufacture of food containers. With Ambassador Troyanovsky, he visited the New York Stock Exchange, where the Soviet flag, with hammer and sickle, was raised for the first time in history.

After becoming commissar of Foreign Trade in 1938, Mikoyan apparently played an active role in foreign policy deliberations as a member of a special subcommittee of Politburo members which tightly controlled the work of the Commissariat of Foreign Affairs. This subcommittee, referred to as a "sextet" in Khrushchev's "secret speech," probably included Stalin, Molotov, Zhdanov, Bulganin, Beria, and Mikoyan. In 1939 Mikoyan participated in the negotiations leading to the Nazi-Soviet Pact of August 23. He was also active in the negotiations with Finland immediately prior to the outbreak of the Russo-Finnish War of 1939–40.

During the Second World War Mikoyan worked from February 1942 as a member of the State Defense Committee created in June 1941. Served by only nine persons, the committee was the supreme governing body in the USSR for the duration of the war and stood above all party and governmental organs; it was abolished in September 1945.

During the war and its immediate aftermath Mikoyan served in several other capacities. In July 1941 he was appointed chairman of the committee to supply food and goods to the soldiers of the Red Army. In recent Soviet accounts he is given major credit, with Alexei N. Kosygin and Nikolai A. Voznesensky, in directing the huge tasks of evacuation and resettlement of Soviet industry in eastern areas safe from the advancing German armies. (Earlier accounts stressed the roles of Molotov, Beria, Malenkov, and Kaganovich.) In August 1943 Mikoyan became a member, together with Beria, Voznesensky, and Andrei A. Andreev, of a committee chaired by Malenkov to restore the economy of Soviet territory liberated from the German forces. Later, in 1945, Mikoyan headed an investigating commission on German reparations which recommended the termination of the dismantling of industry in the Soviet zone of Germany; his report, which was adopted, proposed instead the establishment of Soviet-controlled corporations to manufacture goods to be shipped to the USSR. Apparently in this matter Mikoyan opposed Malenkov and supported the latter's chief rival, Andrei A. Zhdanov. For his wartime work in supplying the Soviet armed forces with goods, food, and other supplies, Mikoyan in 1943 was awarded the title Hero of Socialist Labor.

As commissar of Foreign Trade, Mikoyan took an active role in Allied negotiations throughout the war. He was a participant with Stalin and Molotov in the September 1941 talks with Averell Harriman and Lord Beaverbrook that resulted in the initial lend-lease agreement. Mikoyan was the Soviet official responsible for the receipt of American aid and in this capacity had frequent contacts with Major General John R. Deane, head of the U.S. Military Mission in Moscow. Toward the end of the war, Mikoyan joined with Molotov in the unsuccessful negotiations with Ambassador Harriman respecting American aid for Soviet postwar reconstruction.

In the postwar years down to the death of Stalin in March 1953, Mikoyan consistently supported Stalin in his public utterances, namely, his speeches as a candidate for election to the Supreme Soviet in 1946 and 1950 and his speech in honor of Stalin's seventieth birthday in December 1949. Despite his resignation as minister of Foreign Trade in March 1949, Mikoyan continued to play an important role as economic adviser in foreign affairs. He took part in the lengthy negotiations during late 1949 and early 1950 with the Chinese Communists, which resulted in the Sino-Soviet Treaty of February 14, 1950.

Some Kremlinologists have concluded that Mikoyan and other old Politburo members, such as Molotov and Kaganovich, actually enjoyed little or no real power for several years prior to Stalin's death. Khrushchev's "secret speech" of February 1956 offers considerable basis for this view. It is argued, then, that Stalin effectively cut off the senior Bolsheviks from access to the main machinery of power and was, in fact, preparing to purge them during the last months of his life.

At the Nineteenth Congress, meeting in October 1952, the last congress that assembled during Stalin's lifetime, Mikoyan was not elected to the sixteen-man Presidium of the congress. Eight of the eleven Politburo members were so honored, but not Mikoyan, Andreev, and Kosygin. Nor was Mikoyan elected to membership in the committee to revise the party program of 1919. But he did deliver a major address to the congress, marked by his praise of Stalin's recently published *Economic Problems of Socialism in the USSR* ("that treasure house of ideas") and by his own wit (references, evoking laughter and applause, to the need "to increase the production of all sorts of beverages that whet the appetite").

Among the organizational changes produced by the congress was the expansion (and renaming) of the old Politburo of eleven members and one candidate to a new Presidium of twenty-five members and eleven candidates. Mikoyan and the other members of the old Politburo, except Andreev and Kosygin, were carried over into the new Presidium as full members. They constituted, however, a minority. Khrushchev's "secret speech" reports that, at the first meeting of the Central Committee after the Nineteenth Congress, Stalin suggested that Molotov and Mikoyan were guilty of certain charges. "Stalin," Khrushchev remarked, "evidently had plans to finish off the old members of the Politburo." And he suggested that, had Stalin lived longer, Molotov and Mikoyan would have been eliminated.

Mikoyan's estrangement from Stalin may have begun before the war, if Mikoyan's words in 1956 to Louis Fischer (as recorded in the latter's *Russia Revisited*) are to be believed. Fischer reports Mikoyan as saying: "I not only ate supper with him [Stalin], I was very close to him. But now and then at Politburo sessions I spoke my mind and that ended our friendship. How many people did I myself save from execution!" In his secret speech Khrushchev stated that his views on certain military operations in 1942, at that time rejected by Stalin, were endorsed by Mikoyan after the war in a Politburo meeting, at which point Stalin became enraged. One additional bit of evidence may be noted—the words of Ivan Shaumyan, who spoke at the funeral of Mikoyan's wife in November 1962. Shaumyan, son of the Baku commissar who had been Mikoyan's mentor in 1917–18, asserted that the younger sons of Mikoyan had been arrested and exiled by Stalin during the Second World War.

On the eve of Stalin's death, the Soviet Union witnessed an intensified mood of insecurity and terror, produced by widespread arrests of economic administrators, intellectuals, Jews, party and youth leaders, and highlighted by the disclosure of the "doctors' plot" in January 1953. It has been suggested that Mikoyan's position was endangered especially by the discovery of graft in the commercial apparatus, for which Mikoyan could be considered the responsible Presidium member.

Thus, on the eve of Stalin's death in March 1953, Mikoyan's position at the top echelons of Soviet power was insecure, if not precarious.

In the fourth, current, phase of Mikoyan's career—which is also the post-Stalin phase—these aspects stand out: (1) Mikoyan's continuous membership for thirteen years in the Politburo of the CPSU; (2) his long association with and support of Khrushchev during 1954–64; (3) his political acumen, and perhaps luck, in judging rightly during periods of intra-Presidium debate and crisis in 1954, 1957, and 1964; and (4) his considerable activity as a trouble-shooter in foreign affairs.

The following may be cited as the major developments in the history of the Soviet Union during these years: in domestic politics, the unstable regime of Malenkov (1953–55), de-Stalinization and the Khrushchev era (1955–64), and the current ascendancy of the team of Kosygin and Leonid I. Brezhnev; in economics, the great expansion of Soviet heavy industry and a lesser but appreciable growth in consumer goods, coupled with continued weakness in agriculture; in the sphere of culture, a limited and partial relaxation of party controls; in technology, the advent of the nuclear and space ages; in international Communism, the evolution toward polycentrism and the Sino-Soviet split; and in relations with non-Communist countries, the promotion of "peaceful coexistence," i.e., limited cooperation accompanied by persistent rivalry on all fronts and by all means short of nuclear war.

We may note first Mikoyan's positions during this period in the Communist Party of the Soviet Union. He was a delegate to the last four party congresses and was regularly elected by each as a full member of the Central Committee. Also, he was throughout the post-Stalin era until April 1966 a full member of the highest party organ, the Presidium (which reverted to its former name of Politburo in 1966).

In the governmental structure Mikoyan was elected a deputy to each of the four Supreme Soviets (in 1954, 1958, 1962, and 1966). From March 1953 until July 1964 he was a member of the Council of Ministers. In this body he served as minister of Foreign and Domestic Trade from March to September 1953; as minister of Domestic Trade from September 1953 to January 1955; as deputy chairman from March 1953 to March 1955 and again during a short period in 1957–58; and as first deputy chairman from March 1955 until July 1964, with the exception of the brief period during 1957–58. In April 1962 he was elected to a commission entrusted with drafting a new Soviet constitution. On July 15, 1964, Mikoyan terminated his thirty-eight-year career in the Council of Ministers and became chairman of the Presidium of the Supreme Soviet, i.e., titular head of the Soviet state, resigning on December 9, 1965, whereupon he was immediately elected an ordinary member of that body.

We may now trace Mikoyan's career chronologically through the following episodes: Stalin's death and the immediate aftermath, the Malenkov era to early 1955, the early Khrushchev era, the antiparty crisis of June–July 1957, the later Khrushchev era until October 1964, and the current phase.

On Stalin's death, the Presidium of the CPSU was at once constricted from twenty-five to ten full members, which included Mikoyan and seven veterans, plus the newcomers Maxim Z. Saburov and Mikhail G. Pervukhin. Mikoyan also became on March 6, 1953, minister of Foreign and Domestic Trade (after September, minister of Domestic Trade). On March 15 he was also named deputy chairman of the Council of Ministers. (Ranking above him were four first deputy chairmen—Beria, Bulganin, Kaganovich, and Molotov—and the chairman, Malenkov.) Mikoyan was one of the eight pallbearers at Stalin's funeral, but not one of the three orators (who were Malenkov, Molotov, and Beria).

During his chairmanship of the Council of Ministers (March 6, 1953 to February 8, 1955), Malenkov espoused a sharp increase in consumer goods. Mikoyan appeared initially to have supported this line, e.g., in his speeches of October 17, 1953, and of March 11, 1954. In the developing rivalry between Malenkov and Khrushchev, who had assumed the title of first secretary of the CPSU in September 1953, Mikoyan seems to have endorsed half-heartedly the latter's "virgin lands" program, announced at the end of February 1954. Sometime during 1954 Mikoyan switched his support to Khrushchev, perhaps before September when he traveled to Peking as a member of a delegation including Khrushchev, Bulganin, and Dimitri T. Shepilov. Shortly before Malenkov's fall in February 1955 on charges of administrative inexperience, especially in agricultural matters,

Mikoyan resigned on January 22 as minister of Domestic Trade, possibly to avoid further identification with Malenkov's economic policy. But he retained his post as one of the deputy chairmen of the Council of Ministers, and on March 1 was promoted, along with Saburov and Pervukhin, to the rank of first deputy chairman (joining Kaganovich and Molotov). Bulganin replaced Malenkov as chairman.

During 1955 Mikoyan supported Khrushchev's *rapprochement* with Marshal Tito of Yugoslavia and accompanied Khrushchev, Bulganin, and others to Belgrade in late May 1955. At a meeting of the Central Committee in July, Mikoyan joined Khrushchev in criticizing the Ministry of Foreign Affairs, then headed by Molotov, who continued to oppose the reconciliation with Tito. At the same meeting the question of improving economic relations between the USSR and her East European satellites was discussed. Mikoyan denounced, as blatant and ill-conceived Soviet interference, the joint Soviet-satellite companies that had been established following the war, and demanded their abolition.

The Twentieth Congress of the CPSU, now famous for Khrushchev's de-Stalinizing secret speech, met during February 14–25, 1956. Mikoyan's role at the congress has been variously interpreted. On February 16, following other speakers including Khrushchev who had mentioned Stalin in not unfriendly terms, Mikoyan became the first Presidium member to attack Stalin openly. Besides a general denunciation of a twenty-year period of the "cult of the individual" in the party's history (presumably, the years 1933–53), Mikoyan explicitly attacked Stalin's *Economic Problems of Socialism in the USSR* for containing erroneous theses, and Stalin's authorized 1938 party history, known as the *Short Course*. In his speech Mikoyan supported major elements in Khrushchevian doctrine, e.g., the concepts of peaceful coexistence and nonviolent proletarian revolution. Mikoyan's speech was not immediately published in the Cominform journal. Only nine days later, after a postponement from February 24 to February 25, did Khrushchev deliver his lengthy broadside against Stalin. Was Mikoyan forcing Khrushchev's hand? Or was Mikoyan selected to send up a trial balloon to test the reaction of the congress? Perhaps Mikoyan was chosen because as a Transcaucasian his criticism of Stalin would be more acceptable. But Khrushchev later (1959) denied that his hand had been forced. In his speech Khrushchev referred to Mikoyan three times: once as criticizing Stalin to his face, once as Stalin's prospective victim, and once as an unprotesting witness of a slight injustice. In any case, it seems evident that Mikoyan in 1956 and thereafter was among the most consistent anti-Stalinists. Somewhat ironic is that on November 25, 1955, the date of Mikoyan's sixtieth birthday, he had been hailed as Stalin's comrade-in-arms.

During the succeeding months of 1956—a year of flux in the Communist world—Mikoyan emerged as an active participant in relations between the Soviet Union and other Communist-ruled states. His role obviously became greater than that of a mere economic adviser. During March and April Mikoyan made an Asian tour that included North Vietnam, Communist China, and the Mongolian People's Republic, as well as India and Burma. He was present at the Soviet-Yugoslav talks during Marshal Tito's visit to Moscow in June. In July Mikoyan went to Budapest and presided over the dismissal of the veteran Matyas Rakosi as first secretary of the Hungarian Workers party and his replacement by Ernö Gerö. From Budapest he journeyed to Yugoslavia. In September, heading the Soviet delegation to the Eighth Congress of the Communist Party of China, Mikoyan conceded the right of the Chinese Communists to a measure of independence and praised Mao Tse-tung as an outstanding Marxist-Leninist. On October 19, confronted by the Polish posture of defiance in electing Wladyslaw Gomuka as first secretary of the Polish party, a Soviet party delegation flew to Warsaw, composed of Khrushchev and Mikoyan, who might be considered advocates of compromise, and Molotov and Kaganovich, supporters of a more rigid line. In the even more dramatic case of the Hungarian Revolution, Mikoyan and Mikhail A. Suslov (possibly another pair representing compromise and hard line) were in Budapest during the tense days of October 24–31; they achieved the replacement of Gerö with Janos Kadar, and held several conferences with the Hungarian leaders, the exact nature of which is not known. Following the departure of the Soviet emissaries, the Soviet armed forces in Hungary proceeded to destroy the Hungarian bid for independence from the Soviet Union. During November 15–18, 1956, Mikoyan participated in Soviet-Polish talks in Moscow.

In mid-1957 Mikoyan made one of his most fundamental political decisions—to support Khrushchev against a hostile majority (of seven to four) in the party Presidium. The anti-Khrushchev majority, subsequently known as the "antiparty group," was composed of Malenkov, Molotov, Kaganovich, Voroshilov, Bulganin, Saburov, and Pervukhin. Disturbed by Khrushchev's policies and decisions in several fields, including especially foreign policy and domestic economic reorganization, the Presidium majority sought his removal as first secretary. Mikoyan chose to stand with the minority (Suslov and Alexei I. Kirichenko) in defense of Khrushchev. As is well known, Khrushchev was able to obtain decisive support from members of the Central Committee and easily overcame the Presidium majority. After this crisis he was stronger than ever. Into the reorganized and expanded Presidium of fifteen, Khrushchev brought nine new full members and retained only six (including himself) former members. It may be noted that the members of this new Presidium subdivide into those who were primarily *apparatchiki,* or party apparatus people (a majority) and those who were, like Mikoyan, primarily governmental people (a minority). Mikoyan was not, however, overshadowed by the *apparatchiki.* Henceforth, he was clearly Khrushchev's chief aide in foreign affairs and was assigned to the most sensitive tasks.

Apparently in August 1957 the Soviet government abolished the rank of first deputy chairman of the Council of Ministers, which Mikoyan and others had held at various times. But in late March 1958, with the convening of the newly elected Fifth Supreme Soviet, this rank was re-established. Only Mikoyan and Frol R. Kozlov were then promoted to it. Mikoyan was to retain this rank until 1964, when he became chairman of the Presidium of the Supreme Soviet.

Mikoyan's record of activity as a spokesman, negotiator, and trouble-shooter in international affairs following the antiparty crisis of mid-1957 is indeed impressive. In late July 1957 he was present with Khrushchev at the secret talks in Romania with Marshal Tito. In early August 1957 he accompanied Khrushchev to East Berlin and East Germany. During April 1958 in Bonn he signed several agreements with the German Federal Republic, which provided, among other things, for the establishment of consular relations. Subsequently, during 1958, Mikoyan was in East Berlin (warning West Germany against nuclear rearmament), at the Brussels World Fair, and in Poland.

In January 1959 Mikoyan paid a two-week "holiday" visit to the United States, a trip widely interpreted as preparatory to Khrushchev's later visit in September. Mikoyan conferred with President Eisenhower, Vice President Nixon, Secretary of State Dulles, Adlai Stevenson, Harold Stassen, Eric Johnston, Cyrus S. Eaton, and various business, financial, labor, and civic leaders. Permitted to travel freely about the United States, Mikoyan offered in speeches and news conferences a variety of opinions, warnings, and hopes; he stressed the themes of peaceful coexistence, expansion of Soviet-American trade, and limitation on nuclear testing. Ending his trip on January 20, he expressed the view that his experience had made him more optimistic for the fate of mankind. Later in 1959 Mikoyan met with Prime Minister Harold Macmillan during the latter's ten-day visit to the Soviet Union in February and March, and apparently acted to assuage an affront to the British statesman by Khrushchev. In July Mikoyan talked with Vice President Nixon at the opening of the American Exposition in Moscow. In November, Mikoyan again travelled to North America, this time to open the Soviet Trade Exhibition in Mexico City.

At the Twenty-first Congress of the CPSU, which met in Moscow from January 27 to February 5, 1959, Mikoyan's speech is noteworthy for at least two reasons. First, he devoted over half of his remarks to American-Soviet relations and his recent trip to the United States, and emphasized the friendliness of the welcome accorded him. Second, with reference to the renewed discussions at the congress of the antiparty group of 1957, Mikoyan associated himself with the most moderate, least vengeful camp, and clearly sought to prevent any further reprisals against members of the group. Whereas Khrushchev, Nikolai V. Podgorny, and others viciously attacked members of the antiparty group, Mikoyan, and others like Suslov and Kosygin, sought to close debate on the subject. It has been suggested that Khrushchev wanted to bring the antiparty group to trial and was successfully opposed in this effort by the moderates, including Mikoyan, who felt that further persecution would only discredit the USSR internationally.

During 1960 Mikoyan's position seems to have suffered temporarily as a result of the U-2 incident on May 1. Having identified himself fully with a relaxation in East-West tension, Mikoyan may have become a scapegoat; the break-up of the Paris summit meeting on May 17 reflected possibly a victory of a majority in the Presidium over the line previously pursued by Khrushchev and Mikoyan. At any rate, several indicators in mid-1960 suggest Mikoyan's temporary downgrading: his low position (sixth) in the order of May Day photographs, omission of his name from an article on the establishment of Soviet power in Azerbaijan (which appeared in *Party Life* in May), and references during May to Mikoyan as deputy chairman, rather than *first* deputy chairman, of the Council of Ministers. But if Mikoyan's position was shaken by developments in foreign policy, he was not directly downgraded or attacked, and all official biographical accounts credit him with retaining the rank of first deputy chairman throughout 1960.

During 1960 Mikoyan visited Cuba in February and signed an economic-aid pact. In April he opened a Soviet industrial fair in Baghdad. In June he opened another exhibition in Oslo, and took the opportunity to levy strong attacks against the United States, emphasizing American espionage activities.

At the important Conference of Eighty-one Communist Parties, which met in Moscow during November and December 1960, Mikoyan was a member of the Soviet delegation. This conference has been the last, up to the present, to produce a broad declaration on ideology, strategy, and tactics to which all Communist parties (excepting the Communist League of Yugoslavia) have officially subscribed.

In 1961 Mikoyan paid a state visit to Japan during August. He was the first high-ranking Soviet official ever to visit that country. Among other things, he opened a Soviet trade fair, attacked the United States–Japanese military alliance as the main obstacle to improved Soviet–Japanese relations, and rejected a Japanese proposal for direct Tokyo–Moscow air service. In October he was in East Berlin, honoring the twelfth anniversary of the East German Republic and repeating the Soviet intention to sign a separate peace treaty within a short time.

At the Twenty-second Congress of the CPSU in Moscow during October 1961, Mikoyan, as at the preceding congress, stood with the more moderate wing of the Presidium in the renewed attacks on the antiparty group of 1957. His position was again clear: no further reprisals. Mikoyan also backed Khrushchev's attack upon the Albanian Communists and spelled out specific charges against its leaders, Enver Hoxha and Mehmet

Shehu. As a result of changes in the Presidium following the congress, only Mikoyan and Khrushchev remained of Stalin's heirs and pallbearers of 1953.

Early in 1962 Mikoyan toured several African states, including Guinea, Ghana, Morocco, and Mali. In a speech at Accra on January 16, Mikoyan gave specific recognition to Nkrumah's variant of socialism, or "African socialism." In March, possibly to counter a recent visit of Robert Kennedy to West Berlin, Mikoyan journeyed to East Germany, opened the annual Leipzig industrial fair, and signed a new aid-and-trade pact. In July he spent several days in Indonesia, promising support in its dispute with the Netherlands over Western New Guinea. While going both to and from Indonesia, Mikoyan stopped for visits in India. On August 2 Mikoyan received the Most Rev. Dr. Arthur Michael Ramsey, the first archbishop of Canterbury ever to visit Moscow, and discussed an exchange of information, students, and delegations between the Church of England and the Russian Orthodox Church.

The major diplomatic activity of Mikoyan in 1962, however, was his role in the Cuban missile crisis, which brought him to Havana during November 2–26. Apparently his task was to gain Prime Minister Fidel Castro's acceptance of the Kennedy-Khrushchev settlement of the crisis. The seriousness and difficulty of Mikoyan's assignment was emphasized by his continued presence in Havana despite the news on November 4 of his wife's death in Moscow the previous day. Mikoyan's son, Sergo, who had accompanied his father to Cuba, returned for the funeral. At the end of his Cuban talks, Mikoyan traveled to New York and participated in the American-Soviet negotiations that led to the election of U Thant on November 30 as secretary-general of the United Nations. He also had lengthy discussions with President Kennedy and Secretary of State Rusk.

Doubtless because of his close acquaintance with Fidel Castro, Mikoyan was on hand to greet the Cuban leader in April 1963 on his arrival in the USSR for the May Day celebrations. On July 4, at the American Embassy in Moscow, Mikoyan reaffirmed the Soviet desire for a test-ban accord on nuclear devices. He also took part in the Sino-Soviet talks in Moscow in July, which were the last effort at reconciliation prior to Khrushchev's downfall more than a year later. On the assassination of President Kennedy on November 22, Mikoyan was sent to Washington to attend the funeral as the official Soviet representative. He later talked with President Johnson and returned to Moscow on November 28.

In 1964 Mikoyan made two major trips to the Far East. During May he visited Japan for two weeks as the head of a delegation of members of the Supreme Soviet. Conversing with high government officials, trade union leaders, and others, Mikoyan also made a number of speeches. Among other pronouncements, he rejected Japan's request for the return of certain of the southernmost Kurile Islands and vowed Soviet retaliation if the

United States attacked Cuba. In late June and early July Mikoyan again visited Indonesia, and promised new Soviet weapons and experts to train Indonesians in the use of these weapons.

On July 15, 1964, Mikoyan succeeded Brezhnev as titular head of the Soviet state with his election, after being nominated by Khrushchev, as chairman of the Presidium of the Supreme Soviet.

Three months later, in October, Khrushchev was removed from his posts as first secretary of the CPSU and chairman of the Council of Ministers. Mikoyan had been with Khrushchev at the resort of Gagra on October 12, and with Khrushchev spoke to the three Soviet cosmonauts then in orbit. Early the next morning, Mikoyan was back in Moscow and certainly was by then informed of the plot to oust Khrushchev, if indeed he had not known of it earlier. Khrushchev returned later on October 13 to Moscow. On October 14 the Central Committee elected Brezhnev to replace Khrushchev as first secretary, and the next day the Presidium of the Supreme Soviet, with Mikoyan presiding, removed Khrushchev from his post as chairman of the Council of Ministers, replacing him with Kosygin. It is too early to ascertain Mikoyan's role—whether a willing or unwilling collaborator, or even initiator—in the plot to remove Khrushchev.

The year 1965 may be viewed as a year of declining activity and influence for Mikoyan. He ceased to travel abroad, but in his capacity as chairman of the Presidium of the Supreme Soviet he received many foreign visitors, including the American industrialist Cyrus Eaton, Marshal Tito, President Nasser, French Foreign Minister Couve de Murville, and British Foreign Secretary Michael Stewart. On Mikoyan's seventieth birthday (November 25) *Pravda* carried his picture, congratulatory messages, and a decree of the Presidium of the Supreme Soviet awarding him his fourth Order of Lenin. But on December 9, at a session of the Supreme Soviet, Mikoyan, in a three-minute speech pleading ill health, stepped down as Soviet head of state. Brezhnev immediately took the floor to praise Mikoyan and to affirm the respect of the Soviet people for his fifty years of service. He thus retired with honor and was immediately elected an ordinary member of the Presidium of the Supreme Soviet. For the time being, also, he retained his position as a member of the Presidium of the Central Committee of the CPSU.

In 1966, at the Twenty-third Congress of the CPSU (March 29–April 8), Mikoyan lost his post in the party Presidium (now renamed Politburo) and thus terminated his forty-year career as a member of that most powerful body. He retained full membership in the Central Committee. Thus, by April 1966, Mikoyan was clearly at the end of his long political career as an influential public figure in the Soviet Union.

Mikoyan seems now, in his seventies, finally past the peak years of his power and activity. He is the last of the Old Bolsheviks to depart from the Presidium (Politburo), and one of the extremely few to depart with full honor. Whether or not this experienced elder statesman will be consulted in the future by the new younger leaders is a moot question. His expert status in domestic and international affairs, both political and economic, may well be ignored. But of all the current members of the Central Committee, he has the greatest firsthand acquaintance with the world outside the Soviet Union. In particular, he has visited the United States more often than any person still influential in Soviet politics (in 1936, 1959, 1962, and 1963). In the last few years, he was the only top-ranking Soviet leader, apart from Khrushchev, who was well known by foreigners.

Mikoyan's career has been that of the practical man in politics and administration. He has not been attracted by problems of Marxist-Leninist theory and never sought to present himself as a theoretician. His publications are almost exclusively reports and speeches on current issues. There is one curious item, an introduction by him to a book entitled *The Don Cossacks,* written by Mikhail Donetsky and published in 1926. He himself apparently reads fairly widely and on one occasion recommended to Khrushchev the book *Not by Bread Alone,* by the controversial Soviet novelist, Vladimir Dudintsev.

In personality Mikoyan evidently possesses a measure of charm and a refreshing capacity for humor. Walter Duranty described Mikoyan as having "unusual charm and agility of conversation and a broad and brilliant mind." Former Ambassador Joseph E. Davies found him "aggressive" and "quick as a rapier." In his memoirs, Gustav Hilger, second counselor at the German Embassy in Moscow from 1918 to 1941, offers several evaluations—"exceptional intelligence," "one of the most agreeable partners in negotiations," and "pleasant manner." Hilger reports: "He knew how to make interesting and witty conversation about a great variety of subjects." Like many others, Louis Fischer found him "remarkably uninhibited" in conversation.

Mikoyan is a widower with four remaining sons, one of whom, Sergo, is an economist. One son, a pilot, was killed in the Second World War. Well known in the Soviet Union is Mikoyan's brother, Artem Ivanovich, born in 1906, who is a talented aircraft designer. With Mikhail I. Gurevich he created the famous MIG aircraft and, among other honors, was elected in 1953 a corresponding member of the USSR Academy of Sciences.

In addition to the awards bestowed upon him by the Soviet government —Hero of Socialist Labor, Order of the Red Banner and Four Orders of Lenin—Mikoyan has been given recognition in another form, the naming of places in his honor. These include the village of Mikoyan in the Armenian republic, Mikoyan settlement on Kamchatka peninsula, Mikoyanabad village and district in the Tadzhik republic, Mikoyanovka settlement in the Mikoyanovsk district of the Russian republic, Mikoyanovsk settlement in the Khabarovsk territory, and the Gulf of Mikoyan in the Arctic.

It is not easy to explain Mikoyan's successful retention for forty years of a place at the center of the Soviet power structure. Undoubtedly great political acumen, coupled at times with a measure of luck, has always played a role. In specializing in such sectors of the economy as trade, food, and light industry, Mikoyan revealed a certain lack of ambition for personal aggrandizement. For if Mikoyan had entrenched himself in the party apparatus, or in such a privileged branch of the economy as heavy industry, he could well have, brought upon himself suspicions that he was an ambitious and dangerous power-seeker. Not wielding authority over a domain of prime importance in the government, party, or economy, Mikoyan did not attract the envious attention that others did. Certainly his willingness to serve obediently first one master, then another, is an element to be considered. And Mikoyan always retained his extreme usefulness to the party as an experienced economic administrator and foreign trade negotiator.

With Mikoyan's departure from the center of political life in the Soviet Union, the Politburo lost its sole member who has had considerable first-hand knowledge of the West, and the West is now confronted with a group of men, by and large a younger generation, about whom it knows little. Whatever history's final judgment on Mikoyan, he proved himself an adaptable, flexible public figure. He may rightly be considered, in relation to other recent and current leaders of the CPSU, a moderate, a modernizer, and an advocate of *détente* with the West.

SELECTED BIBLIOGRAPHY

For Soviet sources on Mikoyan's career, one should begin with the biographies in the *Bol'shaia sovetskaia entsiklopediia,* vypusk 1, XXXIX, Moskva, 1938, cols. 343–48 and vypusk 2, XXVII, Moskva, 1954, pp. 430–31. For additional references to Mikoyan, the indices to both editions of the *Bol'shaia* should be checked. More recent biographical data are found in *Ezhegodnik bol'shoi sovetskoi entsiklopedii,* which has appeared since 1957. Also useful and up-to-date is the biography in the *Sovetskaia istoricheskaia entsiklopediia,* IX, Moskva, 1966, cols. 428–430. Shorter biographical sketches are included in the three editions of the *Malaia sovetskaia entsiklopediia.* See also *Deiateli soiuza sovetskikh sotsialisticheskikh respublik i oktiabr'skoi revoliutsii, avtobiografii i biografii,* Moskva, 1929, part II, cols. 37–38. Some slight information on the Caucasian period of Mikoyan's career is given in the following accounts: Ia. Ratgauzer, *Revoliutsiia i grazhdanskaia voina v Baku,* Baku, 1927; A. Dubner, *Bakinskii proletariat v gody revoliutsii, 1917–1920,* Baku, 1931; M. D. Bagirov, *Iz istorii bolshevistskoi organizatsii Baku i Azerbaizhana,* Moskva, 1946; and Suren Shaumian, *Bakinskaia kommuna,* Baku, 1927.

Many details of Mikoyan's activity after 1921 can be gleaned from the official Russian-language reports of meetings of such leading organs of party and state as the party congresses (from the Tenth through the Twenty-third), the All-Union Central Executive Committee, the All-Union Congress of Soviets, and the Supreme Soviet. Certain of these records are available in English, notably the proceedings of the party congresses beginning with the Nineteenth (*Current Soviet Policies,* 4 volumes, New York: Praeger, 1953–62). Mikoyan's report on January 16, 1936, to the All-Union Central Executive Committee, has been separately printed as a pamphlet, *The Soviet Food Industry*, Moscow, 1936.

In English there is a convenient short sketch, now somewhat dated, by Charles Malamuth, "Mikoyan—Kremlin Trouble-Shooter," in *Communist Affairs*, I, 4 (1962), pp. 19–22. See also the data in *Who's Who in the USSR, 1961–1962*, New York: Scarecrow Press, 1962, p. 509. Indispensable for an understanding of the over-all development of Soviet politics are three studies: Merle Fainsod, *How Russia Is Ruled*, 2nd edition, Cambridge: Harvard University Press, 1963; Leonard Schapiro, *The Communist Party of the Soviet Union*, New York: Random House, 1959; and John S. Reshetar, *A Concise History of the Communist Party of the Soviet Union*, 2nd edition, New York: Praeger, 1964. Valuable specialized studies deserving mention are the following: Robert V. Daniels, *The Conscience of the Revolution*, Cambridge: Harvard University Press, 1960; John A. Armstrong, *The Politics of Totalitarianism*, New York: Random House, 1961; Robert K. Conquest, *Power and Policy in the U.S.S.R.*, New York: St. Martin's Press, 1961 and *Russia after Khrushchev*, New York: Praeger, 1965; Roger Pethybridge, *A Key to Soviet Politics*, London: George Allen and Unwin, 1962; Myron Rush, *The Rise of Khrushchev*, Washington, D.C.; Public Affairs Press, 1958 and *Political Succession in the USSR*, New York: Columbia University Press, 1965; George K. Schueller, *The Politburo*, Stanford: Stanford University Press, 1951; and Howard R. Swearer, *The Politics of Succession in the U.S.S.R.*, Boston: Little, Brown, 1964. Certain memoir accounts shed light on Mikoyan's personality: Louis Fischer, *Russia Revisited*, Garden City, N.Y.: Doubleday, 1957; Joseph E. Davies, *Mission to Moscow*, New York: Simon and Schuster, 1941; and Gustav Hilger and Alfred G. Meyer, *The Incompatible Allies*, New York: Macmillan, 1953. To be treated with caution is the study by the Soviet emigré, Abdurakhan Avtorkhanov, *Stalin and the Soviet Communist Party*, New York: Praeger, 1959.

Mikoyan's publications are few and are largely in the form of short pamphlets containing a single speech or report. He contributed the preface to a study of the Don Cossacks: Mikhail Donetskii, *Donskoe Kazachestvo*, Rostov-on-Don, 1926. And he edited, with L. Z. Mekhlis, L. P. Beria, and Z. G. Ordjonikidze, a volume of selected articles and speeches by his fellow Transcaucasian, Grigorii Ordjonikidze, *Izbrannye stati i rechi, 1911–1937*, Moskva, 1939. Mikoyan's report to the Moscow party organization in January 1936 on the Cheka-chief, Felix Dzerzhinsky, was printed as a separate pamphlet, *Feliks Dzerzhinskii*, in 1936 and again in 1937. Other useful items are *Mikoyan in Cuba; full texts of the speeches made by Anastas I. Mikoyan, First Vice-Chairman of the USSR, on his tour of Cuba, February 4–13, 1960*, New York: Crosscurrents Press, 1960, and Victor Perlo, *How the Soviet Economy Works; an Interview with A. I. Mikoyan, First Deputy Prime Minister, the USSR*, New York: International Publishers, 1961. Mikoyan's important speech at the party's Twentieth Congress is available in English as a separate pamphlet, *Speech at the 20th Congress of the C.P.S.U.*, Moscow, 1956. Of interest are his memoirs, "Iz vospominanii o Sergo Ordjonikidze," *Iunost'*, XII, 10 (October 1966), 9–21.

Nikolai Viktorovich Podgorny

by Grey Hodnett

At the June 1963 plenary meeting of the Central Committee of the Communist Party of the Soviet Union (CPSU), two men were promoted to the party Secretariat. Both had been recruited from the Ukrainian party apparatus, and both were considered followers of and potential successors to Nikita Khrushchev as first secretary of the party. One was Leonid Brezhnev, who in fact did win the highest post in the Soviet political system —and sooner than many anticipated; the other was Nikolai Podgorny, until June 1963 first secretary of the Communist Party of the Ukraine.

Nikolai Viktorovich Podgorny was born on February 18, 1903, in Karlovka, a small town in the agriculturally rich Ukrainian province of Poltava. Podgorny's father, an ethnic Ukrainian, was a worker in a foundry. Little else is known of Podgorny's childhood. At fifteen, in 1918, he took his first job, as a mechanic in a workshop in Karlovka. He held several similar positions, it seems, during the next few years—a period in which some of the more adventurous youths his age were fighting in the Civil War.

Nothing is known of the political sympathies of Podgorny's parents during the confused battles and guerrilla warfare that swept the Ukraine following the collapse of the Austro-German occupation in 1918. Podgorny himself revealed a certain early enthusiasm for political activity by joining and participating actively in the Komsomol (Young Communist League) during the Civil War. After acting as a volunteer Komsomol organizer, Podgorny served between 1921 and 1923 as a secretary of the Karlovka District Komsomol Committee and then of other Komsomol organizations in Poltava Province. Thanks to this display of political initiative, and to his properly proletarian social background, the Komsomol sent Podgorny to Kiev in 1923 to receive an accelerated secondary education at a *rabfak* (workers' faculty) organized by a polytechnical institute. He completed his studies in 1926 and went on to acquire a higher education at the Kiev Technological Institute for the Food Industry, from which he graduated in 1931.

Most contemporary leading party officials spent only a short time in other professional occupations during the early part of their careers before becoming full-time political functionaries. But there are exceptions to this rule, including several persons of non-Russian extraction who have been prominent leaders in the national republics. Podgorny may be counted among them. It was indeed fortunate for him during the repeated purges in the Ukrainian party apparatus in the 1930's that he did not occupy a sensitive position. He remained unscathed, although the sugar industry, where he worked, with its high percentage of ethnic Ukrainians, was apparently hit very hard.

From 1931 to 1937 Podgorny served as senior assistant chief engineer, deputy chief engineer, and chief engineer at the Andrushevka, Monastyriska, and Kozhanka sugar refining factories. His rise in the period between 1937 and 1939 to deputy chief engineer (or perhaps chief engineer) of the sugar trust in Vinitsa, and then to chief engineer of the sugar trust in Kamenets-Podolsk, was modest in comparison with the enormous leaps made in the same years by many of his contemporaries. It is probable, therefore, that Podgorny is not responsible for a mass of ruined lives, unlike many party officials his age.

When Khrushchev was confirmed as first secretary of the Ukrainian party in January 1938 at a meeting of its depleted Central Committee, he proceeded to complete the purge that was sweeping away thousands of appointees of the former Ukrainian leadership. Nowhere among the non-Russian Soviet republics was hunting for the heresy of "bourgeois nationalism" taken more seriously than in the Ukraine. Stalin, who had experienced recalcitrance among Ukrainian Communist leaders even in the middle 1930's developed a near-pathological distrust of Ukrainians, and Khrushchev was only half-jesting in his "secret speech" at the Twentieth Congress of the CPSU when he stated that Stalin would have deported the entire Ukrainian population had this been physically feasible. Stalin's fears were seemingly confirmed when many Ukrainians revealed themselves to be less than loyal to Moscow during the Second World War.

There are, of course, valid reasons for any Soviet leader to be apprehensive about the potentially explosive force of nationalism in an area of such enormous economic and geographical importance to the Soviet Union as the Ukraine. A loosening of the bonds between the Ukraine and Russia would impinge seriously upon the over-all pattern of economic development desired by the Soviet leadership, thus affecting the military-industrial might of the Soviet Union; it would have a contagious effect on attitudes among the native leaders of other Soviet national republics; it would set off shocks that would shake the party in the Russian republic to its roots; and it would seriously embarrass the Soviet Union both in the international Communist movement and in the world at large. These ultimate considerations are not and cannot be openly expressed; yet they are very much present when appointments are made to high positions in the Ukraine. In such appointments, loyalty to Moscow takes precedence over professional competence.

It may be assumed, then, that Khrushchev attempted to conform to the criterion of loyalty in selecting replacements for posts vacated by the purges of 1937 and 1938. Among those chosen was Podgorny, who in February 1939 was appointed deputy people's commissar for the Food Industry of the Ukrainian republic. Precisely what Podgorny's responsibilities were is unknown, although it is not unlikely that he directed the Ukrainian sugar refining industry. He apparently performed whatever tasks were assigned to him satisfactorily, for in 1940 he was promoted to deputy people's commissar for the Food Industry of the USSR. Moving from the Ukraine to Moscow, from the local level to the center, was a big step. Presumably Podgorny was now responsible on a nationwide basis for whatever aspect of the food industry he had supervised in the Ukraine—which, as indicated, may well have been the sugar industry.

Podgorny spent only a year or two as an all-union deputy commissar —perhaps because the German conquest of the Ukraine, one of the main centers of sugar production, made his job superfluous. In 1941 or 1942 (his official biographers are inconsistent) he was appointed director of the Moscow Technological Institute for the Food Industry. While most of his future political associates were at the front, either fighting or encouraging others to fight, or else were involved in spurring on war production, Podgorny spent the bulk of the war performing humdrum activities in a job of minor importance.

As the German armies were being expelled from the Ukraine, Podgorny left the food institute and returned to Kiev in May 1944 to resume his former post of deputy commissar for the Ukrainian Food Industry. Because of the enormous loss of manpower, livestock, and farm machinery during the war, the food situation in the Ukraine during the early postwar years was extremely tense and at times in some areas approached near-famine conditions. All officials connected with agriculture or food processing were under the most stringent compulsion to increase food output— without, however, being given adequate resources. The food crisis reached a peak in 1947, the year Lazar Kaganovich replaced Khrushchev for several months as first secretary of the Ukrainian Communist party. According to a later statement by Khrushchev, Kaganovich was barely restrained in these months from undertaking a new blood purge of Ukrainian "bourgeois nationalists."

During the years immediately following his return to the Ukraine, Podgorny was also engaged in a job that most of his official biographers have neglected to mention. As the Soviet armies were driving the Germans out of the Ukraine and back across Eastern Europe, the Ukrainian Insurgent Army, a large underground military force closely affiliated with the Organization of Ukrainian Nationalists (a political movement known more for its desire to establish an independent Ukraine than for its commitment to liberal democracy), intensified its struggle against the Communists both in the western Ukraine and across the border in Poland. The partisan activity of the Insurgent Army—which at times attained a scale of almost

open warfare and was combated by the Soviets with extreme ruthlessness
—drew much of its support from the indigenous Ukrainian population on
both sides of the border. Ukrainian nationalist sentiments had traditionally
been stronger in this region than in the eastern Ukraine.

One of the methods used by the Communists to suppress this revolt,
in addition to armed force, terror, and offers of amnesty, was to uproot and
resettle large numbers of people. According to agreements reached between
Polish and Soviet authorities in September and October 1944, Poles on the
Ukrainian side of the border (which had already been shifted westward)
were to be "repatriated" to Poland and Ukrainians, Byelorussians, and
other Soviet nationals were to be returned to their "homeland" in the
USSR. From 1944 to 1946 Podgorny, besides being deputy commissar for
the Food Industry, was also chief commissioner of the Government of the
Ukrainian Soviet Socialist Republic for the Repatriation of the Ukrainian
Population on Polish Territory to the Fatherland.

How much authority Podgorny's title conveyed is impossible to determine. The actual transfer of people was undoubtedly handled by the security police. Without knowing the facts, one might speculate that he
worked as a liaison with the Polish government and helped to coordinate
the various republic and local governmental agencies involved in relocating
the 518,000 people who were uprooted from Polish territory and moved
to the Ukraine (largely into the Stanislav, Lvov, and Nikolaev oblasts).
Under any circumstances, this mammoth transplantation would have been
a difficult undertaking; with much of the Ukraine laid waste, the difficulties
must have been greatly amplified. To complicate matters even further, the
Ukrainian nationalists, who had attempted to block the removal of Ukrainians from Poland, were making the most of the migration by infiltrating
personnel and propaganda into the eastern Ukraine. Podgorny's position
was thus highly political, requiring him to deal with a very delicate issue.
One false step might have cost him his career, perhaps even his life. That
he survived and performed his duties to the apparent satisfaction of both
the Soviet secret police and his bosses in the Ukraine is a tribute to his
toughness and political acumen.

Podgorny's work had apparently pleased Khrushchev sufficiently for
him to support Podgorny's nomination in April 1946 to a position in Moscow—that of permanent representative of the Ukrainian Council of Ministers to the Government of the USSR. If the Soviet Union had possessed
a genuinely federal form of government, this quasi-ambassadorial office
might have been vested with a certain amount of real power. But neither in
the years 1946 to 1950, when Podgorny was permanent representative,
nor today can the Soviet Union be considered anything other than a highly
centralized state. In those years of harsh repression, whatever bargaining
may have occurred between Stalin and the Ukrainian leadership could not
have involved Podgorny's active participation. At most, his job entailed

technical coordination. Still, the work carried with it an impressive-sounding title, involved a broader range of problems than those of sugar-beet growing, and brought Podgorny into regular contact with people of greater authority than those he had previously encountered. To some extent the Ukrainian leadership may also have relied upon Podgorny as its eyes and ears in Moscow—as a person who could pass on whatever current political intelligence or rumors may have been circulating in the capital. From the standpoint of the leadership in Kiev this was undoubtedly a position of trust, for its occupant, through design or ineptitude, could easily embarrass them. Thus it was an important step forward in his career.

However, it was not until 1950, at the advanced age of forty-seven, that Podgorny held his first job in the party apparatus. In May of that year he was appointed first secretary of the Kharkov Oblast Party Committee—one of the top half-dozen party posts in the entire Ukraine. The timing of this promotion is of some interest, occurring as it did after Khrushchev had left the Ukraine to become a secretary of the Central Committee of the CPSU and first secretary of the Moscow Oblast Party Committee (December 1949). The new first secretary of the Ukraine, Leonid Melnikov, an ethnic Russian and apparently not Khrushchev's choice, was to pursue a harsh Russifying policy during his three and one-half years in office. Although Khrushchev was a member of the Secretariat of the CPSU, at this time Malenkov was the secretary who supervised personnel appointments; it is not clear therefore whether Podgorny was indebted for this initial boost into the ranks of the party elite to Khrushchev, Melnikov, or Malenkov, or whether he simply offended nobody and for this reason was an acceptable candidate. In Kharkov, a large manufacturing city in the northeast Ukraine, Podgorny acquired his first experience with heavy industry.

Stalin's death in March 1953 soon produced a major shake-up in the Ukrainian party leadership. On June 12 Melnikov was charged with agricultural failures and violation of the national sensibilities of the Ukrainian people, and he was replaced as Ukrainian first secretary by Alexei Kirichenko, an ethnic Ukrainian who had been second secretary of the Ukrainian party since December 1949 (and who consequently may also have helped Podgorny in 1950). Podgorny in turn replaced Kirichenko as second secretary. After Stalin's death, Khrushchev, as the sole member of the Secretariat who also held a seat in the party Presidium, was in a position to exert strong influence in personnel appointments. Nevertheless, in 1953 he was not powerful enough actually to appoint the first and second secretaries of the Ukraine. Final decision rested with the Presidium of the CPSU, and Kirichenko and Podgorny were presumably acceptable to at least a majority of its members.

If the extent of Podgorny's indebtedness to Khrushchev in 1953 is thus not absolutely clear, it is clear that by this time Podgorny had, at the very least, strong support from above. Whereas most second secretaries of re-public party organizations spend years working up through the party to attain a position this high, Podgorny achieved it in three years, barely enough time for him to familiarize himself with the habits and procedures of the party apparatus.

Kirichenko came to his position as boss of the Ukraine with a mandate, however indefinite, to pursue a more conciliatory nationality policy than that of his predecessor—who had been accused, among other faults, of "gross errors in the selection of cadres" (i.e., discrimination against Ukrai-nians). As second secretary of the Communist Party of the Ukraine, Podgorny supervised the activities of the Ukrainian party apparatus and implemented the party's day-to-day personnel policy. He therefore occu-pied a pivotal position in carrying out the new nationality policy. In prac-tical terms this meant that Podgorny, a Ukrainian, had the ticklish mission of creating a more equitable balance of Ukrainians and Russians in im-portant jobs in the Ukraine.

Podgorny apparently handled the situation with finesse, for he was elected to the Central Committee of the CPSU at the party's Twentieth Congress in 1956—a sign that he had at last arrived as an important Soviet leader. After Khrushchev's victory over the "antiparty group," Podgorny moved up in December 1957 to become first secretary of the Ukrainian party—a position of great power and responsibility. Coming so soon after Khrushchev's stunning triumph, this promotion was an unmistakable sign of Khrushchev's benevolence. At the same time Podgorny's superior, Kirichenko, a member of the Presidium of the CPSU since 1955, was pro-moted to the Secretariat, becoming the de facto second secretary of the party and heir apparent to Khrushchev. Not long after, Podgorny received the recognition due his office and was elected (June 1958) to candidate membership in the Presidium of the CPSU. Two years later (May 4, 1960) he became a full member. In ten years he had ascended to the highest organ of the Soviet political system.

Podgorny's promotion to full membership in the Presidium came soon after the U-2 affair, a moment when, some Western observers suspect, Khrushchev was politically embarrassed and on the defensive. As Podgorny rose, his former chief, Kirichenko, was in the process of falling into com-plete disgrace, to be replaced as number-two man by Frol Kozlov. Kiri-chenko is widely believed to have been a close follower of Khrushchev, and his downfall is still a major mystery; no explicit accusations were ever lodged against him. It is thought that he may have been charged with not having conscientiously implemented the party's harsher nationality policy (in evidence since 1958). Given Podgorny's background, not to mention his association with Kirichenko, it is likely that he too—justly or not—is vulnerable to the charge of laxity with respect to nationalist devia-tion.

No such difficulties, however, arose for Podgorny in 1960, nor in the four years preceding Khrushchev's fall. He received increasing publicity in the Soviet press, and some Western speculation focused on the possibility of his succeeding to Khrushchev's position, despite the handicap of his nationality. During these years Podgorny was exposed to foreigners, at least to some degree, and to the problems of managing the Soviet Union's international relations—neither of which had previously been part of his experience.

Podgorny's stature in the Soviet elite was almost surely enhanced by the promotion in February 1961 of his subordinate of many years, Vitali Titov, to head of the party Organs Department of the Central Committee— a key position involving personnel-assignment powers. Titov was advanced once more in November 1962 to become a secretary of the Central Committee and chairman of the newly created Commission for Organizational-Party Questions. In June 1963 Podgorny followed Titov into the Secretariat, relinquishing his position as first secretary of the Ukrainian party to a subordinate, Pyotr Shelest. He was accompanied into the Secretariat by Leonid Brezhnev, also a member of the Presidium and graduate of the Ukrainian party apparatus, who assumed the heir apparency to Khrushchev —a role illness had recently compelled Frol Kozlov to give up.

In retrospect it appears that June 1963 may have been the zenith of Podgorny's career. Khrushchev is thought to have elevated Podgorny both to augment his own political support (which had shown signs of erosion in the winter of 1962–63) and to counterbalance Brezhnev's possible premature pretensions. Although Podgorny's credentials were not as impressive as Brezhnev's, it would not have been unreasonable at this point for him to have entertained hopes for the future. But it seems that his base of political support was too narrow, his appointive powers far too limited, his experience too circumscribed, and his nationality too much of a drawback for him to make a bid for supreme power.

More than Brezhnev, Podgorny appears to have needed Khrushchev's backing to keep rising in the Soviet elite. This circumstance may explain Podgorny's being the last top Soviet leader to lavish praise on Khrushchev before the latter's overthrow. Although Podgorny maintained his position after Khrushchev's fall, he is not thought to have been a participant in the conspiracy that gave rise to the coup that ousted Khrushchev. The subsequent demotion of Vitali Titov in March 1965 to second secretary of the Communist Party of Kazakhstan did not bode well for Podgorny's political future. Podgorny's own departure from the Central Committee Secretariat and appointment as chairman of the Presidium of the Supreme Soviet in December 1965 seemed to signify a further erosion of his power. His failure to endorse, in his speech at the party's Twenty-third Congress (March– April 1966), the major proposals to restore the term "Politburo" in place of "Presidium," revive Stalin's title "general secretary" (for Brezhnev), and "reform" the Party Rules strongly suggested that he opposed these measures—thereby opposing any increase in Brezhnev's authority. In the same speech he, unlike most speakers, endorsed the general policy line (including de-Stalinization) pursued by the party since the Twentieth Congress in 1956. These and many other signs made it appear that fundamental disagreements existed among the top Soviet leaders. How long Podgorny will be able to retain his present high position in the leadership under these circumstances cannot be predicted.

SELECTED BIBLIOGRAPHY

In Russian, the main sources of biographical information about Podgorny are the following: *Bol'shaia sovetskaia entsiklopediia,* vypusk 2, LI, Moskva, 1958, pp. 224–25; *Ezhegodnik bol'shoi sovetskoi entsiklopedii 1958,* Moskva, 1958, p. 639; *Ezhegodnik bol'shoi sovetskoi entsiklopedii 1962,* Moskva, 1962, p. 610; *Malaia sovetskaia entsiklopediia,* vypusk 3, VII, Moskva, 1959, p. 265; *Deputaty verkhovnogo soveta SSSR,* Moskva, 1959, p. 317; *Deputaty verkhovnogo soveta SSSR,* Moskva, 1963, p. 339; *Ukrains'ka radians'ka entsiklopediia,* XI, Kiev, 1963, p. 185. A Western source is J. Marin, "Podgornyj, Nikolaj Wiktorowitsch," *Porträts der UdSSR-Prominenz,* München: Institut Zur Erforschung der UdSSR, 1960.

In English, information about Podgorny can be found in *Biographic Directory of the USSR,* New York: Scarecrow Press, 1958, pp. 497–98 and *Who's Who in the USSR, 1965–1966,* New York and London: Scarecrow Press, 1966, p. 656. Podgorny's career is discussed by Myron Rush in *Political Succession in the USSR,* New York: Columbia University Press, 1965, pp. 171–74, and by Robert Conquest in *Russia after Khrushchev,* New York: Praeger, 1965, pp. 140–42.

Vladimir Efimovich Semichastny

by Robert M. Slusser

Vladimir Efimovich Semichastny was born in 1924, of Ukrainian working-class parents. No information is available on his early years. His secondary education, interrupted by the Second World War, was limited to study in the period 1941–42, at the Kemerovo Chemical and Technological Institute. In 1941 he began work as a Komsomol (Young Communist League) committee secretary and joined the Communist Party of the Soviet Union (CPSU) in 1944. In 1945 he was elected second secretary of the Donetsk Oblast Committee of the Ukrainian Komsomol and in 1946 became its first secretary. In the same year he was elected secretary for cadres of the Ukrainian Komsomol, and in 1947 first secretary, a post he held until 1950.

Semichastny's steady rise in the Komsomol brought him to the attention of the party leadership. He was elected to membership in the Ogburo of the Ukrainian party Central Committee immediately following the Sixteenth Congress of the Ukrainian party in January 1949 and the following April, at the plenary session following the Eleventh Congress of the all-union Komsomol, he was elected a member of the Buro of the all-union Komsomol. The career thus launched was closely identified with the Ukrainian Komsomol and party, at that time dominated by Nikita Khrushchev, first secretary of the Ukrainian party.

In 1950 Semichastny was elected a secretary of the all-union Komsomol and served as cadres secretary until 1958. His government career began in 1951, when he was elected deputy to the Supreme Soviet of the Ukrainian republic.

Although Semichastny was re-elected to the Central Committee of the Komsomol at its Twelfth Congress in April 1954, and shortly thereafter secretary and member of the Buro, he was sharply criticized, along with other Komsomol officials at the congress, for neglect of agriculture. In response he contributed an article to the Komsomol's journal *Molodoi Kommunist* (Young Communist) in September 1954: "Penetrate more profoundly into the economic affairs of kolkhozes, MTS [Machine Tractor Stations], and sovkhozes." Among Komsomol officials criticized in the article were those of Azerbaijan, an area in which Semichastny was later to work as a party functionary.

In the February 1955 issue of *Molodoi Kommunist,* Semichastny reported on an "International Meeting of Rural Youth" held in Vienna (December 9–15, 1954) to which he was evidently a delegate. The article reveals an intense hostility to the United States: "One of the principal causes of the deterioration of the living and working conditions of the rural youth," he wrote, ". . . is the preparation for a new war which is being conducted by reactionary circles of the U.S.A. and other imperialist countries."

With his election to the Supreme Soviet of the Russian republic in 1955, Semichastny moved from the Ukraine to the Russian republic and his government experience was broadened. At the Twentieth Congress of the CPSU (February 1956) he was elected to candidate membership of the Central Committee. In March 1958 he was elected to the Council of the Union, Supreme Soviet of the Soviet Union, and was appointed to the council's Commission for Foreign Affairs. During 1958 he was also named a member of the Soviet parliamentary group.

Semichastny's opportunity for advancement in the Komsomol came with the transfer of First Secretary Alexander Shelepin to a party post. At the Komsomol's Thirteenth Congress (April 15–18, 1958) Semichastny presented the report of the Credentials Commission and presided over the two final sessions, delivering a tribute to his departing colleague, Shelepin, whom he characterized as "a talented leader, a good organizer of Komsomol members and youth, a Communist of principle, a sincere and sensitive comrade." At the plenary session of the Komsomol's Central Committee immediately following the congress Semichastny was elected first secretary.

In his relatively brief tenure in this post Semichastny continued Shelepin's policy of close collaboration with Khrushchev in mobilizing the resources of the Komsomol for the economic projects initiated or sponsored by Khrushchev. For example, at a plenum (July 29, 1958) of the Komsomol's Central Committee, Semichastny delivered a report calling for accelerated development of the chemical and plastics industries, a policy favored by Khrushchev.

In October 1958 Semichastny achieved international notoriety with a speech delivered at a ceremonial meeting of the Central Committee of the Komsomol marking the organization's fortieth anniversary. Boris Pasternak, author of *Doctor Zhivago,* had at this time become the center of a major political storm in the Soviet Union following the award to him of the Nobel Prize for literature. Semichastny used the occasion to launch a crude personal attack on Pasternak, comparing him unfavorably with a pig and publicly inviting him to leave the Soviet Union. The strong criticism that the attack drew from abroad may have been a factor in the regime's subsequent modification of its policies toward Pasternak and intellectuals in general, but it had no unfavorable consequences for Semichastny's career. Two months later, at a session of the Supreme Soviet, Semichastny gave a belligerent speech supporting Khrushchev's demand for a nuclear test ban and settlement of the Berlin question on terms favorable to the Soviet Union: "Our young people," he said, "demand with ever greater determination that nuclear tests be discontinued forever and that the abnormal situation caused by the continued occupation of Berlin be eliminated." At the same session he submitted a draft resolution approving the foreign policy of the Soviet government.

Semichastny's continued good standing in the party following the Pasternak incident was further demonstrated by his attendance at the plenary session of the Central Committee in December 1958, where he spoke in support of Khrushchev's policy of extending grain production to the untilled or virgin lands in Asia. He described the work of Soviet young people in the "virgin lands" program as "an irreplaceable school of life and upbringing, a school of bravery and heroism for youth."

His position in the opening stages of the Sino-Soviet dispute is clarified by an article he contributed to *Komsomol'skaia pravda* on January 25, 1959, directed against a Yugoslav critic of the Komsomol. He not only accused the Yugoslav of "revisionism" but took the opportunity to praise the Communist Chinese youth organization.

At the Twenty-first Congress of the CPSU (January 27–February 5, 1959) Semichastny was a voting delegate representing the Kazakh Communist party. He was named a member of the Credentials Commission (a continuation of his experience as Komsomol secretary) and also of the commission to draft a congress resolution on Khrushchev's report on control figures for the national economy, covering the period 1959–65. In his speech to the congress Semichastny praised Khrushchev and gave assurance that the Komsomol would always be ready to fulfill any task set for it by the party. Foreshadowing his later assignment as secret police chief, he declared that the upbringing of Soviet youth in a spirit of collectivism, as opposed to selfish individualism, was a prerequisite for the building of Communism. He continued his support of Khrushchev's policies at a plenary session (February 24–25, 1959) of the Komsomol Central Committee, promising the organization's participation in the drive to achieve the production level called for in the Seven-Year Plan presented by Khrushchev at the party's Twenty-first Congress.

On March 25, 1959, at a plenary session of the Komsomol's Central Committee, Semichastny was released as first secretary and elected an honorary member of the organization. Following in Shelepin's footsteps, he was transferred to a post in the Central Committee of the CPSU, which was later identified as that of head of the Department of Party Organs for the Union Republics.

In July 1959 Semichastny headed a party delegation to Hungary. On August 11, 1959, shortly after his return, he was elected second secretary of the Azerbaijan party's Central Committee. Azerbaijan had just undergone a purge of "nationalist elements," following the intervention there of Nuritdin K. Mukhitdinov, one of Khrushchev's principal troubleshooters. Semichastny's transfer to Azerbaijan, under these circumstances, can be taken to indicate that at this time Khrushchev regarded him as a loyal follower.

Semichastny's service in Azerbaijan was terminated in November 1961 when he was named Shelepin's successor as secret police (KGB) chief (*Pravda,* November 14, 1961).

From that date to the present (1966), Semichastny's career merges with the organizational history of the secret police. His public appearances and writings have been limited, with the exception of his continuing work as a deputy to the Supreme Soviet, to occasions related to secret police functions. It is therefore legitimate to include in his biography facts concerning the recent evolution of the secret police itself.

Under Semichastny the secret police has been implicated in a number of episodes which indicate that it has been used for political purposes, involving questions of both domestic and foreign policy, by individuals or factions in the party Presidium who were opposed to Khrushchev. Thus it would appear that, like Shelepin, Semichastny was not a consistent and loyal supporter of Khrushchev. A striking example was the arrest, trial, and execution, in the period from October 1962 to May 1963, of Oleg Penkovsky, a Soviet Army intelligence official convicted of engaging in espionage for the United States and Great Britain. The Penkovsky case was exploited in the Soviet press in a way which suggests that one of its major aims was to impede Khrushchev's attempts at improved relations with the United States. The conviction of Penkovsky was followed by the ouster of his chief in military intelligence, General Ivan A. Serov, a victory for the KGB, and by the fall of the Soviet rocket chief, Marshal Sergei S. Varenstov, on the charge of "loss of political vigilance."

The secret police was again employed for factional ends in Soviet foreign policy in September 1964, when Khrushchev was maneuvering for improved relations with West Germany. A mustard-gas attack on a West German diplomat was perpetrated near Moscow, under circumstances which indicate the complicity of the secret police, and it was only on the eve of Khrushchev's fall in October 1964 that a formal apology was tendered to the West German government.

Beginning in late August 1964 a major propaganda campaign was launched in the Soviet press and other media to create a more favorable image of the secret police. A series of books and articles appeared in which former secret police officials, especially spies, were glorified and a number of the most prominent wartime Soviet spies, including Richard Sorge in Japan, were mentioned for the first time in the Soviet press. The campaign reached a high point in the spring and early summer of 1965, Semichastny himself contributing an article (*Pravda,* May 9, 1965) in which the exploits of Soviet secret police officials during the Second World War were glorified.

While serving as secret police chief Semichastny continued his work as a deputy to the Supreme Soviet. In March 1962 he was elected to the Council of the Union from the Novotorzhsky Election District, Kalinin Oblast, in the Russian republic.

Although Semichastny had supported a number of Khrushchev's internal policies, his career was not adversely affected by the fall of Khrushchev in October 1964. At the first plenum of the Central Committee of the CPSU held following that event (November 1964), he was raised from candidate to full membership in the Central Committee, a promotion which may be taken as an indication that he had effectively mobilized the secret police during the factional intrigues preceding Khrushchev's ouster. At the Twenty-third Congress of the CPSU in March 1966, Semichastny won reelection to membership in the Central Committee.

Semichastny is less well educated, probably less intelligent, and perhaps less ambitious than Shelepin, on whose career his own has been closely modeled. There has been nothing in his public actions to suggest that he contemplates using the secret police as the basis for further political advancement, in the manner of Shelepin; rather, his actions and statements indicate that he has found a congenial position and is willing to use the secret police apparatus for the support of policies advocated by Shelepin and those associated with him.

SELECTED BIBLIOGRAPHY

There are short biographical sketches of Semichastny in *Ezhegodnik bol'shoi sovetskoi entsiklopedii 1962*, Moskva, 1962, p. 614, and *Deputaty verkhovnogo soveta SSSR, shestoi sozyv*, Moskva, 1962, p. 381. For non-Russian-language biographical sketches, see *Biographic Directory of the USSR*, New York: Scarecrow Press, p. 563; Osteuropa Institut, Munich, *5000 Sowjetköpfe*, Köln, 1959; and H. E. Schulz and S. S. Taylor, eds., *Who's Who in the USSR, 1961–1962*, New York: Scarecrow Press, 1962, p. 664. An important source for the understanding of Semichastny's ideas and policies is a group of articles he published while serving as secretary of the Komsomol: "Glubzhe vnikat' v khoziaistvennyc dela kolkhozov, MTS, sovkhozov," *Molodoi Kommunist*, 9 (1954), 21–30; "Mezhdunarodnaia vstrecha sel'skoi molodezhi," *ibid.*, 2 (1955), 26–33; "Vernyi i nadezhnyi pomoshchik kommunisticheskoi partii," *ibid.*, 10 (1958), 11–24; and "Semiletka i komsomol," *ibid.*, 3 (1959), 3–12.

For speeches by Semichastny at congresses of the Komsomol and CPSU and at plenums of the Central Committee of the CPSU, see *XIII s'ezd vsesoiuznogo leninskogo kommunisticheskogo soiuza molodezhi, 15–18 aprelia 1958 goda, stenograficheskii otchet*, Moskva, 1959, pp. 91–94, 291–99; *Vneocherednoi XXI s'ezd kommunisticheskoi partii sovetskogo soiuza, 27 ianvaria—5 fevralia 1959 goda, stenograficheskii otchet*, I, Moskva, 1959, pp. 236–43; and *Plenum tsentral'nogo komiteta kommunisticheskoi partii sovetskogo soiuza, 15–19 dekabria 1958 goda, stenograficheskii otchet*, Moskva, 1958, pp. 325–31. References to Semichastny, relating him to the general trends of Soviet politics and policies, will be found in John A. Armstrong, *The Soviet Bureaucratic Elite, A Case Study of the Ukrainian Apparatus*, New York: Praeger, 1959; Robert Conquest, *Power and Policy in the USSR*, New York: St. Martin's Press, 1961; *idem*, *Russia after Khrushchev*, New York: Praeger, 1965; Ralph T. Fisher, *Pattern for Soviet Youth*, New York: Columbia University Press, 1959; and Wolfgang Leonhard, *The Kremlin Since Stalin*, New York: Praeger, 1962.

Alexander Nikolaevich Shelepin

by Robert M. Slusser

Alexander Nikolaevich Shelepin was born in Voronezh, Russia, in 1918, the son of a railroad employee. Although little or nothing has been published in the Soviet Union on his family background or early years, available evidence suggests that he comes of middle-class parents and was reared in a cultured and patriotic Russian provincial milieu. It may be significant that his birthplace is only 125 miles from Kalinovka, where Khrushchev was born; it has been reported that both men speak Russian with the same local accent.

Between 1936 and 1939, during the height of the "great purge," Shelepin studied at the Moscow State Institute of History, Philosophy, and Literature, but left before he had completed the full program to join the Red Army. In the war against Finland (1939–40), he served as political instructor (*politruk*) and squadron commander, positions that suggest he was considered not merely a man of political reliability in the testing period of the purge years, but also a militant exponent of Stalinist views.

Shelepin joined the Communist Party of the Soviet Union (CPSU) in 1940 and in the same year began his career in the Komsomol (Young Communist League), which he served for eighteen years and which proved to be the springboard for his later career. His higher education was completed in 1941 when he graduated from the Institute of History, Philosophy, and Literature. From 1940 to 1943 he served in the Moscow Committee of the Komsomol as instructor, department head, and secretary for propaganda and agitation. (It is noteworthy that throughout his career Shelepin has maintained close ties with the Moscow branches of the Komsomol and the party and has never served in the party or Komsomol branches of any other city, province, or republic.)

In 1943 Shelepin was elected a secretary in the all-union Komsomol, a post he held until 1952. At the Eleventh Congress of the Komsomol in 1949, as one of five secretaries, he presided over a session of the congress, presented the report of the Credentials Commission, and was elected both to the presidium of the congress and to the Central Committee of the Komsomol.

From 1945 to 1953 Shelepin was a member of the National Committee for Affairs of Physical Culture under the Council of Ministers of the Soviet Union. Emphasis on competitive sports and arduous training by Soviet athletes in order to establish records characterized his work in both this organization and the Komsomol.

During these years Shelepin also held posts in various Communist-sponsored international youth and student organizations. In August 1949 he attended the World Festival of Youth and Students in Budapest as vice president of the International Union of Students, one of the organizations sponsoring the festival, and in August 1950 he headed a Soviet delegation to the Second World Congress of Students in Prague. Between 1952 and 1958 Shelepin served as deputy chairman of the Communist-sponsored World Federation of Democratic Youth, and in 1957 was elected vice president of the Executive Committee of the Federation at its Fourth Congress.

More significant for his later career was his growing stature in the CPSU, marked by his election to the Central Committee of the party at its

Nineteenth Congress in October 1952. The following month he was elected first secretary of the Komsomol, replacing Nikolai A. Mikhailov. During his years in this office—1952–58—Shelepin worked closely with leading party officials, particularly Nikita Khrushchev, in mobilizing young people, Komsomol members and nonmembers alike, for work in industry and agriculture and for service in the Soviet armed forces. Hundreds of thousands of young people were sent to industrial, mining, and construction jobs and to the virgin and idle lands in Kazakhstan and Siberia, and Shelepin bore primary responsibility for directing the manifold operations which these large-scale movements entailed: recruitment, housing, social services, training, and ideological supervision.

At the Twelfth Congress of the Komsomol (March 19–26, 1954) Shelepin was re-elected to the Central Committee and, at the committee plenum immediately following, first secretary. In his report to the congress Shelepin criticized sharply the spiritual and moral situation in the Komsomol, particularly the political apathy of many members and their tendency to be influenced by "alien" ideologies. At the same time he noted with satisfaction the growth in membership to a total of over 18 million members.

During this period Shelepin launched a career in government work. In March 1954 he was elected to the Council of Nationalities of the Supreme Soviet of the Soviet Union, as a deputy from the Northern District of the Russian republic. At the session of the Supreme Soviet in April 1954 he was assigned to the Foreign Affairs Commission of the Council of Nationalities and during the same year joined the Slavic Committee of the Soviet Union. As a deputy Shelepin stressed the problems of youth with which his work in the Komsomol had made him familiar (speech of May 1957). His participation in the Supreme Soviet's foreign affairs activities was attested by his signature on an interpellation to the Soviet government requesting clarification of its position on the proposal (May 1957) for a ban on nuclear tests. Close relations with the armed forces were fostered by a number of speeches (Soviet Army Day, February 22, 1954; Soviet Navy Day, July 24, 1954). In May 1955 Shelepin was elected a member of the Soviet Committee for the Defense of Peace.

Shelepin's characteristic world outlook, rooted in the experiences of his formative years during the great purge, took shape and found expression in his work as the first secretary of the Komsomol. Intense devotion to the ideology of Communism; loyalty to party leadership combined with an ability to maneuver adroitly in intraparty conflicts and pick the winning side; and a messianic sense of Russian patriotism combined with an unrelenting hostility to the non-Communist world viewed through the prism of a rigid party ideology—these characterize Shelepin's views.

In February 1956, at the Twentieth Congress of the CPSU, Shelepin was re-elected to the Central Committee, and was named a member of the commissions to draft resolutions on Khrushchev's report for the Central Committee and Bulganin's report on the Sixth Five-Year Plan. In his speech at the congress Shelepin supported Khrushchev's demand for a sweeping reorganization of secondary and higher education, emphasizing technical and vocational training.

At the same congress Khrushchev's attack on Stalin, in his "secret speech," presented Shelepin with his greatest challenge as first secretary of the Komsomol. The challenge was twofold: first, the attack on the Stalin cult led to a widespread crisis of belief and values among Komsomol members and other young people; second, the struggle for power between Khrushchev and his rivals which the secret speech helped to precipitate threatened to involve the Komsomol as a power factor on one side or the other. Shelepin weathered the crisis by stressing the loyalty of the Komsomol to the party leadership as such; at the same time his support of projects initiated or sponsored by Khrushchev gave him a claim to the latter's gratitude. Both factions tried to enlist the support of the Komsomol. In November 1956 Khrushchev sponsored the award of the Order of Lenin to the Komsomol and spoke at the meeting in Moscow at which it was given. The opposing faction followed suit rather lamely on March 1, 1957, staging a formal session of the Central Committee of the Komsomol at which a second Order of Lenin was awarded. The meeting, from which Khrushchev was absent, amounted to a formal bid by what was later called the "antiparty group" for the Komsomol's support. Shelepin avoided any formal commitment and merely stated that the Komsomol would support the party and the Soviet government "still more closely."

Following the plenary session (June 1957) of the Central Committee of the CPSU which gave Khrushchev victory over the antiparty group, Shelepin threw the full weight of the Komsomol's propaganda apparatus into the campaign to discredit the group. At the Thirteenth Congress of the Komsomol (April 1958), he continued his close working relations with Khrushchev and praised him in his report to the congress as "an outstanding leader of the Communist party," stressing those functions and tasks of the Komsomol which were most directly relevant to Khrushchev's programs. In return, Khrushchev commended Shelepin's report as "good in form and content." Shelepin's final speech at the congress was an emotional farewell to the organization, in which he said, "To the Komsomol, to our party, I owe literally everything."

Shelepin was replaced as first secretary of the Komsomol by Vladimir E. Semichastny, but was elected an honorary member of the organization. His new post, first definitely identified in early May 1958, was that of head of the Department for Party Organs of the Union Republics in the Central Committee of the party. In this capacity he continued to concern himself with Komsomol affairs, attending a plenary session of its Central Committee on July 29 and 30, 1958. He retained his party post less than a year, however, and on December 25, 1958, was named chairman of the Committee of State Security (KGB, the secret police) of the Council of Ministers of the Soviet Union, replacing General Ivan A. Serov, a veteran secret police official and a former close associate of Khrushchev in the Ukraine.

The appointment to head the secret police was a turning point not only in Shelepin's career but also in the history of the secret police, the party, and the Soviet Union itself. It marked the successful culmination of a drive, originally launched in the early 1950's by a faction in the party associated with Alexander N. Poskrebyshev, to capture control of the secret police.

Shelepin's service as head of the secret police was marked by extensive personnel changes, in which young party and Komsomol members replaced older secret police veterans; a reduction of personnel, to a considerable degree offset by a vigorous drive to establish close working ties with ordinary Soviet citizens; and a well-publicized return to the principles of work which had allegedly guided the secret police in its early years, as formulated by Lenin and Felix E. Dzerzhinsky, for the purpose of refurbishing the somewhat tarnished public image of the secret police. Another major policy, re-establishment of morale which had been shaken by the revelations of Khrushchev's secret speech, found expression at a national conference of leading workers in the state security organs held in Moscow in May 1959. Although Shelepin's speech to the conference has not been published, its tone and content can be inferred from the resolution adopted by the conference, which expressed the determination of the state security service to deliver decisive counterblows "to the subversive activities of the aggressive imperialist states."

Shelepin also bore primary responsibility for the investigation of secret police archives to decide on questions concerning the rehabilitation of victims of repression under Stalin. This work, carried out in close cooperation with party historians working under the direction of Boris N. Ponomarev, enabled Shelepin to provide evidence that lent strong support to Khrushchev's renewed attack on the Stalin cult and the antiparty group at the Twenty-second Party Congress in October 1961.

During his two-year tenure as secret police chief, Shelepin laid the foundations of a territorial and organizational machine which later facilitated his move to positions closer to the center of power. Available evidence indicates that he was able to establish a working alliance with a number of influential ideologists and political figures in the party, including Mikhail A. Suslov, Frol R. Kozlov, and Ponomarev. He also established links with the party organizations of several of the union republics, notably those of Georgia, Uzbekistan, and Byelorussia.

Shelepin was careful, however, to cover the traces of his factional activities—understandably, since they would have been regarded as disloyalty by Khrushchev, against whom Shelepin ultimately used the strength of the position he had systematically built up. Shelepin himself condemned factionalism in strong terms in his speech to the Twenty-first Congress in February 1959, saying with regard to the antiparty group, ". . . the factionalists were overtaken by the fate that awaits all factionalists. The party threw them aside. . . ."

During these years Shelepin took an increasingly active part in Soviet foreign policy, not only in his official capacity but also as a politically significant figure in his own right. The Sino-Soviet rift, which began to emerge as a major determinant of Soviet policy in 1959, engaged his special attention, as suggested, among other indications, by his presence on the delegation which accompanied Khrushchev to Peking in September 1959. It appears probable, in fact, that the principal causes of the split between Shelepin and Khrushchev, which can be dated approximately to late 1959, concerned foreign policy and that the disagreement centered particularly on Khrushchev's handling of the Sino-Soviet dispute and his policy of seeking a limited *détente* with the United States.

At the plenary session of the Central Committee of the CPSU held immediately following the party's Twenty-second Congress in October 1961, Shelepin was elected to the party Secretariat. Two weeks later (November 14), he yielded his post as secret police chief to his former close associate and successor in the Komsomol, Semichastny. Subsequent events make it clear that this change represented no loss of power for Shelepin; rather it can be interpreted as a shrewd move to free himself from the onus of being too closely identified with the secret police—a serious handicap in the bid for supreme power, as Beria's fall sufficiently indicates—while at the same time maintaining close control of the secret police through a trustworthy protégé.

As a secretary of the Central Committee, Shelepin's special spheres have been identified as "the police, the law, the procuracy, and the judicial organs, as well as party-state control functions."[1] It was the latter function which provided him with the opportunity for his next major move. An extensive publicity campaign in the Soviet press in 1961 and 1962 culminated, at the November 1962 plenary session of the Central Committee, in the establishment of the Party-State Control Committee of the Central Committee and the Council of Ministers of the Soviet Union. This body combined for the first time since 1934 the investigative and supervisory agencies in the party and government and recreated under a new name the Commissariat of Workers' and Peasants' Inspection (*Rabkrin*) which had served as one of Stalin's principal organizational bases in his drive for power in the 1920's. Shelepin was named chairman of the committee and at the same time a deputy chairman of the Council of Ministers. The appointment of a network of subordinate control officials throughout the Soviet Union, which followed in late 1962 and early 1963, provided

[1] Merle Fainsod, *How Russia Is Ruled* (2nd ed., Cambridge: Harvard University Press, 1963), p. 221.

him with a widely ramified political machine in the party and government that enjoyed extensive rights of investigation and supervision.

Meanwhile Shelepin maintained his working-level ties with the Soviet government. In the elections to the Supreme Soviet of the Soviet Union held in March 1962, he stood as a candidate for the Council of Nationalities from the October Election District in the city of Tashkent, in the Uzbek republic. In his pre-election campaign, he emphasized the improvement of living conditions in Uzbekistan as the result of Communist rule; the approaching end of colonialism throughout the world; and the need to strengthen Soviet defenses in the face of "imperialist aggression."

During 1963 and 1964 Shelepin broadened his political base in a number of areas. His repeated appearances at Moscow City Party Committee meetings (December 1963, March 1964) indicate his continuing strong influence in that key organization. In addition he extended his ties with outlying regions. In July 1963 he participated in a plenary session of the Moldavian party Central Committee and delivered a major speech to a meeting of party-economic administrators of Moldavia. In March and April 1964 he spoke on the Sino-Soviet dispute to party gatherings in Armenia, Georgia, and Yaroslavl, and participated in a meeting of party-state control personnel in Tashkent.

It can be assumed that Shelepin was a prime agent in the ouster of Khrushchev in October 1964, although the secrecy which surrounded that event, together with Shelepin's customary reticence and circumspection, makes proof difficult. Indirect confirmation, however, is provided by events subsequent to Khrushchev's fall. In November 1964, at the plenary session of the party's Central Committee, Shelepin, bypassing the candidate stage, was named a full member of the Presidium. Sharp differences of opinion between him and Khrushchev on two key issues—relations with Communist China and with the United States—emerge clearly from Shelepin's subsequent statements. With regard to China, he told a conference of the Mongolian Workers' party at Ulan Bator in February 1965, "We have considered and still consider that no matter how great our differences have been they cannot and must not serve as the basis for a split in the socialist camp and the entire Communist movement." With regard to the United States, Shelepin delivered a sharp attack on its foreign policy, from Hiroshima to Vietnam, at a meeting in Pyongyang in August 1965.

In addition, Shelepin has pointedly criticized Khrushchev's characteristic loquacity and unsystematic working methods: in a Navy Day speech on July 24, 1965, he condemned the "jabbering" allegedly characteristic of "some party leaders" in the recent past, clearly a reference to Khrushchev, and expressed his own preference for "careful, profound, comprehensive working out" of current problems, an accurate characterization of his own work methods. Shelepin prefers quiet negotiations behind the scenes to noisy public demonstration. It is noteworthy in this connection that he avoided speaking at any of the plenary sessions of the Central Committee whose reports were published during the period of Khrushchev's ascendancy.

The course of Shelepin's career since Khrushchev's fall provides evidence both of his ambition and of the determination of other party leaders to block his further advancement. In the late summer of 1965 Western correspondents in Moscow reported persistent rumors that a shift in the top party leadership would soon take place in which Anastas I. Mikoyan would retire as chief of state (chairman of the Presidium of the Supreme Soviet), yielding this position to Brezhnev, who would turn over his job as first secretary of the party to Shelepin. Instead, Shelepin's position was systematically weakened during the autumn of 1965, a process which culminated in December 1965 in the reorganization and weakening of the Party-State Control Committee; Shelepin's replacement as its chief by his former deputy, Pavel V. Kovanov; and his ouster as a deputy premier of the USSR. Proof that these changes actually constituted a weakening of his position was provided in January 1966 when former subordinates of Shelepin in the Party-State Control Committee were shunted aside to less important jobs.

The changes of December 1965 deprived Shelepin of his base in the government, but left him in a strong position in the party, as one of only three men (Brezhnev and Suslov being the others) who were members of both the Secretariat and the Politburo (as the Presidium was renamed in March 1966). True, this distinction was somewhat weakened when Alexei I. Kirilenko, already a Politburo member, was named to the Secretariat at the party's Twenty-third Congress in April 1966.

In the field of foreign policy, Shelepin has consistently displayed an energy and resourcefulness which indicate his determination to play a leading role in Soviet policy formulation. In December 1964, shortly after Khrushchev's fall, he made a trip to Cairo, possibly to reassure UAR President Nasser of continued Soviet support from the new regime in Moscow. In 1965 he headed government and party missions to the Mongolian People's Republic (February) and North Vietnam (August), both key centers in the maneuvering between Moscow and Peking for support in the international Communist movement. During the Twenty-third Congress of the CPSU in April 1966, Shelepin and Ponomarev met with representatives of the Swiss Communist party and the Arab Socialist Union, the only party leaders other than Brezhnev whose activities in this field were noted at the time by the Soviet press.

As of June 1966, Shelepin's drive for the top appears to have been somewhat blunted, but it would be premature to consider him eliminated or neutralized in the struggle for power. Eleven years younger than Brezhnev, he can claim to speak for a new generation in the party, and moreover enjoys close relations with old-line Stalinists in the party who were temporarily pushed aside by Khrushchev but whose influence remains strong. In addition Shelepin commands great potential strength through his extensive contacts in two of the principal political hierarchies in the Soviet Union, the Komsomol and the secret police.

SELECTED BIBLIOGRAPHY

There are brief biographical sketches of Shelepin in *Bol'shaia sovetskaia entsiklopediia*, izdanie 2–e, XLIX, Moskva, 1957, p. 648; *Ezhegodnik bol'shoi sovetskoi entsiklopedii 1962*, Moskva, 1962, p. 622; *Deputaty verkhovnogo soveta SSSR, shestoi sozyv*, Moskva, 1962, p. 467; *Entsiklopedicheskii slovar' v dvukh tomakh*, II, Moskva, 1963, p. 665; and *Ukrains'ka radians'ka entsiklopediia*, XVI, Kiev, 1964, p. 302. The only fairly extensive biographical treatment by a Western scholar is A. B. Osadczuk-Korab, "Schelepin, der neue Sicherheitschef Chrushchtschows," *Osteuropa*, IX, 2–3 (1959), 151–53. Almost all Western studies of recent Soviet political history mention Shelepin, but without adding anything significant to the known facts concerning his career.

Speeches at congresses and plenary sessions: *XX s'ezd kommunisticheskoi partii sovetskogo soiuza 14–25 fevralia 1956 goda, stenograficheskii otchet* I, Moskva, 1956, pp. 603–10, English translation in *Current Soviet Policies II. The Documentary Record of the 20th Communist Party Congress and its Aftermath* (New York, 1957), pp. 144–46; *Vneocherednoi XXI s'ezd kommunisticheskoi partii sovetskogo soiuza, 27 ianvaria—5 fevralia 1959 goda, stenograficheskii otchet*, II, Moskva, 1959, pp. 249–55, English translation in *Current Soviet Policies III. The Documentary Record of the Extraordinary 21st Congress of the Communist Party of the Soviet Union* (New York, 1960), pp. 176–78; *XXII s'ezd kommunisticheskoi partii sovetskogo soiuza, 17–31 oktiabria 1961 goda, stenograficheskii otchet*, II, Moskva, 1962, pp. 399–409, English translation in *Current Soviet Policies IV. The Documentary Record of the Twenty-second Congress of the Communist Party of the Soviet Union* (New York, 1962), pp. 180–82. *Plenum tsentral'nogo komiteta kommunisticheskoi partii sovetskogo soiuza, 18–21 iiunia 1963 goda, stenograficheskii otchet*, Moskva, 1964, pp. 111–12. *XIII s'ezd vsesoiuznogo Leninskogo kommunisticheskogo soiuza molodezhi, 15–18 aprelia 1958 goda, stenograficheskii otchet*, Moskva, 1959, pp. 12–56, 288–90, 298–99.

Pyotr Efimovich Shelest

by Grey Hodnett

On a trip to Hungary in April 1964, Nikita Khrushchev visited a Budapest optical plant where he was to deliver a speech. To his embarrassment he learned from the manager that the plant's inability to realize its plan was attributable to a Soviet Ukrainian factory's failure to comply with a contract to deliver electric motors. Turning to one of his entourage, Khrushchev demanded to know how the latter could in good conscience sit in Budapest eating Hungarian goulash while the Ukraine was failing to meet its obligations to Hungary. In an increasingly loud voice, Khrushchev continued to humiliate publicly this bald, heavy-set subordinate, whose reddening face made him look as if—in Khrushchev's words—he had "swallowed a porcupine." The man thus brought to the Western public's attention was more accustomed to give than to receive such "comradely" criticism, albeit from a reputed friend and political benefactor. He was Pyotr Efimovich Shelest, first secretary of the Communist Party of the Ukraine.

An ethnic Ukrainian, Shelest was born on February 14, 1908, in the village of Andriivets, in what is now the district of Balakliisk in Kharkov Oblast. Like many leaders of his generation, Shelest came from a poor peasant family. In 1921, at the end of the war, revolution, and civil war that shook the Ukraine for seven years, he was hired out to a rich, local peasant (*kulak*) as a farmhand. A year later, at fourteen, he took a job on the Ulianovka state farm in the neighboring Poltava region. A brief interval here proved to be his sole experience in an agricultural enterprise. Shelest left the state farm in 1923 to work on the railroad, first as a repair worker at the Osnova railway station, then as a mechanic in the Kharkov locomotive-repair factory. In 1923 he joined the Komsomol (Young Communist League).

During the 1920's attempts were made to draw larger numbers of bench workers into the Communist party. Shelest seems to have been moving in this direction, for in 1927 he enrolled in a Soviet-party school (*sovpartshkol*) in Izium, a city in the southeastern corner of Kharkov Oblast. The purpose of such schools was to train junior party, Komsomol, and state officials. In 1927 or 1928 Shelest held his first full-time political position: he became a secretary of the Borovsk District Komsomol Committee in Kharkov Oblast. And in 1928, at the beginning of the "revolution from above" that was destined to transform Soviet industry and agriculture, he became a member of the Communist party.

As a secretary of a district Komsomol committee in 1928, and thus a leading local activist, Shelest would have found himself on the firing line in the campaign to collectivize agriculture—a campaign against the peasantry that was to be fought with extraordinary brutality in the Soviet Ukraine. But for unknown reasons, he was not forced to undergo this trying experience, being sent instead, that same year, to study at the Artem Communist University in Kharkov. Not actually a university, this institution was a political school, somewhat higher in level than the *sovpartshkol,* providing accelerated secondary education with stress on ideological indoctrination, and designed to turn out cadres for the party and state bureaucracies. Shelest was thus never to receive a general education. He subsequently left the Communist University for a higher technical education at the Kharkov Engineering and Economic Institute where, it is officially said, he "participated actively in the life of the party organization." It is not unlikely that he took some part in the struggle in the villages, but without the responsibility shared by party and state officials.

Without graduating from the Engineering and Economic Institute, Shelest took a job in 1932 in the Ilich Factory in Mariupol (now Zhdanov), an iron and steel producing center on the Sea of Azov in the southeastern Ukraine. He now had lifted himself from the working class, rising in the next four years from shift engineer, to deputy shop chief, to shop chief. At the same time, he continued his higher education at the Mariupol Evening Metallurgical Institute, graduating in 1935.

In 1936 and 1937 Shelest served in the Red Army where, given his education and previous Komsomol and party activism, he probably performed political functions. Returning to civilian life in 1937, he became a shop chief at the Hammer and Sickle plant in Kharkov. During the next few years, at the height of the terror of the 1930's, he was promoted to production chief and then chief engineer of the plant. He was also named a member of the plant's party committee, a routine appointment in view of his occupational status, but one that nevertheless enhanced his position within the party.

In contrast, therefore, with many Soviet political leaders whose claims to a technical-managerial past cannot stand serious scrutiny, Shelest may legitimately boast of having spent at least some years working in industry. It is most unlikely, to be sure, that he could have risen to factory chief engineer at thirty without some assistance from the "great purges." Nevertheless, he apparently emerged from the worst years of the 1930's bearing less guilt than many contemporary party officials.

Khrushchev was formally installed as first secretary of the Communist Party of the Ukraine in January 1938. He had been sent from Moscow to complete the removal of those followers and appointees of the former Ukrainian leadership that Stalin considered untrustworthy. Execution and deportation to remote corners of the Soviet Union necessitated new recruits. This new generation of officials was to provide a pool from which Khrushchev drew generously in staffing key positions throughout the Soviet political system. Among its most illustrious members were Nikolai Podgorny and Leonid Brezhnev. Shelest also belonged to this group.

Shelest's career reached a turning point in 1940, when, at thirty-two, he was appointed to one of the most important second-rank posts in the Ukrainian party apparatus: secretary of the Kharkov City Party Committee. Because the position carried with it responsibility for the defense industry, its occupant almost certainly had to have received Khrushchev's prior approval. Kharkov was one of the largest centers for armaments production in the Soviet Union; and armaments production had the highest priority among all forms of industry. Among the key plants located in Kharkov were the Locomotive and Construction Works, the Diesel Factory, and the famous Tractor Factory, making the city one of Russia's major tank-production centers. As Stalin strove in 1940 to avert, or at least postpone, the German blow from the West, it is certain that party and economic officials accountable for armaments production—particularly tank production—were under the most intense pressure to expand output at any price. Shelest's appointment to this sensitive and demanding position, his first in the party apparatus per se, showed that he was considered both politically trustworthy and professionally competent.

Following the German invasion on June 22, 1941, one of the more spectacular Soviet feats of the entire war occurred—the evacuation of thousands of factories and their personnel from western Russia and the Ukraine to the Urals, western Siberia, Kazakhstan, and Central Asia. Much of Kharkov's industry was routed to the city of Cheliabinsk in the Urals, where parts of it were merged with shops from the Kirov Factory in Leningrad and the Cheliabinsk Tractor Factory to form a new Kirov Factory (known locally as "Tankograd"), one of the three largest tank-producing centers in the Soviet Union. Shelest undoubtedly played a significant role in facilitating the 1,200-mile move from Kharkov to Cheliabinsk and the rapid re-establishment of production there—a task accomplished under exceedingly difficult circumstances. In Cheliabinsk he became chief of the Defense Industry Department of the Cheliabinsk Oblast Party Committee, a crucial position in the oblast party apparatus. His department kept watch over the vastly expanded defense industry in this key Urals province. When difficulties arose, or an important delivery of arms had to be hastened, he was among the first to feel the pressure from Moscow, which in turn had to be transmitted to the factory directors and party organizers, who, with their workers, were already making superhuman efforts to increase production.

Later during the war Shelest was shifted to a number of other jobs. He was made an instructor of the Central Committee of the party, that is, he became a junior—but powerful—member of the party's central apparatus, a roving trouble-shooter and information gatherer. He then worked as party organizer for the Central Committee at a number of factories (one of which may have been an important ball-bearing works) in the city of Saratov, also a wartime center of armaments production. As such, Shelest was directly subordinate to the central party apparatus in Moscow and, next to the manager, was the most influential man in the plants where he worked. By the end of the war, apparently, he had been promoted to deputy secretary for the defense industry of the Saratov Oblast Party Committee, a position similar to his former post in Kharkov. Although Shelest did not serve in the armed forces or perform a glamorous role during the war, his work involved great responsibility.

Whether Shelest stayed on at Saratov between the end of the war and 1948 is unknown. Sometime in 1948 he was appointed manager of a factory in Leningrad, thus rounding off his prewar career in industry and revealing once again that he was considered reliable in both party and economic-managerial functions.

That same year the Leningrad party boss Andrei Zhdanov died, and there followed, early in 1949, the liquidation of many of his followers, especially in Leningrad itself. This purge, the so-called "Leningrad affair," is thought to have been inspired by Georgi Malenkov. Since the date of Shelest's arrival in Leningrad is unknown—as, for that matter, are the date of his appointment to the factory managership, the type of plant involved, and the date of his departure from Leningrad—it is impossible to say how this critical event in the postwar political life of the Soviet Union affected him personally. But whether he was a potential victim or an intended beneficiary or simply a neutral observer, he must have been influenced by what he almost certainly saw happen in Leningrad.

Some time between 1948 and 1954 Shelest became manager of a factory in Kiev, the capital of his native Ukraine. The date of his return would be of interest not only for the light it might shed on his stay in Leningrad, but on his relations with Khrushchev as well. Shelest did not serve under Khrushchev during the war; and Khrushchev left the Ukraine for Moscow in December 1949. Even if Shelest did reside in the Ukraine as early as 1948, which seems most unlikely, his personal ties with Khrushchev could hardly have been very strong. It is therefore questionable how much of a role Khrushchev played in Shelest's return to the party apparatus after Stalin's death.

In 1954 Shelest became second secretary of the Kiev City Party Committee, an important position in the Ukrainian party apparatus involving partial responsibility for job assignments in Kiev, and probably in Shelest's case, a responsibility for industry as well. It is highly unusual for such a significant post in the party apparatus to be given to a factory director, however large the factory. Shelest, however, was no ordinary director, but a man with rich prior experience in party work, an activity to which henceforth he was to devote undivided attention, and one in which he was to attain an eminence granted to very few. Shelest may well have been indebted for this re-elevation into the ranks of the Ukrainian party elite to the first secretary of the Ukrainian party, Alexei Kirichenko, and perhaps also to the second secretary, Nikolai Podgorny. His appointment, of course, required approval by the central party apparatus in Moscow, but there are grounds for believing that Khrushchev had not yet consolidated his control over top-level personnel appointments. As a Ukrainian, Shelest benefited from the post-Stalin tendency not to give exclusive preference to Russians in key appointments in the Ukraine.

Once he had established himself in the Kiev City Party Committee,

Shelest began to rise steadily through the Ukrainian party apparatus. He soon became second secretary of the Kiev Oblast Party Committee, a post comparable to the one he had just left, but more involved with rural affairs and agricultural production. His upward movement was duly certified by election in 1956 to full membership (he had been a candidate member since 1954) in the Central Committee of the Ukrainian party.

The following year—a year in which Khrushchev became the pre-eminent figure in the Communist Party of the Soviet Union (CPSU)—Shelest took over the position of first secretary of the Kiev Oblast Party Committee. He was elected to this post on February 1, 1957, months before Kirichenko handed over the Ukrainian first secretaryship (in order to become Khrushchev's second-in-command in Moscow) to Podgorny. Presumably, Shelest was therefore indebted to Podgorny not so much for his appointment as for his continuity in office, especially after Kirichenko's abrupt fall in 1960.

Shelest's status in the Ukrainian party was now high; he could be counted among its top ten leaders—a success achieved in the remarkably brief span of three years. As one of the elect, he sat on the platform behind the dais at all important Ukrainian ceremonial occasions and was a prominent speaker. His duties brought him into contact with the increasing number of foreign Communist and non-Communist delegations that flowed through Kiev, although probably he remained a man of less than cosmopolitan outlook. In February 1960, just as Kirichenko was being pushed into political retirement, Shelest was nominated to candidate membership in the Presidium of the Ukrainian party's Central Committee—anticipating by several months Podgorny's election to full membership in the Presidium of the Central Committee of the CPSU. At the Ukrainian party congress held in late September 1961, Shelest was raised to full membership in the Presidium of its Central Committee, and several weeks later, at the Twenty-second Congress of the CPSU he became a member of the Soviet party's Central Committee, signifying his arrival as a national, not merely republic-level, Soviet leader.

During the late summer of 1962 preparations were under way for the major reorganization of the Soviet party announced at the November plenum of its Central Committee. The reorganization created parallel self-contained industrial and agricultural party hierarchies at the oblast and lower levels, each hierarchy being supervised at the top by a bureau of the republic central committee: one for industry, the other for agriculture. The object of this radical reform, Khrushchev stated, was to increase the efficiency of party supervision of the economy, particularly industry. He emphasized that while both bureaus would be subordinate to the presidium of the republic Communist party, they should be granted broad operational autonomy. The reorganization was clearly distasteful to many party officials, including oblast committee first secretaries, for not only was it likely to produce an administrative muddle, but it considerably reduced the power of the first secretaries. A majority of these incumbents gravitated toward the agricultural branch of the apparatus, whereas the industrial oblast party committees were headed largely by newcomers.

In the Ukraine the industrial branch was supervised at the top by Shelest, who had been elected a secretary of the Ukrainian party's Central Committee on August 11, 1962, and confirmed four months later (December 6, 1962) as chairman of its Bureau for Industry and Construction. In effect he was now Podgorny's powerful deputy for industrial affairs, and consequently, for the next two years, bore immediate over-all party responsibility for the gigantic mining, metallurgical, and heavy engineering complex of the eastern Ukraine, as well as industry scattered elsewhere throughout the republic. His responsibility came at a time when Soviet industry had begun to display alarming symptoms of stagnation, and instances of labor unrest occurred, it is reliably reported, in the Ukraine as well as other regions of the Soviet Union.

Shelest's star continued to rise with his election on July 2, 1963, to the highest post in the Ukraine—first secretary of the Communist Party of the Ukraine. At the same time, Podgorny moved up to become a secretary of the Central Committee of the CPSU and, it is believed, a counterweight to Brezhnev, who was also made a secretary. Ordinarily the second secretary of a republic party organization may expect preference over the other secretaries when there are changes in the top leadership of a republic. In this case, however, Shelest was promoted over the head of the second secretary, Ivan Kazanets, also an ethnic Ukrainian, who became instead chairman of the Ukrainian Council of Ministers. It is widely thought that these personnel changes in the summer of 1963 reflected an attempt by Khrushchev to strengthen his own position by elevating new and old supporters from the Ukraine. Some proof of this contention—as far as Shelest is concerned—is provided by a speech Shelest delivered in September 1963 praising Khrushchev in the warmest of terms.

It would seem in fact that Shelest owed this promotion in no small measure to Khrushchev, who doubtless was influenced in his choice by the opinion of Podgorny. On the other hand, after he had shouldered the burdens of the Ukrainian first secretaryship, he became subject to a variety of new pressures, some of which must have worked against whatever sense of personal loyalty to Khrushchev he may have felt. The summer and autumn of 1963 witnessed a serious crisis in Soviet grain production, leading Khrushchev to adapt the politically dangerous expedient of purchasing wheat from the capitalist West—a confession of serious failure. As he was being forced into this uncomfortable posture, Khrushchev was in turn tightening the screws on the Ukraine, a key grain surplus region, in the hope of extracting greater state grain purchases.

According to Shelest's speech at the Central Committee plenum in March 1965, demands were made in 1964 that the Ukraine deliver one billion poods of grain to the state, or 300 million more than actual deliveries in 1964. But just as it was in Khrushchev's interests to increase delivery quotas, so it was presumably in Shelest's to keep them down—not only in order to report "success" in fulfilling the agricultural plan, but to avert serious food shortages in the Ukraine and a disastrous decline in livestock production. At the meeting in March 1965 of the Central Committee of the CPSU, Shelest specifically criticized Khrushchev's agricultural policies for leading to a state of affairs in which "there were lines for bread." The situation in the Ukraine may have been worse than Shelest hinted.

Once he became top man in the Ukraine, it would have been odd for Shelest not to receive the minimum political recognition accorded his predecessors and thereby the Ukraine as the second most important republic of the Soviet Union. Hence, on December 13, 1963, at a plenary meeting of the Central Committee he was elected to candidate membership in the Presidium of the CPSU replacing Vladimir Shcherbitsky, former chairman of the Ukrainian Council of Ministers.

It is ironic, if not surprising in the context of Soviet political life, that Shelest, a man substantially (although not entirely) indebted to Khrushchev, should have attained the peak of his power as a result of the bargaining that followed Khrushchev's ouster. It appeared in the immediate aftermath that Shelest's position too might be shaken. Probably it was Podgorny's intervention that permitted Shelest not only to retain candidate membership in the party Presidium, but to rise to full membership on November 16, 1964.

Shelest's promotion and the coopting of several other Ukrainians into Central Committee membership led to speculation in the Western press as to the existence of a strong "Ukrainian faction" within the top Soviet leadership. As long as Podgorny remained the senior secretary who bore over-all responsibility for personnel matters, and Vitali Titov (also ethnically a Ukrainian) remained a secretary of the Central Committee with power in the personnel field, there may have existed an informal "Ukrainian" grouping; but its strength has probably been exaggerated. In March 1965 Titov's demotion to second secretary of Kazakhstan dealt a serious blow to whatever collective hopes the Ukrainians conceivably entertained. In December 1965 Podgorny left the Central Committee Secretariat to replace Mikoyan as chairman of the Presidium of the Supreme Soviet, thus relinquishing his influence in organizational and personnel affairs. Thus despite the indeterminacy of the present Soviet political situation, it seems highly unlikely that Shelest will ever be able to repeat Khrushchev's rise to the top via the Ukraine. Not only does his Ukrainian birth count strongly against him on the national political scene, but he is himself a relative newcomer even in the Ukraine. The important ties of allegiance in the Ukrainian apparatus run to Brezhnev, Podgorny, and Titov. Moreover, Shelest lacks the popular stature of a Podgorny, much less of a Khrushchev. The best that he can probably hope for is to maintain his present, not insubstantial power.

SELECTED BIBLIOGRAPHY

In Russian, the main sources of biographical information about Shelest are *Deputaty verkhovnogo soveta SSSR*, Moskva, 1959, p. 447; *Deputaty verkhovnogo soveta SSSR*, Moskva, 1963, p. 468; *Ezhegodnik bol'shoi sovetskoi entsiklopedii 1962*, Moskva, 1962, p. 622; and *Ukrains'ka radians'ka entsiklopediia*, Kiev, 1964, pp. 302–3.

In English, biographical sketches can be found in *Biographic Directory of the USSR*, New York: Scarecrow Press, 1958, pp. 581–82 and *Who's Who in the USSR, 1965–1966*, New York and London: Scarecrow Press, 1966, p. 754.

Mikhail Solomonovich Strogovich

by John N. Hazard

Mikhail Solomonovich Strogovich, Soviet jurist, was born in St. Petersburg (now Leningrad) on September 18, 1894. Although facts on his education and early years are unknown, former associates report that while still a nonparty man he began his career as a state official in the position of Investigator for Especially Important Cases in the office of the Cassational College of the Supreme Court of the Russian republic, to which were sent requests from convicts or disappointed prosecutors for review on political or legal grounds of convictions and sentences in lower courts. His task was to determine procedural errors and to brief the procurator, the official charged by statute with the duty of presenting for the Court's consideration a proposed decision. His first writing assignment was as co-author of the first commentary on the code of criminal procedure, published in 1923. Thereafter he advanced to become the leading Soviet specialist on criminal procedure, lecturing in the law faculties, writing the textbooks, consulting in the office of the procurator general of the Soviet Union, and chairing the committee which drafted the code of criminal procedure adopted by the Russian republic in 1960.

Throughout his career Strogovich has taken the traditional Marxist position, established in the *Communist Manifesto,* that law at any time and any place is a class instrument designed to preserve the power of a ruling class over all other elements of the population. Following this proposition, law for Strogovich and other Marxists became, after the Russian Revolution fought in the name of the proletariat, an instrument utilized by those who led the state to keep themselves, as the "vanguard of the proletariat," in power. At this point Strogovich departed from the view of many colleagues that if law were a proletarian class tool, judges might make quick decisions against bourgeois elements without careful scrutiny of facts because their careers made guilt probable. Strogovich argued that the accused, regardless of his social origin, should be given an unemotional trial with careful review of the evidence relating to guilt. In legal language this meant that judges should "presume an accused innocent until he was proven guilty." Further to assure the presentation of all pertinent evidence, Strogovich urged that the accused be permitted a lawyer, not only during the public trial but also from the outset of the secret preliminary investigation while the investigating official gathered evidence on which to base his decision to terminate the case or to file an indictment stating the criminal charge.

Controversy over Strogovich raged in the Soviet Union for many years. As a member of the Communist party, which he joined in 1943, he was accused of violating party discipline by arguing his points on procedural protection after the Supreme Soviet's legislative committee had rejected them. He was sometimes thought to be too theoretical, too divorced from practice in spite of his practical experience.

Strogovich reached the position for which he became renowned by degrees. The first edition of his textbook *Criminal Procedure,* published in 1934, stated a conventional Marxist position, declaring that although a court must evaluate evidence objectively, it "is an instrument of class struggle, and the evaluation of evidence, on the basis of which the court draws its final conclusions may not be separated from that class struggle."

His position at the time was orthodox, being partly doctrinal to conform to the official position that law is an instrument of proletarian suppression of class enemies, but also practical in keeping with the view then held that class enemies were liars necessitating severe verification of evidence presented by those who had themselves or through their families associated with propertied elements of Tsarist times or of the period of the New Economic Policy of the early 1920's. In the second edition (1935) of *Criminal Procedure* this position was restated, but by 1938 Strogovich had changed his mind, perhaps in rebellion against the purge techniques of Stalin as evidenced in 1935 and 1936. In the edition of 1938, he eliminated words emphasizing the role of law in a society characterized by class struggle and substituted in its place, in a paragraph otherwise the same, "The Soviet court, the Soviet state as a whole, is interested in the correct resolution of the criminal case in all of its aspects, in the discovery and punishment of those really guilty, in guaranteeing to the honest Soviet citizens that they will not be prosecuted and convicted without foundation in fact." In making this change, Strogovich reflected in part the position taken in the 1936 constitution that Soviet society had outgrown its turbulent struggle with class enemies and had become a socialist society without bourgeois elements.

By 1940 Strogovich had established fully the position for which he later became the symbol both at home and abroad. He added four pages to his new edition of *Criminal Procedure,* explaining the concept of "burden of proof on the prosecution" and "presumption of innocence": "In Soviet criminal procedure the presumption of innocence is one of the guiding procedural principles. It means that a person against whom a criminal charge is brought shall not be supposed guilty until he has been unmasked with mighty and convincing proof." After Stalin's death in 1953 Strogovich became even more forceful. In his edition of 1958, which he entitled *Course in Soviet Criminal Procedure,* he expanded his argument into what amounted to a lawyer's brief in support of his stand.

Opposition to Strogovich's position stiffened in the legislative committee of the Supreme Soviet of the USSR, when it held hearings prior to adoption of a reform of criminal procedure. In 1958 after he had presented a position similar to the one taken in his textbook, he was opposed by Professor Dimitri S. Karev, Dean of the Law Faculty of Moscow University. The committee struck from the draft the precise statement of the presumption of innocence which Strogovich favored, and the Fundamentals of Criminal Procedure, adopted on December 25, 1958, kept only the provision that the burden of proof rests with the prosecutor. Strogovich's book suffered: compared to the 20,000 copies printed for the edition of 1940, only 5,000 copies were printed for the edition of 1958 and its price was seven times as high. This is significant in a planned economy where books are printed in editions and given prices conforming not solely to market demands but bearing relationship to the political ends to be served. Thus a small edition and a high price were tantamount to a vote of little confidence in the political value of the text.

In 1964, after Nikita Khrushchev's ouster, Strogovich's position on the presumption of innocence was vindicated indirectly in a suit for libel brought against the newspaper *Izvestiia* and one of its columnists. A prosecutor from Siberia who had argued that Strogovich's position on the presumption of innocence was wrong and a slur on the work of prosecutors claimed that the newspaper, in circulating a criticism of the prosecutor's stand, had harmed his reputation. The court held that since the presumption existed in fact although not specifically stated in the law, the newspaper and its columnist had not libeled the prosecutor. Strogovich was jubilant in subsequent comment on the case.

Strogovich had other interests as well. In 1940 he co-authored with Professor Sergei A. Golunsky the textbook *The Theory of State and Law.* The authors sought to develop a new approach to Soviet legal theory following denunciation by Stalin's confidant, Andrei Y. Vyshinsky, of the views of Eugene B. Pashukanis. The latter, as a legal theorist of great influence because of his position as director of the principal institution concerned with the formulation of legal theory in the USSR, had argued in the 1920's and early 1930's that law was a product of the bourgeois market economy and must wither away as socialism was established in the Soviet Union. Stalin had begun to undermine the foundation of this theory in 1930, attacking the concept of progressive withering away of the state, asserting that the state must remain strong right up to the time of the achievements of Communism. In 1938 Vyshinsky, as Pashukanis' successor and having achieved wide notoriety as prosecutor in Stalin's purge trials, led an attack on Pashukanis after the latter had been removed from his position of director of the Institute of Law and executed as a traitor. Vyshinsky set forth in detail the positions that needed to be taken in each branch of the law, and this became the guide to research in his Institute.

After Vyshinsky had set the line, Strogovich and Golunsky sought to elaborate an acceptable general theory of the role of law for a Soviet Union whose peoples were emerging from the terror of Stalin's purges which even Stalin had come to realize as unsettling to the stability of social relationships required to prepare for the war with Hitler which was commonly believed to be close at hand. They restated the Marxist concept of law as an instrument of the state, and of the state as an instrument of the dominant class, but they emphasized the gradualness of the transition to a socialist-oriented society. They made no attempt to devise a new theory, as did Khrushchev in 1961, which would fit orthodox ideas of the state as a class instrument to a situation in which classes were presumed to have disappeared with the achievement of socialism. They were intent only upon creating a theoretical base for a stable society, and this they did by denying that there would be any sudden withering away of the state and law as Pashukanis had implied. Strogovich anticipated in the transition further changes in the Soviet state along the line of broadening of socialist democracy, characterized by mass participation in state administration. In this he proved to be prophetic of the post-Stalin leadership's policy expressed after 1957 as mass participation in public administration while preserving the single party political system to assure retention of power by Communists.

While Strogovich's contribution was primarily in the stabilizing of criminal procedure and legal philosophy, he also published a textbook on logic which was widely used in the higher schools. At the time of his seventieth birthday he was credited with about 300 published works, many in foreign translation. He received many honors, the most coveted being election to the Soviet Academy of Sciences as a corresponding member. Few jurists reach such eminence. He was also a titular member of the Academy of Sciences of the Polish People's Republic and a founder of the Marxist-oriented International Association of Democratic Lawyers.

Strogovich's support of the principle of stable criminal procedure and respect for devices useful to the accused in proving innocence provided sharp contrast to Stalin's technique of terror. This contrast had given rise outside the USSR to questions. How did Strogovich survive Stalin's purges? Professor Dimitri S. Karev, in a bitter post-Stalin criticism of Strogovich, hinted that the latter had toadied to Vyshinsky as Stalin's principal legal officer by writing laudatory reviews of Vyshinsky's book on evidence. Strogovich's long part-time practice in the procurator general's office with Vyshinsky may also have protected him; Strogovich may have been valuable to Vyshinsky for his encyclopedic knowledge or for the image of Soviet law he projected both within the Soviet Union and abroad. There may have been personal reasons. In any case, Strogovich made use of his survival to plead his position during Stalin's most dictatorial period and to train the next generation as head of the departments of Criminal Procedure in Moscow's Juridical Institute and in the Law Institute of the USSR's Academy of Sciences. In these posts he influenced many young specialists in the direction of the view that a Communist-oriented society is not incompatible with a fair trial.

From the ranks of Strogovich's students came many who participated in the formulation of policy for law after Stalin's death. Not all of them accepted Strogovich's position, but many defended him and the principles for which he stood. He became a favorite among lawyers of the People's Democracies of Eastern Europe, who saw in his ideas the epitome of what they expected of a Marxist-inspired legal system, for few East European lawyers found Stalin's terroristic methods compatible with the humanistic influences of their youth.

Further, Strogovich was a model of an educated man: he knew not only the history of Soviet law and its Marxist theoretical base, but foreign law as well. This attracted respect from scholars in the academies of Poland, Hungary, Czechoslovakia, Romania, and Yugoslavia where respect for the knowledge of many of those graduated from Stalin's law schools has been minimal. His influence was, therefore, a moderating one in the development of Marxian socialist law. Time may prove him to be credited with having kept alive humanistic legal scholarship during Stalin's destructive years from 1930 to 1953. This scholarship was preserved, to emerge after 1953 when Stalin and Vyshinsky were no more.

SELECTED BIBLIOGRAPHY

A brief biography was published on the seventieth birthday of Strogovich as "K 70-letiiu M. S. Strogovicha," *Sovetskoe gosudarstvo i pravo,* 10 (1964), 141. An even briefer statement is given in the introductory materials to V. I. Lenin *et al., Soviet Legal Philosophy,* translated by Hugh W. Babb, Cambridge: Harvard University Press, 1951. This material has been augmented by an interview with one of Strogovich's colleagues of the 1920's who has since come to the West, and by personal recollections of my own as an American exchange student in his classes for three years in the mid-1930's.

Only one work of Strogovich has been translated into English, and that only in part. It appears as S. A. Golunskii and M. S. Strogovich, "The Theory of State and Law," in V. I. Lenin *et al., Soviet Legal Philosophy,* pp. 351–425.

His books in Russian are: D. Karnitskii and M. Strogovich, *Ugolovno-protsessual'nyi kodeks RSFSR: Prakticheskoe posobie dlia rabotnikov iustitsii, i iuridicheskikh kursov,* Moskva, 1934; M. S. Strogovich, *Ugolovnyi protsess,* Moskva, 1934. Subsequent editions of the latter appeared in 1935, 1936, 1938, and 1940. The enlarged and final edition appeared as *Kurs sovetskogo ugolovnogo protsessa,* Moskva, 1958. Other works are *Priroda sovetskogo ugolovnogo protsessa i printsip sostiazatel'nost',* Moskva, 1938; *Ugolovnoe presledovanie v sovetskom ugolovnom protsesse,* Moskva, 1951; *Material'naia istina i sudebnye dokazatel'stva,* Moskva, 1955; *Proverka zakonnosti i obosnovannosti sudebnykh prigorov,* Moskva, 1956; and with S. A. Golunskii, the text entitled *Teoriia gosudarstva i prava,* Moskva, 1940. It is part of this text which has been translated into English as indicated above.

Mikhail Andreevich Suslov

by Grey Hodnett

Few more dramatic encounters have occurred in the world Communist schism than the Moscow meeting between the Soviet Union and China in July 1963, where it became clear that the gulf between the two most powerful Communist parties in the world could no longer be bridged with compromise declarations of unity. Heading the Chinese delegation was Teng Hsiao-ping, a member of the Politburo and general secretary of the Communist Party of China. Heading the Soviet delegation was Mikhail Suslov, a member of the Presidium and a secretary of the Central Committee of the Communist Party of the Soviet Union (CPSU). The fact that Suslov was selected for this sensitive task revealed more than the Soviet leadership's trust in him. For Chinese polemics against Soviet policies had been couched in highly ideological terms—a style of political combat at which the Chinese Communists excelled—and in Suslov the Soviet leaders nominated the one authoritative member of their ranks equipped to battle the Chinese with their own weapons.

Mikhail Andreevich Suslov was born on November 21, 1902, in the village of Shakhovskoe in Saratov Province (now Ulianovsk Oblast) which lies in the steppe region of the southeastern part of European Russia, bordering on what is now Kazakhstan. Before the Revolution, agriculture was the main occupation of most of Saratov's inhabitants. There is still a large rural population today, although Saratov itself, which is on the right bank of the Volga midway between Kuibyshev and Volgograd, is now an important industrial city with a population of over 600,000.

Like many other current leading party officials, Suslov comes from a peasant family. His biographers stress that his parents belonged to the poorest stratum of the peasantry—a politically respectable social origin for a Soviet leader. Little is known of Suslov's childhood, though he is one of the few contemporary Soviet leaders who spent his teens in a village. Soon after the Russian Revolution in 1918, when he was sixteen, it is known that he linked his future to that of the Bolsheviks by joining the Komsomol (Young Communist League). As a youthful political activist he participated from 1918 to 1920 in the local village "committee of the poor"—one of thousands of such bodies established throughout the countryside by the Soviet regime for the purpose of fanning the rural class war and forcing the peasantry to relinquish food to feed the cities and the Red Army. In these same Civil War years he also played some role in the affairs of the district Komsomol committee, although no details have been made public about this first affiliation with the political apparatus.

In 1921, at the early age of nineteen, Suslov joined the Communist party, and in the same year went to Moscow for an accelerated secondary education at the Prechistensk Rabfak (workers' faculty). Graduating in 1924 he immediately enrolled in the G. V. Plekhanov Institute of National Economy in Moscow. This Institute was a new type of educational establishment, designed to meet the need for professional economic planners, and to produce a corps of ideologues well versed in theoretical political economy. More than likely, Suslov chose to follow the latter course of study. In 1928 he graduated from the Plekhanov Institute, thus having spent the entire period of the New Economic Policy in school. At the very moment when the Soviet Union stood on the threshold of the First Five-Year Plan, he went on to undertake graduate studies at the Economics Institute of the Communist Academy in Moscow and, while still studying, began to teach at both Moscow University and the Industrial Academy.

During these years of his early maturity—a period when all overt opposition to Stalin's rule was being relentlessly crushed—Suslov spent a great deal of time as a "propagandist," making speeches and leading study circles on ideological themes in Moscow factories. Like thousands who lacked any experience of revolutionary activity before the Revolution, he eagerly climbed onto the Stalinist bandwagon, and is officially credited with having "actively participated in the struggle against the Trotskyist opposition in the party, against the Zinovievists, and also against the right opportunist elements, firmly upholding and propagandizing the general line of the party."[1]

Recognizing his talents as an ideological watchdog, Suslov's party superiors appointed him in 1931 to the joint Central Control Commission of the Party and People's Commissariat of Worker-Peasant Inspection (CCC-WPI). This agency had been established in 1923, at Lenin's urging, to act as a center for administrative reform and a check on the party apparatus. Lenin, unfortunately, did not live long enough to ensure that his intentions were carried out, and Stalin packed the CCC-WPI with his own followers, using it until 1934 as a major instrument for purging his opponents from party and state positions. The CCC-WPI was thus an early institutional nucleus for spreading Stalinist totalitarianism.

Having proved himself a trustworthy guardian of political purity, Suslov was sent on missions to the provinces to "cleanse" the local party organizations. In 1933 and 1934 he was a member of the commissions set up by the Central Control Commission to purge the party membership in the Ural and Chernigov oblasts. This work involved close collaboration with the secret police and entailed responsibility for destroying the careers, health, and—as it turned out—the lives of hundreds of men. In 1934 the CCC-WPI was divided into two independent organs—party and state. Suslov served in the new state control agency, the Soviet Control Commission, until 1936.

During 1936 and part of 1937 Suslov enrolled for further study— so it is officially said—in the Economics Faculty of the Institute of Red Professors. Both the Communist Academy and the Institute of Red Professors were party, not lay, schools, in which the primary goal was to prepare ideological cadres; thus Suslov's graduate studies, to which he devoted a total of four years, took place exclusively in a party milieu. In the economics departments, the writings of Marx, Engels, Lenin, and Stalin absorbed most of the students' time, with stress falling on abstract theory and the political implications of economic action. A man exposed to this type of training should be regarded as an ideologue, not an economist in either the Western or the contemporary Soviet sense.

At the height of the terror in 1937, when a sharp need for dependable cadres was felt, Suslov was sent out to be first a department chief, then secretary, of the Rostov Oblast Party Committee. There can be no doubt that he was implicated on a local level in what are now euphemistically called the "errors of the period of the cult of personality."

In recognition of his work in Rostov, Suslov was promoted by Stalin in 1939 to first secretary of the Stavropol Territory and City party com-

---

[1] *Bol'shaia sovetskaia entsiklopediia*, XLI (1956), p. 320.

mittees, a position which made him boss of Stavropol. The Stavropol Territory is located in the fertile agricultural region of the North Caucasus. Suslov was held accountable for the economic and administrative, as well as the ideo-political, well-being of a large area—a responsibility he had hitherto lacked. This shift from an agitational-propaganda career to general organizational work would today be most unusual for a person with Suslov's training and prior experience, indicating that he cannot be considered a typical Soviet ideological specialist. Along with the first secretaryship went election to the Central Revision Commission in 1939, and then election in 1941 to full membership in the Central Committee of the CPSU—a sign that Suslov, at thirty-nine, could count himself within the top stratum of the Soviet elite.

Suslov's routine duties as a territorial first secretary were cut short by the German invasion of the Soviet Union. Beginning in 1941 he performed political functions as a member of the Military Council of the North Caucasus Front. But he remained a party leader in the unoccupied part of the Stavropol Territory and never actually served in the army as Brezhnev did. He was also made head of the partisan detachments for the German-occupied area of Stavropol Territory—a job involving close coordination of operations with the NKVD (secret police). He later helped to supervise the mass deportation of various North Caucasus nationalities, including the Chechen-Ingush, conducted early in 1944 by NKVD troops under General Ivan Serov, an affair that has since been repudiated as a criminal deed by the Soviet government. As the German armies were pushed back into the Ukraine, Suslov played a part in restoring the devastated economy of Stavropol Territory.

Suslov's performance in the North Caucasus evidently convinced Stalin that he had found a man of aggressive orthodoxy, cool nerves, and minimal sentimentality—exactly the qualities required to cope with nationality difficulties in another corner of the Soviet empire, Lithuania. In November 1944 he appointed Suslov head of the Central Committee's Bureau for the Lithuanian Soviet Socialist Republic. Because of the Soviet Army's conquest of Lithuania in 1940, and the subsequent mass terror and deportation of thousands of Lithuanians, a strong Lithuanian partisan movement had begun armed resistance against Sovietization immediately after Soviet troops reoccupied Lithuania in mid-1944. The resistance reached almost pitched warfare on occasion between 1944 and 1948, and from 1945 to 1947 the partisans controlled large areas of the Lithuanian countryside, despite concerted efforts by secret police and regular army troops. Military operations against the partisans were conducted with extreme brutality by General Sergei Kruglov, a deputy chief, under Beria, of the Commissariat of Internal Affairs.

Along with Suslov, who was charged with assuring the political integration of Lithuania into the Soviet Union, there arrived in Lithuania over six thousand Russian officials to institute the reprisals, deportations, and mass purges, which, combined with military pressure, eventually led to the pacification of this small Baltic republic. Having seen this task well on the way to completion, Suslov went to Moscow in March 1946 to work in the Central Committee apparatus and to serve as a member of the Orgburo. His specific position at this time is unknown, though probably it was connected with party propaganda and ideological activities. He was never again to leave the national scene.

Suslov's ascent to the uppermost levels of the Soviet elite occurred in 1947 when Stalin made him a secretary of the Central Committee, and in June of that year Suslov replaced G. F. Alexandrov as head of the agitation and propaganda department of the Central Committee. From this base in ideological work he took his first step into the realm of international Communism (and the world outside the USSR), participating in the founding of the Communist Information Bureau (Cominform) in September 1947. The Cominform was intended to coordinate the actions of the Communist parties of France, Italy, Poland, Bulgaria, Romania, Czechoslovakia, Hungary, and Yugoslavia with those of the Soviet party. At the first meeting, Soviet representatives voiced an aggressive policy toward the West, declaring that the world was now divided into two warring camps—the "peace-loving," headed by the USSR, and the "imperialist," headed by the United States. Less than a year after its inception, Suslov assumed a more prominent role in the Cominform, acting as one of the main Soviet representatives at its second convocation in Bucharest in June 1948. At this meeting Yugoslavia was excommunicated from the Soviet bloc and her leaders anathematized.

In 1949, the year thousands of followers of the deceased Andrei Zhdanov were purged in the so-called "Leningrad affair," Stalin entrusted Suslov with a post requiring the utmost discretion—the editorship of *Pravda*—which Suslov held through 1950. From 1951 through most of 1952 Suslov's activities were confined to his duties of a secretary of the Central Committee in charge of ideological matters.

During 1952 and early 1953 sharply increasing arrests and executions, culminating in the disclosure in January 1953 of the arrest of the Jewish "doctor plotters" accused of designs against the lives of some high Soviet leaders, foretold the onset of a new tidal wave of purges and terror. Stalin's motives in preparing to unleash this storm are obscure; but apparently they included a desire to smooth the way for the introduction of certain economic and other policies hinted at in his last major ideological pronouncement, *Economic Problems of Socialism in the USSR*. Stalin evidently intended to set the stage for this process by linking, in some devious way, the fabrications of the "doctors' plot" with those of the earlier Leningrad affair. The economic aspect of this scheme apparently hinged on an attack against the "anti-Marxist" views attributed to the deceased Nikolai Voznesensky—the famous head of the State Planning Commission, associate of Zhdanov, and best-known victim of the Leningrad affair. This attack took the form of a vitriolic article—undoubtedly commissioned by Stalin—which appeared in *Pravda* on December 24, 1952. It was written by Suslov.

Suslov was not only well equipped to provide the ideological rationalization for the prospective purge; he was especially beholden to Stalin at this moment for an important promotion. At the Nineteenth Congress of the CPSU in early October 1952, Suslov had been among the group of younger officials elevated to membership in the large Presidium, newly created to supplant the former Politburo and Orgburo. It has been suggested, by Khrushchev among others, that Stalin intended to prepare new cadres to replace the top leaders, some of whom he was about to exterminate. This plausible interpretation is reinforced by the fact that in the distribution of power immediately after Stalin's death, Suslov was not permitted to keep his seat in the party Presidium, though he did remain a secretary of the Central Committee (a position he has retained without interruption to the present). Nor does his official biography include mention of his brief membership in Stalin's Presidium—an omission probably indicative of a desire that this episode be forgotten.

After Stalin's death Khrushchev was the sole member of the Secretariat who was also a member of the party Presidium, until Suslov recaptured his Presidium post in July 1955, following Georgi Malenkov's fall. Suslov has been a member of the Presidium continuously since then. It is unclear precisely where he stood in the policy debates that divided the Presidium between 1955 and 1957, or what his relations were with Khrushchev. When the moment of truth arrived in June 1957, Suslov chose to side with Khrushchev against Khrushchev's opponents, yet he was never a "Khrushchevite." In his early career he had infrequently, if ever, crossed paths with Khrushchev and he was indebted to Stalin, not Khrushchev, for his position as secretary of the Central Committee. Entering the Presidium before Khrushchev's consolidation of power, Suslov had in fact helped to assure Khrushchev's victory in June 1957 and, as well perhaps, in the October 1957 purge of the minister of defense and popular military hero, Marshal Zhukov.

In the decade following Stalin's death, Suslov assumed an increasingly large role in formulating and executing Soviet policy in the areas of his jurisdiction—foreign affairs, international Communism, and ideological matters. Together with Anastas Mikoyan, he represented the Soviet leadership in negotiations in Hungary immediately before the explosion of the Hungarian Revolution. He played an important role in applying the brakes to cultural liberalization in 1957, after Khrushchev's February 1956 "secret speech" in denunciation of Stalin had helped to unleash political ferment throughout the Soviet empire. Suslov was an important participant in the Moscow meetings (1957, 1960) of Communist parties which unsuccessfully attempted to reconcile divergent Soviet and Chinese views and interests, and as indicated above, he led the Soviet delegation in the long anticipated but inconclusive bilateral talks with the Chinese in July 1963. Coinciding with the signing of the nuclear test-ban treaty by the Soviet Union, Britain, and the United States, these talks reflected the near rupture of Sino-Soviet relations.

During Khrushchev's reign, Suslov was considered by many Western observers to be the mysterious *eminence grise* of Soviet politics—an unregenerate "Stalinist" and leader, together with Frol Kozlov, of a "conservative" opposition to Khrushchev. He was widely rumored to be violently anti-Western. His gaunt figure, grim expression, and lack of contact with non-Communist foreigners contributed to the image. Though exaggerated, this evaluation probably contains a substantial core of truth. To expect Suslov to be anything but a "Stalinist," literally, would be to ignore the cumulative effect of most of a lifetime spent in the service of Stalinist orthodoxy. In contrast with Mikoyan, Kosygin, or Khrushchev, Suslov has spent little of his career having to worry professionally about production problems. His life has been occupied, by and large, either in bringing into being the essential structural elements of Soviet-style rule or in defending the basic values of this political system.

Suslov's political orientation has not proved incompatible with advocacy of Russian national interests vis-à-vis the Chinese, or with participation—up to a point—in the attack on the "cult of personality." In dealing with the latter Suslov has accepted and engaged in criticism of Stalin insofar as it reinforces the long-run interests of the political apparatus. On the other hand, there are signs that he resisted Khrushchev's attempts to manipulate the "cult" issue in ways that threatened other members of the "collective leadership" or seemed to endanger the cohesion of the existing political system. Likewise there are indications that Suslov tended to be in favor of greater investment in heavy industry and military preparedness and, therefore, did not always agree with Khrushchev's views on resource allocation. To what extent Suslov actively and openly resisted Khrushchev's policies and to what extent, if any, he was able to deflect unwanted innovations are matters which are still unclear. Contrary to the expectations of some observers, Suslov apparently did engage, to an unknown extent, in plotting against Khrushchev and—what is more important—emerged unscathed. It was he who delivered a major speech indicting Khrushchev at the Central Committee plenum in October 1964 that ratified Khrushchev's ouster.

Suslov's prospects are limited by increasing age, reported poor health, and an unappealing public image. Further, his base of power lacks the special influence that accrues to those able to appoint friends to and remove enemies from positions of consequence throughout the major Soviet elite groups. Nevertheless, among all Soviet leaders, Suslov remains the most literate in a *party* sense. While this consideration is irrelevant as far as making rational decisions is concerned, it is of great importance in the Soviet struggle to assert its leadership in the international Communist movement, particularly in the conflict with the Chinese. Suslov has probably dealt with more foreign Communists than any other Soviet leader, including Brezhnev. His ideological abilities are not only a great asset to himself, but also to the entire Soviet leadership.

SELECTED BIBLIOGRAPHY

In Russian, the main sources of biographical information about Suslov are the following: *Bol'shaia sovetskaia entsiklopediia*, vypusk 2, XLI, Moskva, 1956, pp. 319–20; *Politicheskii slovar'*, Moskva, 1958, p. 563; *Ezhegodnik bol'shoi sovetskoi entsiklopedii 1958*, Moskva, 1958, p. 643; *Ezhegodnik bol'shoi sovetskoi entsiklopedii 1962*, Moskva, 1962, p. 617; *Deputaty verkhovnogo soveta SSSR*, Moskva, 1959, p. 383; *Deputaty verkhovnogo soveta SSSR*, Moskva, 1963, p. 408; *Malaia sovetskaia entsiklopediia*, vypusk 3, VIII, Moskva, 1960, p. 1255; *Ukrains'ka radians'ka entsiklopediia*, XIV, Kiev, 1963, p. 190. A Western source is J. Marin, "Suslow, Michail Andrejewitsch," *Porträts der UdSSR-Prominenz*, München: Institut Zur Erforschung Der UdSSR, 1960.

In English, information about Suslov can be found in *Biographic Directory of the USSR*, New York: Scarecrow Press, 1958, pp. 97–98, and *Who's Who in the USSR, 1965–1966*, New York and London: Scarecrow Press, 1966, pp. 829–30. Suslov's career is discussed by Myron Rush in *Political Succession in the USSR*, New York: Columbia University Press, 1965, pp. 177–78, by Robert Conquest in *Russia after Khrushchev*, New York: Praeger, 1965, pp. 135–39, and by Boris I. Nikolaevsky, *Power and the Soviet Elite*, New York: Praeger, 1965, pp. 253–75.

Andrei Antonovich Grechko

by Severyn Bialer

When Stalin died in March 1953 it was natural that his successors to the leadership of the Soviet Union should brace themselves to meet any troubles that might arise. The problem of keeping intact that vast empire built by Stalin after the Second World War in eastern and central Europe was a source of particular concern. Nowhere was the task of preserving stability and securing a powerful and vigilant Soviet presence more immediate than in East Germany and the German Democratic Republic.

Here, in the heart of Europe on the borders dividing East and West Germany, the two major adversaries of the cold war confronted each other with seasoned troops kept in the highest readiness.

In 1953 the Soviet Union maintained in East Germany twenty of its best equipped, best trained, and most highly mobile divisions. As shown by the events of June 1953, when workers and students of East Berlin demonstrated against the Ulbricht government and the Russian occupation, the presence of Soviet armed forces was necessary to keep East Germany within the Soviet sphere of influence. At that time a little-known Soviet general with the typical Ukrainian name of Grechko was appointed by the Soviet government to be the commander in chief of the Soviet Army Group in East Germany. In the following five years, in one of the most rapid advancements of any Soviet military leader in the post-war period, Grechko rose to the number-two position in the Soviet military hierarchy.

Andrei Grechko was born on October 12, 1903, in the village of Golodaevka (now Kuibyshevo) in Rostov-on-Don Province, a vast territory located largely in the steppe region of southern Russia, bordering the Ukraine. Grechko's father, according to official Soviet biographers, was a Ukrainian peasant, though according to other sources he was a Cossack who, while making his living from farming, brought up his son in the tradition of military service by teaching him from childhood how to ride a horse and use a sword.

When Grechko was eleven the stable and traditional life of his youthful environment was shattered with Russia's entry into the First World War. Village men were conscripted in increasing numbers; agriculture declined. In 1917 frustration with the continuing war, the bitterness of crushing defeats, the staggering loss of life, and increasing hunger reached a peak and exploded in a violent revolution that overthrew the tsar. The revolution soon reached a new stage; the Bolshevik party with its radical program took power in Petrograd (now Leningrad), in Moscow, and in other large urban centers. The next three and one-half years of Russian history saw violent, brutal, all-encompassing civil war between the Bolsheviks, who created a Red Army, and their numerous opponents.

In Rostov-on-Don Province some of the biggest and bloodiest battles of the Civil War were fought. In 1919, at the age of sixteen, Grechko volunteered for a Red Army detachment and from that time on his life was inseparably connected with the Soviet armed forces. He fought as private and as noncommissioned officer in the Civil War, at the end of which he remained in the army, and finished his seven-year primary education. In 1925 he went on to a cavalry school, graduating a year later as a junior officer. From Civil War days until the outbreak of the Nazi German war, Grechko served primarily in the cavalry. After graduating from officer-candidate school, he became a platoon commander and then a squadron commander. As a young officer in 1928 he entered the Communist Party of the Soviet Union (CPSU).

At thirty-one Grechko was singled out as a promising junior officer and given an appointment to the Frunze military academy in Moscow, the major Soviet military school for the middle ranks of the officer corps. After graduating from the academy in 1936, he was appointed a regimental cavalry commander and served in this position until the "great purges" of 1937–38 almost annihilated the higher echelons of the Soviet military establishment. In the later 1930's high military careers built up over decades were broken, and possibilities for rapid advancement (for those lucky enough not to be on the list of officers marked for liquidation) were greatly increased. Grechko became chief of staff of a division.

The lack of higher-ranking commanders was felt exceptionally keenly by the Soviet Army in the postpurge period. The lower-ranking officers who replaced their killed or jailed superiors had neither the experience nor the education necessary to command large military units. To remedy this situation at least partly, those considered most talented and loyal—among them Grechko—were sent to the Voroshilov Academy of the General Staff —the highest military school in the Soviet Union.

When the Germans attacked the Soviet Union in 1941, Grechko, then thirty-eight, was just graduating from the Voroshilov Academy. He went immediately as a colonel to command the 34th Cavalry Division on the Southern Front in the Ukraine. He distinguished himself in the defensive fighting in the summer months of 1941 and by the end of that fall already commanded a corps.

The advance of German troops into Russia ground to a halt with the advent of winter, 1941. The increasing resistance and growing experience of the Soviet fighting forces, and the inexhaustible human resources mobilized by the Soviet government, plus the unpreparedness of the German army to fight under the extremely difficult conditions of the Russian winter, stopped the German offensive and produced a relative lull in the fighting and a stabilization of the front. In the spring of 1942 the German offensive recommenced with renewed ferocity. This time the Germans chose not to attack Moscow directly; instead, their two main thrusts were toward Stalingrad and the rich oil fields of the Caucasus. On September 8, 1942, Major General Grechko received the high military post of command of the 47th Army, which participated in repulsing the German advances toward the Caucasus that fall. The 47th Army, Grechko's first command of a large operational unit, was composed of the 216th Mountain Infantry and the 77th Infantry Divisions, the 103rd Infantry Brigade, and the 255th and 83rd Marine Brigades. It was a part of the Black Sea Army Group, under the command of Colonel General Ya. T. Cherevichenko, whose task was to stop the German movement toward the Caucasus along the shore of the Black Sea.

By the end of 1942, after many German victories, the Soviet armies were finally able to stop once and for all the German advance toward Stalingrad and the Caucasus. At Stalingrad the tide of the German-Soviet war turned. In 1943 the major Soviet offensive began. General Grechko, in command of the same army he had led in the defense of the Caucasus, participated in pushing the Germans out of the Black Sea region. On October 9, 1943, Grechko, in the meantime promoted to lieutenant general, reported to the headquarters of the North Caucasian Army Group that, after twenty-five days of heavy fighting, the army under his command had cleared the strategic Taman Peninsula of the enemy. In the winter of 1943–44 Grechko was promoted to colonel general and assumed command of the First Guard Army, an elite operational unit, larger, better equipped, and used for more demanding assignments than his former command.

Until August 1944 the First Guard Army was a part of the First Ukrainian Front (Army Group). Grechko's superiors, the Front chiefs, changed often, and this gave him a chance to become personally acquainted with some of the greatest Soviet military leaders. Until February 1944 he served under Army General Vatutin, from March to May under the greatest of them all, Marshal Zhukov, and until July under Zhukov's great competitor, Marshal Ivan Konev. With the First Ukrainian Front Grechko fought the Germans, Hungarians, and Romanians in the southern Ukraine, participated in a large encircling operation of Korsun Shevchenkovsky, and approached the Soviet-Slovakian borders.

On August 5, 1944, Grechko's army was transferred to the Fourth Ukrainian Front, where his commander was Army General Petrov, a lesser figure in the Soviet military hierarchy. The tasks assigned in the plans of the Soviet high command to the Fourth Ukrainian Front were clearly secondary to those of the First, Second, and Third Ukrainian Army Groups. Positioned on the mountainous borders of Slovakia, the Fourth had the jobs of preventing a transfer of German reserves to the main sectors of the Soviet offensive and of attacking the enemy in a very difficult terrain that precluded quick advance and assured heavy losses. Throughout the fall and winter of 1944, Grechko's army moved slowly ahead in the Slovak-Carpathian mountains. In early 1945 it pushed its way through the southernmost region of Poland and the Polish Tatra mountain range. In the spring it entered Czechoslovakia and by May engaged in its last operation of the Second World War, the encirclement of German troops of the Army Group "Center" near the city of Olomuts (east of Prague).

In the great school of the Second World War, General Grechko advanced from an unknown cavalry division commander to the high rank of colonel general and commander of an elite army. While he could hardly compete for recognition with such names as Zhukov, Konev, Rokossovsky, or Vasilevsky, at the age of forty-two—younger than any of these men —he stood on the threshold of a very promising military career.

Peace, however, has destroyed many promising military careers; and for a long while it looked as if it would destroy Grechko's. By the end of June 1945 the Soviet troops (with the exception of one army) had left Czechoslovakia. Grechko was recalled and appointed commander of the Kiev Military District (one of the Soviet Ministry of Defense's eighteen territorial administrative units). While Kiev was an important military district in the Soviet Union, the fact that General Grechko served in it for eight years would seem to indicate that though he was regarded as a reliable commander and capable administrator, he was not considered a candidate for the uppermost stratum of the Soviet military command. At the Nineteenth Congress of the CPSU in October 1952, the last congress held during Stalin's lifetime, Grechko was elected a candidate member of its Central Committee. Although this was a sign of trust and a high distinction for a military leader, it also showed that he could be ranked only among the second echelon of the Soviet high command. The top stratum has always been elected to full membership in the Central Committee, as it was at the Nineteenth Congress.

But if his military career, as it seems, was temporarily retarded, Grechko's service as commander of the Kiev Military District, with permanent headquarters in the Ukrainian capital, Kiev, offered one consolation, the full value of which was only later to be appreciated. That is to say, the area under Grechko's command, from the end of the war to the end of 1949, was also the domain of the future premier of the USSR and first secretary of the CPSU, Nikita Khrushchev. At that time Khrushchev was the boss of the Ukraine, and Grechko—in view of both his military duties in the Ukraine and his membership in the Presidium of the Communist Party of the Ukraine, over which Khrushchev presided—came into continual contact with him.

It may have been a coincidence that after Stalin's death in 1953, when Khrushchev became the leader of the party and one of the most powerful figures among the small group that at first collectively administered the affairs of the Soviet state, Grechko's military career took a sudden upturn. But his rapid advance in the years to follow so closely paralleled the advance of Chairman Khrushchev himself that coincidence is highly unlikely. Grechko's rise appeared to be the result of two factors. On the one hand, with the death of Stalin, the Soviet political leadership tried to keep the professional military establishment satisfied by granting it more autonomy and influence and by reshuffling its top command, downgrading those military commanders who had been closest to Stalin and advancing or bringing back from forced semiretirement those whom Stalin had disliked or feared. A case in point is the return of Marshal Zhukov and his appointment to the high position of deputy minister of Defense. On the other hand, such powerful political leaders as Khrushchev were interested in having in the key military positions people whom they knew well and upon whose personal loyalty they had reason to count. Thus General of the Army Grechko was appointed in 1953 to the vital and sensitive post of commander in chief of the Soviet military forces stationed in East Germany. While serving in this position, Grechko was promoted in 1955 to the highest Soviet military rank, marshal of the Soviet Union—a promotion that made it almost certain that when his turn of duty in Germany came to an end he would receive a position in the central military establishment in Moscow.

In 1957 Grechko returned to Russia. This was a crucial year not only in Grechko's career, but in Khrushchev's as well. In June 1957 a final showdown occurred between Khrushchev and his major opponents— Molotov, Malenkov, Kaganovich, and others. Khrushchev emerged as the most powerful political leader. Only a few months later, in October 1957, a man who had helped Khrushchev to achieve this victory, Marshal Zhukov, was dismissed. Khrushchev had made sure of the defeat of his enemies, and now he wished to make sure that his too popular and powerful friend would not become as dangerous as those enemies. As the post-Zhukov Soviet military era began, Marshal Grechko assumed the second highest post in the Soviet high command: in November 1957 he was appointed first deputy minister of Defense of the USSR. His only military superior was the minister himself, Rodion Malinovsky.

From 1957 until 1960 Grechko was simultaneously the commander in chief of the Soviet ground forces.[1] In 1960 during a reshuffling of responsibilities among top Soviet military leaders, he became the commander in chief of the United Armed Forces of the Countries of the Warsaw Pact—the Communist equivalent of NATO. This meant that he was in charge of directing and controlling the armies of Poland, Czechoslovakia, Romania, Hungary, Bulgaria, and East Germany. In this capacity he coordinated the strategic plans, training, and weaponry of these armies with those of the Soviet Army—unquestionably a job of the highest trust, requiring not only great military capabilities but a high degree of diplomatic and political skill. Symbolizing his new high status was his election to full membership—after having been a candidate member for ten years— in the Central Committee of the CPSU at the party's Twenty-third Congress in October 1961.

Marshal Grechko is in his sixties, hardly a time at which most military leaders still think of advancing their careers. But the average age of the Soviet high command is very high—much higher than in Western armies. The number-three man in the Soviet military leadership, Marshal Zakharov, and Grechko's superior Marshal Malinovsky, are both older. The chances are good, therefore, that Grechko will be next commander of the Soviet military establishment.

---

[1] On the fortieth anniversary of the Soviet armed forces in 1958, he was awarded the Golden Star and title Hero of the Soviet Union.

SELECTED BIBLIOGRAPHY

For biographical information about Grechko, see the following: *Radians'ka Ukraina,* February 5, 1946; *Krasnaia zvezda,* January 19, 1946; *Deputaty verkhovnogo soveta SSSR,* Moskva, 1959, p. 105; *Deputaty verkhovnogo soveta SSSR,* Moskva, 1963, p. 111; *Sovetskaia istoricheskaia entsiklopediia,* IV, Moskva, 1963, pp. 781–82; *Bol'shaia sovetskaia entsiklopediia,* vypusk 2, LI, Moskva, 1958, p. 88; *Ukrains'ka radians'ka entsiklopediia,* IV, Kiev, 1962, p. 443; *Malaia sovetskaia entsiklopediia,* vypusk 3, III, Moskva, 1959, p. 154; *Politicheskii slovar',* vypusk 2, Moskva, 1958, p. 142.

For description of Grechko's career and activities, see S. P. Platonov, *Vtoraia mirovaia voina,* Moskva, 1958, pp. 408, 496, 597, and *Istoriia velikoi otechestvennoi voiny sovetskogo soiuza 1941–1945,* Moskva, 1963–65, II, pp. 462–63; *ibid.,* III, pp. 90, 356–59; *ibid.,* IV, pp. 77, 217, 322, 386; *ibid.,* V, pp. 301, 322. See also the memoirs of Colonel General L. M. Sandalov, *Perezhitoe,* Moskva, 1961, p. 24.

Nikolai Ivanovich Krylov

by Severyn Bialer

In the Second World War the airplane and the tank were the weapons of destruction the possession of which was ultimately regarded as the most crucial element in achieving victory. Today the dominant weapon, the status symbol of military might, is clearly the missile. Of the numerous types of missiles—the air defense missile, the air attack missile, the tactical ground support missile, the naval support and deep-charge antisubmarine missile—the strategic intermediate range and intercontinental ballistic missiles (IRBM and ICBM) are the principal weapons, and in a true sense the ultimate means of destruction. Their introduction and development as nuclear weapons have reshaped the strategic thinking of military and political leaders in both West and East. The responsibility for their deployment and readiness overshadows all other concerns. Of even more significance, while the ultimate decisions to use those weapons remains everywhere the prerogative of the supreme political leadership, the awesome possibility remains that through error or design a commander may unleash this terrifying force. No nation can therefore remain indifferent either to the quality of supreme leadership in those countries which possess the weapon or to the character of the military men who exercise direct charge over this fearsome weapon. In the Soviet Union the military commander in chief of the strategic rocket forces is Nikolai Ivanovich Krylov.

The most recent photographs of Marshal Krylov show a corpulent man with a double chin, a receding hairline and, but for his hard eyes, a rather unmilitary look. An earlier photograph, however, taken during his fighting days in Stalingrad probably reflects his character more faithfully. It shows a solid, thickset man with strong, energetic face and square jaw. Age and peacetime may have changed Krylov, but it is highly unlikely that the change is more than physical. What little is known about his biography reveals an experienced, tested, and forceful military professional, whose entire life is inextricably enmeshed with the growth of the Red Army.

Krylov was born in 1903 in Goliaevka village, Saratov Province, in south-central Russia, not far from Stalingrad where he later fought. While his social origin cannot be determined with exactitude, it is known to be neither proletarian nor peasant. His father's occupation is identified in the official source as "employee," which can mean anything from clerk or civil servant to manager of an estate. A Russian by nationality, his father was probably able to provide his son with an education so that young Krylov, unlike many of his military colleagues, was not forced to work for support. In any case Krylov failed to complete his formal high school education owing to the Revolution and the Civil War.

In 1918 opposition to the Bolshevik takeover erupted into a civil war in which contending armies of Red, White, and intermediate hues clashed on a territory stretching from the Central European plains to the Pacific Ocean. Barely sixteen in April 1919, Krylov volunteered for service in the Red Army. This same year he fought in the Caucasus, and in the second half of 1920 he participated in the last big campaign of the Civil War in the European part of Russia in which the Red armies defeated the troops of Baron Wrangel and captured the Crimean Peninsula. It would appear that Krylov had enlisted in a regular army unit, for at the end of the Civil War in European Russia he was sent almost 4,000 miles away to the Russian Far East where military engagements with native opponents and Japanese expeditionary troops were still taking place.

In 1921 the future marshal became a military professional; he received a junior officer's commission in the Red Army. Not yet twenty years old, he was already an experienced soldier, a vèteran of two campaigns. The details of Krylov's service in the Red Army from the end of the Civil War until the German attack in 1941 are more sparse than for most of his colleagues, simply, it would appear, because his career during that period advanced more slowly than those of almost all other marshals of the Soviet Union. Some important facts about his interwar activities compiled from various sources provide, however, a general and in some respects an atypical picture.

The most striking element in Krylov's prewar biography concerns his education or, rather, the lack of it. Krylov did not attend either the Frunze military academy, the Voroshilov general staff academy, or any of the branch academies of the Soviet armed forces. Soviet biographers attribute to him a secondary school education, although it is unclear when he was able to complete high school. Most probably he pursued special evening classes or a correspondence course. His only military schooling seems to have been a short infantry course for junior commanders from which he was graduated in 1926. In view of the fact that his service in the Second World War began with staff activities which require systematic and extensive knowledge of military science, it may be suggested that he acquired his preparation for this work through experience and self-education and thus should be regarded as an officer of exceptional ability. Alternatively, he may have attended a military academy without completing his course of study, a circumstance which would explain both his skill in staff work and the absence of any reference to his graduation in official biographies. One can only speculate that during the "great purges" of the late 1930's his schooling and career were interrupted. Such a possibility would also explain his slow promotion before the Second World War. After twenty-two years of military service he achieved only the rank of lieutenant colonel.

It would appear from all available accounts that Krylov served in the Far Eastern territories of the Soviet Union almost until the beginning of the Germano-Russian war. Whether he took part in the 1939–40 clashes between the Soviet Army and the Japanese forces which attempted to occupy a part of the Soviet protectorate, the Mongolian People's Republic, is not known, but his official biographers note that he took part in a much earlier clash on the Far Eastern borders of the Soviet Union in the so-called Chinese Eastern Railway incident in 1929. The only other pertinent fact of Krylov's prewar service mentioned by his biographers is his entry into the Communist party in 1927.

Shortly before the war Krylov was transferred to the southwestern borders of the Soviet Union. At the start of the war he occupied a staff position in the garrison of the Izmail fortress on the Russo-Romanian border. Under overwhelming German attack the Red Army withdrew in the south along the Black Sea coast. The remnants of the defeated divisions tried to hold the German advance at the main Russian naval base of Odessa in the western part of the Black Sea. Here the Special Maritime Army under General Petrov was ordered to stop the German advance at all costs. During the defense of Odessa Colonel Krylov served as deputy chief of staff and head of the Operational Department of the Odessa Defense Region. The two and one-half month defense of Odessa was marked by extremely fierce fighting. The attacking German and Romanian armies severed the port from the Russian mainland, leaving open to the defenders only sea communications with the Crimea and the Caucasus. On October 16, 1941, the last Soviet troops left Odessa under heavy German bombardment for the main Crimean port of Sevastopol.

Krylov participated in what military historians describe as one of the most glorious and heroic defeats of the Soviet Army during the war. The siege of Sevastopol began on October 30, 1941, when the Eleventh German Army under von Manstein reached the outer defense perimeter of the city. It lasted until July 3, 1942, when after a siege of 250 days the Soviet troops abandoned Sevastopol under order of the high command. Krylov, already a brigadier general, served throughout this period as chief of staff of the defending army. In the last days of the defense a Soviet submarine picked up Admiral Oktiabrsky and other top-ranking army and party personnel including General Krylov and brought them to the Caucasus.

The fall of Sevastopol came during the over-all summer offensive of the Germans in southern Russia that brought the German troops closer and closer to their major objective, the great Volga city Stalingrad. General Krylov took part in the battle of Stalingrad, a major turning point in the Germano-Soviet war, from the beginning. He was appointed chief of staff of the 62nd Army, the divisions of which occupied the center of the city itself and against which the main German thrust was directed. In the critical days of September 1942 when the Germans threw seven crack divisions, over five hundred tanks, more than a thousand pieces of artillery, and hundreds of airplanes into the city, the commander of the 62nd Army, Lieutenant General Lopatin, was disabled, and General Krylov assumed temporary command. After a short period, however, he returned to his previous post of chief of staff under a new commander of the 62nd Army, one of the major heroes of the Stalingrad battle, the future Marshal Vasily Chuikov. The Stalingrad Front (Army Group) was at that time commanded by General of the Army Andrei Yeremenko whose deputy and chief political commissar was Nikita Khrushchev. In his memoirs Yeremenko explained his decision to retain Krylov as chief of staff rather than as commander of the 62nd Army: "After the disabling of Lopatin I and Nikita Sergeivich [Khrushchev] made a careful assessment of General Krylov who assumed temporary command of the army. At the beginning we even considered asking the high command to leave him as commander; as a good staff officer he undoubtedly possessed qualities which would have permitted him to grow considerably as a battle commander and to occupy worthily the post of commander. We were restrained, however, by the consideration that it would be very difficult to find for the 62nd Army a chief of staff comparable to Krylov with his enormous experience of defensive fighting gained in Odessa and Sevastopol."

In the battle of Stalingrad Krylov was promoted to the rank of lieutenant general and received the Golden Star and title Hero of the Soviet Union. Soon after the battle, in May 1943, he received his own command at last. For the remainder of the war he served as commander of the Fifth Army, which in the winter of 1945 was the first to reach the border of East Prussia. After VE Day the entire Fifth Army was transferred under

Colonel General Krylov's command to the Far East where in August 1945 it participated in the Soviet attack against the Japanese enemy in Manchuria.

General Krylov spent the first ten postwar years in the Far Eastern territories of the Soviet Union where his military career had begun. He served first as deputy to the present minister of Defense, Marshal Malinovsky, and then as the commander of the entire Far Eastern Military District. In 1956 he was transferred to the command of the Ural Military District where he remained for over a year. In 1957 he assumed command of the second most prestigious military district in the Soviet Union, that of Leningrad. And finally in 1960 he advanced to the top area command in the Soviet military establishment, that of the Moscow Military District. In 1962 he achieved the highest military rank, marshal of the Soviet Union.

Marshal Krylov's most recent assignment (April 1963) to the position of commander in chief of the Strategic Rocket Forces and deputy minister of Defense of the Soviet Union resulted from the purge which followed the dramatic revelation of espionage within the Soviet military establishment. He succeeded Marshal Varentsov whose protégé, Oleg Penkovsky, was exposed as a spy for Western intelligence.

SELECTED BIBLIOGRAPHY

For biographical information about Krylov, see the following: *Bol'shaia sovetskaia entsiklopediia,* vypusk 2, LI, Moskva, 1958, p. 167; *Ukrains'ka radians'ka entsiklopediia,* VII, Kiev, 1963, p. 378; *Sovetskaia istoricheskaia entsiklopediia,* IV, Moskva, 1963, p. 405; *Deputaty verkhovnogo soveta SSSR,* Moskva, 1959, p. 213; *Deputaty verkhovnogo soveta SSSR,* Moskva, 1963, p. 234; *Ezhegodnik bol'shoi sovetskoi entsiklopedii 1964,* Moskva, 1964, p. 604; *Liudi bessmertnogo podviga,* vypusk 2, I, Moskva, 1965, pp. 112–18. For descriptions of Krylov's career and activities, see *Istoriia velikoi otechestvennoi voiny sovetskogo soiuza 1941–1945,* Moskva, 1963–65, II, p. 447; *ibid.,* IV, p. 161; *ibid.,* V, pp. 109, 554, and the following works of memoirs: *Polki idut na zapad,* Moskva, 1964, pp. 184–208; Marshal V. S. Chuikov, *Nachalo puti,* Moskva, 1962; Marshal A. I. Eremenko, *Stalingrad,* Moskva, 1961, pp. 177–78, 182–83; Vice Admiral I. I. Azarov, *Osazhdennaia Odessa,* Moskva, 1962, pp. 72–73, 166–67, 178–79, 185–86; Lieutenant General E. I. Zhidilov, *My otstaivali Sevastopol,* Moskva, 1960.

Rodion Iakovlevich Malinovsky

by Severyn Bialer

When in 1957 Khrushchev terminated the career of the Soviet minister of Defense, Marshal Zhukov, the person he selected to head the military establishment was a stocky man with white hair, beetle brows, and peasant features—the former first deputy of Zhukov and marshal of the Soviet Union, Rodion Malinovsky. The life and career of Marshal Malinovsky are in many respects typical of that generation of Soviet military leaders who came into prominence during the Second World War and who are now—and will be for some time to come—in complete charge of the second most powerful military machine in the world.

Malinovsky was born in 1898 in Odessa, the largest Black Sea port of Russia. It was a bustling port, with a population of about 300,000, through which Ukrainian grain was exported to Western Europe and machinery for the mushrooming industrial complex of the Donbas was imported. It was a cosmopolitan city, multinational in character (Russians, Ukrainians, Romanians, Jews, Tatars), with a colorful mode of life, brilliantly described in the stories of the famous Soviet writer Isaac Babel, very different from that of the stagnant cities of inner Russia.

Malinovsky's father was a worker who probably was employed in the port of Odessa. Any further details about his family are lacking in the official Soviet biographies. It is known that Malinovsky is ethnically a Ukrainian, and that while he normally uses the Russian language, he is fluent in Ukrainian. Nothing indicates, however, that he feels any special allegiance to the Ukrainian nation. His life has been spent mostly among Russians, and his basic allegiance seems to be to the Soviet state, which has been traditionally dominated by Russians and centrally directed from Moscow. Nothing definite is known about Malinovsky's early youth. It seems that he stopped his schooling after finishing primary school in Odessa.

When the First World War broke out in 1914, Malinovsky volunteered for the Tsarist Army at the age of sixteen. He was sent to the front as a private, and by the end of 1915, as a machine-gunner, was promoted to the rank of corporal. In early 1916 for the first—but not the last—time, Malinovsky went abroad. That year the Tsarist government organized a Russian Expeditionary Corps of 20,000 soldiers that was sent to France by way of Vladivostock and the Suez Canal and placed at the disposal of the French military command. This force, in which Malinovsky served as a noncommissioned officer, fought on the Western Front against the Germans. Malinovsky later told the British journalist Alexander Werth that he had taken part in the fighting at Laon and Arras. He had been impressed, so he said, with the British troops: "They are slow, but they are reliable." In his published memoirs Malinovsky recounts that he was wounded while participating with the Second Regiment of the Corps in the battle around the fort Breman.

After the victory of the October Revolution in Russia in 1917, Bolshevik propaganda in the expeditionary force led to the force's almost total disorganization. For all practical purposes it ceased to exist as a fighting unit and could not be used by the French in the war against Germany. A large number of the Russian soldiers, among them Malinovsky who was a member of the Soldiers' Committee (*soviet*) of his company, were interned at Courtine, a French military camp, until the end of war in 1918. A disturbance among them was brutally suppressed by the French authorities, who shot several hundred of Malinovsky's comrades—an event etched deeply in his memory. It seems, however, that Malinovsky left the camp before the conclusion of the war. He mentions in his memoirs that he participated in the closing stages of the war against Germany on the Western Front as a soldier of the French Foreign Legion.

After the armistice of November 1918, those soldiers in the expeditionary corps who demanded to be sent home were accommodated. Apparently Malinovsky also succeeded in being released from service in the Foreign Legion. In 1919, the ship carrying him arrived in a Far East port of Russia.

Malinovsky started out through Siberia on the trip home, but never reached Odessa. In Siberia he joined a Red Army detachment that was fighting the White Army of Admiral Kolchak, and since then he has served uninterruptedly in the Soviet armed forces. Throughout the Civil War until 1920 he fought in the Red Army, during which time he was promoted to junior officer rank.

When the Civil War ended, Malinovsky was sent to an officers' school and became a professional commissioned officer in the Red Army. As far as is known, neither before nor after did he serve as a political commissar in the Soviet armed forces. From the beginning he was first and foremost a military professional. This does not mean, of course, that he was apolitical. He made clear his commitment to the Communist cause by joining the Communist Party of the Soviet Union (CPSU) in 1926. From that time on, except for a short period during the "great purges" of the late 1930's, he was never in any political trouble and his personal loyalty to the Soviet system was never questioned.

During the 1920's the motley, undisciplined, unschooled military detachments of the Civil War Red fighters were being built into an efficient, professional military machine. A great demand existed for new, middle-level commanders—especially staff officers—who would combine proved loyalty to the new regime with technical military proficiency. The Red Army officers who had been commissioned on the battlefields of the Civil War, and had later in peacetime only passed through accelerated officer courses, were being sent to military academies to acquire the knowledge necessary to command a modern army, principally to the Frunze military academy in Moscow (named after M. V. Frunze, the people's commissar of Military and Naval Affairs in 1925). Modeled upon the former Tsarist general staff academy, the Frunze academy was staffed to a large degree by high officers of the former Tsarist Army who served, voluntarily or otherwise, the new regime.

In 1927 the thirty-year-old Red Army officer, Malinovsky, commander of an infantry battalion, was admitted to the Frunze military academy, from which he graduated with distinction in 1930. In his education in the academy, Malinovsky specialized in staff work, and afterward received a direct appointment to the position of chief of staff of a Red Army cavalry regiment. In the mid-1930's he was already serving in the much higher position of chief of the Operational Department of a military district staff. Later he was identified as a chief of staff of a cavalry corps.[1]

On July 18, 1937, the daily newspaper of the People's Commissariat of Defense, *Krasnaia zvezda* (*Red Star*), carried a decree of the Supreme Soviet of the USSR awarding Colonel R. Malinovsky the Order of Lenin for his achievements in the military preparation of the troops under his command. The reason for the decoration had in fact, however, little to do with his achievements in the peacetime training of the Red Army. At the time the decree was published, Malinovsky was many thousands of miles from Soviet borders and, unlike most of his colleagues, already participating in a bloody encounter with a modern, regular army.

Civil war had broken out in Spain in July 1936. The Spanish Republican forces, in which the Spanish Communists from the beginning played an important role (and which at a later stage they dominated), clashed in a full-scale, massive, and highly destructive military encounter with the armies of General Francisco Franco, who was being helped by expeditionary forces from Fascist Italy and Nazi Germany. From the fall of 1936 the Soviet Union was actively engaged in the Spanish War. Stalin decided to send war equipment and military personnel to strengthen the Republican side. The Soviet officers who were delegated to Spain, among them Malinovsky, participated either as pilots or tank commanders or, more often, as advisers to Spanish commanders of large units or instructors in the training of Republican soldiers and officers. Only 500 or 600 Russians

---

[1] In the Red Army at that time the corps was a self-sufficient field unit, including two or three infantry, motorized, or cavalry divisions, with all supporting troops except air support.

were there at one time, it is estimated, though there was a fairly quick turnover. This quick turnover was closely related to the "great purge" that was raging in Russia, and many, if not most, of the Soviet officers fighting in Spain were recalled to Russia—never to be heard of again. Those who went to Spain were not permitted to inform even their families where they were going or to talk about their experiences after their return. In Spain they wore the uniform of the Spanish Republican Army and assumed Spanish pseudonyms.

Little was known until recently about Malinovsky's activities in Spain. Official Soviet sources first admitted his presence there in August 1956 in an article published in the Soviet historical journal, *Problems of History*. Also, a famous military leader of the Spanish Republican Army, El Campesino, reported Malinovsky's participation in the Spanish Civil War. In 1965 Malinovsky himself told the story of his Spanish experiences in memoirs published in Moscow.

According to his own story, Malinovsky petitioned the Soviet Ministry of Defense to be sent to Spain. His request accepted, he went in civilian clothes, alone, by train to Finland, then by ship to Sweden, from which a plane took him to Holland and Paris. After receiving instruction from the Soviet embassy in France, he went by train to the Spanish border and to Madrid.

Now "Colonel Malino," Malinovsky was sent by the Madrid high command in the first half of January 1937 to the front, northwest of the Spanish capital. His first assignment was as deputy to the Soviet General G. I. Kulik (a future marshal of the USSR), who commanded a whole sector of the northwest defense of Madrid. The troops at that sector consisted of Spanish Republican Army units and the twelfth and fourteenth International Brigades (foreign volunteers who had come to Spain to fight Fascism). As Kulik's emissary in various divisions and brigades, Malinovsky participated in the battles of Mahodeont and Haram. In his later assignments he was an adviser to the commander of the Second Madrid Corps, which was entrusted with ensuring the inner perimeter of Madrid's defense, and an adviser in the staff of the Central Front. For some time in the summer of 1937 he participated in the Republican General Staff in planning the "Brunet operation," a Republican offensive to be carried out south of Madrid. His last assignment in Spain, in the late winter and spring of 1938, was as adviser to the commander of the Army of Maneuver on the Eastern Front, in Catalonia, where General Franco's major spring offensive, directed toward cutting off the Republican forces from the Mediterranean Sea, took place.

The circumstances of Malinovsky's return to Russia, as recounted in his memoirs, are worth relating. His tour of duty in Spain had already come to an end in the summer of 1937. He was, however, reluctant to go back to the Soviet Union and approached the senior Soviet officer in

Spain, General G. M. Shtern (the future commander of the Far Eastern Army whom Stalin had shot a few weeks before the Nazi attack in 1941), to intercede for him in Moscow. Shtern succeeded and Malinovsky's tour of duty was extended another six months.

Malinovsky reports that both duty and conscience dictated that he remain in Spain. He adds, however, that like most of the Soviet personnel in Spain, he was troubled and worried by rumors about the purge of military leaders in the homeland. In fact, at exactly that time, July 1937, the top leaders of the Soviet Army—Tukhachevsky, Yakir, Uborevich, Kork, Putna, and others—were sentenced to death by a military tribunal. Malinovsky's reluctance to return to Russia seems, in these conditions, to have been natural and prudent.

By the end of 1937 his second term of duty expired. In the Soviet Union the military purge had reached its height and Malinovsky secured another extension of his stay in Spain under obscure circumstances. In his words: "Again I was faced with a dilemma: to return to the Soviet Union and abandon my Spanish comrades-in-arms . . . or to follow the dictates of my heart and my sense of duty and stay in Spain wittingly provoking the displeasure of my superiors? I chose the latter." It is unclear, however, why his superiors in Moscow let him have his way. One wonders if they were reluctant to press their order for his return for fear that he would not obey.

In the late spring or early summer of 1938, for the third time, Soviet military authorities issued an order for Malinovsky's return. The telegram from Moscow, Malinovsky recounts, was unequivocal: "If you do not obey the order immediately you will be considered a *nyevozvrashchenets* (non-returnee, defector)." "To be frank"—adds Malinovsky—"this threat made my flesh creep." This time without delay he went back to Russia, arriving in early summer of 1938.

Malinovsky's absence from Russia in 1937–38 may well have saved his life. In those two years the Soviet military establishment was exposed to the hardest test of its short existence. A bloody purge, initiated by Stalin and conducted by his assistants, decimated the Soviet officer corps. When Malinovsky returned to Russia, the most devastating part of the purge was already over. Yet a danger still existed, and simply the fact that he had been in Spain—that is, abroad—in contact with foreigners and outside the area completely controlled by the Soviet secret police, made him suspect. Instead of being given a new command, to which his former service and actual fighting experience in Spain entitled him, Malinovsky was appointed, in the fall of 1939, a senior lecturer in the Frunze military academy. Of course, his teaching appointment may be explained by the Soviet high command's desire to utilize his Spanish experience for training new Soviet commanders. But Malinovsky himself describes this period of his life as one of frustration, uncertainty, and insecurity.

Malinovsky's interval as a teacher came quickly to an end. In the early spring of 1941 he was placed in command of an infantry corps on the southern borders of the USSR in the Odessa Military District. His rank was major general (the lowest general-officer rank in the Soviet Army, equivalent to the American brigadier general). The turning point in his career—and the major test of the Soviet armed forces, with whose fate his life was so intertwined—was shortly to come. On June 22, 1941, the Nazi military machine attacked the Soviet Union.

When the war broke out, the 48th Infantry Corps, composed of three not yet fully mobilized infantry divisions and commanded by General Malinovsky, was located on the Romanian border. As the German and Romanian armies advanced, Malinovsky's troops were assigned the task of holding a 240-kilometer (150-mile) sector of the front, without many troops in reserve. Engaged in continuous fighting and many times breaking out from encirclement, the 48th Corps suffered heavy losses and retreated deep into the Ukraine, unable to withstand the force of the advancing enemy.

Throughout the end of 1941 and until the summer of 1942 Malinovsky commanded front-line troops in the southern sector of the 1,500-mile front that extended from the Black Sea to Finland. In August 1941 Malinovsky was promoted, in the importance of his assignment rather than in military rank, from a corps to an army commander. From August until September he directed the 6th Army in defensive battles on the river Dnieper in the Ukraine. In the winter of 1941, still in command of the 6th Army, he kept a stationary front against the Germans on the North Donetsk River, some 200 miles deeper in Russian territory than his September defensive line.

In January 1942 Malinovsky was promoted to lieutenant general and assigned to the highest operational field command in the Soviet Army, that of a Front (Army Group) commander. The sector under his command, the Southern Front (Army Group), covered over 200 miles in the southernmost corner of the Ukraine, its left flank being the port of Taganrog on the Black Sea. The major operational units in his charge were the 9th, 37th, and 57th Field Armies and the 1st and 5th Cavalry Corps.

In the winter of 1941–42 the Soviet Army was able to force the German troops to a standstill. The success of the winter counterattacks outside Moscow built up hopes in the Soviet high command that Soviet troops would be able to turn the tide during the winter and regain the losses of the previous months. Under orders from Moscow, Malinovsky's Army Group, in concert with the Southwest Army Group, attacked on a broad front in mid-January 1942. The offensive, however, was unsuccessful. By early February, after only local breakthroughs, the Soviet advance stopped. Considering the conditions of the operation, it seems that the failure was not at all a result of Malinovsky's lack of determination and talent, but of

Stalin's unrealistic hopes. The lack of success of Malinovsky's Army Group in the winter offensive paled, however, in comparison with its fate during the spring and summer German offensive, when the Germans repeatedly broke the front, encircled large units, pushed his armies hundreds of miles back to the mountains of the North Caucasus.

By the second half of July 1942 Malinovsky was in command of the greatly weakened 37th, 12th, and 18th Field Armies. His 56th Army had to be placed in the second echelon, as unfit to engage in combat. Of his 9th and 24th Field Armies only the staff and some support and supply units were left—and they were sent to the rear to be completely reformed. On July 28, 1942, the Southern Army Group was abolished as an independent command and incorporated into the North Caucasus Front. Lieutenant General Malinovsky was appointed a deputy to the Front (Army Group) commander and put in charge of the 51st, 37th, and 12th Field Armies (supported by the 4th Air Army), which formed the "Don Group." This command also brought Malinovsky failure. Only a few days after the Don Group was created, the Germans broke through its lines and in forty-eight hours pushed eighty miles forward. The 51st Army was completely separated from the Don Group and from Malinovsky's headquarters and was subsequently detached and transferred to the Stalingrad Front. The 37th and 12th Field Armies suffered heavy losses, retreated, and were finally separated from each other. In early August the Don Group as a separate operational command ceased to exist.

The spring and early summer battles of 1942 did not bode well for the Soviet Army. After being halted, even set back, during the winter, the regrouped, still better equipped, and more experienced German forces thrust deeper and deeper into Soviet territory. At a terrible cost of millions killed, wounded, and captured and millions of square miles of homeland laid waste, the most that the Soviet Army could achieve was to make the Germans pay dearly for their victories and to delay the timetable established by the German General Staff. In the battles of this period, Malinovsky acquired great tactical experience in defensive operations against a confident and seemingly invincible enemy. Shortly he was to become a major participant in one of the most crucial offensive operations of the Soviet Army in the Second World War, the turning point in the Nazi-Soviet war—the battle of Stalingrad.

After occupying the whole of the Ukraine, the German armies in the south advanced strongly into the Russian territory proper. Whereas in the 1941 offensive their main goal had been Moscow, in the summer of 1942 it was the city of Stalingrad. On July 17 the great battle of Stalingrad began. In the first stage (July 17–August 10) the Soviet armies tried to hold, or at least delay, the Germans-in the steppes between the river Don and the city. From August 15 to September 12 the fighting was concentrated in the close approaches to the city and even its outskirts. During this period Malinovsky commanded the 66th Army. In the third stage, through November 18, the city itself became a battlefield. Here the German armies achieved their deepest penetration into Russian territory and reached the banks of the river Volga. Beyond Stalingrad and the Volga there were no natural barriers to stop the advance of the Germans, only endless steppes on which the German armor could roll over the Soviet infantry. At Stalingrad the Soviet troops halted the advance of the German armies. In the ruins of this industrial city stretching along the banks of the Volga for some thirty miles, battles for every building and every yard of territory raged with unequaled ferocity for over three months.

Malinovsky had been assigned to the command of the 66th Field Army by the end of August 1942. This command was a unit only slightly more important than the one he had had exactly a year before. His failures as leader of the large operational groups must have created doubts as to his abilities to be in charge of larger units. His assignment to the 66th Field Army not only halted his military career, it was clearly a setback. Having previously had numerous army commanders as subordinates, to be again one of this group himself was probably a bitter pill to swallow.

The 66th Army, consisting of the 49th, 99th, 120th, 231st, and 299th Infantry Divisions and 10th, 69th, 148th, and 246th Tank Brigades, and composed largely of inexperienced recruits, was kept for a short period in the reserve of the Soviet high command. On August 30 the 66th Army was transferred to the command of the Stalingrad theater and on September 5 was thrown against the German forces in an unsuccessful attack north of the city. Malinovsky remained in command of the 66th Army until October 14. During that period his army did not participate in the battle in the city itself, but occupied a front sector of secondary importance north of Stalingrad.

In early December 1942 Malinovsky took over the command of the newly formed Second Guards Army. This army was formed in October 1942 in the Tambov District (about 300 miles southeast of Moscow) and consisted of the 1st and 13th Infantry Corps (each including three divisions), a mechanized corps, and a number of smaller supporting units. While not a promotion (he had formerly been in charge of an army) Malinovsky's assignment carried the distinction of commanding a Guards Army, i.e., an elite unit whose soldiers were better paid, had certain privileges, were equipped with firepower and equipment superior to those of the "normal" army units, and which included in its ranks a high percentage of experienced, battle-wise and decorated soldiers and officers. On December 8 his army was sent to Stalingrad.

After fighting the Germans to a standstill in Stalingrad, the Soviet high command put into action its counteroffensive, designed not only to push the Germans back, but primarily to encircle Field Marshal Paulus' entire army group, a half-million strong, and by concentrated blows from all directions to annihilate it or force it to surrender. In the performance of this operation, four Soviet Fronts (Army Groups) participated. Malinovsky, commanding the 10th Army, was assigned the task of repulsing the attempt by Manstein's Army Group from the West to break through the circle of Soviet troops and open a corridor to Paulus' army, through which supplies and reinforcements could be sent and the ambitious designs of the Soviet high command thwarted. Malinovsky's army, through a counteroffensive (December 24–31), played a decisive role in preventing the breakthrough of the Manstein Army Group.

In the Stalingrad battle, Malinovsky neither commanded the most important sectors nor participated in planning the over-all strategy. Neither during nor after was he praised as a major hero of Stalingrad, as his present subordinates, Chuikov and Yeremenko have been. Still, he commanded a major operational unit in a crucial battle, and he proved himself a talented leader of offensive military action.

Reward was not long in coming. Besides being decorated for his Stalingrad exploits, on February 2, 1943—shortly after the end of the Stalingrad battle—Malinovsky was appointed commander of the Southern Front, composed of four armies. Under his command, the Southern Front, and then the Third Ukrainian Front, participated in the offensive against the Germans in the Ukraine. From the summer of 1943 to May 1944 they expelled the Germans and their allies from the biggest Ukrainian industrial complex, the Donbas, crossed the major Ukraine river, the Dnieper, and participated in the German defeat west of the Dnieper.

In the early summer of 1944 Soviet troops in southern Russia reached the prewar borders of Romania and prepared to carry the war into the Balkans. In May 1944 General Malinovsky assumed command of the troops of the Second Ukrainian Front, whose task was to destroy the German Army Groups that blocked the road to the Balkans and to carry the Soviet flag into that part of Eastern Europe. The Second Ukrainian Front was composed of an impressive number of troops. Its main force consisted of the 27th, 52nd, and 53rd; the 6th Tank Army, and the 5th Cavalry Corps.

In 1944 the high point of Malinovsky's wartime service occurred. Troops under his command, in cooperation with the troops of the Third Ukrainian Front (under the command of General Tolbukhin) and the Black Sea and Danube fleets, performed one of the most impressive feats of the Russo-German war, the so-called Yasa-Kishinev operation. On August 20, 1944, Malinovsky's troops attacked the German Army Group, "Southern Ukraine," and the main forces of the Romanian Army—altogether over forty divisions. By August 24 the main part of the enemy troops was encircled. By September 3 the Yasa-Kishinev operation was over; the German and Romanian troops had been defeated, and the road to the Balkans was open. During the battle, Malinovsky already held the highest general-officer rank in the Soviet Army, general of the army (equivalent to four-star rank in the United States Army). On September 10 he was promoted to the highest Soviet military rank, marshal of the Soviet Union. From September 1944 to May 1945 the Second Ukrainian Front, under Marshal Malinovsky's command, fought successfully in Romania, Hungary, Czechoslovakia, and Yugoslavia and finally participated in the occupation of Vienna.

On May 9, 1945, the war with Germany came to an end. The main commanders of the Soviet armed forces received the highest decorations. Marshal Malinovsky was awarded the highest military decoration of the Soviet Union, the Golden Star, which entitled him thereafter to the official designation Hero of the Soviet Union.[2]

On May 15, 1945, Marshal Malinovsky, along with other Soviet military leaders, stood on the platform beside the Lenin Mausoleum from which Stalin and his closest associates reviewed the victory parade. But for Malinovsky the war was not yet over. At Yalta the Soviet Union had taken upon itself the obligation of entering the war against Japan three months after the end of war with Germany.

The Soviet high command, immediately after ending the war with Germany, started to concentrate large numbers of troops along the eastern borders of the Soviet Union, across from Japanese-occupied Chinese territory. The Soviet troops in the Far East, under the general command of Marshal Vasilevsky, were subdivided into three Fronts (Army Groups). Marshal Malinovsky was appointed to command one of these, the Trans-Baikal. On the night of August 9 Soviet troops went into action. Malinovsky's armies attacked the Japanese Kwantung Army Group and in a short time defeated the Japanese in western and central Manchuria, occupied Chan-chun, the capital of Manchuria, and seized the major industrial center, Mukden. In successive attacks the Soviet troops under Malinovsky forced the Japanese out of the southern part of northeast China and out of the Liaotung Peninsula, and occupied the seaport and the fortifications of Port Arthur. By August 30, 1945, the Far Eastern operation against the Kwantung Army was over.

From the end of the war with Japan to 1956 Malinovsky remained in the Far Eastern territories of the Soviet Union, first as the commander of a military district, and then as the commander in chief of all Soviet troops in this vast area. It may be significant that during the Korean conflict he commanded the Soviet armies in the areas closest to the Korean War theater. But during this whole postwar period, little was seen of him in the high councils of the Soviet military establishment. His command,

[2] In 1958 at the fortieth anniversary of the Soviet Army, Malinovsky was awarded the Golden Star a second time, which then gave him the right to the title Twice Hero of the Soviet Union. This is a distinction that only 104 Soviet citizens have ever achieved. Of all the marshals of the Soviet Union, only five have twice received the Hero award, and only one—Zhukov—has received it four times.

however important, was far from Moscow, and hardly anybody would have predicted the lightning advance that he achieved in little more than a year.

In March 1956 Marshal Malinovsky was appointed first deputy minister of Defense of the USSR and commander in chief of all Soviet Ground Forces. He was second in the Soviet military establishment only to the renowned Marshal Zhukov who, while Malinovsky was still an unknown infantry corps commander, had already (in 1941) been appointed chief of the Soviet General Staff. Zhukov's fame, experience, authority, and popularity so far exceeded Malinovsky, and the difference in age was so insignificant (Malinovsky is three years younger), that had events taken their natural course, Malinovsky could hardly have expected to reach the peak of power in the Soviet armed forces. But in Soviet politics, matters frequently do not proceed in the expected manner. The fame, experience, authority, and popularity that made Zhukov's position within the military establishment so strong became a danger, real or imagined, to the party leadership. In October 1957 Zhukov was summarily dismissed from all his positions, and Malinovsky achieved the top reward of his military career: he assumed command of a military machine so powerful and technologically advanced that it finds its match only in the armed forces of the United States of America.

It is difficult to say why Khrushchev selected Malinovsky to be Zhukov's successor. It is also unclear as to whether the choice was completely in Khrushchev's hands. It seems, however, that the Soviet party leadership wanted to see at the head of its armed forces a man who lacked the broad popularity, flamboyance, and ambition of a Zhukov, but who at the same time would be thoroughly professional, whose expertise could be relied upon by the political leaders, and who would be able to reconcile the conflicting demands and doctrines of various military groupings. In other words, they sought a man who would accept party leadership and pose no threat to the political leaders themselves, yet who would still be an experienced and efficient military leader.

From this point of view it seems that the party leadership selected the right man. Outside the military establishment, in party councils, Malinovsky is much less active than Zhukov was. He was elected a candidate member of the Central Committee of the CPSU in 1952, and in 1961 was promoted to full membership. The party leadership made sure, however, that the Zhukov precedent would not be repeated, and Malinovsky—despite the fact that his formal power position is equal to Zhukov's—has never been admitted to the real decision-making center of the party, its Presidium, as either a full or a candidate member.

In the internal military discussions between "conservatives" and "modernizers," the "bigger bang for a buck" advocates and supporters of conventional warfare preparedness, Malinovsky occupies a "centrist" position, trying to reconcile the prevailing doctrine—according to which the rocket forces are the main component of Soviet military might—with efforts to maintain massive and technologically up-to-date conventional forces.

It would be wrong to consider Malinovsky a simple "yes man" of the Soviet party leadership. To be sure, there is no evidence that he has any ambition to deny the leadership's right to make the final decisions regarding Soviet foreign policy, allocation of resources for military preparedness, and strategic plans, and even less evidence that he or his colleagues have ever engaged in a plot to supplant the party leadership. But there is sufficient proof that as head of the powerful Soviet military establishment, and as the man entrusted with the military security of the Soviet Union, he is ready and willing to fight for his point of view and that of the professional officer corps he represents, whenever they differ from the opinion of the political leaders. The Soviet military establishment, while acting mainly in the background and not participating in the deliberations of the party Presidium, is a force that can influence these deliberations. In the present, unstable political situation in the Soviet Union when no new successor to Khrushchev's mantle is yet recognizable and a precarious balance of power among various factions in the Soviet hierarchy can be easily upset, the support of the Soviet military establishment and its leader, Malinovsky, cannot be dismissed lightly by any contenders for leadership over the Soviet Union. Nor can it be dismissed lightly by the Western analyst who would understand what is going on in the Soviet Union.

SELECTED BIBLIOGRAPHY

For biographical information about Malinovsky, see the following: *Bol'shaia sovetskaia entsiklopediia*, vypusk 2, XXVI, Moskva, 1954, pp. 149–50; *Malaia sovetskaia entsiklopediia*, vypusk 3, V, Moskva, 1959, p. 877; *Politicheskii slovar'*, vypusk 2, Moskva, 1958, p. 331; *Deputaty verkhovnogo soveta SSSR*, Moskva, 1959, p. 247; *Deputaty verkhovnogo soveta SSSR*, Moskva, 1963, p. 266; *Voprosy istorii*, No. 7, August 1956, p. 16; *Ezhegodnik bol'shoi sovetskoi entsiklopedii 1958*, Moskva, 1958, p. 636; *Liudi bessmertnogo podviga*, vypusk 2, II, Moskva, 1965, pp. 6–21.

For evaluations of Malinovsky's career and activities, see Alexander Werth, *Russia at War*, New York: Dutton, 1964, pp. 468, 492–95; Walter B. Kerr, *The Russian Army—Its Men, Its Leaders and Its Battles*, New York: Knopf, 1944, pp. 21–24; and *Krasnaia zvezda*, July 18, 1937.

Memoirs by Malinovsky and his colleagues may be found in *Pod znamenem ispanskoi respubliki 1936–1939*, Moskva, 1965, pp. 139–91; Marshal R. I. Malinovskii, ed., *Budapesht, Viena, Praga*, Moskva, 1965; Marshal K. K. Rokossovskii, ed., *Velikaia pobeda na volge*, Moskva, 1965; Marshal S. S. Biriuzov, *Kogda gremeli pushki*, Moskva, 1961; Marshal S. S. Biriuzov, *Sovetskii soldat na Balkanakh*, Moskva, 1963; Marshal R. I. Malinovskii, ed., *Iassko-kishinievskie kanny*, Moskva, 1964; Marshal R. I. Malinovskii, "Pamiatnye gody," in *Sorok let voennoi akademii imeni M. V. Frunze*, Moskva, 1958, pp. 163–69; *Voenno-istoricheskii zhurnal*, No. 5, Moskva, May, 1960, pp. 11–25.

Konstantin Andreevich Vershinin

by Severyn Bialer

At present the Soviet Air Force is the second strongest air power in the world. According to some expert Western estimates, its present strength is 10,500 operational aircraft and 510,000 military personnel (excluding the Naval Air Force and the Air Defense Command). The responsibility for the organization, training, and battle-readiness of this tremendous power rests with a former fighter pilot, veteran of combat in the Second World War, the present chief air marshal of the Soviet Union, Konstantin Vershinin.

Vershinin was born in 1900 in the village of Borkino in the central Russian province of Kirov. Like most of his colleagues in the Soviet high command his parents were peasants. It would appear that young Vershinin knew real poverty. After completing his elementary education, he left the village and from the age of fourteen worked as a laborer, then as a carpenter, in a shipbuilding yard. He left the factory in June 1919 to volunteer for the recently created Red Army in which he was to serve without interruption for the next several decades. In 1919 he also became a member of the Communist Party of the Soviet Union (CPSU).

When Vershinin joined the Red Army, it was engaged in civil war which lasted three years. Vershinin was selected to attend courses for junior commanders after having served as a private for only a few months. Following several months of schooling Cadet Vershinin was promoted to officer rank and appointed company commander. He took part as a battalion commander in the war against Poland during the summer of 1920. He fought also against the peasant guerrilla armies of Antonov in Tambov Province. At the end of the Civil War he chose a professional military career. As the ranks achieved during the war were not always respected in the greatly reduced peacetime army, Vershinin, it would appear, had again to start close at the bottom of the officer ladder. Until 1925 he served in the infantry.

In the period between the two world wars all major European powers progressively mechanized their armed forces, thus providing for the incorporation of the two new weapons—the tank and the airplane—which had revolutionized the conduct of war a few years earlier. The military forces of the Soviet Union at the end of the Civil War were far inferior to those of the other major powers. Both tank and air forces were virtually

nonexistent. The war, moreover, profoundly decreased the industrial potential of Russia without which the modernization of its armies was impossible. To create an industrial base for such modernization was the
principal goal of the Soviet government in the first Five-Year plans which
were inaugurated late in the 1920's. Special attention was paid to the production of airplanes, and already in the 1930's Russia was listed among the
great air powers of the world, possessing numerous wings of heavy and
light bombers as well as fighter planes. Of equal priority in the modernization of an air force was the arduous task of training military cadres from
an overwhelmingly peasant society in the use of new weapons. Orders were
issued as early as the mid-1920's to transfer volunteers from all branches
of the military to the air force training program. In addition, party organizations in the armed forces were instructed to seek out and recommend
likely candidates for training, to persuade these candidates to abandon their
respective branches of service in favor of the air force.

Vershinin, as a volunteer or through recommendation, entered a school
for military flyers in 1925 and was graduated two years later. He became
a fighter pilot and as such was sent in 1929 to a higher military educational
establishment, the Military Air Academy named after the pioneer of Russian aviation, Zhukovsky. In the academy middle- and high-ranking officers
were trained for the Soviet Air Force. Vershinin was graduated in 1932.
In the ensuing years he commanded a squadron and then a regiment of
fighters. In the year before the German attack on Russia, he commanded
a special fighter regiment in which usual military training was combined
with the testing of new types of fighter planes. At the beginning of the war
he was in command of a fighter division (three regiments).

The technical superiority of the German armed forces at the beginning
of the Nazi-Soviet war was nowhere more striking than in the case of the
air force. While the Germans possessed the most modern combat-tested
Messerschmitts, Junkers, and Henkels, the Soviet Air Force was armed with
planes of much older vintage. In addition to technological inferiority, the
Soviets were handicapped still further by the destruction of a large percentage of Soviet aircraft in the very first days of the war, before many had
left the airfields. The Germans were in complete command of the air at
the beginning of the war. Even after their armies were soundly beaten by
the Soviets from the offensives of winters 1942 and 1943, German superiority in the air continued, if to a somewhat lesser degree than in 1941.

The initial losses of experienced pilots in the first months of the war
could explain the rapid advance of Vershinin from divisional commander
at the start of the war to chief of the Air Force for the entire Southern
Front (Army Group) in September 1941. He remained in this post until
May 1942 when he assumed command of a newly created Air Army (four
divisions) attached to the same front. Although the title may sound impressive, it should be noted that a Soviet Air Army at that time possessed

at times fewer modern airplanes than a German air division. In any case, during the fighting over the Don steppes Vershinin's pilots were no match for the Germans. In September 1942 Vershinin was transferred to the post of chief of the Air Force of the Transcaucasian Front where in the winter of 1942–43 the German offensive finally broke down. With the increased production from Soviet airplane factories and the deliveries of airplanes under Lend-Lease from the United States, the Soviet high command was able to form large air force units which from this time on met the Germans on more equal terms. In April 1943 Vershinin was appointed to command one such unit, the Fourth Air Army, composed of both fighter units and tactical bomber regiments. He remained in command of the Fourth Air Army until the end of the war and participated with it in battles over southern Russia and the Crimea (1943–44), Byelorussia (1944), Poland and East Prussia (1945). On August 19, 1944, he received the Golden Star and the title Hero of the Soviet Union, the highest Soviet military decoration.

In 1946 Air Marshal Vershinin was appointed to the top air force position of deputy minister of Defense of the USSR and commander in chief of the Soviet Air Force, over the heads of his wartime superiors and especially Chief Air Marshal Novikov. He remained in this position until 1949, when he was dismissed for unknown reasons. For the next two years his assignment cannot be discovered. In 1951 he was appointed to a much lower position, commander of the Air Defense District of Azerbaijan with headquarters in Baku. After Stalin's death in 1953 he again received a high position—head of the Air Defense of the USSR. (In the Soviet Union air defense is independent of the air force and directly responsible to the minister of Defense. The command includes fighter units, antiaircraft artillery, radar stations, and ground-to-air missile units.) Vershinin remained in the position for only a year. From 1954 to 1956 he again commanded the Azerbaijan Air Defense District. The reasons for the vicissitudes of his career remain obscure. In 1956 he returned to Moscow and advanced in the military hierarchy to the position of deputy head of the Soviet Air Force. Finally, in January 1957 he again resumed the position that he had formerly occupied—that of deputy minister of Defense and commander in chief of the Soviet Air Force, a post in which he continues to serve. To crown his ascent to the top of the military hierarchy he was promoted to the highest air force rank in 1959—chief air marshal—and in 1961 was elected to the full membership in the Central Committee of the Communist Party of the Soviet Union.

SELECTED BIBLIOGRAPHY

Biographical data on Vershinin may be found in the following: *Bol'shaia sovetskaia entsiklopediia,* vypusk 2, VII, Moskva, 1951, p. 541; *Deputaty verkhovnogo soveta SSSR,* Moskva, 1963, p. 79; *Malaia sovetskaia entsiklopediia,* vypusk 3, II, Moskva, 1958, p. 343; *Ukrains'ka radians'ka entsiklopediia,* II,

Kiev, 1962, p. 328; *Sovetskaia istoricheskaia entsiklopediia,* III, Moskva, 1963, pp. 390–91; *Ezhegodnik bol'shoi sovetskoi entsiklopedii 1960,* Moskva, 1960, p. 595; *Pravda,* May 20, 1960; *Bakinskii rabochii,* February 25, 1954.

For descriptions of Vershinin's career and activities, see S. P. Platonov, *Vtoraia mirovaia voina 1939–1945,* Moskva, 1958, p. 681, and *Istoriia velikoi otechestvennoi voiny sovetskogo soiuz 1941–1945,* Moskva, 1963–65, III, pp. 391–94; IV, pp. 89, 163; V. pp. 106, 120.

Memoirs, by Vershinin and his colleagues, include the following: Chief Air Marshal K. A. Vershinin, "Vozdushnoe srazhenie nad Severnym Kavkazom," in *Voenno-istoricheskii zhurnal,* Moskva, August 1959, No. 8, pp. 17–29; Colonel-General A. I. Pokryshkin, *Nebo voiny,* Moskva, 1966; and Air Marshal S. A. Krasovskii, *Zhizn' v aviatsii,* Moskva, 1960.

Alexei Alexeevich Yepishev

by Robert M. Slusser

Alexei Yepishev was born in May 1908 of Russian parents; his political career, however, was for many years closely identified with the Ukrainian party apparatus. No information is available on his early years. From 1923 to 1927 he worked in the fishing industry. In 1927 he became an instructor in a district committee, and then head of a department, in the Komsomol (Young Communist League). He joined the Communist Party of the Soviet Union (CPSU) in 1929. Yepishev served in the Red Army from 1930 to 1938, and in 1938 finished his higher education at the Military Academy for Mechanization and Motorization of the Red Army. (His long association with the army and his military-technological education must be taken into account in assessing his qualifications for his present [1966] position as chief of the Main Political Administration of the Armed Forces.)

Yepishev's first party assignment, in 1940, was in the cadres department of the Central Committee of the Ukrainian party, working under Nikita Khrushchev, who had been sent to the Ukraine as first secretary in 1938. From 1940 until the fall of Kharkov to the Germans in October 1941, Yepishev held the post of first secretary of the Kharkov City and Oblast Party Committee. From 1941 to 1943 he served as a member of the Military Council of the Stalingrad Front and then as deputy commissar for Medium Machine Construction.[1]

---

[1] The commissariat should not be confused with the ministry of the same name which was established after Stalin's death in March 1953 as the cover organization for the Soviet atomic energy program. The commissariat was presumably charged with munitions production, work for which Yepishev's technical training had prepared him.

Immediately following the Red Army's victory at Stalingrad and the re-capture of Kharkov in February 1943, Yepishev resumed his duties as first secretary of the Kharkov City Party Committee and began to re-establish the party organization. With German reoccupation of Kharkov on March 15, however, this phase of his career was ended. From that point until 1946 Yepishev served in the Red (Soviet) Army as member of the Military Councils of several armies, including the Thirty-eighth Army under General Moskalenko.

In 1946 Yepishev returned to party work in the Ukraine, serving from 1946 to 1948 as secretary for cadres of the Ukrainian party. In 1948, following extensive reorganization of the Central Committee staff, Yepishev became first secretary of the Odessa City and Province Committee, a post he held until 1950.

In the Ukrainian party apparatus Yepishev again worked under Khrushchev, a fact that has caused most Western analysts to conclude that he became and remained Khrushchev's loyal follower. Yepishev's subsequent career, however, and his increased prominence since Khrushchev's fall, fail to support this analysis.

In 1951, three years after Khrushchev had been replaced as first secretary of the Ukrainian party by Leonid G. Melnikov, Yepishev was appointed deputy minister of State Security of the USSR (MGB, the secret police). He was thus a leading official in the Soviet secret police at a time when it was being used as a weapon in the factional intrigue within the CPSU. The fact that this appointment was made when Khrushchev was no longer responsible for direction of the Ukrainian party apparatus provides perhaps the best available evidence that Yepishev's primary political allegiance at this time and subsequently was not to Khrushchev but to the faction in the party hierarchy associated with the chief of Stalin's Private Secretariat, Alexander N. Poskrebyshev. Further evidence of Yepishev's rising stature in the party at this time was his election to candidate membership in the Central Committee of the CPSU at its Nineteenth Congress (October 1952).

Following Stalin's death in March 1953 Yepishev resumed his post as first secretary of the Odessa City Party Committee. In March 1954 he was elected to the Central Committee of the Ukrainian party at its Eighteenth Congress, and in the same year a deputy to the Supreme Soviet of the Russian republic.

In August 1955 Yepishev was appointed Soviet Ambassador to Romania, replacing L. G. Melnikov. Presumably because of his work abroad, he did not attend the Twentieth (1956), Twenty-first (1959) or Twenty-second (1961) congresses of the CPSU, although he was re-elected as a candidate member of the Central Committee at the first and third of these.

Yepishev served as ambassador to Romania from 1955 to 1961, and from 1961 to May 1962 as ambassador to Yugoslavia. Satisfactory performance of his diplomatic duties is indicated by awards given him: the Order of the Red Banner of Labor on his fiftieth birthday in May 1958, "for his services in diplomatic work," and a Yugoslav decoration in May 1962, on the eve of his departure from Belgrade, "for services in connection with the development and strengthening of peaceful cooperation and friendly relations" between Yugoslavia and the Soviet Union.

Yepishev's period of duty in Belgrade was marked by increasingly cordial relations between Tito and the Soviet Union. In facilitating this trend, Yepishev was helping Khrushchev execute a difficult and important maneuver in the struggle between Moscow and Peking for international Communist support in their ideological dispute. His successful performance of this responsible task prepared the way for his return to a position of greater influence in the Soviet Union.

In May 1962, when Khrushchev was under strong pressure from army and party leaders to increase the budgetary allocations for the Soviet armed forces, Yepishev was appointed chief of the Main Political Administration (PRU), the agency subordinate both to the armed forces and the party's Central Committee which has the function of ensuring the political reliability of the armed forces. At the same time he was given the rank of general of the army.

Shortly after his return to the Soviet Union, Yepishev resumed work as a deputy in the Supreme Soviet. In a by-election on September 9, 1962, he was elected to the Council of the Union, replacing General Alexei I. Antonov, who until his death on July 18, 1962, had been chief of staff of the Combined Armed Forces of Nations Participating in the Warsaw Pact; in the list of signatories of Antonov's obituary, Yepishev's name was given a prominent position.

As chief of the Main Political Administration, Yepishev has been able to identify himself closely with the interests of the armed forces. For example, at a series of conferences in the summer of 1962, he urged improvement of the material conditions of service in order to raise morale. He has been active as speaker and writer to a degree unusual in his predecessors, stressing "the growing role of the Communist Party of the Soviet Union in the leadership of the armed forces" (title of an article he contributed to the journal *Questions of the History of the CPSU,* February 1963). As spokesman for the interests of the armed forces vis-à-vis Soviet intellectuals and artists, he has called for the composition of works glorifying the "military-patriotic theme" (speech at the plenary session of the Central Committee of the party, June 1963). On November 25 and 26, 1963, he took part in a session of the committee's Ideological Commission devoted to questions of atheist upbringing; a week later he spoke at a meeting of the party leaders of the Baltic Military District in Riga. Toward the end of January 1964 he addressed a conference of editors and secretaries of party organs of the central military publishing house, calling for a rise in the number of publications. Early in February 1964, at a meeting of officials of the Ministry of Defense and the Main Political Administration with writers and artists, he reiterated his demand for the production of artistic and literary works glorifying patriotism and the martial virtues, and warned against the danger that a mood of pacifism might result from artistic and literary treatment of the physical horrors of war. He stressed the same theme in a meeting with Moscow journalists on February 18, 1964, and again at a meeting of Soviet military commanders with journalists from *Izvestiia* (the organ of the Supreme Soviet) on February 25, 1964.

At this meeting he sounded another theme which was to assume increased prominence in subsequent speeches and articles: the continued and undiminished importance of the individual soldier, notwithstanding the technological revolution which has transformed military affairs in recent years. In an article published in *Kommunist,* No. 5, 1964, the same theme was repeated. The article was noteworthy for its praise of Khrushchev's wartime record as a military figure, and for identifying him as "supreme commander of the armed forces."

The theme of the importance of the individual soldier was the principal subject of an article by Yepishev in *Izvestiia* on August 9, 1964, one of the most important statements of Soviet military policy in recent years. Although the article sought to dismiss reports of United States military superiority as propaganda, its entire argument was an implicit admission that the superiority is a fact with which Soviet military men and policymakers are obliged to reckon. Yepishev argued that notwithstanding American military power, the final outcome of a war between the Soviet Union and the West would be determined by the morale of the Soviet soldier, based on his ideological conviction that he is fighting for a better social and political order.

Yepishev was apparently not forewarned of Khrushchev's impending fall in October 1964; an article by him marking the twentieth anniversary of the liberation of the Ukraine, in which Khrushchev was praised, appeared in *Komsomol'skaia pravda* (the organ of the Komsomol) on October 14. Nevertheless Yepishev not only survived Khrushchev's fall without losing his post, but was raised to full membership in the Central Committee of the party at the November 1964 plenary session. He was re-elected to this position at the Twenty-third Congress of the CPSU (April 1966).

Since Khrushchev's fall there has been no slackening of Yepishev's activity as speaker and writer, and—except for the omission of Khrushchev's name—no significant change in the themes of his articles and speeches. At the end of November 1964 he addressed a military conference of ideological leaders in Moscow. Continued attention to the problem of enlisting the support and cooperation of writers is indicated by his presence at a reception in the Kremlin, March 8, 1965, arranged by the Board of the Union of Writers of the Russian republic following the Second Congress of Writers of the Russian republic. At a Ukrainian republic seminar of lectures organized in connection with the twentieth anniversary of victory over Germany, in April 1965, he gave a lecture entitled "The Communist Party of the Soviet Union, the inspirer and organizer of the victory of the Soviet people in the Great Patriotic War." Later in the same month he addressed a meeting of propagandists, lecturers, and reporters in Moscow on the anniversary of the victory over Germany.

At the Twenty-third Congress of the CPSU in April 1966, Yepishev restated his earlier views on the role of the armed forces in Soviet society and advanced some new ones. Particularly interesting was his statement that Soviet soldiers and military units were volunteering for service in Vietnam, "in order to fight for the freedom of the long-suffering Vietnamese people." In a significant echo of Stalinist policies he said, "Our path to Communism lies not through the weakening but rather through the strengthening of the sense of responsibility of the individual toward society, the strengthening of organization and discipline, the raising of the authority of our state and social organs in the solution of the tasks of Communist construction." He warned writers that the party would not permit attacks on "the cult of personality" (i.e., on Stalin) "to undermine the Soviet people's confidence in the triumph of the cause of Communism."

Yepishev is an able, well-trained, experienced, and highly articulate man. His survival in a key post during a period of extensive party changes, as well as his promotion in the party apparatus, indicates that he enjoys excellent relations with powerful figures in the party leadership. The systematic attention he has devoted in recent years to the ideological preparation of the Soviet armed forces for a possible war against the United States constitutes a sober warning that responsible officials in the Soviet leadership consider it necessary to make definite preparations for that eventuality.

SELECTED BIBLIOGRAPHY

There are brief biographical sketches of Yepishev in *Deputaty verkhovnogo soveta SSSR, shestoi sozyv*, Moskva, 1962, pp. 147–51; *Entsiklopedicheskii slovar' v dvukh tomakh*, I, Moskva, 1963, p. 361; and *Ezhegodnik bol'shoi sovetskoi entsiklopedii 1962*, Moskva, 1962, pp. 594–95.

Speeches and articles by Yepishev: "O vozrastaiushchei roli KPSS v rukovodstve vooruzhennymi silami," *Voprosy istorii KPSS*, 2 (1963), 3–14; "Yadernoe oruzhie i chelovek," *Izvestiia*, August 9, 1964, p. 3; "Vospitanie voina-grazhdanina," *Kommunist* 5 (1964), 64–73; "Kommunisty v avangarde," *Partiinaia zhizn'*, 7 (April 1965), 21–28. Yepishev's speech at the Twenty-third Congress of the CPSU, April 1966, is given in *Pravda*, April 4, 1966; for a partial translation, see *Current Digest of the Soviet Press*, XVIII, 18 (1966), 18–19. See also his pamphlet, *Delo ogromnoi vazhnosti. O nekotorykh voprosakh voenno-patrioticheskogo vospitaniia*, Moskva, 1965.

There are brief but useful references to Yepishev in the following works by Western scholars: John A. Armstrong, *The Soviet Bureaucratic Elite, A Case Study of the Ukrainian Apparatus,* New York: Praeger, 1959, pp. 75, 133–34; Robert Conquest, *Russia after Khrushchev,* New York: Praeger, 1965, p. 180; Merle Fainsod, *How Russia Is Ruled* (2nd ed.), Cambridge: Harvard University Press, 1963, p. 498; and Roman Kolkowicz, *Conflicts in Soviet Party-Military Relations, 1962–1963* (RAND Corporation, 1963), pp. 46–47.

Matvei Vasilevich Zakharov

by Severyn Bialer

On October 19, 1964, a few days after Khrushchev's overthrow, the front pages of all Soviet dailies printed the obituary of Marshal Sergei Biriuzov, chief of the Soviet General Staff, who died in an airplane crash en route to represent the Soviet Union on the occasion of the twentieth anniversary of the liberation of Yugoslavia from German occupation. Some six weeks later the name of his successor was announced. It was Matvei Vasilevich Zakharov, who had been forced into semiretirement from this very post by Khrushchev only a year and a half earlier.

The early biography of Marshal Zakharov exemplifies the ideal of official Soviet propagandists. He was born in 1898, the son of a worker in the largest industrial center of Russia, St. Petersburg (now Leningrad). At the age of seventeen he became a mechanic in one of the largest factories of prerevolutionary Russia, the German-owned Siemens-Halske plant in St. Petersburg. Zakharov joined the Bolsheviks after the establishment of the Russian republic in February 1917. In the fall of 1917 when the Bolshevik *coup d'état* succeeded, Zakharov was serving as a soldier in the Red Guards, armed detachments of industrial workers, the precursors of the Red Army. He took part in the November 8 storm of the Winter Palace, the residence of the republican government. He fought throughout the Civil War in the ranks of the Workers' and Peasants' Red Army, which was formed in the winter of 1918.

When the Civil War came to an end in 1921 Zakharov continued to serve as a junior commander in the artillery. The most striking characteristics of his pre-Second World War military service was his excellent training in Soviet higher military schools. Compared to other senior commanders in the Soviet Army his military education is distinguished by its duration and depth. In 1925 he entered the Frunze military academy, which trained middle-ranking Soviet commanders, and was graduated in 1928. In 1931 he returned to this academy for one year of study in the Operations Department where a select group of the most gifted Soviet staff officers were prepared. In the summer of 1936 he was sent to the newly established Voroshilov general staff academy for training as a high-ranking officer. His colleague at the academy, General Leonid Sandalov, noted in his memoirs that Zakharov was already regarded justly at that time as one of the most experienced and talented staff officers in the Soviet Army.

In addition to his talent and extensive education Zakharov's advance in the 1930's owed not a little to the "great purge" which all but destroyed the upper ranks of the Soviet officer corps. In the words of General Sandalov, as a result of the purge "there arose the necessity to assign students from the academy of the General Staff to the positions of chiefs of staff of military districts and sometimes even to very responsible positions in the General Staff itself." In the summer of 1937 the thirty-nine-year-old Zakharov was appointed chief of staff in the second most important military district in the country, that of Leningrad.

Beginning the war as a major general, Zakharov served for the next four years only in high staff positions. He occupied the position of chief of staff of a number of Fronts (Army Groups), the largest operational units of the Soviet Army, working as closest assistant and deputy under some of the most famous Soviet Front commanders, most notably Marshal Ivan Konev and Marshal Rodion Malinovsky, the present minister of Defense. He participated in battles with the Germans in the Ukraine, and with the Second Ukrainian Front (Army Group) crossed Romania, Hungary, Austria, and Czechoslovakia. In August 1945 again as chief of staff to the commander of the Transbaikal Front (Army Group) Marshal Malinovsky, Zakharov took part in the Soviet offensive against the Japanese Army in Manchuria.

After the victory over Germany Zakharov's first assignment returned him to the general staff academy where he had studied only eight years earlier. Now general of the army, Zakharov, as head of the academy, sought to incorporate the experience gained over long years of fighting into the training of future army commanders. In the postwar years the students at the academy were for the most part highly decorated officers who owed their high ranks less to formal education than to skill in battle. Zakharov headed the academy until 1949 when he was named to an unspecified department in the Soviet General Staff. It would appear that during the period from 1949 to 1952 he was in charge of the Operational Department. By the end of 1952, only a few months before Stalin's death, a reshuffle in the Soviet high command had placed Zakharov in the important post of inspector-general of the Soviet armed forces. It should be noted that Zakharov's duties after 1945 related either to staff work or to training, and he remained without a command of his own until after the death of Stalin.

In 1953 Zakharov was appointed commander of the Leningrad Military District where he had served as chief of staff prior to the war. Four years later he was appointed commander in chief of the Group of the Soviet Forces in East Germany, the westernmost Soviet military base in Europe. While in this position he was promoted in 1959 to the highest Soviet military rank, marshal of the Soviet Union. In April 1960 he was promoted to the third (or perhaps the second) most important military office in the Soviet Union, chief of the Soviet General Staff and first deputy minister of Defense. According to protocol, this position yields precedence to the commander in chief of the Warsaw Pact forces who is also first deputy minister of Defense (Marshal Andrei Grechko). In terms of practical influence, however, it would appear that only the minister of Defense ranks above the chief of the General Staff.

Zakharov's nomination to the position would indicate that he enjoyed if not the favor, then at least the tolerance of Khrushchev. As some Western military analysts have pointed out, however, he tended to be somewhat more oriented toward professional military values and somewhat less demonstrably inclined than such men as Marshals Biriuzov, Chuikov, or Grechko in a pro-Khrushchev direction. In this professionalism he rather closely resembled his superior, Marshal Malinovsky. At the end of 1962 and the beginning of 1963 rumors began to bruit the actual or impending dismissal of Marshal Zakharov and on March 28, 1963, it was announced that Marshal Sergei Biriuzov had replaced him. It would appear that Zakharov's dismissal was connected with the Cuban missile crisis of October 1962 when Premier Khrushchev was forced to retreat in the face of the American determination to rebuff his threat. It is generally believed that Khrushchev's handling of the Cuban missile crisis created dissatisfaction within the Soviet military establishment. Zakharov may well have become the spokesman for the disaffected, thus impelling Khrushchev to substitute him with a more malleable officer.

The fate of Marshal Zakharov following his dismissal cannot be compared to that of purged generals under Stalin. His articles continued to appear from time to time in the military press. His name was listed among those present at important celebrations and parades. He received, however, no positions of responsibility; his status could best be described as dignified semiretirement. His active military career appeared to be at an end. It seemed likely that at the next party congress he would lose also his membership in the Central Committee to which he was elected in 1961.

Zakharov's return to his former position as chief of the Soviet General Staff may be attributed to the fortuitous coincidence of Khrushchev's fall from leadership and Biriuzov's accidental death. His selection by Brezhnev and Kosygin would appear to represent a compromise, an attempt to unify divergent views in the military establishment. Zakharov's appointment would offend fewer military and political leaders in Russia than perhaps almost any other choice. He was neither a supporter of the extreme modernist viewpoint among the military, with its "one weapon" emphasis on ballistic missiles to the detriment of conventional forces, nor an endorser of "hard rock" traditionalism and conservatism, with its defense of the old weapons systems. A prominent American analyst of the 'Soviet military scene, Thomas W. Wolfe, suggests further that "Zakharov might strike the Brezhnev–Kosygin leadership as a figure calculated to avoid rocking the boat unduly during the shakedown cruise of the new regime. Zakharov is sixty-six—the same age as Malinovsky and six years older than Biriuzov at the time of the latter's death. The very fact that Zakharov is approaching the end of an active career thus tends to give his appointment something of a caretaker flavor."

There is little likelihood that any revolutionary changes in the structure or the strategic plans of the Soviet military establishment will occur during Zakharov's tenure. Nor is it likely that he will achieve supreme military leadership. Basic changes can, rather, be expected after his retirement when the younger generation of Soviet generals whom he taught in the Voroshilov general staff academy inherit leadership from the old men of the Soviet military, from the Malinovskys and the Zakharovs.

SELECTED BIBLIOGRAPHY

For biographical data about Zakharov, see *Deputaty verkhovnogo soveta SSSR*, Moskva, 1963, p. 163; *Ezhegodnik bol'shoi sovetskoi entsiklopedii 1960*, Moskva, 1960, p. 597; *Ezhegodnik bol'shoi sovetskoi entsiklopedii 1962*, Moskva, 1962, p. 595; *Ukrains'ka radians'ka entsiklopediia*, V, Kiev, 1962, p. 206; *Leningrad, entsiklopedicheskii slovar'*, Leningrad, 1957, pp. 520–21; *Krasnaia zvezda*, February 16, August 20, and November 29, 1964. For descriptions of Zakharov's career and activities, see Thomas W. Wolfe, *Note on the Naming of a Successor to Marshal Biriuzov*, RAND Paper, P-3025, December, 1964; *Istoriia velikoi otechestvennoi voiny sovetskogo soiuza 1941–1945*, Moskva, 1963–65, III, p. 249; *ibid.*, IV, pp. 60, 261, 379; *ibid.*, V, pp. 205, 300, 552; and the memoirs of Colonel General L. M. Sandalov, *Perezhitoe*, Moskva, 1961, pp. 18–20, 22, 24.

Georgi Konstantinovich Zhukov

by Severyn Bialer

On May 9, 1965, at festivities celebrating the twentieth anniversary of the German defeat in the Second World War, a figure long absent from Soviet public life appeared in Red Square in Moscow among the small group of marshals who command the Soviet armed forces today. Western journalists and Soviet citizens were surprised to recognize among rows of bemedaled uniforms the familiar face of the undoubtedly most popular Russian military leader of the Second World War, marshal of the Soviet Union Georgi Zhukov. This was Zhukov's first official appearance since October 1957, when he was stripped of all his power and influence by the then supreme leader of Russia, Nikita Khrushchev. On May 9, 1965, Khrushchev was nowhere to be seen in Red Square. It was only proper that the man whom he disgraced should again be in the limelight. While the career of Georgi Zhukov is typical in its dramatic zigzags of the present generation of Soviet military leaders, the heights of Zhukov's achievements and the depths of his defeats are unequaled in the history of the Soviet military establishment in the last quarter of a century.

Zhukov was born in 1896 in a small village about 100 miles southwest of Moscow, the son of a poor peasant who made his living also as the village shoemaker. While he was still a child both his parents died, and from the age of eleven Zhukov was brought up by his grandfather, a worker in a metallurgical factory in Moscow. Thus, while of rural origin, his youth was spent among workers in Moscow. At thirteen he left school and started to work for his living. He tried his hand at various menial jobs and from the ages of sixteen to eighteen was apprenticed to a tanner and furrier. It may well be that if the First World War had not broken out in 1914, this would have remained his life's occupation. As it happened, however, in 1915, shortly after Russia declared war on Germany and Austria, Zhukov voluntarily enlisted in the army. It is not known what induced him to take such a step. It may be that he was carried away by the surge of patriotic feelings that initially made acceptance of war with Germany almost universal in Russian society. It may be that he saw in enlistment a way to escape the drudgery and boredom of everyday existence. His behavior and experience as a soldier at the front during the war showed clearly that the spirit of adventure was strong in him, and that whatever his talents may have been as a furrier, the military profession was his natural calling. From that time on—that is, from the age of eighteen—his life was devoted to military endeavor.

Zhukov was inducted into a dragoon regiment that, after a short period of training, was sent to the front and fought almost uninterruptedly from 1915 to 1917 against the German and Austrian armies. He was quickly promoted to corporal and during his service in the Tsarist Army achieved the highest noncommissioned rank. He served in the same regiment as another Soviet marshal and well-known military leader of the Second World War, Rokossovsky, who was a noncommissioned officer. Zhukov was well known in his regiment, the Tenth Novgorod Dragoons of the Tenth Cavalry Division, for his bravery and initiative. His biographer in the Soviet military daily, *Krasnaia zvezda,* calls him "the favorite of the dragoons regiment." According to some sources, Zhukov was one of the most decorated soldiers, not only of his regiment but of the whole division.

Official Soviet sources stress that he was twice given the highest military decoration available to noncommissioned officers, the Cross of St. George, and twice the St. George medal for bravery. As Zhukov later recounted in a newspaper interview, some of the awards were received for capturing German officers during night reconnaissance. The Cross of St. George was a rare distinction that, it may be noted, only a few of the high-ranking Soviet military leaders who fought in the Tsarist Army during the First World War achieved.

There is no record of Zhukov's participation or interest in political activities while serving in the Tsarist Army in the period before the Russian Revolution of February 1917. His record would indicate, rather, that his preoccupations were purely military and that in the battles of the First World War he found a sufficient outlet for his energy and his talents. His prestige among the soldiers of his regiment must have been high, because after the Revolution of February 1917, when the Tsarist government was overthrown, establishing a republic in Russia, Zhukov was elected by his fellow soldiers to be chairman of the Squadron Council and a member of the Regimental Council of Deputies (Regimental Soviet). In the unstable revolutionary situation, marked by a growing alienation of officers and noncommissioned ranks, slowly but surely the soldiers' councils (soviets) took control of the military units. While active in the soviet, Zhukov probably came under the influence of Bolshevik representatives. At that time he himself was not a member of the Communist Party of the Soviet Union (CPSU).

In November 1917 the Bolshevik *coup d'état* took place under the slogan of "peace and bread." The Communist party under Lenin's leadership took over the government of Russia. Russian armies on the front rapidly disintegrated. The new Bolshevik government was almost immediately faced with military opposition from numerous Tsarist generals who organized strong armies in almost every region of the Russian empire, and it desperately needed to organize its own army and defend its rule against the increasingly powerful White armies and the danger of a German occupation. In February 1918, by decree of the Soviet government, the Red Army was officially established.

To form disciplined detachments from untrained civilians and masses of demoralized, tired, and ill-equipped soldiers of the former Tsarist armies was an extraordinarily difficult task. One of the greatest difficulties lay in creating a new officer corps that would be loyal to the new government and at the same time possess the necessary knowledge of and experience in military affairs. While a large number of former Tsarist officers, some of high rank, entered the Red Army, they could not be trusted because of their past associations. Equally important, they could not be expected to gain the confidence of the mass of Red soldiers who had an ingrained mistrust for their former superiors. New commanders of the Red Army had to be found among the lower ranks, especially among the noncommissioned officers of the old army. Zhukov was among those selected. He participated in the organization of the Red Army from October 1918. In the ranks of the Red Cavalry he fought for over two years in the bloody Civil War between the Red Army and the opponents of the Soviet regime.

The cavalry detachment in which Zhukov served as platoon, and later squadron, commander was a part of the Second Cavalry Brigade of the famous First Cavalry Army, the shock force of the Soviet republic. The commander of his brigade was the future marshal and defense minister, Timoshenko, who for the next twenty-three years played an important part in Zhukov's military career. Under Timoshenko, Zhukov fought against the Don Cossacks, and against the armies of the White general, Denikin, in southern Russia and at Tsarityn (later Stalingrad). After recovering from a wound, he participated during the summer of 1920 in the war against Poland in which, following initial successes, the Soviet troops that had come almost within sight of the Polish capital, Warsaw, were forced to fall back to the Russian border. The last Civil War campaign in which Zhukov participated with the Second Cavalry was the operation against General Wrangel in the fall of 1920.

To his First World War crosses and medals Zhukov added, during the Civil War, the highest military decoration of the new Soviet Army, the Order of the Red Banner, numerous citations in orders of the day, a gold watch with a laudatory inscription from the Defense Council of the Soviet republic, and an engraved saber that he received from the commander of his army group after a successful cavalry attack. During the Civil War, in 1919, Zhukov, already a Red officer, entered the Communist party.

When the Civil War ended, the bulk of the Red Army was demobilized, and large numbers of officers were directed back to civilian occupations. Zhukov, however, chose a professional military career. He started the arduous climb as a brave, decorated, intelligent but unsophisticated, wartime squadron commander with no political connections of any importance and no background of underground Bolshevik activity—one of many thousands of young officers in the new army, in a period during which previous bravery and merits would count for little, while formal military schooling, organizational talent, and unquestionable acceptance of military rules and discipline would count more and more.

Zhukov continued his peacetime service in the same unit he fought in during the Civil War and served under the same commander. As an officer of the Fourth Cavalry Division (part of Timoshenko's Third Cavalry Corps) he was stationed until 1928 in the Byelorussian Military District on the western borders of the USSR. In 1928 he was sent to the Frunze military academy in Moscow—the school for higher-grade commanding staff —from which he graduated in 1931.[1] With his experience and talent now

[1] It is noteworthy that only a few of the past and present field marshals of the Soviet Army did not attend the Frunze academy.

reinforced by basic military knowledge, the road to a command career was open.

Zhukov returned to the Byelorussian Military District as an assistant to a regimental commander in the Sixth Cavalry Division (a part of Timoshenko's Third Cavalry Corps), and by 1932 he took over a regiment in this same division. In two years he rose to division commander in the same corps, having the satisfaction of commanding the same Fourth Cavalry in which he started as a squadron commander. In 1936 he assumed the former position of Timoshenko himself (who was promoted to head of a military district), the command of the Third Cavalry Corps. Zhukov's advancement in the early 1930's was exceptionally rapid according to standards of the Soviet military prepurge period. While having a powerful supporter in Timoshenko was probably of no little importance, Zhukov's ability, determination, and especially his enthusiasm for the new, modern types of mobile warfare being introduced into the Soviet Army, played a decisive role. Zhukov was one of the first in the Red Army to experiment with armored forces, especially with combined, highly mobile cavalry-tank units. His attempts to work out firm operating procedures and a stable method of command in the new mobile units brought him recognition in military circles. His troops were singled out as a model unit and Zhukov himself was praised in the pages of the military newspapers.

The year 1937—the darkest hour in the history of the Soviet military establishment—was approaching. In the ensuing two years, according to reliable estimates, about 30,000 senior- and medium-grade officers (forty per cent of their total) were either executed, imprisoned, or sent to concentration camps. As far as can be ascertained, about ninety per cent of the generals and eighty per cent of the colonels disappeared. Zhukov was not touched throughout the purge. His immunity is best explained by his close relation to the former commanding officers of the First Cavalry Army, his Civil War unit, among whom Timoshenko was a major power, and including the minister of Defense, Marshal Voroshilov. This was the only group that Stalin protected from the onslaught of accusations and liquidation. In the bewildered and disorganized Red Army younger and, frequently, immature officers were hastily promoted to fill vacancies. Under these conditions Zhukov's talent was to stand out in the years to come.

In 1937 Zhukov was appointed deputy commander of cavalry of the Byelorussian Military District. His activities in 1938 and early 1939 are somewhat unclear. According to some reports, he was sent to China with a Soviet military mission and observed at firsthand Japanese military methods in the conduct of war. The later 1930's saw a rapid and dangerous intensification of tensions in the Far East between Japan and Russia. Clashes on the Russo-Chinese borders and especially in the Mongolian People's Republic (a Soviet protectorate) between Japanese and Red Army troops multiplied. In 1938 a fierce battle occurred in Mongolian territory near Lake Khasan. In July 1939 a Japanese army of 40,000 (later increased to 75,000) supported by tanks and airplanes crossed the river Khalkhin-Gol, occupied a part of Mongolian territory, and threatened to encircle the defending Soviet-Mongolian troops. Soviet counteroffensives were unsuccessful and showed a none too competent command and lack of coordination. Zhukov was ordered to take over the Far East First Army Group, defeat the Japanese, and restore the Mongolian border. On August 20, 1939, he started an all-out offensive against the Japanese Sixth Army, a brilliant but costly operation that, in eleven days of fighting, destroyed some of the Japanese forces and pushed the rest clearly beyond Mongolian borders. It was the first action in which Zhukov directed a large, combined operational unit. His forces included many infantry and cavalry divisions, about 500 tanks, and 500 aircraft.

Zhukov passed the test of Khalkhin-Gol with flying colors, and the name of the rising new leader became known to the country. On August 29, 1939, the Presidium of the Supreme Soviet of the USSR awarded him the highest Soviet military decoration, the Golden Star and the title Hero of the Soviet Union. It was the first of four Golden Stars he was to receive.

From the summer of 1939 Zhukov was firmly established in the higher ranks of the Soviet military hierarchy. After his Far Eastern success he was appointed deputy, and shortly afterward head, of Kiev Military District, and he commanded the troops of his district in June 1940 in the occupation of the Romanian territory of Bessarabia and Bukovina. This same month, when the ranks of general and admiral were restored in the Soviet Army, he was promoted to general of the army, the highest-ranking general in the Soviet military hierarchy and only one step removed from marshal.

February 1941 marked a decisive advancement in Zhukov's military career. Only recently have the details of this event been made public. That month Stalin ordered a conference of top Soviet military leaders in the Kremlin to review the state of preparedness of Soviet armed forces in the increasingly unstable international situation. Special stress was placed on the strategy and tactics of Soviet military planning in the light of the German victories in the war in the West. War games were played on the highest staff level. Demonstrations of new weapons and new tactics were given on nearby proving grounds and the chief of the General Staff, General Meretskov, was assigned to report to the Politburo and to Stalin personally about the results and implications of this important top military conference. For reasons unknown, Stalin allegedly ordered the report twenty-four hours earlier than planned. The results could have been expected. Meretskov's performance was less than brilliant. According to military participants at this meeting, he stammered; his conclusions were contradictory and his proposals far from original. He was dismissed on the spot by Stalin and in twenty-four hours it was announced that Georgi

Zhukov, the brilliant commander of the Far East Special Army, had been appointed in his place. Thus at forty-four, Zhukov had achieved the second highest position in the Soviet military establishment and was undoubtedly by far the youngest chief of staff of any modern army in the world at that time. The minister of Defense of the USSR, under whom he was to serve, was none other than his patron, Timoshenko, now a marshal of the Soviet Union, who had taken over this job from Voroshilov after the disastrous conduct of the Soviet-Finnish war in 1940. To cap Zhukov's ascent, on February 20, 1941, at the Eighteenth Congress of the CPSU he was elected to alternate membership in the party's Central Committee.

Not much is known about Zhukov's activities from February 1941 to the outbreak of the Nazi-Soviet war. Official Soviet historians describe this period as one of feverish activity on the part of Soviet authorities to eradicate the destructive influence of the "great purges" on the Soviet military machine. New modern arms were being introduced into fighting units at a stepped-up rate, though at the outbreak of hostilities with Nazi Germany the best Soviet weapons—such as the T-34 tank, the new YAK bomber and Ilyushin fighter, the Tokarev antitank gun, and the Shaposhnikov tommy gun—were still available only in small quantities. Zhukov can hardly be blamed for the situation. It seems that both from his own experience in the Far East and especially from a close reading of the experiences of the blitzkrieg in the West, he was strongly impressed by the German departure from positional warfare methods, and he supported the re-education of the Soviet Army in the spirit of maneuver, flanking attack, and massive deployment of armor. He probably had a hand in the reorganization of Soviet armored troops into large units (corps, armies) in place of the decentralization during the 1938–41 period. But whatever attempt he made to improve the quality of the Soviet armed forces in this short period was doomed to failure. Aside from the unfavorable armament conditions, the major reason for the Soviet Army's unpreparedness to conduct modern warfare was the quality of the Soviet officer corps. Most of the Soviet commanders on the regimental level had no more formal military training than was demanded of a second lieutenant. Rarely was a divisional commander a graduate of a military academy, and even commanders with the rank of general on the highest operational level, such as military district commanders, had only a few years earlier been in command of tactical units, with neither the formal education nor the necessary peacetime (not to mention wartime) experience to perform their duties adequately. The production of necessary modern arms and the requisite education and experience that transformed the Soviet Army into one of the strongest fighting forces in the world were achieved under the adverse conditions of actual combat against overwhelmingly superior German forces.

There can be no doubt that of all the Soviet commanders who became known to the Soviet population and the world as a result of victories during the Second World War, Zhukov is the most famous, and, it seems, deservedly so. From the start of the war, when as chief of the General Staff he was responsible for the over-all war plans of the Soviet Union, to the end of the war in Europe when he commanded the troops that took Berlin, Zhukov's name is associated with all the major battles and campaigns of the German-Soviet fighting. Throughout the war he intermittently occupied command positions in the Supreme Command Headquarters in Moscow, from which he devised campaign plans and commanded the major Army Groups in crucial battles. In addition, he was a representative of the Soviet high command and a personal emissary of Stalin, with enormous power of decision-making, at various times, at almost all sectors of the Nazi-Soviet Front. Thus he not only personally commanded the Soviet defense of Moscow and the Soviet attack on Berlin, but as a delegate from Moscow he participated with decisive influence in the organization of the defense of Leningrad and in the planning and execution of the biggest tank battle of the Second World War, Kursk-Orel. He also organized the defense of the Caucasus in 1942 and the offensives of 1944.

The period from June to November 1941 brought nothing but German defeat of the Soviet forces. In tremendous sweep the experienced German armies occupied the whole of the Ukraine and Byelorussia, reached the suburbs of Leningrad and the outskirts of Moscow, captured millions of prisoners, and by November 1941 were preparing for what they considered the final push of the war, the capture of the capital city of the Soviet Union, Moscow. By early September the threat to Moscow was not yet an immediate danger. In the second largest city of the Soviet Union—the birthplace of the Revolution, Leningrad—the situation became critical. Because Voroshilov and the party secretary Andrei Zhdanov were unable to stabilize the front and organize the inner perimeter of defense, Leningrad was in danger of being taken by the Germans. On September 11, 1941, Zhukov took over the command of the Leningrad Front and, as a Western writer has observed, ". . . not until General Zhukov was rushed to Leningrad . . . and reorganized the troops on the spot did the defense of Leningrad begin in real earnest." In another place the same author adds: "Zhukov had literally saved Leningrad in the nick of time by taking over from Voroshilov when all seemed lost."

On October 8, 1941, Zhukov was recalled to Moscow. The position of the capital was becoming acutely dangerous. Two days later Zhukov assumed command of the Western Front (Army Group), which unified all troops defending Moscow from the West. On October 19 the State Defense Committee, headed by Stalin, declared a state of siege and put Zhukov in charge of the entire defense operation.

The defense of Moscow became, from a purely military as well as political and symbolical point of view, the decisive battle of the Nazi-

Soviet war in 1941. There was a fear among Russian leaders that the loss of Moscow might be a signal for the disintegration of their authority over the Soviet population. It should be added that the capture of Moscow by the Germans could also have led to a change in the Japanese attitude toward its nonaggression pact with the Soviet Union.

Under these conditions, placing Zhukov in the supreme command of all Soviet armies defending Moscow must be considered a sign of Stalin's highest confidence in Zhukov's patriotism and talent as a military leader. Zhukov designed and executed the plan to defend Moscow, the success of which exceeded all expectations of military commentators of that period. The crux of his plan was that the Moscow defense could not be limited simply to halting the German troops—in other words, to positional warfare. While the holding operation was of basic importance in the first stage of the battle, and had as its major goal the exhaustion of the attacking German armies and the dissipation of their reserves, the defense was to be accomplished by a counteroffensive which, using the favorite German method of a pincer movement, was to push the Germans back, and of more importance, destroy their manpower and materiel. The key to the plan's success was the strong will and steady nerve needed to keep the newly arrived divisions from Siberia in reserve, wait for the right moment to counterattack, and not send them piecemeal into battle to hold the German advances. When the time came, when exhausting, uninterrupted battle and the barbarous Russian winter conditions had weakened the German push forward, Zhukov started the counteroffensive. In weeks of continuous, brutal fighting, the Germans were pushed back from seventy to 170 miles, leaving behind tens of thousands of dead and war materiel sufficient to arm numerous divisions. The German threat to Moscow from the western approaches had disappeared; the myth of the invincibility of the German Army in ground fighting was damaged; and the Soviet Army had won its first major battle of the Second World War. And nobody contributed more to this success than Zhukov.

In the defense of Moscow Zhukov had under his command about forty per cent of all Red Army troops engaged along the gigantic front from the Baltic to the Black Sea. Among the generals directly subordinate to him were the future leading figures in the Soviet military establishment, such as Konev, Rokossovsky, Sokolovsky, Govorov, Boldin, Golikov, and Lelyushenko. Zhukov, however, became *the* leading figure.

From various accounts, both Soviet and Western, one can surmise that Zhukov's position with Stalin was exceptional, given Soviet conditions. It was never to be repeated, and Zhukov had to pay the price for it later in his career. It appears that the reins of military command in the period of the battle of Moscow rested not in Stalin's hands but in Zhukov's, that Zhukov's opinions and decisions were decisive, and that Stalin may have relegated to him his supreme power in regard to military affairs for this short period. Of great interest is the account by Colonel General Belov, the commander of the Second Guards Cavalry Corps who participated actively in the battle of Moscow. In his recently published memoirs, Belov describes an audience with Stalin, to which he was invited by Zhukov. According to General Belov, Zhukov behaved in Stalin's study as if he were the supreme commander and Stalin his subordinate. He frequently interrupted Stalin's talk, questioned some of his conclusions, and generally made the impression of being the man in charge, without any sign of opposition to such behavior from Stalin. Belov recounts his astonishment at this unexpected situation.

The Soviet high command hoped that the Red Army's early winter counteroffensive would be the turning point in the war with Germany. It planned to continue the attack on German positions throughout the winter and spring. Its estimates of the relation of forces were faulty, however, and by trying to push the offensive in too many directions it scattered its own forces and achieved only very limited, local successes. In that period, from February 1, 1942, Zhukov was in charge of the so-called Western Fronts Theater (*Zapadnoye Napravlenye*), which encompassed four Fronts (Army Groups)—Western (the command of which he simultaneously held), Ukrainian, Northwestern, and Bryansk. The success of the early Moscow counteroffensive was not repeated in the remainder of the winter of 1942. .

In the late spring and early summer of 1942 the regrouped German armies began anew their rapid advance into Soviet territory, this time concentrating on the southern sector. Zhukov at this time was back in the Soviet General Staff in Moscow. In August Stalin's closest military assistant, the former Tsarist colonel and marshal of the Soviet Union, Shaposhnikov, retired due to grave illness. Zhukov officially took over the number-two spot in the Soviet military chain of command. He was appointed first deputy commander in chief of all Soviet armed forces, that is to say, first deputy of Stalin himself.

Again, as in October 1941, a grave danger hung over the Soviet Union. The Germans had reached the river Volga at Stalingrad and stood on the threshold of the rich Caucasus oil fields. Zhukov was assigned as Supreme Command representative to the Stalingrad Theater. He was in charge of coordinating the defensive actions of the Army Groups defending this city and of preparing the counteroffensive plans, which were not only to halt the German advance but to destroy the German Army Group in Stalingrad led by Field Marshal Paulus. While his role in the Stalingrad victory, which marked the turning point of the Nazi-Soviet war, was probably not so direct and all-embracing as the one which he played in the battle of Moscow, Zhukov was apparently more responsible for the brilliant design of the battle and its victorious conclusion than any other single military leader in Russia. The main encounter of the war in 1942, like the main encounter of 1941, was therefore immediately associated with Zhukov. In January 1943, right after the completion of the Stalingrad battle, Zhukov received the highest military rank, marshal of the Soviet Union. It seemed that there was hardly any way for him to ascend further.

In 1943 the initiative passed decisively into Soviet hands. The expulsion of the German invaders from Soviet territory began. In the summer of 1943 Zhukov planned and directed, as the delegate of the supreme commander in chief, the first Soviet summer offensive of the Nazi-Soviet war. Knowing that the Germans planned an all-out attack, chiefly by armored forces, in the area between the cities of Kursk and Orel in central Russia, Zhukov designed imaginative plans to concentrate great reserves of armor and infantry in this area, to wait until the German offensive was well under way and the enemy troops weakened by heavy resistance, and then to counterattack with fresh divisions. The plan succeeded completely. The Kursk-Orel battle of 1943 was the greatest engagement of armor in the history of modern warfare, with some 6,000 tanks and 4,000 aircraft involved. In the opinion of many military analysts, it was also one of the best planned and executed battles of the Second World War. Germany was unable to replenish its devitalizing losses of equipment, and experienced personnel suffered in this battle. In Kursk and Orel Hitler lost his last chance of turning the tide.

From December 1943 to February 1944 Marshal Zhukov assumed responsibility for the campaign in the Ukraine designed to push the southern German armies out of Soviet territory. He became the supreme commander in chief's coordinator, and supervisor of the First and Second Ukrainian Fronts, commanded by Generals Vatutin and Konev, respectively. In the winter of 1944 the two Fronts performed an encircling operation, known as the Korsun-Shevchenkovo battle, which in many respects—though on a smaller scale—resembled the Stalingrad operation. A German force of close to 75,000 was trapped and by February 18, 1944, all its men were either killed or captured.

On March 1, 1944, Zhukov took over direct command of the First Ukrainian Front, Vatutin having been fatally wounded by Ukrainian nationalists. In the spring offensive Zhukov's troops reached the western Ukrainian territory. By May, however, Zhukov had already left the Ukrainian sector of the Front. Together with Marshal Vasilevsky he was put in charge of the largest operation of 1944—the battle for Byelorussia —in which four Soviet Army Groups, 166 divisions in all, participated. Zhukov coordinated the action of two Army Groups—the First and Second Byelorussian Fronts—which were on the line of the main attack. In an almost uninterrupted swoop, the Byelorussian Army Groups completely cleared Soviet territory, crossed into Poland, and finally, by September 1944, stopped on the Vistula River short of the Polish capital of Warsaw. On July 29 Marshal Zhukov was decorated with his second Golden Star and awarded the title Twice Hero of the Soviet Union.

Zhukov returned briefly to Moscow to participate in completing the plans for the final drive into Germany. In the winter of 1945 he took over command of the First Byelorussian Front, which was designated as the main force of the Soviet push toward the German capital. On January 14, 1945, Zhukov's front, with Konev's Army Group to the south and Rokossovsky's to the north, crossed into German territory and reached the last natural barrier before Berlin—the river Oder. From here, at 4 A.M. on April 16, Zhukov's armies, with an unprecedented concentration of 4,000 tanks, 5,000 planes, and 22,000 guns on a fifty-mile-wide front, were launched on Berlin. On May 2 the German capital surrendered to Zhukov's and Konev's troops. By the end of this battle Zhukov had received his third Golden Star and the title Thrice Hero of the Soviet Union—an honor shared by no Soviet marshal before or since. It was fitting that Marshal Zhukov, on May 8, 1945 in Berlin, accepted from Field Marshal Keitel in the name of the Soviet Union, the unconditional German capitulation.

Zhukov's first peacetime appointment reflected his great prestige and his position as the foremost professional military leader of the Soviet Union. He took over the administration of the Soviet-occupied part of the defeated Germany and became the Soviet chief representative in the Four Power Control Council. In Germany he met the top military leaders of the Western Alliance. He became acquainted with General Eisenhower, then commander of the American occupation forces in Germany, who later was to call him a "splendid military leader." The stocky marshal, with close-cropped gray hair and brown eyes, a man whom General Walter Bedell Smith, former United States Ambassador to USSR, called "a man with dignity and character," became to the West the symbol of the Soviet military victory over Germany. Despite the fact that he was known to be a strict disciplinarian, his popularity among Soviet troops—if not among some of his lesser, and therefore envious, colleagues among the top Soviet brass—was unequaled.

However, Zhukov was able to revel in the glory of his Second World War achievements for only a very short period. In January 1946 he was replaced as the supreme commander in East Germany by General Sokolovsky and recalled to Russia. His first appointment back home could still conceivably be regarded as appropriate to his stature, applying the minimal standards: commander in chief of the Soviet Ground Forces, with offices in the Ministry of Defense in Moscow. Only months later, however, when the news of his replacement in Germany quieted down and the image of the war hero became somewhat less sharp in the popular mind, Zhukov lost his post and was forced to leave Moscow. He was appointed to the command, first of the Odessa Military District, and then the Ural Military District. The last was in fact an exile to the least important, most provincial Soviet military area command usually reserved for young generals on their way up or for superannuated commanders on their way to retirement. For all practical purposes, despite his high rank, great popularity, and professional prestige, Zhukov disappeared not only from public, but also from military, life. While his name still appeared in Soviet accounts of the Second World War, it was mentioned less and less frequently and his merits were described in terms not unlike those applied to a few dozen other military commanders. The unlimited credit for the planning and the operational direction of every major battle fought by Soviet armies in the Second World War was assigned to one man only: Stalin.

Zhukov's career seemed to have reached its end. Yet his greatest peacetime victory (and defeat) was still to come. As in the case of so many careers in recent Soviet history, it was brought about by Stalin's death.

While Zhukov's fate in the post-Stalin period is a matter of public record, his whereabouts and activities in the months immediately preceding the dictator's demise are clouded by an air of mystery. There are no indications that as of October 1952, when the Nineteenth Congress of the Communist Party of the Soviet Union (CPSU) convened, anything had changed in his situation. Although numerous military commanders, some his wartime subordinates, were elected to full membership in the party's Central Committee, Zhukov was named only an alternate member. A suspicion exists, however, that in the period between the Nineteenth Congress and Stalin's death in March 1953, Stalin had embarked upon a reorganization of the Soviet high command and a revision of Soviet strategic thinking, and that Zhukov figured prominently in both. Important signs of a reshuffling in the Soviet high command were noted. Marshal Sokolovsky, a highly professional military leader, was mentioned in January 1953 as the new chief of the Soviet General Staff, replacing General Shtemenko, who was better known for his political skills than his professional abilities. What Zhukov's role was in the military turmoil of that period is unknown, and aside from speculations and rumors no new evidence has come to light in the last decade to clarify matters. Zhukov's return to the Moscow limelight after Stalin's death, however, was almost immediate.

In March 1953, in the ranks of the Soviet government constituted three days after Stalin's death, Zhukov was listed as second-in-command of the Soviet armed forces, and the highest-ranking military professional in the Soviet military establishment. He had been brought from virtual exile to be first deputy to the minister of Defense, Nikolai Bulganin—a political marshal who had served his entire career in the party and government administration. Zhukov's appointment was symbolic both of the desire of the post-Stalin leaders to placate and court the Soviet military establishment and of the Soviet marshals' growing influence in the turmoil that followed Stalin's death (and was to end for a while with Khrushchev's assumption of full control in June 1957). Indeed, one can hardly think of anything more suited to symbolize those trends than the re-emergence of the exiled war hero Zhukov in Moscow.

In July 1953 after the arrest, with the army's help, of the secret police chief Beria, Zhukov was coopted to full membership in the Central Committee of the Communist party. Less than two years later, in February 1955, when Bulganin was elevated to the chairmanship of the Soviet Council of Ministers in place of the disgraced Georgi Malenkov, Zhukov's career reached its high point. He took over the top post in the Ministry of Defense, which effectively controls all branches of the Soviet military forces.

His authority in the Soviet military establishment unchallenged, Zhukov began to play an important role in the general political life of the Soviet Union. He attended, with Khrushchev and Bulganin, the first general summit meeting with President Eisenhower in July 1955. His support was eagerly sought by contending factions of the ruling Communist party. At the Twentieth Congress of the CPSU in February 1956, where the party's first secretary, Khrushchev, made his famous "secret speech" against Stalin, Zhukov was elected not only to full membership in the Central Committee, but to alternate membership in the uppermost council of Soviet power—the party's Presidium. This same year, on his sixtieth birthday, he became the first and only man in Soviet history to wear four Golden Stars and be awarded the title Four Times Hero of the Soviet Union.

In the summer of 1957 Zhukov became clearly one of the most powerful men in the Soviet government. The struggle between Khrushchev and his opponents in the party leadership had reached its climax in a series of meetings in June of that year. For the first time not squabbling with each other, Khrushchev's enemies were able to bring over to their side some of his former supporters (for instance, Bulganin) and to achieve an anti-Khrushchev majority in the ruling Presidium. Only by appealing to the 175-member Central Committee did Khrushchev manage to survive and to defeat decisively his adversaries. Zhukov's support in attacking, with the whole authority of the armed forces behind him, the leaders of the opposition and, according to some reports, in using military transport to bring the Central Committee members quickly to Moscow to Khrushchev's rescue was perhaps the single most important element in the June crisis. An indication that this interpretation is correct came at the same plenary session of the Central Committee in June, when Zhukov attained something that no professional soldier before or after has achieved in the Soviet Union. He was elected a full, voting member of the party's Presidium.

The rest of Zhukov's career is short and well known. During his absence from Moscow on an official visit to Yugoslavia and Albania only a few months later, he was dismissed from his military posts and removed from the party Presidium and even from the Central Committee. On October 26, 1957, the second and, it seemed, final exile of Zhukov began. The official reasons for his disgrace were given as "Bonapartist tendencies" (i.e., dictatorial aspirations) and his attempt to exclude the armed forces from party control. The party daily, *Pravda,* carried a statement allegedly made by Zhukov at the party meeting where his errors were discussed, in which he expressed his agreement with the accusations made against him. While Zhukov certainly was not enthusiastic, to say the least, about the party's intrusion in military affairs, the chief reason for his dismissal in 1957 was, as in 1946, his great popularity among the people and authority among the military—which created a potential danger to the political leadership.

In the whole period from the autumn of 1957 until the ouster of Zhukov's detractor, Khrushchev, in the autumn of 1964, very little good was said about Zhukov in the numerous war memoirs and histories of the Nazi-Soviet war published in the Soviet Union. He disappeared completely from public life and was seen only on a few occasions, e.g., in a theater, at an art exhibition, etc.

Today the official treatment of the world-famous marshal is more balanced than it was under Khrushchev. As mentioned before, he appeared at the parade celebrating the twentieth anniversary of VE day. Some articles noting, even favorably, his wartime exploits have appeared in print. He himself wrote in June 1965, in a military journal, an account of the battle of Berlin in which he sharply questioned the views expressed by the present deputy minister of Defense, Marshal V. I. Chuikov. Perhaps the time is not far distant when the Russian leaders will learn to give due respect and gratitude to their wartime military leaders even when they are afraid of their political influence and do not want to grant them peacetime power.[1]

SELECTED BIBLIOGRAPHY

For biographical data about Zhukov, see the following: *Komsomolskaia pravda,* February 1, 1946; *Krasnaia zvezda,* January 24, 1946; *Pravda,* October 20, 1941; *Sovetskaia istoricheskaia entsiklopediia,* IV, Moskva, 1963, p. 402; *Bol'shaia sovetskaia entsiklopediia,* vypusk 2, XVI, Moskva, 1950, p. 223; John Erickson, *The Soviet High Command 1918–1941,* London, 1962, pp. 847–48; *Entsiklopedicheskii slovar',* I, Moskva, 1953, p. 618. For descriptions of Zhukov's career and activities, see Alexander Werth, *Russia at War,* New York, 1964, pp. 897–901 and *U.S. News and World Report,* March 4, 1955. Also see the following works of memoirs: Marshal G. K. Zhukov, "Na berlinskom napravlenii," *Voenno-istoricheskii zhurnal,* No. 6, Moskva, June

---

[1] In 1966, Zhukov was awarded the Order of Lenin, the country's highest award, in recognition of "services to the armed forces."

1965, pp. 12–23; Marshal A. I. Eremenko, *V nachale voiny,* Moskva, 1965; Marshal A. I. Eremenko, *Na zapadnom napravlenii,* Moskva, 1959; P. Rustanov, "Marshal Zhukov," *The Russian Review* (July 1956), 186–95, and (April 1956), 122–29; General P. A. Belov, *Za nami Moskva,* Moskva, 1963, pp. 40–44; General I. V. Boldin, *Stranitsy zhizni,* Moskva, 1961; Marshal A. I. Eremenko, *Stalingrad,* Moskva, 1961, pp. 163, 209–10, 449; Marshal of Artillery V. I. Kazakov, *Na perelome,* Moskva, 1962, pp. 33, 41–43; and *Pravda,* November 4, 1957.

Andrei Andreevich Gromyko

by Severyn Bialer

Of the many confrontations between the United States and the Soviet Union in the cold war, probably none was more serious than the Cuban missile crisis of 1962. And in the early stages of this crisis no incident conveyed more strongly the sense of drama than the meeting on Thursday afternoon, October 18, between the president of the United States, John F. Kennedy, and the foreign minister of the USSR, Andrei Gromyko, who was at the time attending a session of the United Nations. Without disclosing the evidence that he possessed, President Kennedy asked the Soviet foreign minister repeatedly if the Soviet Union had placed intermediate-range ballistic missiles on Cuban soil, and received repeated denials. It is reported that those denials convinced President Kennedy of the necessity to act quickly, not by means of the usual diplomatic channels, but through an open and public confrontation with Soviet power. It is not known if Gromyko, foreign minister of the USSR from 1957, uttered his denial in good faith, not having been informed by Premier Khrushchev of what was happening in Cuba, or whether having full knowledge of the facts, he was simply following instructions. In either case, his credibility as a spokesman for the Soviet Union was seriously damaged, and the fact that as Soviet foreign minister—nominally the chief architect of Soviet foreign policy—he is a technician, implementor, and adviser rather than a decision-maker, was strongly underscored.

In modern nations, the diplomatic service traditionally has highly selective standards of recruitment, employing a larger share of individuals of patrician upbringing, exclusive education, etc., than do almost all other branches of government. Gromyko's background, however, does not conform to this norm at all. He was born in 1909 in the village of Starye Gromyki (Old Gromyki) in the Vetko district of Gomel Province in Byelorussia, which is on the northwest border of the USSR and is the fourth largest republic by population in the Soviet Union. His father was a peasant, more well-to-do, according to some sources, than the average peasant in the region. Most of the population in his area were Byelorussians. There was, however, a strong Russian minority to which the Gromykos belonged. The region itself was one of the more backward western areas of the Tsarist empire (and later of the Soviet Union), predominantly agricultural and provincial to the extreme. Until the age of seventeen Gromyko lived with his parents on the farm, helped with farm chores, and attended the local primary school.

In 1926, after graduating from primary school, Gromyko left the farm and was admitted to a professional secondary technical school in the city of Gomel, the province of his birth. At that time Gomel was a city of around 50,000 people, lacking any big industry—a typical administrative center of a typical, backward, rural area. At the age of twenty Gromyko entered an agricultural vocational high school (*tekhnikum*) in Borisov, also in Byelorussia, a town northeast of Minsk on the road to Smolensk. After graduating from the *tekhnikum,* he took higher agricultural courses in the same town until 1932. The courses were designed to accelerate the flow of trained agronomists into the newly collectivized Soviet agriculture and were meant as a substitute for prolonged higher education, providing only a superficial training.

Normally the road led from such courses to employment on state or collective farms, machine tractor stations, or at best, in the lower administrative organs of agricultural management. But this was not the case with Gromyko. Immediately after graduating, the first big break in his career occurred; he was admitted to the Agricultural Institute in Minsk the capital of Byelorussia. Studying agricultural economics at the institute from 1932 until 1936, he was admitted to graduate studies—the so-called *aspirantura,* that is, candidacy for a higher degree. His next great break came in 1936 when he moved to Moscow. He was admitted to the Moscow Research Institute for Agricultural Economics, where he continued to work on his thesis and received the degree in agricultural economics of candidate of Economic Science, roughly equivalent to a Western Ph.D. Later he was to receive the highest Soviet degree, doctor of Economic Science, which has no Western equivalent.

After concluding his graduate studies, Gromyko was employed in Moscow as a senior research associate at the Soviet Academy of Sciences' Institute of Economics, and as responsible secretary of the editorial board of the leading Soviet economics journal, *Problems of Economics.* It seemed that he had embarked upon a research career and that his prospects for success in this field were bright indeed. The Institute of Economics was one of the most prestigious research establishments in the Soviet Union; to be a senior research associate there before the age of thirty held high promise for the future. It would be wrong, however, to regard the institute as a staid academic institution removed from the political turmoil which the country was then experiencing. Soviet economic research at that period was anything but dispassionate theoretical investigation. In part it involved an inquiry into the best solutions to problems broached by the party and government leaders; in part it was simply propagandistic discourse justifying the party's socioeconomic policies and praising the results; in part it involved the popularization of Marxist economic theory. In any case, Soviet economic research in the 1930's was a highly politicized discipline, both in its substance and in the involvement of its practitioners.

Nothing is known about Gromyko's political activities at this period of his life. Nor do official biographies provide information about his political involvements while in Byelorussia. It is not known, for example, whether he was active in the Komsomol (Young Communist League). The only information available is that he became a member of the Communist Party of the Soviet Union (CPSU) in 1931, when he was only twenty-two, while attending the higher agricultural courses in Borisov.

In 1939 it became evident, however, that the party authorities had the highest regard for Gromyko's political loyalty, for they vested in him the greatest trust of which the Soviet government is capable—they allowed him to serve abroad. At the age of thirty, with his recruitment into the foreign service, the present career of Andrei Gromyko began. His sudden switch from research in agricultural economics into the foreign service, without any preparation in languages or any other discipline related to diplomacy, extraordinary as it seems, was typical at that time in the Soviet Union. In the "great purges" of the late 1930's, Soviet foreign-service personnel was thoroughly decimated, being, in the prevailing paranoiac atmosphere of spy-hunting, especially suspect due to their everyday contact with foreigners. Having an opportunity to participate in conspiracies instigated from abroad, they were suspected of such participation. Thousands of the lowest, intermediate, and highest positions, both in the Commissariat of Foreign Affairs and in the embassies and delegations abroad, became vacant. The normal channels of recruitment from institutes training foreign-service personnel were insufficient, not the least important reason being the fact that these institutes were also exposed to the purges. Hundreds of people were recruited, therefore, from other areas (especially the social sciences and secret police). The authorities were above all interested in their political loyalty, and hoped that recruits would acquire the necessary knowledge on the job.

From the standpoint of the time he entered the diplomatic service, Gromyko is typical of the majority of present Soviet high-ranking, foreign-service personnel. Aside from a small group of party and government officials whom Khrushchev recruited after Stalin's death, and who had previously achieved recognition in other Soviet hierarchies, the bulk of Soviet officials who today occupy ambassadorial posts started their foreign-service careers in the years between 1938 and 1940, and came directly from universities or from junior positions in the Soviet bureaucracy.

When Gromyko set forth on his present career he had in all probability never exchanged a single word with a foreigner. It is also doubtful whether he had any prior connections in high places. He was an agricultural economist with a bright future in his own profession, but indistinguishable from thousands of others with similar provincial backgrounds. He must, therefore, have worked very hard and either shown above-average ability or acquired a powerful patron in his new place of employment (or both), because at the end of 1939, after a short interval in Moscow as deputy chief, then chief, of the Department for American Countries of the Commissariat, he was assigned to one of the major Soviet embassies abroad—that in the United States. He served there as a counselor until 1943.

When America and Russia became allies in the struggle against Nazi Germany, Stalin appointed one of the best-known Soviet diplomats, Maxim Litvinov, as ambassador to Washington. Litvinov, a Jew, was previously the Soviet commissar for Foreign Affairs from 1930 to 1939, when, in the cause of amity with the Nazis, he was dropped from his post. Litvinov's name was associated with the anti-Fascist course in Soviet foreign policy in the mid-1930's and his appointment to Washington was symbolic of the change in Soviet foreign alliance from the Nazis to the Western democracies. In the first difficult years of the war, Stalin considered Litvinov the proper man to evoke American good will toward Russia, but as the Soviet leadership regained its confidence in its ability to defeat the Germans, its position hardened, and its interest in international politics came to be increasingly directed toward the arrangements of the postwar world and toward securing the spoils of victory. In 1943 Litvinov was recalled to Moscow and replaced by Gromyko, his former embassy counselor. Gromyko also became the Soviet representative accredited to Cuba. His promotion was remarkable, taking his past experience (or inexperience) into consideration, and yet typical of Stalin's personnel policies in the period after the "great purges." It showed clearly that Gromyko was a man to watch in the Soviet foreign service.

Undoubtedly the embassy in Washington, at the time of Gromyko's appointment, was the most important diplomatic post in the Soviet foreign service. As the major ally of Russia in the war with the Axis powers, as the arsenal, main supplier, and creditor of all the nations fighting the Nazis, the United States received more attention from Soviet foreign policy-makers than any other Soviet wartime allies. The ambassadorship in wartime Washington involved extensive administrative functions related to the activities in America of numerous high-ranking Soviet delegations and missions engaged in coordinating the Soviet-American war effort, facilitating American help to Russia and, incidentally, laying the groundwork for future espionage activities; but it involved much more. In Stalin's strategy for dealing with his Western wartime allies, the United States was assigned the role of counterweight to England, with its suspiciousness about Soviet postwar intentions, and was seen as the nation which could swing the Western allies to a speedier commitment of massive ground forces in the struggle with Germany on the European continent. Gromyko's position thus entailed playing a highly delicate political game—a game of lulling suspicions, splitting the Western allies whenever Soviet interests were involved, and generating a climate of public opinion favorable to the Soviet Union despite its delinquent record in the past. In pursuit of these aims Gromyko headed, in 1944, the Soviet delegation to the Dumbarton Oaks Conference, at which the future United Nations organization was discussed, and he participated in the Yalta and Potsdam conferences in 1945. He also attended the United Nations conference in San Francisco in the spring of 1945.

Gromyko must have performed his duties as ambassador to the United States to the highest satisfaction of his Kremlin bosses, because in 1946 he received a promotion to deputy minister of Foreign Affairs of the USSR and was appointed permanent representative of the USSR in the Security Council of the United Nations. In those formative years of the UN, which were also the years when the Soviet Union reneged on its wartime promises and extended its control over Eastern Europe, Gromyko's job in this international body was to preside over the dissolution of the wartime alliance and to prevent any intervention by the new organization into Soviet dealings with neighboring states. The major battles of the cold war were still to come. The menace of Soviet expansion had yet to be fully recognized by the Western powers, and encounters in the United Nations between these states and the Soviet Union were at most skirmishes. In those early days of the UN Gromyko cast twenty-six vetoes in the Security Council. Again his performance must have impressed his superiors, because in 1948 he was recalled to Moscow, and promoted in 1949 to the second-ranking position in the Soviet Foreign Ministry, that of first deputy minister of Foreign Affairs.

From 1949 to 1952 Gromyko was the principal assistant to Andrei Vyshinsky, the former architect of Stalin's stage trials, and at that time the foreign minister of the Soviet Union. In this role Gromyko became one of the chief implementors of the most aggressive phase of Soviet cold war policy. His boss Vyshinsky was nicknamed "Mr. No" by Western diplomats for his abundant negatives in answer to Western proposals, requests, and suggestions. During this period Gromyko could well have been called "Mr. Little No."

In 1952 Gromyko's career suddenly veered off on a tangent. He was appointed ambassador to the Court of St. James in London. It is difficult to establish to what extent his assignment was related to some new plan of Stalin's in regard to England, or to what extent it was simply a sign of disfavor. One cannot say what Gromyko's future might have been had Stalin not died ten months after Gromyko arrived in London. It may be noted, however, that Gromyko was first elected a candidate member of the party's Central Committee at the Nineteenth Congress of the CPSU in October 1952. (He became a full member in February 1956.) This honor would suggest that his London assignment did not mean that his career was in jeopardy.

Stalin's death radically changed the Russian scene. In the reshuffling of the Soviet government announced a few days after Stalin's demise, Gromyko returned to his former position of first deputy minister of Foreign Affairs, this time under the newly appointed minister, Vyacheslav Molotov. In this position, but with increased prominence and growing influence, Gromyko was to remain until 1957. During these years he saw the decline and departure of the once powerful Molotov, and he served for a short time under Molotov's successor, Dimitri Shepilov. In February 1957, a few months before the final defeat and expulsion of Khrushchev's major opponents from the party's decision-making bodies and from executive jobs in the government, Gromyko received the top post in the Soviet foreign service, minister of Foreign Affairs. His predecessor, Shepilov, a young, energetic, and outspoken head of the Foreign Ministry with a brilliant career that had already included being a secretary of the party's Central Committee, was soon disgraced as a renegade who had joined the "antiparty group" in its attempt to unseat Khrushchev in June 1957.

Gromyko's rise to the top was a reward not only for his experience, ability, and diligent work, but for his special skill in accommodating his superiors, whoever they were. His career in the Soviet foreign service spanned such diverse phases of Soviet external policy as the Nazi-Soviet alliance; the wartime Western-Soviet alliance; the 1946–53 period of territorial expansion, rigidity, total enmity toward the West, and indifference toward the national revolution in the underdeveloped areas; and the tortuous, complicated period after Stalin's death, in which Soviet policy attempted to combine limited accommodation with the Western powers, especially the United States, with extension of Soviet influence into the underdeveloped areas, and in which changes in tactics occurred with bewildering rapidity and the temperature of the cold war rose and fell erratically. Throughout all of these changes Gromyko's career advanced almost uninterruptedly. He was not committed to any particular line of foreign policy; his only commitment was to the decision-makers in the Kremlin. He was able to serve and to advance under both Stalin and Khrushchev, and it is to be expected that he will continue in his present position under Khrushchev's successors. Before he achieved the top position he was able to act as the closest assistant to such diverse Soviet foreign policy-makers as Molotov, Vyshinsky, and Shepilov, managing to outlast them all. This record has led one veteran observer to assert that "Andrei Gromyko is just possibly the best informed foreign minister in the world today. He's been around so long, and he has a good memory. . . ."

One can only speculate about the extent of Gromyko's influence on the making of basic policy decisions in Soviet foreign affairs. In no major country at the present time is the role of foreign minister an independent one; nowhere can he be called an architect of the foreign policy. Only seldom has a foreign minister had as much power in shaping the international conduct of his country as John Foster Dulles had during the Eisenhower administration in the United States. Viewed in this perspective, Gromyko's role as an implementor, administrator, and technician does not seem exceptional. His power stems from his being an expert adviser who has ready access to the top leadership. He controls no apparatus that can play a role in internal Soviet affairs or act as a pressure group. He has little influence on political appointments, one suspects, even in his own hierarchy. His freedom of action even in executive and administrative matters is circumscribed by the powerful and authoritative branches of the central party apparatus, which, during the last ten years, have greatly expanded and are now directed by men much closer to the source of Soviet power than Gromyko, e.g., Suslov, Ponomarev, and Andropov. In addition the style of personal diplomacy introduced by Khrushchev and continued by his successors tends to put the foreign minister in a shadow, even in representing the Soviet Union at international gatherings.

In the past fifty years of Soviet history the post of Soviet foreign minister has been occupied by three kinds of men: by men of imagination and independent judgment whose character and outlook were formed in the revolutionary days of the Bolshevik movement, as for example, with the first two foreign ministers, Chicherin and Litvinov; by men whose personal prestige admitted them to the small circle of top decision-makers, as was the case with Molotov and probably would have been the case with Shepilov; or by men who were entirely the creatures of the supreme leader, chosen in repayment for extraordinary services performed in the leader's interest, as was the case with Vyshinsky. Gromyko, however, is the product of a bureaucratic career in a bureaucratic hierarchy. His ascendancy reflects the bureaucratic transformation of Soviet society. The attributes which he most cherishes are probably caution and exactitude. His style of work, his countenance, his behavior toward Western colleagues—all lack the affability and suaveness of such new Soviet diplomats as Dobrynin,

Fedorenko, or Menshikov. He conforms to the old proverb: *Tishe edesh, dal'she budesh'*, which might be roughly translated as "He who goes in his own quiet way will go farther."

SELECTED BIBLIOGRAPHY

In Russian, the main sources of biographical information about Gromyko are the following: *Malaia sovetskaia entsiklopediia*, vypusk 3, III, Moskva, 1959, p. 174; *Deputaty verkhovnogo soveta SSSR*, Moskva, 1959, p. 108; *Deputaty verkhovnogo soveta SSSR*, Moskva, 1963, p. 115; *Sovetskaia istoricheskaia entsiklopediia*, IV, Moskva, 1963, pp. 798–99; *Bol'shaia sovetskaia entsiklopediia*, vypusk 2, XXXIX, Moskva, 1956, p. 529; *Ezhegodnik bol'shoi sovetskoi entsiklopedii 1958*, Moskva, 1958, p. 629; *Ezhegodnik bol'shoi sovetskoi entsiklopedii 1962*, Moskva, 1962, p. 592; *Diplomaticheskii slovar'*, vypusk 1, 1, Moskva, 1948, p. 519; *Diplomaticheskii slovar'*, vypusk 2, I, Moskva, 1960, pp. 413–14; *Sovetskaia Belorusiia*, March 4, 1958. See also a press release of the Embassy of the USSR, Washington, D.C., No. 269, September 11, 1959.

Vasily Vasilevich Kuznetsov

by Severyn Bialer

The term "bureaucracy," so often applied to the Soviet system of government, conveys an image of petrified, superorderly procedures, slow advancements of officials in the bureaucratic hierarchy, and eventual prolonged service for the official who reaches his personal zenith of authority. While the Soviet government is undoubtedly bureaucratic, these traditional attributes of bureaucracy do not describe its procedures. It is especially noteworthy that one can seldom find an official in a position of very high authority whose tenure of office goes beyond a few years. Vasily Kuznetsov can clearly be regarded as one of these exceptions. For ten years, an exceedingly long period under Soviet conditions, he served as head of the Soviet trade unions. He has occupied for over ten years the office of first deputy minister of Foreign Affairs of the Soviet Union. As second in charge of Soviet foreign relations, Kuznetsov conveys the impression of a man who is not only extremely efficient, but who has learned well the most vital lesson of Soviet politics, that of survival. While he seldom makes speeches and is much less visible in the international arena than his chief, Gromyko, Western chanceries believe that he exercises important influence on the conduct of Soviet foreign affairs.

Kuznetsov was born in 1901 in the village of Sofilovka, in what is now Gorky Oblast. His father was a peasant. Kuznetsov probably spent his boyhood on his father's farm, but by the time he was fifteen he had moved to the nearby town and never again lived in the countryside (if one does not count his frequent stays in his "dacha" or villa near Moscow). Like many peasant boys of his generation, Kuznetsov left his village to work in a factory. In 1916 he went to work in a large metallurgical factory in Moscow, which after the Bolshevik Revolution was renamed The Red Nailmaker. For the next twenty-seven years his career was bound up with the metallurgical industry. While employed in the factory, he attended an evening vocational school and finally took preparatory courses for higher education.

Nothing is known about Kuznetsov's sociopolitical activity at this stage of his life. One can surmise that he was not very active politically, since such activity would have been duly noted by his numerous official biographers. But it appears that he was a member of the Komsomol (Young Communist League) and showed the proper "proletarian" spirit, because in 1921 he was sent to study engineering in a leading technological school —the Politechnical Institute of Leningrad. He graduated from the institute in 1926 as a metallurgical engineer. By completing his higher education and becoming a technical specialist at the age of twenty-five, he had taken the first important step in a professional career a few years earlier than most of the men of his generation who later became colleagues in the top management of Soviet industry. In his senior year at the institute he took a further necessary step toward a Soviet managerial career—he entered the Communist Party of the Soviet Union (CPSU) as a candidate for a one-year trial period. In 1927, while employed in steel production, he was admitted to full membership in the local Communist cell.

Kuznetsov's first assignment after graduation was to the Makeevka Metallurgical Factory in Moscow, where he was employed until 1931— first as a production engineer and then as shop chief in the blast furnace department. His work must have been highly regarded not simply in the plant but in the Ministry of Heavy Industry as well, because in 1931 he was entrusted with an assignment given only to a select group of Soviet engineers: he was sent to the United States to study American methods of steel production for their possible benefits to Soviet steel production. Kuznetsov stayed in the United States for two years. Until 1932 he worked in the open-hearth division of the Ford Motor Company's River Rouge Plant in Dearborn, Michigan; during the next year he studied at Carnegie Tech in Pittsburgh, where he received an M.S. in metallurgical engineering.

At first, after his return to the Soviet Union, Kuznetsov's experience in the United States did not have any apparent impact on his professional career. From 1933 to 1937 he was employed at the Elektrostal metallurgical factory in the city of Noginsk, twenty miles east of Moscow; first as a deputy shop chief in the steel furnace division, then as head of the plant laboratory. It seems that the Noginsk factory was producing for the armaments industry and that Kuznetsov's duties were related to the fabrication of special types of steel for armor-plates.

The first important break in Kuznetsov's career came in 1937 when, along with many thousands of production engineers, he was recruited to replace officials in Soviet industrial ministries who had been killed or arrested by Stalin in the "great purge." Kuznetsov was assigned to what his official biography describes as "leading work" in the People's Commissariat of Ferrous Metallurgy in Moscow. This ministry, controlling the entire pig iron and steel production of the Soviet Union, was the fastest growing branch of Soviet heavy industry and enjoyed the highest priority in investment plans of this period.

The Commissariat of Ferrous Metallurgy at that time was divided into a number of "main administrations" (*glavky*), each responsible for either a particular phase or a particular type of iron or steel production, and each administering a number of factories and other establishments (e.g., research institutes, laboratories). Kuznetsov's appointment was to the *Glavspetsstal* (Main Administration for Special Steels)—the department in charge of steel production for military needs and undoubtedly the most important main administration in the entire Commissariat. At first Kuznetsov headed a department in the *Glavspetsstal*. Subsequently (probably 1938) he was appointed chief engineer of the whole organization, that is, the man in charge of technological aspects of the steel production for which the *Glavspetsstal* was responsible. As chief engineer, Kuznetsov participated with other engineers in devising improved processes of steel-making. For his successful technological innovations in the Soviet steel industry, he received in 1941 a prestigious and profitable Stalin Prize.

Kuznetsov's status at this time can be regarded as that of both technical expert and high government official. While his position was not as important or prominent as that of some of his colleagues (e.g., Ustinov, who rose from director of a factory to people's commissar of the Armaments Industry; Kosygin, who in two years jumped from director of a textile factory to commissar of the entire Soviet textile industry), it nevertheless established him in a responsible position in the central bureaucracy. One can speculate that his advancement to more responsible and political (and less technical) positions in the national government was slowed during the purges because of his two-year residence in the United States. In the prevailing atmosphere of that time in the Soviet Union, when foreign agents were seen behind every bush and the mere fact of having a relative abroad or receiving a letter from a foreign country was more than enough to send a man to a concentration camp, Kuznetsov's stay in the United States must have caused him considerable trouble. That he survived these critical years of 1937 to 1939 and even advanced his career showed, as nothing else could, that his skills were considered of the highest order by people who had enough influence to prevent his persecution by the secret police.

Kuznetsov's employment in the Commissariat of Ferrous Metallurgy lasted three years. Finally, in 1940, at the age of thirty-nine, he received his first really big promotion, one which made him an important member of the national government. From the rank of medium-level bureaucrat and technical expert he was assigned to the elite position of deputy chairman of the State Planning Commission of the USSR (Gosplan), a ministerial post that brought him into contact with the political leadership of the country.

As deputy chairman of Gosplan, Kuznetsov was apparently responsible for the planning, coordination, and supervision of the program that was basic to Soviet economic development in general and military preparedness in particular: iron and steel production. It is clear that Kuznetsov enjoyed the trust of the political leadership and that he was regarded as a very talented administrator, for at the beginning of the war with Germany, he was appointed additionally to the post of deputy member of the State Defense Committee, a position reserved for top Soviet leaders. The State Defense Committee was the supreme governmental agency that, under Stalin's personal chairmanship, coordinated the Soviet economic war effort. Kuznetsov's fellow committeemen were leaders of such prominence as Mikoyan, Malenkov, and the chief Soviet planner, Voznesensky. Khrushchev, already a member of the supreme political authority, the Politburo, was not appointed to this agency.

By 1943 Kuznetsov could well be regarded as one of the top economic managers of the Soviet Union. Unexpectedly, however, his advancement in the economic administration came to a complete halt, and he was transferred to a position that required greater skill in high-level political maneuvering than in knowledge of economic administration. He was appointed a secretary, and in 1944, chairman of the All-Union Central Council of Trade Unions. In other words, he became the head of the entire trade union establishment of the Soviet Union. He remained in this position until Stalin's death in 1953. His high status among the Soviet political elite was underscored by his election at the Nineteenth Congress of the CPSU in 1952 not only to full membership in the Central Committee of the Communist party, but to the party Presidium as well.

To appreciate Kuznetsov's function from 1944 to 1953 requires an understanding of the role of trade unions in Soviet society. Foremost is the fact that they are a governmental organization. During the Stalin era they had no autonomy whatever in organizational and policy matters. In small and large questions they were directed by the party, from the factory level to the Central Council of Trade Unions. In the party apparatus on the oblast, republican, and central levels there was (and is) a special department that supervises the trade unions, as well as other so-called mass organizations. The unions' main task was not to bargain with the employer —that is, the government—for better working conditions and higher wages, but to organize the workers for greater effort in implementing production plans, to secure tight work discipline, and to act as a channel for the limited funds assigned by the government for the workers' vacations, recreation, etc. The trade union leader in a factory was regarded by the worker as a member of the factory administration who was very different from the factory manager or the party leader, although invested with much less power.

The trade unions were not regarded by the Soviet leadership as the major instrument for securing plan fulfillment. Trade union propaganda and supervision were clearly regarded only as a lever which supplemented economic incentives and direct administrative controls. It is, therefore, not surprising that full-time, paid trade union officials were selected in most cases from among those considered unfit for the party apparatus or economic administration. Their education, experience, imagination, and administrative abilities were generally far inferior to those of their colleagues in the other hierarchies. This does not mean, however, that Kuznetsov's appointment—as head of this vast organization, to which almost all Soviet workers belong and which employs hundreds of thousands of full-time officials—was a sign that he was held in low esteem by the Soviet leadership. The fact that he was able to perform his duties for ten years without being disgraced or dismissed demonstrated that he possessed administrative ability, political acumen, and toughness.

In the light of Kuznetsov's post-Stalin career, one feature of his trade union work should be stressed. In addition to their domestic tasks, the unions are used by the Soviet leadership to exploit the myth of the Soviet Union as a "workers' state." Seldom does a Soviet delegation to a foreign country not include a high-ranking trade union official whose duty is to speak in the name of the Soviet worker. Contacts between Soviet trade unions and numerous trade unions in non-Communist countries, and Soviet participation in various international trade union organizations are used by the government to promote Soviet foreign policy. During his tenure, this external activity was one of Kuznetsov's main jobs. He was one of the organizers of the Communist-led International Federation of Trade Unions which, together with the peace movement and the International Federation of Women, was an important supplementary instrument of Soviet diplomacy.

Kuznetsov's career in the Stalin era—his rise from production engineer to technical expert in a government administration, to top economic administrator and planner, and finally to the leadership of the Soviet trade unions—took him gradually farther away from his primary profession and special technical capacities toward increasingly political preoccupations.

Even as head of the unions, however, his past experience in production and economic administration was probably of considerable help. But the death of Stalin and the ensuing fundamental reorganization of the government pushed him into an area of activity in which his technical and administrative experience was of little, and then only indirect, value.

When Stalin died, the triumvirate of Malenkov, Molotov, and Beria that took over the leadership of Russia (Khrushchev was added shortly as first secretary of the party) revealed a serious concern over the people's possible reaction to the change of rulers, half-expecting that the demise of the leader would be a signal for unrest at home. In their first proclamation to the Soviet population the new leadership appealed for calm to avert "disorder and panic." In this situation the trade union leadership acquired a new significance. It was not surprising, therefore, that it was decided to give over the union leadership to a man of higher stature and far greater political experience than Kuznetsov, whose major attribute was above all else that he was an efficient and trusted administrator. Thus in the first line-up of top positions in the government, announced a few days after Stalin's death, Kuznetsov's position was entrusted to Nikolai Shvernik, a veteran Bolshevik, party member from 1905, and until then formal head of state (chairman of the Presidium of the Supreme Soviet). Kuznetsov's name disappeared also from the new, reorganized, and much smaller Presidium of the Communist party. His tenure in this highest Soviet decision-making body had lasted less than five months.

Despite his meteoric career in the period from 1940 to 1953 (or perhaps because of it) it seems that the new Soviet leadership did not regard Kuznetsov as fit for a key appointment. It may well be that had he continued after 1943 as a steel specialist and economic administrator, he would at least have retained his status after Stalin died, as did most of his colleagues in industrial management. His lack of experience in party work on the one hand, and his ten-year absence from economic administration on the other, with the additional handicap—one suspects—of lacking close connections with and support of one of the top contenders for Stalin's throne, cost him both his political job and his previous managerial position. Instead he was transferred in 1953 to a separate Soviet hierarchy, the foreign service, where at the time of this writing he still serves.

Though unexpected, Kuznetsov's transfer cannot be considered an isolated phenomenon in the post-Stalin period. While it sidetracked his career and was anything but a promotion, his assignment was still of considerable importance. At that time a number of high party and government officials with no foreign-service experience were appointed to diplomatic posts abroad or to the Ministry of Foreign Affairs. (The minister of Agriculture, Benediktov, for example, took over as ambassador to India in 1953, and in the same year the first secretary of the Byelorussian Communist party, Zimianin, was appointed as the chief of the Fourth European Department of the Ministry of Foreign Affairs.) In most cases, as in Kuznetsov's, the new job was a demotion; but at the same time these transfers were calculated to reinforce the Soviet foreign service in a difficult and new period.

Part of Stalin's legacy was the virtual isolation of the Soviet Union in the international arena and the almost totally negative approach characteristic of Soviet foreign policy, dating from the halt of postwar Soviet territorial expansion. The veto in the Security Council, the "No" vote in the General Assembly of the United Nations, the offering of solution to disputes so extreme and onesided that rejection was assumed in advance by their authors, the fear of exchanges and contacts between officials across the Iron Curtain (even at the highest level), the unwillingness to abandon or even to moderate the abusive rhetoric of their international intercourse, the ineptitude in differentiating between various shades of opinion in non-Communist countries and the differing policies of their governments, the desire to restrict the role of Soviet diplomats abroad to the bare minimum of entirely formalized activities—all this was typical of the deadly, unimaginative, crude framework within which the Soviet foreign service was forced to work.

Just as the new Soviet leadership wanted to break away from the stagnation of the Stalin era in domestic economic policies and initiate an upsurge in industrial and agricultural development, so in their foreign policies it wanted to break through the Soviet Union's international isolation, abandon the hopelessly rigid methods and take the initiative in the international arena. Their vision was not like that of the last years of Stalin—of a limited, mainly defensive foreign policy—but was unlimited in scope, diversified in methods, differentiating in its approaches to and treatment of foreign countries, and withal highly aggressive. Given the change in outlook and objectives, the quality of Soviet foreign-service personnel became a matter of far greater importance than it had been under Stalin.

One area in Soviet dealings with foreign countries became especially significant almost immediately after Stalin's death—Soviet relations with other Communist states. Even more than they feared turbulence among their own population, the Soviet leaders were concerned that Stalin's death would result in restlessness not only among the people, but also among the leading party strata and leaders of the Communist states established in Europe and Asia after the Second World War. To retain Soviet dominance in these countries and to prevent unpleasant surprises (of which the East German uprising a few months after Stalin's death had provided a timely warning), the improvement of channels of communication between the leaderships of these countries and the Soviet authorities, together with the lessening of accumulated grievances over past Soviet treatment, became imperative.

To carry out these adjustments the Soviet leaders sent to a number of the East European Communist countries ambassadors who, lacking experience in diplomatic work, possessed as a result of their long tenure in party and government positions inside the Soviet Union an authority that could impress foreign Communist chiefs of state far more than could professional diplomats; who were much better acquainted with the internal mechanics of Communist rule and thus better able to spot signs of danger than could a man who had spent most of his adult life in assignments outside the Soviet Union; and who would be able to speak to foreign Communist officials in their own terms. Thus, for example, the secretary of the Central Committee of the CPSU and former first secretary of the Komsomol, Mikhailov, was appointed ambassador to Poland in 1954.

Of all the Soviet diplomatic posts in the Communist countries, none was more important than that of ambassador to the other great Communist power—the Chinese People's Republic. And this was the position to which Kuznetsov was assigned. From 1953 to 1955 he served as the USSR ambassador extraordinary and plenipotentiary in Peking. As if to emphasize the importance of his position, he was given simultaneously the title of deputy foreign minister of Foreign Affairs of the USSR.

While Kuznetsov's years as ambassador to Peking were far less stormy and by no means as crucial to Sino-Soviet relations as the ensuing period (during which the conflict between the two great powers passed from the simmering stage into a private but fierce debate, and then finally into an open battle), they nevertheless should be considered as the prologue to this period. Immediately after Stalin's death both the Soviet Union and Communist China undertook a reappraisal of their mutual relations. The Chinese made it increasingly clear that they expected to be accorded a more nearly equal treatment. They requested a reassessment of Sino-Soviet trade and credit terms. They moved decisively to curb Soviet influence in Manchuria, purging the boss of that province, Kao Kang, in 1955. On their part, Soviet leaders apparently came to the conclusion that the best way to keep the alliance intact was to relinquish some of Russia's advantages, especially economic, in her relations with China. They dismantled the so-called mixed companies in air transport and mining, which were hardly more than a cover for Soviet control and exploitation of segments of the Chinese economy. They began to speak in public about China with a new respect, and went out of their way to pay high tributes to the wisdom and virtues of "Comrade Mao." In other words, they hoped to keep their Chinese allies in hand by a policy of conciliation and concessions to Chinese interests and pride. As ambassador in Peking, Kuznetsov's role of supervising a peaceful transformation in Sino-Soviet relations from a onesided Stalinism to a more nearly equal interdependency was of real importance. His appointment reflected the high trust placed in him by the Soviet leadership.

Kuznetsov's tenure in Peking, however, came to an end at the exact moment that Soviet policies began to follow a direct path toward the ensuing Sino-Soviet clash. In 1955 Khrushchev's star began its rapid ascendancy on the Soviet scene. In February, Malenkov "resigned" under humiliating circumstances from the premiership. Some months later Molotov, the powerful foreign minister, was overruled by his colleagues on such crucial issues as *rapprochement* with Yugoslavia, the Austrian peace treaty, and relations with East European satellites of the USSR. While Molotov was able to hold his office for another year, he was forced to perform the ritual of public self-criticism and apparently lost control of Soviet conduct in world affairs. Khrushchev embarked on a new course in Soviet foreign policy, the two most important features of which were an attempt to re-establish good relations with the heretic Tito and a willingness to engage in bilateral negotiations with the United States—a policy that the Chinese leaders later condemned as "revisionist," and for which no Soviet economic and propaganda concessions to China could compensate. During this important turn in foreign policy, Kuznetsov was brought home to Moscow as first deputy minister in Foreign Affairs. The new appointment was clearly a promotion and an additional sign of Khrushchev's trust, and was made at a time when the acting foreign minister, Molotov, had been pushed aside from effective control of Soviet diplomacy and his deputies' function was not so much to assist him as to attempt to neutralize him. The other post of first deputy at that time was occupied by Kuznetsov's present boss, Andrei Gromyko.

In the last ten stormy years of Soviet foreign policy, Kuznetsov's position as the second man in the Soviet foreign office was solidly established. In the Soviet system of rotating responsibilities for deputy foreign ministers, it seems that for most of his tenure of office Kuznetsov supervised the Second European Department (UK and Commonwealth), the American Department, and Soviet activities in the UN. On various occasions he has headed the Soviet delegations to the General Assembly of the United Nations. He has been an adviser to other Soviet delegations abroad, including the Khrushchev-led one sent to the abortive Paris summit conference in 1960, and has himself headed Soviet delegations to individual foreign countries. In 1957, for example, he led the Soviet delegation to Iran that signed trade agreements and fixed the demarcation of the frontier between the USSR and Iran. Unspectacular, not given to histrionics, Kuznetsov has achieved the reputation of being a hard-working and trusted behind-the-scenes assistant to the group that makes decisions about the direction and methods of Soviet relations with the outside world.

The confidence of Kuznetsov's superiors in his ability and especially, it seems, in his efficiency as an administrator and precision in implementing established policies was underscored by his election to full membership in the Central Committee of the CPSU at both the Twentieth and Twenty-second congresses of the party (1956 and 1961). It may be anticipated that Khrushchev's departure from Soviet leadership will have no influence on Kuznetsov's tenure of office in the Soviet foreign service. His relationship with his boss, Gromyko, seems amicable. His reputation as a technician who avoids entanglements in Kremlin politics would seem to make him acceptable to any contender for supreme power. Solid, efficient, experienced in administration, respected for his even temper—and in his sixties—Vasily Kuznetsov has very little chance to assume the number-one position in the Soviet foreign service when the time comes, whether through natural or political causes, for Gromyko to depart from the scene. On the other hand, the date of Kuznetsov's own retirement will probably be determined more by his age and health than by the normal vicissitudes of public officeholding in the Soviet Union.

SELECTED BIBLIOGRAPHY

For biographical information about Kuznetsov, see the following: *Deputaty verkhovnogo soveta SSSR,* Moskva, 1959, p. 215; *Deputaty verkhovnogo soveta SSSR,* Moskva, 1963, p. 235; *Ezhegodnik bol'shoi sovetskoi entsiklopedii 1962,* Moskva, 1962, p. 602; *Diplomaticheskii slovar',* vypusk 2, II, Moskva, 1960, pp. 152–53; *Bol'shaia sovetskaia entsiklopediia,* vypusk 2, XXIII, Moskva, 1953, p. 606; *Bol'shaia sovetskaia entsiklopediia,* vypusk 2, LI, Moskva, 1958, p. 284; *Malaia sovetskaia entsiklopediia,* vypusk 2, IX, Moskva, 1951, p. 298; *Trud,* January 5, 1946.

Valerian Alexandrovich Zorin

by Severyn Bialer

Few Soviet leaders, including diplomats stationed in the West, are familiar to the American people. The stocky figure and peasant face of Khrushchev became known to the average American largely through Khrushchev's continuous performance on American television during his visit to the United States in 1959. Another exception to the rule is Valerian Alexandrovich Zorin. As permanent Soviet representative (until the end of 1962) to the United Nations at its headquarters in New York he might have been unknown in America still, had it not been for the dramatic events of October 1962 that thrust him into public view and made an episode in which he participated the major symbol of the American-Soviet confrontation in the Cuban missile crisis.

At 4 P.M. Tuesday, October 23, flanked by photo-interpreters and intelligence analysts, Ambassador Adlai Stevenson forcefully presented to the United Nations Security Council evidence that Soviet Russia had clandestinely installed ballistic missiles in Cuba. The entire proceedings of the

UN Security Council were televised by the three national networks. The Soviet delegate, Zorin, countered that the Central Intelligence Agency had manufactured the evidence. Then, said Stevenson, let a UN team inspect the sites in Cuba. In an encounter well remembered by millions of Americans Stevenson addressed himself to Zorin: *Stevenson:* ". . . let me ask you one simple question: Do you, Ambassador Zorin, deny that the USSR has placed and is placing medium- and intermediate-range missiles and sites in Cuba? Yes or no. Don't wait for the translation. Yes or no." *Zorin:* "I am not in an American courtroom, sir. . . ." *Stevenson:* "You are in the court of world opinion right now!" *Zorin:* ". . . I do not wish to answer a question that is put to me in the fashion that a prosecutor does. In due course, sir, you will have your reply." *Stevenson:* "I am prepared to wait for my answer until hell freezes over, if that's your decision."

For the last twenty years Zorin has been a well-known international trouble-shooter for the Soviet leadership. His past career and known abilities would indicate that this was not the last time a representative of the most powerful Western nation would face Zorin as the representative of the most powerful Communist nation. He was born in 1902. Nothing is known about his social origin, birthplace or youth, though the fact of omission in Soviet biographical sources usually indicates something less than the desirable proletarian social background. In Zorin's case, such suspicions may be well founded. There are rumors that before the Bolshevik Revolution he attended a *gymnasium* (a secondary school in Tsarist Russia having only a small percentage of students not of middle-class origin). His first known employment, at the age of eighteen, was on a newspaper in the city of Kremenchug in the eastern Ukraine, which would suggest, on the one hand, that he completed his secondary education without interruption (unlike the majority of Soviet leaders who were forced at an early age to work for their livelihood) and, on the other, that he was sufficiently educated to qualify for newspaper work. This work apparently ended by 1922 when, at twenty, he became a member of the Communist Party of the Soviet Union (CPSU) and was assigned to what his Soviet biographers describe as "leading work" in the Komsomol (Young Communist League). According to some sources he worked as an official in the Central Committee of the Komsomol in Moscow.

Zorin remained in Komsomol work until 1932 or 1933. During this period he was also engaged in what his official biographers call "pedagogical work," which probably involved lecturing on political subjects in Komsomol and party schools and in institutions of higher learning. From about 1933 on he studied in the Higher Communist Institute of Education, from which he was graduated in 1935. This institute was both a higher educational establishment for teacher-training and an advanced party school. The curriculum was designed to produce an elite cadre that would be loyal to the Communist cause, well versed in Marxism–Leninism, and sufficiently trained in pedagogy to be able to supervise the vast program of re-educating Soviet youth in line with the interests of the state.

After graduation Zorin's career was not, however, confined to education. While he still taught and lectured, his major job became that of a full-time, paid party professional. Apparently he worked in Moscow, but the exact nature and location of his work is unknown. In all probability it was either for the Moscow Party Committee, where his boss at that time would have been Nikita Khrushchev, or for the Central Committee of the CPSU, where there was always a need for able, loyal, and educated young men in one of the ideological departments, such as the Agitation and Propaganda Department or the Department of Culture. It may be, however, that his career in Soviet foreign affairs had already begun. Conceivably he was employed in the immense apparatus of the Executive Committee of the Communist International (IKKI), which was the Soviet-directed body for supervising the activities of Communist parties around the world. Whatever his exact employment, there can be no doubt that it was of a political nature and dealt only marginally with education, and that he had become a member of the narrow and powerful caste of Soviet professional politicians.

Zorin's career in the party apparatus was unexpectedly terminated in 1938. One may speculate that this turn of events had something to do with the "great purge" that was then destroying careers and lives by the thousands. Whatever the reasons, from 1939 until 1941 Zorin occupied the relatively unimportant post of deputy director of the Moscow City Pedagogical Institute, a teacher-training establishment. For a man of Zorin's abilities, with his party seniority (dating back to 1922), his long experience in the Komsomol and party apparatus, and his education, to occupy this position at the age of 38 or 39 did not bode well for the future. In this period men ten years younger were moving into posts of greater prestige and responsibility. However, the disfavor in which Zorin found himself ended as unexpectedly as it had begun. And this time the career on which he embarked or, rather, was launched was to be a lasting one.

In 1941, the year Nazi Germany attacked Russia, Zorin was first formally employed in the Soviet foreign service. Until the fall of 1944 he was employed in the Commissariat of Foreign Affairs itself. From the beginning, he performed important tasks that brought him into almost immediate contact with the upper echelons of the Soviet foreign office. In 1941 and part of 1942 he was an assistant to the general secretary of the Commissariat of Foreign Affairs. It seems that the duties of his superior pertained to the internal administration of the foreign service. Later in 1942 he became an assistant to a deputy commissar (vice minister). It is not known, unfortunately, who this man was. In 1943 it became clear that Zorin's affiliation with the highest officials in his ministry had paid off; he received his first independent and leading post: chief of the Fourth European Department of the Commissariat. This department was in charge of relations with Poland and Czechoslovakia—the Soviet Union's immediate neighbors to the west. As chief of a department in the foreign office, Zorin was still, nevertheless, a middle-rank bureaucrat, known in the service itself but not visible to the political leadership of the Soviet state. In 1944, however, he received an appointment of great responsibility which, given the nature of the case, must have been approved by Stalin himself. He was named extraordinary and plenipotentiary representative of the Soviet Union to the Republic of Czechoslovakia.

Before the Second World War Czechoslovakia was the only industrial country in eastern and east-central Europe, and at the same time the only genuinely democratic country. It also became one of the first victims of Hitler, and by 1939 had lost its independence. The Czechs organized a government-in-exile residing in London under the leadership of Eduard Beneš, the president of Czechoslovakia at the time of the German invasion. The Beneš government was democratic and liberal, but while decisively Western in its ideas concerning the internal postwar order of Czechoslovakia, it took a friendly and cooperative view toward relations with the Soviet Union. It may well be that the behavior of the Western governments during the Munich crisis, when Czech freedom was traded for the illusory promise of peace with Hitler, explains in part why the exiled government's attitude toward the Soviet Union was so different from that of, say, the Polish government-in-exile.

The Soviet government had no reason to doubt that after the victorious conclusion of the war with Germany and the return of Beneš to Czechoslovakia, the Soviets would have in Prague a most friendly and responsive government. The Soviet designs upon Czechoslovakia, however, were part of a much more far-reaching plan for eastern and east-central Europe —a plan that went beyond the understandable wish to have neighbors to the west and southwest ruled by friendly governments, which would help to ensure against a resurrection of the German danger. Stalin regarded eastern and east-central Europe as a prize that he had won in the war with Nazi Germany and secured at the bargaining table with the Western "big powers." He wanted to introduce a Communist system of government into these countries and install rulers who would be completely subservient to Russia. In simple terms he planned to create a vast satellite empire, embracing over 100 million people of east and east-central Europe. This was the background to Zorin's nomination as ambassador to Prague.

Stalin's major instrument in his plan to transform Czechoslovakia into a Soviet satellite was to be the Communist Party of Czechoslovakia. Most of the Czechoslovak leaders had spent the war in the Soviet Union, and even those who participated in the Beneš government in London were of unquestioning loyalty to the Soviet Union. After the re-establishment of the Czechoslovak state, the Communist party engaged in feverish activity among the population and soon became the largest party in Czechoslovakia, far superior in organization to its major competitor on the left, the Czechoslovak Socialist party. Communist leaders received high posts in the government, and the top party boss, Gottwald, became prime minister. Most important, the Communists captured the Ministry of the Interior and, behind the façade of a nonpartisan army general, achieved dominant influence in the Ministry of Defense.

The Czechoslovak situation, from Stalin's point of view, was especially complicated in comparison with that of other East European countries because, lacking any pretext for being there, Soviet troops had to leave Czechoslovakia; thus a decisive instrument of direct Soviet intervention and indirect blackmail, which played such an important role in Poland, Romania, Hungary, and Bulgaria, could not be used. Zorin's role as chief Soviet supervisor of the plans to convert Czechoslovakia into a satellite required, therefore, even more skill and shrewdness than were required of his colleagues in other East European countries. While formally accredited to the constitutional government of Czechoslovakia and its president, Beneš, Zorin engaged throughout his stay in Prague in subversive activities designed to prepare a Communist takeover; in his office and with his advice, authorization, and prodding, the subversion evolved. The verdict on the future of Czechoslovakia was delivered by Stalin in Moscow, but Zorin was its chief executioner.

Zorin left Czechoslovakia before the *coup de grâce,* returning to Moscow in December 1947 to become deputy minister of Foreign Affairs of the USSR. His promotion, ranking him directly below the three top officials in the Ministry (the minister and his two first deputies), was undoubtedly a direct result of his success in Czechoslovakia. The actual Communist takeover in Czechoslovakia occurred in February 1948. It seems, however, that as deputy foreign minister in Moscow Zorin's responsibilities included the East European countries, and numerous accounts seem to indicate that he actually supervised the takeover. It has even been reported that he arrived in Prague on February 19 and guided the Czech party in seizing power in the critical weeks that followed.

Zorin occupied the post of deputy foreign minister from 1947 to 1955. It seems, however, that his responsibility was shifted from Eastern Europe, then secure for the Soviet Union, to the main arena of the cold war—relations with the major Western powers. For a brief period in 1952–53, he was simultaneously permanent Soviet representative in the UN Security Council in New York; but after Stalin's death he was recalled to Moscow to reinforce the central apparatus of the Ministry, still with the rank of deputy minister. In 1955 proof appeared that Zorin's star was not in decline as a result of Stalin's death, and that the new Soviet leadership still regarded him as a major trouble-shooter in the Soviet foreign service.

During 1955 it became clear that the man to watch in Soviet politics was Nikita Khrushchev. After disposing of the powerful police chief Lavrenti Beria, in alliance with his two major competitors for Stalin's succession, Khrushchev was able in the winter of 1955 to neutralize one of these competitors, Malenkov, by forcing him to resign from the Soviet premiership. In the summer of that year he neutralized the second, Molotov, and was then able to take over the direction of Soviet foreign policy. The main trend of the new policy was different from the isolationist, negative, and cautious approach of Stalin. One of the new slogans was "You can't win if you're not there." In 1955, in keeping with its new dynamism, the Soviet government established diplomatic relations with the Federal Republic of Germany, after having ignored the West German state for seven years. Because the Soviet government regarded West Germany as a major and growing danger both in its own right and through its alleged influence on American policy, the appointment of the first Soviet ambassador assumed exceptional importance. The job required not only political skill and force of personality, but much imagination in view of the unexplored possibilities of postwar Soviet-German relations. The man selected in December 1955 for this position was Zorin.

Zorin's stay in Bonn was relatively short. In July 1956 he was recalled to Moscow and resumed his former position of deputy foreign minister of the USSR. His election in February 1956, for the first time, to candidate membership in the party's Central Committee had already enhanced his status. (He became a full member in October 1961.) It may be that his appointment to West Germany was meant to be a short one, and that his major function was to break ground and keep things in hand during the initial, most difficult period.

After his return to Moscow Zorin continued to be one of the most visible and prestigious Soviet representatives in the international arena. He was an editor of *The History of Diplomacy,* published in 1958. In August 1958 he was a member of the Soviet delegation to the special session of the United Nations General Assembly. In October 1958 he was again a member of the Soviet delegation to the Thirteenth Session of the General Assembly. He was also active in disarmament negotiations, having been Soviet delegate to the UN's disarmament subcommittee since April 1959; and in 1960 he headed the Soviet delegation to the ten-nation disarmament conference in Geneva.

In the late 1950's and especially the early 1960's, the Soviet approach to the institutional structure of the United Nations was undergoing an important change. Formerly the Soviet government had regarded the UN as a secondary field of battle with the Western powers, dominated to such an extent by the United States that there was little hope that it might be of great service to the Soviet Union. The basic Soviet attitude toward it, therefore, had been one of exploiting its potentialities for obstruction and propaganda. The tremendous increase in UN membership through the admission of newly independent states, the improvement in the Soviet Union's international power position, the decline in American ability to dominate the UN, and the weakening of the postwar Western alliance led the Soviet government to believe that the time had come when American preponderance in the UN could be destroyed and the door opened to expansion, sooner or later, of Soviet influence. While those hopes were not fulfilled, and while the Soviet estimates of UN power relationships were as over-optimistic as their general evaluation of the East-West balance of power, the early 1960's nevertheless saw a much invigorated Soviet activity in the UN. And again Zorin was sent to the main line of fire.

In September 1960 Zorin was appointed permanent Soviet representative in the United Nations and, simultaneously, Soviet representative to the Security Council. He served in these positions without losing his title of deputy minister of Foreign Affairs of the USSR. Both friends and foes of the Soviet Union agree that Zorin's conduct in these offices was highly forceful, effective, and intelligent until the American-Soviet confrontation over Soviet missiles in Cuba in October 1962. It was fateful, perhaps, that both the high and the low points of his career in the UN involved Cuba: the high point coming after he had been at the UN only half a year when the unsuccessful Bay of Pigs invasion created perfect conditions for his attack upon the United States; and the low point when, apparently left without clear instructions and possibly even information from his government, he stalled for time and was exposed to the biting denunciation of his American adversary, Adlai Stevenson. It seems that after October 1962 Zorin's effectiveness in the UN declined to the same extent that the effectiveness and dynamism of Soviet foreign policy in general declined in the last years of Khrushchev's rule.

In December 1962 Zorin was relieved of his UN posts, and returned to the Soviet Foreign Ministry as deputy foreign minister in charge of West European affairs and as a top adviser on disarmament questions. Earlier in 1962 he had represented the Soviet Union at the Geneva disarmament talks, as he was to do again in 1964. He wrote an important article that appeared in *Izvestiia,* June 30, 1964, severely attacking the Chinese for obstructing progress toward disarmament. In March 1965, however, as in the past when a diplomatic post abroad had demanded a tried and trusted representative, the Soviet leadership appointed Zorin as ambassador to Charles de Gaulle's France.

It is very difficult to make any generalizations about the direction of Soviet foreign policy at the time Zorin assumed his ambassadorship. The overthrow of Khrushchev in October 1964 and the ensuing struggle for supremacy in the Kremlin made the Soviet situation fluid; as they introduced competition between contending leaders, so they introduced competition between contending policies. The absence of a supreme leader and arbiter who, weighing various pressures, decides which policy to adopt, makes possible rapid changes in policy. Nevertheless, one can tentatively suggest that in the post-Khrushchev Soviet foreign policy, the trend toward bilateral *rapprochement* with the United States has weakened, while another trend has come to the fore—that of exploitation of the deep divisions within the Western bloc, especially capitalizing on the growing disunity between France and the United States and between France and England. Faced with a forceful American policy in Asia, attacked on its flanks by its Communist enemy China, losing initiative in the international arena, the Soviet leaders, it seems, see a possible wedge of great potential significance in de Gaulle's position on American leadership, on the unity of Western Europe, and on the Asian crisis. It may well be that this new Soviet trend is of only tactical importance and that after the struggle for power in the Kremlin is decided, Khrushchev's policy will be resumed. Whatever happens in the future, however, Valerian Zorin at the moment occupies one of the most crucial positions in the Soviet foreign service, and continues to enjoy the trust of his present Kremlin superiors, as he did of their predecessor Khrushchev.

SELECTED BIBLIOGRAPHY

For biographical information about Zorin, see the following: *Diplomaticheskii slovar'*, vypusk 1, I, Moskva, 1948, p. 658; *Diplomaticheskii slovar,'* vypusk 2, I, Moskva, 1960, pp. 544–45; *Ezhegodnik bol'shoi sovetskoi entsiklopedii 1961*, Moskva, 1961, p. 560; *Ezhegodnik bol'shoi sovetskoi entsiklopedii 1962*, Moskva, 1962, p. 596; *Pravda*, December 22, 1960.

Leonid Vitalevich Kantorovich

by Robert C. Stuart

Leonid Vitalevich Kantorovich, noted Soviet mathematician and economist, was born on January 19, 1912. By 1930 he had completed basic studies at Leningrad University, and by 1935 was awarded the doctoral degree in physical and mathematical science from that institution. From 1930 through 1939 Kantorovich was engaged as an instructor at the Leningrad Institute for Industrial Construction and Engineering, teaching, in addition, at Leningrad University where he was an instructor from 1932 through 1934, and professor from 1934. From 1940 he was engaged in research at the Leningrad branch of the Institute of Mathematics of the Academy of Sciences of the USSR.

In addition to the Stalin Prize awarded to him in 1949 for work in the field of functional analysis, Kantorovich received the coveted Lenin Prize in 1965 for his work on linear programing and economic models. In 1958 he became a corresponding member of the Academy of Sciences of the USSR, and currently holds the title of academician, the highest academic title in the Soviet Union of which there were, in 1958, only thirteen in the field of economics and 172 in all other fields.

Kantorovich is currently deputy director of the Laboratory For the Use of Statistical and Mathematical Methods in Economics of the Siberian Branch of the Academy of Sciences of the USSR, which is located in Novosibirsk; and he is a member of the Steklov Institute, a prominent mathematical research institute in the Soviet Union. He is also a member of the editorial board of *The Siberian Mathematical Journal,* published in Moscow.

Kantorovich's research work has been devoted primarily to mathematics, and in particular, the theory of functions of real variables, functional analysis, approximating methods, the programing of computers, and the application of mathematical methods to economic analysis. He has published widely throughout his career. In 1939, in response to a specific request to solve a scheduling problem, he became the first man to describe the essentials of the technique now known as linear programing. In the Western world and especially in the field of economics, Kantorovich is probably best known for his work in linear programing and especially for his publication in 1959 of *The Best Use of Economic Resources,* in which he refines these techniques and advocates their application to the Soviet economy.

Linear programing is a versatile mathematical technique for the solution of problems involving the most efficient use of available resources. For example, given the desire to produce a certain volume and composition of goods, and given a supply of inputs (land, labor, capital, etc.) and technology (the ability to convert these inputs to output), the linear programing technique makes it possible to specify which combination of these inputs will produce the desired bundle of goods at minimum cost. From the application of the linear programing technique is derived a set of efficiency prices which are those of the inputs used in the economy. These prices are so described because their application as the bases upon which decisions are made in the economy will lead to an efficient allocation of resources, that is, production of the desired bundle of goods at minimum cost. Finally, although these prices have been generated by means of a mathematical technique, their ability to produce an efficient allocation of resources is a very desirable property, and one characteristic of prices formed by the free interaction of demand and supply in a market economy. Like the forces of a competitive market, the linear programing technique has generated a set of prices which takes account of the scarcities of inputs, on the one hand, and the strength of the demand for these inputs for the production of commodities, on the other hand. In a market economy such as the American, prices are automatically determined by the interplay of supply and demand forces, whereas in a planned economy of the Soviet type, prices are centrally determined by a planning agency. Given the need to set prices, it is essential that planners have a means by which this task may be accomplished, and linear programing is in fact such a means, although the results may not conform to Marxian thinking.

In *The Best Use of Economic Resources,* Kantorovich develops the linear programing technique and advocates its application to planning practice in the Soviet Union. To grasp fully the significance of this work and its impact upon the development of economic thought in the Soviet Union, it is necessary to realize that the development of economic science, by which we mean a study of the most efficient use of scarce resources to satisfy competing demands, is largely a product of the post-Stalin era, consisting in part of a rediscovery of many basic positions of non-Marxian teaching. In combination with this re-examination of economic thinking has been the emergence and refinement of mathematical tools and their application to economic analysis. While this process of quantification has lent precision and clarity to many propositions of economic theory, it has also led to uneasiness with traditional Marxian teachings. One such case is the question of price formation, which has been the subject of a remarkable debate during the past decade in which a wide spectrum of Soviet economic thinking has been displayed.

Throughout these discussions of the past decade, one tends to find a spectrum of thinking characterized by the traditional Marxian "political economists," on the one hand, and the modern quantitatively oriented economists, on the other. The latter group, while apparently willing to pay homage to the past, are at the same time looking for, and advocating, experimentation and change. In the sphere of value and price formation, for example, while Marxian teaching suggests that value is created by socially necessary labor only, traditional Western thinking suggests that value is created by all inputs, on the one hand (land, labor, and capital), and the utility of a good to its consumer as expressed through demand, on the other hand. In a practical sense, the result of this thinking has been the continual absence of explicit charges for land and capital in the Soviet economy, and hence a lack of concern for the most efficient use of these inputs.

Mathematical tools are inclined to be ideologically neutral, however, and when Kantorovich set about to solve the problem of how best to allocate resources to achieve plan goals, it soon became evident that all resources were relatively scarce and hence must have prices attached if they were to be efficiently utilized.

When Kantorovich introduced the essentials of linear programing in 1939, the technique did not initially receive widespread attention. It is notable, in fact, that these techniques were independently rediscovered and extended in the United States by G. B. Dantzig and others. In large measure, the lack of initial response in the Soviet Union to Kantorovich's efforts can be attributed to the prevailing Stalinist socioeconomic theories, which envisaged Soviet-style economic planning and management as hardly suitable ground for subtle statistical methods measuring competing resource needs and demands. One must also realize, however, that while Kantorovich had made a very significant discovery, probably few people anywhere understood the potentials of the technique.

Nevertheless, the past decade has been one of remarkable and encouraging debate in the Soviet Union, although Kantorovich's formulations have yet to receive widespread acceptance. In an editorial preface to the volume *The Best Use of Economic Resources,* Academician V. S. Nemchinov, a noted Soviet mathematical economist, was unable to accept the wide powers attributed by Kantorovich to a linear programing system of prices, though he accepted the formulations for a "strictly limited sphere." Among those who would reject the widespread application of mathematical techniques, Academician K. V. Ostrovityanov of Moscow State University, important in both party and scientific circles, has been an outspoken critic noting contradictions with the Marxian labor theory of value. Most recently he was the leading critic against awarding the Lenin Prize for 1965 to Kantorovich, Nemchinov (deceased), and V. V. Novozhilov, three important mathematical economists in the Soviet Union.

The criticisms of mathematical methods and their application to planning in the Soviet Union are not wholly ideological, however. There are indeed many practical problems in attempting to apply theoretically nice, but complex mathematical, constructions to the daily operation of an economic system. It is not surprising, therefore, that resistance to these techniques might arise on purely practical grounds, especially from those who have long and close contact with daily operations of the economy. Such reasoning might in part explain an apparent chasm between the managerial reforms proposed by Evsei Liberman and the harmonious price reforms proposed by Kantorovich. While Liberman has proposed a scheme for decentralization through a profit mechanism, the accompanying discussion has not recognized the degree to which the price reforms advocated by Kantorovich would in fact allow efficient implementation of such an arrangement of decentralization. However, the development of an improved price system is only one sphere of potential application for mathematical techniques. Of even greater interest, perhaps, is the possibility of recasting entirely the system for planning the economy.

The Soviet economic system is guided by a plan, for which there are two basic requirements. First, the plan must achieve balance. For example, if an industrial firm is told to produce automobiles, steel will be needed, and hence a supplier of steel must be told to deliver the correct quantity and quality and at the proper time. As the economy grows, these interconnections become increasingly complex and difficult to plan centrally.

Second, a plan should be efficient, that is, the planned goals should be achieved at minimum cost. The traditional method of plan formulation in the Soviet Union has been the so-called material balance approach, which in essence involves a simple balancing of available resources against the annual demands placed upon those resources for fulfilling the plan targets. The history of this approach indicates that it has become increasingly difficult to maintain consistency in planning, let alone efficiency, as the economy grows more complex.

To achieve a balanced and efficient plan, and to speed up and simplify the process of plan formulation, mathematical economists have been advocating the widespread application of mathematical methods, especially input-output analysis and linear programing beyond present local and experimental applications. There are, however, a number of associated practical problems. First, there is a need to improve data collection and processing, and especially data of the type needed for the new applications. Second, there is a need to improve electronic computers to ensure not only the rapid flow of information, but also its storage and ready availability for use. Third, there are difficulties associated with the mathematical techniques themselves. For example, these methods have been used experimentally at the regional level, but their extension to national planning is both theoretically and practically complex. Further, insofar as the structure of the economy is to be represented in linear programing by a system of equations, it is necessary to consider the introduction of nonlinear as opposed to linear relationships and of a dynamic as opposed to a static or timeless presentation.

In recent years the rate of economic growth in the Soviet Union has declined. In addition, there has been a growing awareness of the need to cope with an economic system different from that prevailing when the system of economic planning was introduced in 1928. The past decade has been one of continuing re-examination of techniques for planning and operating the economy, and especially the role to be played by economic theory, both "Marxian" and "Western." Kantorovich has promoted the development and advocated the widespread application of a powerful mathematical tool. In addition, he has been an ardent crusader for a forceful re-examination of economic theory in the Soviet Union as well as of a broader application of mathematical techniques, electronic computers, and associated methods. Thus Kantorovich must be considered a leading member of the "modernists" who advocate decentralization and a reorientation of the planning structure around these mathematical methods.

There is little doubt that the use of mathematical methods for the elaboration of economic problems will remain an important part of economic thinking in the Soviet Union, though in the immediate future their application may remain within the boundaries of checking and improving existing measures. However, the impact of mathematical techniques and of those who propound them cannot be fully appreciated by a simple explanation of the speed with which specific techniques are adopted, but rather it must be viewed as part of a general process exerting significant pressures upon traditional avenues of thought.

SELECTED BIBLIOGRAPHY

The main biographical source on Kantorovich is *Bol'shaia sovetskaia entsiklopediia,* LI, Moskva, 1959, 140. Similar material can be found in English in a volume by John Turkevich, *Soviet Men of Science,* Princeton: Van Nostrand, 1963, pp. 143–44.

Kantorovich has published widely throughout his career. His initial presentation of the linear programing technique is contained in a monograph entitled *Matematicheskie metody organizatsii i planirovaniia proizvodstva,* Leningrad, 1939. The application of these techniques to problems of transport are considered by Kantorovich and M. K. Gaburin in "Primenenie matematicheskikh metodov v voprosakh analiza gruzopotokov," *Problemy povysheniia effektivnosti raboty transporta,* Moskva, 1949, pp. 110–38. The linear programing technique is extended and its economic implications considered in an important work by Kantorovich, *Ekonomicheskii raschet nailuchshego ispol'zovaniia resursov,* Moskva, 1959. With V. N. Faddeevoi, Kantorovich recently edited the collection *Raboty po avtomaticheskomu programirovaniiu, chislennym metodam i funktsional'nomu analizu,* Moskva, 1962.

A number of simple examples illustrating the best use of resources in production are described in "Ob ischislenii proizvodstvennykh zatrat," *Voprosy ekonomiki,* 1 (January 1960), 122–34. Comments on the role of mathematics in economics are to be found in "Matematika i ekonomika," *Pravda,* August 24, 1965, p. 2.

In the English language, the initial views of Kantorovich on linear programing can be found in "Mathematical Methods of Organizing and Planning Production," *Management Science,* VI, 4 (July 1960), 366–422. His later restatement and expansion of linear programing was translated by P. F. Knightsfield as *The Best Use of Economic Resources,* edited by G. Morton, Cambridge: Harvard University Press, 1965. Finally, his simplified presentation of the best use of resources in production was translated as "On the Calculation of Production Inputs," in *Problems of Economics,* III, 1 (May 1960), 3–10.

For a general treatment of the Soviet economy, Alex Nove, *The Soviet Economy: An Introduction* (revised edition), New York: Praeger, 1966, is excellent. On the problems of planning and the application of mathematical methods, a recent article by John Montias, "Central Planning in Soviet-Type Economies: An Introduction to Basic Problems," is a good treatment and can be found in *The Soviet Economy in Theory and Practice,* edited by Wayne A. Leeman, Columbia: School of Business and Public Administration, University of Missouri, 1964, pp. 1–32. For a concise summary and evaluation of Kantorovich's *The Best Use of Economic Resources,* the reader is referred to an article by Benjamin Ward: "Kantorovich on Economic Calculation," *Journal of Political Economy,* LXVIII, 6 (December 1960), 545–56 and, in addition, to a simpler presentation by John Montias, "Planning and Efficiency: A Note on Kantorovich," *Problems of Communism,* IX, 3 (May-June 1960), 61–64. Finally, R. W. Campbell offers an excellent treatment of the position of Kantorovich and the conflict with traditional Marxian thinking in his article "Marx, Kantorovich, and Novozhilov: *Stoimost'* Versus Reality," *Slavic Review,* XX, 3 (October 1961), 402–18.

Evsei Grigorevich Liberman

by Robert C. Stuart

Evsei Liberman, Soviet economist and statistician, was born on October 2, 1897, in the town of Volyn in the Ukraine. After the completion of public school (*gymnasium*), he attended Kiev University, receiving a law degree in 1920. By 1933 he had earned a degree in engineering from the Kharkov Institute of Engineering and Economics, and finally, in 1957, the doctorate in economics from Kiev University, after presenting a dissertation on the subject of profitability as a guide to enterprise performance. By this time Liberman had already published a number of articles on the subject, drawing on his academic training and on his practical experience as planning chief of a farm machinery works and consultant to industrial firms in Kharkov.

Before the Second World War Liberman taught and conducted research at the Kharkov Institute of Engineering and Economics. Since 1947 he has been director of the Faculty of Economics and the Organization of the Machine Building Industry of the Kharkov Institute of Engineering and Economics, and since 1963 professor in the Faculty of Statistics and Accounting of Kharkov University, holding the chair of Economics of Engineering. He is also a member of the editorial board of the journal *Economic Science,* published in Moscow.

Although Liberman has been actively concerned with problems relating to performance of industrial firms since 1946, it is only recently, and as a result of his publication since 1955, that his name has come to be associated with an important discussion under way in the Soviet Union. A half-dozen years ago, it became obvious even to the Soviet leaders that something was profoundly wrong with the Soviet planning system. There was a time—in the 1930's and 1940's—when it worked, more or less. Although it was clumsy, wasteful, and cruel, it did help in bringing about enormous increases in industrial production and in the development of strategic technology. The old Marxist economic shibboleths appeared really to provide the proper theory for practice. But by the late 1950's, it became obvious that something had gone wrong. Premier Khrushchev and the other Soviet leaders were faced with a frightening slowdown in the rate of growth, a vast accumulation of unwanted and unsalable goods in stores and warehouses, a labor shortage, a growing number of uncompleted construction projects, a proliferation of illegal practices by factory directors bypassing the hopelessly blocked official channels—and, behind it all, Soviet farms unable to increase production by more than a tiny fraction year after year, despite burgeoning needs.

During his years in office, Khrushchev responded to these problems primarily by experimenting with institutional arrangements: changing, for example, the administration of the Soviet collective farms and introducing new forms of regional economic planning and management. But in the face of the persisting problems, the Soviet leadership permitted and indeed fostered wide-ranging discussions not only of the effectiveness of institutional arrangements but—what has proved far more important—of basic Soviet economic theory; all this in a way not permitted since the 1920's. In short, as Robert W. Campbell has pointed out,[1] Soviet planners became aware that the Soviet economy, in which the efficient allocation of resources to achieve competing goals is a constant preoccupation, has muddled through with no body of theory to explain the implications of actual and potential choices.

In the party journal *Kommunist* in 1956, Liberman set forth a concrete proposal designed to secure greater efficiency in the operations of industrial firms through the increased use of profits and the reduction of central directives issued to individual firms. While this proposal did not receive widespread attention at first, Liberman was invited in April 1962 to address a study group of the Academy of Sciences of the USSR headed by the influential Soviet economist, Academician Vasily S. Nemchinov. Shortly thereafter, in September 1962, Liberman's proposal was published in *Pravda* with an editorial call for comment and discussion. At the plenary session of the Central Committee of the Communist Party of the Soviet Union (CPSU) in November 1962, there was a call for "appropriate experimentation," paralleling the response made by the study group of the Academy of Sciences.

These initial developments served to introduce a period of discussion during which there was widespread recognition that efficient operation of Soviet industry, and hence the best marshaling of resources to meet pressing demands, could no longer be guaranteed by prevailing methods of planning and directing the economy.

Since 1928 the operations of Soviet industrial firms have been conducted through a plan, the essence of which is a set of directives, formulated by a central planning agency, outlining for the firm manager the desired level and composition of output, its price and market, the structure and amount of wages, etc. The most important target has been gross out-

[1] Robert W. Campbell, "Marx, Kantorovich, and Novozhilov," *Slavic Review,* XX, 3 (October 1961), 404.

put, and through the system of bonuses rewards are offered to those managers who fulfill and overfulfill it. In any given year, the level at which these targets are set has depended largely upon the level of performance achieved in previous years. The system has become increasingly inadequate, motivating as it does an overconcern with fulfilling plans. Thus, to secure rewards, managers have tended to ignore the details of the plan and to achieve output in the simplest manner, emphasizing heavy products, for example, if gross output is measured in tons. Such practices have led to distortions of both the level and the composition of output. Further, managers tend to underestimate the capacities of their firms in the hope that central planners will set targets that are easy to fulfill. Significant overfulfillment, however, is avoided in the fear that central planners will discover hidden reserves and increase future targets.

Profits as such have always existed, but since financial variables, including prices, are centrally planned, they arise simply as a residual between the planned revenues of the firm and its planned costs of operation. When real profits are achieved (sometimes as a consequence of government subsidy), the manager may use these as bonus payments to workers and staff, reinvestment in the firm, or as credit in the state bank.

During the past decade, increased attention to the problems of economic efficiency has been spurred by recognition of the growing demands that an increasingly complex economy makes on available resources, and in recent years, a recognition of the decline in the rate of economic growth in the USSR. To combat these developments, Khrushchev experimented with changing the institutional arrangements in the Soviet economy, such as the reorganization of 1957 whereby the central direction of the economy through industrial branches was shifted to central direction through regional channels. Such organizational adjustments have not produced notable results, however, for while there has been a recognition of the need to introduce flexibility into the decision-making and reduce what is termed "petty tutelage" over industrial managers, there has also been a continued reluctance on the part of those who plan and direct the economy to preside over an assumed reduction of their influence.

Further, many Soviet economists have come to recognize not only that Soviet economic practice needs changing, but that traditional Soviet planning theory is now inadequate. An increasing number of economists have been advocating the use of mathematical methods in economics, particularly in combination with electronic computers to develop an improved system of central planning. While it is true that mathematical methods might be a decisive aid in the process of decentralization, it is argued that electronic computers, which facilitate high-speed movement and processing of information, are the means by which a system of centralization planning can be perfected.

Finally, there is recognition that the level of performance of industrial firms must be improved, and to achieve this many economists, plant managers, and political leaders have called for a genuine decentralization, the essence of which would involve an expanded role for the managers. Here Liberman's proposals are of great importance.

In his view, the manager of the firm and its personnel must be actively stimulated toward the achievement of the greatest efficiency in production. To reach this goal, he suggested that the success of the firm's personnel, and hence their bonus rewards, be based not upon the fulfillment and overfulfillment of gross output targets but, rather, upon the level of profitability, to be defined as the ratio of achieved profits to the sum of fixed and working capital. Specifically, the centralized setting of targets would be limited to the volume of output, the assortment of output, and delivery schedules. In addition to being a source of revenue for the state budget and for internal investment as before, there would be increased emphasis upon the use of profits as the sole source from which bonus payments could be made. Liberman constructed a system for determining the size of bonuses, which would be conditional upon the fulfillment of central directives for the mix of products and also their delivery to customers. In essence, the size of the bonus would depend upon how profitable the firm had been (in relation to its capital), and norms for industrial branches would be defined.

In Liberman's view, the use of an incentive mechanism with profit playing a central role would ensure that workers and management were motivated toward the achievement of a profitable operation, and in so doing, would stimulate the full utilization of capacity, the satisfaction of consumer wants through greater attention to quality, attractiveness, and usefulness of products, and finally, the fulfillment of delivery schedules to ensure sale of the product. Thus there would be a renewed emphasis upon reducing the cost of production.

Unfortunately, Liberman's proposals still left unsolved a number of problems. How, for example, could the manager of an industrial firm be stimulated to want higher targets that at the same time would correspond with the national interest? Could a single indicator such as profit be used, and if it were, would this imply the abandonment of central planning? In more specific areas, could the distribution of material supplies remain under centralized administrative direction? Could investment be decentralized without a worsening of the existing problem of incompleted or abandoned projects due to the "spreading" of funds? Finally, what changes would be necessary in the price system?

During the latter part of 1962 considerable attention was given in the Soviet press to Liberman's earlier proposal.[2] Of particular interest was the

[2] Liberman may have been successful in gaining recognition through his personal connections with former Ukrainian party personnel, for example, Podgorny, Titov, and Churaev, who had all been at one time secretaries of the Kharkov party organization.

publication of a series of reports delivered to a session of the Learned Council on Economic Accounting of the Academy of Sciences of the USSR, held on September 25–26, 1962. This initial discussion would seem to have contributed little more than a reassertion of the need for change. During 1962 Khrushchev, still engulfed in administrative reorganization in both party and economic hierarchies, attempted to put Liberman's ideas to work in the textile industry and later in the footwear, dairying, and coal-mining industries.

Active public debate had subsided until, on August 17, 1964, an article in *Pravda* signed by Vadim A. Trapeznikov once again brought forward the ideas expressed by Liberman. While Liberman was not specifically mentioned, the article directly concerned his earlier proposal, and once again invited comment and discussion.

While the discussion of 1962 had appeared to produce few constructive changes, the period of discussion initiated by Trapeznikov seemed to begin from the premise that profit was in fact the accepted unitary regulator of operations within the firm, with discussion thereafter focusing upon adjustments necessary for its widespread introduction into planning practice. It was noted that the "financial and economic levers" must be introduced along with profit which ". . . characterizes to the greatest degree the operation of the enterprise and meets the interests of both the national economy and the personnel of the enterprise." The author went further to suggest that by means of price flexibility managers could be induced to introduce new products of higher quality along with more rapid introduction of new technology. Like Liberman, Trapeznikov did not discuss how the price system might be improved, nor how sufficient price flexibility might be achieved in practice. The contributions which followed generally affirmed the views expressed by Trapeznikov, and there was discussion of these and many related issues.

On September 29, 1965, in a speech to the Central Committee of the CPSU, Alexei Kosygin outlined changes to be made in the organization and operation of the Soviet economic system. In the sphere of organization, the system of directing the economy through regional channels, initiated in 1957 by Khrushchev to replace planning through industrial branches was in turn to be replaced by the ministerial system. With regard to operations within the firm, volume of output *sold* would replace gross volume of output as a basic target, with the exception of a group of "important" products for which central targets would be retained. Centralized controls with regard to labor were also to be reduced, with only the size of the wage fund centrally targeted. The essence of these reforms would seem to be greater freedom for the manager, combined with a bonus fund with which to direct managerial behavior into desirable channels. This bonus fund would be derived from profits. Finally, the introduction of charges for capital and emphasis upon the use of credit as opposed to the traditionally free grants would appear designed to spur management to greater efficiency in the use of these funds.

The implementation and assessment of these reforms will be a slow process. To the extent that they represent an attempt to relax central controls and place greater reliance upon a profit mechanism to direct managerial behavior, they reflect a trend advocated by Liberman. Only time will indicate to what degree this attempted relaxation is in fact genuine, and also viable.

It is evident from the discussion to date that in greater or less degree, the Soviet economy will remain under a system of central planning. Given a desire to retain central control over the development of the economy combined with the need to achieve greater efficiency through flexibility in the decision-making process, one must ask under what conditions profit as the basis of an incentive mechanism will serve these ends, and in addition, to what extent a combination of directives from central planners and freedom of operation by local managers is in fact viable in this economic system.

To the extent that central commands are reduced, they must be replaced by means through which equivalent decisions can be independently made at the local level. Further, the bases upon which these local decisions are made must serve two ends. First, managers must be induced to make decisions which satisfy the central planners' wishes. Second, decisions made locally should strive toward economic efficiency, that is, the achievement of the desired products at minimum cost. These local decisions might be made as they are in a decentralized market economy, on the basis of a system of prices and related variables of costs, profits, etc. However, to achieve the kind of result indicated here and apparently desired in the Soviet Union, it is necessary that prices represent the interaction of both supply and demand forces, not merely the supply forces or cost of production as in a Marxian framework. Under a system of prices not based upon the interaction of both demand and supply forces (whether formulated in a market or by mathematical techniques), it is not clear that decisions made locally will conform with the wishes of central planners, nor is it clear that economic efficiency will be achieved. Under a process of genuine decentralization, prices and the associated variables no longer serve only as an accounting measure of how well a manager has carried out the commands of a central planner but, rather, these monetary variables become the bases upon which decisions are made—decisions which will replace those central commands.

While Liberman and subsequent writers in this discussion have suggested in general terms the need for a revision of the Soviet price system, there has been no willingness to spell out necessary improvements. Recently, a State Committee for Prices was formed to investigate the structure of wholesale industrial prices. It is interesting that during the past decade, discussion of the price system has been conducted apart from the discussion of managerial reforms. Further, although the price reforms advocated by the mathematical economists Leonid Kantorovich, V. Novozhilov and Vasily S. Nemchinov would be in harmony with the profit mechanism proposed by Liberman, they have not been united.

To what extent is a system of central directives and decentralized decision-making a viable combination? One area which is illustrative of possible difficulties is that of materials allocation. If a manager is motivated by a profit or other mechanism to achieve economic efficiency and hence minimize costs of production, he will wish to substitute inputs in such a way as to achieve the economically and technologically most desirable combination. Under the present system, materials needed for the production of goods are allocated on the basis of an annual plan, a system which introduces both rigidity and imbalance. While Liberman advocated direct contacts between producing firms and their consumers, recent reforms have only admonished managers to fulfill their delivery requirements and have made this a requirement for the payment of bonuses from profits. This question of extending the decision-making powers of local managers into the sphere of materials allocation illustrates a fundamental practical problem facing a process of decentralization, namely, the establishment of a compatible mix of centralized controls desired by political leaders, with a measure of decentralization sufficient to ensure economic efficiency and progress. In this regard, the experiences of the Eastern European economies are instructive, for they demonstrate that the transition of an economic system from a stage characterized by central directives to local bodies, to a stage characterized by partial or complete decentralization where responses to central directives are replaced by responses to prices, costs, profits, etc., is not only complex in its initial stages, but also tends to be followed by problems relatively new to the planned economies.

SELECTED BIBLIOGRAPHY

The main biographical source for Liberman is *Ukrains'ka radians'ka entsiklopediia,* XVI, Kiev, 1964, p. 583.

Among Liberman's earlier publications are *O planirovanii pribyli v promyshlennosti,* Moskva, 1950, and *Vnutrizavodskii khoziaistvennyi raschet,* Moskva, 1949, and later, his doctoral dissertation, *Puti povysheniia rentabel'nosti sotsialisticheskikh predpriiatii.* Liberman presented his ideas initially in four articles: "Khoziaistvennyi raschet i material'noe pooshchrenie rabotnikov promyshlennosti," *Voprosy ekonomiki,* 6 (January 1955), 24–44; "O planirovanii promyshlennogo proizvodstva i material'nykh stimulakh ego razvitiia," *Kommunist,* 10 (July 1956), 75–92; "Ob ekonomicheskikh rychagakh vypolneniia plana promyshlennost'iu SSSR," *Kommunist,* 1 (January 1959), 88–97; and "Planirovanie proizvodsta i normativy dlitel'nogo deistviia," *Voprosy ekonomiki,* 8 (August 1962), 104–12. Although these articles were directly concerned with the performance of the Soviet industrial firm, widespread discussion on the subject began in the press only after publication of his article "Plan, pribyl', premiia," in *Pravda,* September 9, 1962, p. 3 and Liberman replied to his critics later in the article "Eshche raz o plane, pribyli i premii," *Pravda,* September 20, 1964, p. 3.

Liberman's proposal met with resistance, for example, from A. Zverev in "Protiv skhematizma v reshenii sloshnykh voprosov," *Voprosy ekonomiki,* 11 (1962), 93–97 and G. Kosiachenko in "Vazhnoe uslovie uluchsheniia planirovaniia," *Voprosy ekonomiki,* 11 (1962), 109–12. However, the basic unity in the diverse positions was emphasized by V. Nemchinov in "Zaniteresovat' predpriiatie v bolee napriazhennom plane," *Voprosy ekonomiki,* 11 (1962), 100–102. The discussion was renewed in 1964, and Liberman's general position upheld in an article by V. Trapeznikov entitled "Za glibkoe ekonomicheskoe upravlenie predpriiatiiami," *Pravda,* August 17, 1964, pp. 3–4.

In addition to English translations available in *Problems of Economics,* White Plains: International Arts and Sciences Press and in the *Current Digest of the Soviet Press,* Ann Arbor: Joint Committee on Slavic Studies, six of the contributions by Liberman and many of the related articles are translated and reprinted in a volume edited by M. E. Sharpe entitled *The Liberman Discussion: A New Phase in Soviet Economic Thought,* White Plains: International Arts and Sciences Press, 1965.

Liberman's proposal and its relation to problems of the Soviet firm are ably discussed by B. J. McFarlane and I. Gordijew in "Profitability and the Soviet Firm," *Economic Record* (December 1964), 554–68. Concise description and evaluation of the proposal is given by A. Nove in "The Liberman Proposals," *Survey,* 51 (April 1963), 112–18, and also by A. Zauberman in "Liberman's Rules of the Game for Soviet Industry," *Slavic Review,* XXII, 4 (December 1963), 734–44. A more recent treatment of the proposal including commentary on the experiments conducted in the Soviet Union is given by R. W. Campbell in "Economics: Roads and Inroads," *Problems of Communism,* XIV, 6 (November-December 1965), 23–33. Finally, the most recent reforms contemplated for the Soviet economic system are outlined by A. Kosygin in his statement entitled "On Improving the Management of Industry, Perfecting Planning and Strengthening Economic Incentives in Industrial Production," *Current Digest of the Soviet Press,* XVII, 38 (October 13, 1965), 3–15.

Vladimir Nikolaevich Novikov

by Grey Hodnett

During Stalin's lifetime, few officials, once demoted, were fortunate enough to regain their former rank in the hierarchy. To lose the "great leader's" confidence implied that a man probably suffered from moral and political leprosy; better that he be cast to the bottom of the pit, than contaminate the rest. Today, however, the absence of a single leader possessed of Stalin's political authority and terroristic power has to some extent mitigated the sense of sinfulness attached to demotion, alleviated the social isolation of the victim, and turned what was largely a bizarre manifestation of tribalism into something more closely resembling an episode of bureaucratic politics. The price of demotion in a system with only one employer is still high, but hope now remains, and the political comeback is thus not unusual on the Soviet scene. One of the most spectacular of such cases was the recent appointment of the former high official, Vladimir Novikov, to the posts of deputy chairman of the Council of Ministers of the USSR and chairman of the Supreme Council of National Economy of the USSR (VSNKh SSSR). The promotion of this heavy-set, dark-haired man was announced concurrently with the election (at the Central Committee's March 1965 plenary meeting) of Dimitri Ustinov, former chairman of the VSNKh SSSR, to candidate membership in the party Presidium and secretary of the Central Committee. The two appointments convincingly demonstrated that the "old school tie" is by no means a monopoly of the capitalist West.

Vladimir Nikolaevich Novikov, born in 1907 in the town of Kresttsy, south of St. Petersburg (now Leningrad), in what is now Novgorod Oblast, was a schoolboy of seven at the outbreak of the First World War; ten at the time of the Revolution; and fourteen when the Civil War was finally over. Nothing is known of his childhood, except that his father was a Great Russian. It seems that Novikov spent most of the 1920's acquiring a secondary technical education, graduating in 1928 from a mechanical vocational high school in Novgorod. Like most present-day Soviet officials, he did not have the opportunity to progress immediately from secondary school to some higher educational institution. In 1928, at the very beginning of collectivization and of the First Five-Year Plan, he took a job as a skilled worker in an armaments and steel-fabricating factory in Izhevsk, a city near the major Urals center of Perm. He was to remain associated with this branch of Soviet industry for almost thirty years.

Anticipating imminent war with one or more nations of the "capitalist encirclement," party leaders assigned high priority to armaments production. Every effort was made to develop the war-industrial capability of the Soviet Union, including technical collaboration with the Reichswehr and German industry. Wages in the armaments industry were high by Soviet standards, and working conditions were relatively good at a time of great privation for most Russians.

Novikov soon demonstrated to his superiors that he was a man of promise, and he was sent to Leningrad to attend the Leningrad Institute of Military Technology. The institute, run with the discipline of a regular military academy, was an educational establishment of relatively high standards whose purpose was to produce both technically trained military officers and specialists for the armaments industry. It is likely that here Novikov first came to know Ustinov, the man who was later to loom large in his life.

Both Novikov and Ustinov—who is a year younger than Novikov— graduated from the institute in 1934; both subsequently followed almost identical paths. Ustinov worked in the armaments industry from 1934 to 1941 as an engineer and designer in a research institute, chief of a factory experimental bureau, deputy chief designer, and finally director of the factory. Novikov returned in 1934 to his former armaments factory in Izhevsk, where he worked until 1941 as a designer, chief engineer, and then director. Both men's careers profited immeasurably from the "great purge" of the 1930's; in no other way could they have risen so rapidly, however brilliant an impression they might have created on their own. Novikov can have been no older than thirty-four when he became director of the factory and might easily have been a year or two younger. The purges, acting as a vast—if artificial—social revolution, brought junior officials to positions of high responsibility in the 1930's, causing the Soviet Union to enter the 1960's supplied with numerous leaders who had accumulated long years of experience at the very top of their professions. Novikov is a particularly successful example of the species.

The most important observable difference between the early careers of Ustinov and Novikov is that Ustinov joined the Communist party in 1927, at nineteen, whereas Novikov did not join until 1936, when he was twenty-nine. Ustinov was thus a party member before he occupied a post of any significance or had received his higher education; before collectivization and the drive toward rapid industrialization had begun to transform the pattern of Soviet life; before Stalin's suppression of all opposition; and before the terror of the 1930's. Novikov, on the other hand, became a member after he received his higher education and could foresee a successful industrial career, and after the introduction of terror, which made it unhealthy in any case to refuse an invitation to join. Novikov was elected a deputy to the Supreme Soviet of the USSR the very year he became a party member, an honor which reflected his professional achievement more, perhaps, than it did the fact that he was simply trusted politically. These considerations lend plausibility to the supposition that in his early life, at least, Novikov was the less politically conscious of the two and more narrowly restricted in ambitions and activities to the realm of technical matters.

Whether Novikov and Ustinov saw much of each other between 1934 and 1941 cannot be determined, although it seems highly likely that they had some contact. The advent of the Second World War catapulted both into the ranks of the highest managerial stratum of Soviet society, and placed Novikov in that position of dependency vis-à-vis Ustinov which continued to exist thereafter. In 1941 Ustinov became people's commissar for Armaments and Novikov deputy commissar—the Commissariat for Armaments having responsibility for many, though not all, types of weapons. Their appointments must have raised many an eyebrow—although not in Stalin's presence; Novikov, the older of the pair, was only thirty-four. It should be said in their favor, of course, that however much loyalty to Stalin was the *sine qua non* for holding high office, competence itself counted—particularly during the war and especially in positions requiring high technical skills. There is no reason to doubt that Novikov was qualified to hold this wartime position in one of the vital branches of the government. Early in the war (1942) he was awarded the honorary title of Hero of Socialist Labor.

In 1948 Novikov moved from his position as deputy minister of the Defense Industry (his title had been changed in 1946) to become director of a research institute connected with the armaments industry, thus still serving under Ustinov. In 1953 or 1954 he returned to his old position of deputy minister of the Defense Industry, still under Ustinov, and retained the post for a year. At the same time he headed one of the main administrations (*glavki*) of the Ministry of the Defense Industry.

The few years which had passed since the explosion of the first Soviet atomic bomb (1949) had witnessed a revolution in the means of warfare; besides the new atomic weapons, radical innovations were occurring in aviation, rocketry, electronics, and all other areas of military technology. The ascent of the first Soviet Sputnik lay not far ahead. If the pressures on Novikov were not so immediate as they had been during the war, the ultimate stakes involved in his work were of no less magnitude, and the intellectual demands upon him were probably even greater. That he was able to cope with his responsibilities became evident in 1955 when he was appointed first deputy minister of General Machine Building. This ministry supervised a sector of the conventional armaments industry, although precisely which one has not been revealed. It was headed by Pyotr Goremykin, who became its first minister on April 2, 1955, and remained in charge until the ministry was merged with the Ministry of Defense Industry on May 10, 1957.

By 1957 Novikov had worked in the armaments industry for almost thirty years. Probably he was involved almost exclusively in the production of conventional, nonnuclear weapons; he never received a State (formerly "Stalin") Prize, one of the signs of participation in vital new weapons development programs. Although he held positions of great responsibility, his experiences were probably not entirely those of a typical economic administrator, for the armaments industry has long been a favored child in the Soviet Union. This has meant that its executives have had to worry less about many of the problems that continually plague other industrial administrators, such as unrealistic and uncoordinated plans, constant shortages of raw materials, excessive labor turnover, and so forth. As a highly centralized and secretive branch of the economy, the armaments industry has enjoyed greater autonomy with respect to local party bosses. High armaments officials have dealt with other high government administrators, with certain key party leaders, and with the military establishment. They constitute an important element in the Soviet version of the "military-industrial complex"—a group with a large stake in rapid growth rates for heavy industry and big allocations for military production. Problems of consumer welfare, needless to say, have stood outside the scope of their professional concerns.

In July 1957 Novikov was given an excellent opportunity to broaden his experience: he was appointed chairman of the Leningrad Sovnarkhoz (Council of National Economy). The decision to eliminate many of the existing ministries and decentralize operational control over the economy to more than 100 local *sovnarkhozy* was made official at the meeting in May 1957 of the Supreme Soviet of the USSR. Khrushchev, who initiated the reform, presumably was concerned that the head of the highly important Leningrad economic region should be a man who could make the new structure work. Novikov's appointment was thus probably not a demotion, even though it was a step down in the formal hierarchy and took him out of Moscow. As economic overlord of the second largest metropolitan area of the Soviet Union, Novikov was accountable for much of the planning and supervision of a vast agglomeration of heavy and light industry, including much precision armaments production. His job was to coordinate the actions of the hundreds of enterprises in Leningrad, to integrate the production of Leningrad with that of other economic regions, and to reconcile demands from Moscow with economic realities as seen through the eyes of local managers and party officials.

Novikov handled these tasks successfully. On May 7, 1958, he was brought back to Moscow and made first deputy chairman of the Council of Ministers and chairman of the State Planning Committee (Gosplan) of the Russian republic (RSFSR). He had now become the chief economic planner of an area within the Soviet Union larger than any other country in the world. Although his power was apparently reduced slightly in April 1959, when he stepped down from first deputy chairman to deputy chairman of the RSFSR Council of Ministers, he continued as head of the RSFSR Gosplan until May 1960.

The spring of 1960 may have been a major turning point in the political history of post-Stalin Russia. It has often been argued, though not yet conclusively proved, that Khrushchev was then under strong attack by some of his fellow Presidium members for a variety of reasons, including manpower and budgetary policies that could be interpreted (by those so inclined) as undermining the military security of the Soviet Union. It is contended by some Western observers that a number of leadership changes in May and July 1960 were on the whole unfavorable to Khrushchev. Whatever the merits of this line of speculation, it is a fact that

Novikov—a man who had spent almost his entire adult life in the manufacture of armaments—was promoted on May 4, 1960, to the post of deputy chairman of the Council of Ministers of the USSR and chairman of the State Planning Committee of the USSR (Gosplan USSR).

Novikov's promotion came at a time when the decentralizing reform of 1957 had begun to create serious problems of interregional coordination. These difficulties provided justification for the recentralization of economic administration that was well under way by the summer of 1960. Gosplan USSR itself had retained enormous power after 1957; the recentralization brought it—and Novikov—even greater influence. Although at first glance it might appear that the chairman of Gosplan is merely a technician who implements the priorities decided upon by the party leadership, the actual process of drawing up the economic plan for the Soviet Union is far more complex. Peevish comments which constantly found their way into Khrushchev's speeches abundantly demonstrate that Gosplan possesses a large measure of the power wielded by all "expert" bodies: the opportunity to formulate choices, to say "it can't be done." This power is amplified in the USSR by a price system that, not reflecting real economic scarcity, makes it easier still for the planner to manipulate "objective" data. But even if the most apolitical intentions be conceded to the chairman of Gosplan, the centralized allocation of resources in the Soviet economy makes it impossible for him to avoid presiding over a focal point of political struggle. This circumstance is reflected in innumerable speeches of Soviet officials high and low.

With the advantage of hindsight, it can be said that Novikov was probably not sufficiently apolitical or pliable to suit Khrushchev. Although Novikov had been elected to the party's Central Committee in October 1961, nine months later—in July 1962—he was replaced as chairman of Gosplan by his deputy, Veniamin Dymshits, and downgraded to the posts of permanent representative to Comecon (the Soviet bloc "common market") and representative in the Executive Committee of Comecon. Several months later, in November 1962, he was further humiliated by being stripped of his title of deputy chairman of the Council of Ministers (he remained a minister) and shunted to the position of chairman of the Commission for Economic Relations with Foreign Countries. The latter demotion occurred during the November plenary session of the Central Committee, when Khrushchev vigorously attacked the existing planning system and unveiled a reorganized structure that assigned short-term planning to a USSR Council of National Economy (SNKh SSSR) and long-term planning to the USSR State Planning Committee (Gosplan). As Novikov was not included in this reorganization, it appeared that he was well on the way to premature political retirement.

In March 1963, however, Novikov's hopes for a comeback were probably enlivened by the good fortune of his superior of many years, Dimitri Ustinov. Under obscure circumstances, a new, apparently all-powerful economic coordinating agency was established—the USSR Supreme Council of National Economy (VSNKh SSSR). The planning organs, construction agency, and majority of other state economic bodies (including those responsible for armaments production) were made directly subordinate to it, not to the Council of Ministers. Ustinov, who appeared to have been slighted in November 1962, was appointed its first chairman.

It took Novikov two more years to make his own return from the political wilderness. On March 26, 1965, he became Ustinov's successor as chairman of the VSNKh SSSR, while Ustinov was promoted to a high position in the Communist party. Novikov also became a deputy chairman of the Council of Ministers, which, though not as high as Ustinov's position when he was chairman of the VSNKh, was equal to his own former rank. Western observers speculated at the time that the VSNKh might have lost some of its former real, or at least statutory, authority with this demotion of its head in the "cabinet" of the Council of Ministers. And, indeed, it was indicated at the September 1965 plenum of the party's Central Committee that the VSNKh was to be abolished. Nevertheless, at the age of fifty-eight, and with the timely departure of Khrushchev, Novikov had risen far toward the pinnacle of the imposing state bureaucracy of the USSR. His high rank in the Soviet elite was certified by his being re-elected to membership in the Central Committee at the Twenty-third Congress of the Communist Party of the Soviet Union (CPSU) in April 1966.

SELECTED BIBLIOGRAPHY

In Russian, the main sources of biographical information about Novikov are the following: *Leningrad: Entsiklopedicheskii spravochnik,* Moskva, Leningrad, 1957, p. 632; *Deputaty verkhovnogo soveta SSSR,* Moskva, 1959, p. 292; *Deputaty verkhovnogo soveta SSSR,* Moskva, 1963, p. 313; *Ezhegodnik bol'- shoi sovetskoi entsiklopedii 1962,* Moskva, 1962, p. 607. A Western source is J. Marin, "Nowikow, Wladimir Nikolajewitsch," *Porträts der UdSSR-Prominenz,* München: Institut Zur Erforschung Der UdSSR, 1960. Information about Novikov in English can be found in *Who's Who in the USSR, 1965–1966,* New York and London: Scarecrow Press, 1966, p. 604.

Dimitri Fedorovich Ustinov

by Grey Hodnett

On March 25, 1965, six months after the *coup d'état* that removed Nikita Khrushchev from office, a plenary meeting of the Central Committee of the Communist Party of the Soviet Union (CPSU) elected Dimitri Ustinov a candidate member of the Presidium and secretary of the Central Committee. The appointments capped a brilliant career marked by early and uninterrupted success.

Dimitri Fedorovich Ustinov was born in 1908 in Samara (now Kuibyshev), an old city on the left bank of a large bend in the Volga River, in the steppe region midway between Kazan and Saratov. Before the era of Soviet industrialization, Saratov was a town which boasted some light industry, but served primarily as administrative center of a predominantly agricultural province; it was also a major transportation center, standing as it did at the crossroads of Volga River traffic and movement between western Russia and the Ukraine, and the Urals, Siberia, and Central Asia. Little is known of Ustinov's childhood, except that he grew up in a worker's family. His father was an ethnic Russian. At the time of the Russian Revolution the young Ustinov was nine, but how the Revolution and Civil War affected his life is unknown.

Ustinov received his secondary education during the 1920's, graduating from a technical high school in the city of Makarev (Kostroma Oblast) in 1927. The same year, at the early age of nineteen, he joined the Communist party—an indication of ambition and an omen of future achievements. For the next two years, until 1929, Ustinov worked as a skilled laborer in the Balakhninsk paper-manufacturing combine, in what is now Gorki Oblast, and in the "Zariad" (projectile) armaments plant in the city of Ivanovo-Voznesensk. During the First Five-Year Plan he left factory work in Ivanovo-Voznesensk in order to acquire a higher education at the Leningrad Institute of Military Technology. In these years, establishments like the institute (in which a military atmosphere was maintained) trained both armaments technicians and future regular officers. The institute stressed weapons design and production, and its academic standards were higher than the average. Graduates could either go on to serve in the armed forces, or assume positions in industry.

In 1934, the year the murder of the Leningrad party boss, Sergei Kirov, unleashed the full fury of Stalinist terrorism, Ustinov, along with other carefully screened students, graduated as a mechanical engineer. He was assigned to work as a design engineer in a scientific research institute run by the USSR People's Commissariat for the Defense Industry and stayed in this position until sometime in 1937, when he was assigned to work in the "Bolshevik" armaments factory in Moscow.

Like thousands of others of similar age, social background, and post-Revolutionary loyalties and training, Ustinov benefited from the terror of the late 1930's by ascending the occupational ladder with extraordinary speed. The purge that ripped through the Red Army and armaments industry in 1937 clearly did not spare the "Bolshevik" factory where he then worked. Starting out the year as an ordinary design engineer, Ustinov rose to chief of the bureau for experimental work, and by the end of the year had been appointed the factory's deputy chief designer. The next year he was named director of the factory. Although meteoric careers could be observed on all sides, few of Ustinov's peers could better his record of becoming manager of a high-priority armaments factory at thirty. It is impossible to say, of course, what blend of professional skill, ambition, shortage of older personnel, and luck (or even moral callousness) produced this remarkable achievement.

Stalin once justified the hardships and suffering brought about by collectivization and industrialization on the grounds that the Soviet system had only ten years to overcome the backwardness of centuries before it would be forced into mortal combat with the capitalistic West. The sacrifices imposed on the Soviet people during the 1930's enabled Ustinov and other managers in the armaments industry to be supplied with new plants, capital equipment, the lion's share of scarce raw materials, and the cream of trained manpower.

The feverish military preparations of the Soviet Union, however, had not been completed when, on June 22, 1941, the German Army surged across Russia's western frontier. In this year of supreme trial for the Communist system and the Russian people, Stalin chose Ustinov, then thirty-three, as his new commissar for armaments—one of the critical posts in the Soviet government. Some light has been cast on Ustinov's appointment by the publication in 1962 of an article by B. Vannikov, Ustinov's predecessor in the post.[1] Vannikov was removed from the post (which he had held since 1938) in connection—so he states—with Stalin's decision to cease producing 45 and 75 mm. antitank weapons and to produce only 107 mm. ones. This decision, in which Andrei Zhdanov is also said to have played a part, was made at the urging of the newly appointed chief of the Main Artillery Administration, G. Kulik, a Stalin follower of dubious credentials, who based his re-evaluation of the Red Army's artillery requirements on faulty intelligence estimates of German

---

[1] Cited in M. N. Chernomorskii *Rabota nad memuarami pri izuchenii istorii KPSS,* Moskva, 1965, pp. 130–31.

armor. Kulik's efforts led to the inevitable lodging of accusations of treason against various people in the armaments industry. Vannikov was arrested in June 1941 on the very eve of the German invasion, imprisoned in solitary confinement, and probably tortured, though less than one month later, when the folly of the antitank gun decision became apparent, he was released and soon appointed commissar of Munitions Production. For his tribulations he was granted in 1942 the title Hero of Socialist Labor.

A week after the German attack, a new supreme political organ— the State Defense Committee—was created. Headed by Stalin, its initial membership included Vyacheslav Molotov, Georgi Malenkov, Kliment Voroshilov, and Lavrenti Beria, and later, Anastas Mikoyan, Nikolai Voznesensky, Lazar Kaganovich, and Nikolai Bulganin were added. (Khrushchev was never admitted to this select group.) Under the State Defense Committee was the Economic Committee for Armaments Production, which presumably exercised day-to-day supervision over the Commissariat for Armaments. As commissar for Armaments, therefore, Ustinov was directly responsible to the chairman of the Economic Committee for Armaments Production, a post first held by Voznesensky, chairman of the State Planning Committee (Gosplan), then by Malenkov. Since Gosplan was the main staff agency for coordinating the entire Soviet war economy, it may be assumed that Ustinov worked closely with Voznesensky throughout the war, though like all other top leaders, he also reported to Stalin.

Manpower, the vast expanse of Russian territory, and Lend-Lease made important contributions to the ultimate Soviet victory. But without the successful design and expanding production of tanks and artillery (whose combat performance came to enjoy a healthy respect in all quarters), the Germans could not have been pushed back as they were. No little credit should be given to Ustinov for this achievement. The war was a grueling test of his intelligence, administrative skill, nerve, and stamina. If the decorations showered upon him are any indication, Stalin and his successors had no cause to complain about his wartime performance. In 1942 he was awarded the title of Hero of Socialist Labor for his part in organizing the Soviet war industry in the Urals and Siberia. Later in his career he received seven orders of Lenin, together with the orders of Suvorov and Kutuzov. In 1953 he was given a Stalin Prize, quite possibly for work in rocket design. (Recognition for having contributed materially to the outstandingly successful Soviet rocket program would have added greatly to Ustinov's prestige, not the least among the military.) An even more reliable sign that his superiors were satisfied with his work, however, was his being permitted, after the war, to continue in his position—a position considered of particular importance in all Communist systems. That Ustinov was in Stalin's good graces through the dictator's last days was indicated by his election to full membership in the Central Committee at the Nineteenth Congress of the CPSU in October 1952.

After Stalin's death, Ustinov retained his status as czar of the Soviet armaments industry.[2] He then survived, successively, the fall of Beria later in 1953, the rise and decline of Malenkov from 1953 to 1955, and the rise of Khrushchev, which culminated in the disgrace of Molotov, Malenkov, Kaganovich, and lesser lights in June 1957. By 1957 Ustinov had been a prominent leader in Soviet military production for some sixteen years. Among wartime armaments ministers of the Great Powers, he was unique in having presided over the postwar retooling of the armed forces, by virtue of which conventional weapons were modernized, mechanization vastly increased, and the groundwork laid for atomic warfare. The enormous experience he accumulated in this period undoubtedly made him increasingly valuable to the men in the Kremlin, which in turn helps to explain why he was able to stay on top throughout the infighting of Soviet bureaucratic life. But Ustinov probably also deserves to be credited with a certain amount of the technician's discretion and restraint—with some willingness to go along with basic policy decisions of the current political leadership without seriously balking or intriguing against them. Otherwise it would be difficult to account fully for his survival.

In December 1957, after Khrushchev had consolidated his power, Ustinov was promoted to deputy chairman of the Council of Ministers. In his new position he was still deeply involved in the armaments industry; but the scope of his responsibilities was apparently broadened to cover areas of basic technology as well. His speeches since 1957 have touched upon a wide variety of matters, ranging from automation of machine tool production to complexities of rocket technology—from metallurgy to electronics. Ustinov, who himself holds the military rank of general-colonel in the Engineering and Technical Services, is distinguished by being among those top Soviet state officials who have had frequent long-time contact with the military establishment. Recently, the nature of his duties may have led him to have more frequent relations with "modernist" elements in the armed forces (who emphasize the need to prepare for quick, highly mobile, missile-atomic wars) than with "traditionalist" ground force commanders (who foresee the continued possibility of wars of attrition waged by large conventional armies). His own views are not known, although it is plausible to suppose that in decisions affecting the division of Soviet national income and the allocation of resources, Ustinov's sympathies have lain with those inclined to sacrifice consumer welfare to military preparedness. If so, he probably did not always see eye to eye with Khrushchev, who—while supporting measures designed to replace manpower with firepower—proposed consumer-oriented programs that implied over-all cuts in the armaments budget.

[2] From 1953 his agency was called the Ministry of Defense Industry.

At the plenary meeting of the Central Committee in November 1962, a major reorganization of the CPSU was instituted, with the aim of improving party supervision of the economy. Changes were also made in the structure of the USSR state administration, including a reorganization of the planning apparatus, whereby short-run planning was to be conducted by a new USSR Council of the National Economy (headed by Veniamin Dymshits) and long-term planning by a transformed USSR State Planning Committee (Gosplan, headed by Pyotr Lomako). The impetus behind these changes was clearly Khrushchev's, who seemed to view them as an integrated whole.

Barely four months later (March 13, 1963), a joint meeting of the party Presidium and the USSR Council of Ministers was held, at which it was decided to form a new high-powered economic directing and coordinating agency, the USSR Supreme Council of National Economy (VSNKh SSSR). The broad responsibilities assigned to this body seemed to overlap those of the Council of Ministers itself, and those of the recently restructured planning organs. The VSNKh was to be the "supreme state agency for guiding industry and construction in the country," invested with "all the necessary rights and plenary powers to decide questions connected with the work of industry and construction and with ensuring the successful fulfillment of state plans." While the VSNKh was to be subordinate to the Council of Ministers, it was empowered to issue "resolutions and instructions, the fulfillment of which is binding upon all state agencies regardless of their subordination." The VSNKh, in turn, was placed over Gosplan, the USSR Council of the National Economy, and the USSR State Committee for Construction Affairs, and was told to coordinate their work. A number of other ministerial state committees were also directly subordinated to the VSNKh (rather than to the Council of Ministers) including the entire complement of state committees for military production. Ustinov was chosen to head this imposing bureaucratic edifice.

A number of signs suggest to some observers that Khrushchev's power diminished during the winter of 1962–63, reaching a nadir around March. Khrushchev did not associate himself in the press with the March reorganization, and it is possible that he opposed creation of the VSNKh, and with it, Ustinov's appointment. The reorganization seemed to signify a victory for the economic traditionalists whom Khrushchev had frequently opposed. In later months, as Khrushchev's position, in the opinion of these observers, seemed to improve, the VSNKh received little publicity. It remains unclear to what extent it performed its assigned duties. Ustinov's uncertain political status in the last years of Khrushchev's rule was suggested by the passing of two Central Committee plenums without his own elevation to candidate membership in the Presidium of the party—a logical promotion given his lofty position in the Council of Ministers. He finally did receive this promotion in March 1965, during the phase of "collective leadership" that followed Khrushchev's downfall. Equally important, he was released from his positions of VSNKh chairman and deputy chairman of the Council of Ministers and made a secretary of the party's Central Committee—a sign that, in view of his cooptation into the party Presidium, his star was on the rise, despite forfeiture of his institutional base of power in the state administration. The transfer into the Secretariat—the nerve center of the party apparatus—of a man who had worked for years exclusively as a high state bureaucrat in itself broke almost all precedents. There could be no room left for doubt that this talented military-production administrator spoke with authority in the highest councils of Soviet political life.

SELECTED BIBLIOGRAPHY

The main sources of biographical information about Ustinov are the following: *Bol'shaia sovetskaia entsiklopediia,* vypusk 2, XLIV, Moskva, 1956, p. 404; *Ezhegodnik bol'shoi sovetskoi entsiklopedii 1958,* Moskva, 1958, p. 644; *Ezhegodnik bol'shoi sovetskoi entsiklopedii 1962,* Moskva, 1962, p. 619; *Deputaty verkhovnogo soveta SSSR,* Moskva, 1959, p. 407; *Deputaty verkhovnogo soveta SSSR,* Moskva, 1963, p. 435; *Ukrains'ka radians'ka entsiklopediia,* XV, Kiev,.1964, pp. 170–71. A Western source is J. Swiridow, "Ustinov, Dmitrij Fjodorowitsch," *Porträts der UdSSR-Prominenz,* München: Institut Zur Erforschung Der UdSSR, 1960.

In English, information about Ustinov can be found in *Biographic Directory of the USSR,* New York: Scarecrow Press, 1958, p. 691 and *Who's Who in the USSR, 1965–1966,* New York and London: Scarecrow Press, 1966, p. 887.

Dimitri Ivanovich Blokhintsev

by Albert Parry

Dimitri Ivanovich Blokhintsev, a prominent Soviet atomic physicist, was born on January 11, 1908. He was graduated from the University of Moscow in 1930 and at once placed on its faculty as an instructor, becoming professor in 1936.

From 1935 to 1956 Blokhintsev was on the staff of the Institute of Physics, and he headed construction of the Soviet Union's first atomic power plant (affiliated with the Academy of Sciences of the USSR). From 1956 to early 1965 he gained wide international renown as organizer and director of the Joint Institute of Nuclear Research at Dubna, near Moscow.

Blokhintsev joined the Communist party in 1943. A corresponding member of the Ukrainian Academy of Sciences since 1939, he became a corresponding member of the Academy of Sciences of the USSR in 1958. His awards include the Stalin Prize, 1952; the title of Hero of Socialist Labor, 1956; and the Lenin Prize, 1957. He was made a judge on the Committee for Lenin Prizes for Science and Technology (affiliated with the Council of Ministers) in 1960.

Blokhintsev appeared as a member of the Soviet delegation to the International Conference on Peaceful Uses of Atomic Energy in Geneva in August 1955, where he was co-author of a report on the construction and functioning of the first Soviet atomic power plant. In December 1957 he visited the United States for the first time, as head of a delegation of four Soviet physicists to an international symposium on nuclear sizes at Stanford University, and he read a paper (in English) at the meeting of the American Physical Society. He was chairman of the organizational committee of the Ninth International Conference on High Energy Physics in Kiev in 1960, and of the Twelfth Conference in Dubna in 1964.

An outstanding theoretical physicist and successful nuclear-plant designer and engineer, Blokhintsev has devoted his efforts to problems of solids, optics, acoustics, theory of fields, and quantum mechanics, as well as such general areas as natural philosophy, and atomic physics and atomic technology. In 1934 he developed the first quantum theory of solid-state phosphorescence, as well as the theory of absorption and fluorescence spectra of complex molecules. A number of his works are on semiconductor phenomena, particularly on the theory of solid rectifiers; he was the first to explain the phenomenon on the basis of the concept of nonlinearity of Ohm's Law at the limit of semiconductors' division. From 1944 to 1947 he did research in propagation of sound waves in a mobile heterogeneous medium.

Blokhintsev is the author of the first complete course of instruction for Soviet universities on quantum mechanics based on dialectical materialism. His published works include "On the Theory of Phosphorescence," 1934; "The Spectra of Fluorescence and Absorption of Complex Molecules," 1939; "The Acoustics of a Mobile Heterogeneous Medium," 1946; "Elementary Particles in a Field," 1950; and "Non-Localized and Non-Linear Theories of Field," 1957. His main book is *Foundations of Quantum Mechanics,* 1944 and 1949.

Among Blokhintsev's practical contributions to Soviet science and technology, his part in creating the nation's first atomic energy plant merits particular attention. For several years in the early 1950's he was in charge of a vast staff of physicists, engineers, technicians, and other specialists from a number of research institutes and industrial plants, which under his direction designed and built the plant (with an initial capacity of 5,000 kilowatts). By mid-1954 construction was completed, and on June 27 the plant produced its first nuclear-derived electric power. In his Geneva report Blokhintsev stated: "The successful completion of the atom power plant's construction necessitated overcoming many difficulties, which became apparent only gradually. This success would have been impossible without extensive and many-sided preliminary work carried out by our scientists, designers, and technicians. By the time the power plant was first projected we had already accumulated wide experience in the projecting and calculating of atomic reactors."

Blokhintsev played a still more important role in the formation and subsequent direction of the Joint Institute of Nuclear Research at Dubna. In March 1956 in Moscow, he was the leading participant in the seven days of negotiations by representatives of eleven Communist states that resulted in the agreement to organize the institute. The expressed purpose of the institute was to conduct theoretical and experimental research in nuclear physics and thus create the conditions for wide and peaceful use of atomic energy. Under the agreement of March 26, 1956, the Soviet government presented to the new international scientific body the Soviet Academy's Institute for Nuclear Problems, together with a synchrocyclotron capable of producing 680 million electron volts, as well as the Academy's electrophysical laboratory with its 10,000-million-electron-volt proton synchrotron. The agreement provided for the creation of a laboratory for theoretical physics equipped with electronic computers, a laboratory for neutron physics with an experimental reactor of a very high neutron flux, a cyclotron for accelerating ionized particles, and several other experimental laboratories and installations.

The first eleven participants in the Joint Institute, in addition to the Soviet Union, were Albania, Bulgaria, Communist China, Czechoslovakia, East Germany, Hungary, Mongolia, North Korea, Poland, and Romania. Soon after, North Vietnam was invited to participate. Each member-government was to contribute to the maintenance of the Dubna facilities and to the construction of new equipment in accordance with its country's resources; but all were to share equally in the institute's administration.

Blokhintsev was elected to direct the institute for a term of three years, and twice re-elected. His first deputy directors were two physicists from Poland and Czechoslovakia. The supreme official body of the institute, to which Blokhintsev was accountable, emerged as the Committee of Plenipotentiary Representatives of the Socialist State Governments—a scientific council whose task was to discuss and approve the institute's plans and achievements.

Construction of the new center was begun in 1956, under Blokhintsev's leadership, in the middle of a pleasant, sandy pine forest next to the upper Volga village of Novo-Ivankovo, near the mouth of the Moscow Canal. Eventually the novel science city absorbed the village, and Dubna's new streets bore the names of such foreign celebrities as Frédéric Joliot-Curie, and such native celebrities as the late atomic scientist Igor Kurchatov. Western scientists came on invitation, among them, increasingly, American physicists.

Believing in peaceful international cooperation in science, Blokhintsev (particularly during his visit in 1957 to the United States) proposed new and yet wider agreements on exchanges of physicists and chemists between Dubna and other Soviet science centers, on the one hand, and Western universities and laboratories, on the other. In 1961 he was instrumental in negotiating such an exchange agreement with CERN, the European organization for Nuclear Research in Geneva that united thirteen Western countries. In May 1962, talking to foreign journalists visiting Dubna, Blokhintsev called on the West to cooperate with the Soviet Union in building a gigantic atomic accelerator of a trillion electron volts. Revealing that he had already discussed the project with certain American scientists, he stressed that such cooperation was necessary for financial reasons, among others: it was becoming, he said, "more and more expensive to build increasingly powerful particle accelerators needed to investigate the forces of the atomic nucleus."

An example of the quality of the research produced at Dubna concerns a young Hungarian physicist, a graduate of the University of Budapest, who presented to the Moscow educational authorities a dissertation based on several years of work in Blokhintsev's institute. Instead of the degree of the candidate for which he had applied (higher than the Western degree of master, lower than the doctorate), the Hungarian was granted, in March 1964, the higher degree of doctor of the physical and mathematical sciences.

In late August 1964 Blokhintsev announced that Soviet scientists under his direction at Dubna had synthesized element Number 104, the twelfth radioactive element heavier than uranium created by man since 1940. The synthesis, he said, was accomplished by hitting a plutonium target with accelerated ions of neon 22. If correct, this meant that Soviet scientists had finally achieved a feat that had eluded the best efforts of (among others) the Lawrence Radiation Laboratory of the University of California at Berkeley, the world's leader in studies of elements heavier than uranium.

Results of these and other researches at Dubna under Blokhintsev's leadership were made public, not alone in the Soviet Union, but at various international conferences, e.g., the Eleventh International Conference of High Energy Physics in Geneva in 1962. The Twelfth International Conference was welcomed by Blokhintsev to Dubna in August 1964, and attracted more than 500 scientists from thirty-one countries (including the United States, France, Italy, and India), who delivered nearly 700 reports on various problems of modern physics. Summarizing this conference in the Moscow *Trud* (Labor) of August 16, 1964 ("On the Eve of Great Discoveries"), Blokhintsev hailed such positive results as "active international cooperation and mutual aid, free exchange of scientific information, discussions bereft of any formality whatever, which help their participants to understand the essence of the problems under discussion that much better." He expressed his conviction, founded on the reports made at

Dubna, that "we stand at the threshold of a most profound scientific revolution which, as has always happened before, will usher in a new epoch in the technology and life of mankind."

In January 1965, at the expiration of his third term, Blokhintsev asked to be relieved of the directorship of the Joint Institute of Nuclear Research at Dubna, so as to return to his own research and teaching. The request was satisfied amid high praise by his Dubna colleagues, and the well-known Soviet scientist and academician N. N. Bogolyubov took over Blokhintsev's duties.

SELECTED BIBLIOGRAPHY

For biographical information see "Dmitry Ivanovich Blokhintsev," *Biograficheskii slovar' deiatelei estestvoznaniia i tekhniki,* I, Moskva, 1958, as well as the biographical entry on Blokhintsev, essentially an English translation of the *Biograficheskii slovar'* entry, in *Who's Who in the USSR, 1961–62,* Montreal: Intercontinental Book and Publishing, 1962. Information on his role in Dubna is contained in "Joint Atomic Body Formed, Soviet Research Donated," *Prague News Letter,* April 14, 1958.

Blokhintsev's published work includes "K teorii fosforestsentsii," *Doklady akademii nauk SSSR,* II, 2 (1934); "K teorii tvyordykh vypriamitelei," *Doklady akademii nauk SSSR,* XXI, 1–2 (1938); "Spektry fluorestsentsii i absorbtsii molekul," *Zhurnal eksperimental'noi i teoreticheskoi fiziki,* IX, 4 (1939); "Elementarnyie chastitsy v pole," *Uspekhi fizicheskikh nauk,* XLII, 1 (1950); "Nelokal'nyie i nelineinie teorii polia," *Uspekhi fizicheskikh nauk,* LXI, 2 (1957); *Akustika neodnorodnoi dvizhushcheisia sredy,* Moskva and Leningrad, 1946. *Osnovy kvantovoi mekhaniki* (vypusk 3), Moskva and Leningrad, 1964, was originally published in 1944 as *Vvedenie v kvantovuiu mekhaniku* and appeared in English as *Principals of Quantum Mechanics,* translated by Scripta Technica, Inc., Boston: Allyn and Bacon, 1964.

Vladimir Alexandrovich Fock[*]

by Siegfried Müller-Markus

Vladimir Fock is a leading Soviet theoretical physicist and philosopher of science, as well as one of the most remarkable scientists of our time. He was born on December 22, 1898, in St. Petersburg, into the family of a forestry specialist. In 1916 he enrolled at the University of Petrograd (the

[*] Strictly speaking, this surname should be transliterated "Fok," but at the request of the author and the subject of the sketch, we have used the transliteration "Fock," the more widely known form of his name because of his long residence in Germany. This essay was translated from the German by Scripta Technica, Inc.

former St. Petersburg), but interrupted his studies to volunteer for military service. After completion of his studies at the Artillery School, he served at the front. Fock was released from the service in 1918 and returned to his studies at the University of Petrograd. It is Petrograd—known today as Leningrad—which still retains his love, and it is with that city that his whole academic career is connected. (This continuing loyalty to the city, incidentally, betrays one trait of Fock's character: with all the originality —one may even say radicalism—that Fock displays in his scientific work, he remains a thorough conservative in his private life.) His mathematical brilliance became apparent early in his student years and he attracted the attention of a member of the Academy of Sciences of the USSR, Professor Rozhdestvensky, who took him under his wing. By the time he finished his studies (1922), Fock was already the author of two original papers on quantum theory and mathematical physics. There were only a few theoretical physicists in Russia at the time, and Fock immediately found himself among the foremost. A mere enumeration of the institutions at which he was active shows the broad range of his interests. Thus, he was successively a graduate student (1922–24), an instructor and lecturer (1924–30) and, finally, a professor (1932) of quantum mechanics at the Leningrad University, a chair he still occupies. During the same years he was an associate scientist at the Leningrad Geophysical Observatory (1924–25), then at the Leningrad Institute of Technical Physics (1924–36), working at the same time at the Leningrad Institute of Optics (1928–41) and the Leningrad Institute for Geological Research and Geophysics (1929–31). During the period from 1931 to 1933, he was professor of theoretical physics at the Leningrad Industrial Institute, as well as a research associate at the Leningrad Institute of Physics and Mathematics of the Academy of Sciences, USSR (1931–34). From 1934 to 1941, and again from 1944 to 1953, he was senior research associate at the Lebedev Institute of Physics in Moscow, and since 1954 occupies the same position at the Vavilov Institute of Physical Problems in Moscow. His headquarters remain, however, in Leningrad, where in addition to teaching quantum mechanics, he holds the chair of theoretical physics at the Physics Institute of the university (since 1940).

In addition to the above activities, Fock has always participated in international scientific exchange, both as a student and as a teacher. He is truly a part of international science. Thus, in 1927–28 he worked at Göttingen and Paris, in 1957 he lectured as a guest of Niels Bohr at Copenhagen, and presently (1966) is a visiting professor at New Delhi. He also takes part in many international conferences, his influence proving especially great during the Bern Conference (1955) devoted to the fiftieth anniversary of the theory of relativity.

Soviet scientists are usually reluctant to divulge much information on their professional development. However, in retrospect, one can say that Fock, who went to Göttingen as an already professionally mature young scientist, was greatly stimulated by his stay there. The spirit of Gauss, who was succeeded in 1886 by Felix Klein, still reigned supreme at that university. Klein himself was an innovator. A visit to the United States convinced him that the distinction between pure and applied mathematics was artificial and, although a pure mathematician, he founded the astronomical, engineering, physical and mechanical institutes of the university. He brought in Hilbert and Minkowski, who influenced decisively the mathematical foundations of quantum mechanics and relativity theory, respectively. Among the scholars visiting Göttingen in the 1920's were Sommerfeld, Bohr, Planck, Poincaré, Lorentz, Debye, Nernst, and Smoluchowski, while Max Born taught there since 1921. These men made Göttingen the atomic physics center of the world in an era considered to be the golden age of that science. It was at Göttingen that the professional lives of Oppenheimer, Wiener, Pauling, Compton, Heisenberg, Dirac, and Robertsen were decisively affected, and it is in that circle that Fock has revolved since 1926.

Fock's achievements have been richly rewarded by the Soviet government: In 1939 he achieved the highest academic distinction available to a Soviet scientist, becoming an academician of the Soviet Union (member of the Academy of Sciences of the USSR). He was thrice decorated with the Order of Lenin, and in 1953 received the Order of the Red Banner of Labor. Among the prizes he has been awarded are the Mendeleyev Prize (1936) for his quantum theory of the structure of complex atoms, the Stalin Prize (1946) for contributions to the theory of propagation of radiowaves, the University of Leningrad Prize (1956) for his fundamental work "Theory of Space, Time and Gravitation," and finally, the Lenin Prize (1960) for contributions to quantum field theory. Fock is also a Fellow of the Trondheim Royal Society (Norway), a Member of the Danish Academy of Science, and holds an honorary doctorate from the University of New Delhi.

Few contemporary physicists have worked as creatively in so many disciplines as Fock, whose contributions range from pure mathematics to engineering, and encompass optics, the whole area of quantum mechanics, general relativity, and quantum field theory. This purely technical work is supplemented and crowned by a body of philosophical thought which makes Fock one of the foremost Soviet thinkers on the relationship between physics and philosophy. While he carries great authority in the Soviet Union both as a physicist and as a philosopher, his critique of the basic concepts underlying general relativity theory are opposed by many of his Soviet and foreign colleagues. However, it must be said that such important theoreticians as Alexandrov, Petrov, Wigner, Bondi, and Lichnerowicz adhere to similar views.

Some of the first work done by Fock dealt with difficult problems of mathematical physics, traditionally a favorite discipline of the famous St. Petersburg mathematical school. Thus, between 1924 and 1926 he calculated the illumination of a surface of arbitrary curvature, worked on the theory of mixing of optical glasses during melting, as well as on diffusion of light, and conduction of heat in polyphase (current-carrying) cables. Since 1926 he has returned only sporadically to pure mathematical problems. In 1927 he worked on the heat theory of the (electrical) breakdown of dielectrics,[1] and in 1933 turned to the theory of the skin effect in a curved conductor,[2] the trace techniques for minerals and the theory of electrical well logging.

Fock's professional activity in pure mathematics was followed by work in quantum mechanics. It is this quantum period that brought him international renown. Immediately following the appearance of the first papers by Schrödinger, Fock generalized the Schrödinger equation to the magnetic field and obtained the formula for the normal Zeeman effect (1926). During the same time he solved, by methods of perturbation theory, the problem of splitting of levels of the hydrogen atom in an electrical field. He derived the relativistically invariant wave equation for the behavior of zero-spin particles in an electromagnetic field.[3] These works were significant contributions to quantum mechanics. During his stay at Göttingen and Paris, he made further contributions to quantum mechanics and became one of the leading theoretical physicists in the world. In 1929 he generalized the Dirac equation to Riemannian geometry. In 1932 Fock wrote the first Soviet text on quantum mechanics. In 1930 he applied himself to the problem of calculation of energy levels in many-electron systems, and the result was the famous Hartree-Fock equation. The fundamental novelty of Fock's treatment was the derivation of the one-electron wave function from the variational principle; this approach provided solid mathematical grounding to the Hartree equation,[4] which hitherto was based on purely intuitive considerations. Fock showed that the Pauli exclusion principle leads to a system of equations which differ from those devised by Hartree by additional, exchange terms. These equations enabled Fock and his coworkers to calculate (in 1934) the quantum exchange energy. This method was of fundamental importance in the many-electron theory. In 1935 Fock demonstrated, in an elegant paper, that the level imparted to an electron in a Coulomb field depends upon a four-dimensional rotation group. He was the first to formulate (1940) the cyclic symmetry of wave function of a system consisting of many electrons without spin. Then, in 1954,

[1] Loss of dielectrical properties caused by superposition of supercritical field strength upon an electrical field.

[2] Inhomogeneous distribution of the alternating current over the cross-section of the conductor. Such a distribution is due to conduction electrons, which generate a field inside the conductor under the influence of the externally applied high frequency field. This, in turn, weakens the external field. Also called the surface effect.

[3] Known as the Fock-Klein-Gordon equation.

[4] Hartree, D. R. Proc. Cambridge Phil. Soc., *24*, 89 and 111 (1928).

he presented the exact solution of the Schrödinger equation for an atom of the helium type. The solution is in terms of a power series of the variables, and is of importance in arriving at the radiation corrections of quantum electrodynamics.[5]

The above work led Fock into quantum field theory, many of whose methods, since 1945, rest upon concepts developed by Fock as far back as the 1930's. His ideas on the subject are similar to those of Dirac.

In 1932 he published a fundamental paper on second quantization, in which he dealt with a system of variable number of particles in the space of the configuration. This is the first clear and consistent statement of the method of second quantization as related to the space occupied by the given configuration. This theory is today of great importance in the theory of the meson field. Together with Podolsky, he extended the method for derivation of the Coulomb interaction via exclusion of the longitudinal electromagnetic field, which Dirac proposed for the one-dimensional case. The classical work of Dirac, Fock, and Podolsky established the many-time formalism of quantum electrodynamics and thereby completed its invariant theory: it ascribed a characteristic time to each particle and the field. This method was used in 1946–47 by Tomonaga and by Schwinger to derive their super-many formalisms. The work culminated in the rigorous theory of systems with variable number of bosons, which Fock formulated by means of functionals in 1934. This method is widely used in modern quantum field theory.

During the Second World War Fock worked on radiowave propagation problems. He used approximation methods for solution of infinite series and integrals to find an exact solution of the diffraction problem, and was able to formulate a rigorous theory of propagation of radiowaves on the surface of the earth. Later on, he included in this theory the effects of a nonhomogeneous atmosphere. His classic work, *Electromagnetic Diffraction and Propagation Problems,* was published in 1965 by Pergamon Press.

In 1939 Fock turned his attention to a new area—the general theory of relativity. He was pushed in this direction not only by his mathematical inclinations, but also by philosophical motivations. On the one hand, he was stimulated by the difficulties inherent in the derivation of the laws of motion from the field equations, and on the other he wanted to replace the Einsteinian justification of the general relativity theory by a mathematically and logically more coherent basis. Fock was able to derive the

[5] There is an interaction of the charged particle with its own electromagnetic field. This produces phenomena which introduce corrections to the quantum-mechanical effects. Formally, this interaction arises from the emission and reabsorption of virtual photons and electrons. The necessary corrections may be calculated from a power series of the form $\alpha = e^2/hc \quad \frac{1}{137}$. This procedure gives residual continuous fractions for charge and mass, which are eliminated by renormalization.

laws of motion from Einsteinian field equations. He did this independently of Einstein and his coworkers. Using an approximation method, he solved the equations for the field of an extended spherical mass by assuming that space becomes Euclidean at infinity. Fock showed that Newtonian equations of motion become conditions necessary for the solution of the metric tensor. At the same time, he was the first to use the so-called harmonic coordinates of Lanczos and de Donder. This work immediately placed Fock in that exclusive band of thinkers concerned with general relativity, the most abstract and at the same time the most grandiose of contemporary physical theories. The further papers of Fock in this area deal with the equations of motion of bodies, whereby he takes into account the structure and rotation of such bodies. He finds the ten integrals of motion and discusses the problems of astronomical aberration.

In his principal work, *Theory of Space, Time and Gravitation* (1955), Fock presents a mathematically and logically complete statement of the general relativity theory. This work also proves Fock to be a philosopher who revises the Einsteinian theory from a philosophical point of view.

Fock was forced into philosophy by the attacks of Soviet philosophers on Einstein and Bohr. From 1952 to 1955, the Soviet philosophical press (led by A. Maksimov and I. V. Kuznetsov) conducted what can best be described as a veritable public trial of Einstein and his theory, and in the end convicted this theory in terms of Communist dogma. The signal for this was given by Central Committee member Zhdanov, who in 1947 instituted a fight against the influence of bourgeois ideas in Soviet science. This led to the attack on relativity theory, genetics, cybernetics, the expansion of the universe and the fundaments of quantum mechanics. The more profound reason for these attacks was that dialectical materialism, born in the nineteenth century, brought conflict to the sciences of the twentieth. Einstein was condemned for being both a Machist and a subjective idealist. Soviet philosophy claims radical realism and thinks that the relativity of mass, length, and time implicates the elimination of reality. Einstein was reproached for having made reality a product of thinking. It was at that time that one of the most remarkable exhibitions of personal courage in Soviet intellectual history took place: in an atmosphere poisoned by terror (Stalin was still alive at the beginning of this period), Fock staked his authority on the side of Einstein and rose to defend his theory. As early as January 1953 Fock, in *Voprosy filosofii* (the journal of the Institute of Philosophy of the Academy of Sciences of the USSR), vehemently attacked the "ignorant critique of modern physical theories" and ascribed "errors in physics and philosophy that cry out to heaven" to the philosophical critics of Einstein. In the final analysis, it was Fock who forced official recognition of the relativity theory in the Soviet Union (1955). It is, therefore, Fock who is responsible for the new tone in Soviet philosophy of science, which since 1955 has freed itself increasingly from the preconceptions of philosophers and struggled toward objectivity. The fact that a truly philosophical discussion is today taking place in such areas of Soviet science as physics, astronomy, mathematics, and biology is to a large extent Fock's personal achievement. His harsh insistence on principles—a quality always prized by Russian intellectuals—has permitted him to overcome philosophical adversaries without incurring the stigma of opposition to Communist philosophy. On the contrary, Fock's philosophy is based upon Communist epistemology. Lenin had stated that any scientific truth can be obtained through sense data and abstract thinking, and affirmed the existence of absolute truth which is the sum of relative truths. Soviet philosophy believes in the unlimited power of reason in exploring the world. The categories time, space, causality, and matter have a real basis in things; they are no mere products of thinking. That is the reason that Fock has always leaned toward the real physical situation despite his mathematical genius.

His main achievement in philosophy, then, is explaining the objectivity of relativity. The problem is as follows: We can confirm that two distant events are simultaneous only by using a method of signals from these events to an observer. This implies, as was shown by Einstein, that an observer A judges time distance between two events in another way than observer B moving to A. Events that appear to be simultaneous to A are not so to B. Both observers are physically equivalent in their judgments so long as they are not influenced by external forces. Is simultaneity, therefore, constituted by an observer's statement, or does it exist independently of the observer? In other words, is it subjective or objective? Soviet philosophers like Maksimov and Kuznetsov considered relativity subjective and hence denied it in the name of dialectical materialism. To register the time distance between two events an observer can be replaced by an automatic device. Relativity is therefore objective. Fock derives the relativistic effects from the homogeneity and isotropy of space-time. In this derivation he does not use the concepts of the observer and his definitions of length and simultaneity, but only the concepts of space and time measurement by means of light signals. For Fock, the effects are therefore as objective as the nature of space, time, and light signals. On the other hand, he rejects, for the same reasons, the Einsteinian philosophy, which for Fock carries too many positivistic connotations. According to Fock, Einstein sees time as a subjective determination of duration, and derives the concept of space from the perceptions of the observer. However, Fock thinks that in his role as a physicist, Einstein behaves as a materialist, i.e., a realist, because in his general relativity theory he lets space and time be determined by matter. Fock's interpretation of relativity as an objective phenomenon is today universally accepted in Soviet philosophy.

His interpretation of the equivalence of mass and energy, however, has met another fate. Soviet philosophers disputed the possibility of transformation of matter into energy and vice versa because they detected in this a reversion to the energetism of Ostwald, which was condemned by Lenin. The problem hit directly upon the fundamental thesis of dialectical materialism. It also involved a clash between technical interests (nuclear energy and atomic bomb development) and ideological dogmas. In 1952 (again while Stalin was still alive) Fock produced an original interpretation of the Einsteinian equation $E = mc^2$. Thus, he says, by analogy with the equivalence of the inertial and gravitational masses—each of which represents a fundamentally different species—mass and energy are also equivalent. In the theory of relativity, the energy tensor differs from the mass tensor only by the factor c^2, the laws of conservation governing both species being identical. Fock calls the rest mass which does not participate in the transformation into energy the passive energy, while he calls the mass (or energy) participating in such processes active. That two energy fractions really exist is shown from the equation for the complete mass density of a continuous elastic medium

$$T^\infty = \rho + S/c^2$$

where ρ is the passive energy (or passive mass) and S represents the active counterparts. The fact that the passive energy does not influence the energy balance is probably related (according to Fock) to the existence of discrete energy levels of elementary particles, whose rest mass can undergo only two modes of conversion: complete or zero annihilation by radiation.

The same uncompromising adherence to objectivism which Fock displayed in defending the special relativity theory against attacks of the dogmatists, now forced him to reject the reasoning which Einstein made the basis of his general relativity theory. Fock faulted Einstein for deriving his theory from the general covariance and equivalence of gravitationless accelerated reference frames and gravitational effects. However, Fock does not see in the general covariance a specific feature of the general relativity theory, because even classical mechanics and the special relativity theory can be formulated in arbitrary coordinates without recourse to gravitation. Further, Fock thinks that Einstein is making a mathematical and logical error by introducing the above equivalence as a basis of the theory. Equivalence holds only locally because frameworks falling without incurring deformation cannot be constructed in arbitrary space and time dimensions. Further, not all transformations of coordinates are allowed as formal bases for introduction of gravitational forces, because (forbidden) velocities higher than that of light may thus arise under certain circumstances, and the sign system of the metric is thus violated. In addition, the boundary condition necessary for solution of differential equations must not, in general, be covariant. The very expression "general relativity" is itself inopportune, because the special relativity theory already includes the most general relativity possible. This is due to the fact that the special relativity theory includes a ten-parameter group which corresponds to a space-time domain of maximum homogeneity and isotropy. By contrast, the curvature of space-time in domains endowed with gravitation restricts this homogeneity, that is, it holds only locally in a tangential Galilean space. Thus, the Einsteinian theory of gravitation comprises only a local relativity, a relativity identical to that already present in special relativity, but in no way more general. For these reasons, Fock refused to call this theory anything else but "the Einsteinian gravitation theory."

Accordingly, Fock introduced the so-called harmonic coordinates as privileged frameworks. These serve for derivation of laws of motion. Also, the conservation laws of the general relativity theory may be formulated in these coordinates. This started an interesting discussion with Infeld who disputed the existence of privileged coordinates. Fock retorted that it was precisely such harmonic coordinates that Einstein and Infeld used to derive their equations of motion. However, Fock saw no necessity for retaining harmonic coordinates in the cosmological problem in which the generally covariant formalism is intrinsic. It must be said that Fock's viewpoint is not universally accepted. According to Shirokov, Fock underestimates the reality of inertial fields; according to B. G. Kuznetsov, the concept of "homogeneity" can be so extended that general relativity theory will also give homogeneity. The present author thinks that the theory of inertial systems (special relativity) which only hold as an approximation, and the theory describing the real case of a gravitational system must intersect at some point.[6] The only real inertial systems are the free-falling reference systems, and it is only in these systems that special relativity theory holds rigorously. Its existence is established by the principle of equivalence; while it is feasible only in the infinitesimal case, it is so always, everywhere and, so far, universally. Denying the equivalence principle means to deprive the special relativity theory of its logical basis. For this reason, the laws of nature must also be capable of formulation in a form more general than the Galilean space-time domain: thus, the general theory of relativity encompasses the inertial system as its infinitesimal limiting case. Because of that, the expression "general relativity" is justified. Admittedly, by starting this discussion, Fock has contributed substantially to an objectivistic clarification of Einsteinian theory.

Fock has also led the way to acceptance of fundamental positions of quantum mechanics by Soviet philosophers. In 1948 the concept of complementarity was officially condemned (in connection with the appearance of a book by M. A. Markov). For many years the Copenhagen school's interpretation was held to be incompatible with dialectical materialism. In particular, Soviet philosophers held that atomic processes are (intrinsically) completely determinable (rejected uncertainty). In 1957 Fock was

[6] For better understanding of this concept, cf. S. Müller-Markus, *Einstein und die Sowjetphilosophie,* Dordrecht: Reidel, 1966, pp. 152 ff.

a visiting professor at Copenhagen and held exhaustive discussions on the subject with Bohr. Just as in the case of Einstein, Fock recognized an objectivistic and also materialistic core in Bohr's interpretation. However, he rejected the concept of indeterminable interaction. Indeed, he must have convinced Bohr, because the latter ceased to use this expression in papers appearing after 1958. At the All-Union Conference on Philosophical Problems of Natural Sciences (Moscow, 1958) Fock was the official spokesman of Soviet quantum theorists, and vigorously opposed every attempt to restore determinism in quantum mechanics. According to Fock, quantum-size objects exhibit a relativity with respect to macro instruments. This relativity is described by the Heisenberg relations, and is just as objective as the effects of special relativity. The atomic-size object has a potential of behaving, depending on external conditions, either as a wave or as a particle. Any other literal interpretation of the wave-particle duality, in the form of a model, is wrong. (This is especially true of the models constructed by the school of de Broglie.) The state described by wave function is an observer-independent characteristic which describes the possibilities for some product of interaction of the quantum object with the measuring apparatus. This state holds only for single quantum-size objects. However, the measurement possibilities are still not exhausted, and for this reason this state has still not been reached (that is, the potential for observation of quantum objects has still not been exhausted).

Fock combines physical intuition with a virtuoso's mastery of the available mathematical machinery. He was always successful in winnowing out the essentials of a problem (and he has dealt with some very complex ones). He then always reduced the problem, by means of suitable mathematical transformations, to usable calculations and tables. His interest was equally held by abstract theory and applied technology, and ranged from geological prospecting methods to cosmology. He belongs among the few thinkers who combine the precision of a physicist with philosophical depth. The same diversity and range is also evident in Fock, the man. His pedagogical abilities enabled him to found a most important school of Soviet theoretical physics. He is always in the forefront of work on new problems. His own translations and his work as an editor of translations have made available to Soviet readers a whole series of non-Soviet research works. He propagated these works even though their authors were sometimes under sharp attack by official dogmatists. This is especially true of the work of Bohr and Dirac, whose fundamental works were published in the USSR under Fock's editorship, as well as the philosophical works of Bohr which were subjected to an especially severe ideological attack. Fock's own work comprises over 200 papers. He combines personal modesty with an uncompromising devotion to scientific truth, which he defends against all real and imaginary errors, a defense he mounts not only against Soviet philosophers but also against philosophical concepts of the most important Western physicists.

SELECTED BIBLIOGRAPHY

Biographical data, as well as information about Fock's work, can be found in "V. A. Fok, Akademik," *Vestnik akademii nauk SSSR*, CXCVI, 2/3 (1930); V. I. Smirnova's introductory article on Fock in *Materialy biografii uchenych SSSR*, Akademiia nauk SSSR, seriia fiziki, 7, Moskva, 1956; M. G. Veselov, "Vladimir Alexandrovich Fok (k shestidesiatiletiiu so dnia rozhdeniia)," *Uspekhi fizicheskikh nauk*, LXVI, 4 (1958), 695–99; S. Müller-Markus, *Einstein und die Sowjetphilosophie*, Band 1, Dordrecht, Holland: Reidel Publishing Co., 1960; S. Müller-Markus, *Einstein und die Sowjetphilosophie*, Band 2, Dordrecht, Holland: 1966.

His major work in the field of quantum mechanics includes "Zur Schrödingerschen Wellenmechanik," *Zeitschrift für Physik*, XXXVIII, 3 (1926), 242–50; "Bemerkung zur Quantelung des harmonischen Oszillators im Magnetfeld," *Zeitschrift für Physik*, XLVII, 5–6 (1928), 446–48; "Über die Beziehung zwischen den Integralen der quantenmechanischen Bewegungsgleichungen und der Schrödingerschen Wellengleichung," *Zeitschrift für Physik*, XLIX, 5–6 (1928), 323–38; "Verallgemeinerung und Lösung der Diracschen statistischen Gleichung," *Zeitschrift für Physik*, XLIX, 5–6 (1928), 339–57; "Über eine mögliche geometrische Deutung der relativistischen Quantentheorie," *Zeitschrift für Physik*, LIV, 11–12 (1929), 798–802; "Geometrisierung der Diraschen Theorie des Elektrons," *Zeitschrift für Physik*, LVII, 3–4 (1929), 261–77; "Zur Quantengeometrie" (with D. Ivanenko), *Zeitschrift für Physik*, XXX, 19 (1929), 648–51; "Sur les équations de Dirac dans la theorie de relativité générale," *Comptes Rendus de l'Académie des Sciences de l'USSR*, Paris, CLXXXIX, 23 (1929), 25–28; "L'équation d'onde de Dirac et la géométrie de Riemann," *Journal de Physique et le Radium*, X, 11 (1929), 392–405; "Näherungsmethode zur Lösung des quantenmechanischen Mehrkörperproblems," *Zeitschrift für Physik*, LXI, 1–2 (1930), 148–216; " 'Self-Consistent-Field' mit Austausch für Natrium," *Zeitschrift für Physik*, LXII, 11–12 (1930), 795–805; L. Kubuch, *Nachala kvantovoi mekhaniki*, Kiev, 1932; "O volnovykh funktsiiakh mnogoelektronnykh sistem," *Zhurnal eksperimental'noi i teoret<icheskoi fiziki*, X, 9–10 (1940), 961–79.

Major studies in relativity theory are "O dvizhenii konechnyk mass v obshchei teorii otnositel'nosti," *Zhurnal eksperimental'noi i teoreticheskoi fiziki*, IX, 4 (1939), 375–410; "Ob integralakh dvizheniia tsentra inertsii dvukh konechnykh mass v obshchei teorii otnositel'nosti," *Doklady akademii nauk SSSR*, XXXII, 1 (1941), 20–28; "Das Kopernikanische und das Ptolemäische System im Lichte der allgemeinen Relativitätstheorie," *Sowjetwissenschaft*. Naturwissenschaftliche Abteilung, 5–6 (1953), 805–9; *Teoriia prostranstva, vremeni i tiagoteniia*, Moskva, 1955; "Uravneniia dvizheniia sistemy tiazhelykh mass s uchetom ikh vnutrennei struktury i vrashcheniia. (Izlozhenie doklada na sessii otdeleniia fizikomatematicheskikh nauk akademii nauk SSSR, posviaschennoi 50-letiiu teorii otnositel'nosti 1 dekabria 1956 g.)," *Uspekhi fizicheskikh nauk*, LIX, 1 (1956), 67–69.

Major articles in the field of quantum theory include "Zur Diracschen Quantenelektrodynamik" (with B. Podolsky), *Physikalische Zeitschrift der Sowjetunion*, I, 6 (Kharkov, 1932), 798–800; "On the Quantization of Electromagnetic Waves and the Interaction of Charges on Dirac's Theory" (with B. Podolsky), *Physikalische Zeitschrift der Sowjetunion*, I, 6 (Kharkov, 1932), 801–17; "On Quantum Electrodynamics" (with P. A. Dirac and B. Podolsky), *Physikalische Zeitschrift der Sowjetunion*, II, 6, (1932), 468–79; "Ob energii kvantovogo obmena," *Zhurnal eksperimental'noi i teoreticheskoi fiziki*, IV, 1 (1934), 1–16; "Zur Quantenelektrodynamik," *Physikalische Zeitschrift der Sowjetunion*, VI, 5 (1934), 269–425.

The following comprise his work in diffraction theory and varia: *Diffraktsiia radiovoln vokrug zemnoi poverkhnosti*, Moskva, Leningrad, 1946; "Reshenie zadachi o rasprostranenii elektromagnitnykh voln poverkhnosti zemli po metodu parabolicheskogo uravneniia," in *Issledovanii po rasprostraneniiu radiovoln*, sbornik 2, pod. red. V. A. Vvedensky, Moskva, Leningrad, 1948, pp. 13–39.

His philosophical writing includes "Protiv nevezhestvennoi kritiki sovremennykh fizicheskikh teorii," *Voprosy filosofii*, 1 (1953), 169–74; "Sovremennaia teoriia prostranstva i vremeni," *Priroda*, 12 (1953), 13–26; "Poniatie odnorodnosti, kovariantnosti i otnositel'nosti v teorii prostranstva i vremeni," *Voprosy filosofii*, 4 (1955), 131–35; "Über philosophische Fragen der modernen Physik," *Deutsche Zeitschrift für Philosophie*, III, 6 (1955), 736–57; "Zamechaniia k tvorcheskoi avtobiografii Al'berta Einshteina," *Uspekhi fizicheskikh nauk* LIX, 1 (1956), 107–17; "Ob interpretatsii kvantovoi mechaniki," *Filosofskie problemy sovremennogo estestvoznaniia*, Moskva, 1959, pp. 212–36.

Pyotr Leonidovich Kapitsa

by Albert Parry

Pyotr Kapitsa,[1] one of Russia's foremost physicists, was born on July 8, 1894, at the naval base and fortress of Kronstadt, near St. Petersburg (now Leningrad), where his father, a lieutenant general in the tsar's Corps of Engineers, was stationed helping to modernize the fortifications. His mother was a well-known teacher and collector of Russian folklore.

Young Kapitsa was graduated from a Kronstadt high school that specialized in the physical sciences. At the outbreak of the Revolution of 1917 he was an honor student in the capital's famous Polytechnic Institute. His first scientific paper was published in the journal of the Russian Society of Physics and Chemistry the very month the Bolsheviks overthrew the liberal Provisional government of Alexander Kerensky and proclaimed their Soviet republic. Kapitsa's official Communist biographer commented: "Life pre-

---

[1] Sometimes erroneously transliterated in Western languages as Kapitza.

sents most incredible coincidences. Along with the new state a new scientist was born."

Graduating from the Polytechnic Institute in 1918, Kapitsa worked with Professor Abram Ioffe, one of Russia's earliest atomic scientists, in the newly established State Technical and Physical Institute. Kapitsa also worked with Professor Nikolai Semyonov, the chemist and physicist who many years later (1956) won a Nobel Prize for chemistry. By 1920 Kapitsa and Semyonov arrived at an original method of ascertaining magnetic properties of the atom.

In 1921 Kapitsa left Russia for England on an official mission from the Academy of Sciences of the USSR, to renew contacts with foreign scholars and to purchase sorely needed books and laboratory equipment for Russia's war-depleted scientific establishments. He remained abroad until 1934—as one of Ernest Rutherford's associates in the celebrated Cavendish Laboratory at Cambridge from 1921 to 1930 (assistant director from 1924 on), and as director of the Cambridge University Laboratory from 1930 to 1934.

Under Rutherford's guidance, in addition to the problem of splitting the atom, Kapitsa busied himself with investigating the reaction of matter to the influence of magnetic fields. In 1923 he defended his dissertation and was awarded his doctorate by Cambridge. The same year brought him the Maxwell Prize, one of the world's highest scientific honors. In 1924 he developed unique equipment for work with superpowerful magnetic fields, and in 1929 he was elected to the Royal Society (British), the first foreigner (or so it was reported) to receive this honor in two centuries.

Kapitsa originated a high-production hydrogen liquefier in 1932. In 1934 he began designs of his original apparatus for producing large quantities of liquid oxygen (further developed and constructed in 1938). By the early 1930's he had been elected to the Institute of Physics (British), to the Cambridge Philosophical Society, and to Trinity College. He was presently made a full professor at Cambridge. The Royal Society built a special laboratory to his exacting specifications.

More and more the eyes of the world's scientists were on Kapitsa. Yet a few scientists did not exactly like him—for reasons both personal and political. Among these men were some Russians in England, America, and France. They were definitely anti-Soviet, but young Kapitsa seemed ambivalent about the issue. To a few acquaintances he explained that he was not an *émigré* but an emissary, that is, a Russian scientist still on official mission from Moscow to do research and to purchase equipment and books, with a vaguely acknowledged obligation to return home some day.

Professor Stepan Timoshenko, an *émigré* already making a name in American academic and engineering circles for his work in theoretical and applied mechanics, met Kapitsa at a scientific congress in Edinburgh in September 1921. Years later in his book of memoirs he recalled that even in his first months at Cambridge young Kapitsa "felt no lack of any of his necessities" because "the Bolshevik government furnished him with money fairly generously." It was this money, Timoshenko went on, that indirectly helped Kapitsa gain his initial renown in England.

He could even afford to buy a motorcycle. On this he began experimenting. He wanted to ascertain the utmost speed that could be attained on it. These experiments ended badly for him. On one occasion, while making a turn at high speed, the motorcycle crashed, and Kapitsa found himself in a ditch. The impact was considerable, but his arms and legs survived intact. His face and chest, however, did suffer. Someone picked Kapitsa up and delivered him to a hospital where he had to remain for more than a week.[2]

At their meeting in Edinburgh, Kapitsa related that in the hospital he was bored waiting for a full recovery and so, his head still bandaged, went back to the laboratory, where the effect was dramatic. One after another, his associates came to his cubicle, asked questions in awe, and wished him to get well soon. "Finally," Timoshenko concluded, "Rutherford himself made his appearance, gazed at the bandaged head, and left silently. This made Kapitsa rather well known in the laboratory."

Grudgingly, Timoshenko admitted that the exuberant Kapitsa quickly proved himself to be as popular in the university dormitory at Edinburgh as he had apparently become at Cambridge:

In the evening, when all gathered in the drawing room, he amused the public by his tricks and experiments. He was extraordinarily bold. When, in the course of an experiment, he needed an assistant, he would unceremoniously pull some celebrated scientist by his sleeve and begin to explain to him just what it was he had to do. Solemn, dignified Englishmen lost their gravity of manner and fully submitted to Kapitsa's decisive actions.[3]

Some of Kapitsa's boldness may have come from his inner conviction that he had something of value to offer to these British and their society. And indeed he did. As even Professor Timoshenko conceded, Kapitsa's "superiority over young English scientists came from his passage through the excellent engineering school of the St. Petersburg Polytechnic Institute." Kapitsa therefore could and did design large machinery. "In his scientific work he tended to shift from small physics equipment to big machines, and this change of the experiment's scale gave him a chance to carry out a series of important researches." Further on in his reminiscences, Timoshenko stressed once again the asset of Kapitsa's Russian schooling: "Physics, in its development, demanded large-scale, factory-size experimentation, and Kapitsa, with his engineering education brought from the St. Petersburg

---

[2] Timoshenko, *Vospominaniia,* Paris: Izdanie ob'edineniia S-Peterburgskikh politekhnikov, 1963, pp. 214–15.

[3] Timoshenko, *Vospominaniia,* p. 215.

Polytechnic Institute, had considerable advantage over the theoreticians of the university type."[4]

Throughout the 1920's Kapitsa visited the Soviet Union and each time his return was unimpeded. Professor Timoshenko, entertained "most graciously" by Kapitsa in Cambridge in July 1926, relates:

Kapitsa loved to talk. He told many tales about his trips to Russia, whither he was repeatedly invited to lecture about the development of physics in England. But he was not too burdened by such lectures, and he spent most of his time at Kislovodsk [a resort in the northern Caucasus] . . . . [on his latest trip] he had managed to visit his old family home, somewhere in the Volyn province.[5]

Toward the end of the same summer, in Paris, Timoshenko accidentally met Alexis Krylov, Kapitsa's father-in-law. A prominent mathematician, physicist, astronomer, and above all a first-rate shipwright and engineer, Krylov was abroad on a mission for the Soviet government. In great secret he asked Timoshenko to warn Kapitsa against accepting any more invitations from Moscow. At his next meeting with Kapitsa, Timoshenko relayed the warning, "but he [Kapitsa] paid little attention to it."

Timoshenko saw Kapitsa for the last time in the summer of 1934, at a scientific congress held at Cambridge. Kapitsa told him of his repeated visits to Soviet Russia: ". . . he found such trips most interesting, since following the reports and lectures it was very pleasant to spend the remainder of a summer somewhere in the Crimea or the Caucasus. I remarked that such journeys were not without their dangers; it was quite possible that one beautiful day the Soviet government would detain him, and he would never return to England. But he only laughed. Such a turn of affairs seemed improbable to him."

Soon after, Kapitsa and his wife, leaving their two children in England, sailed for Russia. Their friend Niels Bohr, the Danish atomic scientist, accompanied them. After a while Bohr returned to Denmark, and the Kapitsas drove southward to their beloved Crimea and Caucasus. When it came time for their return to England, they drove north to Leningrad to board a steamer. But here they were told that their exit visas had been canceled. Incredulous, they protested and pleaded, but in vain. They had to turn back to Moscow.

Soviet officials were polite but implacable: Professor Kapitsa was a Soviet citizen and had to stay. His country needed him. Everything would be done to enable him to continue his important researches.

It was reported that for a whole year Kapitsa and his wife lived in their Moscow hotel room, hardly stirring except for a walk, refusing to say yes,

---

[4] And in a conversation with the present writer, C. P. Snow cited the example of Kapitsa (whom he knew well) as proof that in the Soviet Union there is usually less of a gap between scientist and engineer—between researcher and practitioner —than in the West.

[5] Timoshenko, *Vospominaniia,* p. 256.

demanding their right to return to England. Lord Rutherford and other foreign friends of Kapitsa addressed protests and entreaties to the Kremlin. The Soviet government hardly bothered to reply. But Stalin himself sent word that he would see Kapitsa if the professor wanted to talk things over in a friendly mood. In time Kapitsa weakened, discovering that he longed for his work even more than for England. And so the two met and came to an agreement.

At once things began to hum. Not sparing the high expense, the Soviet government bought certain equipment from Kapitsa's Cambridge laboratory—items he had used for producing high magnetic fields. The British sold the equipment in the interests of science, since no one but Kapitsa could use it, and since the money received for it went to buy England's first cyclotron. Many other things were done for Kapitsa. The two Kapitsa children were soon brought from England to rejoin their parents. The Harris tweeds that Kapitsa liked so well were ordered for him. Even his favorite English pipe tobacco was imported.

In 1935 Kapitsa was made director of the Institute of Problems of Physics, a department within the Academy of Sciences of the USSR. A corresponding member of the Academy since 1929, he was made a full member in 1939. An enthusiastic, devoted circle of colleagues and students formed around Kapitsa at the institute in Moscow. His Wednesday evenings "at-home" became a celebrated colloquium. Professor A. I. Kitaigorodsky describes them:

Kapitsa has introduced a severe regime; the colloquium not only begins at the appointed minute exactly, but also ends within half a minute of the set time: after two hours precisely. Should a report run over the time, Pyotr Leonidovich politely interrupts the speaker at any sentence at all. He says that all this is very interesting and we will hear its continuation with pleasure at our next meeting. It is worse when the subject is exhausted, yet the two hours will not be up for another five or ten minutes. But Kapitsa is a skillful helmsman. Maneuvering with questions and reminiscences, he brings the ship into the port at the set time sharply. Not a minute later, not a minute earlier.[6]

But not all was serene around Kapitsa. The purges of the middle and later 1930's struck Russia in a long, agonizing series. Men and women who had ever had any dealings with the West were arrested and deported to concentration camps or executed by the thousand. Many of Kapitsa's friends, associates, and acquaintances were taken from their homes and laboratories. The secret police hit closer and closer to Kapitsa himself. Among others, Lev Landau, a rising Russian physicist and mathematician and a close friend of Kapitsa's, was arrested. Landau was in prison for one year and on the verge of death when Kapitsa finally succeeded in rescuing him—by fearlessly going to the Kremlin and demanding his release. "Otherwise he said he would leave his Institute," Landau was to recall years

[6] *Physics Is My Profession.*

later, in an article in the Moscow *Komsomolskaia pravda* (July 8, 1964).
"It is hardly necessary to say that in those years [the 1930's], for such an
act, one had to have great courage, great humanity, and crystal-clear
honesty."

The fact was that Kapitsa had proved far too valuable for Stalin to
disregard his plea on Landau's behalf. To summarize Kapitsa's achievements: He did research in electron inertia and properties of radioactive
emission. He designed equipment for powerful magnetic fields and observed
splitting of spectral lines in magnetic fields of 320 thousand gauss (a unit
used in electricity, in measuring magnetic induction or magnetic intensity,
representing one line of magnetic force per square centimeter). He discovered linear increase of metal resistivity as a function of magnetic field,
and studied magnetostriction of diamagnetic bodies in the fields. He invented a turbodetander—equipment for temperatures near absolute zero
to be used for the production of large quantities of liquid helium and
oxygen. He developed hydrodynamic theory of bearing lubrication.

From 1935 on, his major accomplishments were in low temperatures
and their application in the liquefying of air. To his credit he added the
first discovery and investigation of hyperfluidity of liquid helium (although
liquid helium as such had been evolved earlier by Dutch and Canadian
scientists). His small, inexpensive turbine, used to take oxygen out of air,
brought him a United States patent as well as new Soviet honors.

During the Second World War Kapitsa returned to the atomic field by
helping other Soviet scientists in their nuclear researches. Following the
news of the American A-bomb he became a member of the Soviet Commission for the Study of Cosmic Radiation. He built new instruments for
the cosmic-ray observations carried on in the high mountains of the Pamirs
and Soviet Armenia by the Armenian brothers, Abram and Artemy Ali-
khanov. At the same time he experimented with uranium and lectured on
atomics in Moscow's military academies.

Yet in the early 1940's the atom did not seem to be Kapitsa's chief
concern. The Faraday Medal he received (1942) from England and the
Franklin Medal awarded him (1944) by the Franklin Institute of Philadelphia were both for his nonatomic work. For his discovery of superfluidity
he received the First Class Stalin Prize twice, in 1941 and 1943. Early in
1945 Stalin gave him the title of Hero of Socialist Labor for his researches
into the turbine methods of oxygen production.

By 1946 he had also the first of his three Orders of Lenin. During
1945 and 1946 he smilingly denied to foreign correspondents that he was
under any duress whatever. Urbane and relaxed, puffing on his briar, he
spoke in his colloquial English of all the facilities and honors he was en-
joying in the Soviet Union. In his public speeches he dwelt at length on the
glories of his fatherland.

Nevertheless, rumors spread abroad that Stalin was not well pleased
with Kapitsa. He was rewarding the scientist constantly, but more in hopes

of spurring Kapitsa on to new atomic discoveries than in recognition of work already done. Early in the post-Hiroshima period, in December 1945, Kapitsa blandly revealed that his most recent work was with peaceful uses of hydrogen. Unofficially however, it was reported that Kapitsa was leading much of the Soviet effort to produce an atomic bomb. Professor Norbert Wiener of the Massachusetts Institute of Technology, who had known Kapitsa in England in the early 1930's, said later (*I Am a Mathematician,* 1956) that he was not surprised. He recalled that in Russia Kapitsa "became the pioneer of that large-scale, factory-like type of laboratory which [was first] employed by Kammerlingh Onnes in the Netherlands for low temperature research, and which is now the standard means of exploring the nucleus and of designing atomic bombs." When Wiener had first heard of the American atom bomb in 1945, he had felt sure that with Kapitsa training

the Russians in the technique of this sort of laboratory it would not be many years before they would have mastered for themselves the principles and techniques of nuclear research, whether or not they might capture our secrets by means of espionage or persuade a group of malcontents to serve their purposes.

In 1945 and 1946, foreigners—particularly Westerners — saw Kapitsa only seldom. In the summer of 1946, to Richard E. Lauterbach, a young American journalist who questioned him about the atom bomb, Kapitsa made a wry face: "To talk of atomic energy in terms of the atomic bomb is like talking of electricity in terms of the electric chair." A man of peace, Kapitsa was hoping for an international agreement to outlaw the atom bomb. Increasingly he criticized the Americans for what he termed unnecessary stubbornness in safeguarding their atomic secrets.

Late in 1946 Kapitsa's name disappeared from official Soviet news. He was no longer head of the Institute of Problems of Physics, nor in the lists of Russian atomic scientists awarded Stalin's prizes and medals. No letter from or about him reached foreign countries. He was surrounded by complete official silence. Then, after two years, in 1948, an article of his was printed in a Soviet journal of experimental and theoretical physics. In February 1949 another was published in the official annals of the Academy of Sciences of the USSR. Both were on liquids.

Out of the welter of reports and rumors circulating abroad about Kapitsa's status, the following facts emerged as most nearly authentic: In Stalin's final years Kapitsa was reluctant to contribute his genius to further improvement of the Soviet atomic bomb or to agree to Stalin's ignorant ideas on science. Stalin, not daring to shoot or even exile the great scientist, had him confined under house arrest, which, according to the Soviet writer Vladimir Tendryakov's remarks to the Yugoslav critic Mihajlo Mihajlov, lasted eight years.[7] Seven years seems more likely. But that Kapitsa was

[7] Mihajlov, *Moscow Summer 1964.*

indeed under house arrest for a lengthy period near the end of Stalin's reign seems indisputable, if only because mention of the arrest was allowed to seep through uncensored and unrefuted in foreign correspondents' dispatches from Moscow in Khrushchev's time.

But the world did not forget Kapitsa even in those bleak years of his detention and forced isolation: in 1946 he was made an honorary member of the Danish Academy of Sciences and of the National Academy of Sciences of the United States; in 1948 he was given similar honors by the academies of sciences in India and Ireland. Years later (in early 1965, in his reminiscences published in the Moscow *Novy mir*), the Soviet writer Ilya Ehrenburg revealed how dismayed Kapitsa's British friends were on hearing of his arrest. At the end of Stalin's era, on a brief mission to England, Ehrenburg was taken on a visit to Cambridge, where a distinguished physicist and his wife cautiously and unhappily inquired about Kapitsa's troubles. Ehrenburg tried to reassure them; he felt, he said, that they "wanted to believe me but did not dare to."

Kapitsa returned to freedom and to the world's headlines soon after Stalin's death. In August 1953, when Russia's possession of a hydrogen bomb of its own became known, Kapitsa's earlier role in the breakthrough was generally recognized. In Washington it was commented that Kapitsa's particular specialty was the major matter of the H-bomb—the behavior of materials at very high and very low temperatures. A statement made in December 1945 by Kapitsa to the effect that he had transformed hydrogen into a hard, visible metal was recalled. The chairman of the United States Joint Committee on Atomic Energy acknowledged Kapitsa's "special competence in the technical problems relating to hydrogen weapons."

In 1955, two years after Stalin's death, Kapitsa was reinstated as director of the Institute of Problems of Physics. In the same year he made public his hypothesis on the origin of ball lightning, which in some scientific quarters is seriously considered for its potential as a military weapon of great force. In 1960 he was awarded the Lomonosov Gold Medal.

On March 26, 1962, the Moscow *Ekonomicheskaia gazeta* printed Kapitsa's lengthy article "Theory, Experiment, Practice," in which he declared that if not for the science of cybernetics Soviet outer-space successes would have been impossible, and that the Soviets had Albert Einstein's theories to thank for the Soviet atomic bomb. Yet, Kapitsa recalled, only eight years earlier certain Soviet dogmatists had denounced both the computers and the theory of relativity as capitalistic and thus worthless, unclean, harmful. He quoted the following, which had appeared as late as 1954: "Cybernetics is a reactionary pseudo-science, emerging in the United States after World War II and widely spreading in other capitalistic countries as well." He wrote:

Had our scientists at the time, in 1954, obeyed the philosophers [i.e., the Stalinist dogmatists]; had they adopted this definition [of cybernetics] as their directive for the further development of this science, we can say that our conquest of outer space, of which all of us are justly proud and for which the entire world respects us, could not have occurred, since it is impossible to guide a spaceship without cybernetic machines . . . . And now physicists confirm the Einstein law, not on separate atoms, but on the scale of the atom bomb. How embarrassed our physicists would have been had they followed those philosophers' conclusions and had they ceased their work on the problem of applying the theory of relativity in nuclear physics!

Kapitsa went on to imply that in the 1940's and early 1950's he had been among the bold ones who shrugged off the Stalinist anticybernetic dogma and anti-Einstein mania and went on with genuinely scientific work. We may conclude that Kapitsa's house arrest may have been caused not so much by his reluctance to work on the atomic bomb as by his disagreement with Stalin's "philosophers" on the validity of computers and relativity.[8]

In the post-Khrushchev era no less than the post-Stalin, Kapitsa continued to raise his voice on behalf of greater freedom for scientists. Early in 1965, in a speech subsequently published in an Academy journal, he said that, although Soviet scientists could get money for their research more easily than their American colleagues, governmental restrictions made the Soviet research less productive. "Let us emulate some of the American practices," he urged. "Give funds to those who can use them fruitfully, not to those in an area of research that may be judged important by the authorities but may lack truly capable scientists."

At about the same time, in an oblique but again unmistakable way, Kapitsa demanded freer travel abroad for those Soviet scholars who really needed it, among them, surely, himself. He made this demand clear in his article in the Moscow *Sovetskaia Rossiia* (April 15, 1965), commemorating the 200th anniversary of Mikhail Lomonosov's death. Here Kapitsa praised "the international friendship of savants" and pointed out: "These days the necessity of personal contacts between scientists is taken for granted as something self-understood by our as well as foreign savants." This was doubtless to call the world's attention to the fact that since 1934 he himself had not once been allowed to go abroad, and to ensure the Soviet government's permission for him to travel to Denmark the very next month in order to receive the Niels Bohr International Gold Medal from the Danish Engineering Society for his work in the peaceful uses of atomic energy.

On May 23, 1965, for the first time in thirty-one years, Kapitsa did leave Soviet soil—to receive the Bohr medal from the hands of King Frederick IX, to tour Danish laboratories, and to deliver a lecture in Copenhagen on high energy physics. A year later, in May 1966, Kapitsa was the guest of the Royal Society for two weeks at Cambridge and London, his first trip to England since he had left in 1934.

[8] For a fuller discussion of the controversy see p. 221 ff.

SELECTED BIBLIOGRAPHY

In addition to the sources mentioned above, see the following: E. V. Shpol'sky, "Pyotr Leonidovich Kapitsa," *Uspekhi fizicheskikh nauk,* LIV, 4 (1964), 505; "Kapitsa, Pyotr Leonidovich," *Biograficheskii slovar' deiatelei estestvoznaniia i tekhniki,* I, Moskva, 1958, p. 394; S. P. Timoshenko, *Vospominaniia,* Paris: Izdanie ob'edineniia S-Peterburgskikh politekhnikov, 1963; and P. L. Kapitsa, *Zhizn' dlia nauki,* Moskva, 1964. In English, see Richard E. Lauterbach, "Russia's Kapitza," *Science Illustrated* (March, 1948), 24–25, 105; unsigned, "Russian Atom Scientist," *Science News Letter,* Sept. 3, 1940, p. 149; and Albert Parry, chapter on Kapitsa in *The New Class Divided,* New York: Macmillan, 1966, pp. 27–45.

Among Kapitsa's major works are *O vozmozhnosti opredeleniia magnitnogo momenta atoma,* with Nikolai Semyonov, Moskva, 1920; *Turbodetander dlia polucheniia nizkikh temperatur i ego primeneniia dlia ozhzhizheniia vozdukha,* Moskva, 1939; *Teploperenos i sverkhtekuchest' geliia II,* Moskva, 1941; and *Issledovanie mekhanizma teploperedachi v gelii II,* Moskva, 1941; *Elektronika bol'shikh moshchnostei,* Moskva, 1962.

Two sizable translations of Kapitsa's work have appeared in English: *High-Power Microwave Electronics,* translated by S. and M. Mikolic, and edited by D. Ter Haar, Oxford and New York: Pergamon Press (distributed in the Western Hemisphere by Macmillan, New York), 1964; *Collected Papers of P. L. Kapitza,* edited and with an introduction by D. Ter Haar, New York: Macmillan, 1964. The collected papers cover the period from 1916 to 1934.

Fedor Vasilevich Konstantinov

by Richard T. De George

Fedor Konstantinov, a Soviet philosopher-ideologist specializing in historical materialism and in the theory of social development, is important less for the originality of his thought than for the orthodoxy of his writings. He has long been a spokesman for the official Soviet positions on historical materialism and has served as the chief editor of many of the most important textbooks and quasi official Soviet publications in philosophy, which form the basis for widespread ideological indoctrination in Soviet schools and intellectual life.

Konstantinov was born on February 8, 1901. He became a member of the Communist party in 1918. While a student at the Institute of Red Professors (a Marxist institute of higher learning founded in 1921 to provide training for intellectuals in research and teaching) he was a bureau member of the institute's party cell. When his training at the institute was completed in 1932 he engaged in party work and teaching, becoming a professor in 1934. From 1931 to 1938 he wrote a number of articles, some of which appeared in *Under the Banner of Marxism* (the leading philosophical journal of the time). His first book, actually a thirty-nine-page pamphlet, appeared in 1938 and was entitled *The Meaning of Personal Property and Work Under Socialism.*

From 1941 to 1942 Konstantinov was a reader (lektor) of the Central Committee of the Communist Party of the Soviet Union (CPSU), and he published a small book containing a popular account of the fundamentals of Marxist-Leninist philosophy. His work, which closely follows Stalin's *Dialectical and Historical Materialism,* begins with a discussion of the principal features of the Marxist dialectical method (which emphasizes the movement and interconnection of all phenomena and the qualitative changes which take place as a result of the internal oppositions in nature) and ends with a section on the role of ideas in social development. For Marx and Engels the economic conditions of a society formed the basis upon which a society's social relations, institutions, laws, philosophy, and religion were built. Ideas were thus secondary, derived from and dependent upon the economic conditions of society as a superstructure upon its foundation. While Stalin admitted the economic origin of ideas, he insisted that their origin should not be confused with their significance. In fact, he asserted, ideas are a potent force in the development of society, and it is this theme—the active role of ideas in social development—which Konstantinov seized upon and developed diligently throughout his career. From 1931 until his death Stalin's few pertinent writings dominated the philosophical and ideological scene in the Soviet Union. Konstantinov developed, explained, and expanded upon Stalin's theoretical innovations, but he did not go beyond them.

During the Second World War Konstantinov was engaged in political propaganda work in the Soviet Army. With the end of the war he became an associate in the Institute of Philosophy of the Academy of Sciences of the USSR, a position he held from 1945 to 1951. During these years he published nine articles, wrote eight books (some of pamphlet size), and edited two others, establishing his reputation in the field of historical materialism (the Marxist interpretation of history). Especially significant was his development of the theme of "the role of progressive ideas in social development," the title of one of his 1947 pamphlets. His essay, "The Role of Socialist Consciousness in the Development of Soviet Society," which appeared originally as one of a number of essays in a volume entitled *Soviet Socialist Society,* was translated into English and published separately as a 114-page booklet by the Moscow Foreign Languages Publishing House. Here he develops the Stalinist thesis that "the new motive forces of the development of socialist society that were unknown to other societies are: the moral and political unity of the Soviet people, friendship among other nations, and Soviet patriotism."[1] In 1951 he published the short booklet *Basis and Superstructure* in which he elaborated the position Stalin had enunciated on this topic in his letters to *Pravda* in 1950 concerning N. Y. Marr and the linguistics controversy.[2]

Konstantinov's most important work of this period, however, was *Historical Materialism* (1st edition, 1950), a joint effort of a number of philosophers of the Academy of Sciences' Institute of Philosophy. Konstantinov was the general editor of the volume and he wrote a significant portion of the work, which was distributed in an edition of 200,000 copies and quickly sold out. The work, a textbook of historical materialism, systematically presented the "Marxist science of the general laws of social development." It attempted to show how the historical development of society from the primitive communal stage, through the slave-holding, feudal, capitalistic, and socialistic stages, to the stage of full Communism, could be explained in terms of laws which govern these succesive economic developments with an iron necessity. The book provoked lively discussion and was formally discussed for three days in Moscow by 600 specialists from various disciplines. A report in the Soviet philosophical journal *Problems of Philosophy,* of which Konstantinov had been a member of the editorial board since the first issue of 1948, listed a great many deficiencies of the book. But these were primarily sins of omission—that it did not sufficiently consider such contemporary events as the revolution in China, that it did not adequately describe the influence of the Communist party, that it did not criticize bourgeois sociology in any depth—and there was no charge of any substantive doctrinal error.

In 1953 Konstantinov successfully defended a dissertation entitled *Some Problems of Historical Materialism* at the Institute of Philosophy and was named a doctor of philosophical sciences. The dissertation systematically presented much that he had already discussed in print on historical materialism: the reciprocal relation of base and superstructure, the variety of forms of social consciousness, the decisive role of the masses in history, and the motive forces in the development of socialist society. He also discussed three basic socialistic phenomena: the way in which the modes of production determine the development of socialist society, the necessary conformity of productive relations to the character of productive forces, and the dialectical development of productive forces and productive relations; with the aid of these he attempted to show how new productive re-

---

[1] *O sovetskom sotsialisticheskom obshchestve,* p. 67; cf. Stalin, *Problems of Leninism* (1954), p. 778.

[2] Cf. J. Stalin, *Marxism and Linguistics* (1951). In this work Stalin denies Marr's contention that language is part of the superstructure of society and claims that language belongs neither to the base nor to the superstructure. In this work Stalin also emphasizes the active role of the superstructure in social development.

lations are a basic motive force in the development of productive forces. In October 1953 Konstantinov was elected a corresponding member of the Academy of Sciences of the USSR, and in the same year was named a member of the editorial board (philosophy section) of the *Large Soviet Encyclopedia.*

The second edition of *Historical Materialism,* appearing in 1954, was considerably modified in the light of previous criticism and included material from Konstantinov's dissertation. Though it met with some criticism, even the "critical remarks" of a group of teachers from Leningrad acknowledged it as an improvement over the previous edition,[3] and it became the standard text on the subject.

With the fifth issue of *Problems of Philosophy* in 1952 Konstantinov was raised to the position of editor in chief, replacing Dimitri I. Chesnokov. He held this position until the fourth issue of the journal in 1954, when he was replaced by Mikhail D. Kammari and was "transferred to other work."[4] But this was by no means a demotion and he remained on the editorial board of *Problems of Philosophy* until after the second issue of 1955.

During 1954–55 Konstantinov was rector of the Academy of Social Sciences of the USSR and in 1955 he headed the Soviet delegation visiting Hungary. In the same year he was also named head of the Department of Propaganda and Agitation of the Central Committee of the CPSU (a position he held until 1958); he joined the editorial staff of *Kommunist,* the theoretical and political journal of the Central Committee of the CPSU; and he became a deputy of the Moscow City Soviet. In January 1956 he served as a Presidium member of the Twenty-second Congress of the Communist Party of Byelorussia and in February he was a voting delegate to the Twentieth Congress of the CPSU, during which he was elected a candidate member of the party's Central Committee.

Konstantinov continued to publish articles and books during these years, notably, in 1958, the basic textbook in Soviet philosophy, *Fundamentals of Marxist Philosophy* of which he was the editor in chief and contributed two of the book's nineteen chapters. This was the first systematic treatment in the post-Stalin era of dialectical and historical materialism. It has been distributed in well over two million copies, and its second edition (1962) still remains the basic Soviet text in philosophy. The treatment of dialectical materialism reverts back to Engels and Lenin in preference to Stalin's truncated and philosophically less adequate version of it. Thus instead of beginning with a discussion of dialectics as a method, as Stalin (and Konstantinov and other Soviet philosophers following Stalin) had, the discussion begins with a consideration of matter as the ultimately real, and then goes on to discuss the three laws of dialectics which govern

[3] *Voprosy filosofii,* 1955, no. 2, pp. 227–28.
[4] *Vestnik* AN SSSR, 1955, no. 1, p. 104.

its development: the law of the transition from quantity to quality, the law of the unity and struggle of opposites, and the law of the negation of negation—the last of which Stalin had completely dropped. Stalin's innovations in historical materialism, however, including the active role of the superstructure, were kept, though references to Stalin (in contrast to the 1954 edition of *Historical Materialism*) are very few. Other than this there is no significant difference between the 1954 (Konstantinov) and the 1958 presentation and discussion of historical materialism. This remains true also of the second edition of the text (1962) which is only slightly revised.

In 1958, with the seventh issue of *Kommunist,* Konstantinov became its editor in chief (a position he held until he left the editorial board with the sixth issue of 1962). Of his articles in *Kommunist,* one on the Soviet intelligentsia is especially noteworthy for its clarification of the official Soviet view of the intelligentsia. Defining it as a social and professional category, he then develops what the role and place of intellectuals in the Soviet Union should be. On his sixtieth birthday, as the editor of *Kommunist,* he was presented the Order of Lenin "for his services in the development of the social sciences."

The first volume of the *Philosophical Encyclopedia,* of which Konstantinov is editor in chief, appeared in 1960, the second in 1962, and the third in 1964, with three more to be published in the near future. The encyclopedia promises to be an excellent philosophical reference work and one that will rival and in some ways surpass the standard Western philosophical dictionaries and encyclopedias, despite its distortions of certain Western figures and positions. The work attempts to cover the gamut of philosophy including logic, the philosophy of science, ethics, aesthetics, the philosophy of religion and atheism, and the history of philosophy.

In 1962 Konstantinov was appointed director of the Institute of Philosophy of the Academy of Sciences of the USSR, a position which he still holds. In 1963 he was a member of the Soviet delegation to the Thirteenth International Congress of Philosophy in Mexico City, where he delivered a paper on "The Individual and Society." He was named an academician of the Academy of Sciences of the USSR in 1964.

A recognized authority in the field of historical materialism, Konstantinov is a prominent member of the Soviet philosophical scene who has long contributed to and often been in charge of many of the major philosophical projects in the Soviet Union since the end of the Second World War. He is known as an official spokesman of the Communist party's ideological line, which he has conservatively expounded throughout his career. An important member of the party, he has in recent years wielded great influence on the Soviet ideological scene particularly through his editorial and administrative positions. He has been the recipient of two Orders of the Red Star.

SELECTED BIBLIOGRAPHY

The most complete and up-to-date source for biographical information in Russian on Konstantinov is: *Filosofskaia entsiklopediia,* III, Moskva, 1964, p. 49. Some material is also available in *Bol'shaia sovetskaia entsiklopediia,* izdanie 2–e, LI, Moskva, 1958, p. 158, and in *Malaia sovetskaia entsiklopediia,* izdanie 3–e, IV, Moskva, 1959, cols. 1156–57. A non-Soviet source is: *Porträts der UdSSR Prominenz,* München: Institut po izucheniyu SSSR, 1960.

Konstantinov's chief works include the following: *Rol' idei v obshchestvennom razvitii,* Moskva, 1940, which is one of the first Soviet works to discuss the active role of ideas in social development; *Chto takoe marksistsko-leninskaia filosofiia,* Moskva, 1941; and *O sovetskom sotsialisticheskom obshchestve,* Moskva, 1948, of which Konstantinov was the editor and a contributing author. These are his most important earlier works. *Istoricheskii materializm kak nauka,* Moskva, 1949; *Formy obshchestvennogo soznaniia,* Moskva, 1951; *O bazise i nadstroike,* Moskva, 1951; and *Rol' peredovykh idei v razvitii obshchestva,* Moskva, 1953, constitute Konstantinov's major contributions to the doctrine of historical materialism. He is a contributing author and editor of *Istoricheskii materializm,* Moskva, 1950 (izdanie 2–e, 1954) and *Osnovy marksistskoi filosofii,* Moskva, 1958 (izdanie 2–e, 1962) which have served as the basic texts in philosophical instruction in schools and institutions of higher learning. The latter work is still widely used. Konstantinov is also the editor in chief of *Filosofskaia entsiklopediia,* Moskva, 1960–64, a valuable and reasonably accurate encyclopedia of philosophy, of which three volumes have been published thus far.

Several of Konstantinov's works have been translated into English and other languages. Most important of these are: *Basis and Superstructure,* Moscow, 1955, and *The Role of Socialist Consciousness in the Development of Soviet Society,* Moscow, 1950. His paper "The Individual and Society," delivered at the Thirteenth International Congress of Philosophy, is contained in *Philosophy, Science and Man,* Moscow, 1963. Though the text *Osnovy marksistskoi filosofii* has not been translated into English it is available in German, Chinese, Japanese, Czech, Hungarian, Bulgarian, Polish, Romanian, Vietnamese, and Spanish editions.

Scattered items of information concerning Konstantinov's career can be found in the Soviet Academy of Sciences' *Vestnik,* 2 (1953), p. 53; *ibid.,* 6 (1953), p. 230; *ibid.,* 9 (1953), p. 104 (this gives a summary of Konstantinov's doctoral dissertation); and *ibid.,* 1 (1955), p. 104. Items concerning Konstantinov have appeared in the Soviet press and can be most readily found by consulting the *Current Digest of the Soviet Press,* beginning with volume 23.

Lev Davidovich Landau

by Albert Parry

Lev Davidovich Landau, or "Dau" to his closest friends, the fourth Russian scientist to win the Nobel Prize in physics, was born on January 22, 1908, in the Caspian oil city of Baku, the son of middle-class Jewish parents. He was a prodigy in mathematics and physics even before he reached his teens.

Landau was eighteen and a student at the Leningrad University when he published his first independent theoretical work. For his subject he chose quantum mechanics, then—in 1926—the newest, least-known, and most difficult route into the unexplored depths of the micro-world. The next year he introduced into physics the concept of *matritsa plotnosti,* or matrix of density, now common in quantum mechanics and statistical physics. At nineteen, in 1927, he was graduated from the university.

After receiving his doctorate, Landau worked for a time at the University of Kharkov in the Ukraine, but presently went to Moscow. In 1930 he predicted diamagnetism of electrons (now called "Landau's Diamagnetism"). In 1935 he did pioneer work in ferro-magnetism; in 1936 and 1937 he did research in phase transformation of solids. His work in the latter 1930's was concerned chiefly with developing and proving his theory of the intermediate stage of superconductivity. In 1937 he began his association with Pyotr Kapitsa at the celebrated Institute of Problems of Physics (in the Academy of Sciences), a fruitful collaboration lasting to the present (1967).

Landau's friendship with Kapitsa was tested and strengthened when Landau was imprisoned in the late 1930's. A Jew, Landau was arrested by the Soviet secret police on charges of pro-Nazi activities. The absurdity of this accusation can be explained only by the hysteria accompanying the mass purges of the time. Nearly three decades later, writing in the Moscow *Komsomolskaia pravda* (July 8, 1964) Landau recalled the ghastly episode: "They charged me with being a German spy. Now, occasionally, this seems amusing to me, but at that time, believe me, I did not feel like laughing. I spent one year in prison, and it was clear to me that I wouldn't last another six months. I was dying, simply dying." Finally Kapitsa saved Landau:

Kapitsa went to the Kremlin and . . . demanded my freedom. Otherwise, he said, he would leave his Institute. I was freed. It is hardly necessary to say that in those years, for such an act, one had to have great courage, great humanity, and crystal-clear honesty.

Restored to freedom, Landau returned to the institute and resumed his work. In 1940 and 1941 he developed the macroscopic theory of superfluidity of liquid helium at temperatures close to absolute zero, following Kapitsa's earlier discovery (1938) of the phenomenon of helium superfluidity. In time Landau would receive the Nobel Prize for his bold experimentation with condensation, particularly for his liquid-helium theory.

In 1943, in addition to his post at the Institute of Problems of Physics, Landau was appointed to a professorship at the University of Moscow. In 1946, when he was only thirty-eight, he was elected a member of the Academy of Sciences of the USSR, an honor that usually went to professors in their late fifties or sixties. The same year he won the Stalin Prize for his work in the thermodynamic theory of phase transformation in solids. In fact, in the immediate post-Second World War period Landau's chief importance to the Soviet government lay not alone in his research in the theory of solids, low temperature physics, and superconductivity, but also in his work in nuclear physics and cosmic rays. There are clear indications that Landau helped the Soviets to evolve their first atomic bomb. In the 1940's and 1950's he also played a top role in the significant Soviet breakthroughs in rocketry.

In January 1958, to celebrate Lev Landau's fiftieth birthday, Russia's most renowned physicists gathered in Moscow. Two of them were delegated to present Landau with a pair of wooden boards modeled after the Tables of the Ten Commandments as pictured by the nineteenth-century French illustrator of the Bible, Gustav Doré, but bearing Landau's celebrated Ten Formulae. A Moscow journalist commented that if it were not for the numerical limit of the biblical pattern, there could have been inscribed on those boards at least thirty such formulae by Landau, "and even then, most likely, the wealth of the researching talent of Academician Landau would not have been exhausted."

Landau has been awarded a number of Soviet medals, including two Orders of Lenin. When the Soviet government gave him the Lenin Prize in April 1962, the official citation enumerated his series of books (1941–60) on theoretical physics: *Mechanics, The Theory of Fields, Quantum Mechanics, Statistical Physics, Mechanics of Solids,* and *Electrodynamics of Solids.* Translated into several languages, his writings have been published in the United States, England, Japan, China, Poland, and Yugoslavia. He has been honored by memberships in the foremost learned societies of America, Britain, France, Holland, and Denmark, and received the Max Planck Medal (established in memory of the father of the quantum theory) in West Germany.

In late 1962 all these honors were capped by the Nobel Prize for physics. Yet Landau could not travel to Stockholm to receive his award from the Nobel Committee and the Swedish king. He could barely move to the next room when, in November 1962, the momentous tidings reached him. "How sad," the Moscow *Literaturnaia gazeta* noted on November 10, "that the news came to Landau in the hospital, and not at his desk, nor amidst the students' tumult of his lecture halls." It was a miracle that he was alive at all—that he was conscious, able to understand the announcement, and able to half-sit up in his bed, however briefly, smile, and raise his hand to Rolf R. Sohlman, the Swedish ambassador in Moscow bringing him the king's first congratulations.

Ten months before, in January 1962, Landau had been given up for dead, not once but four times. Each time, by a supreme effort of modern medical science, he was brought back to life, though not to consciousness. Each time the doctors thought that their success was temporary and useless.

On January 7 of that year, on the icy road leading to the famous institute of atomic research in Dubna, near Moscow, a car had swung to avoid a girl pedestrian and collided with a truck. Landau, the car's passenger, was lifted from the wreck all but lifeless. His skull, ribs, and pelvis were fractured. His heartbeat and respiration were ebbing. In the hospital, injuries to the heart, kidneys, and central nervous system were found. There were eleven bone breaks besides the skull fracture. He was in deep shock. Oxygen was administered. Blood transfusions were tried. An emergency operation lessened the pressure on his brain. His heart stopped on the fourth day after the accident. Quick stimulants revived it. It stopped again on the seventh day, and once more on the ninth, and for the fourth time on the eleventh day. Each time stimulants pulled him back to life. But throughout, Landau remained unconscious, his temperature rising to 107 degrees.

Word of the impending loss to science was flashed to foreign centers of medical skill. The world's foremost neurosurgeons were rushed to Moscow, among them Canada's renowned Dr. Wilder G. Penfield, who flew in to join the brilliant circle of Russian, French, and Czech colleagues at Landau's bedside.

For seven weeks Landau was in a deep coma, and was still unconscious when, late in February, his condition was judged sufficiently improved for him to be moved to the Moscow Institute of Neurosurgery. Soon after, the neurosurgeons met outside the patient's room for one more consultation. Professor Yevgeny Lifshitz, a physicist and close friend and collaborator of Landau's, was in the sickroom. As he later reported, Landau's body was completely inert, but his eyes were open. Attempting communication, Lifshitz told Landau to close his eyes if he recognized him. Landau's eyes closed. Lifshitz burst into the adjoining room with his news: Landau had recognized him.

The recovery, thus beginning, was slow. Months later, in the winter of 1962, a medical report from Moscow read: "Physicians feel that Landau's intellect, his ability to think deeply and logically, have been restored. But his memory is still unreliable. One important positive factor, they feel, is that he himself now realizes his condition. He speaks of his wish to return to his favorite work—theoretical physics—but understands that he is not quite ready to work properly."

A mathematical problem of some complexity was gingerly tried out on Landau. There was dismay when the patient whispered what seemed to be a wrong solution. But the dismay turned to jubilation when a colleague checked the answer once more—and discovered that it was right after all, that Landau had merely come to the correct conclusion in an entirely original way.

He was judged to be strong enough for the official ceremony of December 10, 1962, when Ambassador Sohlman returned to the sickroom bearing the Nobel Prize with its diploma and gold medal. The physicist was made ready. He was fully dressed and sitting, haggard, but quietly joyful. The envoy was accompanied by his staff. Yet more happily, Landau's friends arrived as beaming witnesses—such luminaries of Soviet science as the academicians Pyotr L. Kapitsa, Nikolai N. Semyonov, Igor Ye. Tamm, Mstislav V. Keldysh, and Lev A. Artsimovich. Semyonov and Tamm had been Nobel Prize winners, in 1956 and 1958; Keldysh and Artsimovich represented the Academy of Sciences of the USSR, as president and secretary, respectively. Kapitsa, speaking of his twenty-five-year association with Landau at the Academy's Institute of Problems of Physics, said in an interview:

Landau has done work in all the fields of theoretical physics, and all of it can be described by one word—remarkable. We all love Landau very much. We are proud that his work has now been marked by this worldwide recognition. Seldom can you find another man with such zest for life, so full of camaraderie, such a wonderful friend, such an attentive teacher of young physicists.

Many young Soviet physicists aspired to study under Landau; but he made stern demands on his students. The Moscow *Komsomolskaia pravda* (August 21, 1963) revealed the existence of "Landau's Minimum," his compilation of essential works (dubbed "that terror-inspiring list" by Russian students) on theoretical physics. "The list," said the newspaper, "is by no means mastered by every university graduate in physics." The procedure for those who wanted to study under Landau, according to a colleague, Professor A. I. Kitaigorodsky, in his memoir *Physics Is My Profession,* was as follows: "Any young man could come to his apartment and tell him that he wished to be a disciple of his." If the applicant passed a preliminary interview and examination, Landau "would tell him what he was to read, and what type of problems he must learn to solve." If the candidate performed satisfactorily at the next interview, Landau would give him another assignment. Thus followed "new instructions and increasingly complex assignments." Once a candidate is accepted, Professor Kitaigorodsky continues, "he is given research tasks, he is allowed to come to scientific seminars, he is set on his tracks. The rest depends on his own talent and industry."

Landau's stature in the field has been aptly summarized by Kapitsa:

Landau's clarity of thought and precise style of work have helped him to bring up several generations of physicists. He is one of the few physicists to whom you may address a question on anything in his field at all—and receive a truly thorough answer. Landau's theoretical method has one important feature among others: he does not separate theory from experiment. This is what he teaches to the young ones. And I can confidently say that there is not a single able physicist anywhere who does not know Landau's work, to whom Landau's books are not a kind of modern encyclopedia.

Like his friend Kapitsa, Landau is keenly interested in all sorts of discussion and experimentation, some of which have nothing to do with the precise sciences. In the mid-1950's he was known to frequent private gatherings in the Moscow homes of certain prominent scientists, where deep and far-ranging philosophical problems were considered. By the early 1960's he joined Kapitsa in admiring and encouraging the abstract sculpture of Ernst Neizvestny. The latter, when reproved in December 1962 by Premier Khrushchev himself, suggested Landau's and Kapitsa's support of his sculpture as reason enough for the Communist party to let him experiment freely. The argument, however, failed to impress Khrushchev, who retorted: "But this is not why we admire Landau and Kapitsa."

Lev Landau has operated on several levels—in the laboratories and lecture halls of his own profession, in the art studios and at the philosophical soirées of Moscow's intellectual elite and, not least, as a popular lecturer and writer for the masses in the hallowed tradition of the Russian intelligentsia. In 1963 his book *Physics for Everybody,* written in collaboration with A. Kitaigorodsky, was issued in a large edition by the State Publishing House of Physics and Mathematical Literature. Yet it remains a question to what degree Landau has been able to function in all these ways since his accident of January 1962. On February 14, 1964, *Time* in New York cited "word from Moscow" that Landau, although on the mend, "still appears unable to think in the A-then-B-then-C sequence necessary to scientific theorizing, and his colleagues fear that despite his physical recovery, he will never return to his work."

Public appearances and statements by Landau have been extremely rare since his recovery. A letter to the *New York Times* signed jointly by him and Professor Yevsei Liberman and dated May 31, 1965, was published in that newspaper on June 2. Protesting the circulation in the West of "all kinds of fabrications on the position of the Jews in the USSR," the two scholars repeated the standard Communist party thesis that there is no persecution of any national minority or group in the Soviet Union: "The Jews of the USSR, as the other national minorities, are inseparable from all Soviet multinational people. They enjoy all social benefits in an equal degree, and participate in all economic, political, and cultural life of the country."

Landau and Liberman were answered in the same newspaper on June 21 by Saul Bellow, Richard Hofstadter, and two other American professors (letter to the editor dated June 17). The rebuttal was that "discrimination against Jews has not disappeared" with Stalin's death; that job opportunities are still not equal for Soviet Jews; that the Soviet government even in these post-Khrushchev days still inflicts upon the Jews of that nation "the deprivation of cultural and religious rights which all other similar groups enjoy and without which the survival of the Jewish community is impossible."

It was generally held in the West that neither Landau nor Liberman put his distinguished name to that letter of his own free will. Comment was made about Landau's lack of certain personal freedoms as a Soviet citizen, most particularly freedom of movement, going abroad to foreign universities and laboratories and international conferences, invitations to which the world-famous physicist and mathematician certainly does not lack. Yet it is possible that in these comparatively permissive post-Stalin years Landau would travel, more or less freely, to foreign countries if his health would allow it.

SELECTED BIBLIOGRAPHY

Biographical information about Lev D. Landau can be found in "Talant, trudoliubie, razmakh," *Izvestiia,* November 4, 1962, p. 6, an interview with Academician Pyotr L. Kapitsa on Landau's life and work; Daniil Danin, "Tovarishchestvo," *Literaturnaia gazeta,* July 21, 1962, p. 2, which describes Landau's accident and treatment; Daniil Danin, "Nobelevskaia premiia—sovetskomu fiziku," *Literaturnaia gazeta,* November 10, 1962, p. 2; F. Kedrov, "Nobelevskie laureaty," *Sovetskaia Rossiya,* August 6, 1965, p. 3. In English, see J. G. Crowther, *Soviet Science,* London: Kegan Paul, Trench, Trubner, 1936; Theodore Shabad, "Fifty-Day Vigil Saves Injured Soviet Scientist," *New York Times,* July 20, 1962, p. 2; and unsigned, "Landau, Nobel Prize Physicist, 'Dead' 4 Times, Regains Mind," *New York Times,* December 5, 1962, p. 33.

Landau's Russian-language publications include several books on theoretical physics written in collaboration with E. M. Lifshitz, among them the following: *Mekhanika sploshnykh sred,* Moskva, Leningrad, 1944; *Kvantovaia mekhanika,* Moskva, Leningrad, 1948; *Teoriia polia,* Moskva, Leningrad, 1948; *Statisticheskaia fizika,* Moskva, Leningrad, 1951; *Elektrodinamika sploshnykh sred,* Moskva, 1959. With Iakov Smorodinsky he wrote *Lektsii po teorii atomnogo iadra,* Moskva, 1955 and with G. B. Rumer, *Chto takoe teoriia otnositel'nosti,* Moskva, 1959.

Many of Landau's works have been translated into English, among them the following: *Statistical Physics* (with E. M. Lifshitz), translated by E. and R. F. Peierls, London: Pergamon Press and Reading, Mass.: Addison-Wesley,

1958; *Quantum Mechanics, Non-Relativistic Theory* (with E. M. Lifshitz), translated by J. B. Sykes and J. S. Bell, Oxford: Pergamon Press and Reading, Mass.: Addison-Wesley, 1958; *Fluid Mechanics* (with E. M. Lifshitz), translated by J. B. Sykes and W. H. Reid, London: Pergamon Press and Reading, Mass.: Addison-Wesley, 1959; *Lectures on Nuclear Theory* (with Iakov Smorodinsky), revised edition, New York: Plenum Press, 1959; *Theory of Elasticity* (with E. M. Lifshitz), translated by J. B. Sykes and W. H. Reid, London: Pergamon Press and Reading, Mass.: Addison-Wesley, 1959; *Electrodynamics of Continuous Media* (with E. M. Lifshitz), translated by J. B. Sykes and J. S. Bell, Oxford and New York: Pergamon Press, 1960; *Mechanics* (with E. M. Lifshitz), translated by J. B. Sykes and J. S. Bell, Oxford: Pergamon Press and Reading, Mass.: Addison-Wesley, 1960; *What Is Relativity?* (with G. B. Rumer), translated by N. Kemmer, Edinburgh: Oliver and Boyd, 1960.

Trofim Denisovich Lysenko[*]

by Maxim W. Mikulak

On September 30, 1898, Trofim Lysenko was born of Ukrainian peasants in the village of Karlovka in Poltava Province. His father, Denis Nikanorovich Lysenko, who displayed an interest in agricultural economics, undoubtedly influenced the young Lysenko to enter the field of agriculture, and at the age of fifteen he completed a two-semester program at an agricultural school. Four years later, in 1917, he graduated from the Poltava Primary School for Horticulture and Gardening. He received further training at the Uman School for Horticulture, and in 1921 was assigned to the Belotserkovsky Experimental Station. In the same year he continued his studies at the Kiev Agricultural Institute, conducting several experiments on tomatoes and sugar beets. He graduated from the Kiev Agricultural Institute in 1925, ending his formal training. By and large, his education in horticulture stressed practical accomplishments in selective breeding.

After his graduation from the Kiev Agricultural Institute, Lysenko was sent to the new selection station in Gandzha (now Kirovabad) in the Azerbaijanian Soviet Socialist Republic. Here he concentrated on the theory of the stages of plant development, producing in 1928 an article entitled "The Influence of the Thermal Factors on the Duration of the Phase of Development of Agricultural Plants." He also developed an interest in the presowing treatment of seeds which was first described in

* This study was made possible through a research grant-in-aid from The Research Foundation of the State University of New York.

1929 as vernalization (*iarovizatsiia*). This process of pretreating the seeds decreased the time between seeding and harvesting, a great boon to those areas of the Soviet Union having a short growing season. The results of the researches at the Kirovabad Plant-Breeding Station were presented by Lysenko in January 1929 to the All-Union Genetics Congress in Leningrad. In the same year he introduced the vernalized winter wheat, Ukrainka, to his father, and together they worked out methods of sowing vernalized winter wheat under field conditions. By 1934 the sowing of vernalized winter wheat was practiced on many of the collective farms of Soviet Russia. Lysenko's studies on vernalization were considered of such importance that he was encouraged to produce the *Bulletin of Vernalization,* which first appeared in January 1932. From 1935, in collaboration with the Ukrainian Marxist, I. I. Prezent, Lysenko edited the journal *Vernalization,* and in 1936 released the pamphlet *Vernalization and Agricultural Plants* which contained practical suggestions, in simple language, on vernalizing large quantities of wheat, oat, and barley seeds. Primarily as a consequence of his research in vernalization, in 1929 Lysenko became the senior specialist at the Ukrainian Institute of Selection and Genetics (in 1935 reorganized into the All-Union Institute of Selection and Genetics).

The years 1932 to 1934 were critical ones in the history of Soviet genetics as well as in Lysenko's career. This period marked the start of Lysenko's meteoric ascendancy in the Soviet world of plant selection and theoretical genetics, but even more dramatic was the arrest and subsequent banishment of some of the outstanding Mendelian geneticists of the 1920's: Agol, Chetverikov, Efroimson, Ferry, and Levitsky. By 1934 it was unmistakably clear that the leadership of the Communist party and the Soviet government was unalterably opposed—for reasons never made public—to the genetics developed by Mendel, Weismann, and Morgan.[1] However, the demise of classical genetics required three conferences, a dozen years, and Lysenko.

Had Lysenko restricted his interests to the practical aspects of plant physiology, he probably would have avoided being drawn into the great Soviet controversy on genetics. He was not an active participant in the debates of the 1920's between the "Morganists" and the "Lamarckists." In fact, as late as the beginning of the 1930's the Soviet Michurinist plant breeders (the followers of I. V. Michurin, who is considered Russia's Luther Burbank) and the Morganist geneticists saw no areas of conflict; the former group was primarily concerned with practice and the latter with theory. Furthermore, Lysenko's early works were obscure and hardly conducive to stimulating enthusiasm or criticism. Although Lysenko's program of vernalization was merely another attempt to increase the productivity of collective farms, and vernalization per se has little to do with the science

[1] A. Weismann and T. H. Morgan developed the concept of the gene, and G. Mendel's laws of heredity quantitatively substantiated this concept.

of genetics, his explanation of the process, based on his theory of phasic development, impinged on the question of the inheritance of characteristics. As early as January 1934 his views on heredity and plant development were challenged by scientists at a meeting of the Seed-Growing Farms Union. His response, appearing in *The Theoretical Principles of Vernalization,* to the resistance his notions encountered from the scientists was one he employed against his critics in the years to come. First, he endeavored to link his theory of phasic development to the *Weltanschauung* of Marx and Engels. Second, he claimed that his theory was a continuation of Darwin's theory of natural selection, of Timiriazev's historical method in biology, and of Michurin's contention that hereditary changes can be artificially produced and transmitted to future generations. And third, he pointed out that his theory survived the ultimate scientific test of validity: practice.

Although Lysenko believes that his theory of phasic development represents a major contribution to general biology, the theory at first hardly commanded serious attention within or without the Soviet Union. Critics have maintained that much of Lysenko's theoretical writing defies verification, lacks clarity, and displays inconsistency. In the case of the phasic theory, nowhere in his principal works does Lysenko offer a detailed, step-by-step analysis of each distinct stage of plant development. Perhaps the clearest exposition of his concept of phasic development (which leaves much to be desired) is to be found in *The Theoretical Principles of Vernalization:*

The development of plants consists of separate qualitatively different stages, or phases. To pass through the different phases of development the plants require different external conditions (different nutriment, light, temperature, etc.). Phases are definite, *necessary* stages in the plant's development, and serve as the basis of the development of all the plant's particular forms—its organs and characters. The different organs and characters can develop only at definite phases. On the basis of a given phase various organs and characters may form, but by no means all those the plant is known to possess.

Stressing that a normally growing plant must follow a strict sequence in its development, he made plain that his stages of development do not refer to the traditional definition of the formation of plant organs and parts but to "those states and qualitative turning points in the development of plants that take place at the growing points of the stem and which are essential for their normal progress through the formation of different organs and characters to fruiting." He admits of "first phases of development," "pre-vernalized phase," "vernalized phase," and the "photo phase" (in which light is required for continued growth). He frequently mentions "separate phases," "other phases," "other qualitative (phasic) change," "next phase," "previous phase," and so on without specification. Aside from the vernalized phase, Lysenko virtually neglected the other phases of his theory of plant development. It is a most difficult task to determine precisely what new contribution Lysenko's phasic theory has made to biological theory in general and to plant physiology in particular.

While Lysenko's theory of phasic development stirred little interest among Soviet biologists, his statements on the impact of the environment upon the hereditary properties of an organism created a tempest inasmuch as they smacked of neo-Lamarckism and had great implications for agricultural practice. There are three major aspects to Lysenko's position on the inheritance of characters: (1) his rejection of classical genetics including the gene concept, (2) his acceptance of the Michurinist teaching that, by controlling environmental factors, man can bring about changes in the hereditary characteristics of an organism, and (3) his thesis that the hereditary constitutions of organisms are potentially or actually pliable, plastic, and unstable, making it possible to induce new forms of plants and animals.

In 1935 Lysenko co-authored with I. I. Prezent a volume entitled *Plant Breeding and the Theory of Phasic Development of Plant*s which in part was concerned with the science of genetics. They declared that the explanation of the lag in socialist plant breeding "lies in the critical state of the science of plant biology that we inherited from methodologically impotent bourgeois science." Both suggested an uncompromising fight for "the reconstruction of the genetic plant breeding theory on the basis of the materialist principles of development, which actually reflect the dialectics of heredity." From the methodological point of view, Lysenko and Prezent were troubled by the supposedly obsessive preoccupation of "bourgeois" geneticists with correlating hereditary characters with specific "rudiments," i.e., genes, thereby overlooking the course of a plant's development and the development of its hereditary constitution. From the practical point of view, Lysenko confessed that Mendel's law of "formal" genetics hindered him in his research in improving the seeds of cereals. In a paper entitled "The Intravarietal Crossing of Self-Pollinating Plants," presented in August 1936 at the Grain Department of the USSR Lenin Academy of Agricultural Sciences, Lysenko stated that he was "violently opposed . . . to the Morgan and Weismann corpuscular genetic conception." By the end of 1936 he defined arbitrarily two irreconcilable trends in genetics: Mendel-Weismann-Morgan-ism and Darwin-Timiriazev-Michurin-ism; he unwaveringly supported then, and still continues to support now, the latter trend.

In works such as "The Mentor—A Powerful Means of Plant Breeding" (1938), "Seed Growing Must Be Based on Michurin's Theory" (1938), "The Creator of Soviet Agrobiology" (1939), "Michurin's Theory at the All-Union Agricultural Exhibition" (1941), "What Is Michurin Genetics?" (1940), and "Genetics" (1946), Lysenko clearly expressed his great admiration for the Russian horticulturist, I. V. Michurin (1855–1935). After noting that the correct principles of socialist agriculture could be found only in the teachings of Lenin and Stalin, Lysenko said that "no one else in the history of science of plant breeding and genetics possessed so profound an understanding of the life and development of plants as Ivan Vladimirovich Michurin." In "The Creator of Soviet Agrobiology" Lysenko wrote that Michurin's theory was the Soviet trend in agricultural science, a trend supported by the Communist party and the Soviet government. To Lysenko, Michurinism represented creative Darwinism in agrobiology and the antithesis to sterile "Mendelism-Morganism." In Lysenko's eyes Michurin's motto, "We cannot wait for favors from Nature; we must wrest them from her," was a guide to action. On the basis of Michurin's practical work and theory of the individual development of plants, Lysenko argued that the direction of plant evolution can be controlled "by creating the definite external conditions at definite times." Lysenko was also strongly attracted by the fact that Michurinist genetics permits man to exert an influence on the environmental factors of a plant and that man can therefore impose his will on nature.

As in the case of the phasic theory of plant development, Lysenko's notions on the nature of the "hereditary foundation" of an organism are nebulously formulated. In order to obtain some glimpse of his ideas on heredity, adaptability, and variability, it is useful to consult his articles on "Ways of Controlling Plant Organism" (1940), "New Achievements in Controlling the Nature of Plants" (1940), "Engels and Certain Problems of Darwinism" (1943), and "Heredity and Its Variability" (1943). In rejecting specific mechanisms (chromosomes and genes) for the transmission of hereditary characteristics of organisms, Lysenko evolved an explanation of heredity in which the entire organism and its environs must be considered. He believes that the hereditary constitutions of organisms are either "conservative" and do not readily assimilate conditions that are imposed upon it, or that they are "destabilized" and have a tendency to assimilate certain naturally or artificially contrived conditions. According to Lysenko, the chief task of the plant breeder is to ascertain the moment in a plant's development when its conservative nature can be unstabilized by altering the environment. In "Heredity and Its Variability" he suggested three methods to effect the destabilization of plants: grafting, crossbreeding, and subjecting plants to external influences. After destabilizing the hereditary foundation of a plant, Lysenko recommended that it be "trained" for certain desired traits; these traits must then be stabilized in the plant by future sowing under proper conditions. It is most clear that Lysenko was completely oblivious to the progress of neo-Mendelian genetics; in fact, Lysenko's methods of destabilization predate Lamarck.

The first conference to administer a blow to Mendelian genetics was held in December 1936 at the USSR Lenin Academy of Agricultural Sciences. This widely publicized Congress on Genetics and Agriculture was dominated by Communist party administrators and supporters who were bent on vanquishing Mendelian genetics. Lysenko delivered one of the major addresses entitled "Two Trends in Genetics" in which he attempted to discredit the renowned geneticist and one-time president of the International Congress of Genetics, Nikolai Ivanovich Vavilov. Lenin himself had appointed Vavilov to head the Bureau of Applied Botany (now the Lenin's All-Union Academy of Agricultural Sciences). Despite Vavilov's high scientific standing as a geneticist, Lysenko ridiculed his theories, programs, and accomplishments. Lysenko also sought to discredit the gene concept and doubted that geneticists or cytologists would ever find a gene under the microscope. In presenting the outcome of this congress to the Soviet public, the party-controlled press made it appear as if Lysenko had scored a personal triumph over the specialists in genetics. As a matter of fact, in 1938 Lysenko replaced Vavilov as president of the Lenin's All-Union Academy of Agricultural Sciences.

In October 1939 the second conference was inaugurated by the editorial board of the Soviet Marxist theoretical journal, *Under the Banner of Marxism*. Of the fifty-three active participants at this Conference on Genetics and Selection, Vavilov, Poliakov, and Lysenko presented the most significant reports. Vavilov, whose talk was greeted with constant interruptions and rude heckling, made a feeble defense of Mendelian genetics. I. M. Poliakov endeavored without success to find a common ground between the Mendelian and Michurinist schools of thought. Lysenko continued to hammer away at Mendelian genetics, reiterated his interpretations of Michurinist genetics, and justified his theoretical claims on the double bases of his agronomic achievements and dialectical materialism, the official philosophic outlook of the Soviet Communist party. The Mendelians, if not thoroughly routed, were completely on the defensive at this conference. In 1940 Vavilov was arrested under mysterious circumstances and perished during the war along with Karpechenko and Serebrovsky, two other leading geneticists. But Mendelian genetics was not as yet extirpated from Soviet soil.

The third conference occurred between July 31 and August 7, 1948, at the Lenin's All-Union Academy of Agricultural Sciences. In his presidential address, "The Situation in the Science of Biology," Lysenko described the irreconcilable cleavage between the dialectical materialist Michurinist teaching of the inheritance of acquired characteristics and the idealist, metaphysical Mendelist-Morganist teaching which denies the organism's dependence on its environment for its hereditary traits. For the most part this conference covered the themes of previous congresses on genetics and selection. The Mendelian geneticists were castigated once again for allegedly following in a subservient manner the nonmaterialist, foreign concepts of reactionary, bourgeois biologists. Time and again Lysenko and his colleagues accused the Mendelian geneticists of making no practical and positive contributions to Soviet agriculture. Lysenko believed the principal reason for this grave situation to be the Mendelist doctrine of "unknowability," resting on probability theory, which allegedly denies the possibility of predicting mutations, or, in Lysenko's terminology, "hereditary alterations," and which allegedly precludes the willful selection and breeding of desired characteristics in organisms.[2]

Some of the outstanding scientists of the Soviet Union defended classical genetics, including Ia. A. Rapoport, B. M. Zavadovsky, S. I. Alikhanian, I. M. Poliakov, A. R. Zhebrak, I. I. Shmalgauzen, and V. S. Nemchinov. Generally speaking, the Mendelians tried to explain the gene concept in a most elementary fashion to the predominantly Michurinist audience, as if the followers of Lysenko were completely ignorant of the existing supporting evidence for the gene. It was clear from several of the speeches of the Mendelian geneticists, which concentrated mainly on theoretical problems, that their contributions in solving the practical problems of Soviet agriculture had been meager. And in general they admitted that although Lysenko and some of his followers were unscientific in their theoretical views, Lysenko's forte was practical selection and breeding. From the remarks of the Soviet classical geneticists it was evident that they hoped to pursue their researches independently of the Michurinists. But Lysenko and his supporters maintained that only one genetics school of thought should be permitted to flourish—the one contributing most to socialist agriculture.

At the tenth and final session of the third conference, Lysenko revealed that the Central Committee of the Communist party had read his report and approved it.[3] Lysenko concluded his moment of greatest triumph with these words:

Progressive biological science owes it to the geniuses of mankind, Lenin and Stalin, that *the teaching of I. V. Michurin has been added to the treasurehouse of our knowledge, has become part of the gold fund of our science . . . Glory to the great friend and protagonist of science, our leader and teacher, Comrade Stalin!*

The controversy between the Michurinists and Mendelians was settled not in the laboratories or experimental fields, but inside the Kremlin by the leadership of the Soviet Communist party.

The Lysenkoist victory had some startling aftereffects: (1) Several prominent Soviet classical geneticists, including Alikhanian, Poliakov, Zhebrak, and Zhukovsky confessed their theoretical errors and promised to up-

[2] As early as 1935 Lysenko said that "breeders ought to *know beforehand, before the crossing,* which of the parents' characteristics will dominate in the offsprings"; see his *Plant Breeding and the Theory of Phasic Development.* Actually, the Soviet Mendelists had no opportunity of putting their theories into practice.

[3] The *Large Soviet Encyclopedia,* second edition, under the heading "Genetics," revealed that both Stalin and Molotov personally backed the Michurinist position in biology.

hold the Michurinist line in biology. (2) Academicians Dubinin, Oberli, Poliakov, Shmalgauzen, Zavadovsky, Zhebrak, and others lost their positions. (3) In accordance with the resolution of the Presidium of the USSR Academy of Sciences, dated August 26, 1948, centers of "Weismannist-Morganist genetics," such as the Institute of Cytology, Histology, and Embryology and including its Laboratory of Plant Cytology, and the Laboratory of Phenogenesis of the A. N. Severtsov Institute of Morphological Evolution were liquidated. (4) The same resolution called for the removal of all Weismannists-Morganists from the staffs, councils, and editorial boards associated with biological sciences. (5) S. Kaftanov, USSR Minister of Higher Education, outlined a program of action whereby Michurinists were to fill the ranks formerly held by the Mendelists, Michurinist textbooks on biology were to replace those stressing "Mendel-Morgan theories," and the "practical sterility" of the Mendelian geneticists was to make way for beneficent Michurinist research. And (6) Academician Lysenko was offered the chair of genetics and selection at the Timiriazev Academy of Agriculture. However, it is now known that many Mendelian geneticists continued working surreptitiously or in fields associated with genetics.

That Lysenko, in his struggle against classical genetics, had the backing of Joseph Stalin and the Communist party was evident by his rapid rise in power and prestige. In 1934 he was appointed scientific director of the All-Union Institute of Selection and Genetics, and from 1936 to 1939 he was its full director. In 1934 he was also nominated to the Ukrainian Academy of Sciences and was confirmed the following year as an active or regular member. The next year he became an active member of the Lenin's All-Union Academy of Agricultural Sciences and its president in 1938, a position he held until 1957. It was also in 1938 that Lysenko was elected as an active member of the Presidium of the Academy of Sciences of the USSR. In 1940 he was made the director of the Institute of Genetics at the academy.

During the Second World War Lysenko wrote and lectured extensively on agricultural problems. In his *The Tasks in the Days of the Great Patriotic War,* Lysenko offered suggestions on cultivating grain cereals, potatoes, sugar beets, and dandelions under wartime conditions. For his patriotic efforts and scientific achievements he was given six Orders of Lenin, three Stalin prizes, the medal of the Hero of Socialist Labor, the medal of the Order of Labor of the Red Banner, the I. I. Mechnikov gold medal, and several other awards. He also served as a Ukrainian deputy to and vice president of the Supreme Soviet of the USSR.

From August 1948 on, Lysenko loomed as the supreme authority on practical and theoretical agrobiology. He and the Lenin's All-Union Academy of Agricultural Sciences were assigned the task of aiding the party and government's program on land reclamation. Lysenko offered suggestions for winter sowing outside the Black Soil Belt, and he advised the party hierarchy on the cultivation of virgin and idle lands. He also contributed the article "Vitality of Plant and Animal Organisms" and "Species" to the *Large Soviet Encyclopedia.* In 1950 he published a controversial theoretical work entitled "New Developments in the Science of Biological Species," which concerns the concept of species. Convinced that no precise definition of the term "species" existed, he consequently defined it as the "forms of organisms, which do not interbreed under the ordinary conditions of life that are normal for them or when they interbreed do not produce normally fertile offspring, i.e., forms which are physiologically incompatible." Of greater interest, since it reveals the shallowness of Lysenko's scientific training, is his explanation of how grains of rye were found in the spikes of wheat, how wheat plants were obtained from ryelike grains, and how barley grains developed an external appearance indistinguishable from branched-wheat grains. His thesis called for *"the emergence of one plant species from another species."* According to him, in order for certain species to originate other species, it is necessary to have "suitable environmental conditions." However, he acknowledged that thus far this explanation of species formation applies to the plant world only, but he hoped that Michurinist biology would demonstrate how new species arise in the animal kingdom.

Lysenko's theory on the speciation of the plant world was used by his opponents to rekindle biological debate. The anti-Lysenkoists, who never completely vanished, crystallized their stand around the *Botanical Journal.* Even before the death of Joseph Stalin on March 5, 1953, N. V. Turbin had subjected Lysenko's new species concept to critical analysis in the *Botanical Journal* of November–December 1952. Two Michurinists, K. Ia. Avotin-Pavlov and S. K. Karapetian, were held up as examples of the kind of crude experimenters who provided the empirical evidence for Lysenko's theory of the formation of new species. The former claimed to have discovered a pine tree in the process of being transformed into a fir tree, and the latter described the transformation of a hornbeam tree into a hazelnut shrub. But it was revealed in the pages of *Botanical Journal* that the fir tree self-grafted itself to the pine tree and that a forestry worker in 1923 had grafted the hazelnut shrub to the hornbeam tree. In response to his critics Lysenko denied that he was promulgating a new doctrine of species. Nevertheless, toward the end of 1953 criticism against his theories and "dogmatism" began to mount.

The influential theoretical journal of the party, *Communist,* published in March 1954 an editorial sharply condemning the "dogmatism" in the agricultural sciences so prominent in Stalin's time and gave every encouragement for open scientific discussions such as Turbin's critique of Lysenko's views on species formation. The party's opposition to any form of dogmatism in the natural science became widely known. Between 1954 and

1958 Lysenko's practices and theories came under increasing scrutiny and attack. His "Developments in the Science of Biological Species" was judged to be unsound, erroneous, and useless. His theory that within a given species there is neither overpopulation nor a struggle for survival was proved false. Lysenko's program for controlling erosion by means of cluster planting of trees was viewed not only as costly to the state but detrimental to erosion control. Finally, Lysenko and his Michurinists were accused of critical niggling, smearing labels on their adversaries, and dredging up from the history of biology issues and literature at least a half-century old. On April 10, 1957, *Pravda* announced that Comrade Trofim Denisovich Lysenko had requested that he be released from his duties as president of the Lenin's All-Union Academy of Agricultural Sciences; he was replaced by P. P. Lobanov. Three months later Lysenko was elected to the presidium of the same academy.

If Lysenko was suffering an eclipse in 1957, it was at most momentary. In September 1958, on his sixtieth birthday, he received the Order of Lenin ostensibly for his agricultural contributions to socialist production, and on December 14, 1958, *Pravda* printed a lengthy article denouncing Lysenko's critics who wrote in the *Botanical Journal*. It was stated in the *Pravda* article that the Michurinist school of biology was firmly founded on dialectical materialism and furthered the teachings of Darwin. By January 1959 a new editorial board was organized for *Botanical Journal,* headed by V. F. Kuprevich, president of the Byelorussian Academy of Sciences. Meanwhile, Lysenko had won over Nikita Khrushchev and the party to Michurnist biology. By August 1961 Lysenko had been re-elected president of the Lenin's All-Union Academy of Agricultural Sciences, but eight months later he asked to be relieved of this position for reasons of health although he continued to pursue his agricultural research.

As long as Khrushchev remained in power, Lysenko enjoyed the high esteem of the party. However, the Central Committee of the Communist party and the USSR Council of Ministers, while recognizing the practical achievements of the Michurinists in genetics, selection, and seed growing, expressed dissatisfaction with several branches of biology and medicine. The Central Committee in January 1963 adopted the resolution "On Measures for Further Developing Biological Science and Strengthening Its Ties with Practice." Although the Michurinists interpreted this resolution as party approval of their school of biology, the classical geneticists saw in it the party's acceptance of the gene concept as necessary to the continued progress in agriculture and medicine; this time the Mendelian geneticists could point to the spectacular developments in biology occurring outside the Soviet Union, a development which revealed a wide gap between Soviet and Western biologies.

With the expulsion of Khrushchev from the highest bodies of the party and the Soviet government, the Michurinists were definitely on the defensive. The president of the Academy of Sciences of the USSR, Academician M. V. Keldysh, admitted that certain groups of scientists had impeded the development of molecular biology and genetics. Keldysh was not prepared to reject completely Lysenko's theory of phasic development, but he did indicate that Lysenko and his followers had neglected experimentally verified facts and recent developments in modern biology. *Komsomolskaia pravda,* organ of the Komsomol (Young Communist League), and *Pravda* began to publish a stream of articles exposing the inadequacies of Michurinist biology. The party leadership made it obvious that the resolution "On Measures for Further Developing Biological Science and Strengthening Its Ties with Practice" signified the end of the monopolistic position of Lysenko and his adherents in Soviet biology. Lysenko's diminishing position in theoretical biology was further reduced when he was relieved of his directorship of the Institute of Genetics and of the Biological Department of the Academy of Sciences of the USSR. Leonid Brezhnev, first secretary of the Communist party, dispelled any doubts about the party's attitude toward Lysenko's leadership in Soviet biological development when he stated on March 24, 1965, at a plenary session of the party's Central Committee that Soviet success in biology would have been more noteworthy "if the fallacious theories and dogmas that came into being without adequate scientific basis and that were supported by administrative methods had been eliminated in time."

During May 1965 the new journal, *Genetics,* published by the Academy of Sciences of the USSR, made its first appearance; its entire issue was devoted to the 100th anniversary of Mendel's laws of inheritance. It contained articles on Mendel written by N. I. Vavilov and A. R. Zhebrak. Academician P. M. Zhukovsky was appointed as editor in chief and the editorial collegium reads like a *Who's Who* in Soviet Mendelian genetics. While the publication of *Genetics* marked a new era for Soviet biology, the November 1965 edition of *Vestnik* (Herald), the organ of the Academy of Sciences of the USSR, marked the demise of Lysenko's professional reputation as an experimentalist. In the latter publication a commission of agricultural experts noted that Lysenko had actually falsified his records and misled Soviet leaders into believing that he had made impressive achievements in cattle breeding and in soil fertility. Even though Lysenko has been exposed for his poorly conceived theories and inadequate control methods in experimentation, he still heads a laboratory at the Institute of Genetics. Of late the campaign against Lysenko's genetics theories and practices is becoming intensified; if this trend continues unabated, it is merely a question of time before Lysenko's biology will be completely ignored in the Soviet Union.

A vital question which merits consideration, even though a definitive answer cannot be obtained at present, is: How did Lysenko achieve his dominant position in Soviet biology? In the Soviet press there is a tendency to cite the personality cult of Stalin as the only factor leading to Lysenko's becoming the final authority in biology, and Lysenko openly admitted in 1948 that Stalin had personally approved of his program. Between 1954 and 1957 there was a lukewarm effort to undo the impact of the personality cult in theoretical genetics, but after 1957 and until 1964, with Khrushchev's support, Lysenko recovered his prestige and managed to retain several key scientific and agricultural posts. Many factors played a role in Lysenko's rise from seed man to chief spokesman of Soviet biology, but one stands out: the general backwardness of Soviet agricultural science and technology. Beset with an archaic agricultural economy, Soviet leaders sought one-shot solutions that would bridge Russia's agrarian primitiveness and twentieth-century modern agricultural productivity. Lysenko believed, and undoubtedly convinced Stalin and Khrushchev, that he could bridge this gap. He failed. According to the Soviet geneticist, Sos Alikhanian, Lysenko had handed out many promissory notes to Soviet agriculture *without meeting one*. The Lysenko experience has proved to be a bitter lesson for Soviet agricultural authorities: there are no miraculous solutions for Soviet agrarian woes.

SELECTED BIBLIOGRAPHY

Although one-sided in their treatment, the following Soviet sources are useful in obtaining the biographical background of T. D. Lysenko: B. A. Keller, *Preobrazovateli prirody rastenii,* Moskva, 1944, pp. 55–94; M. S. Voinov, *Akademik T. D. Lysenko,* Moskva, 1950; and M. S. Voinov, *T. D. Lysenko,* Moskva, 1953. A French source, which is sympathetic to Michurinist doctrines, is J. Segal, *Mitchourine, Lyssenko et le problème de l'hérédité,* Paris: Les Editeurs Français Réunis, 1951.

Many of Lysenko's important writings have been translated into English, the most important being *Agrobiology,* Moscow, 1954, and it includes a bibliographical index of all of Lysenko's works from 1923 to 1951. Also available in English is *Soil Nutrition of Plants,* Moscow, 1957. Of the English works that deal with Lysenko, some important ones are: J. Huxley, *Heredity East and West (Lysenko and World Science),* London: Chatto and Windus, 1949; C. Zirkle, ed., *Death of a Science in Russia,* Philadelphia: University of Pennsylvania, 1949; T. Dobzhansky, "The Crisis of Soviet Biology," *Continuity and Change in Russian and Soviet Thought,* edited by E. J. Simmons, Cambridge: Harvard University Press, 1955, 329–46; H. J. Muller, "Science in Bondage," in *Studies in Genetics (The Selected Papers of H. J. Muller),* Bloomington: Indiana University, 1962, 550–59; D. Joravsky, "Lysenko's Maize," *Survey,* 52 (July 1964), 91–99; D. Joravsky, "The Debacle of Lysenkoism," *Problems of Communism,* 6 (November–December 1965) 2–12; and S. Alikhanian, "Soviet Genetics," *Soviet Life,* 1 (January 1966), 26–27.

The chief collections of Lysenko's works in the Russian language are: *Raboty v dni Velikoi Otechestvennoi voiny,* Moskva, 1943; *Agrobiologiia,* Moskva, 1948; *Stadiinoe razvitie rastenii,* Moskva, 1952; and *Pochvennoe pitanie rastenii,* Moskva, 1955.

Nikolai Nikolaevich Semyonov

by Albert Parry

Nikolai Semyonov, 1956 Nobel Prize winner in chemistry (first Soviet citizen to be so honored), and current vice president of the Academy of Sciences of the USSR, was born into a nobleman's family on April 15, 1896, in the Volga River city of Saratov. He began his first scientific researches in 1912, at the age of sixteen, one year before graduating from a Samara (now Kuibyshev) secondary school specializing in the physical sciences. In 1913 he enrolled in the Physics and Mathematics Department of the St. Petersburg (now Leningrad) University, where he participated in the work of the Physics Club organized by Abram Ioffe, one of Russia's earliest atomic scientists. In 1916, at twenty, Semyonov published his first paper—on collisions of electrons and molecules.

After graduating from the university in 1917, he moved to the University of Tomsk in western Siberia, where he worked as an assistant in the department of physics; but in 1920, at Dr. Ioffe's invitation, he returned to Petrograd to become associated with the new State Institute of Physics and Technology, first as head of its Laboratory of Electronic Phenomena. In the same year he evolved, with Pyotr Kapitsa, an original method of ascertaining magnetic properties of the atom.

Semyonov was named a professor of the Leningrad Polytechnic Institute in 1928 and helped to organize its department of physics and mathematics. In 1931 he became scientific chief of the Institute of Physical Chemistry (formerly the Institute of Physics and Technology) of the Academy of Sciences of the USSR, later becoming director. In 1929 he was made a corresponding member of the Academy of Sciences, and in 1932 was elevated to full membership. He aided in launching several scientific journals, and in 1944 became a professor at the Moscow University.

Semyonov won the Stalin Prize in 1941 and again in 1949. He has been awarded the Order of the Red Banner of Labor and four Orders of Lenin. His Nobel Prize for chemistry in 1956, shared with Sir Cyril Hinshelwood of England, was for his work on the kinetics of chemical reactions. In 1957, in addition to being named director of the Academy's Institute of Physical Chemistry, Semyonov was made secretary of its Division of Chemical Sciences. The next year he became director of the Academy's Laboratory of Anisotropic Structures and a member of the Royal Society (British). His other honors have grown to include a membership in Britain's Chemical Society, the National Academy of Sciences of the United States, and the academies of sciences of India, Hungary, Romania, and Czechoslovakia. He also holds honorary doctorates from the universities of Oxford, London, Brussels, and Budapest, as well as from the Milan Polytechnic Institute.

Semyonov's mission in science has been characterized by his Russian colleagues as the passionate investigation of chemical phenomena with the aid of the methods of physics. His supreme belief is that physics is the key to the most significant, yet least studied, problems of chemistry and that a close combination of physics and chemistry must inevitably result in new achievements of science. Some of Semyonov's Soviet admirers hold that he, and no one else, is the originator of physical chemistry as a new science.

His most outstanding pioneer work has been on the mechanism of chemical transformations. He did successful research in molecular physics and electronic phenomena pertaining to electric disruption of dielectrics, particularly the electronic phenomena of vapor condensation on solid surfaces. He investigated ionization of salt vapors under the action of electronic impulses, probed the theory of the sparkover of insulators, and studied flame expansion, detonation, and combustion of explosives. In his researches on the propagation of explosion wave—for a long time better known in the Soviet Union than abroad—he connected his theory of dielectric disruption to the theory of thermal explosion of gas mixtures. While working on chain reactions he discovered a new type of chemical process called "branching chain reactions"—considered to be a major contribution to science, as a result of which a comprehensive theory of branching, as well as nonbranching, chain reaction has evolved.

Of the English translations of his work, the best known is *Chemical Kinetics and Chain Reactions* (1935), based on his Russian monograph which came out the year before, and by now a classic reference work in kinetics. A partial list of his other Russian-language publications includes "Chemistry and Electronic Phenomena," 1924; "About a Single Sum," and "On some chemical reactions," 1926; "The Thermal Theory of Combustion and Explosions," 1940; and "About Some Problems of Chemical Kinetics and Reaction Capacity," 1954.

A gifted and inspiring teacher, Semyonov has brought forth a brilliant school of young chemists and physicists under his tutelage, encouraging them and sharing credit with them for many of his own achievements. In 1956, as his sixtieth birthday was being celebrated in Moscow, the official Soviet journal of experimental and theoretical physics commented: "His excellent intuition in physics, the clarity of his thought, and his inventiveness aid him in his leadership of a large collective of collaborators."

Semyonov joined the Communist Party of the Soviet Union (CPSU) in 1947 and became an alternate member of its Central Committee in 1961. He is currently a deputy in the Supreme Soviet, his country's parliament. In November and December 1960 he was a Soviet delegate to the Sixth International Pugwash Conference of World Scientists in Moscow. While in such capacities he often voices the official policy of his party and government, nonetheless on numerous occasions he has shown that he is a scientist first and a Communist next. In his frequent public statements in the late 1950's and early 1960's he has demonstrated his readiness to defend the interests of progress and the Academy of Sciences against industrial backwardness and bureaucratic encroachments; he has spoken up for the necessity of giving Russia's scientists still greater freedoms than they gained after Joseph Stalin's death; and he has even demanded liberty of experimentation for Soviet artists. Nor has he restrained himself from just criticism of his academic contemporaries who appear to be narrow careerists and place handicaps in the path of research and advancement on the part of young scholars—whose fiery advocate Semyonov has repeatedly proved to be.

His article "Science Today and Tomorrow," published in the Moscow *Izvestiia* on August 9, 1959, created a stir and led to a lively discussion in both governmental and scientific offices and other groups of the Soviet Union. In the article he deplored the fact that at the time many Soviet production processes lagged behind the latest achievements of Soviet scientific and technical genius. New discoveries should be applied in industries much more rapidly, he urged. "For this purpose it is essential to have a good basis for experimentation, for the development of new equipment and technological processes and the elimination of snags; we must give thought to machine-designing offices, laboratory-plants, and scientific institutions. Only then shall we be able speedily to renovate our industrial plant and replace outmoded equipment. . . ." Semyonov argued that science should not be regarded as a mere "appendage to production," that its independent task "is to study nature, the inner mechanism of natural phenomena, deeply; and consequently to harness the hidden forces of nature in the interests of man." He cited "two sources of industrial progress: first, the logical development of technology and production and, second, the logical development of science" and saw both processes as interdependent: ". . . it is impossible to develop technology without utilizing scientific data and vice versa."

But for Semyonov science was clearly foremost. In the same article he stressed the importance of the Academy of Sciences of the USSR and defined its primary task as leading the way "to establish new properties of matter, to penetrate the unfathomed mysteries of nature in order to make new forces available to man." The Academy, like research laboratories and universities, should also concern itself with "a deep scientific investigation of separate fields of knowledge which are of particular importance to new industries (such as the chemistry of polymers) so that new, more economical technological processes, new materials, new principles of machinery

can be suggested to industry." Improvement of knowledge in already existing fields "should be mainly the job of the laboratories of universities and
some other higher schools," and should occupy the time and effort of the
Academy "in part only."

Yet, in Semyonov's opinion, the Academy was not beyond reproach.
Semyonov pleaded with the Academy members for an improved attitude to
young talent. Older or established scientists, he wrote, should train their
eventual replacements gladly, aye, eagerly. But unfortunately, "some leading scientists deliberately choose incapable assistants, who, they are sure,
can never become their rivals."

Returning to this subject in his article "Talent and Youth" in *Izvestiia*
(December 16, 1961), Semyonov reminded the academic community and
the country at large: "We must not forget that our elder generation of
scientists was moved to leading positions much faster than this is being
done now. Why have we by now become so cautious in pushing the young
ones forward? In my opinion a young scientist must be fostered swiftly,
energetically; he should be imbued with a determination to overcome difficulties." Semyonov appealed to the elder academicians to remember that
"a scientist's most creative period is the span between 30 and 45 years of
his age," and decried the fact that many Soviet scientists were being held
back so cruelly that this fertile time was being wasted, or at least not properly utilized. He called upon the Academy to search for young talent and
encourage it imaginatively, not only in Moscow but also the provinces, and
mapped out other practical proposals. The ideal Soviet scientist, he wrote,
"contributes all the strength of his mind and feeling to science and, through
it, to people," rejoices in his colleagues' and pupils' successes no less than
his own, and in short, is ready "to work not for the sake of glory, of his
career, but in order to bring good to society."

Acting on his preachment, Semyonov became chairman of the All-
Union Society for the Dissemination of Political and Scientific Knowledge,
which by late 1961 had a membership of more than one million volunteer
lecturers. In an interview published in *Pravda* (December 25, 1961), he
criticized the Soviet press for failing to give the Society and its activities
sufficient coverage.

While professing to be a true Marxist-Leninist, Semyonov nevertheless
deplored Stalinism and warned against reviving outdated Stalinist methods
of repression. Thus in late 1962, when Premier Khrushchev led a stern and
vociferous campaign against abstractionist experimentation in Russia's arts,
Semyonov was one of seventeen prominent Soviet chemists and physicists
who addressed a personal letter to Khrushchev defending the experimenting
artists and asking the premier "to stop the swing in the representational
arts to past methods which are alien to the whole spirit of our times."

Also at this time, Semyonov reminded readers of *Pravda* that Lenin
had in fact realized the importance of science and scientists from the very

start of the Soviet regime—"right after the victory of the great October Revolution."[1] Semyonov praised Khrushchev's deference to, and fostering of, Soviet science as a reaffirmation "of Leninist principles."

A few months later, in *Izvestiia,* Semyonov made plain his belief that although the Academy of Sciences should actively and practically help the Soviet industries in many of their important needs, it "should not fritter its strength away on those tasks of technology which are comparatively secondary." The Academy should be spared for "the main tasks of production . . . [for] those that have a decisive meaning for the nation's economic potential."[2]

Hailing increased freedom for Soviet scientists in the post-Stalinist era, Semyonov stressed the great importance of international contacts for further successes of science. In his article "The Chain Reaction of Success," published in the Moscow *Trud* (Labor) of July 13, 1965, he welcomed the Twentieth World Congress of Theoretical and Applied Chemistry, which had opened in the Kremlin Palace the day before. Praising the frequent exchange of visits and correspondence among the scientists of many countries in recent times, he wrote: "In the second half of our century, when contacts among scholars are very well organized, discoveries become instantly known to almost all researchers. The new data are checked and supplemented by scientists of all countries. . . ." He declared that the cause of peace was well served by the freedom and frequency of international scientific congresses and other such contacts.

On August 1, 1965, in *Pravda* ("Notes on Modern Chemistry"), Semyonov characterized the work of the congress that had just closed as highly fruitful. During its sessions, he wrote, "the participants learned of one another's resources in greater depth," and the congress undoubtedly contributed to the cause of "strengthening the creative collaboration of scientists of different countries." On April 15, 1966, at the celebration in Moscow of Semyonov's seventieth birthday, the Academy's president, M. V. Keldysh, lauded the scientist for his deep understanding of "the great role of science in the development of man's intellect," and of "the noble humanistic goals of the betterment of human existence."

SELECTED BIBLIOGRAPHY

For information about Semyonov's life and career, see "Nikolai Nikolaevich Semenov," *Zhurnal experimental'noi i teoreticheskoi fiziki,* XXX, 4 (1956); N. M. Emmanuel', "Krupnyi vklad v mirovuiu nauku," *Priroda* (February 1957); and "Semenov, Nikolai Nikolaevich," *Biograficheskii slovar' deiatelei estestvoznaniia i tekhniki,* II, Moskva, 1958.

Semyonov's published works include his classic *Tsepnye reaktsii,* Moskva, 1934, which was translated into English by Ia. I. Frankel' and J. R. Schmidt-

[1] "Science and Production," *Pravda,* November 26, 1962.
[2] "This Day in Chemistry," *Izvestiia,* February 8, 1963.

Chernysheva as *Chemical Kinetics and Chain Reactions,* Oxford: Clarendon Press, 1935. Other Russian language publications include *Khimiia i elektronnyie iavleniia,* Moskva, 1924; *Ob odnoi summe* and *O nekotorykh khimicheskikh reaktsiiakh,* Moskva, 1926; "Teplovaia teoriia goreniia i vzryvov," *Uspekhi fizicheskikh nauk,* XXIII, 3 (1939) and XXIV, 4 (1940); *O nekotorykh problemakh khimicheskoi kinetiki i reaktsionnoi sposobnosti,* Moskva, 1954. In addition to Semyonov's statements on Soviet and world sciences cited in the text, see also the English translation of his article in *Izvestiia,* August 9, 1959, which was published as "Science Today and Tomorrow," *Soviet High lights, a Survey of Soviet Thought and Development,* New York: International Arts and Sciences Press, October 1951.

Vladimir Dimitrievich Dudintsev

by Ronald Hingley

The Soviet novelist and short story writer Vladimir Dudintsev owes his reputation to a single work, the novel *Not by Bread Alone.* First published in 1956, the novel became the center of a sharp politico-literary controversy in Soviet Russia in the late 1950's when Dudintsev stood out as a leading symbol of reform, "liberalism," de-Stalinization, and the aspirations of the younger generation.

The novel also created a considerable stir outside Russia, after being translated into many European languages and receiving a somewhat mixed reception. Acclaimed by some Western writers—as "epoch-making" (John Wain) and "in the great Russian tradition" (Sir Charles Snow)—it has been condemned by authorities more directly concerned with Soviet literature as "undistinguished . . . not really a novel" (Edward J. Brown) and as a "barely more than mediocre" work from a literary point of view (Gleb Struve). But on its significance as a political and social document all commentators are united, and Dudintsev is everywhere accepted at least as an important symbol if not as a great writer.

Apart from the novel, Dudintsev's only other work of importance is "A New Year's Tale," published in 1960, an extended short story of even more doubtful literary merit than *Not by Bread Alone.* Yet as a child Dudintsev had been regarded, at least in his own family circle, as a literary prodigy. He was born on July 29, 1918, in Kupiansk in the Ukraine, and came of a cultured Russian family, though his mother and father were more interested in music than in writing. The father, an engineer by profession, would have preferred to be a professional singer, while the mother actually had sung in opera. Music-making was a common family activity, but Dudintsev himself showed marked literary leanings from his early years. In an extended interview given to the German journalist Gerd Ruge in 1958, Dudintsev assigned his own first written composition to the time when he was six years old, and said that he had a poem published in 1931. In Rusakova's article in the official *Small Literary Encyclopedia,* his first publication is assigned to 1933, but no details are given.

Dudintsev studied at the Faculty of Law of Moscow State University, where he graduated in 1940. He chose law in order to "gain more experience of life," as he informed Ruge. His desultory early literary activities, later to be described as "feeble" by the author himself, were interrupted by the war, when he served in the infantry, rising to command a company for a time and being severely wounded near Leningrad. From 1942 until the end of the war he worked as a public prosecutor on a court martial in Siberia.

Between 1946 and 1951, Dudintsev worked as a writer of articles (*ocherkist*) on the newspaper *Komsomolskaia pravda,* the organ of the Komsomol (Young Communist League). In 1952 he published a collection of short stories, *With Seven Heroes.* He had already started work on *Not by Bread Alone* in 1950, but progress was hindered by a nervous breakdown in about 1952 caused by, or at least connected with, a decision to stop smoking. Dudintsev described this period to Ruge as a time of despair when he fell into debt and thought of giving up the writing profession. But in 1953 he published a story called "In Its Proper Place" in the leading "liberal" monthly *Novyi mir* (*New World*), which was to bring out *Not by Bread Alone* three years later. In 1959 *With Seven Heroes* and "In Its Proper Place" were brought out in a collection of stories entitled *Tales and Stories* which also includes other stories from the years 1946 to 1951 called "Friends' Hands" and a later story, "The Mad Boy," first published in 1958.

Ruge has recorded the somewhat nondescript impression made by Dudintsev during the interview mentioned above. That Dudintsev wore a suit "provincial even by Moscow standards" is interesting in the light of the persistence with which he describes the approved characters in his fiction as poorly and carelessly dressed. But his own lengthy account of his aims and achievements, as reported by Ruge, is heavily larded with pretentious, trite, and disconnected theorizing about aesthetics and the special role of Russian literature, from which it is difficult to abstract much in the way of meaning or illumination. It seems curious that one so apparently unenterprising and undistinguished (intellectually as well as sartorially) could have become the center of impassioned argument and controversy, and that an author of such modest attainments could regard himself to some extent as the direct heir of Tolstoy and Dostoevsky, or speak of being influenced by such literary models as Proust, Isaac Babel, Pasternak, and Hemingway.

In wearing the unfashionable clothes remarked by Herr Ruge, Dudintsev was only conforming with the practice of Lopatkin, the hero of *Not by Bread Alone*. Lopatkin is an ascetic, a fanatical idealist devoted to the welfare of the people. Having invented a device for welding pipes, he sees his invention blocked by members of the industrial and party Establishment, of whom the most prominent is the villain of the story, Drozdov. It is this duel between the selfless idealist Lopatkin and the complacent careerist Drozdov which forms the core of the novel. Dudintsev's implied onslaught on the Soviet Establishment was rendered highly dramatic by the period when the novel appeared—in the second and more outspoken half of 1956, the "year of protest" in which Soviet writers enjoyed unusual freedom to express political criticism.

Alike in its central clash and in its concentration on technological detail, *Not by Bread Alone* echoes numerous Soviet novels about industrialization dating back to before the First Five-Year Plan. Lopatkin was by no means the first "sincere" and thwarted inventor, any more than Drozdov was the first self-seeking villain of his particular stamp—though, as often happens with fictional villains, Drozdov is a lot more convincing than his idealistic opponent. The question thus arises: what quality in *Not by Bread Alone* (apart from the fact that it appeared in 1956) singled it out to become the center of fierce argument and even to be alternately berated and praised in public by Nikita Khrushchev, then first secretary of the Central Committee of the Communist Party of the Soviet Union (CPSU)?

The main point is that the novel goes a little further in the same direction than other works with a similar theme, such as Daniil Granin's *Seekers*. Criticism of inefficiency has always been legitimate activity for a Soviet author, but with the unspoken qualification that it must be criticism of detail. It is thus permissible to point out flaws in the grand design of Soviet society—but without casting doubts on the design itself. Not that Dudintsev goes quite so far as that. But his novel comes near to doing so. It also has an ambivalent ending. Lopatkin is successful in pushing through his invention, but Drozdov and his allies are still triumphantly in the saddle when the novel ends. Moreover, Dudintsev had committed the error of implying that Drozdov was a typical member of Soviet society rather than a regrettable exception.

Dudintsev had also insistently portrayed the superior way of life of a privileged group and had stressed the existence of marked class distinction in Soviet society. He was, in fact, making much the same point as had been made in the theoretical work *The New Class* by the Yugoslav writer and former political leader Milovan Djilas, and this parallel between Djilas's and Dudintsev's message has impressed several critics of *Not by Bread Alone*. Dudintsev may not use the deadly word "bourgeois" to describe Drozdov and his associates but it is as members of a smug bourgeoisie that he portrays them. He dwells heavily, for instance, on the preferential conditions given to Drozdov's wife Nadya when she is in hospital—as opposed to the offhand treatment meted out to the rank-and-file Soviet citizen. Nadya, incidentally, later deserts Drozdov for Lopatkin (a love intrigue not very interestingly portrayed in the novel), so she is on the side of the angels. This ranging of characters into uncompromising white and black is an artistic defect of the book.

Among its merits are its ringing passion and rhetorical intensity, and Dudintsev's sincerity comes over very successfully—for instance, in a notable interview between Lopatkin and a female assistant prosecutor called Titova, to whom he has been denounced by enraged members of the managerial Establishment. It is, perhaps, Lopatkin's powerful defense of "heresy" in this scene that brings Dudintsev nearest to being a political heretic himself, as well as something of an Old Testament prophet. Referring to his enemies as "silk worms spinning cocoons out of their own saliva," Lopatkin goes on to accuse them of "beating up all heretics. But heretics and dissenters mustn't be destroyed. They are just as necessary to people as their conscience." Lopatkin claims to pursue a different aim from that of his enemies. "They're looking backwards, not forwards. Their aim is to hold tight to their armchairs and carry on making money. But an inventor serves the people. An inventor is always a heretic—in any brand of knowledge."

Initial reactions to *Not by Bread Alone* suggested that it might become a *cause célèbre,* but not that the author himself would be the target for sustained attack. The novel appeared in the August, September, and October 1956 volumes of *Novyi mir* and was thus still being serialized at the time of the Hungarian rebellion. As will be remembered, events in Hungary produced a strong reaction in Soviet Russia, where the protest of 1956 gave way to the severe crackdown on the arts presided over by Khrushchev in early 1957. Before that Dudintsev had even found backing, apparently, in the pages of *Kommunist,* the leading party ideological journal, where an article by G. Glezerman cited an actual instance of the suppression of an invention through the agency of interested parties actuated by self-seeking motives under conditions closely paralleling those described in *Not by Bread Alone.*

Support for Dudintsev was naturally also forthcoming from liberal-minded writers, especially at an enthusiastic meeting of the prose section of the Moscow branch of the Union of Soviet Writers, held on October 22, 1956. The meeting was packed and some young people are even said to have put ladders to the window in order to be able to take part. Konstantin Paustovsky made the most outspoken speech (not accurately reported in the USSR to date), in which he claimed that a "new petty-bourgeois caste" of Drozdovs had indeed arisen in the Soviet Union, just as Dudintsev had shown. Paustovsky backed up this assertion with observations made of the indecorous behavior of privileged Soviet tourists during a pleasure trip to Western Europe on the Soviet liner *Pobeda.* Others too spoke in favor of

Not by Bread Alone and the meeting turned out a personal triumph for its author.

The reaction came in early 1957 with a series of meetings, some presided over by Khrushchev himself, in which pressure was put on Dudintsev and other artistic "rebels" to confess their errors in accordance with longstanding Soviet tradition.

The campaign began in March, when Dudintsev found himself arraigned on the pages of *Pravda,* and also took part in a meeting of the Moscow branch of the Union of Soviet Writers. This was a comparatively peaceful occasion, on which Dudintsev and other rebels (Kaverin, Aliger, Kirsanov, and Yevtushenko) felt few inhibitions about defending themselves. Dudintsev stood up for himself as a champion of Soviet technological progress, describing the demoralizing effect on him at the beginning of the war of seeing the ease with which German Messerschmitts could shoot down Soviet planes—despite the contrary claims made by Soviet propaganda. He was trying to stop this sort of thing from happening again, a sentiment which echoes a passage in *Not by Bread Alone* where the hero describes the humiliation of watching fellow citizens gape at some glossy foreign car on a Soviet street.

In May 1957 the pressure became harder. Leading writers were twice harangued by Khrushchev. The secretariat of the Union of Soviet Writers put out a document severely criticizing *Not by Bread Alone* and other dissident works. And at a plenum of the board of the Union of Soviet Writers, also held in May, the authors concerned were attacked personally. They refused to speak at all, a form of political insubordination which became known as the "heroic feat of silence" (*podvig molchaniia*). Dudintsev further resisted pressure by bringing out *Not by Bread Alone* in book form in the same year with no toning-down or alteration of its more heretical passages. Though he had been singled out by Khrushchev as a "calumniator who took a malicious joy in describing the negative side of Soviet life," Dudintsev went no further toward capitulation than to put it about later in the year that he was writing a novel containing "optimistic figures"—in the context a formula of limited recantation.

Dudintsev came into prominence again at the time of the Third Congress of the Union of Soviet Writers in May 1959. It was on this occasion that Khrushchev chose to offer an olive branch to "rebellious" Soviet authors on condition that they agreed to comport themselves with decorum in future and avoid unduly protesting postures. Since Dudintsev remained a leading symbol of protest, it was appropriate that Khrushchev should refer to him personally, and he did so in sympathetic terms which contrast vividly with the bullying and lecturing of two years earlier. Khrushchev said that though Dudintsev's novel was far from being one of the greatest works in Russian literature (as had been claimed by certain foreign "ill-wishers") it did contain matter worthy of attention. Mikoyan, said Khrushchev, had once compared Dudintsev's arguments with Khrushchev's own. Dudintsev might have overstated his case, but "he was never our enemy and was not an opponent of the Soviet system."

Dudintsev's short story "A New Year's Tale" appeared in *Novyi mir* in January 1960. This is an excursion into science fiction set on an unspecified planet, half of which is plunged in perpetual darkness wherein millions of underprivileged humans are engaged in rearing cabbages by artificial light.

The scientists call to mind the managers of *Not by Bread Alone,* consisting partly of slick careerists who wear smart overcoats which they carefully place on hangers after arriving at their place of work in the morning. These, of course, are the villains. The genuine researchers and inventors have no time for such ostentation. The hero of the story, for instance, goes round with two coat buttons missing, an unmistakable indication of Dudintsev's approval. On his pages the glossy status symbol—be it fashionable clothing, smart apartment, car, or television set—is always a badge of shame. His heroes, by contrast, sport the egg stains on their jackets as proudly as the others carry their Orders of Lenin.

All the same, "A New Year's Tale" is not as outspoken as the novel, and it seems that Dudintsev had decided to accept the olive branch proffered by Khrushchev. At any rate, he soft-pedals his attack on the "new class." He also includes some lyrical passages on the joy of work—a safe and unexceptional theme in any Soviet context, and a topic on which Dudintsev's views obviously agree with the urgings of Soviet propaganda. In another way, though, "A New Year's Tale" is an outstandingly provocative piece of writing, since it deserts the flat, straightforward manner which had long been virtually compulsory for all Soviet writers in favor of an approach strikingly at variance with the practice of Socialist Realism. Though it is hard to pin down, a great deal about the story is allegorical— one of the main characters has even been equated with Khrushchev himself. There is much portentous talk about the nature of time, and a great deal of play with such symbols as a lotus flower and a gigantic owl, apparently a token of ability to make the best use of one's time and energy. This sort of thing harks back to the experimentalist and modernist prose of the Soviet 1920's. In offering this specimen of offbeat prose to the public, the editor of *Novyi mir* was certainly flying a kite, and attempting to establish a precedent for freedom to take up experiment in nonrealist forms of writing such as had scarcely been published in Russia for thirty years. Once again, to vary the metaphor, Dudintsev found his work being used as a battering-ram.

In the 1960's this role has been transferred, so far as Soviet prose is concerned, to a more talented writer, Alexander Solzhenitsyn. Rumors are occasionally heard of various projects on which Dudintsev is reputedly engaged—he has been reported as planning work on subjects as diverse as the life of the Muscovite intelligentsia and of fishermen in Siberia. But none of this has been published, and interest in his activities is somewhat on the wane at the time of writing. However, he has shown much perseverance in the past and it would be rash to prophesy that he will not be heard from again.

SELECTED BIBLIOGRAPHY

Among Dudintsev's major early efforts in the field of fiction is the collection of short stories published in 1952 under the title *U semi bogatyrei,* Moskva, 1952. A collection containing these stories as well as some published shortly after the Second World War and in the late 1950's was brought out in 1960 under the title *Povesti i rasskazy,* Moskva, 1960, and reissued in 1963 as *Rasskazy,* Moskva, 1963. *Ne khlebom edinym,* the novel that established his international fame, appeared first in serial form in the literary journal *Novyi mir,* 8, 9, 10 (1956), and then in book form in Moscow in 1957. His fantastic tale *Novogodniaia skazka* appeared in *Novyi mir,* 1 (1960), 78–96.

His novel, *Not by Bread Alone,* has been translated into English by Edith Bone, New York: Dutton, 1957, and his story *A New Year's Tale* has been translated three times: by Max Hayward, London: Hutchinson, 1960; by Gabriella Azrael, New York: Dutton, 1960; and by George Reavey, in *Modern Soviet Short Stories,* New York: Grosset and Dunlap, 1961, pp. 252–85.

Important pronouncements in the Soviet press both defending and denouncing Dudintsev's novel include articles by G. Glezerman, "Moral'no-politicheskoe edinstvo sotsialisticheskogo obshchestva i stiranie granei mezhdu klassami," *Kommunist,* 15 (1956), 28–43; V. Platonov, "Realnie geroi i literaturnie skhemy," *Literaturnaia gazeta,* November 24, 1956, p. 3; N. Kriuchkova, "O romane *Ne khlebom edinym,*" *Izvestiia,* December 2, 1956, p. 3; D. Eriomin, "Chem zhiv chelovek," *Oktiabr,* 12 (1956), 166–73. Konstantin Paustovsky's famous comments on Dudintsev's novel were inadequately and somewhat misleadingly reported in *Literaturnaia gazeta,* October 27, 1956, p. 3. Premier Khrushchev's comments were reported in "Za tesnuiu sviaz literatury i iskusstva s zhizniu naroda," *Literaturnaia gazeta,* August 28, 1957, pp. 1–3; in the protocols of the *Tretii s'ezd pisatel'ei SSSR. Stenograficheskii otchet,* Moskva, 1959; and *Pravda,* March 10, 1963. Materials from the discussion are also contained in English in the *Current Digest of the Soviet Press.* Konstantin Paustovsky's famous speech on "Drozhdovism" before the meeting of the prose section of the Moscow branch of the Union of Soviet Writers on October 22, 1956, has been translated in H. McLean and Walter N. Vickery, *The Year of Protest 1956,* New York: Random House, 1961, pp. 155–59.

There is biographical information on Dudintsev in A. F. Rusakova, "Dudintsev," *Kratkaia literaturnaia entsiklopediia,* II, Moskva, 1964, p. 814, and in Gerd Ruge's interview with the author in his "Zu Besuch bei sowjetischen Schriftstellern," *Der Monat,* 120 (September, 1958), 25–41. Various estimates in English regarding both the author and his work may be found in Edward J. Brown, *Russian Literature Since the Revolution,* New York: Collier, 1963, pp. 260–64; Vera Alexandrova, *A History of Soviet Literature 1917–1962,*

Garden City: Doubleday, 1963, pp. 317–27; Harold Swayze, *Political Control of Literature in the USSR 1946–1959,* Cambridge: Harvard University Press, 1962, pp. 147–87; and Walter N. Vickery, *The Cult of Optimism: Political and Ideological Problems of Recent Soviet Literature,* Bloomington: Indiana University Press, 1963, chapters 4 and 6.

Ilya Grigorevich Ehrenburg

by Maurice Friedberg

A singularly facile and prolific writer and journalist, a man of strong passions and shifting allegiances, at the age of seventy-five Ilya Ehrenburg remains one of the more enigmatic figures in the history of Soviet letters. Now one of the most outspoken champions of the post-Stalin "liberalization" of Soviet life, he was for years a vociferous defender of the late dictator's oppressive policies. By nature a skeptic and debunker of pretensions, he has often been held up by the Soviet Establishment as a paragon of conformist Communist virtues. Perhaps the one trait of Ehrenburg's that has not changed over the decades is his strong feeling of kinship—indeed, love—for Western Europe's culture, particularly that of France. There is no questioning the fact that Ehrenburg is now the Soviet writer most intimately familiar with Western life and mores. If other surviving writers of the older generation (e.g., Konstantin Paustovsky, Victor Shklovsky, Kornei Chukovsky) link today's Russia with her pre-Revolutionary past, Ehrenburg is Russia's bridge with the West, especially with its left-wing intelligentsia, and it is this quality, rather than his literary accomplishments, that most likely will secure him a place in the annals of Russian letters. It is also probable that his memoirs, published in recent years, have, Ehrenburg's evasions and distortions notwithstanding, been one of the decisive contributions to the partial bridging of the gap between Russians and Western Europeans—a gap created by decades of isolation—and as such have rendered significant service to the fostering of an awareness of the outside world among the Soviet citizenry, particularly the younger generation that has no personal memories of the 1920's and the early 1930's, the "golden age" wistfully described by Ehrenburg in considerable detail.

Ilya Grigorevich Ehrenburg was born in Kiev to an assimilated middle-class Jewish family on January 27, 1891. As Ehrenburg put it in an autobiographical sketch written in 1926:

I was born in 1891. A Hebrew. Spent my childhood in Moscow, Khamovniki, near a brewery. Warm, sour beer. The workers curse and fight in the barracks.

. . . In the spring we went to visit grandfather in Kiev. Imitating him, I prayed, my whole body swaying, and I sniffed clove from a silver vessel. Then the First Moscow Gymnasium. The boys around me said: "The little kike sits on a bench, we'll sit the little kike on a fence." At home I raised mischief—more than was necessary. Set fire to a summer house.

The feeling of outrage at anti-Semitism—the more painful because of Ehrenburg's lack of any positive identification with Judaism or Jewish culture—recurs in Ehrenburg's books and journalistic output throughout his career and appears to have been a major factor in his revolt against Tsarist and later against Stalinist injustice.

At first, Ehrenburg's rejection of the dominant social values took the time-honored Russian form of clandestine political activity, which he began at the age of fourteen, during the Revolution of 1905. Arrested two years later, he was released on bail, which he forfeited by fleeing the country. From 1908 to 1917 he lived abroad, mainly in Paris, and his disgust with the Establishment was now to assume a Western European guise: Ehrenburg became a bohemian and a *habitué* of Montparnasse cafés. His intellectual restlessness resulted in a number of other paradoxical shifts as well, such as his infatuation with a kind of mystical Catholicism which brought him to the verge of entering a Benedictine monastery. At the outbreak of the First World War, the one-time socialist and pacifist Ehrenburg tried to enlist in the Foreign Legion. Rejected for reasons of health, he became a war correspondent for *Birzhevye vedomosti* (The Stock Market Gazette), a staid Russian daily. Years later he was still a war correspondent—this time for *Pravda* and *Izvestiia:* it was Ehrenburg who covered the Spanish Civil War for the Soviet press, and subsequently he became Soviet Russia's foremost reporter of the Second World War.

Ehrenburg did not return to Russia from his exile in Europe until the February Revolution of 1917. His original reaction to the Communist *coup d'état* in November of that year, the poem "A Prayer for Russia" (1918), was sharply hostile, and was reprinted and disseminated for propaganda purposes by the anti-Bolshevik armies. During the Civil War Ehrenburg narrowly escaped execution by the firing squads of either the Reds (as a counter-Revolutionary poet) or the Whites (as a Jew with a politically suspect past). A volume of poetry entitled *Meditations* (1921) marked Ehrenburg's halfhearted acceptance of the Soviet regime. Nevertheless, in 1921 he left Russia again, this time as an official Soviet representative. He was to remain abroad for almost twenty years, residing chiefly in Paris, and did not finally settle in the USSR until shortly before the Nazi attack on the Soviet Union in the summer of 1941.

Of the nearly thirty volumes of Ehrenburg's literary and journalistic output, his most successful is the novel first published in Russian in 1922 and only recently republished in the USSR after a lapse of four decades, The novel, an all-out sardonic attack on modern civilization, bore the intriguing title *The Extraordinary Adventures of Julio Jurenito and of His Disciples: Monsieur Delhaie, Karl Schmidt, Mr. Cool, Alexei Tishin, Ercole Bambucci, Ilya Ehrenburg, and Aisha the Negro, in the Days of Peace, War and Revolution in Paris, Mexico, Rome, Senegal, Kineshma, Moscow and Other Places; As Well As Sundry Reflections of the Master on the Subject of Pipes, Death, Love, Freedom, the Game of Chess, the Hebrew Race, Reconstruction, and Likewise Many Other Things.*[1] In an early autobiography Ehrenburg said of the work: "This is the only book I wrote 'in earnest.' Nobody—not the critics, nor the readers, nor even myself—can say precisely where the mockery ends." And it speaks well for Ehrenburg's taste that forty years and almost as many books after its publication, he still considers *Julio Jurenito* his favorite. Ehrenburg's "Master," the Mexican Julio Jurenito, the great *agent provocateur,* aims to destroy the corrupt and hypocritical civilization of Europe. His "apostles" represent the many facets of that civilization—they include a pleasantly dissolute French *rentier,* an efficiently "scientific" and cruel German, a romantic Italian rebel without a cause, a morbidly sentimental Russian, and an American who combines modern business drive with oldtime religion. Nothing escapes Ehrenburg's savage jeers, and it is in this nihilistic, destructive invective that Ehrenburg is in his own element. In the books that followed, Ehrenburg is—even if superficial—interesting and convincing whenever he mocks and attacks. His "positive" heroes and heroines are, as a rule, painfully dull and colorless, and his affirmations of virtues embarrassingly naïve for a writer of his sophistication. Unfortunately, such "uplifting" fare gradually began to predominate in Ehrenburg's fiction. Suffice it to mention *The Life and Death of Nikolai Kurbov* (1923), the saga of an upright and stern Soviet secret policeman ultimately destroyed by the desires of sinful flesh; and *The Love of Jeanne Ney* (1923), a primitive melodrama involving a bourgeois French girl and her Soviet Communist lover. While Ehrenburg never produced a worthy successor to *Julio Jurenito,* during the period of the comparative artistic freedom of the 1920's he completed several works that are reminiscent of his earlier novel. Thus, for example, *The Grabber* (1925) is an account of a young man's idealism, nurtured by the Spartan austerity of the Revolution, crumbling under the corrupting influence of the period of prosperity that followed—a rather common theme in Soviet literature of the period (the best treatment of the subject is found in Leonid Leonov's *The Thief,* 1927). The disenchantment and aimlessness of the era that was characterized by a return to many of the recently denounced bourgeois values was also reflected in *The Summer of 1925* (1926). The milieu of Soviet derelicts, waifs, and *declassé* bourgeois and the petty squabbles of their daily existence were described in *A Street in Moscow* (1927). *The Thirteen Pipes* (1923) is a collection of

---

[1] The abbreviated Russian title of the novel is *Neobyknovennye prikliucheniia Khulio Khurenito.*

skillfully told tales set in different historical periods. *The Conspiracy of Equals* (1928), a story of Babeuf, one of the heroes of the French Revolution, was another excursion of Ehrenburg into the realm of history. Closest in spirit to *Julio Jurenito* was *The Stormy Life of Lazik Roitschwantz* (1927), a biting lampoon of pretense, incongruity, and injustice both under capitalism and in the new Soviet republic. The hero, a pathetic Jewish tailor from the old Pale of Settlement, a direct descendant of characters from Gogol and Sholom Aleichem, is also a close relative of Isaac Babel's Gedali, the old Jewish shopkeeper who dreams of a revolution "of decent men" and cannot understand why both the Reds and the Whites oppress simple folk like himself. Lazik Roitschwantz's aspirations are modest enough. Though outwardly a rogue, all he really desires is to earn a livelihood and to be left alone by the authorities. Though liberated by the Revolution from the yoke of official tsarist anti-Semitism, he is now suspect as a petty bourgeois individualist artisan: his political unreliability is illustrated to the Soviet authorities' satisfaction by the simple fact that his impeccably proletarian pedigree fails to make him immune to the charms of a clergyman's daughter. Lazik Roitschwantz cannot fathom the false grandiloquence of the new Communist idiom which clashes with his critical common sense, and is consequently imprisoned by the Soviet police. Escaping to Western Europe, he finds himself mistaken for a Communist agent and is, of course, thrown in jail, this time as a Jewish Bolshevik. Fortune occasionally does smile on Lazik and bestows on him typically "capitalist" favors—he finds employment as a living advertisement for patent medicines, a saintly rabbi, a private secretary to a degenerate millionaire—but never for long. And when he finally makes his way to Palestine, fate decrees that he die of starvation in the land of his ancestors. Though somewhat hastily and superficially drawn, the eternally puzzled and frightened Jewish tailor Lazik Roitschwantz remains one of Ehrenburg's more attractive creations.

In his recently published memoirs, Ehrenburg explains that at the height of Stalin's terror his continued loyalty to the Soviet regime was made possible by his hatred for the values of the "bourgeois" world. There is strong evidence that this has also been largely true of other times as well, starting with Ehrenburg's belated conversion to Communism through all the vicissitudes of Soviet history down to the present time. In essence, therefore, Ehrenburg's Bolshevism was one of protest and flight from the West, rather than a conscious, "positive" choice, and this makes his Communist ideology "Western" rather than "native" Soviet, negative rather than affirmative. It is also true that whenever a slight divergence of views can be observed between the leadership of the Soviet Communist party and the Communists of Western Europe, one senses that Ehrenburg's sympathies are with the latter. Thus, Ehrenburg's ideological rather than tactical intransigence toward Fascism was more reminiscent of the French than of the Russian Communist pronouncements. Similarly, in his recent insistence on the need to widen the latitude permitted the arts in the USSR, he came closer to the demands voiced by the Italian Communists than to the stand taken by the party's leadership in his native land.

A case in point is the ending of *The Stormy Life of Lazik Roitschwantz,* in which the protagonist's last desire is to return to the Soviet Union—not out of a sudden burst of enthusiasm for the Soviet system, but because of bitter disenchantment with the alternatives encountered in the West. The Russian artist in *Moscow Does Not Believe in Tears* (1930) returns to Russia because life in Paris is unbearable, whereas the Soviet Union is, at least, an unknown quantity.

Ehrenburg's most important novel with a Soviet setting is *The Second Day,* sometimes translated under the title *Out of Chaos* (1933). In many respects a typical "production" novel of the 1930's, it describes the construction of a large metallurgical combine at Kuznetsk and includes such stock characters as the ascetic, single-minded Bolshevik director of the enterprise bent on finishing the job ahead of schedule, an ignorant young peasant turned into a shock worker, and well-paid foreign engineers— American and Western European—who, try as they may, cannot comprehend the ideological zeal that propels their Soviet colleagues and subordinates. Nevertheless, *The Second Day* bears a distinctive imprint of the author's style and continued qualms about the implications of the Soviet idea. Thus, for example, Ehrenburg's vision of the construction project is one of an elemental force harnessed by the intellect of the Soviet authorities:

There were Ukrainians and Tatars, plain folk from Perm' and Kaluga, Buriat, Cheremys and Kazakh nomads, coal miners from Iuzovka, lathe operators from Kolomna, members of the Young Communist League, bearded Riazan' fellows from road construction gangs, unemployed miners from Westphalia and Silesia, black marketeers and embezzlers from Sukharevo sentenced to forced labor, enthusiasts, petty crooks and religious sectarians. . . . None of them knew where they were moving. But they were all moving eastward, and Moscow knew that.

There can be no doubt, however, that it is the stubbornly individualistic intellectual Safonov who serves as a mouthpiece for Ehrenburg. Like Dostoevsky's Ivan Karamazov—or, for that matter, Ehrenburg himself—he wishes to believe with a strong faith, but is hindered by his critical faculties. As if echoing the fears of Yevgeny Zamiatin voiced in his famous antiutopian novel *We* (1924) which, though never published in Russia, was readily available in the West during Ehrenburg's stay there, the young protagonist of *Out of Chaos* declares:

You [the true believers in the Soviet idea] are accustomed to silence. Some are silent because you have frightened them; others because you have bought them. . . . As in the days of Galileo simple truth can be spoken only at the stake. You want to discuss the question of culture. It is unlikely, however, that anyone among you understands what culture is. For some, culture is blowing one's nose in a handkerchief; for others it is buying the Academy publications, which they do not understand, cannot, indeed, understand. You have established universal literacy and equally universal ignorance. After this you gather together and prattle about culture. Of course your not blowing your nose through your fingers deserves praise. But it has little to do with culture. You build a thousand blast furnaces and you are still ignorant. The anthill is a model of reason and logic. But it already existed a thousand years ago. Nothing in it has changed. There are ant workers, and ant specialists, and ant leaders. But there was never an ant genius. . . . The Acropolis was not built by ants. The law of gravitation was not discovered by an ant. Ants have no Senecas, no Raphaels, no Pushkins. They have a hill, and they work. They build, they carry twigs, they lay eggs, they devour one another, and they are happy. They are far more honest than you are—they don't talk nonsense about culture.[2]

Safonov's doubts, meant as a speech to his comrades, were never expressed openly. One cannot help feeling that in this, too, he resembles his creator.

Ehrenburg's next important novel was *The Fall of Paris* (1941). After the appearance of the first two chapters, the novel, which was to be serialized in the literary monthly *Znamia* (*The Banner*), was discontinued because its tenor ran counter to the official Soviet policy of friendship with Nazi Germany. It was not until the outbreak of the Soviet-German war that the publication of the novel was resumed, with some of the work's major characters, hitherto indifferent to France's defeat, turned, virtually overnight, into ardent French patriots. While these are often lifeless, Ehrenburg's satirical portraits of recognizable leaders of the Third Republic are drawn with considerable effectiveness. Together with nostalgic glimpses of the French capital, they make *The Fall of Paris* a novel of some merit, and earned the author the Stalin Prize in 1942.

The ideological tension that characterizes so much of Ehrenburg's output, the all too visible effort to conform to the letter and spirit of current Soviet policies, are happily absent from Ehrenburg's writings during the one period when these policies clearly coincided with the author's feelings. The wartime alliance of the Soviet Union with the Western democracies and their common struggle against Nazi Germany inspired Ehrenburg's most effective journalistic writing—some of it, in fact, of a literary interest superior to most of his fiction. For a time friends and foes were clearly divided into pro-Nazis and anti-Nazis, and there was no need for hesitation, doubts, and ideological sophistry. The goal of the struggle, too, was, for the time being, easily defined: it was the crushing of Fascism. The Francophile, the Russian patriot, the cosmopolitan leftist intellectual, the Jew— all these components of Ehrenburg's mind and heart made his burning

[2] Quoted from Edward J. Brown, *Russian Literature Since the Revolution,* New York: Collier, 1963, p. 252.

hatred of Nazism inevitable. His impassioned diatribes against the German invaders, printed in newspapers or distributed as leaflets—and subsequently also published in two volumes, each of some 400 pages in length, *The War* (1942 and 1943)—played an important role in the war effort. At a time, however, when other Soviet writers appealed to their compatriots' Russian nationalism, Ehrenburg emphasized the fact that the war was a common effort of many nations to save Western civilization itself from destruction by the Nazi barbarians. Ehrenburg pointed to Russia's varied and traditional links with the West—from Peter the Great's apprenticeship in Dutch navy yards to Western Europe's impact on the evolution of Russian revolutionary thought. In an article entitled "We and Europe" written on March 19, 1943, Ehrenburg wrote:

We never set apart our culture from that of Europe, we are bound up with it not by wires, not by rails, but by blood vessels and convolutions of the brain. We have been Europe's diligent pupils and her teachers. . . . Throughout the last century the leading minds of Russia shared in Europe's passions, aspirations and sorrows. They contributed to European mentality Russia's passionate temperament, truthfulness and humaneness. . . . The destinies of European culture are infinitely dear to us. We remember that the Decembrists were inspired by the Declaration of the Rights of Man, that Turgenev was a friend of France's foremost writers. We cannot observe Europe's tragedy with detachment.

By the spring of 1945 the political situation grew more complex; a victory over Nazism was already certain (in fact, a puppet Communist German government had already been formed in the USSR) and the alliance with Western powers began to disintegrate. Ehrenburg's anti-German and pro-Western tirades had outlived their usefulness and the writer was publicly accused of "exaggeration" in a *Pravda* article signed by Georgi Alexandrov, the head of the Propaganda Section of the Communist party's Central Committee. Once again, the time had come for Ehrenburg to re-evaluate all values—at least insofar as these were to be reflected in his printed work and public speeches.

The comrades-in-arms of yesterday, French, British, and American —except the Communists among them—appear as villains in Ehrenburg's two sequels to *The Fall of Paris,* namely, *The Storm* (1947) and *The Ninth Wave* (1952). Both novels owed their limited success with the Soviet public primarily to the "exoticism" of their settings: they were among the few works of Soviet literature to feature believable foreign surroundings and characters. Both were also typical of the crudely propagandistic Soviet writing of the period and both were virulently anti-American.

During the years of the cold war Ehrenburg was one of the pillars of the Soviet-sponsored World Peace Council, an organization aimed at the unilateral disarmament of the West, and continued his travels in many parts of the world, as well as his propaganda and journalistic activity. His physical survival during the sinister anti-Semitic "anticosmopolitan" purges of the late 1940's and early 1950's which claimed the lives of scores of Soviet intellectuals of Ehrenburg's makeup and with far less controversial pasts—indeed, his uninterrupted activity during the period (in 1952, Ehrenburg was even awarded the Stalin Prize)—remains a mystery that is not likely to be solved in the foreseeable future.

Always among the first to sense a shift in political atmosphere and to reflect it in his fiction and journalistic output, Ehrenburg was also the harbinger of the momentous changes in Russia's intellectual climate that became apparent after Stalin's death in March of 1953. This time, however, it may be said that Ehrenburg not only expressed the new spirit, but actually helped to forge it. Ehrenburg's active rather than passive role was favored by the mood of uncertainty surrounding the outcome of the struggle for succession that followed the dictator's death, as well as the writer's advancing age and acknowledged status as one of the grand old men of Soviet letters and the only one with important contacts abroad. Within six months of Stalin's funeral, Ehrenburg came out with an article in the October 1953 issue of *Znamia* which was, by Soviet standards, a courageous appeal for truthfulness in art and for the restoration of a degree of creative freedom, a subject to which Ehrenburg was to return on numerous occasions in the years that followed, notably in his essays on Chekhov and Stendhal.

The relative liberalism that has been—in spite of its narrow limitations and temporary reversals—characteristic of Soviet intellectual life between 1954 and 1965 is frequently referred to as "the thaw," after the title of a programatic novelette of Ehrenburg's *The Thaw* (1954). It is, perhaps, worth noting that the term was originally coined by the great Russian poet Fëdor Tiutchev (1803–73) to describe the relaxation of political terror that followed the death of Tsar Nicholas I in 1855, i.e., nearly exactly a century before that of Stalin.

The story of Ehrenburg's *The Thaw* is simple and its artistic value is scant. It is, however, of enormous significance as a historical document, a manifesto, as it were, of forces in Soviet society that clamor for a rehumanization of human relations in the USSR, for the recognition of the human individual as an autonomous entity with an existence at least partly independent of the official ideology and government decrees. If these demands strike the Western reader as elementary to the point of triteness, the fault is not Ehrenburg's. Since these self-evident truths had been banished for decades during the Stalin era of Soviet history, their restatement by Ehrenburg had the significance of a momentous discovery. Millions of Ehrenburg's readers in the USSR were startled by the descriptions in *The Thaw* of men productive in their public lives but cold and sterile in personal relationships, people broken by years of fear and now seeking solace in cynicism or refuge in loneliness, successful opportunistic purveyors of officially sponsored "art" and stubborn individualists persisting in the belief that artistic inspiration cannot be invoked by bureaucratic orders.

While it is true that as a result of a barrage of criticism Ehrenburg produced a sequel to the novel in 1956 in which some of the injustices described in the novel's first part were at least partly redressed, he never
renounced the grave charges leveled at the Soviet society in the first part
of *The Thaw*.

In recent years Ehrenburg has become, once again, one of the most
controversial figures in the USSR. He has now assumed the role of the
mentor and defender of a generation of younger writers that has come to
the fore since Stalin's death and demands a greater degree of freedom of
expression. His most important achievement of the postwar years are his
memoirs *People, Years and Life,* the best in all of recent Soviet literature,
which were serialized in the monthly *Novyi mir* (*New World*), with some
interruptions, between 1960 and 1965. In these Ehrenburg brings back to
life scores of persons and events unmentioned for decades in any Soviet
sources. As in Ehrenburg's wartime writings, but this time in unhurried,
smooth prose, Soviet readers, and particularly those under the age of forty,
were informed—rather than reminded—of Russia's cultural ties with Europe, of the years of artistic ferment and iconoclasm that followed the
Revolution, of one-time friends of the Soviet regime who, once declared
foes, were reduced to blank spaces in Soviet accounts of the past. Ehrenburg introduced his readers to the French Montparnasse he never ceased to
love, to the polemics that once raged among writers now familiar to all as
musty classics or else never mentioned in the most detailed of textbooks,
to the romantic aura of the Spanish Civil War, to the eccentrics and non-
conformists who had once made Soviet literature of the 1920's one of the
word's most fascinating, even if not necessarily the greatest, bodies of
writing. In spite of their glaring defects, omissions, and apologetics, Ehrenburg's memoirs constitute the closest Soviet approximation of cultural history to date and are an important testimony to the longing after a freer
intellectual life, a longing that was not uprooted by the nearly half-century
of government-sponsored regimentation of thought.

Much honored and decorated (the country's highest award, the Order
of Lenin, was bestowed on him in 1961), the now aging Ehrenburg is,
his highly checkered political past notwithstanding, one of the standard-
bearers of the "liberal" Soviet intelligentsia, and to the younger Soviet
generation, a witness of the times when Russia was, intellectually and cul-
turally, a part of Europe, thus encouraging hopes for Russia's eventual
return to Europe's spiritual and artistic commonwealth.

SELECTED BIBLIOGRAPHY

Publication of Ilya Ehrenburg's collected works, entitled *Sobranie sochinenii
v deviati tomakh,* began in Moscow in 1962, and thus far six of the nine projected volumes have appeared. Despite good coverage—there are short stories

and novels, poetry, speeches, and a number of essays on Russian and foreign writers—and useful arrangement of the works in an approximately chronological sequence, the edition is highly selective. Left out have been such early works of Ehrenburg's as *Burnaia zhizn' Lazika Roitshvantsa*, Berlin: Petropolis, 1927; *Liubov' Zhenny Nei*, Moskva, 1924; *Edinyi front*, Berlin: Petropolis, 1930; *Moskva slezam ne verit*, Paris: Gelikon, 1933; *Ne perevodia dykhaniia*, Moskva, 1935; and *Chto cheloveku nado*, Moskva, 1937, as well as his journalistic work—to mention but a few glaring omissions.

Ehrenburg's memoirs, comprising six volumes, were published in the Soviet Union in serial form in the literary monthly *Novyi mir* between August 1960 and April 1965. Thus far only the first two volumes have appeared in the USSR in book form, under the title *Liudi, gody, zhizn': kniga pervaia i vtoraia*, Moskva, 1961. English translations of the first five volumes of the memoirs have appeared, published by MacGibbon & Kee in London and Alfred A. Knopf and World Publishing Company in New York and Cleveland, respectively. The London edition appeared as *Childhood and Youth, 1891–1917*, 1961; *First Years of Revolution, 1918–21*, 1962; *Truce: 1921–33*, 1963; *Eve of War, 1933–41*, 1963; *The War, 1941–45*, 1964; while the American editions are entitled *People and Life, 1891–1921*, Knopf, 1962; *Memoirs: 1921–41*, World, 1964; and *The War: 1941–45*, World, 1964.

English translations of Ehrenburg's more substantial fictional works include *A Change of Seasons*, New York: Knopf, 1962, which comprises both *The Thaw* and *The Spring; Julio Jurenito*, London: MacGibbon & Kee, 1958; *The Ninth Wave*, London: Lawrence, 1955; *Out of Chaos*, New York: Holt, 1934; *Storm*, New York: Gaer Associates, 1949; and *The Stormy Life of Lasik Roitschwantz*, New York: Polyglot, 1960. A number of his recent literary essays, which constitute an important part of the struggle of Soviet writers to widen artistic boundaries, have been translated as *Chekhov, Stendhal, and Other Essays*, London: MacGibbon & Kee, 1962.

Ehrenburg has not as yet been the object in the Western world of serious critical and biographical study, but brief accounts may be found in Edward J. Brown, *Russian Literature Since the Revolution*, New York: Collier, 1963, pp. 247–57; Vera Alexandrova, *A History of Soviet Literature, 1917–62*, New York: Doubleday, 1963, pp. 110–23; Mark L. Slonim, *Modern Russian Literature*, New York: Oxford University Press, 1953, pp. 347–79; Slonim, *Soviet Russian Literature*, New York: Oxford University Press, 1964, pp. 208–17; Victor Erlich, "The Metamorphoses of Ilya Ehrenburg," *Problems of Communism*, XII, 4 (July–August 1963), 12–24; Olga A. Carlisle, *Voices in the Snow*, New York: Random House, 1962, pp. 104–14; and Hubert Juin, "Interview with Ehrenburg," *Mainstream*, XV, 10 (October 1962), 52–56.

Sergei Apollinarievich Gerasimov

by Robert M. Slusser

Sergei Apollinarievich Gerasimov, Soviet film director, as well as actor, scenarist, and pedagogue, was born on May 21, 1906, in the Urals. His parents were members of the tsarist nobility who had been sentenced to Siberian exile for revolutionary activities, and then permitted to live in the provinces. His father, an engineer and geologist, was drowned when Gerasimov was three, and the family was raised by the mother and an old nurse, who impressed the boy with her love of nature and her devotion to serving the people. Gerasimov received his secondary education at technical schools in Sverdlovsk and Krasnoyarsk, and in 1924 entered the Leningrad Art Academy to study painting, although by his own admission he had little artistic talent. His deepest interests were in literature, the theater, and the socialist ideals inherited from his parents.

Gerasimov's work in the cinema began in 1924 when, on a friend's suggestion, he visited the "Factory of the Eccentric Actor" (FEKS), an actors' workshop organized by two young film directors, Grigori M. Kozintsev and Leonid Z. Trauberg. Gerasimov's first role, a minor one, was in a detective comedy, *Mishka Versus Yudenich*. Between 1924 and 1931 Gerasimov appeared in a number of films directed by Kozintsev and Trauberg, including *The Overcoat, S.V.D.* (*The Union of the Great Cause*), and *The New Babylon*. His work as an actor in these films was strongly influenced by the concepts of stylized satire and cinematic mannerism for which FEKS was noted.

It was during the filming of *The New Babylon* (a story of the Paris Commune) that Gerasimov first experienced the urge to become himself a director, as the result of realizing the power of the director to shape the final form of the film, contrasted with the powerlessness of the actor to control the outcome of his efforts. Gerasimov's first independent effort as a director, however, a film entitled *The Five Marats,* was a failure, and for his next task Gerasimov served as assistant to Kozintsev and Trauberg in the direction of the film *Alone* (1931), one of the first Soviet sound films, in which he also played a major role.

In 1928 FEKS had been incorporated into the State Institute of Scenic Art, and in 1929 Gerasimov began his pedagogic work—one of the most important aspects of his career—with courses at the institute in film art and acting. He later wrote, "Everything which I have been able to write, produce, act, since that time—all of this is the result of creative and pedagogic studies in the Institute."

Between 1931 and 1934 Gerasimov directed a number of films, which, although none were popular successes, helped to establish him as a promising young director. These included *The Forest,* a story of young Communists in the timber industry, which Gerasimov later described as "very pretentious"; *Twenty-two Misfortunes,* a comedy; and *Do I Love You?* a story of contemporary life in which Gerasimov directed a group of young actors whom he himself had helped to train. With the last, produced in 1934, Gerasimov found his style and subject matter—the realistic portrayal of personal relations in the new Soviet society which was emerging.

The advent of sound in motion pictures marked a sharp break in the history of the Soviet cinema, coinciding as it did with the profound transformations wrought in Soviet society and politics by the Five-Year Plans, industrialization, collectivization of agriculture, and consolidation of Stalin's dictatorship. Socialist Realism was officially proclaimed as the only acceptable style in the arts, including the cinema. Gerasimov was one of a number of young directors whose work reflected these changes. In his acting for the cinema, particularly in his portrayal of a peasant bureaucrat in *Alone,* he had already moved away from the FEKS approach toward a more naturalistic style, based on careful observation and shaped according to the political demands of the Communist party.

Gerasimov's first successful film, *The Brave Seven* (1936), with a scenario by himself and Yuri German, showed the effect of these influences. It concerns a group of Komsomol (Young Communist League) volunteers in the Soviet Far North, portrayed by young actors whom Gerasimov had trained. The style is straightforward and natural, without apparent artifice or stylization. Although attacked by some Soviet critics as a "chamber work" which failed to meet the demand of the times for epic drama, the film was praised by the eminent director Vsevolod Pudovkin and enjoyed widespread popular approval.

Gerasimov's next film, *Komsomol'sk* (1938), treats a similar subject (said to have been suggested by Stalin)—the building of a new city on the Amur River by young Komsomol volunteers from all over the Soviet Union. The plot concerns the unmasking of a villainous kulak who has wormed his way into the Komsomol and who attempts to sabotage the work.

In 1939 Gerasimov directed *The Teacher,* a film dealing with the experience of a teacher in a village soviet. The scenario, written by Gerasimov, had won first prize in the 1939 scenario contest and had attracted wide discussion in the Soviet press as a contribution to the debate on urgent problems of Soviet education. Making the film gave Gerasimov an opportunity to explore the role of the intellectual in Soviet society, the life of a collective farm, and the difficulties facing Soviet educators.

Gerasimov's work in the 1930's was characterized by the ability to depict ordinary people engaged in building a new society. His films contained neither principal heroes nor a strong plot line; the emphasis was on collective activities, portrayed naturalistically and with a detailed observation of real life. These characteristics, together with his prudent silence on the darker aspects of Communist policy, earned his work the approval of party ideologists as well as popular success.

Gerasimov's last film before the Second World War, however, marked a sharp departure from his previous work. To honor the centennial of the death of the poet Mikhail Yu. Lermontov, Gerasimov directed *Masquerade* (1941), based on a drama by the poet. He also wrote the scenario and played one of the principal roles, that of "the Stranger." The concept of the film, Gerasimov subsequently stated, was to portray tsarist society in the period after the Decembrist Revolt (1825) as a masquerade hiding the somber realities. In spite of individual details of great beauty, the film was not a success. Gerasimov's talent obviously does not lie in the direction of literary classics and costume dramas.

Immediately after the German attack on the Soviet Union, Soviet film-makers shifted to the production of films designed to strengthen the Soviet war effort. In August 1941 Gerasimov directed a short film, *Meeting with Maxim,* in which the well-known actor Boris Chirkov played the role of the revolutionary fighter, Maxim, a figure he had already made famous in the 1930's in a trilogy of classic Soviet films. For this film and other short pieces, Gerasimov received a Stalin Prize in 1941.

Gerasimov's first full-length wartime feature film was *The Invincible* (1942), direction of which he shared with an older colleague, Mikhail K. Kalatozov. Although it deals with the siege of Leningrad, the film was shot at the Tashkent film studio, and suffers from the resultant staginess of presentation, as well as from an excessive reliance on coincidence in the plot.

In 1943 Gerasimov joined the Communist party, a logical step in view of his long-established acceptance of the goals of Communism. The closer supervision of his work by party overseers which this step entailed, however, may be responsible for the fact that henceforward his work was to undergo a steady decline in quality, at the same time that it manifested his obvious desire to adhere strictly to the party line.

In May 1944 a resolution of the Central Committee of the Communist party was issued criticizing shortcomings in the production of Soviet newsreels and calling for a major reorganization in the film industry. Gerasimov was put in charge of the Central Studio of Documentary Films, a post he retained until the end of the war. In this capacity he supervised the documentary films of a number of prominent Soviet directors, including Alexander Dovzhenko, Yuri Raizman, Joseph Kheifitz, Alexander Zarkhi, and Sergei Yutkevich.

In 1944 Gerasimov wrote the scenario for and directed *The Great Earth* (also known as *Mainland*), the story of a town in the Urals to which a tank factory is evacuated from Leningrad. In the same year he established a workshop for young actors, whom he trained in group presentation and who were to appear in his next major film, *Young Guard*. Gerasimov's work with young actors and directors found further expression in 1947 with his appointment to the teaching faculties of film acting and directing of the State Film Institute in Moscow.

In a speech delivered at the Moscow House of the Cinema in 1947 Gerasimov spoke of his wish to direct films depicting the life of ordinary Soviet citizens. "I would like," he said, "to show the fate of a man not only in the decisive moments of his life but in the detailed process of life, in work, in the failures of life. I am convinced that such films have a right to existence alongside our heroic genre." This aspiration, however, like a wish expressed in 1940 to film the life of the great Russian writer Anton Chekhov, was to remain unfulfilled. In the postwar years the party was engaged in a major ideological effort to reindoctrinate the Soviet people in the concepts and goals of Communism, and the cinema was called on to play its part in this campaign.

Gerasimov's first postwar feature film, *Young Guard* (Part One, 1947), ran into trouble with party ideologists precisely because of the clash between the concepts of realism and naturalism which are Gerasimov's forte and the party's demand for political propaganda on the screen. On December 3, 1947, *Pravda* attacked both the Stalin Prize-winning novel by Alexander Fadeyev on which the film was based and the film itself, which had just been completed, for their unduly candid portrayal of the confusion of wartime conditions and their failure to give prominence to the role of the party in organizing resistance to the German invaders. Part One was accordingly withdrawn for revision, and extensive changes were made in the script of Part Two. In the revised version (1948), the party is represented by a forceful, intelligent party secretary who overcomes all obstacles without losing his kindly human·qualities. The film satisfied party critics—Gerasimov received his second Stalin Prize in 1949—but at a high cost: the naturalness and humanity which had characterized his prewar films are here replaced by an exaggerated, formalized heroism and by unconvincing propaganda. The film is the counterpart in the cinema to the inflated plaster heroics of Soviet architecture in the Stalin period.

In the late 1940's Gerasimov became active in the Communist-sponsored "peace movement," displaying particular energy in attacking United States film-makers and government policies. In December 1949, for example, he launched a scathing attack on Hollywood at a "peace conference" in New York. As a member of the Presidium of the Soviet Peace Committee, he contributed an article to *Izvestiia* on March 12, 1950, in which he charged that "U.S. statesmen have clearly shown that they do not

desire to fight for the cause of peace, that the struggle for peace is something directly opposed to the concept they are defending."

A distinct mark of party approval was the responsible assignment given
to Gerasimov shortly after the Chinese Communist victory in 1949 to make
a documentary film on the Chinese revolution. Working with Chinese
associates Gerasimov in 1950 directed the color film *Liberated China*. The
point of view from which the film was presented, according to Gerasimov,
was that " . . . we realized that it is not [China's] rich heritage of culture,
which has been created over thousands of years, but the new which has
been born as the result of the national-liberation struggle that is valuable
and interesting for us and for those who see the film." The party's approval
was indicated by the award of a third Stalin Prize in 1951; the Chinese
government presented Gerasimov with an honorary scroll.

Less successful was Gerasimov's next film, *Village Doctor* (1952),
despite the fact that it marked a return to his earlier subject matter; the
story concerns a young woman doctor working under difficult conditions in
rural Siberia.

In the partial thaw in the Soviet arts that followed Stalin's death in
1953, Gerasimov found occasion to re-emphasize his basic concepts of the
art of the cinema. Speaking to the Second All-Union Congress of Soviet
Writers in December 1954 he said, "The basic task of the Soviet film industry is still the truthful, profound reflection of contemporary reality—
the portrayal of the ordinary Soviet man." Despite the fact that he was
speaking to an audience made up primarily of writers, and despite his own
recognition of the profound importance of literature, he praised the cinema
as a more influential art form than literature: "However great the role of
books in drawing people together, it must be admitted that in this respect
the potentialities of film art surpass even those of literature."

During 1956 and 1957 Gerasimov undertook his most ambitious and
responsible task, the filming of Mikhail Sholokhov's epic novel, *The Quiet
Don*. Once again, Gerasimov wrote his own scenario. The film, shot in
color, fails to reach the level of Gerasimov's best prewar work; it suffers
from poor casting in the principal roles, as well as from the obtrusive party
ideology which reduces Sholokhov's complex, full-blooded characters to
stock figures serving to illustrate the inevitable triumph of the Communist
cause. The film was praised, however, by Soviet critics.

Gerasimov was not yet secure against criticism from party leaders. In
1962 a young director named Khutsiev began work under his supervision
on *The Gates of Il'ich,* a film that was to deal with one of the most urgent
problems of contemporary Soviet society: the difficulty in communication
between the younger generation, born and reared since the Second World
War, and the older generation—in other words, the problem of "fathers
and sons." Although conceived and directed in accordance with what
Gerasimov no doubt believed to be the party line, the film ran into stren-

uous criticism; the party preferred to deny the existence of the problem of conflict between generations in Soviet society. At a meeting between government and party leaders and prominent intellectuals and cultural workers, held in the Kremlin on March 8, 1963, Khrushchev condemned the not yet completed film, saying, "It is a great pity that Gerasimov, who filmed this novel [*Young Guard*], did not advise his pupil Khutsiev to show in this picture [*The Gates of Il'ich*] how our youth keep alive and develop the wonderful traditions of the Young Guards." Following Khrushchev's criticism, work on the film was halted and it was withdrawn from production—though not before it had attracted widespread attention among Soviet intellectuals as a fresh and spirited treatment of contemporary Soviet reality.

Notwithstanding this misstep, Gerasimov has retained his position as a recognized master of the Soviet cinema, though his influence in recent years has been exerted mainly as a teacher of young directors rather than as a director. In a recent interview (*Soviet Film,* November 1965), he stressed the need for workers in the Soviet cinema to master new technical advances but expressed the conviction that man, the artist, rather than machinery and technical devices, will remain the determining factor in the production of worthwhile films.

Gerasimov's best work was contained in his films of the 1930's, in which he gave graphic expression to the ideals of Communism in believable human terms. His efforts to follow every turn in the party line had a negative effect on his later work. He himself may be aware of this decline; reports of the unfinished film, *The Gates of Il'ich,* indicate that in it his protégé Khutsiev succeeded in recapturing some of the freshness which made Gerasimov's earlier work noteworthy. Gerasimov's place in the history of the Soviet cinema is likely to remain that of a prominent exponent of Socialist Realism and a teacher whose influence has been deep and widespread, even though his work falls short of that of such masters as Eisenstein, Pudovkin, or Dovzhenko.

SELECTED BIBLIOGRAPHY

Biographical sketches of Gerasimov may be found in the *Bol'shaia sovetskaia entsiklopediia,* vypusk 2, X, Moskva, 1952, pp. 599–600, and the *Malaia sovetskaia entsiklopediia,* vypusk 3, II, Moskva, 1958, p. 994. Two books have been devoted to Gerasimov's career and work in the cinema: S. Freilikh, *Iskusstvo kinorezhissera: tvorchestvo narodnogo artista SSSR S. A. Gerasimova,* Moskva, 1954, and I. Grinberg, *Sergei Gerasimov,* Moskva, 1939. There is much information on Gerasimov's work, in the context of the development of the Soviet cinema as a whole, in *Ocherki istorii sovetskogo kino,* I and II, Moskva, 1956–59.

In English, there is a brief biographical sketch and some factual data on Gerasimov's films in Paul Babitsky and John Rimberg, *The Soviet Film In-*

dustry, New York: Praeger, 1955. The fullest available critical assessment of Gerasimov's work in English is in Jay Leyda, *Kino, a History of the Russian and Soviet Film,* New York: Macmillan 1960. The fullest treatment of Gerasimov's difficulties with party criticism in 1962 and 1963 may be found in Priscilla Johnson, *Khrushchev and the Arts,* Cambridge: M.I.T. Press, 1964.

Gerasimov is a highly articulate artist, who has written illuminatingly not only of his own career but of his artistic concepts and the techniques of his profession. In addition, he has written much polemical material in support of Communist ideological campaigns. On his career as an actor, see his contribution to the book *Litso sovetskogo kinoaktera,* Moskva, 1935, pp. 103–36. He discusses his decision to become a director in an essay in the collective volume, *Kak ia stal rezhisserom,* Moskva, 1946, pp. 76–94. The same work (p. 330) provides a complete list of his films, including his acting roles. Gerasimov's views on the nature of cinema art may be found in "O professii kinorezhissera," *Voprosy masterstva v sovetskom kinoiskusstve,* Moskva, 1952, pp. 7–42, and *O kinoiskusstve; ocherk dlia molodezhi,* Moskva, 1960, a somewhat popularized treatment.

Noteworthy writings by Gerasimov on the training of cinema actors include "Vospitanie kino-aktera," *Iskusstvo kino,* 4, 5 (1938); "Pervye itogi," *Iskusstvo Kino,* 3 (1947); and "Teoriia proveriatsiu zhizniu," *Sovetskoe iskusstvo* (February 10, 1951), an analysis of the Stanislavsky method of training actors as applied to the cinema. An important statement of Gerasimov's political views in relation to his aesthetic credo is the article "O narodnosti kinoiskusstva," *Voprosy kinoiskusstva, ezhegodnyi istoriko-teoreticheskii sbornik,* vypusk 5, Moskva, 1961, pp. 5–14.

English translations of articles and speeches by Gerasimov in his capacities both as film director and as a Communist ideologist and member of the "peace" movement can be found in *USSR Information Bulletin, News* (Moscow), *Soviet Literature, Soviet Woman,* and *Moscow News,* all published in Moscow. There are translations of a number of his articles and speeches in the *Current Digest of the Soviet Press* (New York, 1949–   ).

Ernst Neizvestny

by Robert M. Slusser

Ernst Neizvestny, sculptor, was born in 1926 at Sverdlovsk in the Urals. It has been reported that his father is a physician and his mother a scientist and writer, and that he grew up in an atmosphere of intellectual tension in a milieu where political exiles were numerous. A Western friend, John Berger, reports him as saying, "My war began in early childhood and it hasn't stopped. I have always had the feeling of being in the front line. Now I've reached the point where I feel really well only when I'm under stress."

Although under age, Neizvestny volunteered for military service in 1942 and was commissioned a lieutenant in charge of a commando platoon. He was parachuted behind German lines during an attack by the Second Ukrainian Front, was severely wounded, and was given up for dead. Actually he survived and was taken prisoner. After the war he was sent to a Soviet prison camp, in line with Stalin's policy of purging soldiers who had undergone German imprisonment.

Following his release Neizvestny entered the Surikov Art Institute in Moscow, where he received his formal training. On graduation he settled in Moscow and joined the "Belyutin circle," a group of artists (mostly younger than he) associated with the art critic Yeli Belyutin.

A female torso, created in 1955 and now in the collection of the Tretyakov Gallery in Moscow, won Neizvestny acceptance into the Artists' Union, but its subject and conventionally academic treatment are less characteristic of his style than a number of works dating from 1955–57, grouped for convenience into the "Concentration Camp" and "War" series. These works, which gave expression to Neizvestny's most profound personal experiences, marked a sharp break not only with his previous sculpture but also with the officially approved canons of Socialist Realism in art. They earned for Neizvestny a reputation among influential circles in the Soviet intellectual and cultural elite as an artist with a formidable talent and striking originality, and secured for him his first private commissions.

In 1960 Neizvestny's work was first brought to the attention of the broad Soviet public by the writer Yuri Nagibin in an article published in *Smena,* an illustrated journal aimed primarily at young people. Under the title, "On the Path of Explorations," Nagibin presented Neizvestny's work as controversial but deserving of serious consideration. Nagibin quoted the sculptor as saying, "For me, beauty lies in power, in tension. Everything living is tense and full, like an apple. Tension can be threatening—that is war; joyous, ecstatic—that is youth. [In art,] tension begins with the compositional concept and finds its solution in form and surface." Nagibin identified four groups of sculptures by Neizvestny: "Working People," "War," "Concentration Camps," and "Grotesques." He stressed the monumentality of the sculptor's concepts, even in small pieces, and praised his efforts to find the most suitable medium for each work, including such unconventional materials for sculpture as pig iron, in accordance with the concept. "That which is most valuable in Neizvestny's work," Nagibin concluded, " . . . is the spirit of contemporaneity which pervades all his best works."

In October 1961 S. V. Markov, in the magazine *Decorative Art of the USSR,* illustrated and analyzed a plaster model by Neizvestny for one of a pair of monumental decorative walls to be erected at the Artek, a recreation home for the Pioneers (Soviet children's organization) in the Crimea. The model depicted "Man's Victory over the Sea"; its counterpart was devoted to "Man's Victory over the Cosmos." While praising Neizvestny's intrepidity in seeking new solutions of the artistic problems of the present era, Markov found evidence of eclecticism in the Artek sketches (justifiably, to judge by the photograph accompanying the article), and warned that the sculptor's eagerness to react to great contemporary events (e.g., space flights) might result in shortcomings in his work.

The first recognition from the West of Neizvestny's growing reputation came in an article by John Berger in the London *Observer* (January 28, 1962) which featured photographs of a number of his sculptures. These included such characteristic works as "Silence: Monument to a Concentration Camp Victim"; "All Clear" (the head of a man removing a gas mask, suggesting the emergence of humanity from the poisonous psychological miasma of wartime); and "Man with an Artificial Limb" (a powerful statement of the physical toll of war, based on classical prototypes of a seated male figure). Notwithstanding their originality, these works showed clear evidence of the influence of artists whose work Neizvestny is known to admire, including Henry Moore, Brancusi, and Zadkine.

Berger reported that Neizvestny had received a number of private as well as official commissions and had been awarded several gold medals. Among his patrons were atomic physicists working at the research center at Dubna, a privileged group not required to observe the generally prevailing restrictions on subject matter and style in their patronage of contemporary Soviet artists, and more directly in touch with artistic developments in the West than the ordinary Soviet citizen.

In the autumn of 1962, at a time when the pendulum of Soviet policy in the arts had swung toward increased relaxation of ideological controls, Neizvestny himself published two articles which constitute the most authoritative available evidence on his artistic aims and concepts. In "A Sculptor Meets the Future,"[1] he set forth his views on art, stressing its autonomy and its relevance to contemporary thought in other fields, especially science and architecture. "Art, like science," he wrote, "is a step into the future . . . . The contemporary artist is first of all a man whose world view is as complex as that of contemporary concepts of the universe." Much of the article was devoted to a consideration of the problems of creating monumental sculptures for urban settings—parks, buildings, and highways. Neizvestny emphasized the importance of scale in producing a monumental effect; the need to take into account the duration of time during which a given piece of sculpture is to be viewed; and the desirability of choosing the appropriate medium for each work. In "Discover the New!"[2] Neizvestny presented his aesthetic credo in more generalized philosophic terms. Again he stressed the kinship of the artist and the scientist, and the exploratory, innovational character of genuine art. "From my point of

[1] *Soviet Culture,* September 4, 1962.
[2] *Art,* October 1962.

view," he wrote, "only a step into the 'unknown' is really creation." This is in part because the contemporary observer expects more from art than the mere repetition of well-known images and concepts: "Only an art of ideas can live for the observer in our time [which is] overburdened with innumerable facts. The observer expects from the artist a concept which has become an image." Neizvestny noted particularly the interest manifested by scientists in experimental art: "Many contemporary scientists (cyberneticists, physicists, and mathematicians) are so much interested in experimental works of art, evidently, because the processes of thought are more apparent in these works of art . . . . The attention of many scholars is attracted to those works of art in which there appears not merely the result but the very process of creation itself. Incidentally, one of the most salient characteristics of contemporary art is *the effort on the part of the artist to involve the viewer in the creative process, almost in collaboration."* (Neizvestny's italics.)

Concerning his goal as an artist, Neizvestny wrote, "I am working on the search for a system of symbols and metaphors corresponding to our time . . . . Today it is not the horse or the lion which are symbols of strength; technology and science give us the strength to be as formidable as the lion, and the possibility of flying more swiftly than the eagle. But how can one organically combine man and technology? Ideally, in the same way that the Egyptian artists combined the face of a man with the body of a lion, or those of antiquity merged the torso of a man with a horse . . . ."

Neizvestny vigorously denied any desire to work only for himself or a small group of admirers, while defending the artist's right to determine his own scale of values: ". . . the artist has the right not to be understood, but to make this into a slogan would be a crime. The artist always wants to be understood by the largest possible circle of people. Not to be understood is always a tragedy for the artist."

Neizvestny was thrust into prominence in November 1962 as a center of political and aesthetic controversy. A number of his works were included in a group exhibit (November 26) by the "Belyutin circle" in Belyutin's studio in Moscow, an exhibit destined to play a fateful role in the dispute over party ideology and the arts which flared up in December. It was at about this time that a number of conservative artists and critics became alarmed at what they considered the party's dangerous laxness in aesthetic questions. Reportedly, a petition by the conservatives asking for party action to halt the spread of "formalist art"—art which does not conform to the approved canons of Socialist Realism—was submitted to the plenary session of the Central Committee of the Communist party which met from November 19 to 23, 1962. The exhibit of works by artists of the "Belyutin circle" was seized on by the conservatives as a welcome opportunity to influence Khrushchev in the direction of tightening party ideological controls in the arts.

On December 1, 1962, the exhibit was moved to larger quarters in the Manezh, a large centrally located exhibition hall, and given wide publicity. Khrushchev attended the exhibit, in the company of party ideologists and conservative artists and critics, and his strongly negative reactions to the works displayed, expressed in comments of earthy coarseness, helped to precipitate a general ideological crackdown by the party not only on artists, including Neizvestny, but on intellectuals and creative artists in general.

A direct encounter between Khrushchev and Neizvestny reportedly occurred at the exhibit, in which Neizvestny mentioned the support his work had received from the scientists Pyotr Kapitsa and Lev Landau, to which Khrushchev replied, "That's not why we admire Kapitsa and Landau." Neizvestny's friend, the poet Yevgeny Yevtushenko, spoke up in defense of him, making a direct appeal to Khrushchev not to permit the reimposition by the party of stylistic uniformity in the arts.

On December 17, 1962, the party's chief ideological spokesman, Leonid F. Ilyichev, delivered a long speech at a meeting between party and government leaders and the "creative intelligentsia," in the course of which he called Neizvestny an "abstractionist" (a fundamental stylistic misconception, since Neizvestny's work usually has a clearly marked realistic basis, the human figure) and said that his work had been "sharply but justly criticized" by Khrushchev. Neizvestny's sculptures, "The Crab," "Classics Demolished," and several others, said Ilyichev, "evoke a feeling of protest."

At a further meeting (December 24 and 26, 1962) between party ideologists and creative workers, Neizvestny mollified his critics by a statement of self-criticism which earned him Ilyichev's subsequent approval as one of three cultural figures (Yevtushenko and the writer Vasily Axyonov were the others) who had given evidence of "civic maturity." Neizvestny's position was further strengthened at about this time by a request from the atomic physicists at Dubna for a one-man exhibit of his works.

New difficulties lay ahead, however. At a meeting between top party and government leaders and artists and writers, held in the Kremlin on March 7 and 8, 1963, Neizvestny spoke on the first day, again in self-criticism, and was characterized by Ilyichev as one of those who had "correctly evaluated their errors." On the following day, however, Neizvestny was attacked directly by Khrushchev, who said:

The last time we saw the nauseating concoctions of Ernst Neizvestny, we were disgusted to notice that this man, who is evidently not devoid of talent, and who has graduated from a Soviet institution of higher learning, is repaying the people with such black ingratitude . . . . We denounce such ugliness openly, giving no quarter, and will continue to do so.

Khrushchev's onslaught, coming at a time of general attack by the conservative faction in party and art circles, forced Neizvestny to make a further statement of self-criticism, which was published in *Pravda* (March 15, 1963) under the title "It Is Necessary to Work More, Better, and with Better Ideas." As a statement of Neizvestny's aesthetic and political credo, it deserves quotation in full:

In these days I have been thinking a great deal about the responsibility of the artist to society, and also about my own work and my own responsibility. One must strive to make works of art expressive and filled with ideas. Actually, ideas always constitute the firmest foundations of expressiveness. It is in the very nature of monumental sculptors to address themselves to the people and to have a comprehensive world view.

We have the Marxist-Leninist world view, the most comprehensive of all those existing in the world.

I say to myself once more: I must work more and better, with better ideas and more expression—only in that way can I be useful to the country and to the people.

This statement was somewhat modified by an addendum, broadcast by Radio Moscow on March 19: "An artist not only has the right to experiment. He *must* experiment."

Neizvestny's self-criticism and his public profession of loyalty to the Marxist-Leninist world view (although he omitted any explicit reference to the party) failed, however, to shield him from renewed attack. A new clash occurred at the plenary session (March 26–27, 1963) of the Board of the Union of Writers of the USSR in Moscow. Neizvestny's defense on this occasion was undertaken by Yevtushenko, himself under strong attack from the conservatives. The report adopted by the board stated:

Our struggle against abstractionism is a struggle against the destruction of art. It was the destruction of art that E. Neizvestny, the sculptor, came to. His semi-dilettantish "Atomic Series" gave one a feeling of nausea and revulsion.

(It might be noted, incidentally, that the conservatives unwittingly paid tribute to the power of Neizvestny's work with these words; nausea and revulsion were among the emotions which his works, depicting the horrors of atomic war, were designed to arouse.) It was presumably at about this time that Neizvestny was expelled from the Artists' Union, a step which deprived him of government commissions and thus jeopardized his material security.

The change in the Soviet cultural climate which coincided roughly with Frol R. Kozlov's heart attack in April 1963 (an event which had the effect of virtually eliminating one of the most ardent proponents of tight ideological controls in the arts) helped to relieve the pressure on Neizvestny, as well as on other cultural figures. At the plenum of the party's Central Committee held from June 18 to 21, 1963, Mme Yekaterina Furtseva, Soviet minister of culture, mentioned an incident dating from the ideological meetings of December 1962. An artist of conservative tastes, she said, had publicly criticized Neizvestny but had privately ordered from him a replica of a sculpture representing a woman "without a head, without arms, without legs." The point of the anecdote, evidently, was to illustrate the inconsistency of an adherent of the conservative position in party-art relations.

Of greater importance for Neizvestny's standing vis-à-vis the party was a fatherly statement by Khrushchev on June 21, 1963:

Many people have spoken about the work of the sculptor Neizvestny. I would like to believe that he is an honest and competent man. Perhaps when we talk about the abstractionists we should not mention Neizvestny alone. Let us see how he carries out his promise, shows by his creative work that he serves the people.

Up to this point the controversy over Neizvestny's work had centered around aesthetic-political questions. A new and ominous note was sounded early in July 1963, in an article in *Sovetskaia Kultura* (*Soviet Culture*) by Marshal Rodion Malinovsky, defense minister of the Soviet Union:

It is especially repulsive when certain artists make the theme of the heroic dead and the defense of the Motherland a subject of formalistic exercises. For example, a feeling of indignation was evoked by the outrageous and ugly sculptures of E. Neizvestny entitled "Casualty," "Retreat," and "Artificial Limb."

Neizvestny's work was thus attacked on a new front, from the point of view of the developing campaign by army leaders and ideologists calling on creative artists to glorify heroism, patriotism, and martial valor in their works. With their emphasis on the physical and moral horrors of war, reinforced by powerful expressionist means, Neizvestny's sculptures clearly failed to support this campaign; rather, by contributing to a determination that war must not recur, they undermined it.

Malinovsky's criticism notwithstanding, Neizvestny had support in high places. In July 1963, Mme Furtseva told a foreign visitor that Neizvestny had been commissioned to do a series of bas reliefs for the Pioneer Palace (a reference to the Artěk project), and several portrait statues for the Ministry of Culture, with the scientists Lev Landau, Mstyslav Keldysh, and Mikhail Lavrentev as subjects.

During the remainder of 1963 and most of 1964 the controversy over Neizvestny and his work subsided. At a session of the Ideological Commission of the party's Central Committee on May 15 and 16, 1964, he reportedly spoke on the subject, "The Ideological-Creative and Business Relations of Artists and Architects." That he had made his peace with the military authorities is suggested by the belated award to him in 1964 of the Order of the Red Star for his wartime service in the Red Army. During this period he was reported to be working on the figure of a cosmonaut.

Neizvestny is evidently not destined, however, to live and work in obscure tranquillity. In the June 1965 issue of *Yunost* (*Youth*), a journal often in the forefront of the movement for greater liberalism in the arts, Neizvestny's friend the poet Andrei Voznesensky published a poem entitled, "Neizvestny—A Requiem in Two Steps, with an Epilogue." The poem recounted the story of the sculptor's wartime exploits and, in the epilogue, presented a picture of him in distinctly Bohemian surroundings:

> When, surrounded by women,
> You sleep on my table,
> Drunk, like an ichthyosaurus
>   . . . . .
> I can feel the monument stirring within you.

The poem referred to critics of Neizvestny—"Fops and goody-goodies [who] squeak about your revels"—but ignored entirely his far more serious difficulties with aesthetic and ideological criticism in 1962 and 1963. It would appear, therefore, that Neizvestny, having successfully weathered the political storm which at one time threatened to wreck his career, now faces criticism from moralists who disapprove of his mode of life. Nevertheless, in September 1965 he was granted permission to visit Yugoslavia—his first trip abroad, and a distinct mark of official favor.

Almost entirely cut off from official commissions and forced to improvise for studio space and materials, Neizvestny has doggedly continued working along his chosen lines. Berger reports that a major feature of his over-crowded studio is a "construction on a huge scale which people will cross like a park or enter like a building," planned as a project for a new research town near Novosibirsk, though not officially commissioned. The theme is said to be "human thought examining its own history."

Neizvestny is still young, both as a man and as an artist. His style incorporates elements of Western expressionist sculpture of the early twentieth century, but gains additional force from the experiences through which he has lived and from his moral sense of obligation to the people. By shifting to more contemporary, regime-approved subjects (e.g., the cosmonaut), Neizvestny has blunted the edge of the criticism from military officials and others, of those earlier works that emphasized the physical horrors of war and imprisonment. The controversy his work aroused can be seen as part of the shock-wave produced in the conservative and traditionalist world of Soviet Socialist Realism by the first tentative reappearance of Western influences after a long interruption of cultural contacts. More serious in their implications are his concept of the autonomy of the artist and his defense of the artist's right and duty to search for his own solutions to aesthetic problems, rather than simply accept the solutions provided for him by party ideologists. The subsequent fate of Neizvestny and his career may thus serve as an index not only to the degree of Western influences on the officially approved aesthetic style, but also to the varying state of the relations between the regime and the individual artist.

SELECTED BIBLIOGRAPHY

Writings about Neizvestny in Russian include Yuri Nagibin, "Na puti poiskov," *Smena,* 13 (1960), 20–21, a pioneering article with photographs of the sculptor and a representative group of sculptures from the series "Working People," and "Concentration Camps." The Artek project is illustrated and analyzed in S. V. Markov, "V poiskakh novogo resheniia," *Dekorativnoe iskusstvo SSSR,* 10 (1961), 26–27. A brief, favorable reference to Neizvestny's work which occurred in an article by the veteran conservative sculptor Sergei Konenkov, published in *Izvestiia* on November 13, 1962, helped to precipitate the ideological attack on "abstractionism" in Soviet art in December 1962.

Several notices of Neizvestny have appeared in English: John Berger, "A Revelation from Russia," *Observer* (January 28, 1962), analyzes and illustrates a number of Neizvestny's works. A recent account is Olga Carlisle, "A Soviet Sculptor, Ernst Neizvestny," *Art in America* (January–February 1966), 104–107, with photographs of the sculptor and some of his works. The clash between "liberals" and "conservatives" in the Soviet arts and the Communist party in 1962 and 1963, in which Neizvestny's work became a principal center of controversy, is analyzed in Priscilla Johnson, *Khrushchev and the Arts,* Cambridge: M.I.T. Press, 1965, and Ralph Blum, "Freeze and Thaw: the Artist in Russia," *New Yorker* (August 28, 1962), 49–81. Of particular value is a study by John Berger, "Familiars of Death," *The Nation,* November 21, 1966, pp. 553–57.

Neizvestny's aesthetic concepts and goals are defined in his articles "Skul'ptor vstrechaet budusshchee," *Sovetskaia kul'tura,* September 4, 1962, and "Otkryvat' novoe," *Iskusstvo,* 10 (1962), 9–11. The latter includes a photograph of a plaster model of the figure of a cosmonaut. For his self-critical statement of March 1963, published in *Pravda,* March 15, 1963, see Johnson, *Khrushchev and the Arts,* pp. 29, 203.

Konstantin Georgievich Paustovsky[*]

by Edgar H. Lehrman

Konstantin Georgievich Paustovsky was born in Moscow on May 31, 1892. His father, Georgi Maximovich Paustovsky, was a railroad statistician. The family also had two older boys, Vadim and Boris, and a girl, Galina. Georgi, who was never able to stay long in one place, soon left Moscow for Pskov and Vilno before moving with his family to Kiev, where Konstantin spent most of his childhood. While Konstantin was a student at the First

* The author would like to thank the Research Committee of Emory University, whose aid greatly facilitated the completion of this article.

Kiev Classical Gymnasium, from which he graduated in 1909, Georgi Paustovsky lost his position after a clash with his superior and abandoned his wife and children.[1] Young Konstantin soon entered Kiev University, but transferred to Moscow University to be near his mother. His two brothers had just been called to active service—it was 1914—and the old woman was almost alone. Konstantin himself was exempted from military service because he was nearsighted, a student, and a youngest son. In Moscow he gave up school to become a streetcar motorman. Moved by the sight of the wounded being brought in from Russian Poland, he enlisted as a medical orderly and was assigned to a hospital train which traveled over much of European Russia. Late in 1916 a letter written somewhat earlier and satirizing the tsar was traced to Paustovsky, and he was discharged from the army.

After a short time at a munitions factory in the south, Paustovsky returned to Moscow and became a reporter. Journalism would be his main profession for the next decade and a half, during which he frequently changed cities and newspapers. He worked in Odessa, Batum, and Tbilisi, before coming north again to Moscow in the middle 1920's. In addition to his newspaper and periodical work, Paustovsky was writing fiction. His first two works of fiction, *Sea Sketches* (1925) and *Minetoza* (1927), were collections of stories. His third book, *Ships that Meet* (1929), was similar. The first novel that he published, *Gleaming Clouds* (1929), enjoyed scant notice and no success.

The turning point in Paustovsky's life came a few years later. *Nashi dostizheniia,* Gorky's monthly, commissioned some articles from him, and Paustovsky went out "after material" for the first time. Largely as a result of that trip, Paustovsky in 1932 published *Kara-Bugaz,* a work which elicited favorable comments from Gorky and from Lenin's widow. After this book, he was able to travel to his heart's content and his journeys often produced new works, such as *The Colchis* (1933), *The Fate of Charles Lonceville* (1933), *The Black Sea* (1937), and *A Northern Tale* (1937). Perhaps the most rewarding of his shorter works at this time are his sketches of the Meshchora, a swampy, forested lowland near Moscow, some of which were published in *Summer Days* (1937). When war came in 1941, he served as a correspondent on the Southern Front. He wrote a war novel, *The Smoke of Our Homeland,* but the manuscript was lost for twenty years and published only in 1964.

After the war, Paustovsky turned to autobiography. *Distant Years* was first published in full in 1946. It was followed years later by *Restless Youth* (1955), *The Start of an Unknown Age* (1956), *A Time of Major Expectations* (1960), *Sprint to the South* (1961), and *A Book of Wanderings*

---

[1] The mother soon moved back to Moscow with Vadim and Galina, but not before the gymnasium had granted her petition to waive tuition fees for Boris and Konstantin.

(1964). The collective title of the entire series may be translated either as
A Story About Life or as *A Story About a Life* since Russian has no grammatical articles. Paustovsky's chief claim to fame may well rest on this
series; translations of the first volume have already appeared in England,
France, Germany, Italy, Sweden, and the United States. Paustovsky's book
about writing, *The Golden Rose* (1955), is also widely respected in Russia.
Some chapters from a second volume of the same work appeared in *Pages
from Tarusa* in 1961 and Paustovsky himself has noticed the close ties between *The Golden Rose* and his autobiography.

In the years since Stalin's death, Paustovsky has also emerged as a
publicist. He has consistently supported the "left" wing in Soviet intellectual life against the efforts of "orthodox" writers and critics to enforce
complete conformity within literature. It is no surprise to see his name
among those who wish to preserve Lake Baikal against pollution or to learn
from the apparent transcript (which somehow reached the West) of the
recent Siniavsky-Daniel trial for un-Soviet activities that the defense tried
unsuccessfully to include a statement by Paustovsky in the record. Inside
Russia, he is greatly respected for his modesty and honesty.

Paustovsky deals with his background in *Distant Years.* Konstantin
feels that he owes at least part of his romanticism to his grandfather,
Maxim Paustovsky, a Ukrainian-speaking Zaporozhe Cossack who had
married a Turkish woman. But Georgi, Maxim's son, was also an "incor-
rigible dreamer." This may help to explain why, to use the writer's words,
"from childhood on, I have wished to see and experience everything that
a human being can." Konstantin's maternal grandmother was a Pole who
always wore mourning for the unsuccessful revolt of 1863. He was appalled
by the fanaticism he saw when she once took him on a pilgrimage to Czesto-
chowa. Thus, the Russian element in Paustovsky's heritage was comparatively weak. Konstantin himself spoke Ukrainian before he spoke Russian.
This makes his achievement as a master stylist in Russian all the more remarkable.

The first chapter of *Distant Years,* the first volume of his autobiographical series, describes a Russia as far from us today as Tolstoy's characters
were from him when he was finishing *War and Peace.* Georgi Paustovsky
lay dying, and Konstantin had come from the Gymnasium to see him, accompanied by a priest and transported by a Jewish driver. But the Russia
of Gymnasiums, priests, and Jewish drivers has disappeared, like that of
Natasha Rostova and Pierre Bezukhov. Paustovsky's first chapter creates
tension between the landscape of the present and the people of the past.
Paustovsky has stated, "I have never been able to write about people outside of the landscape and the most ordinary phenomena of nature." This
tension helps to give the book the double perspective which Soviet critics
have commented on, as the mature man lives again—this time vicariously
—the years of his childhood and youth. The countryside he describes is

that of Bunin and Chekhov; Gorky too began his autobiography by telling of his father's death. One of the accomplishments of *A Story About a Life* is the brilliant description of the change from Bunin's and Chekhov's Russia to the Soviet Union of the post-Stalin period and the effect of that change upon the life of an intellectual whose career began in 1912 and continues to the present. Levitsky[2] feels that Paustovsky almost typifies the Russian intelligentsia.

The rest of *Distant Years* deals mainly with Paustovsky's school days. His longing for faraway places was stimulated by contact with Uncle Iuzia (the family traveler), by the imaginative geography teacher Cherpunov, by reading *Tristan and Isolde,* and even by seeing a midshipman on the streets of Kiev. Perhaps part of the reason Paustovsky has so little to say about his home life was the slow moral and financial disintegration of his father, told with carefully controlled clarity, empathy, reserve, and simplicity. When Georgi formed other "attachments," Konstantin was puzzled and hurt, although a quiet and almost furtive love for his father remained. After Georgi left his family, they survived by selling their household goods. Years after Georgi's death in the narrative, the reader shares the author's joy when the widow tells her son, "He was a wonderful man. The most wonderful man on earth. I have forgiven him everything. You do so too!" Georgi's desertion brought his family closer to Uncle Kolia, a metallurgist who lived in Briansk. Visits to Briansk, and to the people who loved him there, awakened Paustovsky's love for central Russia. One of the most moving moments in *Distant Years* occurs when, on the train moving away from Briansk, he opens a letter just given him by his uncle at the station; in it he finds best wishes, money, and a freely offered promise of further help when it is needed.

Paustovsky was now attending school without paying the usual fees. Perhaps this is another reason why the Gymnasium so stimulated his interest, and why he recalls with such glee the visit of King Peter of Serbia, the fights between the "democrats" (led by the future writer Mikhail Bulgakov) and the "aristocrats," the classes in religion, and all the rest of it. He helped support himself by giving lessons to the spoiled and stupid daughter of a retired general.

One of the chapters in *Distant Years,* "The Inn on the Braginka," forms a perfect short story. It tells of the vengeance taken by the *maistry,* or guild of blind beggars, when the boy guide of one of them was killed by a landowner's dog. This chapter first appeared separately and won the unsolicited praise of Ivan Bunin, who considered it among the best short stories in Russian literature.

Paustovsky, whose first sketch, "On the Water," appeared over a pen name in 1912, attended the university in Kiev until war broke out in 1914.

---

[2] Lev Abelevich Levitskii, *Konstantin Paustovskii,* Moskva, 1963, p. 256.

The period of his college days, his life in wartime Moscow, and his military service are described in *Restless Youth,* the second volume of his autobiography. Paustovsky gives a fine picture of Moscow as it then was, with the passenger who always tried to pay his fare with a hundred-ruble bill, with Igor Severianin (the ego-futurist poet so famous at the time), and above all with the wounded coming in from the west. On the hospital train to which he was assigned after he volunteered, he became very friendly with a young nurse named Lelia—close enough to meet her family on a trip to Moscow. These contacts with her prepare us brilliantly for the shock of her later sickness and death in a smallpox-ravaged Russian village. In what may be the best part of the book, he evokes a sense of impending doom as he describes the sullen and reluctant retreat of the Russian Army before von Mackensen in 1915, while some of its men muttered to themselves about treason. Paustovsky captures the horror of the war in the incidents he describes: a little boy killed by panic-stricken refugees; a woman pausing a few hours in her flight from the Germans to give birth, and his own discovery in the newspapers that both his brothers have been killed in action on the same day on different Fronts.

Paustovsky learned of the February Revolution of 1917 when he was in Elets, and he describes well the euphoria that possessed Russia at the time. The next stage was, as the title of the third volume suggests, *The Beginning of an Unknown Age.* This volume is impressive for its painful honesty: Paustovsky admits that most intellectuals were against the Bolsheviks, and that he himself was a bystander who became convinced that the Communists were right only in 1920. To say such things in the Soviet Union requires courage, particularly since the earlier volumes of his work had already been attacked by Soviet critics as too liberal and insufficiently oriented toward Communism; this volume, as Yegorova pointed out in 1960, was completely ignored in Soviet criticism, and only the appearance of Levitsky's study of Paustovsky in 1963 broke the silence.

When the Communist government closed the Socialist-Revolutionary newspapers in the summer of 1918, Paustovsky lost his position. He then went south to see his mother and sister and moved on to Kiev in the late fall. Kiev was anarchy. There was a weird series of occupying armies: Skoropadsky, Petliura, the Bolsheviks, and Denikin were among those to take the city before the Communists returned to claim it permanently. It was a city of ten-year-old prostitutes, where cocaine was sold openly on the streets, and counterfeit money accepted at par. There Konstantin was drafted, first by Skoropadsky and then by the Bolsheviks. He fled to Odessa, and the trip—which had taken twelve and a half hours by express in 1914—took eighteen days. There is a feeling of muffled horror in his description of how Pomoshnaia (about two hundred miles from Odessa) was deserted before the anarchist leader Makhno's train passed through— and how a railroad man working at the station was shot dead by Makhno for no reason whatever. In Odessa, Paustovsky had to decide whether to leave Russia. He had already left both Moscow and Kiev after the Communists had taken them. In Odessa he met Bunin, many of whose writings Paustovsky knew by heart, and Bunin was leaving Russia forever. But Paustovsky stayed, feeling that his place was in his country. And thus, with Paustovsky's "third October Revolution," the volume ends.

The fourth part of the autobiography, like its successors, has not yet appeared in English (as of the end of 1966). Called *A Time of Major Expectations,* it deals with Odessa and the Soviet Black Sea shore in and after 1920 during the "intermission" of Odessa's meteorlike path of glory across the Russian literary scene. Kuprin had emigrated, and the new writers—Katayev, Ilf and Petrov, Babel, Bagritsky, etc.—were not yet famous. He catches well the mad, irreverent atmosphere of what was then Russia's Brooklyn.[3] Odessa then had such runaway inflation that money was printed on the backs of playing cards. Here Paustovsky met Isaac Babel, who gave him excellent advice about keeping *prichastiia* and *deeprichastiia* out of his writing.[4]

In those exciting but difficult times, when typhus and famine were rampant, merely to stay alive was a major project, but Paustovsky still had a bad case of wanderlust. The fifth volume of his autobiography—*Sprint to the South*—describes his two years in the Caucasus and on the Soviet Black Sea coast, especially in Poti and Batum. Abkhazia at this time was so plagued by vendettas that his editor rejected as too dangerous an article by Paustovsky denouncing blood feuds. At this time, Paustovsky was robbed of his wedding ring in the Klukhor pass. This is the first hint that he is married, and the reader may very well feel puzzled by it. If puppy love on the Crimea and the death of Lelia can occupy whole chapters, why does Paustovsky avoid any mention of that love which was requited? He describes being on the verge of falling in love with Misha Siniavsky's wife; one wonders where his own wife was at the time. In this reticence about his emotional life as a mature adult, Paustovsky is writing in the Russian autobiographical tradition of Vladimir Korolenko, Maxim Gorky, and his own contemporary Ilya Ehrenburg (if not that of Alexander Herzen). And there is always the possibility that Paustovsky may take up his inner life as a man in future volumes.

Like the earlier parts of the autobiography, *Sprint to the South* has many vivid descriptions of people and events. One example will suffice: Someone in rat-infested Batum tried to get rid of the vermin by spraying

---

[3] The Odessa accent sounds as funny to Russians as the so-called Brooklyn accent does to Americans. Both cities are lively ports whose local jargons have been noticeably influenced by their large Yiddish-speaking populations.

[4] These grammatical terms signify respectively, adjectives and adverbs derived from verbs, the widespread use of which imparts a Germanic heaviness to so much Russian writing, particularly scholarship.

them with kerosene and igniting them. The rats ran to their nests, and the massive fire that resulted lasted two days. (No one remembered the Old Russian story of Olga's vengeance on the Derevlians!) *Sprint to the South* is perhaps the weakest of Paustovsky's autobiographical works. It lacks the thrills of growing up, the horrors of the war and famine, and the fascinating descriptions of teeming cities that had enlivened the earlier works.

The unity collapses in the sixth volume, *A Book of Wanderings,* which includes a description of a trip Paustovsky made to France in 1957. This chapter is set at least two decades later than the rest of the book. Worse than the violation of chronology is the lack of connection between his visit to the France of the Fourth Republic and his life in the Soviet Union of the 1920's and the 1930's, when he was again based in Moscow. He was writing fiction as well as journalism, but his work was too hurried and sometimes primitive in its execution. The best parts of *A Book of Wanderings* deal with his memories of his old schoolfellow, the writer Mikhail Bulgakov, who was driven out of Russian literature by Stalin, but continued to tell his fantastic inventions to those he trusted. His favorite oral narratives dealt with his "friend," the Georgian dictator, depicting that paranoid tyrant as kind, generous, outgoing, and human. The macabre overtones of the Stalin passages contrast sharply with the chapter on Lenin preceding them, which transmits genuine grief over Lenin's death.

Paustovsky's autobiography, published over almost two decades, also gives us some indication of the slight easing of Soviet censorship since 1945, when such a treatment of Stalin would have been unthinkable. So too, perhaps, would have been Paustovsky's admiration of Bunin, who was a White *émigré*. Paustovsky can admit now in the sixth volume that he prettified Poti when he described it in *The Colchis*. On the other hand, the censorship is still very much alive. The speech which Paustovsky made in 1956 against the "Drozdovs" (Soviet Philistines in positions of power, named for the villain of Dudintsev's novel *Not by Bread Alone*) has yet to be published in the Soviet Union, although French and English translations of it are easy to obtain in the West. Again, *Literaturnaia gazeta* for March 23, 1963, indicates that the title of Paustovsky's sixth volume was to be *Over a Slow Fire*. Inasmuch as the book concentrates on life in Russia during the 1920's, some readers may assume that the author felt living in Russia then was like being roasted over a slow fire. No explanation has been given in the completed book for the change in title.

Poor health during the winter of 1965 interfered with Paustovsky's hopes to write a seventh volume of his autobiography. (He has suffered from asthma in the past.) If he is able to discipline himself as he did in describing the Russian retreat of 1915, he may yet give us additional distinguished work. Of all major Soviet autobiographies, only Ehrenburg's approaches Paustovsky's in length. But Paustovsky does not have on his record the stigma of wholehearted collaboration with Stalin that Ehrenburg has been trying to erase for over a decade. Even with its shortcomings, Paustovsky's autobiography is one of the few reasonably honest and fascinating records we have of what it has been like to be a Russian in Russia during the first half of the twentieth century.

About 1930, Soviet writers began to feel pressure from the party and the government to create works with which to inspire people along the officially prescribed political lines. This trend was reflected in Paustovsky's *Kara-Bugaz* (1932), the title of which is Turkish for "Black Gulf" and refers to a body of water on the eastern shore of the Caspian Sea, where there are great deposits of Glauber's salt. The hero of Paustovsky's tale is not a human being but rather the technical progress made possible by the Soviet regime. Like Karel Čapek (or Vasily Axyonov), Paustovsky tells the story from different viewpoints, shifting his first-person narrative from the letter of a tsarist naval officer to an old traveler, to a Bolshevik geologist, etc. (He made up many of the scientific "observations" given here himself.) The work is full of heady ideas for the future so appealing to Russians. One character suggests turning the gulf into a laboratory for catching solar energy; another wants to build a railroad from Aleksandrov Gai to Khiva. The book is the work of an enthusiast, trying hard to integrate Communist attitudes of zest for construction, belief in the future, hatred for the Whites, and a religious faith in the idea that only a Communist regime can bring the local people out of their age-old backwardness into the modern, industrialized world. To deal with the changing position of women, Paustovsky introduces a female chemist, a female engineer, and a widow named Nachar who escapes from the persecution of the local men to the protection of the Soviet regime. Read today in the West, the work has glaring defects: it is too schematic; there is little unity of character development; one scarcely sees interpersonal relationships or skillful plotting at all. But *Kara-Bugaz* was not read from a Western point of view. Gorky praised the work as one of a number of pieces which boldly and successfully gave children and adolescents a good attitude toward future construction. And Krupskaya, Lenin's widow, also praised the work as a socialist answer to Fenimore Cooper, declaring that such books as *Kara-Bugaz* were "very necessary." The work does have some interest. There is a clean, classical style in the writing of the tsarist officer, Lieutenant Zherebtsov. The spirit of Jules Verne, popularized science, an almost geological treatise on Glauber's salt ($Na_2SO_4 \cdot 10H_2O$), and descriptions of the desert all combine to give the Soviet reader—particularly the child or adolescent—a real sense of wonder at the miracles of nature which exist inside his own vast country and a wish to capture nature's resources and to put them to work on behalf of Soviet man. *Kara-Bugaz* has also at least one other claim to distinction: it brought its author fame. This is the book of Paustovsky's which has attracted the most attention in his native land, and the most favorable reviews. As a result of its success, he was able to give up journalism and to concentrate on creative writing.

Only after Stalin's death was Paustovsky able to see the West—France, Holland, Greece, Sweden, and Italy—but wherever he has traveled, he has had a special affection for two spots. One of these is a village called Tarusa on the Oka River, where he has done much writing; it is this spot, beloved by Russian painters and by the poetess Marina Tsvetayeva, that gave its name to the recent anthology, *Pages from Tarusa,* which caused such a stir in Moscow. His other favorite area is his "second native land," the Meshchora country.

There are no special beauties or riches in the Meshchora territory, except for the woods, the meadows, and the limpid air. But this territory is very attractive just the same. It is unpretentious in the way that Levitan's pictures are. But like those pictures, it contains all the charm and all the variety of the Russian landscape, which cannot be appreciated at first glance.

What can be seen in the Meshchora territory? Blooming or reaped fields, pine forest on sandy ground, lakes in the woods and in the water meadows overgrown with black sedge, and ricks smelling of warm, dry hay . . . .

Thus begins some of Paustovsky's best writing: his essay, "The Meshchora Country" (1937). His old friend, the Soviet nature-writer Mikhail Prishvin told him not to describe this area lest tourists come and ruin it. Paustovsky has the generosity to admit that Prishvin's rebuke was deserved. Paustovsky first became interested in this region because some food (or tea) he bought in downtown Moscow was wrapped in a piece of an old map of the Meshchora. His sketches about the Meshchora are written with the deep feeling that only personal experience can engender. The fishing is good there, and that is yet another source of the region's attractiveness. His sentences are short, expressive, vivid, careful, and beautifully written; they create the illusion of transparency and simplicity—until one seeks to analyze them. His writing shows the countryside not only at rest, but in motion. Succinct and memorable descriptions are given of a water-rat catching fish in "The Meshchora Country"; of a badger which burned its nose on some frying potatoes and sought to ease the pain by using the damp and rotten wood of a tree stump, in "The Badger's Nose" (1937); of a peasant sure that a devil—which turns out to be a pelican escaped from a zoo—has attacked him, in "The Last Devil" (1936); of a puppy gnawing at the air valve of a rubber boat until the escaping air lifts him off his feet, in "The Rubber Boat" (1936), and of a predatory tomcat tamed by food and good treatment to the point where he voluntarily drives away chickens from his new master's cereal, in "The Thieving Tomcat" (1935). Next to his autobiography, the Meshchora tales represent Paustovsky's best writing. Particularly vivid, for example, are his cats jumping toward the catch of fish that has been strung along a line and hung from the branch of an old apple tree (in "The Meshchora Country"). In his Meshchora tales, Paustovsky shows that he knows how to find a whole miracle in each blade of grass, and to share his awe with his reader. True, he sometimes adds a happy little moral, but this does not negate his achievement.

Soviet critics, and Paustovsky himself, have noticed Joseph Conrad's influence on his writings about the sea. Thus, his *Black Sea,* as Levitsky observes, has some connection with Conrad's *The Mirror of the Sea.* The influence is there but, in my opinion, is not fruitful. The reason is that Conrad wrote from his own experience of many years as a ship's officer, whereas Paustovsky's fascination for the sea is always that of a landsman or a passenger, based largely upon what he has read and never concerned with the real ocean. It is more productive, I think, to talk about the influence on Paustovsky of Russian writers of the preceding generation, particularly Anton Chekhov, Alexander Grin, and Ivan Bunin. Paustovsky has written lovingly about all three. From Grin he took his early "exoticism" —an attitude based on dreams, with overtones of unreal heroism (preferably from sailors), and simplistic psychology. (One of the best articles on Paustovsky was entitled "A Journey from the Land of Grin" and appeared in 1938—one year after Iuri Olesha had asked Paustovsky to leave Grin behind.) Paustovsky admired Bunin's interest in central Russia, in the carefully crafted sentence, in color, lighting, travel, tone, and honesty. In Chekhov, Paustovsky admired the analytical, precise style with its abhorrence of needless non-Russian words, and Chekhov's quiet humanity.

Paustovsky never talks of Korolenko in a special essay (as he does of Grin, Chekhov, and Bunin) but the points of contact between the two men are very real. Both came from middle-class families and grew up in the Ukraine. Both were part Polish, but won fame for their writings in Russian. The most extended achievement of each is his autobiography, and each viewed his own life as typifying in some very important ways the story of his own generation. Both men considered themselves romantics and showed kindness in their relations with others. They have both taken seriously their roles as publicists, and the sentimentality which sometimes mars their other work is absent in their publicistic pieces. Their humanitarianism in their writings is not abstract but very specific; their attitude to individual Jews furnishes a case in point. Korolenko suffered along with his Jewish friend Simkha as they read together Ukrainian literature containing anti-Semitic passages, and Korolenko wrote articles in defense of the persecuted Mendel Beilis. Paustovsky suffered along with Babel as the latter discoursed on anti-Semitism, and the main character in what may be Paustovsky's best story, "Labels for Colonial Products" (1928), is a wandering Jew who has lost everything. Korolenko's brief introduction to his autobiography sounds in spots as if Paustovsky could have written it. But one must not exaggerate the similarities between the two writers. In Korolenko's time, a publicist could be much more independent of official Russian government attitudes than he can today. And the literary situation in Russia today is considerably better than it was in Stalin's time. It is to Paustovsky's credit that he managed to survive the Stalin period with so little damage to his ethics and his soul. No doubt one source of his strength and equilibrium has been his love for the Russian countryside of Briansk, Tarusa, and the Meshchora.

Paustovsky's love for the Russian countryside also shines through his potpourri on writing, *The Golden Rose*. This is an elusive book, which contains odd thoughts on writing and on the beauty of Russian words along with some fiction and commentaries on famous authors. But, as a Soviet critic has pointed out, the fiction that most concerns Paustovsky here was written by others.

Paustovsky has his shortcomings as a writer, many of them stemming perhaps from his very productivity: the six-volume set of his *Selected Works* contains, in addition to the first three volumes of his autobiography, well over 100 works, including short stories, essays, a few plays, and some short novels. Since its appearance in 1957–58, he has published three more volumes of autobiography, another novel, and various tales and essays.

Among Paustovsky's weaknesses is his difficulty in constructing credible plots; they are often so disjointed that they simply fall apart, as in *Gleaming Clouds, The Fate of Charles Lonceville,* and *The Lake Front* (1933). His attempts at explaining human motivation are frequently primitive, and many of his works, such as the stories "Valuable Cargo" (1931), "Valor" (1935), and "Snow" (1944), drip with sentimentality. His fondness for the exotic, especially in his early work, has led him to write sentences like the following in "Fever" (1924): "Night fell suddenly, slippery, like the skin of a hippopotamus." He has been accused of a cavalier disregard for known facts, such as toward events in the lives of the poet Shevchenko and the girl friend of the 1905 hero Lieutenant Schmidt, toward Captain Robert Scott's Antarctic expedition, and toward the geography of Pushkin's Mikhailovskoe. And his description of the "interventionists" in the American army in *The Lake Front* is at best unintentionally funny to anyone familiar with the army of the United States.

Paustovsky also relies too frequently on the same devices. The optimistic letter from someone who has since died is used in "Sorang" (1932), *The Fate of Charles Lonceville,* "The Constellation of Hunting Dogs" (1936), and "A Northern Tale" (1937). And he loves to invent sentimental incidents in the lives of famous men. The musician who plays the piano for a dying cook in "The Old Chef" (1940) turns out to be Mozart, and the gentleman who writes a song for a little Norwegian girl who meets him in the woods in "The Basket with Pine Cones" (1954) is none other than Grieg. Peter Tchaikovsky is similarly sentimentalized in *Povest' o lesakh.*

As Belinsky said of the early Turgenev, Paustovsky's talent enables him to depict meaningfully what he has seen, but "he cannot create characters and place them in such mutual relationships in which they form themselves of their own accord into novels and stories." This is why Paustovsky's best work—his autobiography, and his sketches of the Meshchora country—so often deals with his own experiences.

No discussion of Paustovsky would be complete without mention of his role as a "leftist" publicist. Soviet writers in the mid-1960's are generally divided into two groups: the orthodox, conservative, Stalinesque hardliners, and the "leftists." Both groups are devoted Communists, but the "leftists" would like more leeway in writing because they are convinced that Soviet artists will not "abuse" whatever artistic freedom the party gives them. Paustovsky, even in 1933, believed that it was not necessary for Soviet art to sugarcoat reality, but rather that men could learn by being shown along with their stupidities and their errors. Some three years later he declared that literary politics and other petty concerns interfered with the mood needed for writing. But Stalin's reign was no time to develop such ideas and most of Paustovsky's important publicistic thinking dates from after 1953. Thus, in his *Golden Rose,* he remarks about writers' "brigades" that it is just as impossible for two or three people to play the violin at once as to write the same book. Again, when he observes that he rarely saw a malicious and arrogant bureaucrat in Poland, he is not thinking merely of Poland. His voice sounds refreshing too when he states simply and sensibly that a writer's job is to write and not to make declarations about how one ought to write. But his outstanding achievement as a publicist so far has been the courageous article he wrote in connection with the Congress of Union of Soviet Writers in 1959, "Unarguable and Arguable Ideas." This may well be even more important than his contributions to the "leftist" anthology, *Pages from Tarusa.* In his 1959 article he attacked the Soviet convention of the happy ending, remarking how lucky Tolstoy was to have finished *Anna Karenina* before that fetish became widespread. He denounced also the "harmful tradition" of ignoring suffering and sorrow in Soviet literature and attacked the unwavering and infallible heroes of Soviet books and films for their empty hearts. Complaining about the lack of variety and breathing space in Soviet literature caused by arbitrary and vulgar criticism, he stated, "Perhaps we shout so much and so loudly about truth in literature precisely because we do not have enough of it." The article closes with a panegyric on Soviet patriotism, but that does not change what has gone before. Kochetov, Metchenko, Pertsov and other members of the "orthodox" group soon attacked Paustovsky, and early in 1960 the Ukrainian writer Maxim Rylsky attempted to depict Paustovsky as a Ukrainophobe—an effort at defamation which Paustovsky was able to brush off with consummate ease.

Paustovsky is regarded with great affection by his countrymen. They love his kindness; perhaps that is one reason they so often think of him as a children's writer. He is a master at describing the details of sight (even though he is nearsighted), sound, and smell. Believing that every autumn is his first and last, he not only can actually listen to the quiet rustle of a falling leaf, but describe it so well that we can hear it too—through his ears. He still betrays a sense of childlike wonder at the variety, beauty, and newness of the world. There is feeling for the romance of faraway places, even if he had to wait until his seventh decade before he was able to see Europe for himself. Babel and Bulgakov are dead now, but they— and many others—will live on in Paustovsky's descriptions of them, as well as in their own works. His greatest achievement is his bringing to life through brilliant vignettes and reminiscences the Russia of a young intellectual just before and after the October Revolution.

SELECTED BIBLIOGRAPHY

There are no real biographies of Paustovsky, but there are several worthwhile Soviet critical studies, including Lev Abelevich Levitskii, *Konstantin Paustovskii*, Moskva, 1963; Liudmila Petrovna Egorova, "Konstantin Paustovskii: ocherk tvorchestva" (a dissertation for the degree of Candidate of Science at the Moscow State Pedagogical Institute named for Lenin), Moskva, 1960; A. Roskin, "Puteshestvie iz strany Grina," *Literaturnyi kritik*, 5 (1938), 167–87; and perhaps Sergei L'vov (pseudonym of Sergei L'vovich Gets), *Konstantin Paustovskii, kritiko-biograficheskii ocherk*, Moskva, 1958. See also G. P. Trefilova, "Konstantin Paustovskii," in Akademiia nauk SSSR, *Istoriia russkoi sovetskoi literatury v trekh tomakh*, III (Moskva, 1958–1961), 341–62.

The basic collection of Paustovsky's writings is his *Sobranie sochinenii v shesti tomakh*, Moskva, 1957–58 (hereinafter referred to as *Sobsoch*). This contains the first three parts of his autobiography (comprising volume III), the first volume of his book on writing *Zolotaia roza*, such novels and novellas as *Romantiki, Blistaiushchie oblaka, Kara-Bugaz, Kolkhida, Chernoe more, Severnaia povest', Povest' o lesakh*, plus eight long short stories including *Meshchorskaia storona*, eight fairy tales, sixteen "literary portraits and notes," three plays, two articles on art, thirty essays, and eighty-nine short stories.

His autobiographical writings include the six parts of *Povest' o zhizni* now published: *Dalekie gody*, first published in *Novyi mir*, 10 (1945), and available in *Sobsoch*, III, 7–299; *Bespokoinaia iunost'*, first published in *Novyi mir*, 3, 4, 5, and 6 (1955), and available in *Sobsoch*, III, 299–567; *Nachalo nevedomogo veka*, first published in *Sobsoch*, III, 567–789; *Vremia bol'shikh ozhidanii*, Moskva, 1960; *Brosok na iug*, Moskva, 1961; and *Kniga skitanii*, Moskva, 1964. Autobiographical information can also be found in his preface to *Sobsoch*, I, 5–18, and in "Korotko o sebe," *Sovetskie pisateli: avtobiografii v dvukh tomakh*, compiled by B. Ia. Brainina and E. F. Nikitina, II (Moskva, 1957–58), 208–15.

Paustovsky's publicistic writings occupy a special place in his canon. No Russian version is available of the speech he made about the "Drozdovs," but an English version (called "The Drozdovs" and unavoidably taken from a French translation), may be found in *The Year of Protest 1956*, edited by Hugh McLean and Walter N. Vickery, New York: Vintage, 1961, pp. 155–60.

Paustovsky's most important and courageous article is "Besspornye i spornye mysli," *Literaturnaia gazeta,* May 20, 1959, p. 4. He is also an editor of the anthology *Tarusskie stranitsy,* Kaluga, 1961. An abridged translation of this volume is available in English: *Pages from Tarusa,* edited by Andrew Field, Boston: Little, Brown, 1964.

The major English translations of Paustovsky's work include *The Story of a Life,* translated by Joseph Barnes, New York: Pantheon, 1964, which contains "The Faraway Years," (*Dalekie gody*), pp. 3–254; "Restless Youth," (*Bespokoinaia iunost'*), pp. 257–478; and "The Start of an Extraordinary Era" (*Nachalo nevedomogo veka*), pp. 481–661. Translations of *Dalekie gody* and *Bespokoinaia iunost'* have also been made by Manya Harari and Michael Duncan: the first is *Story of a Life,* London: Harvill, 1964; the second is *Slow Approach of Thunder,* London: Harvill, 1965.

The Golden Rose, translated by Susanna Rosenberg and edited by Dennis Ogden, was published by the Foreign Languages Publishing House in Moscow, but the year of publication was not given. The same publishers issued his *Selected Stories* in 1949. *The Black Gulf (Kara-Bugaz),* translated by Eugenia Schimanskaya, was published by Hutchinson in London in 1948, and another version of this is included in his above-mentioned *Selected Stories. Selected Stories* also contains *The Colchis* and five short stories.

Two of Paustovsky's most popular stories are "Snow" (which can be found in *Selected Stories*) and "The Telegram" (available in *Soviet Short Stories,* edited by Avrahm Yarmolinsky, Garden City, New York: Doubleday Anchor, 1960, pp. 132–45.

I know of no critical work on Paustovsky yet written in English. Perhaps the best and most extensive treatment of him now available in English is the chapter on Paustovsky in Vera Alexandrova (or Aleksandrova), *A History of Soviet Literature, 1917–1962,* translated by Mirra Ginsburg, Garden City, New York: Doubleday, 1963, pp. 260–72. This chapter is largely based on the same author's article "Konstantin Paustovskii," *Mosty,* I (München, 1958), 181–93.

Mikhail Alexandrovich Sholokhov

by David H. Stewart

Acclaimed in his homeland and abroad as the greatest prose writer of the first Soviet generation, Mikhail Sholokhov is at once the most typical and the most exceptional representative of Russian literature since 1917. He is typical because he combines political activity and social service with his profession of writing, thus complying with Communism's ideal of fostering many-sided development rather than specialized individualism, as well as with an older Russian propensity among writers for fervid extra-literary commitments. He is, therefore, a distinguished citizen: member of the Communist Party of the Soviet Union (CPSU) since 1932, elected deputy to the Supreme Soviet of the USSR, and member of the Academy of Sciences of the USSR. He is exceptional because by birth and inclination he is identified with a minority people, the Don Cossacks, and because his work occupies a distinctive but not central position in the evolution of Soviet literature. Recognition of his achievement in fiction can be measured by the Stalin and Lenin prizes awarded to all his major works and by the Nobel Prize for literature that he received in 1965.

A mixture of the commonplace and the unexpected characterizes Sholokhov's entire life as well as his work. His grandfather came to the Don from Ryazan and married into a local merchant family, said to be a model for the Mokhovs in *The Quiet Don.* He prospered and raised a large family himself, four daughters and four sons, the second of whom fell in love with a domestic servant, Anastasiya Danilovna Chernikova, an illiterate but attractive peasant girl. To prevent a disadvantageous marriage, the Sholokhov family compelled the girl to marry a retired noncommissioned Cossack officer and sought a suitable bride for the son. He, however, frustrated their design by leaving his parents and establishing his own home, with Anastasiya Danilovna as his servant. Their son, Mikhail, was born May 26, 1905, one of Russia's prophetic years; but he was not technically a Sholokhov until 1912 when his mother's legal husband died, freeing her to marry his father.

Sholokhov's father was apparently an enterprising businessman who tried his hand at numerous occupations until his death in 1925. In addition, he was concerned enough about his son to procure a modest library for him, to engage the services of tutors, and to send him to school. In 1914 and 1915 young Mikhail was in Moscow undergoing treatment for an eye ailment, and he attended school there, transferring later to Boguchar in Voronezh Province because education in the capital became too expensive. But his formal education ended in 1918 with the Revolution and the German occupation. Sholokhov spent the next two years in an area controlled by Whites.

By 1920 the Red Army established Soviet rule in his region, and he promptly went to work for the local Revolutionary Committee. His main occupation was apparently to assist in establishing schools and theaters, but he also served with grain requisitioning detachments, often a dangerous and brutal occupation. To seize grain from irate peasants was dangerous in itself, but the region was infested with armed bands of brigands and disaffected remnants of anti-Soviet forces who executed Communist sympathizers with alacrity. On one occasion Sholokhov avoided hanging at the hands of Nestor Makhno only because he was thought to be too young to know what he was doing. Elements of this adventure are probably incorporated in his short story, "The Way of the Road" (1925).

Sholokhov's serious commitment to literature began when he moved to Moscow in 1922 and joined a group of young writers who called themselves Young Guards and obtained for their quarters one floor of a third-rate hotel. To be sure, he had tried his hand at writing dramatic skits and brief sketches earlier, and he had spoken to friends about a large novel on the life of the Don Cossacks during the Civil War as early as the summer of 1922. He could not, however, be called a true apprentice until he began attending the Young Guard "seminars." One for poets was conducted in Mikhail Švetlov's apartment by Nikolai Aseev; one for prose writers was supervised alternately by Osip Brik and Viktor Shklovsky in the apartment of Mark Kolosov.[1] Sholokhov's exposure to the instruction of these men, brief as it was, must have been invaluable because of their emphasis on the *craft* of writing, the forms and techniques of fiction, rather than exclusively on content.

There are indications, however, that Sholokhov disliked coterie-life among the intellectuals. In a preface to the story "Azure Steppe" (1926) he scorned the verbal ostentation and patriotic naïveté of literary meetings. In a letter to Marc Kolosov he implied that certain magazine editors belong to the "slobbering intelligentsia" because they failed to accept a realistic account of class murder in his story "Food Commissar" (1925).[2]

Unlike many Soviet writers, who found their way to the capital from the farthest ends of the old empire and who plunged enthusiastically into cosmopolitan life, Sholokhov resisted the city. Already in the winter of 1923–24 he returned home briefly in order to wed Maria Petrovna Gromoslavskaya, a local teacher, and took her for their honeymoon to Moscow. But they remained only until May 1924, when they returned to the Don, settling first in Karginskaya, then Bukanovskaya, and finally Veshenskaya. "I wanted," he later said, "to write about the people among whom I was born and whom I knew."[3] To do this, he felt he must remain on native ground. Like the American novelist William Faulkner, whose early career is comparable, Sholokhov derived his greatest inspiration from the regional muse. His attachment to a distinctive land area and culture guaranteed him an independence denied many Soviet writers; it led him to create inimitable fiction, much of which belongs somewhat outside the main stream of Soviet literature but belongs, on the other hand, to a classical Russian tradition by its very rurality.

As one would expect, Sholokhov's life, like that of any busy writer, was relatively uneventful from the time he returned home. During 1924 and 1925 he wrote most of his short stories, and he began *The Quiet Don* in 1925, working at it more or less constantly until 1930 when he composed the first volume of *Virgin Soil Upturned*. He first rented a room

---

[1] I. Lezhnev, "Molodoi Sholokhov," *Izbrannyi stat'i* (Moskva, 1960), 38, 41.

[2] I. Lezhnev, *Put' Sholokhova,* Moskva, 1958, p. 46.

[3] I. Eksler, "Kak sozdavalsia *Tikhii Don,*" *Izvestiia,* June 12, 1940, p. 5.

beneath the blacksmith's shop beside his father-in-law's establishment. To the accompaniment of hammer and anvil, he worked steadily. Later he wrote in a room in his father-in-law's home where, according to his wife, he worked days and nights. His own father is said to have teased him about "scribbling" for a living, but Sholokhov was not to be diverted.[4] The six years from 1925 to 1930 were by far his most productive.

Unfortunately he had become involved in a controversy that very nearly ruined him and, as we see now, did inestimable damage to the creative impulse, which had sustained him up to that time. The difficulty he had had with publishers from the start increased; so that by 1927 the first part of *The Quiet Don* was rejected by the editorial board of *Oktiabr* because it was a chronicle which allegedly lacked political pertinence. The rejected manuscript went finally to Alexander Serafimovich, an honorary editor, who insisted on publication without the radical abridgment that the board demanded. Publication ensued in 1928. But that winter Sholokhov became seriously embroiled because of a rumor that he had purloined the manuscript of the novel from a dead White officer. On March 29, 1929, in *Pravda,* Serafimovich, Alexander Fadeyev, and other prominent writers repudiated the charge as calumny, but the slander did not stop. In the fall a certain Nikolai Prokofev published an article in a Rostov Komsomol paper charging that Sholokhov stood "aside from politics . . . , took no part at all in the life of society . . . ," and hid behind "the little shutters of his house." Further, Sholokhov was accused of conniving with kulaks and interceding on their behalf.

Sholokhov's distress at this time can be determined from a letter he wrote to Serafimovich in April 1930:

I received a number of letters from lads in Moscow and from readers in which they inform me of and inquire about the rumors that are again abroad to the effect that I stole *The Quiet Don* from the critic Goloushev—a friend of L. Andreev.

What am I to do Alexander Serafimovich? I'm sick to death of being a "thief." They've slung so much mud at me. And now a lucky break for all the slanderers: my third volume of *The Quiet Don* won't be printed. This will give them . . . a chance to say: "Look, he's silent; he wrote while he fed on Goloushev; but then the source dried up!"

I've had a productive time just now, finished Volume III; but such a situation will not advance the work. My hand has ceased; I feel wretched. What kind of ill-will is there toward me that my brother-writers should take arms against me . . . ? It all comes from literary circles.[5]

In the fall of 1930 Sholokhov attempted to visit Gorky in Sorrento, obviously hoping for counsel and assistance, but he could not obtain a visa from Mussolini's government. Nine months later, in May 1931, Sholokhov sent Gorky the manuscript of volume III with a plea for help and

---

[4] Willi Bredel, *Sieben Dichter,* Schwerin, 1950, p. 8.

[5] V. V. Gura and F. A. Abramov, *M. Sholokhov seminarii,* Moskva, 1962, p. 177.

a complaint that editors wanted to mutilate his text. The intercession of Gorky and Serafimovich helped; the writing of *Virgin Soil Upturned,* with its immediate relevance to the collectivization campaign, helped more. This novel and the continuation of *The Quiet Don* appeared in serial form simultaneously in 1932. In November Sholokhov became a full member of the Communist party.

Virgin Soil Upturned was enormously popular, in a stage version as well. Negative criticism of Sholokhov's work rapidly diminished, so that he no longer heard himself called a "confused middle peasant" or "a reactionary defender of kulak interests." Instead, he saw his books added to the required reading lists for Soviet school children and used for indoctrination in factories and on farms across the land.

At the same time party bureaucrats managed agriculture so incompetently and abused farming people in Sholokhov's area with such impunity that he tried to oppose them by writing Stalin. His letters were scorned and his own loyalty again impugned. Not until the summer of 1934 were his party credentials verified, and we are obliged to surmise that he barely avoided arrest.

Little wonder, therefore, that writing occupied a secondary place. The 1930's became Sholokhov's first period of silence, a condition familiar to almost every major Soviet writer during some part of his career. To be sure, he slowly completed *The Quiet Don,* the last installment appearing in 1940. For the most part, he busied himself with political and editorial work, making speeches, counseling novice writers, and interviewing visiting dignitaries and ordinary people who sought his advice or advised him how to conclude his novel.

For Sholokhov, as for many other Russians, the Second World War brought relief from the tensions of the purge years. That Sholokhov survived the purges at all may be accounted to his recognition already in 1930 that "scapegoating" was essential in Stalin's order. Having witnessed Stalin's administrative style firsthand during collectivization, Sholokhov learned that prominent leaders often vanished while the inconspicuous remained. He stayed far from Moscow.

Like the majority of writers, Sholokhov served during the war as a correspondent. His contribution was slight, though one of his stories, "The Science of Hatred," is noteworthy for its didactic detestation of Germans and was honored by publication in *Pravda,* June 22, 1942. The war was no less trying for Sholokhov than for other Soviet citizens. While his wife and four children survived, his mother was killed, almost before his eyes, when German planes destroyed his home. Many of his manuscripts perished at the same time. Losses notwithstanding, Sholokhov availed himself of this period of relaxed political discipline to insist that he was not a journalist but a writer of extended prose fiction. The distinction is important in a nation where censors often appear to insist that journalism suffices as a substitute for serious literature.

The repressive measures against literature initiated by Andrei A. Zhdanov after the war drove Sholokhov once again into silence. Passages from his war novel, *They Fought for Their Country,* appeared first in 1943 and 1944, but there was no continuation until a few chapters appeared in 1949, a few more in 1954 and 1959. The work remains uncompleted. Contrary to his own expressed inclination, he relapsed into journalism until the death of Stalin, and the essays he wrote rarely enhance his reputation. Marred by sentimental patriotism and anti-Western vituperation, they would seem to be grudging admissions of Stalin's power to control a nation's mind rather than expressions of independent thought.

These harsh years saw Sholokhov relegated to the role of harmless "classic." If he could not, or would not, publish new fiction, he was obliged to consent in 1952 and 1953 to the publication of bowdlerized editions of *Virgin Soil Upturned* and *The Quiet Don.* In these, Red heroes were systematically purified while the villains were blackened. Even his distinctive idiom was adulterated with grammar school Russian, so that the rural, Cossack flavor faded.

Stalin's death signaled the restoration of these works to their earlier form. Equally important, Sholokhov once again began to publish fiction: chapters of the second volume of *Virgin Soil Upturned* began to appear in 1955, and the novel was finished in 1960. The long story "A Man's Fate," devoted to a Soviet citizen's capacity for suffering and his enduring hope for the future, appeared in 1956. Sholokhov's fiftieth birthday in 1955 occasioned a celebration approximating a national holiday.

During Premier Khrushchev's tenure, the party lionized Sholokhov. Instead of summoning him to the Kremlin, Khrushchev traveled to the Don to visit him, and he invited Sholokhov to accompany him to the United States in 1959. Sholokhov responded to this treatment in kind, trading witticisms and wisecracks with the premier in public as gustily as a court jester.

His role guaranteed certain immunities, so that at the Second Writers' Congress in 1954 he dared to demand that control of literature be in the hands of writers, not bureaucrats. And he has been known to treat the principle of Socialist Realism with jocularity, observing that *The Quiet Don* was first labeled anti-Soviet but presently became a sterling example of the officially endorsed literary form.

In the post-Stalin polarization of writers into liberals, on the one hand, and reactionaries, on the other, Sholokhov's position is ambiguous. He endorses neither extreme: he published no defense of Pasternak, yet he castigates party hacks fiercely; thus neither the youthful innovators nor the old-guard disciplinarians seems particularly fond of him. At the Twenty-third Congress of the CPSU in 1966, he incurred the wrath of many Soviet intellectuals by endorsing legal reprisals against his fellow writers, Sinyavsky and Daniel, whose crime was publishing abroad works critical of Soviet life.

In 1957 he traveled and lectured in Sweden, Norway, and Denmark, making a clear bid for the Nobel Prize, but the trip was not productive. As in 1946 his candidature failed, the award going instead to Boris Pasternak. It began to appear that this particular prize would be denied Sholokhov if the Swedish Academy waited until he produced another distinguished work. Time and the endless demands upon him for social service had taken their toll, and the second volume of *Virgin Soil Upturned* lacked both the audacity and the skill of the first. Sholokhov himself may have lost patience with the Academy when in 1963, at a celebration of the hundredth anniversary of Serafimovich's birth, he observed that the *émigré* Bunin received a Nobel Prize but not Gorky or Serafimovich. "As you see, in the international arena as well, valuations are motivated by class interest. And even in this light, in the light of valuations, there is a false ring to the assertions of bourgeois theoreticians that art is by its very nature above classes . . . ."[6] To his own and the world's surprise, however, the Swedish Academy honored him in 1965.

No comprehensive estimate of his work is yet possible. Soviet critics point with pride to, roughly, fifty million copies of his books printed in more than sixty languages. They acclaim him as a writer of and for the people, an ardent Soviet patriot and a transmitter of Communist party spirit. Too often they merely observe that Sholokhov's major work treats the three great events of Soviet history—the Revolution, collectivization, and the Second World War—so that immediate relevance seems to be the crucial criterion. In recent years, however, critics and scholars have analyzed Sholokhov's work extensively in terms of plot, character, style, and structure, as well as ideological content.

Western critics have been perhaps too cursory and sometimes motivated by political rather than literary concerns. Thus the West German, Jürgen Rühle, implies that Sholokhov is, inadvertently, an anti-Communist in *The Quiet Don*. Sholokhov, he claims, inherited from his middle-class father the revolutionary ideals of the liberal intelligentsia and from his mother the ideals of plebeian, peasant insurrection. This unique union of upper- and lower-class ideologies enables him to express the longings of the *Volk* and the old humanitarian democrats—both ultimately opposed to Bolshevik tyranny. Thus Grigory Melekhov becomes a premature "freedom fighter" instead of an enemy of the people.[7]

Most literary historians in the West avoid ideological polemics of this kind and prefer to see Sholokhov as a second-rate Tolstoy, anachronistically reproducing the "family chronicle" or *Bildungsroman* through the medium of an obsolete and pedestrian realism.

That Sholokhov is a traditionalist, not an innovator, in style and form seems obvious enough. His models are Gogol, Tolstoy, Gorky, and Chekhov, though, as he has explained, he tried to learn something from *all* great

---

[6] *Pravda,* January 22, 1963, p. 2.
[7] *Literatur und Revolution,* Köln, 1960, p. 93.

writers.[8] Yet Soviet and Western critics alike will misgauge him as long as they confine him within an ideological or a perfunctorily traditional frame. His masterpiece, *The Quiet Don,* justifies examination in terms of the European historical novel, the regional novel, and the folk epic. Such a variety of approaches will convey a clearer impression of Sholokhov's scope and will help to explain why his half-literate hero, Grigory Melekhov, has become one of the monumental figures in twentieth-century fiction, appealing to readers of all classes in all nations.

While none of his other works approaches the magnitude of *The Quiet Don,* all contain characters worthy of inclusion in Sholokhov's gallery of fully realized and distinctive human beings. Nagulnov and Uncle Shchukar in *Virgin Soil Upturned* or Andrei Sokolov in *A Man's Fate,* to name only three, are as memorable as any of the portraits in *The Quiet Don.* We may legitimately conclude that Sholokhov's first qualification as a master is his creation of characters who dramatize themselves through significant actions.

The Don cycle is perhaps the most convincing celebration of man in the twentieth century. Its appeal to many Western readers seems restricted by the fact that none of the characters knows enough about the world to sense the full implication of events. Intellectuals never qualify for the hero's role in Sholokhov's novels. Moreover, the absence of cities with their industry and technology precludes any treatment of urban problems, which appear to be crucial in this century of war, revolution, and the loss of individuality. The absence of these things, however, has advantages; without them Sholokhov can concentrate not only on the original stability of his rural society, but precisely upon the process of disintegration during its most climactic moments—a process that typifies the condition of a vast majority of humankind, though not of the middle-class citizen in the West.

Inadequately educated, Sholokhov had to learn as he worked, and the improvement between his clumsy and imitative first compositions and the final sections of *The Quiet Don* testifies to his development. His early stories, often surprisingly sentimental, and his two other novels do not rival it. His genius is best seen first in his judicious selection of detail and sense of proportion, second in the compassion that suffuses his work and animates his characters, third in his poetic diction and the decorous vigor of his figures and descriptions, and last in his syncretic power and his breadth of vision, which permit him to contain Dostoevskian contradictions in a single, steady conception that is Tolstoyan, but without Tolstoy's mechanistic or religious justifications. In addition, his is the first great portrayal of rural Russian life from the viewpoint of rural Russia itself rather than that of the aristocracy or intelligentsia. If he began as a mere chronicler of the Cossack debacle in the Revolution, his *Quiet Don* developed into an autonomous literary work whose characters and actions

[8] I. Eksler, "V gostiakh u Sholokhova," *Izvestiia,* December 31, 1937, p. 3; and M. Soifer, *Masterstvo Sholokhova,* Tashkent, 1961, p. 67.

achieve universality. With good reason has its hero, Grigory Melekhov, been compared with legendary *bogatyrs,* with Hamlet and Don Quixote, though he began as a composite portrait of actual participants in actual events on the Don.

Nowhere in contemporary fiction is there an equally insistent vindication of individual right that does not degenerate into madness and egocentrism or founder on paradoxes between the claims of reason and emotion or between the individual and the community. At the same time, nowhere in contemporary fiction is the individual subjected so ruthlessly to the demands and needs of the community, nor are the rights of "the people" more fiercely championed. It is precisely Sholokhov's seeming contradictions that have provoked critics to quarrel whether he is an optimist or pessimist. Having apparently learned that, in the words of the poet Calderón, "the greatest crime of man is that he ever was born," Sholokhov nonetheless faces the future with equanimity. Such is the measure of his faith in humanity.

Sholokhov's distinction is that he confronts man's fate in terms accessible to all people; thus he occupies a lonely eminence. Few other authors in the twentieth century are both great and popular.

SELECTED BIBLIOGRAPHY

With the exception of published interviews, almost all recorded biographical information about Sholokhov is contained in three books: I. Lezhnev, *Put' Sholokhova, tvorcheskaia biografiia,* Moskva, 1958; V. V. Gura, *Zhizn' i tvorchestvo M. A. Sholokhova,* Moskva, 1955, revised 1960; and F. A. Abramov and V. V. Gura, *M. Sholokhov seminarii,* Leningrad, 1958, revised 1962. Only two non-Russian works deserve mention: Willi Bredel, *Sieben Dichter,* Schwerin, 1950, and Jürgen Rühle, *Literatur und Revolution,* Köln, 1960.

There is no extensive biographical sketch in English. The most reliable information is in Ernest J. Simmons, *Russian Fiction and Soviet Ideology,* New York: Columbia University Press, 1958, and Olga Andreyev Carlisle's *Voices in the Snow,* New York: Random House, 1962. Additional material must be gleaned from the standard histories of Soviet literature and occasional notes in the journal *Soviet Literature* (formerly *International Literature*).

Almost all of Sholokhov's works are available in two translations: Mr. Henry C. Stevens (pseudonym, Stephen Garry) has translated the major works for Putnam and Co., Ltd. in London (reprinted by Alfred A. Knopf in New York); Mr. Robert Daglish has both revised Stevens and translated independently for the Foreign Languages Publishing House (FLPH) in Moscow. Thus *The Quiet Don* appeared in England and the United States in two volumes (abridged by approximately twenty-five per cent), entitled *And Quiet Flows the Don* (1934) and *The Don Flows Home to the Sea* (1940)—Knopf's two-volume boxed edition is called *The Silent Don* (1941); the FLPH edition in four volumes (uniform with recent Russian editions) is called *And Quiet Flows the*

Don, undated. *Virgin Soil Upturned:* volume I appeared in England and the United States in 1935 (retitled *Seeds of Tomorrow* in the Knopf edition); volume II, entitled *Harvest on the Don,* in 1960. The FLPH edition in two volumes is called *Virgin Soil Upturned,* undated. Although fragments of *They Fought for Their Country* appeared earlier, the most accessible translation is in *Soviet Literature* (July and August 1959), 3–56 and 3–72. "A Man's Fate," retitled "The Fate of a Man," translated by Robert Daglish, appeared in *Atlantic,* CCIV (November 1959), 41–45; but it was published earlier as "A Man's Lot" in *Soviet Literature* (May 1957), 3–30. Mr. Stevens translated a substantial selection of Sholokhov's early stories in *Tales from the Don,* London: Putnam, 1961 and will add another volume (to include essays as well as stories) in 1967.

The definitive edition to date in Russian is *Sobranie sochinenii,* eight volumes, Moskva, 1956–60, though it will be supplanted by a nine-volume edition (1965–67) which includes *They Fought for Their Country,* volume I. It is always valuable to compare Sholokhov's most recent texts with those published earlier because revision has been virtually continuous, especially in *The Quiet Don.* For an adequate though incomplete bibliography, see V. V. Gura and F. A. Abramov, *M. Sholokhov seminarii,* Moskva, 1962, pp. 328–64.

The first editions (after serialization) of principal works are: *Donskie rasskazy,* Moskva, 1926; *Lazorevaia step',* Moskva, 1926 and 1930; *Tikhii Don,* four volumes, Moskva, 1928, 1929, 1933, and 1940; *Podniataia tselina,* two volumes, Moskva, 1932 and 1960; *Nauka nenavisti,* Moskva, 1942; *Oni srazhalis' za rodinu,* Moskva, 1945 and 1959; *Sud'ba cheloveka,* Moskva, 1957; stories from the Second World War, essays, and speeches are collected in the eighth volume of *Sobranie sochinenii.*

Dimitri Dimitrievich Shostakovich

by Robert M. Slusser

Dimitri Dimitrievich Shostakovich, Soviet composer, pianist, and public figure, was born in St. Petersburg (now Leningrad) on September 25, 1906, of Russian, Polish, and Greek ancestry. His parents were members of the gentry who had served a term of Siberian exile for revolutionary activities. The boy grew up in a musical environment: his father, a chemical engineer, had a good though untrained tenor voice, and his mother had studied piano at the St. Petersburg Conservatory. Shostakovich's musical talent manifested itself and was recognized early. In 1916 he entered the Glyasser school of music in Petrograd, and in 1917, moved by the stirring events of war and revolution, composed a "Hymn to Liberty" and a

"Funeral March for the Victims of the Revolution." His talents attracted the attention of the composer Alexander Glazunov, who advised him to study composition and who provided financial aid. In the autumn of 1919 Shostakovich entered the Petrograd Conservatory. When his father died in 1922, the young musician helped support his family by playing the piano in movie houses. The physical hardships of the years of revolution and civil war had an adverse effect on his health, and in 1923 he underwent an operation for the removal of tubercular glands in his neck.

At the Petrograd Conservatory Shostakovich studied piano until 1923 and composition, under Maximilian Steinberg, a pupil of Rimsky-Korsakov, until 1925. His unmistakable talent helped him to overcome the prejudice against his "bourgeois" background, but did not prevent hostility from politically militant fellow students, which impeded his career. While at the conservatory he composed a Scherzo for Orchestra (Op. 1) and Eight Preludes for piano (Op. 2), but of the works of this period only *Three Fantastic Dances* for piano (Op. 5) and the First Symphony (Op. 10) were published at the time. In 1966 L. Danilevich published a number of Shostakovich's early works: settings of two Fables by Krylov, and five Preludes for Piano. Toward the end of 1923 Shostakovich made his debut as a performer of his own works. Glazunov, Director of the Petrograd Conservatory, described him at about this time as "one of the best hopes of our art."

The premiere of the First Symphony on May 12, 1926, was a major event. The work achieved immediate popularity, despite certain marks of immaturity, and remains in the active repertoire in the Soviet Union and abroad. The late 1920's were a period of avid experimentation in Soviet music, particularly in Leningrad. The influence of avant-garde composers —Stravinsky, Hindemith, Křenek, Prokofieff, and others—was strong. Shostakovich's early music shows the effect of these influences, combined with a sincere desire to serve the cause of socialism as he understood it. This admixture characterizes the Second Symphony, "Dedicated to October" (Op. 14), first performed on the tenth anniversary of the October Revolution (November 6, 1927), and the Third Symphony, "May Day" (Op. 20), first performed on January 21, 1930, neither of which has retained its initial popularity. Characteristically modernist in style were the First Piano Sonata (Op. 12, 1926) and *Aphorisms* for piano (Op. 13, 1927). On January 18, 1930, the premiere took place, in Leningrad, of Shostakovich's opera, *The Nose* (Op. 15), based on the satirical fantasy by Nikolai Gogol.[1] The music reflects a bewildering mixture of daring experimentation, technical ingenuity, and lighthearted antitraditionalism. During this period Shostakovich also wrote much occasional music for

---

[1] The score of an earlier opera, on Pushkin's poem *The Gypsies,* was destroyed by the composer.

the theater, ballet, and film, working for a time in close association with the Leningrad Theater of Working Youth, where he served as musical director.

It was at about this time that Shostakovich made the difficult choice between the careers of a composer and a pianist. In 1927 he had earned a Certificate of Merit in the First International Chopin Festival in Warsaw; three years later he gave his final public concert as a piano soloist, in a recital at Rostov-on-Don. Subsequently, nevertheless, he continued to appear in public and private performances of his own works.

Dissatisfaction with the concepts and practice of experimental modernism in music, as well as with his journeyman labors in the theater and cinema, led to a crisis in Shostakovich's creative development. A turning point was his opera *Lady Macbeth of Mtsensk District* (Op. 29), composed between 1930 and 1932, and based on a story by Nikolai Leskov. The music of the opera is conceived in broadly symphonic terms, and while manifesting strong modernist influences, emphasizes the psychological and sociological aspects of Leskov's tale of crime and punishment in nineteenth-century provincial Russia. The composer planned the opera as the first part of a tetralogy which would depict the fate of women in tsarist and Soviet Russia, but he was not destined to carry out this ambitious concept.

.A warning that the party intended to take a more active part in directing the activities of creative artists, including composers, was the resolution of the Central Committee of the Communist party in April 1932 dissolving "proletarian" associations in the arts. Henceforward, it was made clear, the individual artist would be given less leeway to choose his subject and style, no matter how much he might consider himself a sincere advocate of socialism. The immediate effect of the turn in the party line with regard to art, as far as Shostakovich was concerned, was to cause him to lay aside an ambitious programmatic symphonic cycle on which he had embarked in 1932, to be entitled *From Marx to Our Days,* based on texts from the founders of Marxism-Leninism. Instead, he turned his attention increasingly toward instrumental music, composing Twenty-four Preludes for piano (Op. 34, 1933), a Sonata for cello and piano (Op. 40, 1934), and the First Piano Concerto (Op. 35, 1933). In these works Shostakovich found inspiration in the music of late romanticism, a dominant influence that was to continue to be of major importance in his later career being that of Gustav Mahler. The concepts of music as a vehicle for emotions both personal and civic, and of the composer as a philosopher responsible for embodying the aspirations and experiences of the society of which he forms a part emerged as the basis of Shostakovich's work. Characteristically, however, he continued to give particular emphasis to humor in music: in an article published in November 1934 he wrote, "I want to defend a legitimate *right to laughter* in so-called serious music."

The Fourth Symphony (Op. 43), composed in 1935–36, was conceived on an ample scale under the immediate influence of Mahler. It was completed and in rehearsal when, on January 28, 1936, *Pravda* launched a devastating attack on *Lady Macbeth of Mtsensk District,* characterizing it as " 'leftist' confusion" both because of its unconventional musical style and its alleged preoccupation with bourgeois crime and sexual intrigue. Although it had been successfully playing for two years in Soviet opera houses, Stalin, in the company of his principal ideological adviser Andrei Zhdanov, had just got around to attending it, and the attack in *Pravda* was generally interpreted as the direct expression of Stalin's personal views— views which in the Soviet Union of the developing "great purge" were tantamount to an authoritative expression of party policy in music. Two weeks later *Pravda* published a similar diatribe against *Bright Stream* (Op. 39), a ballet composed by Shostakovich in 1934 on the subject of life on a collective farm. These articles marked the first direct intrusion of Stalin and the party leadership into the realm of musical aesthetics. Shaken by the attack on his work, Shostakovich withdrew the Fourth Symphony before its first performance; it was not to receive its belated premiere until 1961.

The *Pravda* attacks, coming at a time when Shostakovich was already engaged in a profound critical examination and re-evaluation of his art, had the effect of crystallizing new tendencies in his work and forcing him to resolve his creative dilemma. Having already concluded that for him the path of modernist experimentation in music was a blind alley, and convinced of the artist's duty to serve society as represented and led by the Communist party, Shostakovich accepted as valid *Pravda's* criticism of his work. At the same time the criticism undoubtedly had a traumatic effect on Shostakovich, reinforcing his tendency to introspection and to a tragic view of life. Nor can one ignore the evidence that he interpreted *Pravda*'s attacks as being in some sense a personal affront to him by Stalin; in this connection it is noteworthy that among the friendships which Shostakovich had formed, a particularly warm one was with the Red Army leader Marshal Tukhachevsky, whom Stalin purged on false charges of treason in June 1937.

Shostakovich's "creative answer to criticism" took the form of a new symphony, his Fifth (Op. 47), first performed on November 21, 1937. The Fifth Symphony was at once hailed by Soviet critics as a masterpiece; the influential novelist Alexei Tolstoy, for example, wrote, "Glory to our people, who have given birth to such artists!" Despite its outward conformity to the approved tenets of Socialist Realism in music, including the obligatory affirmative final movement, the Fifth Symphony is basically tragic in conception, though it provides a resolution for personal grief in the protagonist's acceptance of his larger duty to society. The creative balance it achieves is missing from the Sixth Symphony (Op. 54; premiere,

November 5, 1939), in which a long, slow first movement, somber and contemplative, is followed by two short, hectically bright and lively movements amounting to an almost deliberate parody of the party's demand for "positive" elements in music.

In 1938 Shostakovich embarked on an ambitious programmatic symphony, dedicated to the memory of Lenin. The work, whose concept dated back to 1924, was to incorporate folk music and poetry on Leninist themes, but it remained uncompleted, probably because of the fact that during the "great purge" the Stalin dictatorship discouraged any artistic glorification of Lenin. Meanwhile Shostakovich had found a fertile new field of expression in chamber music. His First String Quartet (Op. 49, written in 1935 but first performed on October 10, 1938) was a modest though attractive work, but the Piano Quintet (Op. 57, 1940) has been generally recognized as a masterpiece. A popular favorite as well as a critical success in the Soviet Union, it earned the composer a Stalin First Prize in 1940.

In 1939–40 Shostakovich prepared a new orchestration (Op. 58) of Mussorgsky's opera *Boris Godunov,* designed to replace the customarily performed Rimsky-Korsakov orchestration by one closer to the composer's intentions. Plans for performance were interrupted by the German attack on the Soviet Union in June 1941, and the work remained unperformed until 1959. Soviet participation in the Second World War marked a major epoch in Shostakovich's career. Choosing to stay in his native Leningrad despite the extreme hardships imposed by German attack and blockade, Shostakovich combined service as a volunteer fire warden with work on a new symphony. Between July and December 1941 he composed his Seventh Symphony (Op. 60), dedicated to Leningrad and depicting in musical terms the onslaught and repulse of the Germans. Following its premiere in Kuibyshev on March 5, 1942 (to which the composer had been evacuated), the symphony was enthusiastically acclaimed in the Soviet Union and abroad as a masterpiece which embodied the determination of the Russian people to defend their native land against aggression. With the passage of time and the dimming of wartime fervor, the symphony may have lost some of the emotional appeal it held for contemporaries, but it remains the work in which the composer most successfully solved the problem of combining the expression of individual and civic emotion with artistic mastery.

The Eighth Symphony (Op. 65; premiere, November 4, 1943) also reflects the experiences of the war, but whereas the Seventh is an affirmation of the will to resist the aggressive forces of evil, the Eighth is a distillation of the human tragedy of the war. Less widely popular than the Seventh, the Eighth has retained its power undiminished. A third major work in which the experiences of the war found expression was the Piano Trio (Op. 67; 1944), dedicated to the memory of the composer's close friend Ivan I. Sollertinsky (d. 1944). Despite its more restricted scope, in craftsmanship and emotional profundity the Trio fully matches the wartime symphonies. It is also noteworthy as the first major work in which Shostakovich sought for musical means (thematic, harmonic, and rhythmic) to give expression to the tragedy of the Jewish people in Europe, a search which was to set a distinctive mark on later phases of his career.

A number of smaller works in various genres also date from the war years: an orchestral suite, *Native Leningrad* (Op. 63; 1942), written for the NKVD Ensemble of Song and Dance, the Second Piano Sonata (Op. 61; 1942), the Second Quartet (Op. 68; 1944), and a number of scores for the cinema and theater. A notable project of this period was the unfinished opera *The Gamblers* (originally numbered Op. 63, later withdrawn), on a story by Gogol, which, to judge by available reports, represented the continuation of the experimental vein dating back to *The Nose*.

With the completion of the heroic Seventh and the tragic Eighth symphonies, it appeared to many observers that Shostakovich had blocked out a gigantic symphonic trilogy which only needed for its completion a triumphant Ninth. Perhaps these expectations, reinforcing the composer's characteristic diffidence in challenging comparison with Beethoven and Mahler, help to explain the troubled genesis and unexpected character of his Ninth Symphony (Op. 70). After two unsuccessful starts, Shostakovich wrote the work during the summer of 1945 and it received its premiere on November 3, 1945. It proved to be a short, lighthearted, almost jocular work, mirroring the mood of festivity and release from tension that accompanied the end of the war. Brief quotations from Beethoven's Ninth Symphony in the score serve as a jokingly deprecatory reference to the inevitable comparison. (It should be noted, incidentally, that quotations from his own and other composers' works, as well as less direct stylistic borrowings, have long served Shostakovich as semantically meaningful compositional devices, so that analysis of his compositions often takes on the character of musical detective work. The practice is justified in Shostakovich's usage, however, because it is never used mechanically or arbitrarily; the borrowed or quoted material is organically incorporated into the texture of his own musical thought.)

Shostakovich's wartime services to his native land and the growing recognition in the Soviet Union and abroad of his stature as a major composer did not shield him from undergoing a new period of personal travail and politically motivated attack in the immediate postwar years. Unmistakable signs of tension appeared in the somber, agitated music of the Violin Concerto (composed in 1947–48, but not performed until 1955, when it was identified as Op. 99, although the composer prefers to list it as Op. 77, relating it to the works of the postwar period). More explicit in its identification of some of the tensions which wracked late Stalinist Russia is the song cycle *From Jewish Folk Poetry* (Op. 79; 1948), in which Shostakovich impressively demonstrated his ability to assimilate new stylistic influences and enter into the emotional life of an entire people. As an unequivocal expression of sympathy for a persecuted minority which faced new repression in late Stalinist Russia, the composition of this work was an act of courage which may have helped bring down the party's wrath on the composer.

On February 10, 1948, as part of the postwar Zhdanov campaign for increased ideological purity in the Soviet arts and tightened party controls over the creative intelligentsia, the Communist party's Central Committee adopted a resolution on music which condemned Shostakovich's recent works, along with those of other leading Soviet composers, as "formalist," and which called for the writing of music with explicitly political texts suitable for propaganda exploitation, in place of the textless and "abstract" genres of the symphony and chamber and instrumental music—exactly those forms in which Shostakovich had established himself as a recognized master. For Shostakovich the new party attack was far more serious than that of 1936, for not only were certain tendencies in his music condemned, but the entire basis on which his creative work rested was rejected as unacceptable. The attack was accompanied by the loss of his professorships in the Leningrad and Moscow conservatories (dating from 1937 and 1942 respectively), as well as his membership on the Organizational Board of the Leningrad Section of the Union of Soviet Composers, and by a virtual ban on the performance of his works in the Soviet Union.

Following publication of the decree Shostakovich made valiant efforts to follow the path prescribed for him by the party. He turned to the writing of large-scale choral works with propagandist texts: *The Song of the Forests* (Op. 81; 1949); the chorus, "Glory to Stalin" (1950); and the cantata, *Over Our Motherland Shines the Sun* (Op. 90; premiere November 6, 1952). In addition he devoted increased attention to work for the cinema, with scores for *Young Guard* (1948), *Michurin* (1948), *Meeting on the Elbe* (1948), *The Fall of Berlin* (1949), *Belinsky* (1950, released in 1953), and *Unforgettable 1919* (1951). Recognition of his efforts came with the award in 1950 of a Stalin First Prize.

During the period 1948–53, furthermore, Shostakovich earned his way back into the party's good graces by extensive work in Communist-front organizations, particularly the Communist-sponsored "peace" movement, attending "peace congresses" in New York (1949), Warsaw (1950), and Vienna (1952). In recognition of this phase of his activity he was awarded a Soviet-sponsored International Peace Prize in 1954.

Notwithstanding his apparent acceptance of the party's rebuke, however, Shostakovich continued writing in nonprogramatic forms. Inspired by the 200th anniversary of Bach's death, in 1950–51 he composed a cycle of Twenty-four Preludes and Fugues for piano (Op. 87) which enriched modern Russian music with a work of dazzling structural resourcefulness and thematic invention, although it inevitably falls somewhat short of matching the profundity of its great exemplar, Bach's *Well-Tempered Clavichord*.

He also continued his work in the field of chamber music, with the Third, Fourth, and Fifth quartets (Op. 63, 1946; Op. 83, 1949; Op. 92, 1952).

For Shostakovich the death of Stalin in March 1953 was a major turning point. As though freed from an incubus, during the summer of 1953 he began work on a new symphony, his first in eight years (Tenth Symphony, Op. 93). Even in the *oeuvre* of as subjective a composer as Shostakovich, the Tenth stands out as an intensely personal statement. Not only is its mood tense and tragic, in sharp contrast to the approved concepts of Socialist Realism in music, but the composer has taken pains to emphasize its personal significance by employing as one of its principal themes a four-note sequence based on his own initials, a theme which he had first used in the second movement of the Violin Concerto. Other thematic and stylistic links make it clear that the Tenth Symphony bears a close psychological and emotional relation to the ill-fated Violin Concerto.

The premiere of the Tenth Symphony on December 7, 1953, was the signal for a heated debate in the world of Soviet music, in which ardent admirers of the composer and advocates of greater liberalism in the Soviet arts were ranged against personal enemies and diehard proponents of taut political controls. The outcome of the struggle was decided in the field of politics. The gradual relaxation of party controls in the arts initiated by the Malenkov regime in 1953–55 had a favorable influence on Shostakovich's position, as indicated by the belated appearance of some of his hitherto unperformed major works. The premiere of *From Jewish Folk Poetry* on January 15, 1955, was followed on October 29, 1955, by that of the Violin Concerto. Encouraged by the new atmosphere of relaxation, in 1955 Shostakovich embarked on the revision of his opera *Lady Macbeth of Mtsensk District*.

Further impetus to liberalization in the arts was provided by Khrushchev's attack on the "cult of Stalin" in his "secret speech" to the Twentieth Congress of the party in February 1956, which was hailed as a new charter of liberalism by many Soviet artists and critics, among them Shostakovich. When his fiftieth birthday was celebrated on September 25, 1956, he was awarded the Order of Lenin "for his great contributions to the development of Soviet music." Also indicative of his improved standing was the publication of a number of autobiographical and critical articles at this time, which provide essential materials for the analysis of his creative concepts and artistic evolution. A defense of the tragic in art as life-affirming; outspoken criticism of the bureaucratic administration of Soviet music (but no direct criticism of the party); uncompromising rejection of modernism and avant-garde tendencies in music, especially the atonal or twelve-tone system of composition—these are principal themes in his articles of this period.

For Shostakovich the years 1956–62 witnessed the triumphant vindication of his artistic integrity, as well as new proofs of unimpaired creative vitality. The revival or reworking of old scores was accompanied by a steady succession of new works in a wide variety of genres. The premiere of the Sixth Quartet (Op. 101; 1956), was followed by that of the Second Piano Concerto (Op. 102; composed in 1953), a light, joyful work first performed on May 10, 1957, with the composer's nineteen-year-old son Maxim, to whom the work is dedicated, as soloist. On October 30, 1957, the Eleventh Symphony (Op. 103) was introduced. It is a politically inspired work, with a program based on the 1905 Revolution, and uses themes derived from Revolutionary songs. In the West it has been evaluated as of distinctly minor musical interest; in the Soviet Union, however, it was acclaimed as a masterpiece and in 1958 was awarded a Lenin Prize.

Of great importance for Soviet art generally, as well as for Shostakovich personally, was the resolution of the Central Committee of the party on May 28, 1958, "correcting" its prior resolution on music of 1948, which was now attributed to Stalin's "subjective approach to certain works of art" and to the "extremely negative influence" on him of Molotov, Malenkov, and Beria.

The year 1958 also saw the first performance of *Moskva, Cheremushki,* an operetta in which Shostakovich made a valiant but not wholly successful attempt to acclimatize the American musical comedy in Russia. Of greater significance was the technically demanding Cello Concerto (Op. 107; 1959), dedicated to and first performed by the composer's friend, the cellist M. L. Rostropovich. The Shostakovich reorchestration of *Boris Godunov* received its first performance on November 4, 1959. In 1960 Shostakovich wrote his Seventh and Eighth quartets (Op. 108 and 110), the latter of which is one of his most personal works. Thematically it is based almost exclusively on the theme on his initials, already used in the Tenth Symphony and the Violin Concerto. By skillful handling, nevertheless, the work avoids monotony and serves effectively, in the words of the dedication, as "a memorial for the victims of fascism and war."

Shostakovich's Twelfth Symphony (Op. 112; premiere October 15, 1961), like the Eleventh, was programmatic in character, being dedicated to the memory of Lenin; creatively it marked a falling-off of inspiration, or perhaps the recurrence of the composer's old difficulty in combining a political program with creative freshness. A long-deferred triumph was the premiere of the Fourth Symphony on December 30, 1961, and its enthusiastic reception by a generation which was able to understand and sympathize with the composer's long struggle for his right to expression.

The cycle of programmatic symphonies was continued with the Thirteenth Symphony (Op. 113, 1962), which included a setting of Yevtushenko's poem "Babi Yar" in which Soviet anti-Semitism is condemned; the work thus forms a link in the cycle dating back to the wartime Piano Trio. This time, however, the composer found himself out of step with the party, which had no desire to call attention to the Jewish question in the Soviet Union. Furthermore, the appearance of the Thirteenth Symphony coincided with the swing, late in 1962, toward increased party control in the arts. The work was authoritatively criticized for "substantial defects" in the field of ideology, and the composer hastened to make changes designed to render it more acceptable to the party. Despite this misstep, his position remained strong, and in January 1963 Soviet critics and the public gave a cordial welcome to the premiere of *Katerina Izmailova* (Op. 29/114), the revised version of *Lady Macbeth of Mtsensk District*.

For the 1963 centennial of the annexation of Kirgizia by Russia, Shostakovich composed a short *Overture on Russian and Kirgiz Popular Themes* (Op. 115), and in the same year started work on the score for a film version of *Hamlet* (over thirty years earlier he had composed incidental music for an irreverently updated version of Shakespeare's tragedy for the experimental Vakhtangov Theater in Moscow). The new *Hamlet* score (Op. 116) was completed in 1964, as were the Ninth and Tenth quartets (Op. 117 and 118) and a tone poem, *The Execution of Stenka Razin* (Op. 119), to a text by Yevtushenko. During 1964 Shostakovich was also reported to be working on an opera based on Mikhail Sholokhov's epic cycle of novels about the Don Cossacks.

Shostakovich's most recent works are reported to be the Eleventh Quartet, a cycle of five humoresques, and a satirical composition entitled *Prelude to the Complete Collection of My Works, and Brief Reflections on This Prelude*. In October 1966 the premiere took place of his Second Cello Concerto.

In his personal life Shostakovich has been intensely devoted to his family—in the early years, the Leningrad home created and sustained by his mother, with the composer's sisters Mariya and Zoya; later, following his marriage in 1932 to Nina V. Varzar, a physicist, his own family, including his daughter Galya (born 1936) and his son Maxim (born 1938). (Maxim Shostakovich was trained as a pianist, and in February 1966 made his debut as conductor of the Moscow Philharmonic Orchestra.) In 1954 Shostakovich's wife died and in 1955 his mother; the following year he married Margarita A. Kainova, a secondary school teacher. Despite the physical privations of his early years, he has enjoyed good health and the ability to work with intense concentration for extended periods. In May 1966 he was reported to have suffered a slight heart attack, from which, however, he soon recovered.

At the age of sixty Shostakovich may well have years of creative work ahead of him; even if he does nothing more, however, his place in the history of Russian and world music is secure. In the course of his development he has participated actively in politics, teaching, and administration while maintaining an uninterrupted and intensely active creative life. For an understanding of the relations between party ideology and the creative arts in the Soviet Union, his career is of cardinal significance. He has been the protagonist of some of the major clashes between party ideologists and the creative intelligentsia, and although at times he has been forced to make concessions to party pressure, in the long run he has succeeded in maintaining both his creative independence and his right to determine the forms and content of his art. Thus he inevitably assumes a major significance for the younger generation of composers and artists in the Soviet Union, to whom his career serves as a rich source of instruction, inspiration, and warning.

The sincerity and integrity of Shostakovich's music, combined with his great technical skill and thorough knowledge of the craft of composition, have brought him worldwide recognition as a contemporary master. His foreign honors include election to the American Institute of Arts and Literature (1943); honorary membership in the Swedish Royal Musical Academy (1954) and in the Academy of Santa Cecilia, Italy (1956); honorary doctorate, Oxford University (1958); the Jan Sibelius Prize (1958); appointment as Commander of the Order of Art and Literature, France (1958); membership in the United States Academy of Sciences (1959); and honorary membership in the Mexican Conservatory (1959). In August 1962 he was honored at the Edinburgh Festival of the Arts with the performance of a number of his symphonic and chamber works.

His Soviet honors, in addition to those listed above, include the Order of the Red Banner (1940); Honored Art Worker of the RSFSR (1942); Order of Lenin (1947); People's Artist of the RSFSR (1948); and People's Artist of the USSR (1954). He has served as secretary of the Union of Composers, USSR (1957), first secretary of the Union of Composers, RSFSR (1961), and deputy to the Supreme Soviet of the USSR (1962). He has been a member of the Communist party since 1961. His sixtieth birthday in September 1966 was marked by the award of the Order of Lenin with Gold Hammer and Sickle and the title "Honored Art Worker of the U.S.S.R." in recognition of his services to Soviet music.

SELECTED BIBLIOGRAPHY

The earliest biography in English, V. I. Seroff's *Dmitri Shostakovich, Life and Background of a Soviet Composer,* New York: Knopf, 1943, retains its value as the fullest available account of the composer's family background and early years, prepared with the indispensable collaboration of his aunt, Mme Nadezhda Galli-Shohat. Interesting personal reminiscences are in Nicolai Malko, *A Certain Art,* New York: Morrow, 1966. Soviet biographies, though helpful, must be used critically, since they avoid a candid treatment of the composer's political difficulties. Two have been translated into English: Ivan Martynov, *D. D. Shostakovich* (Moscow, 1946; N.Y., 1947), and D. Rabinovich, *Dmitry Shostakovich, Composer* (Moscow, 1959). There are also studies in German, by Heinz Alfred Brockhaus (Leipzig, 1962); French, by Rostislav Hoffman (Paris, 1963); and Bulgarian, by Venelin Krustev (Sofia, 1954). A short autobiographical sketch written in 1927 is printed in *Sovetskaia muzyka,* September

1966, No. 9, pp. 24–25. The same issue includes studies of the composer and his music by V. Bogdanov-Verezovskii, Givi Ordzhonikidze, and V. Bobrovskii.

The fullest and most accurate guide to Shostakovich's works and to books and articles about him is E. Sadovnikov, compiler, *D. D. Shostakovich. Notografcheskii i bibliograficheskii spravochnik,* 2nd revised and enlarged edition, Moskva, 1965. It includes a list of opus numbers complete through 1964, Op. 119, as well as a list of writings about the composer. The opus numbers are those assigned by the composer himself and sometimes differ from those given elsewhere. A discography is provided, but is limited to Soviet recordings.

Soviet critics and musicologists have done much significant work in analyzing Shostakovich's style and creative evolution. There is an extensive listing in Sadovnikov, *op. cit.,* pp. 202–79. Of particular value are L. Danilevich, *D. D. Shostakovich, sovetskii kompozitor,* Moskva, 1958; L. Mazel', *Simfonii D. D. Shostakovicha, putevoditel',* Moskva, 1960; G. Orlov, *Simfonii Shostakovicha,* Leningrad, 1961; and M. D. Sablinina, *Simfonizm Shostakovicha, put' k zrelosti,* Moskva, 1965. More detailed technical studies include L. Berger (comp. and ed.), *Cherty stilia D. Shostakovicha,* Moskva, 1962; V. Bobrovskii, *Kamernye instrumental'nye ansambli D. Shostakovicha,* Moskva, 1961; and A. N. Dolzhanskii, *24 preliudi i fugi Shostakovicha,* Moskva, 1963. A recent study by L. Danilevich, *Nash sovremennik (tvorchestvo Shostakovicha),* Moskva, 1965, provides valuable documentary and other information on the composer's early years. The early works mentioned above are printed in *Muzykal'noe nasledstvo,* Vol. II, Part 1, Moskva, 1966, pp. 277–298.

For a partial but representative listing of Shostakovich's articles, see Danilevich, *op. cit.,* pp. 185–86. The following are of particular importance: "Deklaratsiia obiazannosti kompozitora," *Rabochii i teatr,* 31 (1931); "Moi tvorcheskii otvet," *Vecherniaia Moskva,* January 25, 1938; "Beseda s molodymi kompozitorami," *Sovetskaia muzyka,* 10 (1955), 10–17; "Dumy o proidennom puti," *ibid.,* 9 (1956), 9–15; and "O nekotorykh nasushchnykh voprosakh muzykal'nogo tvorchestva. Zametki kompozitora," *Pravda,* June 17, 1956.

Alexander Isaevich Solzhenitsyn

by Thompson Bradley

Alexander Solzhenitsyn was born in 1918 to a family of Cossack intellectuals in the city of Rostov-on-Don. Very little biographical information is available and almost nothing is known of his early years. After his father's premature death, Solzhenitsyn was brought up by his mother, a secondary school teacher. He graduated from the University of Rostov-on-Don with a degree in mathematics and physics and later took a correspondence course in literature at Moscow University. During the Second World War he was drafted into the army and reached the rank of artillery captain.

Solzhenitsyn fought at the front from 1942 to early 1945 and was decorated twice for bravery. In February 1945, while in East Prussia, he was arrested on a political charge and sentenced to eight years in a forced labor camp. The charge was based on remarks Solzhenitsyn allegedly had made in a letter to a friend concerning the military shortcomings of the "whiskered one," the latter taken as a derogatory reference to Stalin. His correspondent, an army officer, reportedly received ten years.

Accounts of Solzhenitsyn's activities during the three years following the termination of his sentence in 1953 are in conflict. According to some reports his term was prolonged an additional three years. Other accounts state that he was released in 1953, but kept in exile until 1956. In any case, after more than eleven years he was "rehabilitated" and permitted to return from exile in 1957. (Once again there is a certain confusion over the dates of release and rehabilitation. A probable reconstruction indicates that Solzhenitsyn was freed in 1956, but not rehabilitated, and thus unable to move or travel until the following year.) That year he settled in a village near Riazan, in central Russia, married a chemistry student, and took a position in the local school as a teacher of mathematics and physics.

Solzhenitsyn's biography, at least his public biography, begins more appropriately on November 20, 1962. On that day the Soviet literary journal *Novyi mir* (*New World*) appeared on the newsstands with his short novel *One Day in the Life of Ivan Denisovich*. Within hours of its appearance all copies of the November issue were sold out. This first published work lifted Solzhenitsyn, a complete unknown, to the heights of international fame. Four translations in English alone have been made of the novel. The public reaction to this account of life in a forced labor camp may be compared to that evoked by the revelations of the Communist party's Twentieth and Twenty-second congresses. With the possible exception of Boris Pasternak's *Dr. Zhivago,* no literary work from the Soviet Union has attracted more attention or been subjected to such extensive commentary at home and abroad.

The circumstances underlying the publication of *One Day* are in themselves extraordinary. Solzhenitsyn finished the novel in 1959, but like so many other autobiographical or fictional accounts of prison experiences under Stalin it remained simply another unpublishable manuscript "for the drawer." And so it remained for three years until Alexander Tvardovsky, editor of *Novyi mir,* brought the work to former Premier Khrushchev's attention in the early autumn of 1962. At this time Khrushchev was engaged in a renewed de-Stalinization campaign begun during the Twentieth (1956) and Twenty-second (1961) congresses of the Communist party. To this purpose he personally authorized publication of the novel as written, overruling demands by high party members for cuts in the story and persuaded the Central Committee to approve his decision. Khrushchev's move was not without precedent, for in October he had officially opened the campaign in literature by sanctioning the publication of Yevgeny Yev-tushenko's biting poem "Stalin's Heirs" (*Pravda,* October 21, 1962). Soon after, *Pravda* printed a short story entitled "Good Memory" which tells of a woman Communist's return home after many years in exile. Georgi Shelest's "The Nugget" appeared a week earlier in *Izvestiia.* Chronologically this story was the first published fictional account of the cruel conditions in a forced labor camp. To a degree, therefore, the ground had been laid for *One Day,* by far the most far-reaching and artistically accomplished of the four works.

The significance of this official sanction cannot be exaggerated. It established the novel as ideologically unassailable and virtually guaranteed its critical success. Enthusiastic, superlative reviews by highly placed writers and critics appeared in the journals and newspapers. But the party, and Khrushchev not the least, soon had good cause for regret. In December, with the discovery of semiabstract works by Moscow artists, the campaign for liberalization abruptly ended. A wave of reaction followed with an ideological crackdown in all the arts which lasted from December 1962 to May 1963. Throughout most of this period Solzhenitsyn, as author of *One Day,* enjoyed a special immunity from the sharp criticism leveled at the "liberals." One critic demurred and criticized the novel for its negative, incomplete picture of the time.[1] She was promptly rebuked the following week in the same publication. Official displeasure was couched solely in asides. In an oblique reference to *One Day* not a little tinged with regret, Leonid Ilyichev, the party theoretician, complained that "the journals and publishing houses were swamped with manuscripts on the camp theme." Khrushchev echoed this plaint later and warned of the dangers inherent in such material, particularly vis-à-vis the Western "sensation seekers." Implicit in this warning was a clear recognition of the political danger the novel represented and more importantly the precedent it had set for future literature. What had begun as a useful political maneuver had become an ideological liability. Clearly, the party could not undermine its authority at so critical a juncture by retracting its approval.

Solzhenitsyn's aim in *One Day* is seemingly modest in the extreme. The novel renders a close account of one man's day in a forced labor camp from early morning to lights out and, with a masterful eye to detail, depicts his attempts to survive hunger and cold, escape punishment, and preserve

[1] L. Fomenko, *Literaturnaia rossiia,* No. 3, January 11, 1963. Adverse criticism of *One Day* began to appear only late in the spring of 1963. Up to that time critics contented themselves with attacking Solzhenitsyn's two stories "Matryona's Homestead," and "An Incident at Krechetovka Station," published in January 1963. Interestingly enough, their criticism closely parallels that of Fomenko's earlier article. It is important to note, however, that there would seem to be no direct connection between this criticism of Solzhenitsyn and the general antiliberal reaction of that spring. Solzhenitsyn's name never appeared among those under attack, and he was never called upon to recant or reform.

the strength to live another day. The hero, Ivan Denisovich Shukhov, is a simple peasant. During the war he is captured along with his unit by the Germans. He escapes and with great difficulty makes it back to the Russian lines only to be arrested as a spy and sentenced to ten years of hard labor.

The narrative opens in the camp and follows Shukhov through a day of his life there. Telescoped into that one day are the eight years he already has served. Sharing in his fate are men of highly varied backgrounds and professions—Baptists, Old Believers, non-Russians, artists, party officials, intellectuals, and professional soldiers. The very breadth of its social spectrum reveals the all-inclusiveness of the terror, offering in microcosm a reflection of the society in general. The choice of a peasant for the hero-narrator is doubly ingenious, for it plays upon the traditional Russian empathy for the simple Everyman, the voice of the many, while it subtly precludes criticism for ideological unsoundness by exploiting the over-sentimentalized peasant cliché of Socialist Realism. The difference here lies in Solzhenitsyn's inventive treatment. By extending this method of metaphorical compression into his exclusive focus on the camp as reality, Solzhenitsyn leads irrecoverably to the conclusion that the camp, the prisoners, and the one day were *the reality* of the Stalin years. No one, including Khrushchev, had gone so far in presenting the unvarnished truth. The political implication made sensational news, but few critics noted the immense literary significance of *One Day.*

The narrative resonates with cruel ironies. The prisoners build the walls which imprison them. They work with energy, not out of submissiveness but to keep warm. Moreover, the men are as harsh and intolerant toward malingerers and laggards as are the guards, for their survival demands it. One malingerer may cause an entire brigade to lose its ration; a laggard will keep the prisoners standing in the subzero cold until the guards come up with the right number. As Shukhov puts it with characteristic pithiness: "Who is the prisoner's worst enemy? The guy next to him." The insidiousness of the system lies in its transformation of the victims into willing accomplices.

Above all, the novel is a tribute not simply to the will to survival, but to human dignity and self-respect in survival. Shukhov is a hero because he refuses to be crushed or dehumanized by his fate. In a small but telling gesture he removes his hat at meals, no matter what the temperature. Despite his gnawing hunger, seldom relieved by the meager fare, he will not degrade himself by cadging or stealing scraps from the others' plates and scorns the "jackals" who do. At the building site, in a rare lyrical scene reminiscent of the haymowing episode in *Anna Karenina,* Shukhov works with skill and intense professional pride. Like Levin he loses himself in his work and enjoys a moment of transcending freedom in the pleasant sensation of honest sweat and in the rhythmic motion. Here Solzhenitsyn recalls Tolstoy's theme of the transfiguring nature of physical labor. Shukhov enjoys a natural intimacy with nature, with life and death, and lives in a highly ethical relationship with others. He has a rootedness, a stability, and a freeness which mock his captors and their walls. In the search for classical models critics have compared him to the peasant Karatayev in *War and Peace*. The comparison is appropriate, but the similarity superficial. Both come to stand for man's irreducible freedom and greatness before tyranny. But Karatayev remains a bloodless, disembodied ideal, while Shukhov emerges a fully individualized and dramatically realized human being. To a great extent Solzhenitsyn's success here and in the over-all effect of his tale derives from his choice of narrative method.

One Day unfolds in the *skaz* style of oral narration: that is, the story is told in Shukhov's own words and from his point of view. But it is no ordinary monologue or confessional in the first person. In order to exploit and simultaneously reach beyond the structural limitations, Solzhenitsyn employs a well-integrated combination of first- and third-person narration with certain inventive variations. The traditional first-person narrative is modified by a novel form of indirect speech wherein the narrator, whether Shukhov or Solzhenitsyn, speaks of himself as if in the third person as well as in the first person. Solzhenitsyn further modifies the narrative "I" by replacing it with the more forceful generalized "you" coupled with direct speech, as in:

So he could let his eyes wander a little and look at other bowls around him. The fellow on the left had nothing but water. The way these bastards treated a man! You'd think they were just prisoners too!

These variations help to blur the narrative distinction between author and hero while the *skaz* technique lends dramatic immediacy and credibility to the hero and thereby to his tale. Where the action extends beyond the range of Shukhov's possible experience or knowledge, the third-person narration intervenes quite unnoticeably. Solzhenitsyn effects this easy movement between indirect and direct narration by sustaining Shukhov's *sui generis* style and viewpoint throughout. Only in the tone is it possible to discern a difference between the narrative voice (Solzhenitsyn) and the dramatic voice (Shukhov).

Shukhov's prose style is vivid and racy, mixing peasant colloquialisms and sayings with prison jargon, interlaced with grammatical errors and neologisms. Before us, speaking directly to us, stands Ivan Denisovich vibrant and alive. We know him because we recognize his voice.

This crude expressiveness suits its harsh subject perfectly and is set off by the severely laconic, often axiomatic phrasing. At times, the novel achieves the astringent terseness of a documentary report or a battle plan. Consistent with this mode of expression Solzhenitsyn sustains a restrained, almost matter-of-fact tone. *One Day* is not a compendium of horrors, nor is it a bitter indictment. If anything, it is striking for its apparent objectivity. This very restraint accounts for the novel's devastating effect. And furthermore, by filtering the experience through a naïve and limited consciousness, Solzhenitsyn obtains the maximum impact of understatement, stripped of the obvious and expected indignation. For a sense of the intolerable cruelty and injustice grows in 'the reader's awareness as he discovers the radical difference between the perception and the reality. No Russian writer since Isaac Babel has employed the *skaz* with such power and talent.

In 1963 Solzhenitsyn published three stories. "Matryona's Homestead" and "An Incident at Krechetovka Station" appeared together in the January number of *Novyi mir,* and the third, "For the Good of the Cause," in the July issue of the same journal. The first two gave conclusive proof, if any were needed, of the new writer's fine talent and revealed the breadth of his ability. (Solzhenitsyn is no one-novel writer, as Tvardovsky pointed out in his remarks in *Novyi mir*'s jubilee in January 1965, nor is he limited to one subject.) The stories treat diverse subjects from a variety of narrative approaches.

Some critics consider "Matryona's Homestead" the finest short story written in the post-Stalin period. Without doubt it is the most artistically accomplished of the three. Set in a rural locale in central Russia around the time of Stalin's death, the story has as its central figure a truly eccentric and extraordinary human being. Matryona is a "good" woman in an imperfect world, a kind of half-pagan, half-early-Christian saint who lives and works for others out of an all-embracing selfless generosity. As a consequence of her Christian folly her home is destroyed and she is killed.

In style and language "Matryona's Homestead" closely resembles *One Day*. Matryona speaks with the same peasant laconism which frequently borders on aphorism punctuated with a rich earthiness and warm humor. The narrative represents a story within a story and may be seen as a chronological sequel to the novel. The framing story concerns a returning political exile who comes to live with Matryona while he teaches in the nearby village school. Through him the reader is introduced to the real hero, Matryona, whose story merges with the narrator's and comes to dominate the entire foreground. In its meandering way, overlapping and cutting back on itself, the loose-textured structure traces the narrator's gradual revelation of Matryona as it uncovers the mysteries of this deceptively simple woman's nature. The village in its narrowness and greed remains unable to comprehend her other than as an object of ridicule and exploitation. Only an outsider, the exile, ironically, has the spirit and sensitivity to appreciate her and mourn her tragic death.

The last two works are more explicitly political in statement. "An Incident at Krechetovka Station" exposes the destructive atmosphere of suspicion and fear rampant during Stalin's reign, while "For the Good of the Cause" decries the presence of this legacy and Stalin's heirs in the present.

Lieutenant Zotov, the hero of "An Incident at Krechetovka Station" is a naïve idealist. Denied a frontline assignment, as earlier he had been rejected brusquely as a volunteer to fight in Spain, he languishes behind the lines as an aide to the commandant of a backwater railroad substation. Unlike the others, he shuns the loose off-duty life in the rear and spends his evenings in solitary study of Marx's *Capital,* when not closely following and torturing over the course of the war. Zotov's idealism and principled moral sense cut him off from his compatriots who consider him an eccentric. He is forced into an internal exile.

As in *One Day* the narrative action is restricted in setting and time to one room during part of the day. Toward evening an extravagantly mannered older man, who introduces himself as Tveritinov, comes to Zotov for permission to continue his journey on the next train out. The stranger's manner and his bizarre, wholly unseasonal dress capture the lieutenant's imagination. In the ensuing conversation a feeling of kinship develops between the two men, and for the first time in months Zotov is reprieved from his loneliness. A chance remark by Tveritinov puts Zotov on his guard and abruptly destroys the mood. Just to be safe the lieutenant has the man retained for questioning by the NKVD as an enemy agent. Later, plagued by Tveritinov's parting cry and his own doubts, Zotov makes inquiries with the secret police. The NKVD agent cuts him off and drily comments: "We never make mistakes."

"An Incident at Krechetovka Station" has been overshadowed by the other works, yet it is a thoughtful, artfully constructed piece of writing. Solzhenitsyn retards the central moment of the story while he carefully establishes Lieutenant Zotov as a sensitive man of principle and integrity. Through flashback to earlier experiences and more immediately by a succession of encounters he reveals the hero's eccentric justness and goodness. While they are integral to the story and enhance the action these scenes are in truth only preparation for the major encounter with Tveritinov and Zotov's act. Solzhenitsyn goes to the extreme, once again, to make his point: If the best of men could not escape the insidious web of fearful suspiciousness, is it strange that lesser men did not? In this principal scene the sustained conversation between Zotov and Tveritinov further demonstrates Solzhenitsyn's impressive, creative handling of language and dialogue for creating mood and character. Tveritinov's peculiar theatrical manner and the tone and resonance of his voice are so vividly brought out that he emerges fully differentiated and individualized. Yet we know Tveritinov not only by what he says and does, but also from Zotov's inner reactions and responses. We are compelled to share directly every shade of emotion and every sensation as Zotov experiences it. The effect is a double, complementary portrait of Tveritinov and simultaneously an expanded insight into the hero. Although the body of the story unfolds in an impersonal third-person narration, Solzhenitsyn shifts here to a combination of direct and indirect narration—a counterpoint of Zotov's inner thoughts and the objective account—which augments the tempo and sharpens the emotional and psychological poignancy of the scene.

"For the Good of the Cause" is Solzhenitsyn's first published work to deal with the contemporary scene in Russia. It is most noteworthy for its liberal and moral stance. The story takes place at a technical institute which has had to operate in makeshift quarters since its founding. At the beginning of the new semester the entire institute is caught up in a fever of excitement over the long-anticipated move into a new building under completion nearby. When the institute's director attempts to obtain final approval to move, he encounters unexplained delays and endless temporizing. Despite his appeal to the party the promised building is taken away from the institute. A group of bureaucrats motivated solely by political expediency gain the building rights through devious means "for the good of the cause." The director is told to wait and given more dubious promises for the future.

Artistically, the story is inferior to the earlier writing. The prose is pedestrian and the characters are flat and rather superficially treated. Fedor Mikheevich, the hero, bears a certain resemblance to his predecessors, but is pale in comparison. It is as if Solzhenitsyn had become so involved in his argument that he sacrificed artistic execution to the moral, political point. Most likely the story will be remembered best for the sharp debate it provoked on the pages of *Novyi mir* and *Literaturnaia gazeta* during the fall of 1963.

After his dramatic appearance with a novel and three stories in less than a year Solzhenitsyn quietly disappeared from the literary scene. The editors of *Novyi mir* prominently advertised more stories for 1964. A new novel was scheduled for the following year. No new works materialized. Then, after more than two and a half years of silence Solzhenitsyn brought out "Zakhar-kalitá" in the January 1966 issue of *Novyi mir*. This last work is little more than an anecdote, an occasional piece. The author recalls a visit to Kulikovo Pole (Snipes' Field) the scene of a famous Russian victory over the Mongol and Lithuanian armies in 1380. There he and his traveling companion meet and spend the night with Zakhar, the strange and irascible caretaker of the monument and grounds. Outside of a few vivid touches in the portrait of Zakhar and some dextrous word play "Zakhar-kalitá" reveals little of Solzhenitsyn's earlier talent and it is too slight to form any judgment of his future promise.

Solzhenitsyn breaks radically with Socialist Realist literary tradition. He eschews the factory and collective farm theme with its glorification of joyful collective labor and concentrates instead on the neglected and hitherto forbidden areas of Russian life. His heroes are loners and outsiders. They are motivated by a moral view of life which suffuses their every act with a spirit of individual dignity and generosity. The venal world around them victimizes them as eccentrics and fools. This characterization has led some to see a Christian symbolism concealed in the works and particularly in the characters Shukhov and Matryona. There is some evidence to support this interpretation; Solzhenitsyn's essential concern clearly extends beyond the Russian political reality to the universal theme of good and evil. But it is more probable that he is working within the established humanist tradition, developed in Russian literature over the past hundred years, without any specific reference to Christianity or religious values. Whatever the case, whereas other contemporary Russian writers, such as Kazakov, Aksyonov, and Tendryakov, have depicted the outsider quite effectively, none has gone as far as Solzhenitsyn. In the naïve spontaneity and simple justness of their lives his major characters challenge not only the political system but the entire civilization. Nowhere is this expressed with more biting irony than in the final lines of "Matryona's Homestead":

We all had lived side by side with her and had not understood that she was that righteous one without whom, as the proverb says, no village can stand.

Nor any city.

Nor our whole land.

These lines have the ring of a credo and must be considered the key to the works.

Solzhenitsyn does not experiment with the basic structure of the story or the novel. Events are presented in a rational, logical order. Nor does he attempt new insights into the subconscious and the state of alienation through distorted perception of reality or fragmented point of view. Solzhenitsyn is no innovator. Rather, he is a synthesizer. At their best, his works represent a fusion of the nineteenth- and early twentieth-centuries' literary themes and moral values with the contemporary Russian consciousness. His recently translated "prose poems" offer a further excellent example of this synthesis, where historical and cultural continuity is revealed in a series of parallels between Peter's "intentional city" and Stalin's Leningrad and between Soviet Moscow and "the Third Rome."[2] Solzhenitsyn's literary forebears are the great writers and stylists Tolstoy, Leskov, and

---

[2] Translated by Harry Willetts in *Encounter* (March 1965), 3–9. "Prose poems" seems an appropriate description for these short prose studies which draw so heavily on past literary tradition and bear a striking resemblance in style and form to Turgenev's cycle of prose poems "Senilia" (1877–82). They have not been published in the Soviet Union and circulate in typescript under the title "Etiudy i krokhotnye rasskazy" ("Studies and Sketches"). Copies have been brought out to the West with varying numbers of "poems," which makes it difficult to ascertain how many were written. The typescript with the largest number contains eighteen, all but three of which appear in *Encounter*. The missing "poems" are "A Prayer," "The Old Bucket," and "Means of Travel" ("Molitva," "Staroe vedro," and "Sposob dvigat'sia").

Babel, and their influence is felt everywhere in his writing. His extraordinary appearance on the Russian literary scene marks a crucial point in the renaissance of Russian literature through this revival of the classical heritage to render the new Soviet experience.

Outside of the bare facts nothing else is known about Solzhenitsyn's life before the appearance of *One Day,* and very little has come to light since that time. The major cause lies in the writer himself. He is an extraordinarily taciturn and shy man who values privacy above all else. Like the heroes of his stories he keeps his own counsel. He refuses to give interviews and does not take part in public reading or literary debates. Notwithstanding his great popularity at home and his international fame Solzhenitsyn has remained in the same little village near Riazan. He has given up teaching to write and is said to be working on a play. There are reports that he is writing verse and possibly a second novel based on his experience in concentration camp.[3]

SELECTED BIBLIOGRAPHY

Since Solzhenitsyn has refused to grant interviews, the only source for biographical information is an officially sanctioned one-page biography released by the Soviet News Agency, TASS. This release was composed for journalists and is exceedingly short on details. The best Soviet critical studies are: V. Lakshin, "Ivan Denisovich, ego druz'ia i nedrugi," *Novyi mir,* 1 (1964), 223–45; T. G. Vinokur, "O iazyke i stile povesti A. I. Solzhenitsyna *Odin den' Ivana Denisovicha,*" *Voprosy kul'tury, rechi,* Moskva, 1965, pp. 16–32. The debate over "For the Good of the Cause" is contained in the following publications: Iu. Barabash, "Chto est' spravedlivost'," *Literaturnaia gazeta,* August 31, 1963; "O rasskaze A. Solzhenitsyn dlia pol'zy dela," *Novyi mir,* 10 (1963), 193–98. Several non-Soviet articles deserve mention: R. Gul', "A. Solzhenitsyna, sotsrealizm i shkola Remizova," *Novyi zhurnal,* 71 (1963), 58–74; V. Zavalishin, "Povest' o 'mertvykh domakh' i sovetskom krest'ianstve (Ob *Odnem dne Ivana Denisovicha*)," *Grani,* 54 (1963), 133–50; H. Zamoyska, "Soljénitsyne et la grande tradition," *La Table ronde,* 185 (1963), 61–81.

There is no extensive biographical sketch in English. Critical articles depend heavily on the TASS release for background information. A reconstruction and analysis of the publication of *One Day in the Life of Ivan Denisovich* is presented in several sources: P. Benno, "The Political Aspect," *Soviet Literature in the Sixties,* edited by Max Hayward and Edward L. Crowley, New York and London: Praeger, 1964, pp. 189–93; P. Johnson, "The Regime and the Intellectuals," *Problems of Communism: Special Supplement,* 4 (July–August 1963), II-X passim; T. P. Whitney (ed. and tr.), *The New Writing in Russia,* Ann Arbor: University of Michigan Press, 1964, pp. 432–36; B. Rubin, "The Decade Since Stalin," *Soviet Literature in the Sixties,* pp. 89–96. (This collection contains very useful commentaries on Solzhenitsyn by other contributors);

[3] It is possible that the verse mentioned here refers to the unpublished "prose poems."

G. Zekulin, "Solzhenitsyn's Four Stories," *Soviet Studies,* XVI, 1 (1964–65), 45–62; N. Zisserman, "The Righteous Ones: A Study in Figural Interpretation," *Landfall,* XVIII (1964), 140–51.

One Day in the Life of Ivan Denisovich is available in four translations: the best known are by Max Hayward and Ronald Hingley, New York and London: Praeger, 1963, and by Ralph Parker, New York: Dutton and London: Victor Gollancz, 1963. Mr. Parker's translation was published in *Soviet Literature,* 2 (1963) and appeared serially in *Moscow News* in December 1962 and January 1963. Thomas P. Whitney's translation for Crest Books (Fawcett) in New York (1963) has a fine introductory essay and contains an early attempt at an interview with Solzhenitsyn in the appendix. The fourth translation, by Bela Von Block with an introduction by Jacques Katel, was published in New York by Lancer Books in 1963. Harry T. Willetts' translation of "Matryona's Homestead" appeared in *Encounter* (May 1963), 28–45, and was republished in *Half-way to the Moon: New Writings from Russia,* edited by Patricia Blake and Max Hayward, New York: Holt, Rinehart, and Winston, 1964, pp. 51–91. A second rendering by Paul W. Blackstock, retitled "Matryona's House," appeared under the general title *"We Never Make Mistakes": Two Short Novels,* Columbia: University of South Carolina Press, 1963, which contains, in addition, the only translation of "An Incident at Krechetovka Station," also by Blackstock. "For the Good of the Cause" exists in a single translation by Max Hayward and David Floyd, New York and London: Praeger, 1964. The great majority of the "prose poems" was translated by Harry T. Willetts in *Encounter* (March 1965), 3–9. A small selection of these had appeared earlier in *New Leader,* January 18, 1965. "Zakhar-kalitá" has not been translated.

With the exception of the "prose poems," which remain unpublished in the Soviet Union, all of Solzhenitsyn's works were printed in the literary monthly *Novyi mir: Odin den' Ivana Denisovicha, Novyi mir,* 11 (1962), 2–68; "Dva rasskaza" ("Sluchai na stantsii Krechetovka" and "Matrenin dvor"), *ibid.,* 1 (1963), 9–63; "Dlia pol'zy dela," *ibid.,* 7 (1963), 58–90; "Zakhar-kalitá," *ibid.,* 1, (1966), 69–76. *Odin den' Ivana Denisovicha* was republished in book form in Moscow in 1963. There is no edition of the collected works. Flegon Press in London has made photo copies of *Odin den' Ivana Denisovicha* and "Sluchai na stantsii Krechetovka" and "Matrenin dvor" and put them out in paperback. By a similar process Russian Language Specialties in Chicago has reprinted "Dlia pol'zy dela."

Alexander Trifenovich Tvardovsky

by Vera S. Dunham

> Without the slightest artifice
> Tvardovsky sang in nocturnal Florence
> as one sings in Smolensk
> and, transfigured like a tear,
> his closed face
> soared
>   over the tapestries. . . .

These are the opening lines of Andrei Voznesensky's poem in which he recollects an evening Alexander Tvardovsky and he had spent together in a hotel in Florence with Italian friends. He suggests that Tvardovsky managed to reach the foreigners present with his songs, even the hotel porters downstairs . . . but not in the fullest measure, not entirely.

> . . . They cannot understand that the hideous face
> of the Great Patriotic,
> reflected in modernist mirrors,
> touches ground among us.
> An anxious bird, it lands.
> Staring into the eyesockets of the bird
> one of us knows
> that he sings for the last time. . . .[1]

Though it may be rude to use only a fragment of a good poem for introductory purposes, the justification lies in the shorthand manner with which poetry communicates. A dozen short lines speak of Tvardovsky's values: the simplicity of an ancient peasant chant which expresses his own unmannered self; the solemn earnestness with which he commemorates the war; his controlled and tired face.

Tvardovsky, now in his late fifties, is a grandee among the Russian literati. Soviet textbooks insist on the resemblance between his poetry and that of the populist giant of the nineteenth century, Nikolai Nekrasov (1821–78). The resemblance might even be more striking in their public roles as editors of influential journals. The work of literary midwives is of very special importance, but it is primarily national and does not readily

---

[1] A. Voznesensky, "Pochta so stikhami," *Znamya,* 11 (1963), 50.

lead to world fame. If an editor is an editor par excellence, his commitment to the search of new talent keeps him in the shadow. Important as his activity is to the life of literature, especially in a society known for things other than freedom, it is nevertheless "untranslatable." Thus, Tvardovsky is as unknown abroad as he is famous in Russia. But consensus about him is far from being "monolithic." If the liberal Soviet intelligentsia has made up its mind about him, indeed, this cannot be said of that branch of the power elite which is still charged with the control of the literary output. Soviet liberals respect Tvardovsky, and their adversaries are uneasy about him because he has been so far a most successful strategist of the literary cause. Tvardovsky's advocacy of greater freedom in literature is implemented by his consistent support and protection of the young practitioners of a liberated literature. Granting all the differences in goals and behavior between the leaders of the opposition against the Establishment in periods as different as the mid-nineteenth and the mid-twentieth centuries, the least one can say is that Nekrasov challenged authoritarianism in his time and so does Tvardovsky today.

His career started some thirty years ago with the publication in 1937 of *Land Muravia,* a folk tale devoted to the vicissitudes of collectivization. At that time Tvardovsky was still a student. The work was considered at once a major literary event and included on the required reading list of students majoring in literature. As a Soviet critic remarked, Tvardovsky could have easily drawn an examination question about his own poem in the institute in which he was enrolled.[2] Since then a great deal has been written about him, condemnation and praise both, depending on the period, repressive or less so. Because he has been under fire and because he occupies a key position in the literary struggle of the left against the right, it is not surprising that an objective full-scale study of his work does not yet exist in Russia. Unquestionably, however, he is a powerful man. And power of a humane and humanitarian kind becomes him well. This is borne out even by his external appearance. Anything but a hermit poet, Tvardovsky the public tribune is much photographed. One sees strong, large features, a powerful forehead, the broad and handsome face of a successful middle-aged kolkhoz chairman, rather than that of a harassed urban intellectual. The eyes seem kind, sad, and skeptically intelligent, the eyes of a wise peasant.

Tvardovsky is chief editor of *Novyi mir* (*New World*), the most influential and prestigious of the Soviet literary journals; and it should perhaps be noted that literary journals are charged with an importance in the life of the Soviet intelligentsia not readily understood in the West. *Novyi mir* possesses its own tone and profile, the shaping of which in recent years has been largely Tvardovsky's achievement. The editorial board welcomes

[2] N. Vil'iam-Vil'mont, "Zametki o poezii A. Tvardovskogo," *Znamia,* 11/12 (1946), 198.

conventional writers more cordially than modernists, prefers prose to poetry, and sponsors a cognitive Chekhovian style in fiction. On occasion sharp and daring social criticism is launched in *Novyi mir* through a genre it especially favors, namely, the sketch (*ocherk*). Different from its counterpart in the West, this genre is rather monumental and, because of its length, represents journalistic reportage organized formally as fiction. As civic literature, the sketch turns out to be an effective blend of *Dichtung und Wahrheit* (poetry and truth). *Novyi mir* stands for the emphasis on *Wahrheit*. Above all, the journal has acquired under Tvardovsky's tenure that rare quality that might be called dignity, a quality that he himself possesses as a public figure.

As a result of his editorial courage—and these are only a few examples—the following publications in *Novyi mir* can be cited; Yuri Bondarev's novel, *Silence* (1962), openly treating of wartime denunciations; Alexander Yashin's *Wedding in Vologda* (1962), a candidly naturalistic account of the isolation and of the backward mores of northern peasants; Victor Nekrasov's relaxed, perceptive, and sophisticated travelogue of Italy and the United States, *Both Sides of the Ocean* (1962), which enraged Khrushchev because of its pro-Western spirit. In spite of its semi-candid nature, Ilya Ehrenburg's monumental memoirs managed to reveal in a sensational way the maiming fear of the intelligentsia under Stalin. The reactionaries of the literary apparatus attacked the book twice. The combination of Tvardovsky's dogged determination and patience brought about the major literary event of "the thaw" period. It was the publication of Alexander Solzhenitsyn's *One Day in the Life of Ivan Denisovich* (1962). When reactionary forces collided with the new left over the evaluation of this work, Tvardovsky backed his stand by publishing, at a propitious moment, a commodious and magnanimous defense of Solzhenitsyn, written by a member of *Novyi mir*'s editorial staff, V. Ya. Lakshin, under the title of "Ivan Denisovich, His Friends and Enemies." This might be an appropriate place to mention that *Novyi mir* launched Andrei Sinyavsky (Abram Tertz) as a critic and literary scholar. Before and after Sinyavsky and Daniel were tried and sentenced for having published fiction abroad, Tvardovsky's journal continued to champion the cause of truth with which literature in his view is entrusted. For instance, the February 1966 issue of *Novyi mir* contained a remarkable piece, "Legends and Facts" by V. Kardin which dealt head-on with the disparity between standard official myths and historical reality. And both the January and February issues contain the realization of Kardin's demands: a movingly honest, bitter, tragic war novella by the talented, young Byelorussian novelist Vasily Bykov, suggestively entitled *The Dead Feel No Pain*. Establishmentarians once more reacted by opening fire on Tvardovsky and his journal during the spring of 1966.

It needs repeating that the above is only a partial record of Tvardovsky's activity as an editor. But he is also, and in his view, primarily a poet.

However, Tvardovsky the poet is, as we have already suggested, virtually unknown to the general reading public in the West. Furthermore, Western scholars who *do* know him as a poet appraise him variously. The more exacting among them are inclined to dismiss him as a popularizer, a balladeer, a contributor to mass culture only. Curiously, however, even his severest critics find it hard to deny that he has talent.

Tvardovsky's own literary work and his devotion to the general cause of literary independence are so closely related that it seems unwise to separate them. For his muse is a public one and so are his ministrations to the muses of those poets and writers who are helping the revival of Russian literature.

From the very beginning of his career, Tvardovsky sought to communicate with the general reader by means of his "unsecretive" and conventional poetry and to discuss in it the most important social issues of the last thirty years. In so doing, he posited and defended values which have consistently been those of a neo-populist who pleads for tolerance, personal loyalties, compassion; in short, his is a humanist posture in the traditional Russian sense.

The civic tradition, to which Tvardovsky's *oeuvre* clearly belongs, presents an equally traditional obstacle in the way of a fair evaluation of his poetry. The difficulty looms especially large when the appraisal is made outside the confines of this civic tradition itself. Whatever the vantage point, the primacy of aesthetic considerations is unquestionably legitimate. But legitimacy is not always free of narrowness. Nor is aesthetic absolutism the best possible ally for historical sensitivity. By supporting the primacy of aesthetic standards, one supports the primacy of the aesthetic function of literature and one tends to denigrate the concomitant cognitive function which had a long and rich history in Russia. The period of post-Stalinist relaxation of controls marks the collision between the didacticism of Socialist Realism and the newly re-emerging forces of cognitive writing. Tvardovsky helped the latter to come into their own. The discussion of social issues is Tvardovsky's own main theme as well as that of writers he supports. This, above all, makes him a follower of Nikolai Nekrasov, who is considered a major nineteenth-century poet *only* in Russia. In the west, Nekrasov has remained untranslated, uncrowned, and unfree of suspicion of being an unimportant poet altogether. One hundred years later, Tvardovsky shares in the predicament.

Perhaps intransigent critics treat "civic" prose writers with more sympathy than "civic" poets. One such abrasive Western critic recently suggested that, if it were not for the specifically Soviet circumstances, Tvardovsky would not be writing verse altogether. For he is a poet "through his own will" and not "through God's grace." He strives for various external goals, which he consciously poses for himself, rather than for the satisfaction of an inner need.[3]

[3] E. Rais, "Sorokoletie russkoi poezii v SSSR," *Grani,* 50 (1961), 144–65.

It has sometimes been claimed—and disavowed—that a narrative poet subsists on a lesser amount of grace than a lyrical poet; whatever the case may be, Tvardovsky is a narrative poet par excellence. He also writes distinguished prose for which, one should assume, some minimum amount of grace is also necessary. In his well-known autobiographical sketch, both brief and rich, he even suggests that prose begins to compel him more and more.[4] Why, then, has the long narrative poem been, until now, his favorite form? An attempt to answer this question evokes the larger problem of the relationship of talent, genre, and intent in Soviet letters. And although this problem is so complex that it falls beyond the scope of this sketch, it might be suggested that, despite the frequent incompatibility between contents and genre in Soviet literature, Tvardovsky's case is different. The very themes of his narrative cycles point to the adequate relationship between his favorite genre and the kind of thing he communicates.

His topics are simple, concrete and popular. They are expressed in simple, conventional, folklike verse. Here are several examples. In *Land Muravia,* Tvardovsky relates the pitiful odyssey of a recalcitrant peasant searching for his very own spot of land in the face of impending collectivization of agriculture in the early 1930's. In *Vasily Tyorkin* (1946), his most famous work, he commemorates the will of a simple soldier to survive the Second World War in decent communion with his comrades, but without declaratory heroics. In *House on the Road* (1946), his second war book, he traces the hardships of a humble peasant family, torn apart by the war. In both these works he admonishes the reader never to forget the people's martyrdom. And after the war, in *Horizons beyond Horizons* (1961), Tvardovsky embarks on a double voyage. One of them is real enough, as he crosses the country by train from Moscow to Vladivostok, while the other journey is not exactly geographic. It is in time that he travels back to test his conscience in a retrospective confrontation with Stalin's dictatorship. In his last long poem, a brilliant satire entitled *Tyorkin in the Other World* (1963), Tvardovsky returns once more to the subject of the excesses of Stalinism and lampoons its sacred cows, such as total control over human nature and punitive vigilance of top bureaucrats over their subjects.

Neither a recluse nor a visionary, neither a prophet nor an iconoclast, Tvardovsky, perhaps, is best described as a chronicler, one who is both honest and of his time. He contributed to the critique of Stalinism rather early in the period of de-Stalinization and, because of his prestige, his contribution became a bulwark for the independent writers of the generation younger than his own.

Why has the major portion of his *oeuvre,* including some salient confessional chapters in *Horizons beyond Horizons,* been written in verse? Perhaps because Tvardovsky's kind of prosody—narrative, lucid, chronicle-

---

[4] A. Tvardovskii, *Sobranie sochinenii,* four volumes, Moskva, 1959, p. 16.

like, and frequently leaning on folklore stylization—happens to be an optimum vehicle for his kind of message. Its main impact contributed unobtrusively and "naturally," as it were, to the humanistic uprising against the vestiges of Stalinism.

The basic truths of the human condition were violated under Stalin ruthlessly enough. But Stalinist literature had devised a double talk to cover these violations. The initial rehabilitation of humanist values was not all too spectacular and loud in the kind of poetry Tvardovsky writes. And yet, perhaps, it was at the time more effective than anything that could have been done in prose. Compared with the longevity of folk poetry with its stylization which Tvardovsky imitated, Stalinism, after all, was but an incident. Thus, Tvardovsky's populist and "folksy" poetry, easily understood and easily remembered, had communal and corporate overtones. It was not then, nor is it now, a private and personal poetry. And some of its illuminating and confessional passages—lulling, incantatory, traditional —offered, perhaps, an organic and, at the same time, less embarrassing and less aggressive synthesis of protest against the excesses of totalitarianism than the sharp i-dotting argumentation of prose. The latter is specific; the former is general. To put it differently, folk stylization succeeds at times in transforming that which is unique and "unnatural" in history into that which is self-evident and "natural." For one of its main devices is to lend an aura of fatalism to the accident. In folk stylization the ebb and flow of Stalinism became "singable" as fathomable phenomena. Thus, in the startling and chaotic days of early de-Stalinization, simple and popular verse was both a plausible and an effective vehicle for the public exteriorization of wounds inflicted by the Stalinist regime. Among them, the personal guilt of association with Stalinism was one of the severest, as far as the intelligentsia was concerned. And that is precisely what Tvardovsky chose to disclose in simple, traditional, that's-the-way-it-was verse, paving the way for far more bitter exposés that were to follow his.

A civic poet without an audience can not perform his task. Tvardovsky has been eminently public and publishable. The conditions in which Soviet literature functions are equally trying for those poets who do publish as for those who do not. And an honorable posture of spiritual survival is, of course, more of a problem for those who do. The Soviet new left worships the victims of Stalinism. Tvardovsky is not one of them. On the contrary, as suggested in the beginning, he is not a victim, but a powerful man. The very fact that the new left accepts him as a leader indicates, perhaps, that it cannot be the job of an outside observer to pass judgment as to what has been more honorable: to have been sent to a concentration camp under Stalin for the voicing of one's own opinion; to have been placed for similar behavior in an insane asylum under Khrushchev's modified style of punishment; or to have escaped either treatment in either period through judicious maneuvering, as Tvardovsky has so far succeeded in doing. One may well conjecture that it was not easy.

Tvardovsky has been in serious jeopardy twice: first, for the publication of his war sketches; second, for promulgating early heresy, prior to Khrushchev's more liberal decisions in regard to literature, through such essays as A. Pomerantsev's famous "On Sincerity in Literature" (December issue of *Novyi mir,* 1953). The punishment for Tvardovsky was his dismissal as chief editor of *Novyi mir* in 1954. He was, however, reinstated in 1958. The relative innocuousness of reprisals against him indicates that punitive periods are not alike.

In the aftermath of the Twenty-second Congress of the Communist Party of the Soviet Union (CPSU), the climax of liberalization on the cultural scene was marked by Tvardovsky's triumph. It happened in the fall of 1962, when, in one issue of *Novyi mir,* he printed both Solzhenitsyn's *One Day in the Life of Ivan Denisovich,* and Nekrasov's *Both Sides of the Ocean.* Thereupon, however, he was once more severely attacked. But once more he managed to maintain his composure.

In the period of new adversity at the end of 1962, when Khrushchev began to vacillate in regard to the new concessions liberal writers were demanding, Tvardovsky neither pressed for more nor retreated from the positions already taken. Doggedly, but tactfully, he insisted on quality in literature, which in the Soviet setting amounted to a covert plea for artistic freedom and pluralism of self-expression. Tvardovsky's speeches, editorials, and interviews of the last ten years are reasonable on the surface. This means that his pronouncements have been a characteristically ambiguous mixture of "Leninist" pieties and covert pleas for artistic freedom. Thus, the limits of the permissible are not violated in Tvardovsky's public language. But in this manner he has managed to keep claiming and reclaiming the new gains. He does it in a matter-of-fact fashion and, one might say, even casually. This kind of *tour de force* seems to be possible only when courage and diplomacy are well blended; this, perhaps, is precisely the forte of Tvardovsky's generation, which has served as a bridge between Stalinism and its aftermath.[5]

Tvardovsky was reared under Stalinism and he, too, was hurt by it. For he, too, had sung his hosannas to the Big Brother and, remarkably, has not denied it. But he was not maimed. A good and strong man, he managed to save his integrity and, in so doing (fortunately for others) he did not become a recluse which, in Soviet circumstances, is perhaps the easier of the ways out. He has protected others and has accomplished more than anyone else for the creation of a better atmosphere for the growth of a new literature. And it is likely that he will be better known for this civic deed on behalf of the values of decency than for his poetry. Even in Russia.

Perhaps, because of the traditional adversities befalling independent

[5] As examples of his tactical prowess, the interview with Henry Shapiro which appeared in *Pravda* (May 12, 1963) might be cited, as well as Tvardovsky's editorial statement in *Novyi mir,* 12 (1965).

thought and creativity in Russia, Russian literature has been granted miraculous trustees, totally devoted to its maintenance. It needs them. They fret and cluck and implore and discover new talent and edit and push and publish and wait and advise and sit on manuscripts until the propitious moment and care about literature in a way almost incomprehensible to the West. Tvardovsky belongs among them, among the Belinskys, Nekrasovs and Gorkys of the past, as he is flanked today by other tested guardian angels such as Paustovsky and Chukovsky, his seniors.

There fortunately exists an unprepossessing autobiographical sketch of some ten pages in which Tvardovsky candidly and saliently speaks of his origin, roots, and some of his personal values.[6]

He was born in 1910 in Zagorye, a village in the Smolensk region where his father was a blacksmith. Tvardovsky started writing early, but his formal education was interrupted after he finished elementary school in his native village. At the age of eighteen he went to Smolensk, where he not only failed to enter school, but could not even find work. The late 1920's and early 1930's were no easier for Tvardovsky than for anyone else. He made his appearance in the capital when his first poems were published in *Oktiabr'* (*October*), then as now a leading, but relentlessly orthodox, literary journal. But in Moscow also he failed to find work or to enroll in a school. He had, as he himself recalls, the good sense to return to Smolensk, where he was admitted to the pedagogical institute without having to pass entrance examinations. He made up on his own the preparatory courses he lacked and then completed two years of training, graduating later from the Moscow Institute of History, Philosophy and Literature (MIFLI), where he studied from 1936 to 1939.

It seems to me that my literary generation grew and developed with great difficulty. To some of my contemporaries the obstacles encountered were destructive. We were obsessed with writing. We started to appear in print. But having become "professional" writers, we lacked education and general culture. Instead, our reading was superficial. And a certain familiarity with the "small secrets" of the craft only nurtured in us dangerous illusions.[7]

It is customary in the West to attribute all the ills that befell Soviet literature in the 1930's and 1940's primarily to the theory and practice of Socialist Realism. Tvardovsky suggests here in a forthright way that the literary sensitivities of writers of that period were either non-existent or became atrophied, and for a number of reasons. The arrogance, parochialism, and lack of education of the aspiring young literati were as detrimental to them as the dogmatic prescripts imposed from above. But in Tvardov-

---

[6] Tvardovsky's modest autobiographical sketch ("Avtobiografiia") has been widely printed. It introduces the 1959 edition of his collected works and is included in the selective two-volume collection of autobiographies of prominent writers, *Sovetskie pisateli: avtobiografii*, Moskva, 1959.

[7] "Avtobiografiia," *op. cit.*, p. 11.

sky's case, his fundamental respect for culture, his insistence on craftsmanship, and his tactful but firm remonstrations all contributed to the debt that the literature in the 1960's owes him.[8] As to his own youth,

Those years of study and of work in Smolensk are marked for me forever by a high spiritual soaring. I could not possibly exaggerate the joy, experienced then for the first time, of entering the world of ideas and images which revealed themselves to me from the pages of books, the existence of which I had not known until then.[9]

Land Muravia was published in 1936. Tvardovsky, a narrative poet from the beginning, deals in this tale with the initial phase of the agricultural revolution. The pilgrim peasant, Morgunok, inseparable from his horse, fails to find a private green paradise. Both the itinerant horse and peasant have since then entered the Soviet assembly of successful folk characters, never too crowded.

That period is perhaps the most decisive and significant in my literary life. Those were the years of the great reconstruction of the village on the basis of collectivization, a period that became for me what the October revolution and the civil war had been to the older generation.[10]

In an early tribute to Tvardovsky's talent, the futurist poet Nikolai Aseev (1889–1962) pointed to Tvardovsky's ability to control subject matter and narrative scope:

The serious, and at the same time joyous, voice of the poem, the pleasant youthful bass timbre attracts one's attention because of the real, artistic, truthful soundness of the narrator who knows what he is talking about and who speaks without falseness and pretensions.[11]

The simplicity and sincerity discovered here in the young Tvardovsky are the same qualities the young poets admire in him today. And he himself has always been aware of his inclination to communicate rather than explore:

That which I knew about life—it seemed to me then—I knew better, in greater detail and more authentically than anyone else alive in the world and I had to tell what I knew.[12]

---

[8] In an important speech delivered at the Twenty-second Congress of the CPSU in 1959, Tvardovsky accused the literary bureaucracy, in a poignant but undramatic tone, of flagrant misunderstanding of the nature of literature. *Sobranie sochinenii,* IV, 453–62.

[9] "Avtobiografiia," *op. cit.,* p. 12.

[10] "Avtobiografiia," *op. cit.,* p. 12.

[11] N. Aseev, "Aleksandr Tvardovskii," *Komu nuzhna poeziia,* Moskva, 1961, p. 212.

[12] "Avtobiografiia," *op. cit.,* p. 14.

In this first important work of his, in *Land Muravia,* the arch peasant, Morgunok, combines traditional traits with new responses to social change. Partly because of his own peasant origin and partly because of the predominance of rural themes in his early work, Tvardovsky has been frequently labeled in textbooks as a peasant poet. Whereas this label seems to have applied to such poets as Sergei Yesenin and Nikolai Kluev, it appears less felicitous in the case of Tvardovsky. For firsthand knowledge of subject matter need not be connected with a commitment to one's own origins or class values, or with their denial, for that matter. Unlike the great lyrical peasant poets of the Russian apocalyptic years, he is neither obsessed nor tormented with the need to imbue his poetry with the spiritual legacy and mystique of the Russian peasant culture. And if it is indeed the lyrical poet who more readily submits to the traditionally Russian divisive nomenclature of "urban" and "peasant," a narrative poet is primarily what he is, a storyteller. Tvardovsky's posture, therefore, has hardly ever been that of a mythmaker or martyr defending the endangered peasant ethos. No matter how folklike his early prosody, throughout his life his style was always that of a sober, thorough chronicler.

Tvardovsky moved to Moscow in 1936 and became a party member in 1938. In the fall of 1939, he was drafted and took part in the Byelorussian campaign. He became a war correspondent during the Finnish war and served in the same capacity during the Second World War.

A book about the adventures of a Russian soldier, *Vasily Tyorkin,* was the result of his war experience. It is his best-known work and one of the most popular pieces of literature in Soviet Russia. He started writing this cycle, chapter by chapter, in the beginning of the war, and it was serialized during the period 1941–46 in various journals, including publications for the front-line soldiers. Vasily Tyorkin rapidly became as well known in Russia as the cartoonist Bill Mauldin's G.I.'s did in the United States. The Russian reader pledged allegiance to Tvardovsky's cheerful and humble hero long before the work received the Stalin Prize in 1946. Tvardovsky's ordinary soldier—successfully and somewhat paradoxically sharing some traits not only with Tolstoy's Platon Karatayev, but also with Hashek's good soldier Schweik, and Bill Mauldin's Joe and Willie—was caught up in the initially disastrous retreat of the Soviet armies; survived all the unspeakable hazards and hardships of a combat soldier; grieved over the loss of his family, which perished under the German onslaught; was severely wounded, but managed to mend for the participation in the final attack on Berlin. And it is right at the end of the war, with Tyorkin in a boxcar bound homeward from Germany, that the poet bids him a warm and melancholy farewell. With a somewhat uncanny clairvoyance, Tvardovsky feels that both poet and hero are to become at once obsolete. Andrei Zhdanov, in the trying period which spanned war and peace, enthroned as controller of the creative intelligentsia, was indeed just about to anathematize the very theme of war as defeatism.

The period of Zhdanov's postwar repressions notwithstanding, much has been written about this long folk tale by critics and readers alike. Front-line soldiers who were avid readers of Tyorkin's peregrinations sent open letters to the poet demanding' that their friend and buddy, Tyorkin, not be abandoned. Some readers even undertook to write their own sequels to the Tyorkin saga. In one of his important essays, Tvardovsky finally answered his readers. He shared with them the story of the conception of the work and the reasons why it had to end when it did.[13]

The Tyorkin cycle, as compared with Tvardovsky's prewar poems, showed an enlarged narrative scope which now provided elbow room for the exteriorization of the poet's own values and thoughts. The poet, Tyorkin's faithful companion and interpreter, now becomes as prominent as the unassuming hero, and so does the reader with whom the poet converses directly throughout the long poem in the Pushkinian manner. As Tvardovsky put it:

Tyorkin was to me my lyric poetry and my journalism, song and sermon, anecdote and proverb, an intimate conversation and repartee on a special occasion.[14]

Tyorkin has become a folk hero, not so much because of the vernacular in which the book was written, but through the immediate affection he won from the mass reader.[15] This dogface is Everyman in the garb of a humble Russian soldier. His Russian "antecedents" are not hard to find. Tenacious vitality, common sense, resigned humor, and masculine givingness make him a worthy successor of Tolstoy's soldiers and a no less worthy precursor of Ivan Denisovich Shukhov, Solzhenitsyn's stoic and humble hero. Tyorkin is articulate, warm, and cheerful without being a buffoon; disciplined without servility; resourceful against all odds. Quite credibly, neither devil nor death can take him, not even when later, in peculiar circumstances, he was to visit the Stalinist "other world" and escape from it successfully.

·The poet depicts Tyorkin during the catastrophic first period of the war. Hungry and cold, "our brother" the soldier trailed behind the government strategically "retreating" eastward, as it was appropriate to say at the time. But in depicting Tyorkin thus, the poet himself was tormented by gnawing guilt, and it became important to him to portray Tyorkin's soldierly endurance in the face of everything without sugar-coating it.

> And we didn't know why
> And we didn't ask the reason
> Why it was that at the time
> They didn't give him a medal.[16]

    [13] "Kak byl napisan Vasilii Terkin: Otvet chitateliam," *Sobranie sochinenii,* IV, pp. 412–62.
    [14] "Avtobiografiia," *op. cit.,* p. 15.
    [15] "Pis'ma frontovikov o Vasilii Terkin," *Znamia,* 12 (1944), 194–202.
    [16] *Vasilii Terkin* in *Sobranie sochinenii,* II, p. 206.

The generic traits that form the soldier's image show him as a Russian and not as a Soviet soldier. Identification with the hero presaged already toward the end of the war the poet's alienation from the ruling ideology.

It is Tyorkin's stylization as a type that makes him akin to the idea for which Tolstoy's Karatayev stands. Tyorkin is less a study of an individual than of the idea of the people's courage. His personal characteristics are not emphasized; he has no visible family ties, no personal friends. His separate life makes no sense, as he is totally dissolved in the army unit in which he serves. He is a postulate of neo-populism. The poet chuckles over him, admires him, grieves for him and, after the war, openly does not know what to do with him. Since this character represents anonymous heroism, sentimentality does not mar the poet's ornate and overt compassion. But when, elsewhere, Tvardovsky undertook to write the story of individuals, the folksiness of the diction subsided and the characterization became unadorned and terse.

The House by the Roadside (1946), written almost simultaneously with *Tyorkin,* portrays the hardships of one young peasant family. The war separates Anna and Andrei Sivzov. The soldier's wife is now the heroine. She is treated as an individual and not as a type; thus, her destiny is special, even if it was, in actuality, repeated millionfold. After her husband's conscription, she is driven into captivity. She gives birth to their last child far away from their destroyed house, on the straw of a German barrack. And her "house by the roadside" is flimsy, indeed, for it is nothing but a pathetic hand cart that she pushes surrounded by the other children, with little Andrei in her arms. She is on her improbable way "home" after the end of the war. The story is not finished. The Sivzovs do not know whether they will find each other, and the reader is left in uncertainty. Thus, the work joins many others in sounding one of the richest war themes: the heroism of the Russian woman.

Tvardovsky's work, dedicated as it was to the tragedy of war, marked his estrangement from orthodoxy and his resistance against the militant spirit of "partyness." By the end of the war, when victory was in sight, the intelligentsia was required once more to produce ideological orthodoxy and political vigilance. In this perilous atmosphere, Tvardovsky's Tyorkin had managed already to irritate some watchful critics who were assisting Zhdanov in his punitive actions against those writers who were either unable, or unwilling, to terminate their participation in the national War Requiem. It was Tyorkin's ageless "Russianness" that angered them.[17]

The growing forces of reaction openly branded Tvardovsky a defeatist and "slanderer" when his war sketches were published, under the title *Native and Foreign Land* (1946). In simple and informal prose fragments he recorded what he saw. His pioneering truthfulness on the subject of the

---

[17] For instance, F. Gladkov's attack in *"Zapiski pisatelia," Novyi mir,* 4 (1945), 152.

disaster that the first phase of the war actually turned out to be was pitched against the corrective ideological program recommended by Andrei Zhdanov and culminating in the purges of the late 1940's. Tvardovsky's war sketches struck a sore point, since they depicted the debacle of unpreparedness and the resulting agony of the helpless population. If he had already permitted himself some daring *bon mots* in *Vasily Tyorkin* ("Cities are surrendered by soldiers,/Generals recapture them"),[18] he treats here even an "honest-to-goodness de-kulaked kulak" with sympathy. Not only does the "arch enemy" of the people who had served a long sentence in Siberia not turn into a traitor under German occupation, but he saves the life of a Soviet guerrilla fighter. The ex-kulak's motivation, however, is more patriotic than ideological. As Tvardovsky surely knew, the difference between patriotism and proper faith in Stalinism had become at that time a rather touchy matter.

Thus, during the years of Zhdanov's reprisals, Tvardovsky turned to virtual silence. It is doubtful whether he could have assumed leadership among the liberals quite so effectively in our time if he had not been in such disfavor at that time. Having remained silent, Tvardovsky came into his own soon after Stalin's death. His main literary contribution to the period of the so-called thaw is *Horizons beyond Horizons*, the first chapters of which started appearing as early as 1953 in *Novyi mir*. For the completed cycle he was awarded the Lenin prize in 1961.

Several chapters of this book, which is notable for its coverage in time as well as for its depth, come close to important confessional literature. As already suggested, several parts of it appeared here and there from 1953 through 1960, in journals, newspapers, and even on the first page of *Pravda*. Fortunately, each chapter is a self-contained unit in the form of either a well-rounded narrative or a pensive reminiscence. The over-all framework is provided by the poet's train journey from Moscow to Vladivostok. The sixteen chapters are uneven in quality and interest. One is devoted to childhood reminiscences, whereas another rhapsodizes about birch forests, the majesty of the Volga, and the breathtaking shores of Lake Baikal. Other chapters comprise a hymn to new construction projects on the Angara River as well as sympathetic sketches of fellow travelers, young and old. One of the weightiest chapters presents an incisive critique of the system of controls imposed on Soviet literature and the conformism and cowardice it breeds. Above all, however, there reigns in this book the exhilarating spirit of travel and of escape from the doldrums—a pleasure Russian literature has commemorated from Pushkin to Pasternak. The release and transfiguration that a long railroad journey offers to an eager Russian passenger make its express purpose irrelevant. Tvardovsky, patient and gregarious, curious and melancholy, joins a noble romantic tradition,

---

[18] *Vasilii Terkin, op. cit.*, p. 347.

namely that of finding peace in the long-distance railway car. This favorite Russian conveyance is, as it has been for a long time in literature, a comfortable Noah's ark, a shelter rather than a vehicle. In this book, the hero is clearly the poet himself, and he speaks about himself at great length. The work is, in fact, a personal diary with topical digressions—the story of an intellectual of the mid-generation, and of his conscience. In the long meditative passages the folkloristic vernacular is abandoned. But clarity remains.

Three chapters deserve special attention. They are well known in Russia by Tvardovsky's friends and foes alike, and they represent his contribution to the current struggle of liberal forces against reaction. The first of these chapters, "Conversation about Literature," created a sensation already in 1956, when it was published separately. It describes how a traveling companion in the train compartment scolds the poet for the entrenched literary defects: cowardly prudence, soullessness, falsity. The poet admits these defects, but blames the censors, editors, and the literary apparatus. At this point, an unexpected voice chimes in from the upper berth and makes sarcastic fun of the poet. The sudden stranger turns out to be an editor, to be sure . . . but a phantom, no other than the embodiment of the author's own fear. And that's just the point: Certain debates in the Soviet Union, frequent if still risky today, were far more sensational in the mid-1950's.

When some forces in the contemporary intelligentsia took off on the tortuous post-Stalinist road toward truth, it must be emphasized once more that Tvardovsky was one of the first of such pilgrims. Therefore, "A Childhood Friend" is the most significant chapter in *Horizons beyond Horizons*. It is the painful record of the poet's chance encounter with a beloved friend of his early youth. After seventeen years of separation, the poet and the friend run into each other at a Siberian railroad station, pinned by destiny on the platform between two refueling trains about to continue in opposite directions. The poet's friend is going west at last. His seventeen years were spent in a concentration camp. Valor—somewhat bemused and quietistic—dignity, and a touch of wise humor mark the tersely sketched words and gestures of the victim. But it is the depth of the author's self-revelation that is compelling. A searing shame engulfs him. Guilt, heretofore selfishly suppressed, surfaces and turns into clumsy and humiliating embarrassment. The two men separate after a few all too brief minutes without having said anything meaningful to each other.

This painful theme leads to the one which has been acknowledged as the climax of the cycle. The chapter, "That's the Way It Was," appeared on the front page of *Pravda* on a day of ritual, May 1, 1960. Needless to say, Khrushchev made good use of this poem, since it contained a powerful indictment against "the cult of personality" at precisely the time when Stalin's remains were being taken from the mausoleum. But

Tvardovsky said more, perhaps, than Khrushchev needed. In this, a major statement of the anti-Stalinist credo, two points distinguish Tvardovsky's position from that of the new power elite and from that of the younger poets. Tvardovsky speaks for his own generation, the tainted generation in its fifties. On the one hand, he treats the all-absorbing and ambiguous paternalistic phenomenon of Stalin's deification commensurately, without a retrospective attempt either to minimize or to ridicule it and, on the other, he confesses his generation's active involvement with idolatry and stands prepared to share in the responsibility for the crimes of Stalinism.

> Thus, he lived on earth and ruled
> Holding the reins in his hard hand.
> Just try and find the man who
> Did not praise and glorify him,
> Just try and find him!
> Probably not in vain
> The son of the East
> To the very end
> Fulfilled the traits
> Of his hard,
> Of his cruel
> Wrongness
> And rightness.
> But who of us is fit to be a judge,
> To decide who is right, who is wrong?
> We speak of people. And people.
> Do they not create gods themselves?[19]

Tvardovsky speaks here clearly enough for the generation which was damaged by its servility to the dictator and of the retribution that appeared as inevitable. Significantly, he also implies that the attempts at whitewashing one's own involvement and of dissociating oneself from the past are dishonest.

But Khrushchev, having once more become alarmed over the efforts of both the extremists of truth and the explorers of modernism to overstep the accepted boundaries, once again attacked the independent writers and artists in the winter of 1963. The final consequences were unforeseen and somewhat paradoxical. In that winter of 1963, the liberals closed ranks as never before; in fact Tvardovsky's usual steadfastness provided a model.

Having again weathered the storm, Tvardovsky helped to break the tension of possible serious reprisals by publishing *Tyorkin in the Other World*. It appeared first in *Izvestiia* with an astounding preamble by Alexei Adzhubei, Khrushchev's son-in-law and then chief editor of this ranking governmental daily with the circulation of 4,500,000. In it Adzhubei de-

---

[19] *Za dal'iu dal'* in *Sobranie sochinenii*, III, p. 341.

scribed his father-in-law's merry laughter as the poet read his work to him in the presence of foreign visiting literary dignitaries. This hilarious satirical poem, to which readers responded with an avalanche of approving letters to the editor, appeared thereafter in the August issue of *Novyi mir,* as well as in a popular paperback (1963). It is a breakthrough in both genesis and contents. Prior to publication, it had been widely circulated in the Moscow literary underground and was published anonymously in the *émigré* almanac, *Mosty (Bridges),* in Munich in 1963.

In *Tyorkin in the Other World,* Tvardovsky returns to his earlier swift, folksy, rollicking vernacular. The resurrected Tyorkin descends to the Soviet purgatory and examines it with subdued incredulity. He is shown over the grounds by a *sui generis* Vergil, the phantom of one of his old war comrades. Spies, censors, ideological drill masters, punitive agents, bureaucrats—they are all here. And so is the grotesque version of Red Tape, subdivided into Departments, Combines, and Systems. The Special Section is here too, behind barbed wires, ruled by the Supreme One himself. But Tvardovsky's most daring satirical whimsy, directed against ideological shibboleths, places the Soviet afterworld adjacent to the capitalist one. In fact, delightfully enough, the "two other worlds," or nether worlds —the Soviet and the capitalist—are housed under one and the same roof, and their "coexistence" is separated merely by a wall, so transparent as to permit the respective inhabitants to observe each other. The proximity of the capitalist establishment turns out to be not without seduction for the Soviet inmates, for the former is far less dreary (by implication) than "the best and most advanced" Soviet establishment. For one thing, as the guide explains, there is a modicum of romanticism and dynamism on the capitalist side of the flimsy divide. Over there, they at least have both hell and paradise. The comparison, in general, seems whimsically cathartic.

> They are old-fashioned over there
> With their foolish delusions
> Of refreshing waters and hellish steam.
> Remember what I say:
> Our other world is natural.
> We have neither hell nor paradise.
> We have science. They have opium.
> Our foundation is indestructible.
> We have shortcomings, of course,
> But, on the other hand, we have a system.
> First of all, their discipline
> Is weak compared with ours.
> The picture is this, if you please:
> Over here we form a column,
> Over there they have a mob.[20]

[20] *Terkin na tom svete,* Moskva, 1963, pp. 49–50.

There is a transparent hint in the opening passages that what is about to be described is not *only* the "other" Soviet world and that the story has realistic points to make in regard to "this" world. In the end, the poet helps Tyorkin to escape and to return back to life above. Thereupon, the poet anticipates the outrage of some of his readers and critics for having been taken on a ride into the realm of useless, frivolous, dangerous fantasy (which allegedly undermines the "foundations") by a rebuttal in which he neatly underscores his own conception of his task. Tvardovsky did not wish to trap the reader. Far from it. He wished to make him think about the allegorical nature of this fantastic tale, without panicking about the "treasonable" potentiality of thought itself.

> I undertook my own offensive,
> Possessed by one thought alone:
> Should I succeed with this story,
> Any other will be easy.[21]

At the present time Tvardovsky's position has become precarious again. The aftermath of the Sinyavsky and Daniel trial does not presage anything but the continuation of uncertainty, confusion, and new perils for the liberals and modernists among writers. Tvardovsky's stand remains uncompromising. As the attacks on him (and on *Novyi mir*) from the right become louder his editorial policy remarkably continues on its unaltered course. However, quite ominously, he was missing from the delegation of the Union of Writers of the Russian Federation to the Twenty-third Congress of the CPSU, which opened on the last day of March of this year (1966). In contrast to the Twenty-second Congress of five years ago, where Tvardovsky delivered a key speech on the state of literature, he was not invited this time. Instead, the Nobel Prize winner, Mikhail Sholokhov flanked by the arch reactionaries, villified not only the two last martyrs of thought control but all those who dared to sympathize with them abroad and at home. This was a serious threat. But his was not the only performance to evoke memories of a hideous past. Leonid Brezhnev himself reiterated the traditional canons regarding the relationship between the party and literature:

The party has directed the activities of creative organizations and institutions in the past and will continue to do so in the future . . . We are guided by the principle of partyness of art, of the class approach toward the evaluation of everything transpiring in the domain of culture.[22]

And, if there is nothing new in this statement, it is all the more alarming for *Novyi mir,* the liberal cause, and Alexander Tvardovsky.

[21] *Ibid,* p. 103.
[22] *Literaturnaia gazeta,* April 5, 1966.

SELECTED BIBLIOGRAPHY

The most succinct biographical information on Tvardovsky is contained in his own autobiographical sketch which introduces his *Sobranie sochinenii*, four volumes, Moskva, 1959. The same sketch appears also in the prestigious *Sovetskie pisateli avtobiografii*, two volumes, II, Moskva, 1959, 410–17.

According to the habit of blending work with life, Soviet scholarship heavily admixes biographical information into the following standard and orthodox critical studies: F. Lubareva, *A Tvardovskii: Kritiko-biograficheskii ocherk*, Moskva, 1957. A revised version of this study appears as an essay, "A. Tvardovskii," in *Istoriia russkoi sovetskoi literatury* Moskva, 1963, pp. 376–471. Not too imaginative either, but perhaps more widely known because of its place in an authoritative reference work is L. Shvezova's essay "A. Tvardovskii" in *Istoriia russkoi sovetskoi literatury*, three volumes, III, Moskva, 1961, 499–539. The last two items are equipped with bibliographies.

A biographical study of Tvardovsky does not exist in English. His own brief autobiographical sketch, mentioned above, was translated into English under the title "About Myself" in *Soviet Literature Monthly*, 4 (Moscow, 1961). In the recent histories and surveys of Soviet Russian literature published in the United States, such as Mark Slonim's *Soviet Russian Literature, Writers and Problems,* New York: Oxford University Press, 1964, and Vera Alexandrova's *A History of Soviet Literature, 1917–1962*, Garden City: Doubleday, 1963, Tvardovsky is treated with respect and understanding, but certainly not as a major writer.

As to translations of his poetry and prose, the situation is even worse. Snippets of his poems have been published here and there in anthologies and readers but since they are no more than that, it would be foolish to enumerate them here. For one thing, the inventory would look far more impressive than it really is. However, *Terkin na tom svete* (*Tyorkin in the Other World*) has been well translated by Leo Gruliow for the *Current Digest of the Soviet Press,* 1963, and published as a separate pamphlet.

Curiously, Russian critical literature of a sustained and scholarly nature on Tvardovsky is not plentiful. The Tvardovsky specialist so far is P. Vykhodtsev and his long essay "Tvardovskii i russkaia klassicheskaia poeziia," published in the collection *Problemy sovetskoi literatury,* III, Moskva, 1956, pp. 199–244, is thorough and convincing in disclosing Tvardovsky's connections with the Nekrasov tradition. Tvardovsky's themes and style are analyzed in Vykhodtsev's book *Poeziia A. Tvardovskogo,* Moskva, 1958, and the most complete study to date is the same author's *A. Tvardovskii seminarii,* Leningrad, 1960. But it was the septuagenarian poet Samuil Marshak, the late master of the classical epigram and one of Russia's best writers for children, who has paid the warmest and most commensurate tribute to Tvardovsky the man and the poet in a short and informal book *Radi zhizni na zemle,* Moskva, 1961.

The definitive edition of Tvardovsky to date is *Sobranie sochinenii,* four volumes, Moskva, 1959. A new five-volume edition is currently in preparation. The dates of the major works, according to publications of entire cycles in book form are *Strana muraviia,* Moskva, 1937; *Vasilii Terkin,* Moskva, 1946; *Dom u dorogi,* Moskva, 1946; *Na rodine i na chuzhbine,* Moskva, 1946; *Za dal'iu dal',* Moskva, 1961; *Terkin na tom svete,* Moskva, 1963.

Andrei Andreevich Voznesensky

by Patricia Blake

The Russian poet Andrei Andreevich Voznesensky was born in Moscow May 12, 1933. His great-grandfather was a Caucasian who was captured as a child by the Russians and placed in a monastery in Murom where he ultimately became an Orthodox priest. As was often the case among sons of priests, Voznesensky's grandfather became a doctor. His father is a professor of engineering and a designer of hydroelectric stations.

Voznesensky spent a part of his early childhood in the ancient Russian city of Vladimir. During the war, from 1941 to 1944, he lived with his mother and younger sister in Kurgan, in the Urals, while his father was in Leningrad, engaged in evacuating factories during the blockade. Both Voznesensky's parents have literary and artistic interests. His mother read poetry to him from his earliest childhood—Severyanin and Pasternak, he remembers in particular. Voznesensky recalls seeing his father once during the war when he flew to Kurgan on leave from the front. He carried nothing with him but a small rucksack containing some food and a little book of reproductions of etchings by Goya which powerfully affected his small son. Voznesensky's childhood apprehension of war in Russia, heightened by Goya's grotesque and terrible visions, ultimately gave rise to his most famous poem, "I Am Goya."

After the war the family returned to Moscow. As an adolescent Voznesensky thought of becoming an artist, and then he studied architecture. "I was already writing," he says, "but mainly I painted. Yet poetry was flowing in me then like a river under the ice." Shortly before his graduation from the Moscow Architectural Institute in 1957, an event occurred which is the subject of the poem "Fire in the Architectural Institute." Like other senior students Voznesensky had spent his last year on an elaborate design project. His he describes, with all due modesty, as "a spiral-shaped thing, a bit like the Guggenheim Museum." "One morning," he says, "we found that a fire had destroyed a year's work. Whole cities and countries on blueprints had vanished. We were so tired that we were glad that final examinations now had to be postponed. But for me it was more than a fire. I believe in symbols. I understood that architecture was burned out in *me*. I became a poet."

Voznesensky's interest in painting and architecture is seen in all his poetry, most explicitly in his choice of themes and symbols. In "Master

Craftsmen" he invokes the legend that Barma, the architect of St. Basil's Cathedral in Moscow, was blinded by Ivan the Terrible so he might never again design anything so beautiful. Architectural images predominate in a number of his poems such as "The Torches of Florence" and "Italian Garage." "New York Airport at Night" is one sustained metaphor of the airport as the self-portrait of the poet.

Voznesensky often speaks of poetry in terms of the architect's craft. "Modern technical advances in poetry and architecture are very great," he says. "You can now build a house on the head of a pin. To construct a room in the old days you had to have four columns and transverse beams which inevitably produced a rectangular room. Now that these technical requirements have disappeared, one can build a room of any shape at all. But men don't know what shape to give their rooms. They haven't found the form they are looking for. Therefore their rooms remain rectangular. The artist must find the shape that suits him. Only then is technique justified. In my poetry I am searching for a new shape."

Certainly the decisive event in Voznesensky's life came soon after his abandonment of architecture. This was his meeting with Boris Pasternak. He sent his first poems to Pasternak, who replied with a letter of praise and an invitation to visit him. "From that time on I never left his side," he has said. "I moved out to Peredelkino and stayed near him until his death. . . . He was my only master."

Voznesensky's earliest writings are said to be derivative of Pasternak, but judging from his first published poems (1958) he quickly found his personal and wholly original idiom. He shares, however, Pasternak's fondness for the pathetic fallacy. And his sense of the unity of all organic life is quite Pasternakian:

> I know we shall live again as
> Friends or girl-friends or blades of grass,
> Instead of us this one or that one will come:
> Nature abhors a vacuum.[1]

But above all Voznesensky bears the mark of Pasternak's moral intelligence which has formed and armed him, as it has so many others, in the struggle to recreate a genuine literature for Russia, devastated by Stalin. In *Dr. Zhivago,* Pasternak described the enemy:

It was then [during the First World War] that falsehood came into our Russian land. The great misfortune, the root of all the evil to come, was the loss of faith in the value of personal opinions. People imagined that it was out of date to follow their own moral sense, that they must all sing the same tune in chorus,

---

[1] "Autumn in Sigulda," translated by W. H. Auden in *Antiworlds: Poetry by Andrei Voznesensky,* edited by Patricia Blake and Max Hayward, Basic Books: New York, 1966. All citations in English translation from Voznesensky's works are taken from *Antiworlds.*

and live by other people's notions, the notions which were being crammed down everybody's throat. And there arose the power of the glittering phrase, first tsarist, then revolutionary.

Pasternak's celebration of individual values, his passionate insistence on the right of privacy, and his exaltation of the life of the heart provided the moral climate—above the miasma of Stalinism—in which Russian literature was revived and restored in the post-Stalin period.

Moreover, Pasternak's forty-seven years of creative work, from 1913 to 1960, bridging, as they do, the sterile years of Stalinism, have provided a point of departure from which Voznesensky, and other young poets and writers, have been able to proceed to their principal task: to resurrect the language which had been corrupted by the "power of the glittering phrase." Not only were such abstract nouns as "freedom," "justice," and "truth" debased, but the language of life itself was extinguished; this was perhaps one of the most terrible indictments contained in *Dr. Zhivago*.

It is in this context that Voznesensky's immense popularity (inconceivable in the West for a "serious" modern poet) may be fully understood. If 14,000 people congregated (as they did in 1962) in a sports stadium to hear Voznesensky read his poetry, and 500,000 subscribed to buy his most recent book, it is because countless Russians have ceased to attend to the "glittering phrase," turning instead to the language of symbol and fantasy for the truths they seek. One result has been the rage for poetry readings which seized Russia in the post-Stalin decade. Until the antimodernist campaign of 1963 severely curtailed poetry readings, these had become the principal entertainment of intellectuals and students in Moscow, and in provincial towns as well, where poets traveled—literally by the truckload.

Voznesensky's readings display to the fullest advantage the assonances, rhythms, and modulations of pitch and intensity which he uses with such virtuosity in composing his poems. Such devices serve his intention rather as a brilliant orchestration serves a central musical idea. ("Form isn't what counts," he says. "Form must be clear, unfathomable, disquieting, like the sky in which only radar can sense the presence of a plane.") "I Am Goya," begins one of his most extraordinary poems: "I am Goya/of the bare field, by the enemy's beak gouged/till the craters of my eyes gape/I am grief/I am the tongue/ of war, the embers of cities/on the snows of the year 1941/ I am hunger. . . ." In Russian the assonances are devastating: *"Ya Góya . . . nagóye . . . ya góre . . . ya gólos . . . góda . . . ya gólod . . . ya górlo . . . góloi. . . ."*

Most characteristic of Voznesensky's idiom are the abrupt shifts of tone and intention within the same poem or even the same line; he is tender, playful, mocking, and finally, and most compellingly, ironic. He is a master of irony and to this end employs not only his technical resources (for example, punning, juxtaposing or rhyming internally a pompous word with

far-out slang) but also his alarming associations, fantasies, and images, as
in "The Skull Ballad" where the decapitated head of Anna Mons, the mis-
tress of Peter the Great, speaks to the tsar in these terms:

> love is so small who cares for love
> in times like these men build
> and set a world on fire—you kiss
> me State in blood in blood[2]

Even before the cultural campaign of 1963 released a torrent of abuse
against Voznesensky, conservative critics often accused him of "formalism"
(experimentalism) and ambiguity. To the first charge he answered, in his
poem "Evening on the Building Site": "They nag me about 'formalism.'/
Experts, what a distance/You are from life! Formalin:/You stink of it,
and incense." And again, in the poem "Antiworlds," he wrote, "Ah my
critics; how I love them./ Upon the neck of the keenest of them,/ Fragrant
and bald as fresh-baked bread,/There shines a perfect anti-head. . . ." To
the charge of ambiguity, he replied in "Who Are We?": "I am myself/
Among avalanches, like the Abominable/Snowman, absolutely elusive."

To his enemies Voznesensky appears elusive indeed, but to his tremendous following he speaks more clearly than any writer in Russia. Voznesensky often talks of his responsibility to the people who have given him
their confidence: "When a man writes, he feels his prophetic mission in the
world. The task of the Russian poet today is to look deep inside man. When
I read my poetry to a great number of people, their emotional, almost sen-
sual, expression of feeling seems to me to reveal the soul of man—now no
longer hidden behind closed shutters, but wide open like a woman who has
just been kissed."

Voznesensky's popularity has made him enemies in the literary and
political establishment. The hacks who built their careers on writing odes
to Stalin now feel threatened when huge printings of Voznesensky's books
sell out in a single day, while their own books molder away unsold in the
bookstores. The bureaucrats, whose careers and tastes were formed by
Stalin, are scarcely more attuned to Voznesensky and other modern poets;
their authority is undermined, they feel, when people are seen to respond
with more enthusiasm to poetry than to *agit-prop*.

Criticism of Voznesensky became most menacing in 1963, during the
vast official campaign against Russia's liberal-minded modern writers and
artists. The campaign was launched by Khrushchev at the now-famous
Manege exhibition of abstract art where he denounced the painters in a
torrent of scatalogical abuse and equated modern art with homosexuality—
"and for that," he said, "you can get ten years." Khrushchev's fury turned
quickly to the writers, whom he abused—in roughly the same terms as the
painters—at closed meetings held between government leaders and writers,

---

[2] "The Skull Ballad," translated by Stanley Kunitz in *Antiworlds*.

artists, and other intellectuals. In its public aspect, the campaign raged for seven months in the press and at writers' meetings held all over the country. Here Stalinist mediocrities proceeded to vent their pent-up anger and jealousy on nearly every young writer who had received public acclaim during the last decade—particularly Voznesensky and Yevtushenko. They called for an end to the editions of 100,000 copies, the favorable reviews, and the trips abroad for writers who, they claimed, flout party opinion, and play the game of the Western bourgeois ideologists ("with one foot on Gorky Street and the other on Broadway") in their "rotten, overpraised, unrealistic, smelly writings."

In classic purge style, recantations were demanded of the writers. Here Voznesensky, together with most of the other writers, proved to be "absolutely elusive." Many maintained silence, or defended themselves; although the writers were hardly offered a forum in the Soviet press, reports from foreign Communist observers indicated widespread defiance at the writers' meetings. Even the excerpts of recantations deemed fit to print in the newspapers were often ambiguous or ironic. After a savage attack on Voznesensky by Khrushchev, the poet responded as follows: "It has been said at this plenum [of the board of the USSR Union of Writers] that I must never forget the stern and severe words of Nikita Sergeevich [Khrushchev]. I shall never forget them. I shall not forget not only these severe words, but also the advice which Nikita Sergeevich gave me. He said 'work.' I do not justify myself now. I simply wish to say that for me now the main thing is to work, work, work. What my attitude is to my country, to Communism, what I myself am, this work will show."[3]

The campaign petered out in late June 1963. It had failed utterly in its objective to cow and humiliate the writers, and to re-establish controls, on the Stalinist model, over literature. The writers had clearly won a moral victory. The authorities had to settle for an undeclared truce with the liberal writers, which was maintained (with some grave lapses) during the first year of the post-Khrushchev era. Voznesensky and the other writers under fire in 1963 gradually reappeared in print, and poetry readings were ultimately resumed.

Whatever the outcome of the campaign, the force and character of the attack on Voznesensky, and other writers, were bound to be profoundly wounding. Voznesensky was at first sent into virtual exile (it was announced that he was spending his time in factories near Vladimir), and for many months he wandered about the country:

> Beware my darling. Hush. Not a sound,
> While I charge noisily
> From place to place around Russia,
> As a bird diverts the hunter from its nest.[4]

---

[3] *Pravda*, March 29, 1963.
[4] From "My Achilles Heart," translated by W. H. Auden in *Antiworlds*.

His poems of that period are often love poems. It is love that defends and saves man from that which oppresses him:

> When trouble licked at me like flame,
> I dived into Riga, as one would into water,
> And through a straw as fair as your hair,
> You gave me your breath and your breath was air.[5]

Among his most affecting poems are a group suffused with the raging pain of that period. Among these are "Dead Still" (*Zamerli*), "Give me Peace" (*Tishiny*), "My Achilles Heart" (*Shest' strof s ironei*), several poems in the long work in verse and prose, "Oza," "The Ballad of Pain," and "The Monologue of Marilyn Monroe." Most of these poems appeared, however, a year or two after the denunciations had subsided. His first major poem to be published after the campaign was "Longjumeau,"[6] a tribute to Lenin. While the subject is, of course, eminently "acceptable," and the poet is extremely respectful of Lenin, he is by no means sycophantic. Moreover, the poem shows clearly that Voznesensky was not disposed to yield in any way to criticism of his use of language. "Longjumeau" offers splendid examples of Voznesensky's inventiveness in this regard: he has Lenin, while playing a Russian form of skittles (*gorodki*), throw a stick and smash "empires,/churches, future Berias" (*tak chto vdrebezgi imporii,/ tserkvi, budushchie berii*). Bold and startling in its play with the grimmest of names, *imperii-berii* is also characteristic of Voznesensky's semantic exploitation of rhyme, as opposed to purely phonetic rhyming. (Beria had, of course, an empire himself.) Another instance of his use of this "rich" sort of rhyme was singled out by the writer Samuil Marshak in a posthumously published article (*Novyi mir*, No. 9, 1965) on the work of young Russian poets. This is the rhyme *vaiateli* (sculptors) and *voiteli* (warriors) in "Master Craftsmen" (*Mastera*), a poem about embattled artists. Such rhymes, besides being ingenious phonetically, reinforce the whole meaning of the poem.

In general, Voznesensky stands out among the other poets who have emerged in the post-Stalin era for the resourcefulness with which he handles language. Probably none has a greater range than he. Together with Yevtushenko he has pioneered the emancipation of Russian poetic language from the restriction from which it has long suffered and given back to it some of the freedom which it enjoyed in the 1920's. Where necessary for his poetic purposes he never hesitates to introduce slang, neologisms, and the jargon of modern technology. In "Oza" he complains that his "throat is sore from technical terms." His use of slang and technical jargon is, however, quite disciplined. There is no question of his using this language, as lesser poets

---

[5] From "Oza," translated by William Jay Smith in *Antiworlds*.

[6] *Pravda*, October 13, 1963. The poem later appeared in *Antimiry* and *Akhillesovo serdtse*. Longjumeau was the party school near Paris associated with Lenin.

sometimes do, to flaunt his "emancipation," which has become all too common during the sort of poetic revolution which is going on in Russia at this time. If he chooses an unusual word or expression, it is not for its own sake, but because he thinks it is best suited to achieve a particular effect. Apart from his superb mastery of contemporary Russian idiom, Voznesensky also brings to his craft an impressive knowledge of his native poetic tradition. His own original manner is enhanced by an easy familiarity with Mayakovsky and Pasternak, both of whom have influenced him, as well as with the classical Russian heritage. In "Oza" particularly there are some echoes of Pushkin, Lermontov, and Blok.

His most ambitious work thus far is the long poem "Oza," in which he makes an elaborate statement of his view of the world. The poem's structure is highly complex. It alternates prose and verse. Its abrupt changes in mood range from the lyrical to the satirical, with elements of mystification and parody. The work has nonetheless certain unifying themes. One is the chronicle of an ill-starred secret love affair. Never wholly abandoning this crucial personal theme, the poet moves from time to time to a purely speculative plane, expressing ideas on the state of the world in general, the history of his country, and man's condition. He is at once fascinated and repelled by modern technology, which is personified by the cyclotron and its master. On this theme, the poem in section XII is most explicit: "All progress is retrogression/If the process breaks man down." In "Oza," as in many of his other poems, Voznesensky is engaged in a defense of love and of the free human spirit against "pseudo-progress" and the "goddamned Machine," which, when it gets into the hands of the soulless and heartless, begets oppression. Here it is the poet who comes forward as the essential guardian of human values.

SELECTED BIBLIOGRAPHY

No extensive biographical sketch of Voznesensky exists, in English or in Russian. There is a brief sketch in Russian in *Kratkaia literaturnaia entsiklopediia*, Moskva, 1962. Major articles in Russian in which his work is discussed include A. Menshutin and A. Siniavskyi, "Za poeticheskuiu aktivnost'," *Novyi mir*, 1 (1961); V. Nazarenko, "Nastuplenie ili otstuplenie?", *Zvezda*, 7 (1962); and S. Marshak, "Molodym poetam," *Novyi mir*, 9 (1965).

A good deal of biographical material is contained in "Eloquent New Voice in Russia" by Peter Young (*Life*, April 1, 1966) based on several interviews with Voznesensky. Voznesensky discusses his views on poetry (his own and others') in an interview conducted by Robert Lowell, Stanley Kunitz, and William Jay Smith (*Atlantic Monthly*, July, 1966). A succinct statement about the poet's life and work appears in "Young Writers about Themselves," *Soviet Literature*, 12 (Moscow, 1962). This article was translated into English from *Voprosy literatury*, 9 (1962).

Voznesensky's poetry has been published in Russian in the following collections of his work: *Mozaika,* Vladimir, 1960; *Parabola,* Moskva, 1960; *Scrivo come amo* (*Pishetsia kak liubitsia*), Milan: Feltrinelli, 1962; *Treugol'naia grusha,* Moskva, 1962; and *Antimiry,* Moskva, 1964; and *Akhillesovo serdtse,* Moskva, 1966.

Forty-six poems in English translation, including "Oza," appear in *Anti-worlds: Poetry by Andrei Voznesensky,* edited by Patricia Blake and Max Hayward, and translated by Auden, Garrigue, Hayward, Kunitz, Moss, Smith, and Wilbur, New York: Basic Books, 1966. Other collections in English translation are: *Selected Poems of Andrei Voznesensky,* translated by Anselm Hollo, New York: Grove Press, 1964; *Voznesensky: Selected Poems,* translated by Herbert Marshall, New York: Hill and Wang, 1966.

Other English translations have appeared in various anthologies and magazines. Among the anthologies are: twelve poems translated by George Reavey in *Modern European Poetry,* New York: Bantam Books, 1966; fifteen poems translated by George Reavey in *The New Russian Poets, 1953–66,* George Reavey, ed., New York: October House, 1966; seven poems translated by Babette Deutsch in *Two Centuries of Russian Verse,* edited by Avrahm Yarmolinsky, New York: Random House, 1966. Translations of Voznesensky's poems have appeared in the following periodicals: *Stand,* Quarterly 7 (Leeds, England, 1962); *Odyssey Review,* II, 4 (New York, 1962); *Modern Poetry in Translation,* No. 1 (London, 1965). A translation of "Oza" by George Kline appeared in *Tri-Quarterly* (Evanston, Illinois, Spring 1965). Three translations by Robert Conquest appeared in *Encounter* (London, April 1963). A prose sketch, "A Portrait of Plisetskaya," translated by Max Hayward, appeared in *The New York Review of Books,* Nov. 17, 1966.

Major articles in English in which Voznesensky's work is discussed are: P. Forgues, "The Poetry of Andrei Voznesensky," *Survey* (London, October 1963); P. Forgues, "Russian Poetry, 1963–65," *Survey* (July 1965); P. Forgues, "The Young Poets," a chapter in *Literature and Revolution in Soviet Russia, 1917–62,* edited by Max Hayward and Leopold Labedz, London and New York: Oxford University Press, 1963; Patricia Blake, Introduction to the anthology *Halfway to the Moon: New Writing from Russia,* New York: Holt, Rinehart and Winston, 1965; Patricia Blake and Max Hayward, Introduction to *Antiworlds: Poetry by Andrei Voznesensky,* New York: Basic Books, 1966.

For a discussion of Voznesensky's role on the political-literary scene in Russia during 1962–64, see Priscilla Johnson's Introduction to *Khrushchev and the Arts,* Cambridge: M.I.T. Press, 1965. Documents pertaining to Voznesensky during this period also appear in this book.

A valuable interview with Voznesensky appears in French in *Les Lettres Françaises* (Paris, December 20–26, 1962).

Yevgeny Alexandrovich Yevtushenko

by R. R. Milner-Gulland

Yevgeny Alexandrovich Yevtushenko was born on July 18, 1933, at Zima (literally *Winter*), a small town on the trans-Siberian railway. He uses the surname of his mother's family, which is of Ukrainian origin: his great-grandfather was a peasant from Zhitomir Province who had been exiled to Siberia for taking part in a fire-raising insurrection. His father's family, by contrast, were intellectuals, with the Latvian name Gangnus. Russian and Tartar blood also flows in his veins.

In *A Precocious Autobiography* Yevtushenko describes his early life in some detail. In the late 1930's both his grandfathers—the soldier-peasant Yevtushenko and the mathematician Gangnus—vanished in the purges; his parents separated, and he went with his mother to Moscow. In 1941 he was evacuated back to Zima. In 1944 (not 1941, as English editions of the *Autobiography* confusingly state) he returned to Moscow, and did not revisit his birthplace until a time of both public and personal crisis, in the summer of 1953, shortly after Stalin's death and its concomitant upheavals. This visit is the background to the long poem "Zima Junction" (1956), a key work in the poet's development.

Meanwhile he had been a precocious versifier from childhood on; the journal *Soviet Sport* first published his work in 1949. He joined geological expeditions to Central Asia, and he has always been a considerable athlete, with ambitions at one time toward becoming a professional goalkeeper; instead he devoted himself to copious and indiscriminate versifying. By 1952 he was able to produce his first collected volume *Prospectors of the Future*—an immature work whose light-blue cover, as Yevtushenko says, matched the spirit of its contents.

Authorship of a published book gave him entry into the Moscow Literary Institute. Many poems referring to this period reflect an apparently nostalgic attitude to it; but he was by no means a model student, and eventually left without a diploma. Meanwhile his style as a poet was beginning to gain a distinctive and assured touch. One or two poems from 1952 and 1953 have lasting merit. His second collection *Third Snow,* published in 1955, marks him as a significant writer; his popular reputation came in 1956, with the completion of "Zima Junction" (published in the literary journal *Oktiabr'* [*October*] but not in book form in the USSR).

Yevtushenko dates the maturing of his attitudes to life and poetry to the year 1953, and more specifically to the shock of Stalin's death and the sinister events at his funeral (described in a splendid set-piece passage of the *Autobiography*). No doubt this is an oversimplification, but it is nevertheless from that time that we notice the particular mixture of private and public themes, often within a single poem, which he has made so much his own. Among his contemporaries it was probably the more intimate aspects of his work that brought him popularity. His love poems were fresh, lyrical, and above all came straight out of an unashamedly youthful heart. "This is what is happening to me . . ." was the most successful; "You asked in a whisper . . ." the most notorious, since it deals directly with an amorous situation that tends to be avoided by the mealy-mouthed. Parodies of the latter poem (facilitated by its outrageously memorable use of rhyme) have passed into Russian popular lore.

Notoriety of a political sort first came Yevtushenko's way in 1956. "Zima Junction" ran into heavy criticism and its author was temporarily excluded from the Komsomol (Young Communist League). It may now seem hard to understand the furor the poem occasioned, and indeed it stands up perfectly well as literature without any need for political exegesis. But the immediate response to it showed the precision with which it reflected widespread public feeling in 1956—the height of the so-called thaw period. In a series of vignettes of people he meets in Zima and its countryside, and in his own linking reflections, Yevtushenko presents a modern Russian gallery of characters: some admirable, some reprehensible, most of them between the two, their human weaknesses and inconsistencies nowhere glossed over. The theme that unifies this episodic work, 1,000 lines or so in length, is that of a young man's quest for truth. The world is in flux, and there turns out to be no easy way back to the certainties of his childhood: instead we see growing in him a stubborn conviction of the need for the search for truth in itself, for a return to directness and honesty in personal relations and to simple values generally. These include an uncomplicated Communist idealism of the kind that motivated his revolutionary forebears. But there are concealed difficulties here: both the sophistications of Stalinism and the poet's own intellectuality are facts which cannot be denied or ignored. There is considerable irony in the scene where the poet, turning to his simple peasant relatives for an answer to life's baffling complexities, finds that they turn to him (as an educated Muscovite) to resolve similar difficulties for them.

The poem has no anti-Soviet message—just the opposite—but it touched on tender spots that most writers had preferred to avoid, and so provoked exaggerated hostility, even outrage, in sections of the Soviet press. It is a pattern that has been repeated frequently since then in Yevtushenko's working career. This has never brought it to a complete halt, as might have been the case in the late 1930's or early 1950's. His supporters in the Soviet Union have never been so clamorous as his critics, but they have evidently been authoritative enough to ensure that he has never had to go unpublished for more than a few weeks or months at a time. We shall discuss the pattern of Yevtushenko's career, and the interpretations to which it has given rise, at greater length below.

Excellent new volumes appeared in 1956 and 1957—*Enthusiasts' Highway* and *Promise;* in 1959 he published a book of poems about Georgia and Russian versions from its poets, headed by some minatory stanzas about translation (*"Ne strashen vol'ny perevod / nichto ne vol'nost', yesli lyubish . . ."* "A free translation is nothing terrible / Nothing is a liberty in love . . ."). By the same year he had written enough to publish a retrospective volume *Poems of Several Years,* and in 1960 another slim collection *Apple* appeared. He had written a not unsuccessful short story ("Fourth-Meshchansky Street") and was preparing a film scenario. His considerable productivity as a writer can be assessed from this—it is a quality that has not been altogether to his advantage, since his best lines too often tend to be diluted in a flood of mediocre verbiage.

A newly critical period opened before Yevtushenko in the 1960's. In his personal life there came a divorce from his first wife, the brilliant young poetess Bella Akhmadulina (whom he had married in 1955 when she ·was eighteen), and remarriage, to a fellow Siberian named Galina. There also came the opportunity to travel abroad. In the Western world this may seem a trivial matter. To a Soviet Russian of Yevtushenko's questing temperament it was a crucial and not easily attained stage in his life. He went successively to Eastern Europe, the United States, France, Great Britain, Italy, Cuba, Germany, East Africa, Australia and intermediate parts, sometimes as a plain tourist, sometimes hailed as a celebrity. This new mobility was perhaps a delayed complement to the voraciously indiscriminate reading of his youth: equally an essential part of his development. Early in 1962, by one of the stranger quirks of journalism, he became well known to the public of the Western countries he visited. This can probably first be traced to his being the subject of a major article (with cover photograph) in *Time* magazine, largely under the authorship of Edmund Stevens. Other papers picked up the cue, and by the time of his visit to England as official guest of the British Council in May 1962 he was already a celebrity. Press publicity has spread his fame, but has rendered him subject to certain journalistic excesses, which have scarcely helped his serious reputation as a writer. Like many another public figure, Yevtushenko has suffered from tendentious or slipshod reporting, both inside and outside his own country; he has crossed swords with, for example, *Paris Match, Der Spiegel,* and the *Daily Mail.* These irritations are ephemeral (though a Soviet citizen stands to lose a good deal if his real or supposed indiscretions appear in the foreign press). They are unimportant in comparison with the damage done to his reputation by the frequent absurd attempts to build him up into that which he is not: Russia's Angry Young Man, Soviet international playboy, heir to the greatest Russian poets, or a mixture of the three. Perhaps the most unrestrained examples come from the French press:

Partout où il passe, souffle un vent de génie, de scandale peut-être, d'amour et d'amitié à coup sûr . . . . Mais ce phénomène prodigieux, ce mélange de dinamitéro, d'Elvis Presley et de Pouchkine, ce pin-up boy aux mots chargés de désir ou de foudre, ce promeneur tempêtueux et désinvolte, gourmand et pur, qui est-il vraiment? . . . tous sont d'accord: ce garçon super-séduisant est de feu et de velours, plein de ces cries et de ces caresses qui font de lui le vrai successeur des grands poètes de son pays . . . ."

[Wherever he wanders, he carries an air of genius, of scandal perhaps, of love and friendship for sure . . . But this prodigious character, this mixture of a dinamitero, of an Elvis Presley and of a Pushkin, this pin-up boy whose words are loaded with desire and thunder, this tempestuous and unconstrained walker, greedy and pure, who is he indeed? . . . . they all agree: this super seductive fellow is fire and velvet, full of those cries and caresses which make him the very successor of the great poets of his land . . ."]

How did such an image of Yevtushenko arise? First, because Western writers and readers have been too ready to project their own fantasies onto the more humdrum truth; this is not surprising, since the Soviet Union is scarcely a ready source of "human-interest" news stories: Yevtushenko's individualism and supposed heterodoxy are in equal measure surprising, interesting, and subconsciously reassuring to the West. Second, there is the less easily analyzable power of Yevtushenko's own personality. Those who have come into contact with him (even hard-bitten Kremlinologists) have shown themselves impressed beyond the predictable effect of his work by his striking personal qualities, while his performance as a reciter of his own verse can be electrifying. Third, the somewhat regrettable "Yevtushenko image" is not a Western invention, save in its more rabid development. It is rooted in the enthusiasm (perhaps typically Russian) with which Soviet audiences and readers—particularly of the younger generation—have greeted the poet's books and public readings during the last decade. It is not unusual in the USSR for a literary figure to attain the popularity of a sporting hero, or for his editions to be sold out (under the counter) on publication day. But Yevtushenko's success even by this yardstick has been remarkable, and is no doubt the only such triumph to have come to the attention of his surprised Western admirers.

It has been necessary to describe the cult image that has grown up around Yevtushenko in some detail. An understanding of it is important if one is to assess the worth of his real achievements, the nature of the critical reaction against him, the ambiguities of tone with which his doings continue to be reported (e.g., the London *Times,* April 21, 1966: "He masticates American chlorophyll chewing gum, chain smokes American cigarettes, wears tailor-made European pin-striped suits, and his opinions on everything from politics to women are seemingly limitless. In short, Russia's Yevgeni Yevtushenko—part poet, part showman—is his old self again . . ."), and—most important—the developments in his own career since 1963.

Early that year he was in France, where *L'Express* commissioned and serialized *A Precocious Autobiography.* The work was written hastily, and has a flavor of the midnight oil about it. But it evidently crystallizes numerous ideas which had been forming in Yevtushenko's mind for some time, and had received partial expression previously, both in verbal utterances and in a long article written for the *Observer* during his London visit in 1962. The book contains impressively written set scenes from the poet's experience, encapsuled among uncomplicated, near journalistic passages and aphoristic jottings on Soviet cultural life. It is interesting as a possibly unique attempt by a Soviet writer to explain his world and his credo to a specifically Western audience, in a full-length work not subject to Russian censorship (ironically, the French version was unpardonably distorted).

The last installments of the *Autobiography* had not yet appeared when Khrushchev delivered his notorious speech of March 8, 1963. This speech gave high-level backing to an antimodernist offensive in official artistic policy which had been gathering momentum since the end of the previous year (itself an *annus mirabilis* for the "liberal" school of Soviet writers). The *Autobiography's* appearance could not have been more unfortunately timed. Khrushchev's strictures were comparatively mild and haphazard, missing obvious targets and chasing will-o'-the-wisps. But they immediately gave the cue for a much more systematic intensification of the offensive (organized by Leonid Ilyichev, then chief ideological functionary), during which the leading young "liberal" poets, Yevtushenko and his friend Andrei Voznesensky, were among those vilified. The *Autobiography* (which to a Western reader may well seem a work imbued with the purest Communist idealism) had especially rough handling, apparently because of the author's allegedly individualistic interpretation of Russian history and his generally "egocentric" approach. But the scurrility of the attacks far outweighed the occasion for them, showing plainly that the literary "old guard" was anxious to take its revenge on one who had provoked and lampooned it often enough in the past. The very fact of publication not in the USSR, but abroad, was taken as a sign of duplicity, even treachery.

The antimodernist offensive collapsed rather surprisingly during the summer months; it is probable that the intervention with Khrushchev of such respected figures as Tvardovsky and Paustovsky was a factor in this. In any case, it had never really taken the course that it would have done in Stalin's day. It was reported in the Western press that the various errant writers had "confessed" their misdeeds; but this can hardly be said to have been so, since after a long meeting evidently called in hope of exacting such "confessions," only brief and equivocal statements were printed in the USSR. Yevtushenko's speech "displeased his audience," and apparently little of it was contrite enough to be quotable; the regrets he expressed over his *Autobiography* are scarcely fundamental: "My most serious mistake was that I forgot about the morals of the foreign press, and I have been severely punished for this" (a reference to the fact that *L'Express* distorted his text).

Effects of the offensive, however, lingered on for some time. In 1961 Yevtushenko had given some 250 public recitals of his work; from 1963 to 1965 these were almost entirely eliminated. He could no longer go abroad. But his work was published. A lyric poem uses the lasting beauty of Queen Nefertiti in the ossified world of the pharaohs as a symbol of the living role of art in society. It foreshadows Yevtushenko's most ambitious single work, which appeared in April 1965, "Bratsk Power Station." In this lengthy poem-cycle the Pyramids are used as a symbol of the negative and stultifying tendencies in mankind, while the great hydroelectric scheme at Bratsk in Siberia, near the poet's birthplace, serves as a symbol not only of technological progress, but of human cooperation (*brat* — *brother*) and of enlightenment (light from electricity). It is a digressive work, with many good moments (notably a passage on Mayakovsky), but in this writer's opinion it is not ultimately successful; it is too diffuse and portentous. Yevtushenko would seem to produce his best poetry when not trying too hard to do so.

At the time of writing (1966) Yevtushenko's public position is re-establishing itself. He has traveled to Australia, West Africa and the U.S.; a booklet of a few new poems has appeared, and more can be expected; he has lent poetic but ineffective encouragement to the World Chess Championship contender Boris Spassky; he is again reciting before large audiences. The events of 1963 have been a shock, but a salutary shock, to one who was an admirer of Khrushchev. It can be expected that he will not fade from the public eye, but will outgrow his *enfant terrible* image without retracting his principles. His verse may become all the better for such a development.

How should we sum up Yevtushenko the public figure and Yevtushenko the poet? The two are bound closely together, yet sometimes they war with each other. His public role (traditional among Russian poets) has quite evidently both inspired and hampered him as an artist: he might have been a better poet had he been a less important one. In his poem "About Creativity" (1961) we watch him first battling with himself and with the "frightening dumbness" which descends on a writer when inspiration is withheld from him, then realizing he must as a poet make himself the mouthpiece for all the dumb yearnings of the world (symbolized in the rustle of falling snow, the clanking of lonely trams). It should be noted that his most public poems tend to be couched in personal and particular terms. "Babi Yar," a resounding cry against anti-Semitism, gains in immediacy through its origin in the poet's own response to visiting the neglected site of a massacre near Kiev. "Heirs of Stalin," one of his best-known polemics, is couched in alarmingly tangible detail (particularly the fine opening section, with its perverted echoes of "The Burial of Sir John Moore after Corunna"); as poetry, the generalized latter part tails off. The honesty of Yevtushenko's public position has sometimes been impugned, in the West as well as in Russia. This is unjust. His battles have been real ones, his successes bought at the price of considerable risk. Though we may read, for example, that "Yevtushenko's poetry is interesting in as much as it reflects changes of political opinion in the Soviet Union," we should remember that some of his best-known poems took months or years before anyone would accept them for publication. Politically he is scarcely the enigmatic figure that he has sometimes been made out to be. In his answers to an extremely interesting questionnaire, "Writers' and Artists' Forum" (circulated in 1962) he wrote:

I think of communism as a sort of symbolic state where the president will be Truth, served by the two ministers, Gentleness and Strictness. In my view, these two ministers will be enough. The writer, then, ought to be the prototype of a communist state of that nature. In the first place, he must be gentle in his attitude to people, he must love them and understand them. But he must be something else too: he must be implacably strict both towards his own failings and towards those of others. However, I'd like to say that an author has the right to be merciless and severe with people only if he knows how to treat them gently too.

A simple philosophy, but hardly the worse for that. More generally, he sees a world made up of two nations—the good and the bad—cutting across any national or political allegiances. "Maturity is the ability to see the good in others and to fight for that good. That is why I have remained an optimist. But my optimism is no longer sky-blue or rosy. It is made up of all colours of the spectrum, including black." The struggle is often enough depressing, and some of his most poignant and memorable poetry stems from the almost insuperable difficulties of overcoming *razobshchonnost'* (the negative principle that drives people apart, hinders communication or understanding) in private or in public matters: cf. the poem "Lyudi" ("People"). Revolution—a concept genuinely close to his heart— seems to mean for him the cooperation of good people (overcoming *razobshchonnost'*) in the face of evil. Dr. Ronald Hingley (in *Problems of Communism,* May 1964) misinterprets this attitude as naïvely condoning bloodshed; but Yevtushenko is perfectly aware of the tragedy which revolution has brought in its train—ideally "revolution" is bloodless, indeed universally welcomed.

For a non-Russian-speaking readership, any discussion of the purely artistic quality of Yevtushenko's work must be brief. It has been frequently criticized, and not without reason; all but his best poems contain weak, even jejune passages (as the poet himself will admit). Yet at his best he has far more than temporary or local merit. From Mayakovsky, and even more from Mayakovsky's disciple Semyon Kirsanov, he has learned to use words to their maximum sonorous effect, with strikingly novel rhymes and assonances. From Yesenin he has acquired lightness of touch, love of the countryside, moments of pathos and a touch of sentimentality—sometimes well controlled, sometimes not. The transcendental, highly personal visions of Blok and Pasternak find occasional echoes in his verse—as in "Tainy" ("Secrets")—and one would like to see further developments in this direction. In general both imagery and fantasy are sparse in his verse (as is common—and to a Western reader disconcerting—among Russian poets). He is eclectic, having learned from other writers besides those mentioned; but he has successfully found a recognizable poetic voice of his own. Two short stories and the *Autobiography* show him also to be a promising prose stylist. He could be characterized—not pejoratively—as a middle-brow writer; on the whole he has left the higher subtleties to his friend Voznesensky (this could well be a deliberate act of abnegation; he is genuinely modest about his own literary significance). What his verse has thereby lost in sophisticated critical esteem, it has gained in effect when declaimed aloud—such a poem as "Kar'era ("Career") is a shadow of itself on the printed page. When all the political alarums about Yevtushenko's name have died down, there should still be enough artistic and human merit apparent in his best work for his name to survive.

SELECTED BIBLIOGRAPHY

The volumes of Yevtushenko's poetry published in the Soviet Union include *Razvedchiki griadushchego* (Moskva, 1952); *Tretii sneg* (Moskva, 1952); *Shosse entuziastov* (Moskva, 1956); *Obeshchanie* (Moskva, 1957); *Luk i lira* (Tbilisi, 1959); *Stikhi rasnykh let* (Moskva, 1959); *Iabloko* (Moskva, 1960); *Vzmakh ruki* (Moskva, 1962); *Nezhnost'* (Moskva, 1962); *So mnoiu vot chto proiskhodit* (Moskva, 1966). Among the many poems by Yevtushenko that have been published in various Soviet newspapers and journals, the most important are "Stantsiia Zima," *Oktiabr'*, 10 (October 1956); "Babii Iar," *Literaturnaia gazeta*, September 19, 1961; "Nasledniki Stalina," *Pravda*, October 21, 1962; and, more recently, "Tretiia pamiat'," *Novyi mir*, 7 (July 1964); "Ballada o brakonerstve," *Novyi mir*, 1 (January 1965); and "Bratskaia GES," *Iunost*, 4 (April 1966). Yevtushenko's prose includes the short stories "Kurinii bog," *Molodaia gvardiia*, 1 (January 1963); and "Chetvertaia meshchanskaia," *Iunost' 1955–1965* (Moskva, 1965); and comments in the "Writers' and Artists' Forum," in *Soviet Literature,* 12 (December 1962).

Although it has never been published in the Soviet Union, Yevtushenko's autobiography is now readily available in English translation as *A Precocious*

Autobiography, translated by A. A. MacAndrew, New York: Dutton, 1963. For other English translations of Yevtushenko's work, see Yevgeny Yevtushenko, *Selected Poems,* translåted and with an introduction by R. R. Milner-Gulland and P. Levi, S.J., Harmondsworth and New York: Penguin and Dutton, 1962, and *The Poetry of Yevgeny Yevtushenko, 1953 to 1965,* translated by George Reavey, New York: October House, 1965; *Halfway to the Moon: New Writing from Russia,* edited by Patricia Blake and Max Hayward, New York: Holt, Rinehart and Winston, 1964; *Yevtushenko: Selected Poetry,* translated by R. R. Milner-Gulland and P. Levi, S.J., London and New York: Collins and Dutton, 1966.

Yevtushenko's poetry has also been published in the West in the original Russian, in *Posle Stalina,* introduction by A. M. Gurbich, Chicago: Russian Language Specialties, 1962; Yevgeny Yevtushenko, *Selected Poetry,* edited by R. R. Milner-Gulland, Oxford: Pergamon, 1963; *Soviet Russian Verse: An Anthology,* edited by R. R. Milner-Gulland, Oxford and Long Island City: Pergamon Press, 1964; George Reavey, *op. cit.* (a bilingual edition). And *The Penguin Book of Russian Verse* (bilingual), second edition, edited by D. Obolensky, Harmondsworth and New York: Penguin and Dutton, 1965.

Criticism, both literary and political, may be found in *Vo ves' golos* (Moskva, 1963), a collection of Soviet articles attacking Yevtushenko; Patricia Blake, "New Voices in Russian Writing," *Encounter* (April 1963); Pierre Forgues, "The Young Poets," *Literature and Revolution in Soviet Russia, 1917–1962,* edited by M. Hayward and L. Labedz, London: Oxford University Press, 1963; and Priscilla Johnson, *Khrushchev and the Arts,* Cambridge: M.I.T. Press, 1965.

List of Contributors

SEVERYN BIALER is senior fellow of the Research Institute on Communist Affairs at Columbia University and associate professor in the Department of Government. He is engaged in research on the Soviet political and military elite and has written many articles, most recently, "The Men Who Run Russia's Armed Forces," *The New York Times Magazine*, February 21, 1965, and "An Unstable Leadership," *Problems of Communism*, XIV, 4 (July and August, 1965).

PATRICIA BLAKE has been research associate at the Russian Institute of Columbia University (1964–1966). A specialist on contemporary Soviet literature, she has edited *The Bedbug and Selected Poetry* by Vladimir Mayakovsky and coedited, with Max Hayward, *Dissonant Voices in Soviet Literature; Halfway to the Moon: New Writing from Russia;* and *Antiworlds: Poetry by Andrei Voznesensky.*

THOMPSON BRADLEY is assistant professor in the Department of Modern Languages and Literatures at Swarthmore College. He spent 1961–1962 in the Soviet Union under the official academic exchange. He has translated three stories (by Vs. Ivanov, M. Prishvin, and B. Pilniak) for *Great Soviet Short Stories,* edited by Franklin D. Reeve, and edited *The Gentleman from San Francisco and Other Stories* by Ivan Bunin, the work of whom has been the object of his doctoral research.

RICHARD T. DE GEORGE is professor of philosophy at the University of Kansas. He has served as senior research fellow at the Russian Institute of Columbia University (1965–1966) and as associate of the Institute of East European Studies at the University of Fribourg, Switzerland (1962–1963). In addition to having edited *Classical and Contemporary Metaphysics* and *Ethics and Society,* he has written *Patterns of Soviet Thought,* and is presently completing a book on Soviet ethics and morality.

VERA S. DUNHAM is lecturer in the Department of Slavic Languages and Literatures at Wayne State University and senior fellow at the Russian Institute, Columbia University (1966–1967). She has done extensive research in recent Soviet poetry and has published many articles on Soviet life and literature. She is a book reviewer for *Ost-Europa, Russian Review,* and *The Slavic and East European Journal* and is consultant and reader for the *Current Digest of Soviet Press,* Columbia University.

MAURICE FRIEDBERG is professor of Slavic languages and literatures at Indiana University. He has written *Russian Classics in Soviet Jackets* and *The Party and the Poet in the USSR* as well as many articles and reviews on modern Russian literature. He has edited and translated volume I and, with Robert Maguire, volume II of *A Bilingual Collection of Russian Short Stories.*

JOHN N. HAZARD is professor of public law and a member of the faculty of the Russian Institute at Columbia University. He serves on the editorial boards of leading law journals. Among his best-known books are *Soviet Legal Philosophy; Law and Social Change in the USSR; The Soviet System of Government; Settling Disputes in Soviet Society;* and with I. Shapiro, *The Soviet Legal System.*

RONALD HINGLEY is university lecturer in Russian and fellow of St. Antony's College at Oxford. He has written *Chekhov: A Biographical and Critical Study; Under Soviet Skins; The Undiscovered Dostoevsky; Russian Writers and Society: A Background,* and he is serving as general editor and translator for volumes III and VIII of *The Oxford Chekhov.*

GREY HODNETT is assistant professor in the Department of Government at Columbia College and associate of the Russian Institute, Columbia University. He has written a number of articles on internal Soviet government, his special field of interest, and is doing research on the current organizational and policy problems of the Communist Party of the Soviet Union.

EDGAR H. LEHRMAN is associate professor and chairman of the Russian Department at Emory University. He has translated and edited *Turgenev's Letters: A Selection* and written "Akimov Versus Hamlet," in *Essays of Shakespeare* edited by Gordon Ross Smith. He spent 1962–1963 in the Soviet Union under the official academic exchange, and met Paustovsky there in 1963.

KERMIT E. MCKENZIE is associate professor and director of graduate studies in the Department of History at Emory University. He has written articles on Soviet politics and international Communism, his specialty, and he is the author of *Comintern and World Revolution, 1928–1943: The Shaping of Doctrine.*

MAXIM W. MIKULAK is assistant professor of history at the State University College at Fredonia, New York. He has specialized in the Soviet philosophy of science and contributed articles on the subject to the *Journal of Social Studies, The Scientific Monthly, Philosophy of Science, Slavic Review,* and to the books *Essays in Russian and Soviet History* and *The State of Soviet Science.*

R. R. MILNER-GULLAND is lecturer in the School of European Studies at the University of Sussex, with over-all responsibility for Russian at the university. In 1960–1961 he was a postgraduate exchange student at Moscow University. He has edited *Soviet Russian Verse: An Anthology* and *Yevgeny Yevtushenko:*

Selected Poetry, and with Peter Levi, S.J., has edited and translated *Yevtushenko: Selected Poems* and *Poems Chosen by the Author: Yevtushenko.*

SIEGFRIED MÜLLER-MARKUS is professor and chairman of the Physikalisches Sonderstudium of the East European Institute at the University of Fribourg, Switzerland. During ten years as war prisoner in Russia, he studied physics and Soviet philosophy. He has since published many articles on the Soviet philosophy of science as well as a two-volume work, *Einstein und die Sowjetphilosophie.*

ALBERT PARRY, a native of Russia, is professor of Russian civilization and language and chairman of the Department of Russian Studies at Colgate University. A specialist on Soviet science, he serves as consultant and visiting lecturer to the United States Army War College and the Inter-American Defense College, and he is the author of *Russia's Rockets and Missiles, Russian Cavalcade,* and *The New Class Divided: Russian Science and Technology versus Communism.*

MYRON RUSH is professor of government at Cornell University. Formerly senior research staff member of RAND Corporation, he is the author of *The Rise of Khrushchev, Political Succession in the USSR,* and co-author with Arnold Horelick of *Strategic Power and Soviet Foreign Policy.*

GEORGE W. SIMMONDS is associate professor of history and Russian language at Elmira College as well as co-director of its Russian Studies Program. He has written on Soviet and Russian history and is currently completing a study of the politics of the twentieth-century prerevolutionary Russian gentry.

ROBERT M. SLUSSER is associate professor of history at Johns Hopkins University. He served as associate director of the Research Program on the USSR, East European Fund, Ford Foundation, from 1953 to 1956. He has written *A Calendar of Soviet Treaties, 1917–1957* and *Theory, Law and Policy of Soviet Treaties,* and is co-author of *The Soviet Secret Police.*

DAVID H. STEWART is professor of English language and literature at the University of Michigan. He has written many articles in the field of comparative literature, giving special attention to Mikhail Sholokhov. He has written a number of critical articles on that author and has made translations of his stories. He is presently completing the first full-length study on Sholokhov in English.

ROBERT C. STUART served as teaching assistant in the Department of Economics at the University of Wisconsin in 1963–1964. He was one of four Canadian scholars to spend 1966 in the Soviet Union under the official academic exchange, where he pursued his doctoral study of Soviet agriculture.

Glossary of Political and
Historical Terms

ACADEMY OF SCIENCES OF THE USSR. The chief, central learned society in the Soviet Union. The Academy of Sciences of the USSR serves as coordinating agency for a vast system of academic and research institutions throughout the Soviet Union as well as the principal foundation through which the Soviet government channels funds for research of national importance in all fields of learning. The membership of the Academy, consisting of elected fellows and corresponding members, is divided into nine sections according to fields, each of which is governed by its own administration. The executive authority is in the hands of a presidium headed by the president of the Academy, traditionally a well-known and respected scientist. The Academy has branches in the Russian republic and in other areas of the Soviet Union. In addition, all of the republics, except the Russian, have their own academies which are responsible to the national society. Hundreds of institutes, laboratories, scientific councils, research stations, museums, libraries, and the like participate in the work of the Soviet and republican academies.

AUTONOMOUS REGION. Separate territorial and administrative units within the union republics. Subordinate to the governmental machinery of the union republics in which they are found, autonomous regions are made up of various minor ethnic groups in the USSR, such as the Kalmyk people on the northern Caspian coast, the Cherkess in the northern Caucasus, and the South Ossetians in Georgia. See UNION REPUBLIC; REGION.

AUTONOMOUS REPUBLIC. A territorial and administrative unit in the USSR, twenty in all. Designated formally as Autonomous Soviet Socialist Republics (ASSR), there are sixteen in the central Asian and Siberian parts of the Russian republic alone, where they comprise some of the lesser ethnic groups, such as the Bashkirs, Mordovians, Ossetians, Tartars, Yakuts, and Buriat Mongols. Two autonomous republics—the Abkhazian and Adzharian—are located in the Azerbaijanian republic; the Karelian autonomous republic is situated on the Finnish frontier, and Kara Kalpak autonomous republic is in the Uzbek Soviet Socialist Republic. See UNION REPUBLIC; RSFSR.

CENTRAL COMMITTEE OF THE CPSU. The highest body of the Communist Party of the Soviet Union (CPSU), elected by the party congress and directed internally by the smaller body, the Politburo. The present-day Central Committee of the CPSU is composed of over 250 high party officials from around the country who owe their positions as either full or candidate (probationary) members to the top leadership in the party. The Central Committee concerns itself not only with the organization and supervision of party staffs throughout the Soviet Union, but with every other aspect of Soviet life as well, from literature to production. Basic decisions of policy for the party—and for the country—are made by members of the Politburo and Secretariat of the Central Committee, or in the entourage of the first secretary of the Central Committee. The full membership of the Central Committee is usually summoned to rubber-stamp decisions made by the smaller, leading internal bodies. See POLITBURO OF THE CENTRAL COMMITTEE OF THE CPSU; SECRETARIAT OF THE CENTRAL COMMITEE OF THE CPSU.

COLLECTIVE FARM. In theory, an agricultural producers' cooperative jointly operated by its membership. The collective farm (*kollektivnoe khoziaistvo* or *kolkhoz* for short) is the most widely established form of agricultural organization in the USSR. Essentially controlled by the state, collective farms are distinguished from the so-called state farms (*sovkhoz*) by the fact that the members of the former are permitted to live in their own dwellings and dispose of the products grown on their own tiny private household plots, over and above, of course, their common responsibilities to their collective farm. See MTS.

COMMUNIST PARTY OF THE SOVIET UNION. Originating as a small, left-wing faction (called Bolshevik after 1903) of the revolutionary Russian Social Democratic Labor Party, the Communist Party of the Soviet Union (CPSU) is today the elite corps managing the conventional state machinery as well as all other aspects of life in the USSR. The only legal political party in the USSR, the CPSU is a disciplined, centralized bureaucracy (*apparat*) of some 9,000,000 members whose behavior—which includes operating in concerted groups, subordination to the next higher party units, and rigid adherence to party decisions—is carefully defined in party statutes. Members are recruited especially from youth organizations, such as the Komsomol (see YOUNG COMMUNIST LEAGUE), and membership is considered a privilege earned and retained through service. To join, an applicant must be recommended by three party members and must be approved by the local unit to which he is applying and by the district (*raion*) or city party committee. A probationary period—candidate membership—of at least one year is required during which the applicant has a voice but no vote. Dues are paid according to income. Aside from the approximately quarter of a million full-time paid party professionals, party members, many of whom are highly influential Soviet citizens, have full-time jobs of their own and serve the party during their free time. The hierarchical structure of the party has at its base almost half a million "primary organizations," formerly called "cells." Ranging in size from three to several hundred members, the primary organizations are based on economic entities (rather than on territorial areas) such as factories, farms, offices, and the like. The hierarchy culminates in the fifteen union republics, except in the case of the Russian republic, where each *krai* or territorial unit has its own party structure. Thus, the primary organizations elect delegates to city conferences or district conferences. These elect delegates to regional (*oblast*) conferences, which in turn elect delegates to party congresses of the union republics (*krais,* in the case of the Russian republic). Finally, delegates to the all-union party congresses are chosen at the republican party congresses. Capping the entire structure is the Central Committee with its two major inner bodies, the Secretariat and the Politburo. The work of the central governing institutions of the Soviet Union—including the Supreme Soviet, Council of Ministers, ministries and boards, Judiciary—is supervised and controlled by the parallel organs of the central administration of the party, and indeed by the top party officials themselves who are also members of the central institutions of the government. Thus the basic policies of state are hammered out in the Politburo and Secretariat of the party's Central Committee. See CENTRAL COMMITTEE OF THE CPSU.

COUNCIL OF MINISTERS OF THE USSR. Located at the very top of the vast Soviet state economic structure, the Council of Ministers of the USSR supervises the over-all work of Soviet industry and agriculture and carries out supervision over long-range and short-term planning. Similarly, each union republic has its own counterpart council. The membership of the Soviet Council of Ministers, formally elected by the Supreme Soviet of the USSR but in fact appointed by the top party organs, includes the chairmen of the ministerial councils of the union republics; the chairmen of the committees and ministries controlling the work throughout the country of the conventional sectors of the economy and of special fields; and representatives from the State Planning Committee (Gosplan), the Central Statistical Administration, and other organs of economic management. Most of the leading members of the council are also members of the party. In practice the council follows the policies developed by its small inner directorate, the Presidium of the Council of Ministers of the USSR, which in turn is responsible to the top party organs. A similar relationship exists between the presidium and councils of the union republics. Both the all-union and the republican ministerial councils were charged with supervising the work of the more than one hundred all-union committees and regional councils of the national economy (*sovnarkhozy*), until the latter were abolished in November 1964. See COUNCILS OF THE NATIONAL ECONOMY; MAIN ADMINISTRATION.

COUNCILS OF THE NATIONAL ECONOMY. Instituted for the first time in 1957, and abolished after Khrushchev's fall from power in November 1964, the economic councils (*sovnarkhozy*), operating locally, supervised large sectors of economic life in a given area as opposed to the previous practice whereby ministries ran one industry throughout the entire country. The creation of *sovnarkhozy*, it was hoped, would destroy the typical bottlenecks that resulted from overcentralization of the Soviet economy. The work of the economic councils was supervised by the councils of ministers of the union republics, and at the all-union level, by a Council of the National Economy which in turn was subordinate to a Supreme Council of the National Economy (VSnKh SSSR) established in 1963.

COURT SYSTEM. The court system of the USSR ranges from the People's Courts (composed each of a judge and two nonprofessional "lay assessors") at the grass-roots level, through intermediate courts at each higher step of local government culminating in supreme courts of the union republics, which act largely as courts of appeal and review. The highest court is the Supreme Court of the USSR. At each level there is an office of the procuracy, which has functions similar to those of the attorney general in the United States, except that it combines the function of checking on the legality of court decisions with prosecution of criminal cases and representing the interest of the state in civil cases. Decisions are based on code law formulated by the republics. However, political and criminal cases are still tried by military tribunals, and the judicial system is subject to check by the party. Social or public "comradely courts" have also been revived for minor infractions since 1957.

CPSU. Abbreviation for the COMMUNIST PARTY OF THE SOVIET UNION.

DISTRICT. The district (*raion*), constituting the major subdivision of the region (*oblast'*), may be compared to the American county. Its governing organs are subordinate to those of the region as well as to the pertinent national administrations of which they may be a part. Larger cities are also divided into districts, which then function as urban wards, and some small ethnic groups living within the territory of a more important nationality are governed within their own so-called national districts.

ECCI. The Executive Committee of the Communist International (IKKI) was the Moscow-controlled ruling body of the international union of Communist parties, or Comintern, from 1920 to its abolition on May 20, 1943.

EXECUTIVE COMMITTEE. Constituting the true governing body in the hierarchy of soviets at the local level, from territorial or regional organizations on down, the executive committee (*ispolnitel'nyi komitet* or *ispolkom*) of each local soviet consists of a chairman, vice chairman, a secretary, and other members, usually heads of departments or standing commissions of the organization. This board of directors carries on the main work of the soviets in the intervals between the infrequent plenary sessions of elected soviet deputies. In the larger soviets the executive committee is itself guided by a small board of its top officials (the bureau or presidium). The chairman of the executive committees, who are appointed to office by the party committees and executive committees on the next higher levels, play a major role in all aspects of the work of their organization. Although responsible to some extent to their "electors," since the full plenums of the soviets always vote on the appointments of their officials, the members of the executive committees are basically subordinate to the executive committee on the next higher rung of the hierarchy of soviets, and to the party. See PRESIDIUM; SOVIETS.

FIRST SECRETARY. See PARTY SECRETARY.

GLAVK. See MAIN ADMINISTRATION.

GOSPLAN. See State Planning Committee.

IZVESTIIA. Published by the Presidium of the Supreme Soviet of the USSR, *Izvestiia* (*News*) is the second most important daily newspaper in the Soviet Union, the first being the leading party paper, *Pravda*. Founded on March 13, 1917, as the organ of the Petrograd Soviet of Workers' and Soldiers' Deputies, the newspaper now carries, because of its official nature, the full text of laws and government decrees, notices of official appointments, information about the conventional state machinery, and the like.

KHOZRASCHOT. Economic accountability (*khozraschot*), a system that partially resembles Western business practice, is one of the principles in the management of Soviet enterprises. Each Soviet firm is legally an independent entity, required to make its own economic arrangements and balance its books, though of course the Soviet state and party determine in many ways the nature and direction of enterprise performance. Much thought has been given recently in the Soviet Union regarding the possibility of increasing the autonomy of Soviet industrial management.

KOLKHOZ. See COLLECTIVE FARM.

KOMMUNIST. The theoretical and political journal of the Central Committee of the Communist 'Party of the Soviet Union. Appearing bi-monthly, its pages are devoted primarily to discussion and pronouncements on party theory and history, current party practice, foreign affairs and problems pertaining to international Communism. *Kommunist*'s earlier name (from 1924 to October 1952) was *Bol'shevik*.

KOMSOMOL. See YOUNG COMMUNIST LEAGUE.

KOMSOMOL'SKAIA PRAVDA. The official organ of the Young Communist League (Komsomol), and as such, carefully controlled by the party. It has in the past reflected to some extent the attitudes current among Soviet youth. On its pages are published from time to time the writings of youthful critics, such as the poetry of Yevgeny Yevtushenko, while at other times the paper has served as an instrument for exceedingly rabid official opinion—for example, when it printed violent diatribes against Boris Pasternak after the illegal publication abroad of his novel *Dr. Zhivago*.

KRAI. See TERRITORY.

KRASNAIA ZVEZDA. The central organ of the Ministry of Defense of the USSR. A weekly paper, *Krasnaia zvezda* (*Red Star*) features articles on all aspects of Soviet military theory and practice as well as on the place of the military in Soviet life. The paper has been published since 1924.

KULAK. The term applied to the well-to-do peasant, distinguishing him from the poor peasant (*bedniak*) or middle peasant (*sredniiak*), in the political and economic sociology applied by the Bolsheviks both prior to the Russian Revolution of 1917 and during the NEP and collectivization periods.

LITERATURNAIA GAZETA. Published since 1929, and now appearing three times a week, *Literaturnaia gazeta* (*Literary News*) is the organ of the Union of Writers of the USSR. In the Soviet manner, articles and editorials on important nonliterary domestic and foreign problems appear frequently on its pages. The paper has been moderate and sometimes even liberal in tone since 1953.

MAIN ADMINISTRATION. The work of enterprises in a given area involved in the production of a group of related products or services is coordinated not only by the home office of the pertinent ministry or economic council, or the relevant department in the executive committee of the local soviets, but also by a number of intermediary bodies such as the main or chief administration (*glavk*) in that field. Other types of similar intermediary organs include the trust (*trest*), combine (*kombinat*), department (*otdel*), and administration (*upravlenie*).

MTS. The Machine Tractor Stations (MTS) were state agencies stationed throughout the Soviet countryside which for a fixed fee, usually in kind, provided tractors, combines, and other agricultural machinery as well as service the year round to the collective farms until, in 1958, they were liquidated and their machinery turned over to the collective farms themselves.

NATIONAL AREAS. There are ten so-called national areas (*okrug*) in the Russian republic, each populated by a minor Siberian ethnic group, such as the Buriat-Mongols in southern Siberia, and each administratively subordinate to the region or territory of which it is a part.

NEP. Shorthand designation for the period of the New Economic Policy which was established by the Eighth Congress of the Communist Party of the Soviet Union in March 1921 and superseded by the policy of forced collectivization and industrialization at the end of the 1920's. The economic, social, and cultural policies followed during the NEP period by the party were designed to permit Soviet Russia to recover from the stringent wartime policies of 1917–21, and included restoration of small-scale private industry, farming, and trade (whereas major industry and foreign trade remained in the hands of the government); restoration of traditional methods of diplomacy; acceptance of wide latitude in the fine arts; and expression of cultural nationalism. Politically, however, the period marked a further step in the direction of governmental authoritarianism, a consequence of the abolition of all competing political parties in 1922.

Novyi MIR. Founded in 1923, the journal *Novyi mir* (*New World*) has become, since the Second World War, a major force not only in the USSR's literary world, but in Soviet culture in general. It ranks as the most solid and established liberal literary journal in the country. Sixty per cent of its space is devoted to fiction, poetry, and criticism, and the remainder to the publication of articles on important current issues and—in recent years—of extremely revealing travel accounts and memoirs.

OBLAST'. See REGION.

OKRUG. See NATIONAL AREAS.

ORGBURO. Established, along with the Secretariat and Politburo, as an inner body of the Central Committee of the Communist party at the party's Eighth Congress (March 1919), the Orgburo (Organizational Bureau) was to supervise organizational procedures in the party, including distribution and assignment of personnel. However, the Secretariat, headed after 1922 by Stalin, soon took over many of the Orgburo's functions and the latter was abolished in October 1952 at the party's Nineteenth Congress. See SECRETARIAT OF THE CENTRAL COMMITTEE OF THE CPSU.

PARTY COMMITTEES. The permanent executive bodies of the party organizations, called committees on the local level and central committees at the union republic and all-union levels, are charged with maintaining control over all party undertakings and supervising the work of all other institutions in their areas. Since at higher party levels the staff is organized in specialized departments and is thus often very large, the real direction in each of the larger committees or central committees belongs to an inner body of seven or more top officials, including the party chairmen (secretaries), called the bureau or, at the union republic or all-union level, the presidium. See CENTRAL COMMITTEE OF THE CPSU; PARTY SECRETARY.

PARTY CONFERENCE. See PARTY CONGRESS.

PARTY CONGRESS. The congresses of the party, as they are called at the union republic and all-union levels, and conferences, their designation at regional and district levels, are assemblies of the more important party officials held periodically in accordance with party statutes; thus, the congresses meet not less than every four years, the conferences not less than every eighteen months. Although party rules empower conferences and congresses to elect their executive bodies (committees and central committees) and standing commissions, to choose the delegates to conferences and congresses at the next higher level, and to discuss important problems facing the party, these bodies are not at all "the supreme directing organ of each party organization" as stated in the party rules; rather, since the late 1920's, they are rubber stamps for the more important inner bodies of the party organizations. See PARTY COMMITTEES.

PARTY SECRETARY. The secretaries, or chairmen, of the party organizations at all levels constitute the directorate for the party and all other institutions in their area. They are directly responsible to, and appointed by, the next higher level of the party. The post of first secretary is probably the most powerful single office at any given level throughout the Soviet state, the first secretary taking precedence over all other officials in his area including the chairman of the executive committee of the local soviet. The second secretary, usually responsible for the organization and agitation and propaganda departments, also holds a special place. The first and second secretaries of all party organizations at the regional (*oblast'*) level and up must be considered part of the ruling elite not only of the party but of the USSR, with the first secretary of the Central Committee and his entourage constituting the real policy-making body in the Soviet Union. See CENTRAL COMMITTEE OF THE CPSU.

POLITBURO OF THE CENTRAL COMMITTEE OF THE CPSU. Established formally, along with the Orgburo and Secretariat, as an inner body of the party's Central Committee, at the Eighth Congress of the CPSU in March 1919, the Politburo (Political Bureau) became the policy-making authority not only of the party but of the country for over a decade. Its power gradually declined thereafter as Stalin preferred to make and implement decisions either on his own or in small groups of top party leaders constituting his entourage. In October 1952 the Politburo was superseded by the Presidium, but at the Twenty-third Congress of the CPSU in April 1966, the Presidium was renamed Politburo. See ORGBURO; PRESIDIUM OF THE CENTRAL COMMITTEE OF THE CPSU.

PRAVDA. As the official organ of the Central Committee of the CPSU, *Pravda (Truth)* is the leading daily newspaper in the Soviet Union. Published almost continuously since its establishment as the organ of the Bolshevik faction of the Russian Socialist Democratic Labor Party on May 13, 1912, the newspaper carries in its usual six to eight pages the chief foreign and domestic policy pronouncements of the Soviet leadership as well as information that is circulated to provincial newspapers and other news media throughout the country.

PRESIDIUM. The term is applied to directorates in central and local governing institutions in the Soviet Union. At the federal level, there is the Presidium of the Supreme Soviet of the USSR, the Presidium of the Council of Ministers of the USSR, and the Presidium of the Central Committee of the CPSU. Similarly, there are the presidiums of the supreme soviets, councils of ministers, and central committees of each of the fifteen union republics. Presidiums of executive committees of local soviets have been known to exist, though these have sometimes been designated as bureau (*biuro*). See PRESIDIUM OF THE

CENTRAL COMMITTEE OF THE CPSU; PRESIDIUM OF THE SUPREME SOVIET OF THE USSR.

PRESIDIUM OF THE CENTRAL COMMITTEE OF THE CPSU. At the Nineteenth Congress of the CPSU (October 1952), the Politburo of the Central Committee was replaced by a Presidium consisting of twenty-five full and eleven candidate (probationary) members. In April 1966, at the party's Twenty-third Congress, the Presidium was renamed Politburo. See PARTY SECRETARY; POLITBURO OF THE CENTRAL COMMITTEE OF THE CPSU; SECRETARIAT OF THE CENTRAL COMMITTEE OF THE CPSU.

PRESIDIUM OF THE SUPREME SOVIET OF THE USSR. As the executive committee of the Supreme Soviet of the USSR, the Presidium consists of a chairman, fifteen deputy chairmen (the chairmen of the presidiums of the supreme soviets of the fifteen union republics), a secretary, and sixteen additional members. The chairman of the Presidium, who has always been a respected senior member of the party, performs certain conventional tasks as "head of state," such as receiving diplomatic representatives, presenting decorations, signing legislation, and ratifying treaties. The Presidium carries on the work of the Supreme Soviet in the intervals between the latter's infrequent plenary sessions, issuing decrees, changing laws, or establishing and abolishing government departments, often without approval from the parent body. See SUPREME SOVIET OF THE USSR.

RAION. See DISTRICT.

REGION. The most important administrative subdivision in the union republics. The boundaries of the region (*oblast'*) are usually drawn so as to make possible the most efficient economic management in the area and are frequently changed in accordance with economic needs. In January 1961 there were forty-nine regions in the Russian republic, twenty-five in the Ukraine, six in Byelorussia, eight in the Uzbek republic, fourteen in the Kazakh republic, one in the Tadzhik republic, and three in the Turkmen republic. The regions are themselves subdivided into districts (*raion*), and their governmental, economic, and party organs are subordinate to those of the union republics in which they are located as well as to the national administrations of which they are a part. In addition, a small number of so-called autonomous regions, formed on the principle that smaller ethnic groups should have their own regional institutions, are located primarily in the Russian republic.

RSFSR. Abbreviation for the Russian Soviet Federated Socialist Republic (*Rossiiskaia sovetskaia federativnaia sotsialisticheskaia respublika*), or Russian republic, for short. The RSFSR was established November 7, 1917. It is the largest of the fifteen union republics of the Soviet Union, occupying 6,691,000 square miles or some three quarters of the entire USSR and containing over half of the Soviet Union's population. For that reason its governmental structure is somewhat special, with most of the autonomous republics and regions and all of the national areas of the Soviet Union falling within its borders. Its capital city, Moscow, is also the capital of the Soviet Union. See AUTONOMOUS REGION; AUTONOMOUS REPUBLIC; NATIONAL AREAS; UNION REPUBLIC.

SECRETARIAT OF THE CENTRAL COMMITTEE OF THE CPSU. Instituted by the Eighth Congress of the CPSU in 1919 as the official office organization of the party, the Secretariat was transformed by its first general secretary, Stalin, from a merely administrative organ into one exercising party guidance. Even today the Secretariat is the nerve center of the party—and indeed of the country—by virtue of its control over party appointments, and of the fact that the first secretary has in the past become the chief leader of the country. See CENTRAL COMMITTEE OF THE CPSU; COMMUNIST PARTY OF THE SOVIET UNION; PARTY SECRETARY.

SOIUZ PISATELEI *SSSR*. See UNION OF WRITERS OF THE USSR.

SOVET. The appellation of a unit in the hierarchical system of the formal governmental structure of the USSR. See SOVIETS.

SOVETSKAIA KULTURA. The organ of the Ministry of Culture in the USSR. *Sovetskaia kultura* (*Soviet Culture*) is published three times a week, bringing news and providing editorial comment on all aspects of cultural development in the Soviet Union from the official point of view. The paper first appeared in July 1953.

SOVIETS. The present hierarchy of governmental bodies known as soviets appeared briefly, for the first time, during the Russian Revolution of 1905 in the form of assemblies of delegates from strike committees and then again, permanently, after the Revolution of November 1917, when the Bolsheviks first designated as the government of the future socialist state the nationwide system of organs composed of elected delegates from the socialist parties, the working-class population, the peasants, and the army and navy. Today the system of soviets forms an integral part of the government of the USSR. It appears at the federal level as a national bicameral legislature, the Supreme Soviet of the USSR, which is, to be sure, largely a rubber stamp. Each of the fifteen union republics has a supreme soviet whose functions are similar to those of the Supreme Soviet of the USSR, and there are soviets at each level of local government, from the territory or region on down to the settlement. The major work of the soviets at all levels, in view of the infrequent plenary sessions of the popularly elected delegates, is carried on by permanent departments or in smaller elected or appointed bodies operating under the supervision of a permanent executive committee. At the local level (from the territorial or regional organization on down) the soviets have considerable responsibilities, including the detailed management of production and local services such as education, the militia, public catering, public health, local industry, the communal economy, and agriculture. In the performance of these tasks they are expected to be sensitive to the wishes of the public, but they are also subordinate to the authority of organs in their field at the higher levels (particularly the executive committee of the next higher soviet) and to the party—and the latter two frequently count for more. See EXECUTIVE COMMITTEE; PRESIDIUM; PRESIDIUM OF THE SUPREME SOVIET OF THE USSR; SUPREME SOVIET OF THE USSR.

SOVIET UNION. Abbreviated designation for UNION OF SOVIET SOCIALIST REPUBLICS.

SOVNARKHOZ. See COUNCILS OF THE NATIONAL ECONOMY.

STATE PLANNING COMMITTEE. Planning, a central factor in the Soviet economic system, is in the hands of the State Planning Committee (Gosplan) and its agencies, which is itself subordinate to the Council of Ministers of the USSR.

The planning agency is broken into two sections: those devoted to planning the development of individual branches and sectors of the economy and those dealing with general problems facing the whole of the economy (wages, prices, etc.). Plans are drawn up on a long-range basis (for every five or seven years, for example) as well as annually and even quarterly. Offices of the State Planning Committee exist on every level down to the individual firms, and they are involved in the gathering of information as well as in the formation of plans by all establishments on their level.

SUPREME SOVIET OF THE USSR. The counterpart of the Congress of the United States, but substantially without its power, the Supreme Soviet of the USSR is a bicameral national legislature consisting of a Council (*sovet*) of the Union and a Council of Nationalities. Deputies to the former are elected every two years on the basis of population, roughly one deputy for every 300,000 people, whereas the deputies to the Council of Nationalities are elected on the grounds of nationality in accordance with a complex system of representation from the various ethnic groups. The vast majority of the deputies are members of the Communist party and many hold party or state positions. As the highest formal state organ, the Supreme Soviet of the USSR and its Presidium and standing commissions study and vote on the yearly national budget and economic plan, new legal codification, declarations on foreign policy, and the like, and the officials of its Presidium fulfill ceremonial and diplomatic functions. The Supreme Soviet also elects the members of the Supreme Court of the USSR, the procurator general of the USSR, its own Presidium, and it approves government appointments. It is not a real parliament, however: national policies originate elsewhere; despite hearings and discussions, the Supreme Soviet of the USSR may not essentially alter the nature of basic acts; its effectiveness is curbed by party controls, short sessions, and the custom of unanimity in voting; and many basic laws and state acts passed by other state bodies, such as the Council of Ministers and party Central Committee, never come before the Supreme Soviet. See PRESIDIUM OF THE SUPREME SOVIET OF THE USSR.

TERRITORY. The territory (*krai*) constitutes one of the largest territorial and administrative units below the level of the union republic. At present there are seven territories in the Russian republic and one, the Virgin Lands Territory, in the Kazakh republic.

TRUD. The daily newspaper *Trud* (*Labor*), organ of the official central trade union organization of the USSR, deals with Soviet labor problems and unionism, the impact of new technology, international labor questions, and the like. The paper has a long history, having appeared first in 1921.

UNION OF SOVIET SOCIALIST REPUBLICS. Occupying the largest territory of any country in the world (some 8,640,000 square miles), the Union of Soviet Socialist Republics (*Soiuz sovetskikh sotsialisticheskikh respublik*), often designated as the USSR or Soviet Union, is a heavily centralized state in federal form. The Soviet Union was formally established in December 1922. At present its fifteen constituent republics, or states, are the Russian Soviet Federated Socialist Republic (RSFSR), the Ukrainian Soviet Socialist Republic (UkSSR), the Byelorussian SSR, the Uzbek SSR, the Kazakh SSR, the Kirgiz SSR, the

Tadzhik SSR, the Turkmen SSR, the Georgian SSR, the Azerbaijanian SSR, the Armenian SSR, the Lithuanian SSR, the Latvian SSR, the Estonian SSR, and the Moldavian SSR. See RSFSR; UNION REPUBLIC.

UNION OF WRITERS OF THE USSR. As the official national writers' organization, the Union of Writers of the USSR (*Soiuz pisatelei SSSR*) maintains a central headquarters and permanent staff (*pravlenie*) in Moscow as well as affiliates in all of the localities in the Soviet Union. With a membership of about 6,000, the organization brings out a national paper, the *Literaturnaia gazeta,* as well as additional national and local literary journals and publications. The union operates the Gorky Literary Institute in Moscow for research purposes as well as the Literary Fund, a state foundation providing Soviet writers with travel fellowships, vacations, and other benefits. Since its inception, the organization has held not only innumerable smaller conferences but also three national writers' congresses: in August 1934; December 1954; and May 1959.

UNION REPUBLIC. The territorial and administrative divisions of the USSR have been established primarily on the basis of nationality or ethnic grouping and for the sake of economic efficiency and management, and are thus subject to change. The fifteen constituent or union republics are the chief territorial units, and each is subdivided further into units designated as region (*oblast'*), area (*okrug*), district (*raion*), town, village, and settlement, in descending order of size and importance. Because it comprises over half the population and three quarters of the territory of the Soviet Union, the Russian republic (RSFSR) contains in addition so-called autonomous republics, territories (*krai*), autonomous regions, and national areas, all differing in size and comprising different ethnic groups. All of these units are incorporated into the hierarchical and centralized Soviet governmental system, so that there are organs of the conventional state machinery, the national economic structure, and the party at each level. See AUTONOMOUS REGION; AUTONOMOUS REPUBLIC; DISTRICT; NATIONAL AREAS; REGION; RSFSR; TERRITORY; UNION OF SOVIET SOCIALIST REPUBLICS.

USSR. The abbreviated designation for the Soviet Union, or, more fully, the UNION OF SOVIET SOCIALIST REPUBLICS.

VOPROSY FILOSOFII. In this journal, which appears six times a year, the official view on Soviet philosophy is presented. Published by the Institute of Philosophy of the Academy of Sciences of the USSR, *Voprosy filosofii* (*Problems of Philosophy*) deals in the Soviet manner not only with problems of philosophy proper, but also with general social and political theory. The journal was founded in 1947.

VOPROSY ISTORII. Published by the Institute of History of the Academy of Sciences of the USSR, the monthly journal *Voprosy istorii* (*Problems of History*) serves as chief general official guide for Soviet historians. Dating back in its present form to January 1937, the journal features articles on important aspects of Russian and Soviet history. It also contains considerable material on the publication of new sources, news of the profession, and, in recent times, extensive surveys of historical publication abroad.

YOUNG COMMUNIST LEAGUE. As successor to the Socialist League of Working Youth, established in 1917, the Young Communist League (Komsomol) held its first full-dress national congress in the fall of 1918. Today the organization is not only completely modeled on but also tightly controlled by its parent body, the CPSU. It frankly serves as training ground for future party officials, and although in theory membership is confined to those between the ages of fourteen and twenty-six, more than half exceed the age limit. Close to twenty million young people belong to the organization. Its units, like those of the party, range all the way from a presidium of the central committee of the organization headed by a first secretary, to grass-roots units in schools, factories, and farms. Its central committee is subordinate to the Central Committee of the CPSU and its local organizations under the direct supervision of the corresponding party organs. The chief officials are full-time party professionals.

Index